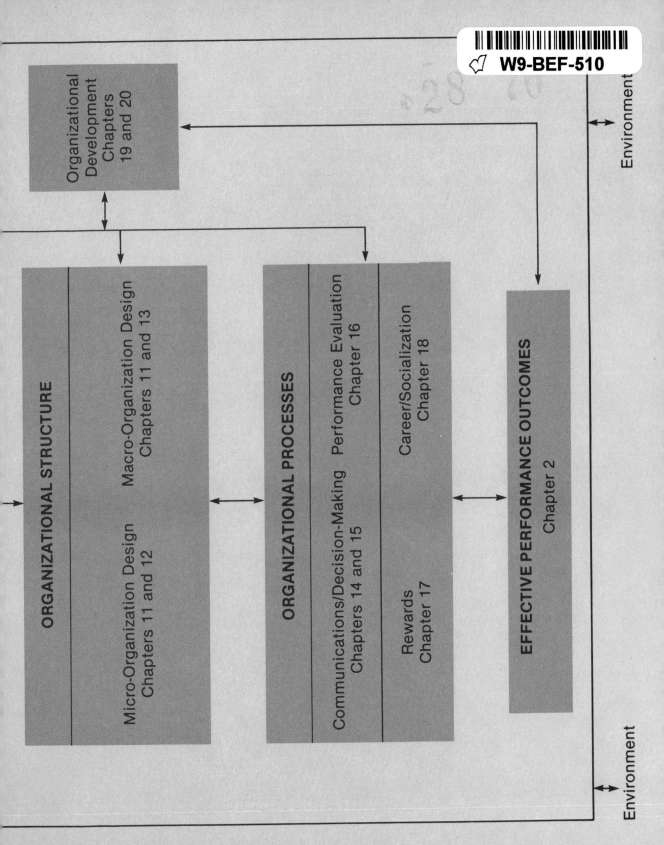

ORGANIZATIONS

Behavior   Structure   Processes

ORGANIZATIONS
Behavior   Structure   Processes

James L. Gibson
Professor of Business Administration
University of Kentucky

John M. Ivancevich
Hugh Roy and Lillie Cranz Cullen
Chair and Professor of Organizational
Behavior and Management
University of Houston

James H. Donnelly, Jr.
Professor of Business Administration
University of Kentucky

1982
Fourth Edition

BUSINESS PUBLICATIONS, INC.   Plano, Texas   75075
Irwin-Dorsey Limited   Georgetown, Ontario   L7G 4B3

ISBN 0-256-02692-0

Library of Congress Catalog Card No. 81–68093

Printed in the United States of America

1 2 3 4 5 6 7 8 9 0 V 9 8 7 6 5 4 3 2

Preface

Objectives of this Edition

The objective of this edition of *Organizations* is the *achievement of individual, group, and organizational performance through enlightened, effective management*. It accomplishes this objective by providing the bases for applying the relevant contributions of behavioral science to the management of organizations.

Accordingly, the continuous thread throughout the book is *the effective management of organizational behavior*. Given this thread, our task was to interpret behavioral science theory and research so that students can comprehend the three characteristics common to all organizations—behavior, structure, processes—as affected by actions of managers. We want to provide a book which will illustrate how behavioral science theory leads to research and how both theory and research provide the basic foundation for practical applications in business firms, hospitals, educational institutions, and governmental agencies.

New Material in this Edition

This edition includes important new subject matter as well as new and additional learning approaches.

First, individual stress, applications of motivation theory, and socialization and career processes are subjects of three new chapters written for this edition. These topics have become especially important in recent years and deserve more intensive treatment than given in previous editions. Each of these three new chapters is based upon the most recent theory, research, and application available in the literature. To make room for these new chapters, several chapters were combined into single chapters and one chapter was omitted.

Second, in addition to new chapters, material in existing chapters was updated. Material on *expectancy theory, groupthink, creativity, attribution approaches to leadership, politics, quality of work life, MAPS approach to organizational design*, and other topics was added to appropriate chapters. In all cases, the new material complements existing material. Comprehensive additional references provide current sources for readers who desire more in-depth discussions of these and other topics presented in the text.

Third, experiential exercises were introduced in the previous edition. Positive reaction to them has encouraged us to increase the number of experiential exercises in this edition to 14. We have retained the short cases included in the previous edition and added three new ones. Each case has been written to emphasize a particular issue or managerial technique. They cover a variety of different types and sizes of organizations and include problems of all levels of management. Feedback was very positive on the four longer cases included in Appendix B, and they have been retained in this edition.

Fourth, new to this edition are "Organizations: Close-Up." These report actual managerial applications of concepts and theories presented in the chapter. They appear at the *exact* point in the text discussion where the concept or theory is being discussed. In classroom testing they were extremely well received. Through the identification of actual managerial applications of text materials, the gap between the classroom and the real world can hopefully be narrowed.

In addition to the practical relevance that the experiential exercises, cases, and close-ups contribute, the text discussion itself carries out our intention to interpret the practical significance of theory and research. Of course, many issues in organizational behavior are unresolved and alternative theories compete. In these instances, issues are presented and readers are encouraged to consider the relative strengths of each. Whenever possible, we acknowledge the tenuousness of both contemporary theory and practice.

To heighten reader interest and to highlight the contingency nature of much of the subject matter, appropriate chapters begin by introducing "An Organizational Issue for Debate." These are short presentations of arguments for and arguments against a popular principle, theory, or application. Introduced in the previous edition, they have been retained and expanded, based on extremely positive feedback.

While the total page length is longer in this edition, the actual number of text pages is not significantly longer. The difference in length is because of additional experiential exercises, cases, and close-ups. We believe this will give instructors greater choice and allow them greater freedom in constructing their own course format.

Framework of this Edition

The framework in which the content of the book is organized is based on the three characteristics cited above as common to all organizations: *behavior, structure,* and *processes.* This order of presentation is in response to numerous adopters who found it easier to discuss the material on human behavior first, followed by structure and processes. It should be mentioned, however, that in this edition each of the major parts is written as a self-contained unit and can be presented in whichever sequence the instructor prefers.

The text is presented in six major parts:

Part One consists of two chapters which together introduce the subject matter. Chapter 1 presents the significance of organizations as a means by which societies produce and distribute goods and services and introduces the reader to ways of acquiring knowledge and understanding about the management of organizational behavior. Chapter 2 develops important ideas concerning the roles of management in achieving effective individual, group, and organizational performance. A framework which integrates the remaining material in the text is presented and briefly described in Figure 2–5.

Part Two includes four chapters which focus on *individual behavior in organizations*. Separate chapters are devoted to individual characteristics and differences, motivation theories, the application of motivation theories (new chapter), and individual stress (new chapter).

Part Three focuses on *group behavior and interpersonal influence in organizations*. It consists of four chapters which focus on group behavior, intergroup behavior, and a two-chapter sequence on leadership.

Part Four includes three chapters which focus on the *structure of organizations*. Separate chapters are devoted to the anatomy of organizations, job design, and organizational design. The latter two follow a micro (job design)-macro (organizational design) sequence.

Part Five includes five chapters dealing with *organizational processes*. Chapters 14 and 15, which deal with communications and decision making, begin this section. The rationale is that these two organizational processes are fundamental to the processes of performance evaluation (Chapter 16), rewarding (Chapter 17), and socialization and careers (Chapter 18). The last is a new chapter written specifically for this edition.

Part Six focuses on *developing organizational effectiveness*. It is a two-chapter sequence that presents the theory of organizational development in the context of an integrated model and then describes and evaluates the more widely used OD techniques.

The book concludes with a short epilogue.

Contributors to this Edition

The authors wish to acknowledge the contributions of reviews of previous editions whose suggestions are reflected throughout the present edition. For this edition we are especially indebted to Richard S. Blackburn, University of North Carolina, Chapel Hill; Carmen Caruana, St. John's University; Sara M. Freedman, University of Houston; Cynthia V. Fukami, State University of New York at Buffalo; and Arthur G. Jago, University of Houston

A special thank you is due Margaret Fenn of the University of Washington and the Fellows of Harvard Business School who permitted us to use cases. We also wish to acknowledge Vic Vroom of Yale University and Art Jago of the University of Houston for permitting us to use their creative ideas and cases to develop a part of our leadership presentation.

Finally, Richard Furst, Dean of the College of Business and Economics, University of Kentucky, and A. Benton Cocanougher, Dean of the College of Business Administration, University of Houston, provided much support for our efforts. Judy Holladay and Erin Sumrall provided immeasurable assistance in preparing the manuscript.

James L. Gibson
John M. Ivancevich
James H. Donnelly, Jr.

Contents

Organizational Programs to Manage Stress: *Role Analysis and Clarification. Companywide Programs.* Individual Approaches to Manage Stress: *Relaxation. Meditation. Biofeedback.*

Case for Analysis
Am I a Success or Failure? 168

Experiential Exercise I
Analysis of Your Type A Tendencies, 169

Experiential Exercise II
Analysis of Job-Related Stress, 173

PART THREE
BEHAVIOR WITHIN ORGANIZATIONS: GROUPS AND INTERPERSONAL INFLUENCE

Organization Design: Conceptualization of the Problem. Division of Labor. Departmentalization: *Functional Departmentalization. Territorial Departmentalization. Product Departmentalization. Customer Departmentalization. Mixed Departmentalization: Divisional Organization.* Span of Control. Delegation of Authority. Dimensions of Structure: *Formalization. Centralization. Complexity.* Matrix Organization Design: *Different Forms of Matrix Organization.*

Case for Analysis
Selecting Between Function and Product as Basis for Departmentalization, 313

An Organizational Issue for Debate: *Job Redesign: Was It Successful?* 315

Quality of Work-Life. A Conceptual Model of Job Design. Designing Job Scope and Job Relationships: *Job Scope. Job Relationships. Scientific Management and Objective Job Scope. Job Content and Individual Differences.* Perceived Job Content and Performance Outcomes: *Job Performance. Job Outcomes. Job Satisfaction.* Motivational Properties of Jobs. Redesigning Job Range: Job Rotation and Job Enlargement: *Job Rotation. Job Enlargement.* Redesigning Job Depth: Job Enrichment. Redesigning Job Range and Depth: Combined Approach. Some Applications of Job Redesign: *The Volvo Experience. The General Motors Experience. Other Experiences with Job Redesign.*

Case for Analysis
Work Redesign in an Insurance Company, 343

Experiential Exercise
Personal Preferences, 344

An Organizational Issue for Debate: *The Technological Imperative,* 348

Universal Design Theories: *Classical Organization Theory. Bureaucratic Organization Theory. System 4 Organization.* Contingency Design Theories. Technology and Organization Design: *The Woodward Research Findings. An Interpretation of Woodward's Findings.* Environment and Organization Design: *The Lawrence and Lorsch Findings. Differentiation, Integration, and Effectiveness. An Interpretation of Lawrence and Lorsch's Findings.* Environmental Uncertainty, Information Processing, and Adaptive Design Strategies: *Strategies to Reduce the Need for Information. Strategies to Increase Capacity to Process Information. Boundary-Spanning Roles.* An Environmental-Contingent Model of Organization Design: *The Output Subenvironment. The Input Subenvironment. The Technology Subenvironment. The Knowledge Subenvironment.* An Integrative Framework.

Case for Analysis
Defining the Role of a Liaison Officer, 384

Experiential Exercise
Organizing a New Business, 388

PART FIVE
THE PROCESSES OF ORGANIZATIONS

mance Evaluation Methods: Traditional: *Graphic Rating Scales. Ranking Methods. Weighted Checklists. Descriptive Essays.* Rating Errors. Performance Evaluation Methods: BARS and MBO: *Behaviorally Anchored Rating Scales. Proposed Advantages of BARS. Management by Objectives.* Performance Evaluation: The Assessment Center: *Purposes of Assessment Centers. Dimensions Measured by Assessment Centers. A Typical Program. Problems of Assessment Centers.* A Review of Potential Performance Evaluation Programs. Developing Employees through Performance Evaluation Feedback.

Case for Analysis
The Evaluation of a Performance Evaluation Program, 470

Experiential Exercise
The Facts of Organizational Life, 471

An Organizational Issue for Debate: *The Pay for Performance Controversy,* **475**

A Model of Individual Rewards. Rewards and Satisfaction. Intrinsic and Extrinsic Rewards: *Extrinsic Rewards. Intrinsic Rewards.* Rewards and Job Performance. Administering Rewards: *Positive Reinforcement. Modeling and Social Imitation. Expentancy Theory.* Rewards and Organizational Membership. Rewards and Turnover and Absenteeism. Rewards and Organizational Commitment. Selected Reward Systems: *Cafeteria-Style Fringe Benefits. Banking Time Off. The All-Salaried Team.*

Case for Analysis
The Effort, Performance, Pay Dilemma at Justis Corporation, 493

Experiential Exercise
Making Choices about Rewards, 496

An Organizational Issue for Debate: *The Socialization Process Is a Major Contributor to Individual, Group, and Organizational Performance,* **498**

Organizational Careers: *Career Effectiveness. Career Stages. Career Paths. Organizational Careers in Perspective.* Socialization: A Linkage between Career Effectiveness and Organizational Effectiveness: *Socialization Stages. The Outcomes of Socialization.* Characteristics of Effective Socialization and Career Processes: *Effective Anticipatory Socialization. Effective Accommodation Socialization. Effective Role Management Socialization.* Socialization as an Integration Strategy.

Case for Analysis
Refusing a Promotion, 520

Experiential Exercise
Reorienting an Excellent Performer, 522

PART SIX
DEVELOPING ORGANIZATIONAL EFFECTIVENESS

PART SEVEN
EPILOGUE

Part One

INTRODUCTION

Chapter 1

The Study of
Organizations

If we were to examine our lives, most of us would conclude that organizations pervade both society and our lives. We come into contact with organizations daily. In fact, most people probably spend the majority of their lives in organizations. If they do not spend a sizable amount of their time as members (work, school, social, civic, church, and so forth), they are affected as clients, patients, customers, or citizens. Our experiences in or with these organizations may be good or bad. Sometimes they may appear to be efficiently run and responsive to human needs, and at other times our experiences with them may be extremely frustrating and irritating. At times they may actually harass us. These personal experiences in or with organizations provide each of us with a commonsense understanding of what it means to be "organized." While our attitudes about organizations may be positive or negative, this commonsense understanding can at least provide us with a good foundation for examining organizations in a more systematic manner.

The primary rationale for the existence of organizations is that certain goals can be achieved only through the concerted action of people. Thus, whether the goal is profit, providing education, religion, or health care, getting a candidate elected, or having a new football stadium constructed, organizations are characterized by their goal-directed behavior. That is, they pursue goals and objectives that can be more efficiently and effectively achieved by the concerted action of individuals. Organizations are vital instruments in our society. Their accomplishments in industry, education, health care, and defense have resulted in impressive gains in our standard of living and international power. They have become models for other nations. The very magnitude of the organizations with which we deal every day of our lives should illustrate to each of us the vast political, economic, and social power that they separately possess.[1]

---

[1]For additional discussion, see L. F. Urwick, "That Word Organization," *Academy of Management Review*, January 1976, pp. 89–91.

Organizations are, however, far more than mere instruments for providing goods and services. They also create the settings in which the majority of us spend our lives, and in this respect have a profound influence on our behavior. However, because of the relative recency of the development of large organizations, we are just now beginning to become aware of some of the psychological effects of this type of involvement and the necessity for studying it. We are just beginning the process of developing procedures to study the behavior of people in organizational settings.

A FRAMEWORK FOR THE STUDY OF ORGANIZATIONS

■ The framework in which the content of this book is presented is based on three characteristics common to *all* organizations: *behavior, structure, and processes*. It has evolved from the authors' concept of what all organizations are. Our chain of logic is presented in Figure 1–1.[2]

Accordingly, the middle three sections of the book contain chapters related to the three characteristics of all organizations: behavior, structure, and processes. These are shown in Figure 1–1 in the middle column. For example, Parts Two and Three contain several chapters on human *behavior* and are concerned with such topics as those in the right-hand column in Figure 1–1. Chapters are included on individual characteristics, individual stress, motivation, groups, and leadership. Part Four contains chapters concerned with various concepts related to the *structure* of organizations (that is, the design of the fixed relationships that exist among the jobs in the organization). Part Five contains chapters on the *processes* which make organizations "tick." Thus, our logic is as follows: people bring with them certain influences on *behavior* (for example, needs, personality, attitudes) when they become part of an organization *structure*, and within this organization structure they engage in the *processes* of communication, decision making, rewarding, evaluating, and socialization.

One might argue, however, that the design of an organization structure should be discussed before human behavior. Admittedly, it is possible to think about an organization in terms of structure and shape without having people in mind. In fact, the ideal organization of early management writers was designed without specific people in mind. They believed it was important to design an organization that was best for achieving the stated goals. People were fit into the design after it was developed. A major belief of the present authors is the importance of human behavior in determining the effectiveness of any organization. People are one resource common to all organizations. There is no such thing as a "peopleless" organization. For this reason we believe it makes good sense to discuss concepts of human behavior in organizations before discussing the design of an organization.

---

[2]Stimulated by the discussion of Geoffrey Hutton in *Thinking about Organizations* (London: Tavistock Publications, 1972).

FIGURE 1–1
A Framework for the Study of Organizations

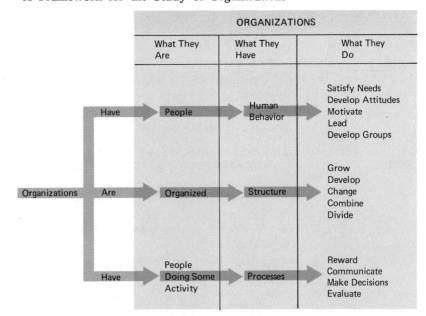

It is people who make organizations work, and it is also people trying to influence other people in organizations that eventually results in either effective or ineffective organizational performance. One thing therefore is certain, a knowledge of organizational behavior requires the understanding of *people* and *organizations* one way or the other.

PURPOSE OF THE BOOK

■ Therefore, the specific purpose of this book is to review available theory and research on what we describe as the behavior, structure, and processes of organizations. While not the sole interest, a major interest of this book will be the behavioral sciences which have produced theory and research concerning human behavior in organizations. However, no attempt will be made here to write a book which will teach the reader "behavioral science." The continuous thread throughout the book will be the *management of organizational behavior*. Given this thread, our task is to *interpret* behavioral science materials so that students can comprehend the behavior, structure, and process phenomena *as affected by actions of managers*. It is our intention to provide the reader the basis for applying the relevant contributions of behavioral science to the management of organizations. Because our continuous thread will be the management of organizational behavior, it is appropriate at this point that we briefly examine this newly developing field of study.

THE DEVELOPING FIELD OF ORGANIZATIONAL BEHAVIOR

■ Why do employees behave as they do in organizations? Why is one group or organization more effective than another? Why do managers continually seek ways to understand and influence the behavior of subordinates? These and other similar questions are important ones in the relatively new field of study known as _organizational behavior_. An understanding of the behavior of people in organizations has become increasingly important as management concerns such as employee productivity, the quality of work life, and career progression have become front page news.

The field of organizational behavior can be defined as:

> The study of human behavior, attitudes, and performance within an organizational setting; drawing on theory, methods, and principles from such disciplines as psychology, sociology, and cultural anthropology to learn about _individual_ perceptions, values, learning capacities, and actions while working in _groups_ and within the total _organization_; analyzing the external environments effect on the organization and its human resources, missions, objectives and strategies.

This definition illustrates a number of points. First, organizational behavior is a _way of thinking._ It views behavior as operating at individual, group, and organizational levels. This approach suggests that when we study organizational behavior we need to clearly identify the level of analysis being used—individual, group, and/or organizational. Second, organizational behavior is an _interdisciplinary field_ that utilizes principles, models, theories, and methods from already established disciplines. Organizational behavior is not a discipline or a generally accepted science with an established theoretical foundation. It is a field that is only now beginning to grow and develop in stature and impact. Third, there is a distinctly _humanistic_ orientation within organizational behavior. People and their attitudes, perceptions, learning capacities, feelings, and goals are of major importance. Fourth, organizational behavior is _performance oriented._ Why is performance low or high? How can performance be improved? Can training enhance on-the-job performance? These are important issues facing practicing managers. Fifth, the impact of the external _environment_ on organizational behavior is recognized as significant. Sixth, since the field of organizational behavior relies heavily on recognized disciplines, the role of the _scientific method_ in studying variables and relationships is important. Figure 1–2 summarizes the main characteristics of the field of organizational behavior.

In order for us to learn about organizations and their functioning, someone has to study them and report about them. Otherwise, the only way we could learn about the functioning of organizations would be to become associated with one for many years and, hopefully, learn from experience. The study of organizations must involve someone using some method and reporting the results in some fashion. It might be a successful executive discussing 25 years of experience or a professor reporting the results of interviews with a group of employees. This section is concerned with how

FIGURE 1–2
Major Characteristics of the Field of Organizational Behavior

Characteristic	Focal Point
Three levels of analysis	Individuals, groups, and the organization are equally important in studying and understanding behavior within organizational settings.
Interdisciplinary nature	Utilizes principles, concepts, and models from the behavioral sciences—psychology, sociology, and cultural anthropology. It uses these disciplines as a basis for theory, methods, and managerial applications.
Humanistic orientation	Stresses the importance of human attitudes and perceptions in understanding behavior, structure, and processes within organizations.
Performance orientation	Places continual emphasis on search for ways to improve, sustain, and encourage effective performance.
Recognition of external environmental forces	The identification and continual monitoring of external environmental forces are important for improving the effectiveness of organizations.
The use of the scientific method	Whenever possible scientific methods are used to supplement experience and intuition.
Application orientation	Knowledge developed in the field of organizational behavior must be useful to practicing managers when they confront individual, group, and organizational problems.

we go about studying organizations. Its purpose is to answer three questions: *who* studies organizations, *how* they study them, and *where* they report the results of what they studied.

How do we know what we know about organizations? In other words, aside from personal experience, how can one learn about the functioning of organizations? Numerous sources of knowledge exist, and each has provided important insights. While some are used more today than others, each has been an important source, and together they form the basis for the knowledge presented in this book. Let us examine each source of knowledge in more or less chronological order. In doing so, we shall answer the first two questions of *who* studies organizations and *how* they study them.

History as a Way of Knowing about Organizations

The oldest approach to the study of organizations is through the history of organizations, societies, and institutions. Organizations are as old as human history. Throughout time, people have joined with others to accomplish their goals, first in families, later in tribes and other more sophisticated political units. Ancient people constructed pyramids, temples, and ships; they created systems of government, farming, commerce, and warfare. For example, Greek historians tell us that it took 100,000 men to build the great pyramid of Khufu in Egypt. The project took over 20 years to complete. It was almost as high as the Washington Monument and had a base that would cover eight modern football fields. Remember, these people had no construction equipment or computers. One thing they did have, though, was *organization*. While these "joint efforts" did not have formal names such as "XYZ Corporation," the idea of "getting organized" was quite widespread throughout early civilizations. The literature of the times refers to such managerial concepts as planning, staff assistance, division of labor, control, and leadership.[3]

The administration of the vast Roman Empire required the application of organization and management concepts. In fact, it has been said that "the real secret of the greatness of the Romans was their genius for organization."[4] This is because the Romans used certain principles of organization to coordinate the diverse activities of the empire.

If judged by age alone, the Roman Catholic Church would have to be considered the most effective organization of all time. While its success is the result of many factors, one of these factors is certainly the effectiveness of its organization and management. For example, the development of the hierarchy of authority with a territorial organization, specialization of activities by function, and use of the staff principle were integral parts of early church organization.

Finally, it is not surprising that some important concepts and practices in modern organizations can be traced to military organizations. This is because, like the church, they were faced with problems of managing large, geographically dispersed groups. As did the church, military organizations early adopted the concept of staff as an advisory function for line personnel.

Knowledge of the history of organizations in earlier societies can be useful for the future manager. In fact, many of these early concepts and practices are being utilized successfully today. However, one may ask whether heavy reliance on the past is a good guide to the present and future. We shall see that time and organizational setting have much to do with what works in management.

Experience as a Way of Knowing about Organizations

Some of the earliest books on management and organizations were written by successful practitioners. Most of these individuals were business executives, and their writings focused on how it was for them during their time with one or more companies. They usually put forward certain gen-

---

[3]For an excellent discussion of organizations in ancient societies, see Claude S. George, Jr., *The History of Management Thought* (Englewood Cliffs, N.J.: Prentice-Hall, 1968), pp. 3–26.

[4]James D. Mooney, *The Principles of Organization* (New York: Harper & Row, 1939), p. 63.

eral principles or practices which had worked well for them. For example:

1. In 1929, Henri Fayol, a managing director of a large coal mining company in France during the early part of the century, described the managerial process by identifying five functions in which managers must engage: planning, organizing, commanding, coordinating, and controlling. He also proposed principles which should guide the thinking of managers in resolving problems.[5]

2. In 1938, Chester I. Barnard, president of New Jersey Bell Telephone, wrote that the basic function of a manager is to provide the basis for cooperative effort, and he defined organization as a system of goal-directed cooperative activities. He believed that a manager's functions include the formulation of objectives and the acquisition of resources and efforts required to meet the stated objectives. He emphasized *communication* as the process for acquiring cooperation.[6]

3. In 1964, Alfred P. Sloan, former chief executive of the General Motors Corporation, wrote on the need for top management not to rely totally on what subordinates tell them (upward communication). He believed management should have independent communication concerning the activities of widely dispersed organizational units.[7]

A great deal of what we know about organizations and their managing has been learned from the experiences of such practitioners, and examples can be found throughout this book. As "practical" as this approach sounds, it does have its drawbacks. Successful managers are susceptible to the same perceptual phenomena as each of us. What we read from them are their own accounts, based on their own preconceptions and biases. No matter how objective the approaches, their accounts may not be entirely complete or accurate. In addition, their accounts may also be superficial since they are often after-the-fact reflections of situations in which, when they were occurring, the managers had little time to think about how or why they were doing something. As a result, their suggestions are often oversimplified. Finally, as with history, what worked yesterday may not work today or tomorrow.[8]

Science as a Way of Knowing about Organizations

We have noted that a major interest in this book will be the behavioral sciences which have produced theory, research, and generalizations concerning the behavior, structure, and processes of organizations. The interest of behavioral scientists in the problems of organizations is relatively new, becoming popular in the early 1950s. It was at that time that an organization known as the Foundation for Research on Human Behavior was

---

[5] See Henri Fayol, *General and Industrial Management*, trans. J. A. Conbrough (Geneva: International Management Institute, 1929), and the more widely available translation by Constance Storrs (London: Pitman Publishing, 1949).

[6] Chester I. Barnard, *The Functions of the Executive* (Cambridge, Mass.: Harvard University Press, 1938).

[7] Alfred P. Sloan, *My Years with General Motors* (New York: Doubleday, 1964).

[8] An excellent article on this subject is W. H. Gruber and J. S. Niles, "Research and Experience in Management," *Business Horizons*, Fall 1973, pp. 15–24.

established. The goals and objectives of this organization were to promote and support behavioral science research in business, government, and other types of organizations.

Many advocates of the scientific approach believe that practicing managers and teachers have accepted many of the practices and principles that preceded them without the benefit of scientific validation. They believe that scientific procedures should be used whenever possible to validate practice. Because of their work, many earlier principles have been discounted or modified, while in other instances they have been validated.

In this section we have examined three important approaches which have been used to gain knowledge about organizations: the *history* of societies and other institutions, the *experience* of practitioners, and *science*. All three are very important, and each has provided knowledge which appears in this book. For the specific purpose of this book, however, behavioral science is by far the most important. Since the majority of the knowledge in this book draws from the behavioral sciences or has been derived from behavioral science research in organizations, we shall examine this approach in detail.

THE BEHAVIORAL SCIENCES

■ To answer the question of *who* studies organizations from the behavioral science viewpoint, one must become familiar with various disciplines. The term *behavioral sciences* refers to the disciplines of psychology, sociology, and anthropology.[9]

Psychology is the study of human behavior. There are many branches of general psychology which have provided concepts useful to the study of organizations. For example, *social psychology* deals with human behavior as it relates to other individuals. It examines how groups and individuals influence and modify each other's behavior. *Organizational psychology* is a relatively new branch which is appearing in many schools of business and public administration. It deals specifically with human behavior in organizational settings and examines the effect of organizations upon the individual and the individual's effect upon organizations. Psychologists have also been concerned with such topics as personnel selection, training, job satisfaction, employee morale, and job performance, which are of interest to students of management. In addition, their concern with more general topics such as human motivation, personality, attitudes, and perception has also provided knowledge useful for the purposes of this book.

Sociology seeks to isolate, define, and describe the behavior of groups. It strives to develop generalizations about human nature, social interaction, and culture. One of the major contributions sociologists have made to our knowledge of organizations has been their focus on small groups. Much has been learned about the behavior of small groups in organizations, the

---

[9]The term *social sciences* usually refers to six disciplines: anthropology, economics, history, political science, psychology, and sociology.

influence of groups on their members, and their impact on the organization. Sociologists have also studied leadership and organization structure as related to organizational effectiveness. They approach the study of organizations as the study of bureaucracy, focusing on bureaucratic behavior as well as the structural relationships in bureaucratic organizations. Finally, sociologists have provided knowledge for this book related to leader and follower roles and the patterns of power and authority in organizations.

Anthropology studies behaviors which have been learned, including all of the social, technical, and family behaviors that are a part of the broad concept of "culture." This concept is the major theme of cultural anthropology, the behavioral science devoted to the study of different peoples and cultures of the world, and is a key idea in all of the behavioral sciences. In fact, the ways in which individuals behave, the priority of needs they seek to satisfy, and the means they choose to satisfy them are functions of their culture. Anthropologists have also provided knowledge for this book with respect to the impact of culture on organizations, individual personality, and perception.

Research in the Behavioral Sciences

Present research in the behavioral sciences is extremely varied with respect to the scope and methods used. However, the common thread found among the various disciplines is the study of human behavior through the use of scientific procedures. Thus, it is necessary to examine the nature of science as it is applied to human behavior. There are those who believe that a science of human behavior is unattainable and that the same scientific procedures used to gain knowledge in the physical sciences cannot be adapted to the study of humans, especially humans in an organization.

The authors do not intend to become involved in these arguments. This is for scholars in the behavioral sciences to decide. However, we believe that the scientific approach is applicable to management and organizational studies.[10] Furthermore, as we have already seen in this chapter, there are means other than scientific procedures which have provided important knowledge concerning people in organizations.

The manager of the future will draw from the behavioral sciences just as the physician draws from the biological sciences. The manager must know what to expect from the behavioral sciences, their strengths and weaknesses, just as the physician must know what to expect of bacteriology and how it can serve as a diagnostic tool. However, the manager, like the physician, is a practitioner who must make decisions in the present, whether

---

[10] A similar debate has taken place for years over the issue of whether management is a science. The interested reader should consult R. E. Gribbons and S. D. Hunt, "Is Management a Science?" *Academy of Management Review*, January 1978, pp. 139–43; O. Behling, "Some Problems in the Philosophy of Science of Organizations," *Academy of Management Review*, April 1978, pp. 193–201; and O. Behling, "The Case for the Natural Science Model for Research in Organizational Behavior and Organization Theory," *Academy of Management Review*, October 1980, pp. 483–90, for relevant discussions.

or not science has all the answers, and certainly cannot wait until it finds them before acting.

The Scientific Approach

Most current philosophers of science define "science" in terms of what they consider to be its one universal and unique feature: *method*. The greatest advantage of the scientific approach is that it has one characteristic that no other method of attaining knowledge has: *self-correction*.[11] It is an objective, systematic, and controlled process with built-in checks all along the way to knowledge. These checks control and verify the scientist's activities and conclusions to enable the attainment of knowledge independent of the scientist's own biases and preconceptions.

Most scientists agree that there is no single scientific method but rather several methods that scientists can and do use. Thus it probably makes more sense to say that there is a scientific approach. Table 1–1 summarizes the major characteristic of this approach. While only an "ideal" science would exhibit all of them, they nevertheless are the hallmarks of the sci-

---

TABLE 1–1
Characteristics of the Scientific Approach

1 *The procedures are public.* A scientific report contains a complete description of what was done, to enable other researchers in the field to follow each step of the investigation as if they were actually present.

2. *The definitions are precise.* The procedures used, the variables measured, and how they were measured must be clearly stated. For example, if examining motivation among employees in a given plant, it would be necessary to define what is meant by motivation and how it was measured (for example, number of units produced, number of absences).

3. *The data collecting is objective.* Objectivity is a key feature of the scientific approach. Bias in collecting and interpreting data has no place in science.

4. *The findings must be replicable.* This enables another interested researcher to test the results of a study by attempting to reproduce them.

5. *The approach is systematic and cumulative.* This relates to one of the underlying purposes of science, to develop a unified body of knowledge.

6. *The purposes are explanation, understanding, and prediction.* All scientists want to know "why" and "how." If they determine "why" and "how" and are able to provide proof, they can then predict the particular conditions under which specific events (human behavior in the case of behavioral sciences) will occur. Prediction is the ultimate objective of behavioral science, as it is of all science.

Source: Bernard Berelson and Gary A. Steiner, *Human Behavior: An Inventory of Scientific Findings* (New York: Harcourt Brace Jovanovich, 1964), pp. 16–18.

---

[11] See Fred N. Kerlinger, *Foundations of Behavioral Research* (New York: Holt, Rinehart, & Winston, 1973), p. 6.

entific approach. They exhibit the basic nature—objective, systematic, controlled—of the scientific approach, which enables others to have confidence in research results. What is important is the overall fundamental idea that the scientific approach is a controlled rational process.

Methods of Inquiry Used by Behavioral Scientists

How do behavioral scientists gain knowledge about the functioning of organizations? Just as physical scientists have certain tools and methods for obtaining information, so do behavioral scientists. These are usually referred to as *research designs*. In broad terms, there are three basic designs used by behavioral scientists: the case study, the field study, and the experiment.

Case Study. A case study attempts to examine numerous characteristics of one or more people usually over an extended time period. For years, anthropologists have studied the customs and behavior of various groups by actually living among them. Some organizational researchers have done the same thing. They have actually worked and socialized with the groups of employees they were studying.[12] Such reports are usually in the form of a case study. For example, a sociologist might report the key factors and incidents which led to a strike by a group of blue-collar workers.

The chief limitations of the case study approach for gaining knowledge about the functioning of organizations are:

1. Rarely can you find two cases that can be meaningfully compared in terms of essential characteristics. In other words, in another firm of another size the same factors may not have resulted in a strike.

2. Rarely can case studies be repeated or their findings verified.

3. The significance of the findings is left to the subjective interpretation of the researcher. Like the practitioner, the researcher attempts to describe reality, but it is reality as perceived by one person (or a very small group). The researcher has training, biases, and preconceptions which can inadvertently distort the report. A psychologist may give an entirely different view of a group of blue-collar workers than a sociologist.

4. Since the results of a case study are based on a sample of one, the ability to generalize from them may be limited.[13]

Despite these limitations, the case study is widely used as a method of studying organizations. It is extremely valuable in answering exploratory questions.

Field Study. In attempts to add more reality and rigor to the study of organizations, behavioral scientists have developed several systematic field

---

[12] See E. Chinoy, *The Automobile Worker and the American Dream* (New York: Doubleday, 1955); and D. Roy, "Banana Time—Job Satisfaction and Informal Interaction," *Human Organization*, 1960, pp. 158–69.

[13] Based in part on Robert J. House, "Scientific Investigation in Management," *Management International Review*, 1970, pp. 141–42. The interested reader should also definitely see G. Morgan and L. Smircich, "The Case for Qualitative Research," *Academy of Management Review*, (October 1980, pp. 491–500, and L. R. Jauch, R. N. Osborn, and T. N. Martin, "Structured Content Analysis of Cases: A Complementary Method for Organizational Research," *Academy of Management Review*, October 1980, pp. 517–26.

research techniques such as personal interviews, observation, and questionnaire surveys that are used individually or in combination. They are used to investigate current practices or events and, unlike some other methods, the researcher does not rely entirely on what the subjects say. The researcher may personally interview other people in the organization—fellow workers, subordinates, and superiors—to gain a more balanced view before drawing conclusions.[14]

A very popular field study technique involves the use of expertly prepared questionnaires. Not only are they less subject to unintentional distortion than personal interviews, but they also enable the researcher to greatly increase the number of individuals participating. For example, Figure 1–3 presents part of a questionnaire used in the Department of Business Administration at the University of Kentucky to measure students' perceptions of their instructor. It enables the collection of data on particular characteristics which are of interest (for example, enthusiasm, originality, and so on). The seven-point scales measure students' perceptions of the degree to which their instructor possesses a given characteristic.

Certain questions, such as student perceptions of teaching, can only be answered by a survey. In most cases, surveys are limited to simply a description of the current state of the situation. However, if researchers are aware of factors that may account for survey findings, they can make conjectural statements (known as hypotheses) about the relationship between two or more factors and relate the survey data to those factors. Thus, instead of just describing student perceptions of teaching, finer distinctions could be made among groups of students (for example, year in school, major area, grade point average). Comparisons and statistical tests could then be applied to determine differences, similarities, or relationships. Finally, there are also *longitudinal* studies involving observations made over time which are used to describe changes that have taken place. Thus, in the situation described here, we can become aware of changes in overall student perceptions over time as well as those relating to individual instructors.[15]

Despite their advantages over many of the other methods of gaining knowledge about organizations, field studies are not without problems. Here again, researchers have training, interests, and expectations which they bring with them.[16] Thus, a psychologist may inadvertently ignore a

---

[14]See G. R. Salancik, "Field Stimulations for Organizational Behavior Research," *Administrative Science Quarterly*, December 1979, pp. 638–49, for an interesting approach to field studies.

[15]The designing of surveys and the development and administering of questionnaires is a skill better left to trained individuals if valid results are to be obtained. The reader interested in an introductory discussion might consult D. W. Emory, *Business Research Methods* (Homewood, Ill.: R. D. Irwin, 1980).

[16]For an excellent article on the relationship between what researchers want to see and what they do see, consult G. Nettler, "Wanting and Knowing," *American Behavioral Scientist*, July 1973, pp. 5–26.

FIGURE 1–3
Student Perceptions of Instructor

PART II: DESCRIPTIVE ITEMS

A. Listed below are 15 sets of items. Place in the box at the right
the number on the scale which best describes your feeling about
the instructor for each of the 15 sets. Please indicate only one
number for each set.

Fair 1 2 3 4 5 6 7	Unfair	▭
Muddled Thinking 1 2 3 4 5 6 7	Clear Thinking	▭
Irresponsible 1 2 3 4 5 6 7	Responsible	▭
Sincere 1 2 3 4 5 6 7	Insincere	▭
Confident 1 2 3 4 5 6 7	Lacks Confidence	▭
Helpful 1 2 3 4 5 6 7	Not Helpful	▭
Unoriginal 1 2 3 4 5 6 7	Original	▭
Enthusiastic 1 2 3 4 5 6 7	Unenthusiastic	▭
Likes Teaching 1 2 3 4 5 6 7	Does Not Like Teaching	▭
Idealistic 1 2 3 4 5 6 7	Realistic	▭
Poor Listener 1 2 3 4 5 6 7	Good Listener	▭
Patient 1 2 3 4 5 6 7	Impatient	▭
Prejudiced 1 2 3 4 5 6 7	Tolerant	▭
Deep 1 2 3 4 5 6 7	Shallow	▭
Humorless 1 2 3 4 5 6 7	Humorous	▭

B. In comparison to faculty members outside of the Department of
Business Administration, how would you rate your instructor?
Place the number in the box at right.

(1)	(2)	(3)	(4)	(5)	(6)	(7)	▭
One of the Worst	Very Poor	Below Average	Average	Above Average	Very Good	One of the Best	

vital technological factor when conducting a study of employee morale while concentrating on the psychological factors. Also the fact that a researcher is present may often influence how the individual responds. This weakness of field studies has long been recognized and is noted in some of the earliest field research in organizations.

Experiment. The experiment is the most rigorous of scientific techniques. For an investigation to be considered an experiment it must contain two elements—manipulation of some variable (independent variable) and observation or measurement of the results (dependent variable) while maintaining all other factors unchanged. Thus, in an organization a behavioral scientist could change one organizational factor and observe the results while attempting to keep everything else unchanged.[17] There are two general types of experiments.

In a *laboratory experiment* the environment is created by the researcher. For example, a management researcher may work with a small voluntary group in a classroom. The group may be students or managers. They may be asked to communicate, perform tasks, or make decisions under different sets of conditions designated by the researcher. The laboratory setting permits the researcher to control closely the conditions under which observations are made. The intention is to isolate the relevant variables and to measure the response of dependent variables when the independent variable is manipulated. Laboratory experiments are useful when the conditions required to test a hypothesis are not practically or readily obtained in natural situations, and when the situation to be studied can be replicated under laboratory conditions. For these situations, many schools of business have behavioral science laboratories where such experimentation is done.

In a *field experiment* the investigator attempts to manipulate and control variables in the natural setting rather than in a laboratory. Early experiments in organizations included manipulating physical working conditions such as rest periods, refreshments, and lighting, while today behavioral scientists attempt to manipulate a host of additional factors.[18] For example, a training program might be introduced for one group of managers but not for another. Comparisons of performance, attitudes, and so on could be obtained later at one point or at several different points (a longitudinal study) to determine what effect, if any, the training program had on the managers' performance and attitudes.

---

[17] For a volume devoted entirely to experiments in organizations, see W. M. Evan, ed., *Organizational Experiments: Laboratory and Field Research* (New York: Harper & Row, 1971). Also see J. A. Waters, P. F. Salipante, Jr., and W. W. Notz, "The Experimenting Organization: Using the Results of Behavioral Science Research, *Academy of Management Review*, July 1978, pp. 483–92.

[18] See an account of the classic Hawthorne studies in Fritz J. Roethlisberger and W. J. Dickson, *Management and the Worker* (Boston: Division of Research, Harvard Business School, 1939). The studies, which were conducted at the Chicago Hawthorne Plant of Western Electric, had as their original purpose to study the relationship between productivity and physical working conditions.

The experiment is especially appealing to many researchers because it is the prototype of the scientific approach. It is the ideal toward which every science strives. However, while its potential still is great, it has not produced a great breadth of knowledge about the functioning of organizations. Laboratory experiments suffer the risk of "artificiality." The results of such experiments often do not extend to real organizations. Teams of business administration or psychology students working on decision problems may provide a great deal of information for researchers. Unfortunately, whether this knowledge can be extended to a group of executives making decisions under severe time constraints is questionable.[19]

Field experiments also have drawbacks. First, researchers cannot "control" every possible influencing factor (even if they knew them all) as they can in a laboratory. Also, here again the fact that a researcher is present may make people behave differently, especially if they are aware that they are participating in an experiment. Experimentation in the behavioral sciences and more specifically in organizations is a complex matter. The interested reader may consult Appendix A of this book for an introductory discussion of the topic.

Finally, with each of the methods of inquiry utilized by behavioral scientists, some type of *measurement* is usually necessary. For knowledge to be meaningful, it often must be compared with or related to something else. As a result, research questions (hypotheses) are usually stated in terms of how differences in the magnitude of some variable are related to differences in the magnitude of some other variable. For example, earlier in our discussion of Figure 1–3 we mentioned that student perceptions of teaching could be compared to grade point averages. This may be meaningful to the instructor.

The variables studied are measured by research instruments. Those instruments may be psychological tests such as personality or intelligence tests, questionnaires designed to obtain attitudes or other information such as Figure 1–3, or in some cases electronic devices to measure eye movement or blood pressure.

It is very important that a research instrument be both *reliable and valid.* Reliability is the consistency of the measure. In other words, repeated measures with the same instrument should produce the same results or scores. Validity is concerned with whether the research instrument actually measures what it is supposed to be measuring. Thus, it is possible for a research instrument to be reliable but not valid. For example, a test designed to measure intelligence could yield consistent scores over a large number of people but not be measuring intelligence. Behavioral science researchers have ways to ensure that as much as possible their research instruments are both reliable and valid.[20]

---

[19] See K. E. Weick, "Laboratory Experimentation with Organizations: A Reappraisal," *Academy of Management Review*, January 1977, pp. 123–27, for a discussion of this problem.

[20] See Kerlinger, *Foundations of Behavioral Research.*

SOURCES OF KNOWLEDGE ABOUT ORGANIZATIONS

■ The vast majority of reports and writing on organizations are contained in technical papers known as journals. Some of these, such as the *Academy of Management Review*, are devoted entirely to topics of management and organization while *Organizational Behavior and Human Performance* is devoted largely to the results of laboratory studies. Others such as the *Harvard Business Review* are general business journals while the *American Sociological Review* and the *Journal of Applied Psychology* are general behavioral science journals. These general business and behavioral science journals often contain articles of interest to students of management. Table 1–2 presents a list of selected journals.

TABLE 1–2
Selected Sources of Writing and Research on Organizations

1.	*Academy of Management Journal*	17.	*Journal of Applied Behavioral Science*
2.	*Academy of Management Review*		
3.	*Administrative Management*	18.	*Journal of Applied Psychology*
4.	*Administrative Science Quarterly*	19.	*Journal of Business*
5.	*Advanced Management Journal*	20.	*Journal of Human Resources*
6.	*American Sociological Review*	21.	*Journal of Management Studies*
7.	*Business Horizons*	22.	*Management International Review*
8.	*Business Management*	23.	*Management Review*
9.	*California Management Review*	24.	*Management Science*
10.	*Fortune*	25.	*Organizational Behavior and Human Performance*
11.	*Harvard Business Review*		
12.	*Hospital and Health Services Administration*	26.	*Organizational Dynamics*
		27.	*Personnel*
13.	*Human Organization*	28.	*Personnel Journal*
14.	*Industrial and Labor Relations Review*	29.	*Personnel Psychology*
		30.	*Public Administration Review*
15.	*Industrial Engineering*	31.	*Public Personnel Review*
16.	*Industrial Management Review*	32.	*Training and Development Journal*

SUMMARY

■ This is a book about organizations written for future managers, but we do not intend to imply that this is the only or best way to learn about organizations. In fact, no book can make one a manager. The only way to become a manager is to "manage." What this book seeks to do is to provide future managers with frameworks and intellectual skills to apply to their experience. So while this book will certainly not make you an effective manager, it will help you accomplish this goal.

In studying the physical and biological sciences, one is fortunate because the real world can be brought into the laboratory. If you wish to test the theory of gravity or observe a chemical process all you need do is perform the required experiments in a laboratory. In this way you can acquire the needed knowledge and skills of the field.

Unfortunately, learning how to manage organizational behavior is much more difficult. It is highly unlikely that a business organization, government agency, or hospital will allow you access to its members so that you may study their behavior and experiment with them and the organization. People must, however, gain knowledge about how organizations work and acquire the knowledge and develop the skills that are essential if they are to become effective managers. The task of writing a book on organizational behavior is, therefore, not an easy one.

This raises the overworked question of theory versus practice. Our experience has shown that most practicing managers are very uncomfortable with the word *theory*. When they refer to something as being "theoretical," they usually mean that it is unrelated to the everyday problems they face. What these managers do not realize, however, is that they themselves are theorists. For example, every manager has a theory of how best to motivate subordinates or of which type of leadership technique is most effective. They may not formally recognize (or wish to admit) it as a theory; they may instead look upon it as their own "concept" or "approach," developed through years of experience.

If you will be taking managerial action at some time, you will be influenced by assumptions (for example, people like to work or don't like to work; money is the best motivator). These assumptions will either be good ones or bad ones, valid or invalid. Our intent is to introduce you to several viewpoints and the support for these viewpoints so that, when the time comes, you will be able to make sense of your experience and develop your own theories in the light of alternatives. We shall not try to convince you that one management technique or approach is more effective than another. Unfortunately, managing an organization has not yet become that easy. Our assumption is a very simple one: Since you are going to have theories one way or another, our mission is to help to be more intelligent about them.

Your behavior as a manager will always reflect a theory. It may be a theory about what an organization is, what people are, or human rights and values. If your behavior as a manager is going to implicitly or explicitly reflect a theory, at least you should make an attempt to ensure that the theory is a good one *for you*. Being exposed to what others say will enable you to evaluate and select what appears to be most useful. This book will help you do this.

As you read this book you will find that there are no neat solutions to most organizational problems. In fact, there are probably very few neat organizational problems. However, the difficulty of achieving organizational effectiveness is not sufficient reason to avoid it. The potential impact of individual managerial decisions and actions (or inactions) has never been more pervasive than it is today. The cost of effective management is very high, but the cost of ineffective management (as well as the potential for error) is even greater.

Since our goal is to help you become a more effective manager, the next chapter deals with this topic: managing organizations effectively. It serves as the foundation for studying the remainder of the book.

DISCUSSION AND REVIEW QUESTIONS

1. Do you believe that organizations pervade your life? List each organization to which you belong. Are there any consequences as far as you are concerned?

2. The word *bureaucracy* is often used as a synonym for red tape, inefficiency, and a generally unresponsive, ineffecient, and ineffective organization. The truth is that these are exactly opposite of what a bureaucracy is supposed to be: an efficient and effective organization. What's happened?

3. What are your attitudes and feelings about organizations? What has influenced your attitudes?

4. Think of a particularly frustrating experience you've had recently with an organization. It may have been at school or at work, or it may have been an organization with which you dealt as a customer, patient, or citizen. Describe the experience and try to outline what may have been some of the causes.

5. "The kind of problems faced by America today are such that they will only be solved by large organizations." Comment.

6. Discuss briefly each of the methods outlined in the chapter for gaining knowledge about organizations. Why is behavioral science research considered the most effective method?

7. Think of something you have had experience in. It might be a particular job, sport, and so on. If you were to tell a group of people about your experience or attempt to teach them what you know, can you see any possible problems? What might be some considerations?

8. A noted baseball player writes a book entitled *My Ten Years as a Major League Pitcher.* How useful is a book such as this to an aspiring major league pitcher? How might it compare to a similar book written by a successful executive?

9. Think of something you believed was true for quite some time only to find out at some later point through experience or some other method that it was not true. Describe it and discuss what happened. Did you learn anything from this experience? What does it point out?

10. Discuss the three basic research designs used by behavioral scientists. Give an example of each type, other than those provided in the chapter. Develop your own if necessary.

11. A popular magazine features an article entitled, "Study and Social Habits of College Males." Upon reading the article you find that it is based on a case study where the reporter lived for two months as a member of a fraternity at a private school in the northeastern part of the country. Evaluate this article based upon your knowledge of the characteristics of the scientific approach.

12. Select and read an article in one of the journals listed in Table 1–2. Which one of the approaches for gaining knowledge about organizations did the author use? Evaluate the article as to its usefulness. What criteria did you use to make your judgment?

ADDITIONAL REFERENCES

Argyris, D. *The Applicability of Organizational Society.* New York: Cambridge University Press, 1972.

Armstrong, J. S. "Advocacy as a Scientific Strategy: The Mitroff Myth." *Academy of Management Review,* 1980, pp. 509–12.

Conner, P. E. "Research in the Behavioral Sciences: A Review Essay." *Academy of Management Journal,* 1972, pp. 219–28.

Downey, H. K., and R. D. Ireland. "Quantitative versus Qualitative: The Case of Environmental

Assessment in Organizational Studies." *Administrative Science Quarterly*, 1979, pp. 630–37.

Emshoff, J. R. *Analysis of Behavioral Systems.* New York: Macmillan, 1971.

Ford, C. H. "A Manager's View of Business Journals." *Business Horizons*, 1978, pp. 219–28.

Frost, P. "Toward a Radical Framework for Practicing Organization Science." *Academy of Management Review*, 1980, pp. 501–8.

Heald, K. "Using the Case Survey Method to Analyze Policy Studies." *Administrative Science Quarterly*, 1975, pp. 371–81.

Kaplan, A. *The Conduct of Inquiry.* San Francisco: Chandler Publishing, 1964.

Lackenmeyer, C. "Experimentation—A Misunderstood Methodology in Psychological Research." *American Psychologist*, 1970, pp. 617–24.

Massarik, F., and B. E. Kreuger. "Through the Labyrinth: An Approach to Reading in Behavioral Science." *California Management Review*, 1970, pp. 70–75.

Meltzer, H., and W. Nord. "The Present Status of Industrial and Organizational Psychology." *Personnel Psychology*, 1973, pp. 11–29.

Miles, M. "Qualitative Data as an Attractive Nuisance: The Problem of Analysis." *Administrative Science Quarterly*, 1979, pp. 590–601.

Mintzberg, H. "An Emerging Strategy of Direct Research." *Administrative Science Quarterly*, 1979, pp. 582–89.

Mitroff, I. I. "Reality as a Scientific Strategy: Revising Our Concepts of Science." *Academy of Management Review*, 1980, pp. 513–16.

Pettigrew, A. "On Studying Organizational Cultures." *Administrative Science Quarterly*, 1979, pp. 570–81.

Schein, E. H. "Behavioral Sciences for Management." In *Contemporary Management*, edited by J. W. McGuire. Englewood Cliffs, N.J.: Prentice-Hall, 1974.

Seashore, S. E. "Field Experiments within Formal Organizations." *Human Organization*, 1974, pp. 164–70.

Snow, C. C., and D. C. Hambrick. "Measuring Organizational Strategies: Some Theoretical and Methodological Problems." *Academy of Management Review*, 1980, pp. 527–38.

Van Maanen, J. "Reclaiming Qualitative Research Methods for Organizational Research: A Preface." *Administrative Science Quarterly*, 1979, pp. 520–26.

Webber, R. A. "Behavioral Science and Management: Why the Troubled Marriage?" *Proceedings of the Academy of Management 1970*, pp. 377–95.

Weiland, G. F. "The Contributions of Organizational Sociology to the Practice of Management." *Academy of Management Journal*, 1975, pp. 318–33.

Chapter 2

Managing Organizational Performance

AN ORGANIZATIONAL ISSUE FOR DEBATE
Employee Satisfaction Leads to Organizational Performance

ARGUMENT FOR

The argument for the idea that satisfied people produce more is firmly established in the human relations literature. "Improve the morale of a company and you improve production," is the oft-stated claim. Or as George Allen, former coach of the Los Angeles Rams, put it: Happy football players win games. The view that satisfaction leads to production was established by the Hawthorne studies and subsequently rooted in the motivation theories of Herzberg and the leadership theories of Likert.

These views are the bases for humanistic leadership training. The training exercises attempt to instill in managers the understanding that they must provide the necessary motivators which satisfy people. Managers must provide the "right" motivators to tap employee productivity through increased satisfaction.

An important part of this argument is that employee satisfaction is important only as it leads to productivity. That is, the sole criterion of organizational performance is efficient production. If there were no relationship between satisfaction and production, there would be no compelling reason to be concerned with the satisfaction and morale of employees.

ARGUMENT AGAINST

The argument against the idea that satisfaction leads to performance cites numerous studies showing no, or negative, relationship between the two. Thus employee satisfaction and performance may be subject to more complex relationships than posed by the supportive argument. For example, employee satisfaction may itself be based upon rewards other than those obtained through production. But if rewards are related to production, then satisfaction may be the *result* of performance not the cause of it. As Dallas Cowboy coach Tom Landry no doubt has said: If the players win football games (and championships) then they are happy.

The implications of this argument is that employees must be selected and trained to perform their assigned tasks; managers must provide positive paths to task completion and assure that rewards are related to performance. Salary structures must clearly reflect differential levels of production.

The counter-argument also includes the idea that both satisfaction and production are criteria of organizational effectiveness. The interactive relationship between satisfaction and production indicates that managers must balance and reconcile the two, rather than assume that one leads to the other.

Managers are accountable for the performance of organizations. This accountability and the authority that goes with it are derived from those who provide resources. For example, property owners supply the resources for business organizations and taxpayers supply the resources for governmental organizations. Of course, both groups can have interests in the same organization or can share their interests with other groups, such as students, patients, and clients. Communications Satellites Consortium (COMSAT) is an example of an organization which is supported by both stockholders and taxpayers; a public university is supported by taxpayers and tuition-paying students. Thus the managers of organizations are intimately linked to the society in which they operate because they are ultimately accountable to those groups which contribute resources to the organizations.

Organizational performance depends upon individual and group performance, managers must achieve high levels of performance from the people within the organization. Society evaluates organizational performance, but managers evaluate individual performance. Organizational, group, and individual performance are separate, but interrelated, concepts.

PERSPECTIVES ON EFFECTIVENESS

■ The foregoing discussion highlights the importance of distinguishing among the several perspectives on effectiveness. At the most basic level is *individual effectiveness.* The individual perspective emphasizes the task performance of specific employees or members of the organization. The tasks to be performed are ordinarily assigned as parts of jobs or positions in the organization. Individual performance is routinely assessed through performance evaluation processes which are the bases for salary increases, promotions, and other rewards available in the organization.

Individuals seldom work alone or in isolation from others in the organization. In fact the usual situation is for individuals to work together in work groups. Thus it is necessary to consider yet another perspective on effectiveness, *group effectiveness.* In some instances group effectiveness is simply the sum of the contributions of all its members. For example, a group of scientists working on individual, unrelated projects, would be effective to the extent that each individual is effective. In other instances group effectiveness is more than the sum of the individual contributions. Such an example is an assembly line which produces a finished product as a result of specific, yet cumulative, contributions of each individual.

The third perspective is that of *organizational effectiveness.* Organizations consist of individuals and groups; therefore organizational effectiveness consists of individual and group effectiveness. However organizational effectiveness is more than the sum of individual and group effectiveness; through synergistic effects, organizations are able to obtain higher levels of performance than the sum of their parts. In fact the rationale for organizations as a means for doing the work of society is that they can do more work than is possible through individual effort.

FIGURE 2–1
**Three Perspectives
on Organizational
Effectiveness**

Source: Adapted from
David J. Lawless,
*Effective Management:
Social Psychological Ap-
proach* (Englewood
Cliffs, N.J.: Prentice-Hall,
1972).

The relationship among the three perspectives on effectiveness is shown in Figure 2–1.[1] The connecting arrows between each level do not imply specific forms for the relationships. That is, individual effectiveness does not necessarily *cause* group effectiveness; nor can it be said that group effectiveness is the *sum* of individual effectiveness. The relationships among the perspectives vary depending upon such factors as the type of organization, the work it does, and the technology used in doing that work.

The fundamental task of management is to identify the *causes* of organizational, group, and individual effectiveness. As noted in Figure 2–2, each level of effectiveness can be considered a variable which is dependent upon other variables; that is, the causes of effectiveness. For example some causes of individual effectiveness are obvious—physical attributes, psychological traits, and motivation can account for differences in performance among individuals. Causes of group performance include group leadership, communication, and socialization. Organizational effectiveness is the result of a vast number of variables including technology, environmental constraints and opportunities, and personnel competence and motivation.[2] These suggested causes of effectiveness at the various levels are discussed

---

[1] The following discussion is based upon David J. Lawless, *Effective Management: Social Psychological Approach* (Englewood Cliffs, N.J.: Prentice-Hall, 1972), pp. 391–99.

[2] One of the more ambitious attempts to identify factors associated with organizational performance is reported in John Child, "Managerial and Organizational Factors Associated with Company Performance—Part I," *Journal of Management Studies*, October 1974, pp. 175–89; and John Child, "Managerial and Organizational Factors Associated with Company Performance—Part II: A Contingency Analysis," *Journal of Management Studies*, February 1975, pp. 12–27. This study did not reach definitive conclusions due, no doubt, to the inherent complexity of the concept, organizational effectiveness.

FIGURE 2–2
Sources of Effectiveness

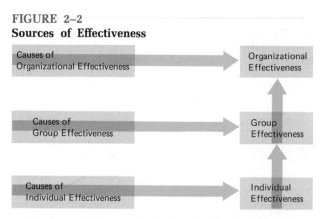

Source: Adapted from David J. Lawless, *Effective Management: Social Psychological Approach* (Englewood Cliffs, N.J.: Prentice-Hall, 1972).

at length in subsequent chapters. Other causes are also presented. But now we must introduce an equally difficult issue, the concept of effectiveness per se. Two approaches will be presented: the goal approach and the systems theory approach. These two approaches are most often contrasted in the literature and practice of organizational behavior.[3]

THE GOAL APPROACH

■ The goal approach to defining and evaluating effectiveness is based upon the idea that organizations are created as means to ends (goals). An organization, so goes this approach, exists to accomplish goals. An early and influential practitioner and writer in management and organizational behavior stated: "What we mean by effectiveness . . . is the accomplishment of recognized objectives of cooperative effort. The degree of accomplishment indicates the degree of effectiveness."[4] The idea that organizations, as well as groups and individuals, should be evaluated in terms of goal accomplishment has widespread commonsense and practical appeal. The goal approach reflects purposefulness, rationality, and achievement— the fundamental tenets of contemporary Western societies.

Yet the goal approach, for all its appeal and apparent simplicity, is not without problems.[5] Some of the more widely recognized difficulties include:

---

[3]Kim Cameron, "Critical Questions in Assessing Organizational Effectiveness," *Organizational Dynamics*, Autumn 1980, pp. 66–80 identifies two other approaches: the internal process approach and the strategic constituencies approach. The former can be subsumed under the systems theory approach and the latter is a special case of the multiple goal approach.

[4]Chester I. Barnard, *The Functions of the Executive* (Cambridge, Mass.: Harvard University Press, 1938), p. 55.

[5]E. Frank Harrison, *Management and Organization* (Boston: Houghton Mifflin, 1978), pp. 404–14, is an excellent survey of limitations of the goal approach.

1. Goal achievement is not readily measurable for organizations which do not produce tangible outputs.
2. Organizations attempt to achieve more than one goal and the achievement of one goal often precludes or diminishes its ability to achieve other goals.
3. The very existence of a common set of "official" goals to which all members are committed is questionable. Various researchers have noted the difficulty of obtaining consensus among managers as to the specific goals of their organization.[6]

Despite the problems of the goal approach, it continues to exert a powerful influence on the development of management and organizational behavior theory and practice. Contemporary discussions reflect the importance of organizational goals in strategic decision making[7] and the distinction between *maximizing* goals and *optimizing* goals.[8] Strategic decision making requires explicit attention to the purposes of the organization as it confronts its environment; the fact that environments are typically uncertain and diverse implies that organizations must be content with achieving feasible rather than ultimate goals.

The actual process of evaluating performance is considerably more difficult than one might suspect. It is easy to say that managers should direct organizations in such ways as to maximize ends with efficient use of resources. It is much more difficult to know how to do this. Our approach to this managerial problem is to acquaint managers with the basic concepts of systems theory. Through systems theory, the concept of effectiveness can be defined in terms that are meaningful to the managers of organizations, whether business firms, hospitals, governmental agencies, or universities.

SYSTEMS THEORY ■ Systems theory enables us to describe the behavior of organizations both internally and externally. Internally we can see how and why people inside organizations perform their individual and collective tasks. Externally, we can relate the transactions of organizations with other organizations and institutions. It is a fundamental principle that all organizations acquire resources from the larger environment of which they are a part and, in turn, provide the goods and services which are demanded by the larger environment. Managers must deal simultaneously with the internal and external aspects of organizational behavior. This essentially complex process can be simplified, for analytical purposes, by employing the basic concepts of systems theory.

---

[6]Terry Connolly, Edward J. Conlon, and Stuart Jay Deutsch, "Organizational Effectiveness: A Multiple-Constituency Approach," *Academy of Management Review*, April 1980, p. 212.

[7]Max D. Richards, *Organizational Goal Structures* (St. Paul, Minn.: West Publishing, 1978).

[8]Richard M. Steers, *Organizational Effectiveness: A Behavioral View* (Santa Monica, Calif.: Goodyear Publishing, 1977), p. 5.

FIGURE 2–3
The Basic Elements of a System

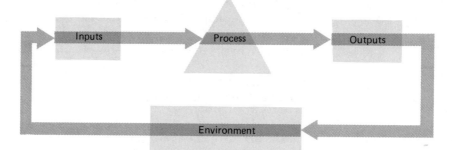

In the context of systems theory the organization is viewed as one element of a number of elements which interact interdependently.[9] The flow of inputs and outputs is the basic starting point in the description of the organization. In the simplest terms, the organization takes resources (inputs) from the larger system (environment), processes these resources, and returns them in changed form (output). Figure 2–3 displays the fundamental elements of the organization as a system.

Systems Theory and Feedback

The concept of the organization as a system which is related to a larger system introduces the importance of feedback. As noted above, the organization is dependent upon the environment not only for its inputs, but also for the acceptance of its outputs. It is imperative, therefore, that the organization develop means for adjusting to environmental demands. The means for adjustment are information channels which enable the organization to recognize these demands. In business organizations, market research is an important feedback mechanism.

In a more general sense, feedback is the dynamic process by which any organism learns from its experiences with its environment. Throughout this text, we will see how important feedback is for reinforcing learning, and developing personality, group behavior, and leadership. In simplest terms, feedback refers to information which reflects the outcomes of an act or a series of acts by an individual, group, or organization. Systems theory emphasizes the importance of responding to the content of the feedback information.

Examples of the Input-Output Cycle

The business firm has two major categories of inputs: human and natural resources. Human inputs consist of the people who work in the firm—operating, staff, and managerial personnel. They contribute their time and

---

[9]This discussion of the organization as a system is based upon E. J. Miller and A. K. Rice, *Systems of Organizations* (London: Tavistock Publications, 1967).

energy to the organization in exchange for wages and other rewards, tangible and intangible. Natural resources consist of the nonhuman inputs which will be processed, or which will be used in combination with the human element to provide other resources. A steel mill uses people and blast furnaces (along with other tools and machinery) to process iron ore into steel and steel products. An auto manufacturer takes steel, rubber, plastics, fabrics, and—in combination with people, tools, and equipment—makes automobiles. A business firm survives as long as its output is purchased in the market in quantities at prices that enable it to replenish its depleted stock of inputs.

Similarly, a university uses resources to teach students, to do research, and to provide technical information to society. The survival of a university depends upon its ability to attract students' tuitions and taxpayers' dollars in sufficient amounts to pay the salaries of its faculty and staff and the other costs of resources. If a university's output is rejected by the larger environment so that students enroll elsewhere and taxpayers support other public endeavors, or if a university is guilty of expending too great an amount of resources in relation to its output, it will cease to exist. Like a business firm, a university must provide the right output at the right price if it is to survive.[10]

As a final example, we will describe a hospital in terms of systems theory. The inputs of a hospital are its professional and administrative staff, equipment, supplies, and patients. The patients are processed through the application of medical knowledge and treatment. To the extent that its patients are restored to the level of health consistent with the severity of disease or injury which they suffered, the hospital is effective. Yet the criterion of efficiency must also be met. The rising cost of medical care has initiated considerable search for alternative forms of medical care delivery. This activity is in direct response to society's discontent with the seeming inefficiencies of the present medical-care delivery system.

The systems concept emphasizes two important considerations: (1) The ultimate survival of the organization depends upon its ability to *adapt to the demands of its environment,* and (2) in meeting these demands, *the total cycle of input-process-output must be the focus of managerial attention.* Criteria of performance must reflect these two considerations and we must define effectiveness accordingly. As Etzioni has observed, the systems framework assumes that "some means have to be devoted to such nongoal functions as service and custodial activities, including means employed for the maintenance of the unit (organization) itself."[11] In other words, *adapt-*

---

[10]For a treatment of university organization in terms of systems theory, see A. K. Rice, *The Modern University* (London: Tavistock Publications, 1970); and Kim Cameron, "Measuring Organizational Effectiveness in Institutions of Higher Education," *Administrative Science Quarterly,* December 1978, pp. 604–29.

[11]Amitai Etzioni, "Two Approaches to Organizational Analysis: A Critique and a Suggestion," in *Assessment of Organizational Effectiveness,* ed. Jaisingh Ghorpade. (Santa Monica, Calif.: Goodyear Publishing, 1971), p. 36.

ing to the environment and maintaining the input-process-output flow re-quire that resources be allocated to activities that are only indirectly related to the organization's social mission.

CRITERIA OF ORGANIZATIONAL EFFECTIVENESS

■ The concept of organizational effectiveness in this book relies upon our previous discussion of systems theory, but we must develop one additional point, the dimension of time. Recall that two main conclusions of systems theory are that (1) effectiveness criteria must reflect the entire input-pro-cess-output cycle, not simply output; and (2) effectiveness criteria must reflect the interrelationships between the organization and the larger envi-ronment in which it exists. From these two points, we can derive two cor-ollaries:

1. Organizational effectiveness is an all-encompassing concept which in-cludes a number of component concepts.
2. The managerial task is to maintain the optimal balance among these components.

Presently, we are proposing a tentative set of ideas. Much additional research is needed to develop knowledge about the components of effec-tiveness. There is little consensus not only about these relevant compo-nents, but also the interrelationships *among them* and the effects of mana-gerial action *on them*.[12] We are attempting to provide the basis for asking the right questions about what constitutes effectiveness and how those qualities which characterize effectiveness interact.

The dimension of time enters into the model when an organization is conceptualized as an element of a larger system (the environment) which *through time* takes, processes, and returns resources to the environment. Accordingly, the final test of organizational effectiveness is whether it is able to sustain itself in the environment. Survival of the organization, then, is the ultimate, or long-run, measure of organizational effectiveness. Yet, management and others who have interests in the organization must have indicators which assess the probability that it will survive. These indica-tors are of short-run nature and include *production, efficiency,* and *satis-faction* measures. Two other criteria which are termed *intermediate,* are *adaptiveness and development.* The relationship between these effective-ness criteria and the time dimension are shown in Figure 2–4. As is true of all classification schemes, the list of short, intermediate, and long-run cri-teria is somewhat arbitrary and dependent upon definitions. Accordingly let us define our meanings.

---

[12]J. Barton Cunningham, "Approaches to the Evaluation of Organizational Effectiveness," *Academy of Management Review,* July 1977, pp. 463–74, and Richard M. Steers, "Problems in Measurement of Organizational Effectiveness," *Administrative Science Quarterly,* Decem-ber 1975, pp. 546–58.

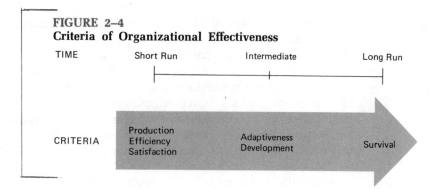

FIGURE 2–4
Criteria of Organizational Effectiveness

Production

As used here, production reflects the ability of the organization to produce the quantity and quality of output which the environment demands. The concept excludes any consideration of efficiency as will be defined below. The measures of production include profit, sales, market share, students graduated, patients released, documents processed, clients served, and the like. These measures relate directly to the output that is consumed by the organization's customers and clients.

Efficiency

This concept is defined as the ratio of outputs to inputs. This short-run criterion focuses attention on the entire input-process-output cycle, yet it emphasizes the input and process elements. The measures of efficiency include rate of return on capital or assets, unit cost, scrappage and waste, downtime, cost per patient, per student, or per client, occupancy rates, and the like. Measures of efficiency must inevitably be in ratio terms; the ratios of benefit to cost or to output or to time are the general forms of these measures.

Satisfaction

The conceptualization of the organization as a social system requires that some consideration be given to the benefits received by its participants as well as its customers and clients. Satisfaction and morale are similar terms which refer to the extent to which the organization satisfies the needs of employees. We will use the term *satisfaction* to refer to this criterion. Measures of satisfaction include employee attitudes, turnover, absenteeism, tardiness, and grievances.

Adaptiveness

Adaptiveness is the extent to which the organization *can and does* respond to internal and external changes. However, contrary to its use elsewhere, adaptiveness is viewed here as an intermediate criterion; it is more abstract than production, efficiency, or satisfaction. This criterion refers to management's ability to sense changes in the environment as well as within the organization itself. Ineffectiveness in achieving production, efficiency, and satisfaction can signal the need to adapt managerial practices and policies; or the environment may demand different outputs or provide different inputs, thus necessitating change. To the extent that the organization cannot or does not adapt, its survival is in jeopardy. The usual measures of adaptiveness for research purposes are provided by responses to questionnaires. But how can one really know whether the organization is effectively adaptive? Unlike the short-run measures of effectiveness, there are no specific and concrete measures of adaptiveness. The management can implement policies which encourage a sense of readiness for change; and there are certain managerial practices which, if implemented, facilitate adaptiveness. Yet when the time comes for an adaptive response, the organization either adapts or does not—and that is the ultimate measure.

Development

An organization must <u>invest in itself to enhance its capability to survive in the long run</u>. The usual development endeavors are training programs for managerial and nonmanagerial personnel, but more recently the range of organizational development has enlarged to include a number of psychological and sociological approaches.

Time considerations enable us to speak of effectiveness in the short, intermediate, and long run. For example, we could evaluate a particular organization as effective in terms of production, satisfaction, and efficiency criteria, but ineffective in terms of adaptiveness and development. A manufacturer of buggy whips may be optimally effective in the short run, but with little chance of survival. *Thus when we speak of optimal balance, we are speaking, in part, of balancing the organization's performance over time.*

Another aspect of optimal balance is *that of achieving the proper relationships among the criteria within a given time period.* There are no fixed relationships among production, satisfaction, and efficiency. Neither research nor actual practice provides the basis for saying that production and satisfaction are positively related. These two measures can move in the same or opposite direction depending upon the circumstances. Therefore it is necessary for managers to recognize what potential relationships they want to affect, prior to implementing policies designed to affect them.

We know that the more distant the future, the more uncertain are our predictions. A forecast of tomorrow's events is, by definition, more certain than a forecast of next year's events. The case of effectiveness criteria is similar. We would expect, for example, measures of production, satisfaction, and efficiency to be relatively more *concrete, specific, verifiable,* and *objective* than measures of adaptiveness and development. Furthermore we know that relative effectiveness is much easier to determine if short-run rather than long-run criteria are used.

THE NATURE OF MANAGERIAL WORK

■ Theories which describe managerial work are many and varied.[13] These theories, produced by academicians and practitioners alike, are intended to provide the bases for research as well as for selecting, training, and devel-

---

[13]Surveys of the history of management thought can be found in Daniel A. Wren, *The Evolution of Management Thought* (New York: The Ronald Press, 1972); and Claude S. George, Jr., *The History of Management Thought* (Englewood Cliffs, N.J.: Prentice-Hall, 1968).

oping managers. The academic purpose of theory is to suggest research questions which, in turn, are the bases for refining existing theory and developing new theory. The practical purpose of theory is to guide decisions. Managers must be identified, selected, trained, evaluated, developed, rewarded, and disciplined. But without a theoretical framework for *describing what managers do* and for *prescribing what they should do,* no basis exists for making those decisions.

The first attempts to describe managerial work were undertaken in the early 1900s by writers of the Classical School of Management.[14] The writers of the Classical School proposed that managerial work consists of distinct, yet interrelated, *functions* which taken together comprise the *managerial process.* The view that management should be defined, described, and analyzed in terms of what managers do has prevailed, but whether the functions as identified by the Classical School are appropriate is a matter of continuing debate.

No doubt management can be defined as a *process,* that is, as a series of actions, activities, or operations which lead to some end. The definition of management should also recognize that the process is undertaken by more than one person in most organizations. This definition should be broad enough to describe management wherever it is practiced, yet specific enough to identify differences in the relative importance of the functions associated with a particular manager's job. A definition which meets these tests has not been fully developed.

The definition of management developed here is based upon the assumption that the necessity for managing arises whenever work is specialized and undertaken by two or more persons.[15] Under such circumstances, the specialized work must be *coordinated* and it is this imperative that creates the necessity for performing managerial work, that is, the managerial process, can be subdivided into three major *functions:* planning, organizing, controlling. It is certainly possible to expand the list to include other functions, but these three can be defined with sufficient precision to differentiate them and, at the same time, to include all others which management writers have proposed.

Managerial Functions

The managerial functions discussed here are found in some degree in every instance where the work of others needs to be coordinated. The logic is fairly simple: If <u>work is to be coordinated there must be</u> some understanding of what is to be done (<u>planning</u>), how it is to be done (<u>organizing</u>), and whether it was done (<u>controlling</u>).

---

[14]The term *Classical School of Management* refers to the ideas developed by a group of practitioners who wrote of their experiences in management. Notable contributors to these ideas include Frederick W. Taylor, *Principles of Management* (New York: Harper & Row, 1911); Henri Fayol, *General and Industrial Management,* trans. J. A. Conbrough (Geneva: International Management Institute, 1929); James D. Mooney, *The Principles of Organization* (New York: Harper & Row, 1947); and Lyndall Urwick, *The Elements of Administration* (New York: Harper & Row, 1944).

[15]This idea is essentially that of James D. Mooney as developed in *Principles of Organization.*

Planning Effective Performance. The planning function includes de-fining the ends to be achieved and determining *appropriate means to achieve the defined ends.* The necessity of this function follows from the nature of organizations as purposive, that is, end-seeking, entities. Plan-ning activities can be complex or simple, implicit or explicit, impersonal or personal. For example, the sales manager who is forecasting the demand for the firm's major product may rely upon complex econometric models or upon casual conversations with salespersons in the field. The intended outcomes of planning activities are mutual understandings about what the members of the organization should be attempting to achieve. These un-derstandings may be reflected in the form of complicated plans which specify the intended results or they may be reflected in a general consensus of the members.

The development of a coherent set of goals and objectives defines the scope and direction of the organization's activities. In fact, the develop-ment of a set of activities (or means) follows from the prior determination of ends. Planning involves not only the specification of where the organi-zation is going, but how it is to get there. In specific terms, alternatives must be analyzed and evaluated in terms of criteria that follow from the mission, goals, and objectives. And once the determination of appropriate means is completed, the next managerial function must be undertaken, or-ganizing.

Organizing Effective Performance. The organizing function includes *all managerial activities which are taken to translate the required planned activities into a structure of tasks and authority.* The interrelationships be-tween planning and organizing are apparent. The planning function results in the determination of organizational ends and means; that is, it defines the "whats" and "hows." The organizing function results in the determi-nation of the "whos," that is, *who will do what with whom to achieve the desired end results.* The structure of tasks and authority should facilitate the fulfillment of planned results, but it is apparent that there can be a bad fit between the two. Yet even with the most appropriate fit, the fact that the organization operates in an environment which may change and with peo-ple who are unique means that variances between expected and actual out-comes may occur.

Controlling Effective Performance. The controlling function includes *activities which managers undertake to assure that actual outcomes are consistent with planned outcomes.* Simply stated, managers undertake con-trol to determine *whether* intended results are achieved and if not *why* not. The conclusions managers reach because of their controlling activities are that the planning function was (and is) faulty or that the organizing func-tion was (and is) faulty, or both. Controlling is, then, the completion of a logical sequence. The activities which comprise controlling include em-ployee selection and placement, materials inspection, performance evalua-tion, financial statement analysis, and other well-recognized managerial techniques.

The concept of management in terms of the three functions of planning, organizing, and controlling is certainly not complete. There is nothing in this conceptualization which indicates the specific behaviors or activities associated with each function. Nor is there any recognition of the relative importance of these functions for overall organizational effectiveness. The point has been made that these three functions conveniently and adequately define management.

A MODEL FOR MANAGING ORGANIZATIONS: BEHAVIOR, STRUCTURE, PROCESSES

■ A model for understanding organizations is presented in Figure 2–5. The model will serve as the focal point for discussion and analysis of behavior structure, processes, performance outcomes, change and development, and environment. At this point, many of the dimensions, relationships, and issues presented may not be clearly defined or understood. By presenting the model at the outset, it can serve as the framework for presenting the material in the book. It will also serve as the framework for analyzing the cases and experiential exercises used throughout the book.

Society and Organizations

Organizations exist in societies; in fact, organizations are created by societies. Systems theory draws attention to the relationships between organizations and the society which creates and sustains them. Within a society, many factors impinge upon an organization, and management must be responsive to them. Every organization must respond to legal and political constraints and to economic, and technological change and development. Figure 2–5 reflects environmental forces interacting with the organization and throughout the discussion of each aspect of the model, the relevant societal factors will be identified and discussed.

Individual Characteristics

Individual performance is the foundation of organizational performance. Consequently managers must have more than passing knowledge about the determinants of individual performance. Psychology and social psychology contribute a great deal of relevant knowledge about the relationship between attitudes, perceptions, personality, and values and individual performance. Individual capacity for learning and coping with stress has become, in recent years, more and more important. Managers cannot ignore the necessity for acquiring and acting on knowledge of individual characteristics of their subordinates and themselves.

Motivation

Motivation to work and ability to do the work interact to determine performance. Motivation theory attempts to explain and predict how behavior of individuals is aroused, started, sustained, and stopped. Not all managers and researchers agree on the "best" theory of motivation. The topic is so complex that it may be impossible to have one, simple, all-encompassing theory. It is more likely that various theories will always compete for acceptance. Yet the complexity of the issue should not deter attempts to un-

FIGURE 2–5

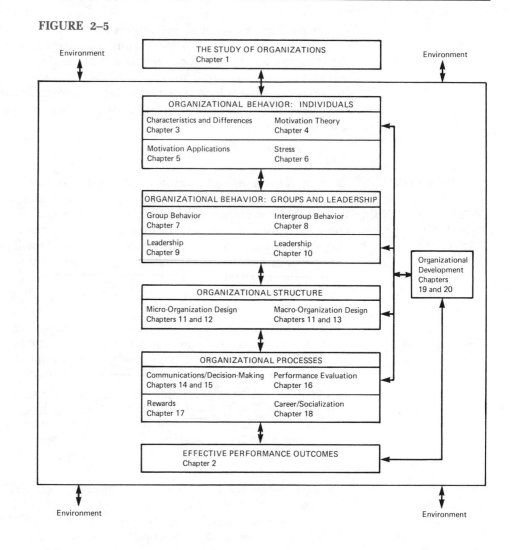

derstand it. Managers must be concerned with motivation because they are concerned with performance.

Stress

An important outcome of the interaction between job performance and the individual is stress. Although the term is used quite freely in ordinary conversation, its precise scientific meaning and implications are not so well understood. Generally, <u>stress refers to a state of imbalance within an individual</u> which manifests itself in symptoms such as insomnia, excessive perspiration, nervousness, and irritability. Whether stress is positive or negative depends upon the individual's tolerance level. People will react differently to situations which outwardly induce the same physical and psychological demands. Some individuals will respond positively through increased states of motivation and commitment to finish the job. Other individuals will resort to less desirable coping responses—alcoholism and drug abuse being the more extreme ones. The role and responsibility of the organization in managing stress are not clearly defined, yet there is growing evidence that organizations are devising programs to counteract the negative effects of job and work-induced stress.

Group and Intergroup Variables

Groups form in organizations because of managerial action, but also because of individual efforts. Managers create work groups to carry out assigned jobs and tasks. These groups are created by managerial decision and they are termed *formal groups*. As these groups function and interact with other groups they develop characteristics, including structure, processes, norms, roles, and cohesiveness. In addition, they may cooperate or compete with other groups; the intergroup competition can lead to conflict.

Groups also form as a consequence of employees actions. Such groups, termed *informal groups*, develop around common interests and friendship. Even though not sanctioned by management these groups can affect organizational and individual performance. The affect can be positive or negative depending upon the intention of the group's members. Effective managers recognize the consequences of the individual's need for affiliation.

Leadership

Leaders exist within all organizations. They may be found in formal and informal groups, they may be managers or nonmanagers. The importance of effective leadership for obtaining organizational, group, and individual performance is so important as to have stimulated a great deal of effort to determine its causes. Theories and research have been advanced which suggest that effective leadership depends upon leaders' traits and behaviors—separately, and in combination. Some managers and researchers believe that one leadership style is effective in all situations; others believe that each situation requires a specific leadership style. The state of knowledge about leadership is still too tenative to permit firm conclusion about the validity of any one leadership theory.

Macro-Organizational Design

An important determinant of effective performance at all levels is the macro-organization design, that is, the overall organization structure. The design of an organization involves the application of principles of division of labor, departmental bases, span of control, and delegation of authority. The result of applying these principles is a *structure* of tasks and authority relationships intended to channel the behavior of individuals and groups toward high levels of performance.

Micro-Organizational Design

Micro-organizational design refers to the process by which managers specify the contents, methods, and relationships of jobs to satisfy organizational as well as individual requirements. This managerial concern has perhaps the longest history since the earliest attempts to develop systematic ways to design jobs can be traced to the scientific management era.

Those early efforts relied almost exclusively on engineering and physiological studies and resulted in jobs which met organizational demands to the exclusion of individual requirements. More recent theory and practice of job design emphasize the necessity to achieve a balance.

Communication Process

Organizational survival is related to the ability of management to receive, transmit, and act on information. Communication processes link the organization to its environment as well as to its constituent parts. Information flows across the boundaries of the organization from the environment. It flows within the organization from individual to individual, from group to group. Thus information serves to integrate the activities of the organization and the demands of the environment, but it also integrates the internal activities of the organization.

Decision-Making Process

The quality of decision making depends upon selecting proper goals and dentifying appropriate means for achieving them. Through optimal integration of *behavioral* and *structural* factors, management can increase the probability that high-quality decisions are made. For example the proper placement of individuals in compatible jobs involves matching the motivations and abilities of the individual with the skill requirements of the job. If properly matched, the decisions of the jobholder should result in proper goal selection. Organizations rely upon group decisions as well as individual decisions. Executive committees, steering committees, and task forces are only a few of the kinds of groups which managers form to make decisions. Effective management requires knowledge about the process of group decision making.

Performance-Evaluation Process

Managers must evaluate the performance of individuals and groups within their organizations. Figure 2–5 indicates that individual, group, and organization performance are the outcomes, or dependent variables, of organizational behavior, structure, and processes. The system which management installs to evaluate performance serves many purposes, including reward decisions (pay, promotion, transfer), identification of training needs, and provision of feedback to employees. Many different methods exist to evaluate performance and the challenge to management is to select the appropriate one.

Reward Process

One of the most powerful processes influencing individual performance is the organization's reward system. Not only can management use rewards to increase performance of its present employees, it can also use rewards to attract skilled employees to join the organization. Monetary rewards are important aspects of the reward system, but not the only aspect. Performance of the work itself can provide employees with *intrinsic* satisfaction particularly if performance of the job leads to a sense of personal responsibility, autonomy, and meaningfulness. To the extent that managers can design work to include these potentialities, the reward system is considerably more powerful than one which relies exclusively on *extrinsic* rewards.

Career and Socialization Process

Individuals enter organizations to work and pursue their personal **career** goals. Organizations employ individuals to perform certain tasks which comprise the jobs of the organizational structure. Thus the <u>individual and organizational interests and goals must be brought into congruence if both are to be effective.</u> Individuals move through time and jobs along career paths that are more or less prescribed by the organization. The extent to which the individual is successful in the career depends, in part at least, on the extent to which he or she adapts to the organization's demands. The process by which the individual is made aware of the organization's expectations is termed *socialization*. The process of socialization may be formal, as in the case of orientation programs for new employees, or informal, as when the manager and the individual's peers provide relevant information about the organization's expectations. The two activities, career development and organizational socialization, are interrelated and the performance of both the organization and the individual is affected by them.

Performance Outcomes: Individual, Group, and Organizational

Performance is the bottom-line consideration, and, as we have noted throughout the discussion it consists of three levels of analysis: individual, group, and organizational. <u>No one measure, or criterion, adequately reflects performance at any level. Systems theory conclusions caution against the use of a single criterion.</u> Rather managers are encouraged to consider multiple measures within a time framework. From the manager's perspective, ineffective performances at any level is a signal to take corrective action. The focus of corrective action are elements of organizational behavior, structure, and processes.

Organizational Change and Development

Concerted, planned, and evaluated efforts to improve performance have great potential for success. <u>The requirements for success include accurate diagnosis of the causes of poor performance.</u> Management often will engage the services of an outside consultant to facilitate the change and development program. The diagnostic efforts will trace the causes of performance problems to structural or behavioral causes. If the diagnosis is accurate and if the method is correctly implemented, the target of the program (individuals and groups) should change toward more effective performance.

SUMMARY

■ Concepts of organizational effectiveness and managerial process have been developed in this chapter. The concepts depicted in Figure 2–5 emphasize the need for balanced perspectives, yet they allow for the identification of differences from manager to manager and from organization to organization. An overriding consideration that is documented in many studies of managerial work is that the managerial process is inherently a human process—people relating to people. The recognition of this fact establishes the importance of understanding human behavior in the workplace. The behavior of individuals and groups is principally important for achieving effective organizational performance, but there is also the behavior of managers themselves to be understood.

This chapter also provides the basis for evaluating managerial practice. Managerial techniques are all directed toward improving effectiveness. But to understand the impact of these techniques, one must evaluate the effectiveness criteria used to judge those techniques. Some techniques affect the short-run criteria of production, satisfaction, and efficiency; others affect the longer-run criteria of adaptiveness and development. Furthermore, as the impact of a managerial technique becomes more distant in the future, the measures of its effectiveness become more subjective, general, and qualitative.

DISCUSSION AND REVIEW QUESTIONS

1. Can the evaluation of the effectiveness of an organization ever be made in absolute terms? Or is it always necessary to state effectiveness criteria in relative terms? Explain and give examples to support your argument.

2. Is the distinction between short-run, intermediate, and long-run criteria meaningful for evaluating the effectiveness of a college course? Explain.

3. "An organization is effective if its employees believe that it is." Discuss.

4. If you were a training director responsible for instructing first-line supervisors in the techniques of supervision, how would you evaluate the effectiveness of your training program?

5. "Effectiveness criteria are relevant only in terms of the evaluator. For example, the state legislators look for some things, the federal people look for other things. I give each group whatever it wants." Comment on this statement which was made by the administrator of a state governmental agency.

6. Explain why effectiveness criteria of subunits tend to emphasize the short run rather than the long run.

7. How would you evaluate the effectiveness of contemporary American society in terms of production, efficiency, satisfaction, adaptiveness, and development? Rate each criterion on a five-point scale and compare your evaluation with that of other classmates.

8. One writer on management theory states that management is aptly defined as "getting work done through out people." Compare this concept of management with the one proposed in this chapter.

9. Describe the process by which society makes known its expectations for the missions of universities. Based upon your knowledge of the university or college you attend, how satisfactorily is it achieving its mission?

10. A public official with a talent for simplifying matters stated: "Planning is concerned with doing the right things, organizing is concerned with doing things right." Comment.

11. Can an organization go out of business even if its management is proficient in the performance of the managerial process?

12. Explain the important differences between managing an investment fund and managing an organization.

ADDITIONAL REFERENCES

Angle, H. L., and J. L. Perry. "An Empirical Assessment of Organizational Commitment and Organizational Effectiveness." *Administrative Science Quarterly*, 1981, pp. 1–14.

Barnard, C. I. *The Functions of the Executive.* Cambridge, Mass.: Harvard University Press, 1938.

Cameron, K. S. "Dimensions of Organizational Effectiveness in College and Universities." *Academy of Management Journal,* 1981, pp. 25–47.

Coulter, P. B. "Organizational Effectiveness in the Public Sector: The Example of Municipal Fire Protection." *Administrative Science Quarterly,* 1979, pp. 65–81.

Deniston, O. L., and I. M. Rosenstock. "Evaluating Health Programs." *Public Health Reports,* 1970, pp. 835–40.

Drucker, P. *Management: Tasks, Responsibilities, Practices.* New York: Harper & Row, 1974.

England, G. W.; O. P. Dhingra; and N. C. Agarwal. *The Manager and the Man: A Cross-Cultural Study of Personal Values.* Kent, Ohio: Kent State University Press, 1974.

Flanagan, J. C. "Defining the Requirements of the Executive's Job." *Personnel,* 1951, pp. 28–35.

Georgopoulos, B. S., and F. C. Mann. *The Community General Hospital.* New York: Macmillan, 1967.

Greenburg, L. *A Practical Guide to Productivity Management.* Washington, D.C.: The Bureau of National Affairs, 1973.

Grusky, O. "Managerial Succession and Organizational Effectiveness." *American Journal of Sociology,* 1963, pp. 21–30.

Hemphill, J. K. "Job Descriptions for Executives." *Harvard Business Review,* 1959, pp. 55–67.

Jones, H. R. "A Study of Organizational Performance for Experimental Structures of Two, Three, and Four Levels." *Academy of Management Journal,* 1969, pp. 351–66.

Katz, D., and R. L. Kahn. *The Social Psychology of Organizations.* New York: John Wiley & Sons, 1966.

Kay, B. R. "Key Factors in Effective Foreman Behavior." *Personnel,* 1959, pp. 25–31.

Kay, E., and H. H. Meyer. "The Development of a Job Activity Questionnaire for Production Foremen." *Personnel Psychology,* 1962, pp. 411–18.

Koontz, H. *Toward a Unified Theory of Management.* New York: McGraw-Hill, 1964.

McGregor, D. *The Human Side of Enterprise.* New York: McGraw-Hill, 1960.

McGuire, J. W., ed. *Contemporary Management: Issues and Viewpoints.* Englewood Cliffs, N.J.: Prentice-Hall, 1974.

Mahoney, T. A. "Managerial Perceptions of Organizational Effectiveness." *Management Science,* 1967, pp. 76–91.

———, and W. Weitzel. "Managerial Models of Organizational Effectiveness." *Administrative Science Quarterly,* 1969, pp. 357–65.

Miner, J. B. *Management Theory.* New York: Macmillan, 1971.

Neuhauser, D. *The Relationship between Administrative Activities and Hospital Performance.* Chicago: Center for Health Administrative Studies, University of Chicago 1971.

O'Neil, H. E., and A. J. Kubany. "Observation Methodology and Supervisory Behavior." *Personnel Psychology,* 1959, pp. 85–96.

Ponder, Q. "Supervisory Practices of Effective and Ineffective Foremen." Ph.D. dissertation, Columbia University, 1958.

Price, J. L. "The Study of Organizational Effectiveness." *The Sociological Quarterly,* 1972, pp. 3–15.

Rice, A. K. *The Enterprise and Its Environment: A System Theory of Management Organization.* London: Tavistock Publications, 1963.

Snow, C. C., and L. G. Hrebiniak. "Strategy, Distinctive Competence, and Organizational Performance." *Administrative Science Quarterly,* 1980, pp. 317–36.

Urwick, L. F. *The Pattern of Management.* Minneapolis: University of Minnesota Press, 1956.

Weaver, J. L. *Conflict and Control in Health-Care Administration.* Beverly Hills, Calif.: Sage Publications, 1975.

Webb, R. J. "Organizational Effectiveness and the Voluntary Organization." *Academy of Management Journal,* 1974, pp. 663–77.

Yuchtman, E., and S. E. Seashore. "A Systems Resource Approach to Organizational Effectiveness." *American Sociological Review,* 1967, pp. 891–903.

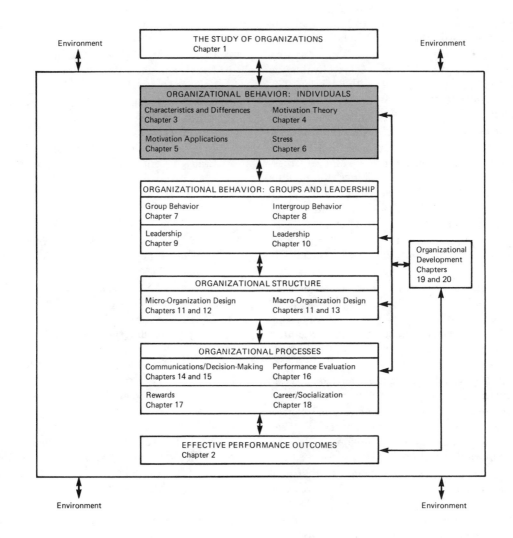

Part Two

BEHAVIOR WITHIN ORGANIZATIONS: THE INDIVIDUAL

Chapter 3

Individual Behavior and Differences

AN ORGANIZATIONAL ISSUE FOR DEBATE
Individual Personality Theories

ARGUMENT FOR

During the first half of the 20 century, theories of personality were almost exclusively concerned with individual differences. The theories also share some common assumptions. The most common of these was that personality is basically a characteristic of the individual human being.

Each individual personality theory attempted to describe people with terms that convey a particular perspective on human behavior. Virtually all the descriptive terms that these theories use refer to the individual alone and rarely to environmental events (e.g., the work group, the organizational structure, the reward system) around the individual. The person being described was complex, internally driven, but isolated from the environment. Terms such as traits, needs, cognitions, motives, and self-perception explain the internal mechanisms of the person.

All individual personality theorists proposed that there are individual differences in personalities. Further, these are not just transient differences but enduring ones. They are consistent over time and across situations. A person who respects and obeys his or her father would probably continue to do so in any situation, and would probably display the same attitude toward other father-like figures. That is, the person would submit to the wishes or orders of authority figures.

Individual differences is the term used by the-

ARGUMENT AGAINST

The individual personality theories are assumed to be too narrow by people like B. F. Skinner. His approach and other similar ones differ significantly, but they share a common set of assumptions that are contrary to individual personality assumptions. The more recently developed social personality theories assume (1) that the major influences on human behavior come from the environment, and therefore, (2) that situational rather than individual differences should be the primary focus of attention.

Skinner and others consider the individual to be open to his or her environment and significantly influenced by it. The major vocabulary used in these more environmental oriented theories include terms like stimulus, interaction, reinforcement, imitation. Terms which describe the individual as having drive, cognition, and needs are used by some of the environmental or social personality theorists. Some refer to the work of Skinner and others as social theories of personality because of the importance of social interactions in an individual's environment. The main theme then of the social personality theories will focus either "outside" the individual or on the individual-in-relation-to-the social environment and only rarely on properties exclusively "inside" the individual.

Some claim that with an emphasis on the en-

ARGUMENT FOR (continued)

orists and researchers to refer to three related as- sumptions about people: (1) individuals do differ from one another in significant ways; (2) that any particular individual's difference from others is true in many situations; and (3) that each individ- ual maintains this characteristic difference over a considerable period of time.

These assumptions are behind all personality tests. The aim of personality measurement is to identify the significant, relatively permanent characteristics of individuals. The test may be ob- jective, subjective, projective, or observational. The purpose of measurement is to find the impor- tant individual differences. We have to first un- derstand the individual before addressing issues such as how the individual interacts with the en- vironment.

ARGUMENT AGAINST (continued)

vironment and situational differences instead of on individual differences, that reinforcement the- ory and social learning theory are not personality theories. Surely personality is more a property of a person and not of say a work environment. Where is the person in these more social-domi- nated theories? The person is where he or she should be is the true answer. The person is inter- acting with the "real world" and not operating in isolation in some kind of "vacuum tube" insu- lated from events, other people, and situations.

Any attempt to learn why people behave as they do in organizations requires some understanding about individual characteristics and behavior. Managers planning and organizing work, or controlling and directing individuals must spend time making judgments about the fit between individuals, job tasks, and effectiveness. These judgments typically are influenced by the manager's, as well as the subordinate's characteristics. Making decisions about who will perform what tasks in a particular manner without some understanding of behavior can lead to irreversible long-run problems.

This chapter focuses on four major individual characteristics that influence organizational effectiveness. These are perception, attitudes, personality, and learning. Each of these factors influences the behavioral patterns of managers and their subordinates. Managers as well as subordinates perceive people and objects, form attitudes about others or the organization, have a personality structure, and learn while working. Thus, effective management includes understanding these four major individual characteristics as well as being familiar with their relationship.

A FRAMEWORK FOR ANALYZING INDIVIDUAL DIFFERENCES

■ The ability to deal with and cope effectively with individuals in work organizations requires a framework for understanding behavior. A framework provides a basis for considering why individuals behave as they do. No framework can provide perfect answers and predictions. However, a systematic and logical framework can initiate thinking about what to look for when attempting to understand performance differences among individual employees.

The analysis of individual behavior requires a consideration of the types of variables shown in Figure 3–1. An examination of Figure 3–1 suggests that people enter organizations with these variables in various stages of development. Many behavior patterns of people have been developed before they join an organization. Whether managers can modify, mold, or reconstruct behaviors is a much debated issue among behavioral scientists and practitioners. It is usually agreed that changing any of the psychological variables requires thorough diagnosis, implementation, evaluation, and modification. There is no universally agreed-upon method that can change personalities, attitudes, perceptions, or learning patterns. People are always changing, although slightly, their behavior patterns. It is the direction and kind of behavior change that managers want to influence.

Obviously human behavior is too complex to be explained by a generalization that applies to all people. Some of the relevant variables which influence human behavior are presented in Figure 3–1. Coverage of each of the variables presented in this figure is beyond the scope of the book. Most of our attention will be on the psychological variables because they form the foundation for our discussion of motivation, group behavior, and leadership.

FIGURE 3–1
Some Variables that Influence Behavior

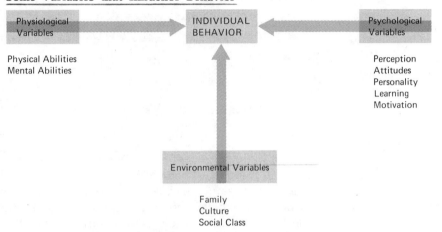

Physical Abilities
Mental Abilities

Perception
Attitudes
Personality
Learning
Motivation

Family
Culture
Social Class

**INDIVIDUAL
DIFFERENCES**

■ Effective managerial practice requires that individual differences be recognized and when feasible taken into consideration when designing jobs, conducting performance evaluation interviews, or developing reward strategies to encourage improved performance. In addition to understanding individual differences, it is desirable to (1) measure the differences, (2) study relationships between variables, and (3) discover causal relationships.[1] Being able to predict behavior and performance is a goal of management in any type of organizational setting. However, prediction is possible without understanding. It is possible to predict accurately that an employee will resist the introduction of new equipment or a new performance evaluation program. These accurate predictions tell little about why the behavior occurred or how the behavior can be altered.

Some researchers believe that many issues concerning individual differences are not being addressed by managers. For example, one study of different groups performing different tasks found the "typical" interpersonal relationships formed a pattern which was described as individuals tending to express their ideas in ways that supported the norm of conformity. There was almost no experimenting with ideas and feelings and also no trust observed in the groups. Individual differences in creativity, understanding, influence, and problem-solving ability tended to be smothered.[2] This finding underlines the relevance of studying individual differences to better understand how people interact within the work environment.

Some specific key factors which account for individual differences in

[1]C. Argyris, "Problems and New Directions for Industrial Psychology," in *Handbook of Industrial and Organizational Psychology*, ed. M. D. Dunnette, (Chicago: Rand McNally, 1976), p. 153.

[2]C. Argyris, "The Incompleteness of Social-Psychological Theory," *American Psychologist*, December 1964, pp. 893–908.

FIGURE 3–2
A Model of Behavior

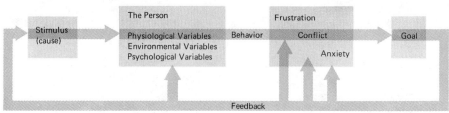

behavior include perception, attitudes, personality, and learning. Figure 3–2 presents a model of behavior which is assumed to be applicable in many respects to all employees, both managerial and nonmanagerial. The particular behavior which develops is certainly unique for each person, but the underlying process is basic to all people. The model makes four important assumptions about individual behavior:[3]

1. *Behavior* is caused.
2. *Behavior* is goal directed.
3. *Behavior* toward goals can be disrupted by frustration, conflict, and anxiety.
4. *Behavior* is motivated.

The model is offered as a starting point for understanding behavior. The important points to note are that (1) the behavior process is similar for all people, (2) actual behavior can differ because of physiological, environmental, and psychological variables, and such factors as frustration, conflict, and anxiety, and (3) many of the variables influencing behavior have been shaped before the person enters the work organization.

PERCEPTION

■ *Perception,* as depicted in Figure 3–3, is the process by which an individual gives meaning to the environment. Because each person gives meaning to stimuli, different individuals will "see" the same thing in different ways.[4] The way an employee sees the situation often has much greater meaning for understanding behavior than does the situation itself.

Since perception refers to the acquisition of specific knowledge about objects or events at any particular moment, it occurs whenever stimuli activate the senses. Perception also involves cognition (knowledge), thus, perception involves the interpretation of objects, symbols, and people in the light of pertinent experiences. In other words, perception involves re-

[3]Items 1, 2, and 4 are proposed by Harold J. Leavitt, *Managerial Psychology* (Chicago: University of Chicago Press, 1978), p. 10.

[4]W. R. Nord, ed., *Concepts and Controversy in Organizational Behavior* (Santa Monica, Calif.: Goodyear Publishing, 1976), p. 22.

FIGURE 3–3
The Perceptual Process

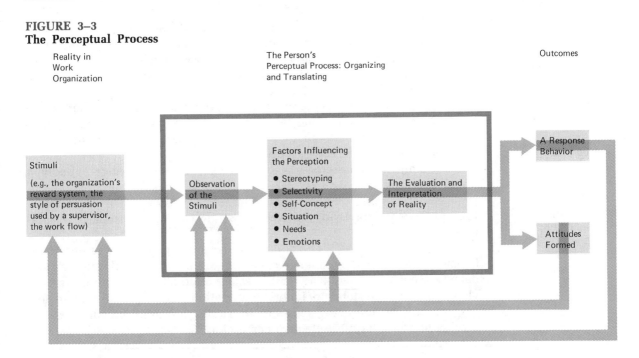

ceiving stimuli (inputs), organizing the stimuli, and translating or interpreting the organized stimuli in such a manner to influence behavior and
form attitudes.

Each person selects various cues that influence his or her perceptions of
people, objects, and symbols. Because of these factors and their potential
imbalance, people often misperceive another person, group, or object. To a
considerable extent, people interpret the behavior of others in the context
of the setting in which they find themselves.

Perceptual
Organization

An important aspect of what is perceived involves organization. One of
the most elemental organizing principles of perception is the tendency to
pattern stimuli in terms of *figure-ground* relationships. Not all stimuli
reach one's awareness with equal clarity. The factor focused on is called
the *figure*. That which is experienced and is out of focus is called the
ground. As you read this text your perceptions are organized in terms of
figure and ground. The printed words are the figure and the white spaces
are the ground. In every perceptual act the figure-ground principle is operating. The mountains stand out against the sky and the dangerous working area stands out in a particular work laboratory.[5]

The organizing nature of perception is also apparent when similar stimuli are grouped together and stimuli in close proximity are grouped. Another grouping principle that shapes perceptual organization is called *clo-*

_____
[5] B. V. H. Gilmer, *Applied Psychology* (New York: McGraw-Hill, 1975), p. 229.

sure. This refers to the tendency to want to close something with missing parts. There is a strong need in some individuals to complete a configuration, a job, or a project. For example, if a person with a high need for closure is prevented from finishing a job or task, this could lead to frustration or a more drastic behavior such as quitting.

Stereotyping. The manner in which managers categorize others often is a reflection of a perceptual bias. The term *stereotype* has been used to describe judgments made about people on the basis of their ethnic group membership. Other stereotypes are also common.

For example, men stereotype women executives, managers stereotype union stewards, and women stereotype aggressive men. Most people engage in stereotyping. Stereotyping of employees can result in implementing improper programs for motivation, job design, or performance evaluation.

Selective Perception. The concept of selective perception is important to managers since they often receive large amounts of information and data. Consequently, they may tend to select information that supports their viewpoints. People tend to ignore information that may make them feel discomfort. The following close-up illustrates how individuals use self-serving bias as a form of selective perception.

ORGANIZATIONS: CLOSE-UP

The Better-than-Average Epidemic

John is a better-than-average salesperson; Donna is a better-than-average Certified Public Accountant; Monty is a better-than-average data processor. Believing ourselves better than "average" is a human tendency. Many experiments disclose a self-serving bias in the way we perceive events. Individuals explain positive behavior in terms of personal traits ("I helped Joe finish the job because I am a considerate person"). On the other hand individuals attribute negative behavior in terms of external forces "I didn't help Joe because my boss made me do another job"). This self-serving bias enables a person to take credit for good behavior and find scapegoats for bad behavior.

Such self-serving bias can cause trouble in organizations by leading employees to expect greater-than-average rewards (e.g., pay) when their organizations do well. If most employees believe they are underpaid and underappreciated, disharmony, poor performance, and even quitting are strong possibilities.

The self-serving bias even spills over into international conflict. Irving Janis noted that one source of international conflict is the tendency of each side to believe in the moral correctness of its acts. Americans say that the United States builds missile bases near the Russian border in Turkey to protect the free world from communism, while the Soviet Union puts missiles in Cuba to threaten our security. The Soviets see the motivation behind building the bases as exactly the opposite.

Source: David G. Myers and Jack Ridl, "Can We All Be Better than Average?" *Psychology Today*, August 1979, pp. 89–90, 96, 98.

The Manager's Characteristics. People tend to use themselves as benchmarks in perceiving others. Research suggests that (1) knowing oneself makes it easier to see others accurately,[6] (2) one's own characteristics affect the characteristics identified in others,[7] and (3) persons who accept themselves are more likely to see favorable aspects of other people.[8]

Basically, these conclusions suggest that managers perceiving the behavior and individual differences of employees are influenced by their own traits. If they understand that their own traits and values influence perception they can probably perform a more accurate evaluation of their subordinates.

The Situational Factor

The press of time, the attitudes of people a manager is working with, and other situational factors influence perceptual accuracy. If a manager believes that certain people in a group are different because of their particular skin color or speech habits, these differences can be magnified and also perceived in other areas. Such perceived differences are likely to lead to inaccurate perceptions of employee performance, loyalty, and commitment. The manager is searching for differences because of a predisposition to believe that they exist.

Needs and Perceptions

Perceptions are significantly influenced by needs and desires. In other words, the employee, the manager, the vice president, the director see what they want to see. Like the mirrors in the fun house at the amusement park, the world can be distorted; the distortion is related to needs and desires.

The influence of needs in shaping perceptions has been studied in laboratory settings. Subjects at various stages of hunger were asked to report what they saw in ambiguous drawings flashed before them. It was found that as hunger increased up to a certain point, the subjects saw more and more of the ambiguous figures as articles of food. The hungry subjects saw steaks, salads, and sandwiches, while the subjects who had recently eaten saw nonfood images in the same figures.

Emotions and Perceptions

A person's emotional state has a lot to do with perceptions. A strong emotion, such as total distaste for an organizational rule, can make a person perceive negative characteristics in most company policies and rules. Determining a person's emotional state is difficult. Yet, managers need to be concerned about what issues or practices trigger strong emotions within subordinates. Strong emotions often distort perceptions.

---

[6] R. D. Norman, "The Interrelationships among Acceptance-Rejection, Self-Other Identity, Insight into Self, and Realistic Perception of Others," *Journal of Social Psychology*, 1953, pp. 205–35.

[7] J. Bossom and A. H. Maslow, "Security of Judges as a Factor in Impressions of Warmth in Others," *Journal of Abnormal and Social Psychology*, 1959, pp. 147–48.

[8] K. T. Omivake, "The Relation between Acceptance of Self and Acceptance of Others Shown by Three Personality Inventories," *Journal of Consulting Psychology*, 1954, pp. 443–46.

ATTITUDES

■ Attitudes are determinants of behavior, since they are linked with perception, personality, learning, and motivation. An *attitude* is a mental state of readiness, organized through experience, exerting a specific influence upon a person's response to people, objects, and situations with which it is related.

This definition of attitude has certain implications for the manager. First, attitudes define one's predispositions toward given aspects of the world. Second, attitudes provide the emotional basis of one's interpersonal relations and identification with others. Third, attitudes are organized and are close to the core of personality. Some attitudes are persistent and enduring. Yet like each of the psychological variables, attitudes are subject to change.

Attitudes: Affect, Cognition, and Behavior

Attitudes are intrinsic parts of a person's personality. However, a number of theories attempt to account for the formation and change of attitudes. One such theory proposes that people "seek a congruence between their beliefs and feelings toward objects," and suggests that the modification of attitudes depends on changing either the feelings or beliefs.[9] It further assumes that people have structured attitudes that are composed of various affective and cognitive components. The interrelatedness of these components means that a change in one will set in motion a change in the other. When these components are inconsistent or exceed the person's "tolerance level," instability results. Rosenberg, the developer of the theory, believes that instability can be corrected by either (1) disavowal of a message which is designed to influence attitudes, (2) "fragmentation" of the attitudes, or (3) acceptance of the inconsistency so that a new attitude is formed.

Rosenberg's theory proposes that affect, cognition, and behavior determine attitudes, and attitudes, in turn, determine affect, cognition, and behavior. *Affect,* the emotional, or "feeling," component of an attitude, is learned from parents, teachers, and peer group members. One study displays how the affective component variable can be measured. A questionnaire was used to survey the attitudes of a group of students toward the church. The students then listened to tape recordings that either praised or disparaged the church. At the time of the tape recordings the emotional responses of the students were measured physiologically with a galvanic skin response (GSR) device. Both prochurch and antichurch students responded with greater emotion (displayed by GSR changes) to statements that contradicted their attitudes than to those that reflected their attitudes.[10]

The *cognitive* portion of an attitude consists of the person's perceptions, opinions, and beliefs. It refers to the thought processes, with special em-

---

[9]M. J. Rosenberg, "A Structural Theory of Attitudes," *Public Opinion Quarterly*, Summer 1960, pp. 319–40.

[10]H. W. Dickson and E. McGinnies, "Affectivity and Arousal of Attitudes as Measured by Galvanic Skin Responses," *American Journal of Psychology*, October 1966, pp. 584–89.

FIGURE 3–4
The Three Components of Attitude: Affect, Cognition, and Behavior

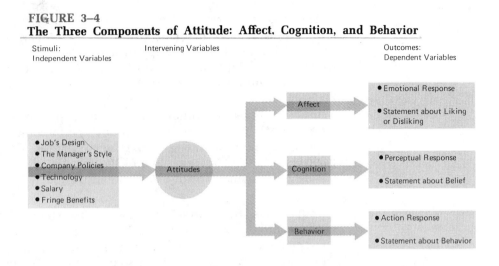

phasis on rationality and logic. An important element of cognition is the evaluative beliefs held by a person. Evaluative beliefs are manifested in the form of favorable or unfavorable impressions a person holds toward an object or person.

The *behavioral* component of an attitude refers to the tendency of a person to act toward something in a certain way, the action component of attitudes. The way a person acts toward someone or something can be friendly, warm, aggressive, hostile, apathetic, or any of a number of different ways. These actions could be measured or assessed to examine the behavioral component of attitudes.

Figure 3–4 presents the three components of attitude in an organizational perspective. Attitudes are linked to organizational stimuli and individual responses in this framework.

The Rosenberg theory of affective, cognitive, and behavioral components as determinants of attitudes and attitude change has significant implications for managers. The manager has to be able to demonstrate that the positive aspects of contributing to the organization outweigh the negative aspects. It is through attempts to develop generally favorable attitudes toward the organization and the job that many managers achieve effectiveness.

Attitude Formation

There are many sources of attitude formation. Attitudes are formed from family, peer groups, society, and previous job experiences. The early *family* experiences help shape the attitudes of individuals. The attitudes of young children usually correspond to those of their parents. As children reach their teen years, they begin to be more strongly influenced by *peers*. Peer groups are able to influence attitudes because individuals want to be accepted by others. Teenagers seek approval by sharing similar attitudes or by modifying attitudes to comply with those of a group.

The culture, mores, and language of a society influence attitudes. The attitudes of French Canadians toward France, Americans toward the Iranians, and Russians toward capitalism are learned in society. Within the United States there are subcultures in the form of ethnic communities, ghetto communities, and religious groups that help shape attitudes of people.

Individuals learn attitudes through job experiences. They develop attitudes about such factors as pay equity, performance review, managerial capabilities, job design, and work group affiliation. Of course, previous experiences can account for some of the individual differences in attitudes toward performance, loyalty, and commitment.

Attitudes and Consistency

Individuals strive to maintain consistency among the components of attitudes—affect, cognition, and behavior. However, contradictions and inconsistency often occur. When this happens a state of disequilibrium occurs. The resultant tension from such a state is reduced only when some form of consistency is achieved.

The term, *cognitive dissonance*, describes a situation when there is a discrepancy between the cognitive and behavioral components of attitude.[11] Any form of inconsistency is uncomfortable, therefore individuals will attempt to reduce dissonance. *Dissonance* then is viewed as a state within a person that, when aroused, elicits actions designed to return the person to a state of equilibrium.

Cognitive dissonance has important organizational implications. First, it helps explain choices made by individuals when attitude inconsistency is present. For example, if the elements underlying the dissonance are of little importance, the person will not be under pressure to reduce the dissonance.

Second, cognitive dissonance theory can help predict the propensity a person has to change attitudes. If individuals are required, for example, by the design of their jobs or occupation, to say or do things that contradict their personal attitudes, they will tend to change these attitudes to make them more compatible with what they have said or done.

Changing Attitudes

Managers are often faced with the task of changing attitudes because previously structured attitudes hinder the job performance of individuals. Although many variables affect attitude change, they can all be described in terms of two general factors—trust in the sender and the message itself.[12] If employees do not trust the manager, they will not accept the message or change an attitude. Similarly, if the message is not convincing, there will be no pressure to change.

---

[11]Leon Festinger, *A Theory of Cognitive Dissonance* (Evanston, Ill.: Row-Peterson, 1957).

[12]Jonathan L. Freedman, J. Merrill Carlsmith, and David O. Sears, *Social Psychology* (Englewood Cliffs, N.J.: Prentice-Hall, 1974), p. 271. Also see D. Coon, *Introduction to Psychology* (St. Paul, Minn.: West Publishing, 1977), p. 626–29.

The greater the prestige of the communicator, the more attitude change is produced.[13] A manager who has little prestige and is not shown respect by peers and superiors will be in a difficult position if the job requires changing the attitudes of subordinates in order to get them to work more effectively.

Liking the communicator produces attitude change because people try to identify with a liked communicator, and tend to adopt attitudes and behaviors of the liked person.[14] Not all managers, however, are fortunate to be liked by all of their subordinates. Therefore, it is important to recognize the concept of liking but to consider the issues of trust and strength of the message as being more controllable variables.

Even if a manager is trusted, presents a convincing message, and is liked, the problems of changing people's attitudes are not solved. An important factor is the strength of commitment to an attitude by the employee. A worker who has decided not to accept a promotion is more committed to the belief that it is best to remain in his or her present position than to accept a promotion. Attitudes that have been publicly expressed are more difficult to change because the person has shown commitment, and to change would be to admit a mistake.

Attitudes and Values

Values are linked to attitudes in the sense that a value serves as a way of organizing a number of attitudes. *Values* are defined "as the constellation of likes, dislikes, viewpoints, shoulds, inner inclinations, rational and irrational judgments, prejudices, and association patterns that determine a person's view of the world."[15]

Certainly the work that one does is an important aspect of one's world. Moreover the importance of a value constellation is that once internalized it becomes, consciously or subconsciously, a standard or criterion for guiding one's actions. Thus, the study of values is fundamental to the study of managing. Some evidence exists that values are also extremely important for understanding effective managerial behavior.[16]

Values will affect not only the perceptions of appropriate ends, but also the perceptions of appropriate means to those ends. From the design and development of organization structures and processes, to the utilization of

---

[13] Ibid., p. 272.

[14] H. C. Kelman, "Process of Opinion Change," *Public Opinion Quarterly*, Spring 1961, pp. 57–78.

[15] Edward Spranger, *Types of Men* (Halle, Germany: Max Niemeyer Verlag, 1928) as quoted in Vincent S. Flowers et. al., *Managerial Values for Working* (New York: American Management Association, 1975), p. 11.

[16] Flowers et al., *Managerial Values*, undertook a questionnaire study of members of the American Management Association. Questionnaires were mailed to 4,998 members and the researchers were able to use 1,707 replies. Based upon these results and other studies, these researchers state that the impact of values on managerial and nonmanagerial behavior is sufficiently important to account for some variation in the relative effectiveness of managers. Also see Andrew F. Sikula, "Values, Value Systems, and Their Relationship to Organizational Effectiveness," *Proceedings of the Thirty-First Annual Meeting of the Academy of Management*, 1971, pp. 271–72.

particular leadership styles and the evaluation of subordinate performance, value systems will be pervasive. An influential theory of leadership is based upon the argument that managers cannot be expected to adopt a particular leadership style if it is contrary to their "need-structures," or value orientations.[17] Moreover, when managers evaluate the performance of subordinates, the effects of their values will be noticeable. For example, one researcher reports that managers can be expected to evaluate the performance of subordinates with similar values as more effective than those with values dissimilar from their own.[18] The impact of values will be more pronounced in those decisions involving little objective information and, consequently, a greater degree of subjectivity.

Another aspect of the importance of values occurs when the interpersonal activities of managers bring them into a confrontation with different, and potentially contradictory, values. Studies have shown that assembly-line workers, scientists, and various professional occupations are characterized by particular, if not unique, value orientations.[19] Day-to-day activities will create numerous situations in which managers must relate to others having different views of what is right and wrong. Conflicts between managers and workers, administrators and teachers, line and staff personnel have been documented and discussed in the literature of management. The manner in which these conflicts are resolved is particularly crucial to the effectiveness of the organization.[20]

PERSONALITY

■ The relationship between behavior and personality is perhaps one of the most complex matters managers have to understand. Personality is significantly influenced by cultural and social factors. Regardless of how personality is defined, certain principles are generally accepted among psychologists. These are:

1. Personality is an organized whole, otherwise the individual would have no meaning.
2. Personality appears to be organized into patterns, These are to some degree observable and measurable.

---

[17] Fred E. Fiedler, *A Theory of Leadership Effectiveness* (New York: McGraw-Hill, 1967).

[18] John Senger, "Managers' Perceptions of Subordinates' Competence as a Function of Personal Value Orientations," *Academy of Management Journal*, December 1971, pp. 415–24.

[19] For example, see Flowers et al., *Managerial Values*, and also Renato Tagiuri, "Value Orientations and Relationships of Managers and Scientists," *Administrative Science Quarterly*, June 1965, pp. 39–51.

[20] In recent years the increasing tendency of American firms to use foreign nationals to manage overseas offices has created a concern for understanding the impact of culture on managers' values. See William T. Whitely and George W. England, "A Comparison of Value Systems of Managers in the U.S.A., Japan, Korea, India, and Australia," *Proceedings of the Thirty-Fourth Annual Meeting of the Academy of Management*, 1974, p. 11; and Richard B. Peterson, "A Cross-Cultural Perspective of Supervisory Values," *Academy of Management Journal*, March 1972, pp. 105–17.

3. Although there is a biological basis to personality the specific development is a product of social and cultural environments.
4. Personality has superficial aspects, such as attitudes toward being a team leader, and a deeper core, such as sentiments about authority or the Protestant work ethic.
5. Personality involves both common and unique characteristics. Every person is different from every other person in some respects, while being similar in other respects.

These five ideas are included in the following definition of personality.

> An individual's personality is a relatively stable set of characteristics, tendencies, and temperaments that have been significantly formed by inheritance and by social, cultural, and environmental factors. This set of variables determines the commonalities and differences in the behavior of the individual.[21]

A review of each determinant that shapes personality (Figure 3–5) should indicate that the manager has little control over these forces. This should not lead the manager to conclude that personality is not an important factor in workplace behavior because it is formed outside the organization. The behavioral responses of an employee simply cannot be thoroughly understood without considering the concept of personality. In fact, personality is so interrelated with perception, attitudes, learning, and mo-

FIGURE 3–5
Some Major Forces Influencing Personality

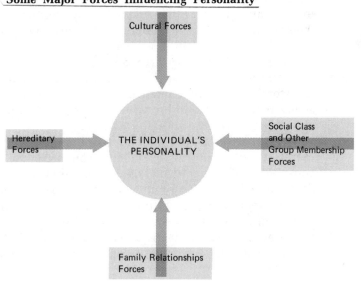

---

[21]This definition is based upon Salvatore R. Maddi, *Personality Theories: A Comparative Analysis* (Homewood, Ill.: Dorsey Press, 1980), p. 41.

tivation that any analysis of behavior or attempt to predict behavior is grossly incomplete unless it is considered.

**Theories of
Personality**

The many theoretical approaches to understanding personality can be classified as: trait, psychodynamic, or humanistic.

Trait Approach.   Just as the young child seems to be always searching for labels by which to classify the world, adults also label and classify people by their psychological or physical characteristics. Classification helps to organize diversity and reduce the many to a few.

Gordon Allport was the most influential of the trait theorists. In his view, traits are the building blocks of personality, the guideposts for action, the source of uniqueness of the individual. *Traits* are defined as inferred predispositions that direct the behavior of an individual in consistent and characteristic ways. Furthermore, traits produce consistencies in behavior because they are enduring attributes and they are general or broad in scope.[22]

Trait theories have been criticized as not being real theories in that they do not explain how behavior is causally determined. The mere identification of traits like tough-minded, conservative, expedient, reserved, or outgoing doesn't offer insight into the development and dynamics of personality. Furthermore, trait approaches have not been successful in predicting behavior across a spectrum of situations. This is due to the fact that situations (the job, the work activities) are largely ignored in trait theories.

Psychodynamic Theories.   The dynamic nature of personality was not seriously addressed until Freud's work was published. Freud accounted for individual differences in personality by suggesting that people deal with their fundamental drives differently. To highlight these differences, he pictured a continuing battle between two parts of personality, the id and the superego, moderated by the ego.[23]

The *id* is conceived as the primitive, unconscious part of the personality, the storehouse of fundamental drives. It operates irrationally and impulsively without considering whether what is desired is possible or morally acceptable.

The *superego* is the storehouse of an individual's values, including moral attitudes shaped by society. The superego corresponds roughly to conscience. The superego is often in conflict withd the id. The id wants to do what feels good, while the superego insists on doing what is "right."

The *ego* is like the arbitrator of the conflict. It represents the person's picture of physical and social reality, of what will lead to what and which things are possible in the perceived world. Part of the ego's job is to choose actions that will gratify id impulses without having undesirable consequences.

---

[22]G. W. Allport, "Traits Revisited," *American Psychologist*, January 1966, pp. 1–10.

[23]Sigmund Freud, "Psychopathology of Everyday Life," in *The Standard Edition of the Complete Psychological Works of Sigmund Freud*, ed. J. Strackey (London: Hogarth Press, 1960).

TABLE 3–1
Some Ego Defense Mechanisms

Mechanism	*How It Is Applied in an Organization*
Rationalization	Attempting to justify one's behavior as being rational and justifiable. (I had to violate company policies to get the job finished.)
Identification	Increasing feelings of worth by identifying self with person or institution of illustrious standing. (I am working for Jim, who is really the best manager in the country.)
Compensation	Covering up weakness by emphasizing desirable traits or making up for frustration in one area by overgratification in another. (I may be a harsh rater but I play no favorites.)
Denial of reality	Protecting self from unpleasant reality by refusing to perceive it. (There is no chance that because of the economy, this company will have to let people go.)

Often the ego has to compromise and try to partially satisfy the id and the superego. Sometimes the compromise involves using ego defense mechanisms. These are mental processes that attempt to resolve conflicts among psychological states and external realities. Table 3–1 presents some of the ego defense mechanisms that are used by individuals.

Even Freud's critics admit that he made contributions to the modern understanding of behavior. His emphasis on unconscious determinants of behavior is important. Furthermore, the significance he attributed to early life origins of adult behavior gave impetus to the study of child development. In addition, his method of the treatment of neurosis through psychoanalysis has added to our understanding of how to get people back on the right track toward effective personal functioning.[24]

Humanistic Theories. Humanistic approaches to understanding are characterized by an emphasis on growth and self-actualization of the individual. These theories emphasize the importance of how people perceive their world and all of the forces influencing them.

Carl Rogers's approach is humanistic or people-centered.[25] His advice is to listen to what people say about themselves. Attend to these views and to their significance in the person's experiences. Rogers believes that the

---

[24] Philip G. Zimbardo, *Psychology and Life* (Glenview, Ill.: Scott, Foresman, 1979), p. 484.

[25] Carl Rogers, *On Personal Power: Inner Strength and Its Revolutionary Impact* (New York: Delacorte, 1977).

most basic drive of the human organism is toward *self-actualization*—the constant striving to realize inherent potential. The self-actualizing person is problem-centered, democratic, highly creative, capable of deep, satisfying interpersonal relations, and can readily accept others for what they are.

It is difficult to criticize theories that are so people-centered. However, some complain that the humanists never clearly explain the origin of mechanisms for attaining self-actualization. Others indicate that people must operate in an environment that is largely ignored by the humanists. An overemphasis on self neglects the reality that an individual must function in a complex environment.

It might help to think how each of the major theories improves our understanding of personality. Trait theories provide a catalog which *describes* the individual. Psychodynamic theories integrate the characteristics of people and *explain* the dynamic nature of personality development. The humanist theories emphasize the *person* and the importance of self-actualization to personality. Each theoretical approach attempts to highlight the unique qualities of an individual that influence his or her behavior patterns.

Assessing Personality

Although the term *personality* is used in a broad sense as indicated by the definition stated above, personality tests are instruments used to measure emotional, motivational, interpersonal, and attitudinal characteristics. There are hundreds of tests available to organizations. Especially numerous are the personality inventories and the projective techniques. One of the most widely used inventories is the Minnesota Multiphasic Personality Inventory (MMPI). It consists of affirmative statements, to which a person responds: "true," "false," or "cannot say." The MMPI items cover such areas as health, psychosomatic symptoms, neurological disorders and social attitudes, and many well-known neurotic or psychotic manifestations such as phobias, delusions, and sadistic trends.[26]

Projective techniques are also used to assess personality. These tests have an individual respond to a picture, an inkblot, or story. In order for the person to freely respond, only brief, general instructions are given. For the same reason, the test pictures or stories are vague. The underlying reason for this is that the individual perceives and interprets the test material in a manner that will display his or her psychological functioning. That is, the person will project his or her attitudes, needs, anxieties, and conflicts.

In general, projective testing requires expert interpretation. It is also less susceptible to faking than self-report inventories. The issue of validity and reliability also should be considered before using personality measurements. In short, any form of inventory or projective test to measure personality variables needs to be carefully examined. The evidence to date suggests that managers should be aware of how personality influences behavior, but to attempt to use inventories or projective tests is for experts and not nonqualified managers.

---

[26] A. Anastasi, *Psychological Testing* (New York: Macmillan, 1976), chaps. 17, 18, and 19.

Personality and Behavior

An issue of interest to behavioral scientists and researchers is whether personality factors such as those measured by inventories or projective tests can predict behavior or performance in organizations. Using a total inventory to examine whether personality is a factor in explaining behavior is rarely done in organizational behavior research. Typically, a few select personality factors such as locus of control, tolerance of ambiguity, Machiavellianism, or androgyny are used to examine behavior and performance.

Locus of Control. Some people believe that they are autonomous—that is, they are masters of their own fates and hence bear personal responsibility for what happens to them. They see the control of their lives as coming from inside themselves. Rotter calls these people *internalizers.*[27]

On the other hand, Rotter proposes that many people believe that they are helpless pawns of fate, that they are controlled by outside forces over which they have little if any influence. Such people believe that their *locus of control* is external rather than internal. These people are called *externalizers.*

A study of 900 employees in a public utility found that internally controlled employees are more satisfied with their jobs, more likely to be in managerial positions, and are more satisfied with a participative management style than are employees who perceive external control.[28]

In an interesting study of 90 entrepreneurs, locus of control, perceived stress, coping behaviors, and performance were examined.[29] The study was done in a business district over a three-and-a-half-year period following the flooding by Hurricane Agnes. Internals were found to perceive less stress, employ more task-centered coping behaviors, and fewer emotion-centered coping behaviors than externals. In addition, the task-oriented coping behaviors of internals were associated with better performance.

Tolerance of Ambiguity. The interest in tolerance-intolerance of ambiguity derives from attempts to establish the relationship of this personality factor to authoritarianism. *Intolerance of ambiguity* is defined as the tendency to perceive (i.e., interpret) ambiguous situations as sources of threat; *tolerance of ambiguity* is the tendency to perceive ambiguous situations as desirable. An ambiguous work situation would exist when it cannot be adequately structured by the individual because of the lack of sufficient cues. In various work situations involving changes in technology, structure, or personnel the tolerance of ambiguity factor could be significant in understanding or predicting behavioral reactions.

Machiavellianism. Imagine yourself in the following situation with two other people. Thirty new $1 bills are laid on the table to be distributed any way the group decides. The game is over as soon as two of you agree

---

[27]J. R. Rotter, "Generalized Expectancies for Internal versus External Control of Reinforcement," *Psychological Monographs* 1, no. 609 (1966): 80.

[28]T. R. Mitchell, C. M. Smyser, and S. E. Weed, "Locus of Control: Supervision and Work Satisfaction," *Academy of Management Journal*, September 1975, pp. 623–31.

[29]C. R. Anderson, "Locus of Control, Coping Behaviors, and Performance in a Stress Setting: A Longitudinal Study," *Journal of Applied Psychology*, August 1977, pp. 446–51.

to how it will be divided. Obviously, the fairest distribution would be $10 for each. However, a selfish party could cut out the third person and each end up with $15. Suppose one person suggests this alternative to you. Before you can decide, the left-out person offers to give you $16, taking $14 as his or her share and cutting out the other person. What would you do?

Niccolò Machiavelli has provided in his writings the origins of a concept called Machiavellianism that helps answer the question.[30] He was concerned with how people can be manipulated and with what orientations and tactics differentiate those who weld influence from those who are influenced.

From ancedotal descriptions of power tactics and the nature of influential people a scale has been constructed to measure Machiavellianism. The questions were organized around a cluster of beliefs about tactics, people, and morality.[31] Examples of each are:

Tactics
High MACH: "A white lie is often a good thing."
Low MACH: "If something is morally right, compromise is out of the question."

View of People
High MACH: "Most people don't really know what's best for them."
Low MACH: "Barnum was wrong when he said a sucker is born every minute."

Morality
High MACH: "Deceit in conduct of war is praiseworthy and honorable."
Low MACH: "It is better to be humble and honest than important and dishonest."

The MACH scales differentiate between high and low Machiavellians on the basis of the extent to which people endorse Machiavelli's rules of conduct. In the money allocation game, the individuals who get the lion's share are those who score high on these scales. The low MACH scorers get only slightly less than would be expected by a fair one-third split.

Androgyny. In our society, males are supposed to be masculine or macho and females to be feminine. We are born with a sexual gender, but we are trained to develop a sexual identity that fits the inherited gender. This training begins before birth with planning clothes, furniture, and room colors for the newborn. Blue for a boy and pink for a girl. When behavior is not in step with the traditional sex role, one's very self-concept is questioned. Masculinity and femininity are viewed as polar opposites in our society.

---

[30] R. Christie and F. L. Gers, eds., *Studies in Machiavellianism* (New York: Academic Press, 1970).

[31] Ibid.

The concept of *androgyny* refers to the blending of the behaviors and personality traits traditionally associated with one or the other sexual identity. The androgynous person is both masculine and feminine, and is able to respond to situational demands with the most effective behavior for the particular situation. The androgynous person can be tender and gentle in one situation and hard-nosed and aggressive in another. That is, androgyny implies an adaptable personality.

Bem has pioneered and influenced the thinking on the androgynous personality. She developed the Bem Sex Role Inventory (BSRI), a series of 60 adjectives to measure androgyny patterns.[32] The BSRI includes 20 masculine adjectives, (e.g., ambitious, self-reliant), 20 feminine adjectives (e.g., affectionate, gentle), and 20 neutral adjectives (e.g., truthful, happy). The person responds on a seven-point scale. The average number of points assigned by the person to the feminine items is the femininity score, while the average number of points assigned to the masculine adjectives constitutes the masculinity score. Androgyny is defined as having high scores on both the masculine and feminine dimensions.

Studies using the BSRI have shown that androgynous individuals are more independent, nurturant, and supportive than those who score high on either the femininity or masculinity scales.[33] It has also been found that androgynous men and women have higher self-esteem, social competence, and achievement orientations.

There are many other popularly studied personality variables including creativity, dogmatism, self-esteem, higher order need strength, and cognitive complexity. These and the four factors discussed above seem to have some influence on behavior and performance in various work situations. The importance of personality variables appears to differ from job to job, person to person, and situation to situation. If they can be measured validly they can provide managers with improved accuracy in predicting behavior and job performance.

LEARNING

Learning is one of the fundamental processes underlying behavior. The majority of behavior within organizations is learned behavior. Goals and emotional reactions can be learned. Skills, such as programming a computer or counseling a troubled employee, can be learned. The meanings and uses of language are learned. Perceptions and attitudes can also be learned.

Learning can be defined as the process by which a relatively enduring change in behavior occurs as a result of practice. The words *relatively enduring* signify that the change in behavior must be more or less permanent.

---

[32] Sandra L. Bem, "The Measurement of Psychological Androgyny," *Journal of Consulting and Clinical Psychology*, April 1974, pp. 155–62.

[33] J. R. Spence and R. L. Helmreich, *Masculinity and Femininity: Their Psychological Dimensions, Correlates, and Antecedents* (Austin: University of Texas Press, 1978).

The term *practice* is intended to cover both formal training and uncontrolled experiences. The changes in behavior which characterize learning may be adaptive and promote effectiveness, or they may be nonadaptive and ineffective. The definition also indicates that learning is a process in which certain changes in behavior occur. The process cannot be directly observed. It must be inferred from changes in behavior.

Types of Learning

Three types of learning are considered important in developing and altering behavior: classical conditioning, operant conditioning, and observational learning.

In understanding each of these types of learning four basic concepts need to be clearly understood. First, the *drive* of the person must be considered. A drive is an aroused condition within the person. It can result from deprivation or some specific stimulation. Primary drives like hunger are unlearned. On the other hand secondary drives like being anxious about meeting a supervisor are learned. Once a drive is learned it serves to trigger behavior.

A second important concept is stimulus. A *stimulus* is a cue that is the occasion for a response. A supervisor's request to complete a report is a stimulus to complete the job. The time on the clock is a stimulus to get up and go to the committee meeting. Stimuli, then, set the stage for a response to a series of responses. Sometimes, the stimulus that calls forth a response is clearly obvious. In other cases, the stimulus for a particular response is obscure.

Another important concept is the response. A *response* is the behavioral result of stimulation. It is any activity of the person, regardless of whether the stimulus is identifiable or whether the activity is observable. Responses become linked to stimuli so that, when stimuli occur, the response is likely to follow. Responses in work organizations may be oral, written, manual, or attitudinal. The attitudinal response is often covert and difficult to detect. The cognitive and affect components of attitude cannot be seen.

The final important basic concept is the reinforcer. A *reinforcer* is any object or event that serves to increase or sustain the strength of a response. Some of the common reinforcers used in organizations are praise from a supervisor, a merit increase in pay, and transfer to a desirable job.

Classical Conditioning. The study of classical conditioning had its beginnings with the work of a Russian physiologist Pavlov around the turn of the 20th century. While studying the automatic reflexes associated with digestion, he noticed that his laboratory dog salivated not only in the presence of food but also at the presentation of other stimuli before food was placed in its mouth. Pavlov reasoned that food automatically produced salivation. This phenomenon was an unlearned association; he therefore labeled food an *unconditioned stimulus* and salivation an *unconditioned response*. Since he believed that the response of salivating to other, seemingly unrelated, stimuli had to be learned, he labeled it a *conditioned response* initiated by a *conditioned stimulus*.

FIGURE 3–6
The Pavlov Procedure for Classical Conditioning

Before training
    Ringing a bell ————————————→ No salivation (no response)
Training
    Bell rings and food (uncon- ——————→ Salivation (unconditioned response)
    ditioned stimulus) is provided
After training
    Bell rings (conditioned stimulus) ————→ Salivation (conditioned response)

As part of his experiments, Pavlov rang a bell (conditioned stimulus) followed by placing food in the dog's mouth (unconditioned stimulus). Soon the bell alone evoked salivation. Thus, salivation produced by food is an unconditioned response, whereas salivation produced by the bell alone is a conditioned (or learned) response. Figure 3–6 graphically presents the Pavlov work on classical conditioning.[34]

Operant Conditioning. The name most associated with operant conditioning is B. F. Skinner. This form of conditioning is concerned with learning that occurs as a consequence of behavior. In classical conditioning, the sequence of events is independent of the subject's behavior. Behaviors which can be controlled by altering consequences (reinforcers and punishments) which follow them are referred to as *operants.* An operant is strengthened (increased) or weakened (decreased) as a function of the events which follow it. Most workplace behaviors are operants. Examples of operant behaviors are performing job-related tasks, reading a budget report, or coming to work on time. Operants are distinguished by virtue of being controlled by their consequences.

In classical conditioning, the response to be learned (salivating) is already present in the animal and may be triggered by the presentation of the appropriate unconditioned stimulus (food). In operant conditioning, however, the desired response may not be present in the subject. Teaching a subordinate to prepare an accurate weekly budget report is an example of operant conditioning. There is no identifiable stimulus that will automatically evoke the response of preparing the budget. The superior works with the subordinate and reinforces him or her for preparing an accurate budget. Figure 3–7 illustrates the operant conditioning process.

The interrelationships of $S_1 \rightarrow R_1 \rightarrow S_2 \rightarrow R_2$ are referred to as the contingencies of reinforcement.[35] This sequence is also described as the A-----

---

[34] An excellent and clear presentation of the conditioning process is given in Bernard M. Bass and James A. Vaughn, *Training in Industry: The Management of Learning* (Monterey, Calif.: Brooks/Cole Publishing, 1966). Also see Alan E. Kazdin, *Behavior Modification in Applied Settings* (Homewood Ill.: Richard D. Irwin, 1980).

[35] See W. Clay Hamner, "Reinforcement Theory and Contingency Management in Organizational Settings," in *Organizational Behavior and Management: A Contingency Approach* ed. Henry L. Tosi and W. Clay Hamner (Chicago: St. Clair Press, 1974), pp. 86–112.

FIGURE 3–7
An Example of Operant Conditioning

S_1 →	R_1 →	S_2 →	R_2
A memo which informs subordinate to prepare budget	Preparing weekly budgets	Receiving valued praise from the superior	A sense of satisfaction
Conditioned stimulus	Conditioned operant response	Reinforcing stimulus	Unconditioned response
(Antecedent)	(Behavior)	(Consequence)	

B-----C operant mode. *A* designates the antecedent or stimuli that precedes the behavior *B*. And *C* is the consequence or what results from the behavior. Skinner believes that the consequences will be acted out in the future.[36] This notion lends itself particularly well to the study of various learning principles such as reinforcement and knowledge of results.

There are a number of important principles of operant conditioning that can aid the manager attempting to influence behavior. Some of these principles are being applied in organizations.

Reinforcement is an extremely important principle of learning. It can be stated that without reinforcement no measurable modification of behavior takes place. Managers often use *positive reinforcers* to modify behavior. In some cases the reinforcers work as predicted, while in other instances they do not modify behavior in the desired direction because of competing reinforcement contingencies. When reinforcers are not made contingent on the behavior desired by the manager, desired behaviors do not occur. Also when reinforcers are given long after desired behaviors have occurred, the probability of the resulting behavior occurring again is decreased.

Negative reinforcement refers to an increase in the frequency of a response following removal of a negative reinforcer immediately after the response. An event is a *negative reinforcer* only if its removal after a response increases performance of a response. A familiar example of negative reinforcement in the summer months in Phoenix and Houston is turning on the automobile air conditioner on a stifling hot day. Turning on the air conditioner (the behavior) usually minimizes or terminates an aversive condition, namely being hot (negative reinforcer). The probability of having an operating air conditioning system in the summer months is increased. Similarly, exerting high degrees of effort to complete a job may be negatively reinforced by not having to listen to the nagging boss.

Punishment is an uncomfortable consequence for a particular behavioral response.[37] It is certainly a controversial method of behavioral modification.

---

[36]B. F. Skinner, *Beyond Freedom and Dignity* (New York: Alfred A. Knopf, 1971); and B. F. Skinner, *Contingencies of Reinforcement: A Theoretical Analysis* (New York: Appleton-Century-Crofts, 1969).

[37]W. E. Craighead, A. E. Kazdin, and M. J. Mahoney, *Behavior Modification* (Boston: Houghton Mifflin, 1976), pp. 112–20.

Some people believe that punishment is the opposite of reward and is just as effective in changing behavior.

Punishment may be a poor approach to learning because:

1. The results of punishment are not as predictable as those of reward.
2. The effects of punishment are less permanent than those of reward.
3. Punishment frequently is accompanied by negative attitudes toward the administrator of the punishment, as well as toward the activity that led to the punishment.

Despite the costs of using punishment it has been and will continue to be used as a method of altering behavior. In situations where the costs of not punishing outweigh the advantages, punishment may be an appropriate approach. For example, punishing a worker who deliberately slows down the flow of work is a costly way of altering behavior. However, there might be ways of dealing with the problem other than punishment. The point is, however, that punishment and its use depend upon the situation and the managers style of altering behavior.

Extinction reduces undesired behavior. When positive reinforcement for a learned response is withheld, individuals will continue to practice that behavior for some period of time. If the behavior continues not to be reinforced, the behavior decreases and will eventually disappear. The decline in response rate because of nonreinforcement is defined as extinction.

Knowledge of results is knowledge of goal accomplishment. Knowing why the behavior is not acceptable and how much modification is needed is important. New management trainees who have no idea of whether they are doing an acceptable job have little chance of improving their performance.

Accurate feedback from a manager furnishes information which can be used to correct mistakes and improve job performance. The knowledge of correct behavior is reinforcing and strengthens the preceding behavior, while knowledge of incorrect responses is not reinforcing and could extinguish the preceding behavior.

Knowledge of results, affects performance only to the extent to which employees set higher performance goals in response to such feedback.[38] In addition other investigators have concluded that providing employees with incomplete or erroneous feedback may actually result in poorer performance than providing no feedback at all.[39] The best job performance can be achieved when employees are provided with accurate feedback on performance based on clear and publicized criteria.

Observational Learning. Many professional golfers and baseball players improve their ability to hit the ball by taking a lot of practice swings. In fact in the professional ranks the best golfers and batters study and observe how others swing the club or the bat. Today most major league base-

---

[38] Edwin A. Locke, "Toward a Theory of Task Performance and Incentives," *Organizational Behavior and Human Performance*, May 1968, pp. 157–89.

[39] L. L. Cummings, D. P. Schwab, and M. Rosen, "Performance and Knowledge of Results as Determinants of Goal Setting," *Journal of Applied Psychology*, December 1971, pp. 526–30.

ball teams film the batting habits of players and then study these films to observe each part of the swing. These teams are using a form of observational learning. This type of learning occurs when an individual observes a model's behavior (it may be his own hitting behavior on film) but performs no overt responses or receives direct consequences.

Major corporations such as Exxon, Westinghouse, Union Carbide, and Federated Department Stores are teaching managers to apply motivation principles on the job through observational learning. More and more attempts and empirical research of such practices are expected to increase in the 1980s. The "how-to" results orientation has impressed those organizations who are in the forefront of using observational learning.[40] An example of applied observational learning is presented in the close-up below.

ORGANIZATIONS: CLOSE-UP

Applied Observational Learning at General Electric

Since observational learning or behavior modeling began as an experiment with a few supervisors at General Electric in 1970, it has grown into an applied learning technique that was utilized in the training of approximately 500,000 supervisors, managers, and employees in 1980. The hardheaded pragmatist is impressed with the numbers but will undoubtedly ask, "How do we know that behavior modeling is an effective learning experience for each of these trainees?" The honest answer is, "We don't know and probably never will know."

The value of applied observational learning in an organization like General Electric is determined by computing the value of correcting a skill deficiency, preventing a problem from occurring, or maximizing an opportunity. The cost of using observational learning to develop, say, a manager's skill at conducting a performance appraisal feedback session with subordinates would include: (1) analysis of skills that need to be developed, (2) purchase of materials and equipment to make videotapes of models using effective skills, (3) salaries of managers while they are in the learning sessions, (4) salaries of instructors, and (5) cost of overcoming barriers in using learned skills on the job. One medium-sized engineering firm in Houston recently calculated the costs of a three-hour observational learning program for 32 managers as $9,240 or approximately $290 a manager.

Observational learning is becoming a popular procedure for improving managerial practices and performance. It is expected that this type of learning will be used in the future to teach sophisticated skills such as problem solving, decision making, team building, conflict resolution, interviewing, and goal-setting negotiation.

Source: James C. Robinson and Dana L. Gaines, "Seven Questions to Ask Yourself before Using Behavior Modeling," *Training/HRD* December 1980, pp. 60–62, 67–69.

---

[40] Bernard L. Rosenbaum, "Common Misconceptions about Behavior Modeling and Supervisory Skill Training (SST)," *Training and Development Journal*, August 1979, pp. 40–48.

Observational learning has significant potential in organizational settings especially in training programs. It can and has been used already in training programs designed to improve interpersonal skills, supervisory practices, and managerial use of positive reinforcement.[41] Other uses which seem to be suited for modeling and observational learning are:

Training managers to conduct performance appraisal sessions.

Training individuals to engage in goal-setting processes.

Training individuals to interview properly.

Training sales personnel to practice sound selling procedures.

MAJOR MANAGERIAL ISSUES

A. Employees joining an organization must adjust to a new environment, new people, and new tasks. The manner in which people adjust to situations and other people will depend largely on their psychological makeup and personal backgrounds.

B. The behavioral patterns of most people are established before joining an organization. To modify these patterns requires time, patience, and understanding. Simplistic assumptions about people are generally incomplete.

C. Individual perceptuial processes help the person face realities of the world. People are influenced by other people and by situations, needs, and past experiences. While a manager is perceiving employees, they are also perceiving him or her.

D. Attitudes are linked with behavioral patterns in a complex manner. They are organized and they provide the emotional basis of most of a person's interpersonal relations. To change attitudes is extremely difficult and requires at the very least trust in the communicator and strength of message.

E. Personality is primarily developed long before a person joins an organization. It is influenced by hereditary, cultural, and social determinants. To assume that it can be easily modified can result in managerial frustration and ethical problems. The manager should try to cope with personality differences among people and not try to change personalities to fit his or her model of the ideal person.

F. A number of personality variables such as locus of control, androgyny, tolerance of ambiguity, and Machiavellianism have been found in research studies to be associated with behavior and performance. Although difficult to measure, these variables appear to be important in explaining and predicting organizational behavior.

---

[41] For a review of behavior modeling uses in organizations, see six articles in *Personnel Psychology*, Autumn 1976, pp. 325–70.

> **MAJOR MANAGERIAL ISSUES** (continued)
>
> G. Learning is a process by which a relatively enduring change in behavior occurs as a result of practice. It is an important process because it is at the very heart of motivation. Adequate motivation not only sets in motion the activity which results in learning, but also sustains and directs it.

DISCUSSION AND REVIEW QUESTIONS

1. What is observational learning?

2. Why does operant conditioning have more practical value to managers than classical conditioning?

3. If a manager were concerned about the job performance of his or her subordinates, would learning principles be important factors to consider? Explain.

4. Explain why managers who are not treated favorably by their superiors would have problems changing their subordinates' negative attitudes toward the organization.

5. Provide some examples of selective perception that would be used in purchasing a new automobile and accepting a new position with an organization.

6. Some critics of operant conditioning believe that it cannot be used in all situations. They believe that many of Skinner's conclusions would result in treating people like animals. Do you agree? Why?

7. Why would it be difficult for a manager to determine the personality, behavior, and performance relationships for his or her subordinates?

8. What reinforcers motivate you to do a better job?

9. Some people state that being too concerned with individual differences can cause chaos in an organization. Do you agree? Why?

10. Why is it difficult to measure such factors as personality and other individual differences?

ADDITIONAL REFERENCES

Andrisani, P. J., and R. C. Muljus. "Individual Differences in Preferences for Intrinsic versus Extrinsic Aspects of Work." *Journal of Vocational Behavior*, 1977, pp. 14–30.

Argyris, C., and J. Schon. *Organizational Learning: A Theory of Action Perspective.* Reading, Mass.: Addison-Wesley Publishing, 1978.

Bartley, S. H. *Introduction to Perception.* New York: Harper & Row, 1980.

Berger, S. M., and W. W. Lambert. "Stimulus-Response Theory in Contemporary Social Psychology." In *The Handbook of Social Psychology*, edited by G. Lindzey and E. Aronson. Reading, Mass.: Addison-Wesley Publishing, 1971.

Drory, A., and U. M. Gluskinos. "Machiavellianism and Leadership." *Journal of Applied Psychology*, 1980, pp. 81–86.

Ewen, R. G. *An Introduction to Theories of Personality.* New York: Academic Press, 1980.

Flaherty, J. F., and J. B. Dusek. "An Investigation between Psychology Androgyny and Components of Self-Concept." *Journal of Personality and Social Psychology*, 1980, pp. 984–92.

Frost, P.; V. Mitchell; and W. R. Nord, eds. *Organizational Reality: Observations from the Firing Line.* Santa Monica, Calif.: Goodyear Publishing, 1978.

"Imitating Models: A New Management Tool." *Business Week,* May 8, 1978, pp. 119–20.

Jones, E. E. "How Do People Perceive the Causes of Behavior?" *American Scientist,* 1976, pp. 300–5.

Lundin, Robert W. *Personality.* New York: Macmillan, 1974.

Luthans, F., and R. Kreitner. *Organizational Behavior Modification.* Glenview, Ill.: Scott, Foresman, 1975.

Mahoney, M. J., and D. B. Arnkoff. "Self-Management: Theory, Research, and Application." In *Behavioral Medicine: Theory and Practice,* edited by J. P. Brady and D. Pomerlean. Baltimore: William & Williams, 1979, pp. 75–96.

Mann, C. C., and H. P. Sims, Jr. "Self-Management as a Substitute for Leadership: A Social Learning Perspective." *Academy of Management Review,* 1980, pp. 361–67.

McConnel, J. V. *Understanding Human Behavior.* New York: Holt, Rinehart, & Winston, 1980.

Watson, D. L., and R. G. Tharp. *Self-Directed Behavior.* Monterey, Calif.: Brooks/Cole Publishing, 1977.

Watson, R. I. *The Great Psychologists.* Philadelphia: J. B. Lippincott, 1978.

AFFIRMATIVE ACTION, INACCURATE PERCEPTIONS, OR A REAL PROBLEM

Nick Troc is the accounting department manager in Mid-States Telephone Corporation, a large telephone utility. Nick is 36 years old and a college graduate. He joined Mid-States one year ago after working for Southern Lines Telephone Company for eight years. The accounting department employs approximately 230 female and 125 male clerks, 8 female and 15 male first-line supervisors, 6 female and 14 male second-line supervisors, and 1 female and 6 male third-line supervisors. Recently Nick has sensed some problems in working with and understanding the third-level supervisors and he believes that the problems may have been caused by the firm's attempts to implement an affirmative action promotion policy. Each of these supervisors has been in his or her present position for less than 15 months. The third supervisory level was created by the executive committee to improve efficiency and provide managers at Mid-States with some additional opportunities for promotion. Prior to this change only two levels of supervision existed. Many of the promotable employees were leaving Mid-States because of no advancement opportunities.

Discussions with various employees have not revealed why the third-level supervisory group does not seem to be working effectively as a team. After searching for answers to his problem, Nick decides to ask the personnel department for some information about each of the third-level supervisors. Below is a listing taken from the labor force inventory data bank. This information is used to acquire a background summary of present employees for promotion and for examining the records of employees who have retired in the past five years.

Labor force Inventory Summary: Third-Level Supervisors

Dennis Balinger: Age 46; time in present position, 12 months; graduate of Myers High School and Lee Junior College. Has worked in Mid-States for 21 years; rated in top 80 percentile for last 5 years of performance appraisal; present salary $27,000

Sam Turkla: Age 51; time in present position, 6 months; graduate of Wilcox High School. Has worked in Mid-States for 8 years; rated in top 65 percentile for last 3 years of performance appraisal; present salary $28,400.

Mark Hardesty: Age 40; time in present position, 15 months; graduate of Midwest University. Has worked in Mid-States for 14 years; rated in top 84 percentile for last 6 years of performance appraisal; present salary $28,250; CPA.

John Jackson: Age 50; time in present position, 8 months; graduate of the University of the South. Has worked in

Mid-States for 8 months; present salary $30,500; CPA.

Doris Riska: Age 44; time in present position, 9 months; graduate of Tuley High School. Has worked in Mid-States for 22 years; rated in top 75 percentile for last 5 years in performance appraisal; present salary $28,400.

Willis Rogers: Age 42; time in present position, 14 months; graduate of Walker High School and Darby Junior College. Has worked in Mid-States for 12 years; rated in top 78 percentile for last 4 years in performance appraisal; present salary $27,600.

Rudy Ramirez: Age 44; time in present position, 12 months; graduate of Northeast University. Has worked in Mid-States for 16 years; rated in top 75 percentile for last 3 years in performance appraisal; present salary $28,200; CPA.

Nick's Analysis

Nick, in carefully reviewing the labor force inventory information, notes that three of the supervisors are CPAs: Doris is female, Willis is black, Rudy is Chicano, and Sam is the oldest at 51. Whether these obvious differences have resulted in the lack of coordination between the supervisors is puzzling Nick. He just doesn't accept the premise that differences like these can influence behavior and performance on the job. This assumption causes him to discuss some of the problems with a few of the third-line supervisors. A summary of three of these discussions is presented. The discussion with Willis is as follows:

Nick: Willis, I'm trying to "dig out" what I believe is a problem among the third-level supervisors in accounting.

Willis: Nick, what problem are you talking about?

Nick: Well, you and the others just do not seem to be working well with each other.

Willis: I don't know what you mean by "working well with each other." I thought that we each worked on our assigned jobs and were performing well.

Nick: Well, I don't know. Perhaps your background is getting in the way of working together.

Willis: Background! I don't know what you mean. I'm from Chicago and I like soul food. Is this what you mean?

Nick: No, Willis. I mean that each of you is so different in age, education, and overall qualifications. Let me think this out a little more and I will get back to you.

Willis: Okay, Nick, but I think you're making something out of nothing. Give us a chance to "click" and we will.

The conversation with Doris proceeded in this manner:

Nick: Doris, I need your help with a problem.

Doris: What kind of problem?

Nick: Well, I've been thinking that the third-level supervisors group is too diverse to work well together.

Doris: Nick, I'm female and the others are male and this is the only difference that I can see.

Nick: Some of you are CPAs and college graduates.

Doris: So what? I do my job and perform any accounting task that has to be done. Are you telling me to get a CPA and a degree? This was not the way this job was presented to me nine months ago.

Nick: Doris, you're jumping to conclusions.

Doris: Nick, you're the one who called me in. Of course I am jumping to conclusions. You call me in and in one swoop you start talking about certificates, degrees, and problems. I think that you are making a problem because you think one is present.

At this time Doris is called out of the session with Nick because of some problems in her unit. The discussion between John and Nick proceeded as follows:

Nick: John, I wanted to discuss some problems that exist with the third-level supervisors.

John: You're right on target, Nick. These guys and Doris are a pain. They just are not top quality people and are bossy and wise. I really can't stand them.

Nick: What problems do you perceive?

John: They want to run their own small world. They are not cooperative and they hold back relevant information from me. If I were you I'd bust them up good and not let these practices go too far. They can become such a problem that accounting services can become a tangled mess.

Nick: John, how long have you been faced with these difficulties?

John: Since the day I set foot in the door. The reception I received was miserable. These people all come on as aristocracy.

Nick: Thanks for your inputs. I'll get back to you later.

Nick sat and thought about his discussions with the supervisors. He just didn't want to accept the thought that Mid-State's affirmative action program which included promoting minority employees was the cause of the problem he felt existed. Willis, Rudy, and Doris were all fine people, but they did not appear to be working as a team. In addition, the other four supervisors were not working as a team.

Questions for Consideration

1. What individual differences do you see in this case that appear to be important and are being overlooked?

2. Why do you believe the differences identified in your answer to the first question are being overlooked by Nick?

3. Do you feel that Nick is effectively communicating the problems he believes exist? Why?

EXPERIENTIAL EXERCISE

SELF-PERCEPTION: ARE YOU ON TARGET?

Objectives

1. To learn how you perceive yourself.
2. To determine the perceptions others have of you.
3. To find areas in which your self-perception and the perceptions others have of you do not match.

Related Topics

The perceptions you have of others, your job, your family are all projected outside toward other people or things. We also have self-perceptions, our own internal picture of what we are. Sometimes we are surprised that others do not perceive us like we think they do.

Starting the Exercise

Individually complete the list by writing on a separate sheet of paper the statements which best describe you. Some of the statements may not apply to you. If they do not do not place them on your sheet.

Have a classmate do the same thing—write down the statements on a separate sheet of paper that describe you. Also have a close friend or family member prepare a list of statements that describe you.

Collect the lists from the classmate and the friend/family member. Analyze the results. What differences in self and others perceptions of you did you find?

Exercise Procedures

1. Form into groups of three members each to discuss what you each found. Did the others find discrepancies in their perceptions versus what others perceived?
2. Discuss why these discrepancies were found. What common errors do we make in perceiving ourselves and the way others perceive us? Are you someone who:
   a. Listens carefully to what others say?
   b. Tends to make snap judgments?
   c. Is rushed by time?
   d. Prefers to work alone?
   e. Daydreams a lot?
   f. Is competitive?
   g. Is argumentative?
   h. Has a good sense of humor?
   i. Is satisfied with life?
   j. Is defensive?
   k. Has trouble relaxing?
   l. Is emotional?
   m. Is warm and friendly?
   n. Wants to finish the job on time?
   o. Is independent?
   p. Becomes upset easily?
   q. Can't keep a secret?
   r. Always asks for help?
   s. Is friendly?
   t. Gets nervous under pressure?

Chapter 4

Motivation: Theories and Principles

ARGUMENT FOR

Some researchers and managers believe that the behaviorism work of Skinner has been overlooked, misinterpreted, and misapplied. Some of the neglect has been pointed out as follows:

Since the major concern of managers of human resources is the prediction and control of behavior of organizational participants, it is curious to find that people with such a need are extremely conversant with McGregor and Maslow and totally ignorant of Skinner.*

The increasing attention in the applied organizational behavior literature to Skinnerian behaviorism should minimize some of the misinterpretation.

At the very heart of Skinnerian behaviorism is a major contention: Behavior is a function of its consequences. Skinner's approach is based on what is called an external approach; it emphasizes the effect of environmental consequences on objective, observable behavior. He believes that behavioral scientists should abandon their preoccupation with the inner thoughts of a person and

---

*Walter Nord, "Beyond the Teaching Machine: The Neglected Area of Operant Conditioning in the Theory and Practice of Management," *Organizational Behavior and Human Performance*, November 1969, p. 375.

ARGUMENT AGAINST

The critics of Skinnerian behaviorism are numerous. One of the most respected and articulate critics is William F. Whyte. It is Whyte's contention that Skinner's operant conditioning theory tells us little about prediction and control of behavior. It also fails to deal with four crucial elements of real-life behavior in organizations. These are:

1. *The Cost-Benefit Ratio*—Skinner, in using pigeons to develop his principles would disregard the costs of the action to the actor. The costs were trifling compared to the benefits (food) the experimental pigeon received as a consequence of action. This is not generally true with people. Individuals weigh what they receive for their efforts in terms of personal investments. Thus, providing positive reinforcers for production is much more complex than giving pigeons food.

2. *Conflicting Stimuli*—Employees face conflicting stimuli of the reward system, requests from subordinates, meeting schedules, and other organizational sources. They do indeed respond, as Skinner argues, in terms of the consequences of past behavior. But many situations provide conflicting stimulus conditions and managers cannot easily predict any

ARGUMENT FOR (continued)

concentrate more on the fit between the person and the environment.

According to Skinner's approach, work behavior is shaped and maintained by its consequences; these consequences (reinforcers) can be either positive or negative, but positive reinforcers are more effective. Through the use of reinforcers, behavior can be learned. A learned behavior is called an *operant* because it operates on the environment to produce a consequence. Skinner called unlearned behavior *respondent behavior*.

The advocates of Skinner's principles have recommended that operant conditioning be applied to motivation attempts, and programs, training and personal development, job design, compensation, organizational design, and performance appraisal. They believe that managers who take the time to study Skinner's principles of behavior control will see the potential managerial applications. The advocates state that even Skinner's critics admit that his behavior principles work in organizations.†

----

†For support for applying behavior modification, see Fred Luthans and Robert Kreitner, *Organizational Behavior Modification* (Glenview, Ill.: Scott, Foresman, 1975); and Everett E. Adam, Jr., "Behavioral Modification in Quality Control," *Academy of Management Journal*, December 1975, pp. 662–79.

ARGUMENT AGAINST (continued)

response simply by analyzing the relationship between the individual and the anticipated reinforcement.

3. *Time Lag and Trust*—Few of a person's acts bring immediate rewards. The time span between behavior and reinforcement in organizations can be quite long. There is also the issue of trust that an individual must have if a time lag must exist. The individual must trust the person applying reinforcers. These are not issues when experimental animals are used.

4. *One-Body Problem*—In the Skinner laboratory experiments, the researcher's attention is only on the environmental conditions that induce the pigeon to behave a certain way. When working with people, the contingencies to which an individual responds are provided by another person or persons. Thus, it is necessary to learn to deal with the contingencies affecting the behavior of the person initiating the reinforcers and the workers.

Whyte does not want to discard Skinner's theory, but asks that it be treated cautiously. He would like Skinner and his supporters to not make grandiose claims since the claims do not serve to develop what is an important set of ideas regarding motivation.‡

----

‡Whyte's position appears in William F. Whyte, "Skinnerian Theory in Organizations," *Psychology Today*, April 1972, pp. 67–68, 96–100, and "An Interview with William F. Whyte, *Organizational Dynamics*, Spring 1975, pp. 51–66.

An important determinant of individual performance is motivation. It is not the only determinant; other variables such as effort expended, ability, and previous experience also infuence performance. This chapter, however, concentrates on the motivation process as it affects behavior and individual performance. First, an integrated model depicting the motivation process and other variables influencing behavior and performance is developed. Second, distinctions between selected theories of motivation are described. The next chapter will address some specific applications of motivational theory in organizations. This sequence permits us to show the close association between theory, research, and practice.

THE MOTIVATION DILEMMA

■ A continual and perplexing problem facing managers is why some employees perform better than others. A number of interesting and important variables have been used to explain performance differences among employees. For example, such variables as ability, instinct, intrinsic and extrinsic rewards, aspiration levels, and personal backgrounds explain why some employees perform well and others are poor performers.

Despite the obvious importance of motivation, it is difficult to define and to analyze in organizations. One definition proposes that motivation has to do with (1) the direction of behavior; (2) the strength of the response (i.e., effort), once an employee chooses to follow a course of action; and (3) the persistence of the behavior, or how long the person continues to behave in a particular manner.[1]

Another viewpoint suggests that the analysis of motivation should concentrate on the factors which incite and direct a person's activities.[2] One theorist emphasizes the goal-directedness aspect of motivation.[3] Yet another states that motivation is "concerned with how behavior gets started, is energized, is sustained, is directed, is stopped and what kind of subjective reaction is present in the organism while all this is going on."[4]

A careful examination of each of these views leads to a number of conclusions about motivation:

1. Theorists present slightly different interpretations and place emphasis on different factors.
2. It is related to behavior and performance.
3. It involves goal directedness.
4. Physiological, psychological, and environmental differences are important factors to consider.

[1]John P. Campbell, Marvin D. Dunnette, Edward E. Lawler III, and Karl E. Weick, *Managerial Behavior, Performance, and Effectiveness* (New York: McGraw-Hill, 1970), p. 340.

[2]J. W. Atkinson, *An Introduction to Motivation* (Princeton, N.J.: D. Van Nostrand, 1964).

[3]D. Bindra, *Motivation: A Systematic Reinterpretation* (New York: The Ronald Press, 1959).

[4]M. R. Jones, ed., *Nebraska Symposium on Motivation* (Lincoln: University of Nebraska Press, 1955), p. 14.

THE STARTING POINT: THE INDIVIDUAL

■ Most managers must consider motivating a diverse, and in many respects unpredictable, group of people. The diversity results in different behavioral patterns that are in some manner related to needs and goals.

Needs refer to deficiencies that an individual experiences at a particular point in time. The deficiency may be physiological—a need for food; psychological—a need for self-esteem; or sociological—a need for social interaction. Needs are viewed as energizers or triggers of behavioral responses. The implication is that when need deficiencies are present, the individual is more susceptible to managers' motivational efforts.

The importance of goals in any discussion of motivation is apparent. The motivational process, as interpreted by most theorists, is goal directed. The goals, or outcomes, an employee seeks are viewed as forces that attract the person. The accomplishment of desirable goals can result in a significant reduction in need deficiencies. In organizational settings, goals can be *positive*, such as praise, recognition, pay increase, promotion; or *negative*, such as being passed over for promotion or being reprimanded for poor performance.

THE MOTIVATION PROCESS

■ Needs and goals are concepts which provide the bases for construction of an integrated model. The initial step in developing a model for clarifying the motivation process is the relate these variables in a sequential manner as shown in Figure 4–1.

As illustrated in Figure 4–1 people seek to reduce various need deficiencies. Need deficiencies trigger a search process for ways to reduce the tension caused by the discomfort. A course of action is selected and goal (outcome)-directed behavior occurs. After a period of time, managers assess that performance. The performance evaluation results in some type of reward or punishment. These outcomes are weighed by the person, and the need deficiencies are reassessed. This, in turn, triggers the process and the circular pattern is started again.

A more complete and integrative model can be developed using the circular model as a foundation. A number of factors such as effort and ability that are extremely important for understanding the motivational process are not represented in Figure 4–1. However, these factors should be included in a more complete motivation model. *Effort* involves the energy a person exerts while performing a job. *Ability* designates the capabilities of a person, such as intelligence and dexterity. The amount of effort expended is related to some extent to ability. An employee who does not have the ability to analyze a problem will probably not exert much effort to solve it.[5]

Organizational variables also influence the motivational process. The job design, span of control, leader's style, group affiliations of the person, and technology are some of the organizational variables influencing moti-

---

[5]L. L. Cummings and Donald P. Schwab, *Performance in Organizations* (Glenview, Ill.: Scott, Foresman, 1973), p. 8.

FIGURE 4–1
The Motivational Process: An Initial Model

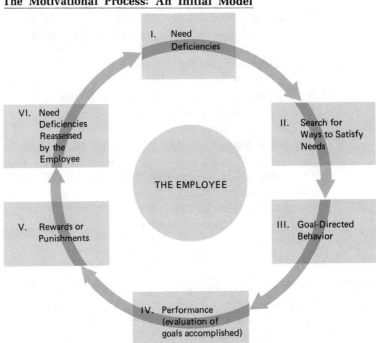

vation. The individual's behavior and performance are significantly influenced by these factors.

Another variable that is part of the motivational process is satisfaction. *Satisfaction* generally means the fulfillment acquired by experiencing various job activities and rewards. The term *satisfaction* is used to analyze outcomes already experienced by an employee.[6] Thus, satisfaction is a consequence of rewards and punishments associated with past performance. The employee can be satisfied, or dissatisfied, with the behavior, performance, and reward relationships that currently exist.

Motivation and satisfaction are related, but are not synonymous concepts. Motivation is primarily concerned with goal-directed behavior. The manager who works extra hours to perfect the budget is displaying a high degree of motivation. A counterpart manager who boasts about "slapping together the important budget" in spare moments just to quiet the accountant is displaying low motivation from the organization's perspective. This manager may enjoy every aspect of the job, and this state represents high job satisfaction. On the other hand, the manager who works long hours to prepare a sound budget may be dissatisfied with the job.

---

[6]John Wanous and Edward E. Lawler III, "Measurement and Meaning of Job Satisfaction," *Journal of Applied Psychology*, April 1972, pp. 95–105.

FIGURE 4–2
An Integrated Model of the Motivational Process

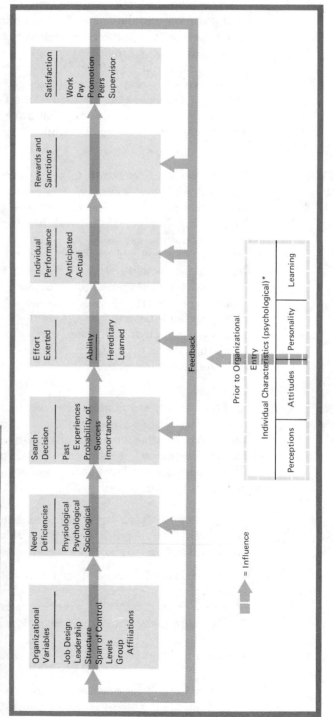

* Note that these variables are also influenced by the person's life in an organization.

Combining the concepts represented in Figure 4–1 with effort, ability, organizational variables, satisfaction, and various psychological concepts results in a more complete model of the motivation process. This model, Figure 4–2, shows how these various factors are linked together. The organizational variables influence needs which initiate the search process until ultimately the employee evaluates rewards and punishments associated with performance. Note that each of the factors is influenced by psychological variables (e.g., perception) that have been shaped primarily before the employee entered the organization.

MOTIVATION THEORIES AND RESEARCH

■ Each person is attracted to some set of goals. If a manager is to predict behavior with any accuracy, it is necessary to know something about an employee's goals, and the actions the person will take to obtain them. There is no shortage of motivation theories and research findings that attempt to provide explanations of the behavior-outcome relationship. Two categories can be used to sort theories of motivation.[7] The *content* theories focus on the factors *within* the person that energize, direct, sustain, and stop behavior. They attempt to determine specific needs which motivate people. The second category includes what are called the *process* theories. They provide a description and analysis of the process of *how* behavior is energized, directed, sustained, and stopped. Both categories have important implications for managers who are by the nature of their jobs involved with the motivational process.

CONTENT THEORIES

■ Three important content theories of motivation are Maslow's need hierarchy, Herzberg's two-factor theory, and McClelland's achievement theory. These theories have stimulated an extensive number of research studies and numerous application endeavors by managers. These theories remain popular and have had an impact on managerial practices years after they were first presented.

Maslow's Need Hierarchy

The crux of Maslow's theory is that needs are arranged in a hierarchy.[8] The lowest level needs are the physiological and the highest level are the self-actualization needs. These needs are defined to mean the following:

1. Physiological: The need for food, drink, shelter, and relief from pain.
2. Safety and security: The need for freedom from threat, that is, the security from threatening events/or surroundings.
3. Belongingness, social, and love: The need for friendship, affiliation, interaction, and love.
4. Esteem: The need for self-esteem, and esteem from others.

---

[7]Campbell et al., *Managerial Behavior*, pp. 340–56.

[8]A. H. Maslow, "A Theory of Human Motivation," *Psychological Review*, July 1943; pp. 370–96; and A. H. Maslow, *Motivation and Personality* (New York: Harper & Row, 1954).

5. Self-actualization: The need to fulfill oneself by maximizing the use of abilities, skills, and potential.

Maslow's theory assumes that a person attempts to satisfy the more basic needs (physiological) before directing behavior toward satisfying upper level needs (self-actualization). The lower order needs must be satisfied before a higher order need begins to control the behavior of a person. A crucial point in Maslow's thinking is that a satisfied need ceases to motivate. When a person decides that he or she is earning enough pay for contributing to the organization, money loses its power to motivate.

The Maslow theory is built on the premise that people have a need to grow and develop. This assumption may be true for some employees, but not for others. An inherent problem with the theory is that it was not scientifically tested by its founder. In a declarative manner, Maslow proposed that the typical adult has satisfied 85 percent of the physiological need, 70 percent of the safety and security need, 50 percent of the belongingness, social, and low need, 40 percent of the esteem need, and 10 percent of the self-actualization need. This assertion is highlighted in Figure 4–3.

An implication of the high degree of need deficiency in the self-actualization and esteem categories (Figure 4–3) is that managers should focus attention on strategies to correct these deficiencies. This logic assumes that attempts to satisfy these deficiencies have a higher probability of succeeding than directing attention to the already satisfactorily fulfilled lower order needs.

Furthermore, the highly deficient needs are a potential danger for man-

FIGURE 4–3
The Typical Person's Need Deficiency and Satisfaction

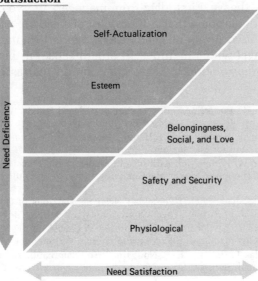

agers. An unsatisfied need can cause frustration, conflict, and stress. The skilled technician in a research laboratory who is given paperwork assignments instead of more challenging project assignments is an example of a person being blocked from satisfying self-actualization needs. This type of blockage in the fulfillment of needs can lead to frustration and stress that may eventually result in undesirable performance. As discussed in the previous chapter, individuals often cope with blockages of goal attainment by using ego-defense mechanisms.

Some Selected Need Hierarchy Research.   A number of research studies have attempted to test the need hierarchy theory. The first reported field research that tested a modified version of Maslow's need hierarchy was performed by Porter.[9] At the time of the initial studies, he assumed that physiological needs were being adequately satisfied for managers and he substituted a higher order need called autonomy, defined as the person's satisfaction with opportunities to make independent decisions, set goals, and work without close supervision.

Since the early Porter studies, other studies have reported

1. Managers higher in the organizational chain of command place greater emphasis on self-actualization and autonomy.[10]
2. Managers at lower organizational levels in small organizations (less than 500 employees) are more satisfied than their counterpart managers in large firms (more than 5,000 employees); however, the managers at upper levels in the large organizations are more satisfied than their counterparts in small companies.[11]
3. American managers overseas are more satisfied with autonomy opportunities than their counterparts working in the United States.[12]

Despite these findings a number of issues remain regarding the need hierarchy theory. First, data from managers in two different companies provided little support that a hierarchy of needs exists.[13] The data suggested that only two levels of needs exist: one is the physiological level and the other a level which includes all other needs. Further evidence also disputes the hierarchy notion.[14] Researchers found that as managers advance in an

---

[9]Lyman W. Porter, "A Study of Perceived Need Satisfaction in Bottom and Middle Management Jobs," *Journal of Applied Psychology*, February 1961, pp. 1–10.

[10]Lyman W. Porter, *Organizational Patterns of Managerial Job Attidues* (New York: American Foundation for Management Research, 1964).

[11]Lyman W. Porter, "Job Attitudes in Management: Perceived Deficiencies in Need Fulfillment as a Function of Size of the Company," *Journal of Applied Psychology*, December 1963, pp. 386–97.

[12]John M. Ivancevich, "Perceived Need Satisfactions of Domestic versus Overseas Managers," *Journal of Applied Psychology*, August 1969, pp. 274–78.

[13]Edward L. Lawler III and J. L. Suttle, "A Causal Correlation Test of the Need Hierarchy Concept," *Organizational Behavior and Human Performance*, April 1972, pp. 265–87.

[14]Douglas T. Hall and K. E. Nougaim, "An Examination of Maslow's Need Hierarchy in an Organizational Setting," *Organizational Behavior and Human Performance*, February 1968, pp. 12–35.

organization, their needs for security decrease, with a corresponding increase in their needs for social interaction, achievement, and self-actualization.

Alderfer condenses the Maslow hierarchy into existence, relatedness, and growth needs which he refers to as the ERG theory. The *existence* needs include Maslow's physiological needs, pay, fringe benefits, and working conditions. The *relatedness* needs include the Maslow social and esteem categories. The *growth* needs include the person's desire to be self-confident and productive. Thus, the growth need overlaps the Maslow esteem and self-actualization needs.[15]

Researchers have examined the ERG theory using nurses, bank employees, and life insurance personnel. The researchers concluded that need satisfaction is "perhaps most appropriately conceptualized as a global construct, in the Gestalt sense, a general state of the organism which may be greater than the sum of its parts."[16] They proposed that Maslow's theory is not specifically applicable to employees in organizational settings.

A review of the research concludes that there is little support for the Maslow theory. There is some support for the notion that physiological needs take precedence over other needs, but there is not sound evidence that the other needs are activated as suggested by Maslow. Furthermore, the concepts of "esteem" and "self-actualization" are not well defined.[17] Maslow's need hierarchy also shows little ability to predict employee behavior. One reason for this is that the model was never intended by its originator to be a predictor of behavior. It was only offered as a simplified approach in understanding human needs.

Herzberg's Two-Factor Theory

Herzberg developed the two-factor theory of motivation.[18] The two factors are called the dissatisfiers-satisfiers or the hygiene-motivators or the extrinsic-intrinsic factors, depending on the discussant of the theory. The original research testing this theory included a group of 200 accountants and engineers. Herzberg used interview responses to questions like, "Can you describe, in detail, when you felt exceptionally good about your job?" and "Can you describe, in detail, when you felt exceptionally bad about your job?" Rarely were the same kinds of experiences categorized as both good and bad. This systematic procedure resulted in the development of two distinct kinds of experiences—satisfiers and dissatisfiers.

The initial Herzberg study resulted in two specific conclusions about the theory: First, there is a set of *extrinsic* conditions, the job context, which

---

[15]Clayton P. Alderfer, *Human Needs in Organizational Settings* (New York: Free Press, 1972).

[16]Benjamin Schneider and Clayton P. Alderfer, "Three Studies of Need Satisfactions in Organizations," *Administrative Science Quarterly,* December 1973, pp. 489–505.

[17]M. A. Wahba and L. G. Birdwell, "Maslow Reconsidered: A Review of Research on the Need Hierarchy Theory," *Organizational Behavior and Human Performance,* April 1976, pp. 212–40.

[18]Frederick Herzberg, B. Mausner, and B. Synderman, *The Motivation to Work* (New York: John Wiley & Sons, 1959).

result in *dissatisfaction* among employees when they are not present. If these conditions are present, this does not necessarily motivate employees. These conditions are the *dissatisfiers* or *hygiene* factors since they are needed to maintain at least a level of "no dissatisfaction." These factors include:

a. Salary.
b. Job security.
c. Working conditions.
d. Status.
e. Company procedures.

f. Quality of technical supervision.
g. Quality of interpersonal relations among peers, with superiors, and with subordinates.

Second, a set of *intrinsic* conditions, the job content, when present in the job build strong levels of motivation which can result in good job performance. If these conditions are not present, they do not prove highly dissatisfying. This set of factors is called the *satisfiers* or *motivators*. They include:

a. Achievement.
b. Recognition
c. Responsibility

d. Advancement.
e. The work itself.
f. The possibility of growth.

Herzberg's model basically assumes the job satisfaction is not a unidimensional concept. His research leads to the conclusion that two continua correctly interpret satisfaction. Figure 4–4 presents graphically two views of job satisfaction. Prior to Herzberg's work those studying motivation considered job satisfaction as a unidimensional concept; that is, job satisfaction on one end of a continuum and job dissatisfaction at the other end of the same continuum. This meant that if a job condition caused job satisfaction it would cause job dissatisfaction if it were removed; similarly, if a job

FIGURE 4–4
Traditional versus Herzberg Satisfaction Continua

Traditional Theory

*High Job
Satisfaction*

*High Job
Dissatisfaction*

|———————————————————————————————|

Herzberg's Theory

*High Job
Satisfaction*

*No
Satisfaction*

|———————————————————————————————|

*No
Dissatisfaction*

*High Job
Dissatisfaction*

|———————————————————————————————|

condition caused job dissatisfaction it would cause job satisfaction if it were removed.

One appealing aspect of Herzberg's work is that the terminology is work-oriented. There is no need to translate psychological terminology to everyday language. Despite this important feature, Herzberg's work has been criticized for a number of reasons. First, the theory was originally based on a sample of accountants and engineers. Critics ask whether this limited sample can justify generalizing to other occupational groups. The technology, environment, and backgrounds of the two occupational groups are distinctly different from such groups as nurses, medical technologists, salespeople, computer programmers, clerks, and police officers.[19]

Second, some researchers believe that Herzberg's work over simplifies the nature of job satisfaction. Dunnette et al. state that:

> Results show that the Herzberg two-factor theory is a grossly oversimplified portrayal of the mechanism by which job satisfaction or dissatisfaction comes about. Satisfaction or dissatisfaction can reside in the job context, the job content, or both jointly. Moreover, certain dimensions—notably Achievement, Responsibility, and Recognition—are more important for both satisfaction and dissatisfaction than certain other job dimensions—notably Working Conditions, Company Policies and Practices, and Security.[20]

Other criticisms focus on Herzberg's methodology which requires people to look at themselves retrospectively. Can people be aware of all that motivated or dissatisfied them? These critics believe that subconscious factors are not identified in Herzberg's analysis. The "recency of events" bias of being able to recall the most recent job conditions and feelings is embedded in the methodology.[21]

Another criticism of Herzberg's work is that little attention has been directed toward testing the motivational and performance implications of the theory.[22] In the original study of engineers and accountants, only self-reports of performance were used and, in most cases, the respondents were reporting on job activities that had happened over a long period of time. Herzberg has offered no explanation as to why various extrinsic and intrinsic job factors should affect performance. The two-factor theory also fails to explain why various job factors are important. In reality, the theory, be-

---

[19] For critiques of the Herzberg theory, see Robert J. House and L. Wigdor, "Herzberg's Dual-Factor Theory of Job Satisfaction and Motivation: A Review of the Empirical Evidence and a Criticism," *Personnel Psychology*, Winter 1967, pp. 369–80, and Joseph Schneider and Edwin Locke, "A Critique of Herzberg's Classification System and a Suggested Revision," *Organizational Behavior and Human Performance*, July 1971, pp. 441–58.

[20] Marvin Dunnette, John Campbell, and M. Hakel, "Factors Contributing to Job Dissatisfaction in Six Occupational Groups," *Organizational Behavior and Human Performance*, May 1967, p. 147.

[21] Abraham K. Korman, *Industrial and Organizational Psychology* (Englewood Cliffs, N.J.: Prentice-Hall, 1971), pp. 148–50.

[22] Edward E. Lawler III, *Motivation in Work Organizations* (Monterey, Calif.: Brooks/Cole Publishing, 1973), p. 72.

cause of its heavy emphasis on job factors, is basically a theory of determinants of job dissatisfaction and satisfaction.

**McClelland's
Learned Needs
Theory**

McClelland has proposed a theory of motivation that is closely associated with learning concepts. He believes that many needs are acquired from the culture.[23] Three of these needs are: the need for achievement (n Ach), the need for affiliation (n Aff), and the need for power (n Pow).

McClelland proposes that when a need is strong in a person, its effect is to motivate the person to use behavior which leads to satisfaction of the need. For example, having a high n Ach encourages an individual to set challenging goals, work hard to achieve the goals, and use the skills and abilities needed to accomplish them.

Measuring n Ach. How is what McClelland has labeled as the need for achievement (n Ach) measured? It is not enough to assume that those who work hard and long hours have it, while those who work slow or in spurts do not. Interestingly, to assess individual differences in n Ach the Thematic Apperception Test (TAT) is used.[24] Individuals are shown pictures and asked to write a story about what is portrayed in the pictures. The achievement, affiliation, or power needs are inferred from how he or she responds to the pictures. The person is asked to answer these questions about the pictures: What is happening? Who are the people? What has led to this situation? What has happened in the past? What are the people (person) thinking? What is wanted?

The story written by the individual is scored by trained evaluators. They develop objective measures of the strength of each of the needs using a scoring technique developed by McClelland.[25] To be coded as a need achievement theme a person's story about the picture has to reveal concern to do better, to improve performance. By contrast, social need affiliation themes reveal concern for establishing, maintaining, and repairing social relations. And power need themes are displayed by concern with reputation, influence, and impact.

An important feature of McClelland's n Ach is his contention that needs can be learned. McClelland cites instances in which individuals with a low initial n Ach were subjected to training or learning experiences that increased the n Ach. He proposes that entire cultures (nations) that are economically backward can be dramatically improved by stimulating the need for achievement in the populace. If McClelland is correct, and some research supports his theory, his approach could have a significant impact

---

[23]David C. McClelland, "Business Drive and National Achievement," *Harvard Business Review*, July–August 1962, pp. 99–112.

[24]R. Murray, *Thematic Apperception Test Pictures and Manual* (Cambridge, Mass.: Harvard University Press, 1943).

[25]David C. McClelland, *The Achievement Motive* (New York: Appleton-Century-Crofts, 1953).

on motivation in general. Motivation could be taught in organizational and nonorganizational settings. The following close-up emphasizes how n Ach can even be a factor in athletic programs.

ORGANIZATIONS: CLOSE-UP

Wanted: Football Players with a High n Ach

Tom Hosier is head football coach at Macalester College in St. Paul, Minnesota. His football team has not won a game since 1974—50 consecutive losses, the all-time NCAA record for organized futility. Productivity is obviously poor. Turnover is high. The team is obviously not competitive with its counterparts in the Conference.

Frederick Kiel, a consultant, has never met Tom Hosier but he offers some ideas about motivation to help turn the fortunes of Macalester around. There is, he observes, a basic culture to losing that must be addressed if the situation is to be improved. Kiel believes that Hosier must get beyond the obvious manpower problem. He will have to attract people who truly want to win.

Kiel believes that the coach should recruit new players from winning backgrounds. He notes that there are distinct value differences between habitual winners and habitual losers. Winners get their feeling of accomplishment by being part of success, those who are high on personal recognition, praise, or social status. Achievement-oriented people are achievement oriented in all aspects of their lives.

Finally, Kiel claims that it is vital to make changes visible to the team. The coach needs to use everything he can—praise, feedback, statistics. They're all forms of psychic income. The way he does it is also important: praise in public, criticize in private.

Coach Hosier seems to be on the same wavelength as Kiel. Hosier always wears a T-shirt that announces "Mac Is Back." He claims that by wearing the T-shirt the players see a visible form of achievement motivation. He further believes that to dream and to anticipate winning are what is needed. Any success in life is based on realism, fun, dreams, and anticipation. Once these dreams are reached it is then necessary to establish a new dream.

Source: Dick Schaef, "Motivating People Who Think They Don't Have a Chance," *Training*, September 1980, pp. 85–86, 88.

Research on n Ach.   The majority of research evidence offered as support for McClelland's learned needs theory has been provided by him or his associates. The research has provided a profile of the high achievers in society.[26] The descriptive profile suggests that:

---

[26]David McClelland and D. Burnham, "Power Is the Great Motivator," *Harvard Business Review*, March–April 1976, pp. 100–111; and McClelland, *Achievement Motive*.

Those who are high n Ach prefer to set their own performance goals.

The high n Ach person prefers to avoid easy and difficult performance goals. They actually prefer moderate goals that they think they can achieve.

The high n Ach person prefers immediate and efficient feedback on how they are performing.

The high n Ach person likes to be responsible for solving problems.

Research has not only provided the basis for developing a profile of those with high n Ach, but it has also pointed out the complexity of the achievement motive. Differences have been found between individuals with high n Ach who focus on attaining success and those who focus on avoiding failure.[27] Those who focus on attaining success tend to set more realistic goals and choose tasks of moderate difficulty.

In the majority of the research on n Ach, the subjects have been men. One study compared achievement needs of college men and women.[28] It was determined in this study that women appeared to fear success more than men. Students were asked to complete a story that began, "At the end of first-term finals, Anne finds herself at the top of her medical school class." For male subjects, John was the name used. When the male and female stories were analyzed, 62 percent of the women expressed conflict over Anne's success, while only 9 percent of the men expressed conflict over John's success. Women had a greater negative imagery about success.

The "fear of success hypothesis" was sensationalized by the popular press as an example of a personality type created by sexist ideology. Since this study over 200 studies were conducted following up on various aspects of women's fear of success.[29] The conclusion reached is that fear of success (achievement) is not a personality attribute of women. Rather, it is better conceived as a strong avoidance reaction by certain social-economic-historic conditions in both women and men.

Based on theory and research McClelland has made specific suggestions about developing a positive high need for achievement, that is, a high n Ach where there is no fear of success. He suggests that (1) people arrange tasks so that they receive periodic feedback on performance, this will provide information to make modifications or corrections, (2) people should seek good models of achievement; search for achievement heros, the successful people, the winners and use them as models, (3) people should modify their self-image; the high n Ach person likes himself or herself and seeks moderate challenges and responsibilities, and (4) people should control their imagination; think in realistic terms and think positively about how they will accomplish goals.

---

[27] W. V. Meyer, "Achievement Motive Research," in *Nebraska Symposium on Motivation,* ed. W. J. Arnold (Lincoln: University of Nebraska Press, 1968).

[28] M. S. Horner, "Fail: Bright Women," *Psychology Today,* November 1969, pp. 36–38.

[29] D. Tresemer, ed., "Current Trends in Research on Fear of Success," *Sex Roles,* Spring 1976, entire issue.

There are a number of criticisms of McClelland's work. First, the use of the projective TAT test to determine three needs has been questioned. While projective techniques have some advantages over self-report questionnaires the interpretation and weighting of a story is at best an art. The validation of such analysis is extremely important and is often neglected.

McClelland's claim that n Ach can be learned conflicts with a large body of literature that argues that the acquisition of motives normally occurs in childhood and is very difficult to alter in adulthood. McClelland acknowledges this problem, but points to evidence in politics and religion to indicate that adult behaviors can be changed.[30]

Third, McClelland's notion of learned needs is questionned on the grounds of whether the needs are permanently acquired. Research is needed to determine if needs that are acquired last over a period of time. Can something learned in a training and development program be sustained on the job?[31] This is the issue that McClelland and others have not been able to clarify.

A Synopsis of Three Content Theories

Each content theory attempts to explain behavior from a slightly different perspective. None of the theories has been accepted as the sole basis for explaining behavior. Although critics are skeptical, it appears that peo-

FIGURE 4–5

Maslow's Need Hierarchy: McClelland's Achievement, Affiliation, and Power Needs; and Herzberg's Two-Factor Theory

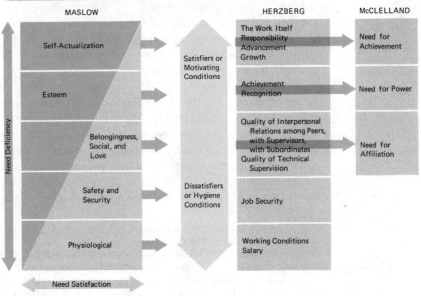

---

[30]McClelland, *Achievement Motive.*

[31]Paul R. Lawrence and Jay W. Lorsch, *Developing Organizations: Diagnosis and Action* (Reading, Mass.: Addison-Wesley Publishing, 1969).

ple have innate and learned needs and that various job factors result in a degree of satisfaction. Thus, each of these theories provides the manager with some understanding of behavior and performance.

The three theories are compared in Figure 4–5. McClelland proposed no lower order needs. However, his needs for achievement and power are not identical with Herzberg's motivators, or Maslow's higher order needs, but there are some similarities. A major difference between the content theories is McClelland's emphasis on socially acquired needs. The Maslow theory offers a need classification system and Herzberg discusses intrinsic and extrinsic job factors.

PROCESS THEORIES

■ The *process* theories of motivation are concerned with answering the question of *how* individual behavior is energized, directed, maintained, and stopped. In this section we shall examine three process theories: expectancy theory, equity theory, and reinforcement theory.

Expectancy Theory

Several theories of motivation have been developed in recent years which have become known as expectancy, or instrumentality theories. One of the more popular versions was developed by Victor Vroom.[32] He bases his theory on three important concepts—expectancy, valence, and instrumentality. Over 50 studies have been done to test the accuracy of expectancy theory in predicting employee behavior.[33]

Vroom defines *motivation* as a process governing choices among alternative forms of voluntary activity. Most behaviors are considered to be under the voluntary control of the person and are consequently motivated.

In order to understand expectancy theory, it is necessary to define the important terms in the theory and explain how they operate. The most important terms are the following:

First and Second-Level Outcomes. The first-level outcomes resulting from behavior are those associated with doing the job itself. These outcomes include productivity, absenteeism, turnover, and quality of productivity. Second-level outcomes are those events (rewards or punishments) that first-level outcomes are likely to produce such as merit pay increase, group acceptance or rejection, and promotion.

Instrumentality. This is the perception of an individual that first-level outcomes will be associated with second-level outcomes. Vroom suggested

[32] Victor H. Vroom, *Work and Motivation* (New York: John Wiley & Sons, 1964). For earlier work, see Kurt Lewin, *The Conceptual Representation and the Measurement of Psychological Forces* (Durham, N.C.: Duke University Press, 1938); and E. C. Tolman, *Purposive Behavior in Animals and Men* (New York: Appleton-Century-Crofts, 1932).

[33] David A. Nadler and Edward E. Lawler III, "Motivation: A Diagnostic Approach," in *Perspectives on Behavior in Organizations,* ed. J. R. Hackman, E. E. Lawler, III, and L. W. Porter (New York: McGraw-Hill, 1977), pp. 26–38. Also see Edwin A. Locke, "Personnel Attitudes and Motivation," *Annual Review of Psychology* (1973), pp. 457–80, and Abraham K. Korman, Jeffrey H. Greenhaus, and Irwin J. Badin, "Personnel Attitudes and Motivation," *Annual Review of Psychology* (1977), pp. 175–96.

that instrumentality can take values ranging from −1, indicating a perception that attainment of the second level is certain without the first outcome and impossible with it, to +1, indicating that the first outcome is necessary and sufficient for the second outcome to occur. Since this reflects an association it can be thought of in terms of correlation.

Valence. This term refers to the preferences of outcomes as seen by the individual. For example, a person may prefer a 9 percent merit increase over a transfer to a new·department, or the transfer over a relocation to a new facility. An outcome is positively valent when it is preferred and negatively valent when it is not preferred or is avoided. An outcome has a valence of zero when the individual is indifferent to attaining or not attaining it. The valence concept applies to first- and second-level outcomes. For example, a person may prefer to be a high performing (first-level outcome) employee, because he or she believes this will lead to a merit increase in pay (second-level outcome).

Expectancy. This term refers to the belief concerning the likelihood or subjective probability that a particular behavior will be followed by a particular outcome. That is, the assigned chance of something occurring because of the behavior. Expectancy has a value ranging from 0, indicating no chance that an outcome will occur after the behavior or act, to +1, indicating certainty that a particular outcome will follow an act or behavior. Expectancy is considered in terms of probability.

In the work setting there is an effort-performance expectancy held by individuals. This expectancy represents the individual's perception of how hard it will be to achieve a particular behavior (say, completing the budget on time) and the probability of achieving that behavior. For example, the person may have a high expectancy that if she works around the clock she could complete the budget on time. On the other hand she may perceive that her chances of finishing on time are about 40 percent if she works only during the day.

Given a number of alternative levels of behavior to finish the budget (working 8 hours, 10 hours, or around the clock 24 hours) she will choose the level of performance that has the greatest motivational force associated with it. In other words, when faced with *choices* about behavior, the person preparing the budget goes through a process of questioning—Can I perform at that level if I give it a try? If I perform at that level, what will happen? Do I prefer those things that will happen?

There is also a performance-outcome expectancy. In the individual's mind every behavior is associated with outcomes (rewards and/or punishments). For example, an individual may have an expectancy that if the budget is completed on time she will receive a day off next week.

Force. The term *force* is equated with motivation. The intent of expectancy theory is to assess the magnitude and direction of all forces acting on the individual. The act with the greatest force is that which most likely will occur.

Ability. The term *ability* designates the person's potential for doing the job or work. It may or may not be utilized. It refers to what physical and mental abilities a person has to do the job and not what the person will do.

Principles of Expectancy Theory.   When the important expectancy theory concepts are integrated three major principles are generated.[34] They are:

1. $P = f (M \times A)$.   Performance is considered to be a multiplicative function of motivation (the force) and ability.
2. $M = f (V_1 \times E)$.   Motivation is a multiplicative function of the valence for each first-level outcome (V_1) and the perceived expectancy that a given behavior will be followed by a particular first-level outcome. If expectancy is low there will be little motivation. Similarly, if the valence of an outcome is zero neither the absolute value nor variations in the strength of expectancies of accomplishing it will have any effect.
3. $V_1 = (V_2 \times I)$.   The valence associated with various first-level outcomes is a multiplicative function of the sum of the valence attached to all second-level outcomes and the instrumentalities that attainment of the first-level outcome has for achieving each second-level outcome.

Figure 4–6 presents the general expectancy model and includes the two expectancy points ($E \rightarrow P$ and $P \rightarrow 0$). However, instead of developing this

FIGURE 4–6
Expectancy Theory Conceptually

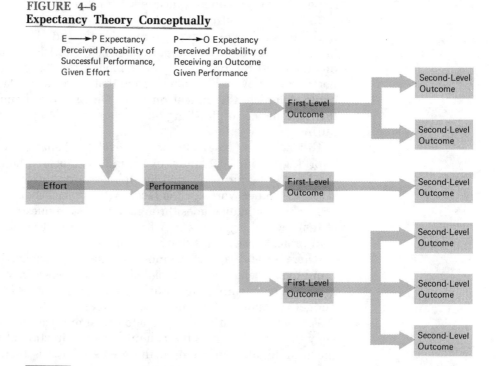

[34]W. Clay Hamner and Dennis W. Organ, *Organizational Behavior: An Applied Psychological Approach* (Plano, Tex.: Business Publications, 1978), pp. 144. © 1978 by Business Publications, Inc.

FIGURE 4–7
Expectancy Theory Applied

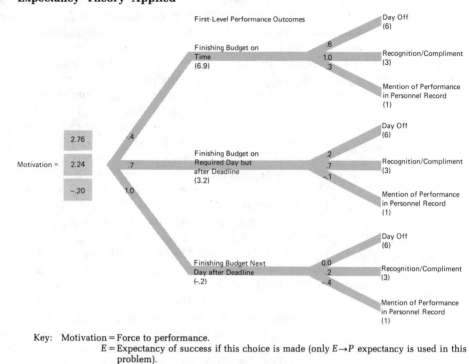

Key: Motivation = Force to performance.

  E = Expectancy of success if this choice is made (only $E \rightarrow P$ expectancy is used in this problem).

  V_1 = Valence of first-level outcomes.

  I = Instrumentality (relationships between V_1 and V_2).

  V_2 = Valence of second-level outcomes

Work problem from right to left to reach motivation values of 2.76, 2.24, and −.20.

complex model we prefer, for illustrative purposes, to use the simpler expectancy-performance ($E \rightarrow P$) version. Thus, Figure 4–7 uses numerical values to illustrate how expectancy theory works conceptually. The situation portrayed involves an employee faced with various first- and second-level outcomes. Starting at the second-level outcome point (the right side), the valence associated with finishing the budget on time is calculated by $V_1 = V_2 \times I$ or $V_1 = [(6 \times .6) + (3 \times 1.0) + (1 \times .3)]$ or 6.9. All these values were assigned by the authors to show how the theory works. The motivational force is calculated by $M = f (V_1 \times E)$ or $M = 6.9 \times .4$ or 2.76. The motivation force for finishing the budget on the required day but after the deadline is 2.24, while finishing the budget the next day after the deadline has a force of −.20. Thus, the strongest force or motivation would be directed toward finishing the budget on time.

Research on Expectancy. The empirical research that purports to test expectancy theory continues each year. A few studies have used students in laboratory experiments. However, the majority of recent research has been conducted in field settings. For example, one interesting study examined performance-outcome instrumentality in a temporary organization.[35] The experiment used either an hourly rate of pay (low instrumentality) or a piece rate (high instrumentality). After individuals had worked for three four-hour days under one pay system, they switched to the other system and worked three more days. Immediately following the shift in pay systems, and for all three subsequent days, the performance of subjects who were shifted to the high instrumentality system was higher than their own performance under the low instrumentality system and higher than the performance of those subjects shifted to the low instrumentality system.

Another area that has been researched focuses on the valence and behavior portion of the model. The results are mixed. However, it appears that three conditions must hold for the valence of outcomes to be related to effort. Performance-outcome instrumentalities must be greater than zero, effort-performance expectancies must be greater than zero, and there must be some variability in the valence of outcomes.[36]

Still today after almost 20 years theorists, researchers, and practitioners (to a lesser extent) continue to work on defining, measuring, and applying expectancy concepts. There are still many difficulties encountered when testing the model. One problem involves the issue of effort or motivation itself. The theory attempts to predict choice or effort. However, there is no clear specification of the meaning of effort and consequently there is no measurement of the variable that possesses acceptable validity. Typically self, peer, or supervisor ratings of effort are used. Unfortunately each study seems to have its own definition, measurement, and research design.

Another difficulty concerns the issue of first-level outcomes. Expectancy theory is a process theory and does not specifiy which outcomes are relevant to a particular individual in a situation. Each researcher is expected to address this issue and does so in a unique way. Consequently, no systematic approach is being used or refined.

Furthermore, there is an implicit assumption in the expectancy approach that all motivation is conscious. The individual is assumed to consciously calculate his or her expected pleasure or pain to be attained or avoided. Then a choice(s) is made. Certainly it is generally accepted that individuals are not always conscious of their motives, expectancies, and perceptual processes. Expectancy theory says nothing about subconscious motivation and this is a point that has been for the most part neglected in the theory.

The majority of available field studies testing the model have relied on employees from a single organization who were doing similar or the same jobs. It seems that these type of studies would seriously limit and restrict the range of expectancies and instrumentalities. This type of research also

[35] R. D. Pritchard and P. J. DeLeo, "Experimental Test of the Valence-Instrumentality Relationships in Job Performance," *Journal of Applied Psychology*, April 1973, pp. 264–79.

[36] J. P. Campbell and R. D. Pritchard, "Motivation Theory in Industrial and Organizational Psychology," in *Handbook of Industrial and Organizational Psychology*, ed. M. D. Dunnette (Chicago: Rand McNally, 1976), pp. 84–95.

raises the issue of generalizing results from these studies to other samples. Is it valid to make these kind of generalizations?

Thus, although the research results have been promising, there are some major problems with the theory, research, and application of expectancy motivation. Over the years, the additions to the original model have made the expectancy theory a complex model to understand, measure, and apply. Some researchers seem more interested in adding to the complexity than improving upon or testing the model.

Equity Theory

The essence of equity theory is that employees make comparisons of their efforts and rewards with those of others in similar work situations. This theory of motivation is based on the assumption that individuals are motivated by a desire to be equitably treated at work. The individual works in exchange for rewards from the organization.

Four important terms in this theory are:

1. *Person:* The individual for whom equity or inequity is perceived.
2. *Comparison Other:* Any group or person used by Person as a referent regarding the ratio of inputs and outcomes.
3. *Inputs:* The individual characteristics brought by Person to the job. These may be achieved (e.g., skills developed, experience, learning) or ascribed (e.g., age, sex, race).
4. *Outcomes:* What Person receives from the job (e.g., recognition, fringe benefits, pay).

Equity exists when employees perceive that the ratios of their inputs (efforts) to outcomes (rewards) are equivalent to the ratios of other employees. Inequity exists when these ratios are not equivalent; an individual's own ratio of inputs to outcomes could be greater than or less than others.[37]

The existence of perceived inequity creates tension to restore equity; the greater the inequity, the greater the tension. Depending upon the source and intensity of the inequity, a number of courses of action can be followed. For example, individuals may attempt to increase or decrease their outcomes if they are lower than those of the comparison person. Or they may increase or decrease their inputs by increasing or decreasing their efforts. If these courses of actions are not possible, individuals may stay away from the work situation so that their perceptions are not continually reinforced. The extreme course of action is to quit the job. Figure 4–8 illustrates the equity theory of motivation.

Research on Equity. Most of the research on equity theory has focused on pay as the basic outcome.[38] The failure to incorporate other relevant

---

[37]J. Stacy Adams, "Toward an Understanding of Equity," *Journal of Abnormal and Social Psychology,* November 1963, pp. 422–36.

[38]Paul S. Goodman and Abraham Friedman, "An Examination of Adam's Theory of Inequity," *Administrative Science Quarterly,* December 1971, pp. 271–88.

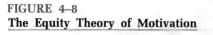

FIGURE 4–8
The Equity Theory of Motivation

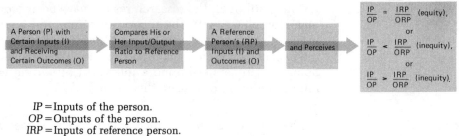

IP = Inputs of the person.
OP = Outputs of the person.
IRP = Inputs of reference person.
ORP = Outputs of reference person.

outcomes limits the impact of the theory in work situations. A review of the studies also reveals that the comparison person is not always clarified. A typical research procedure is to ask a person to compare inputs and outcomes with a specific person. In most work situations, the comparison person is selected after working for some time in the organization. Two issues to consider are whether comparison persons are within the organization and whether comparison persons change during a person's work career.

Several individuals have questioned the extent to which inequity that results from overpayment (rewards) actually leads to perceived inequity ($IP/OP < IRP/ORP$). Locke argues that employees are seldom told they are overpaid. He believes that individuals are more likely to adjust their idea of what constitutes an equitable payment to justify their pay.[39] Campbell and Pritchard point out that employer-employee exchange relationships are highly impersonal when compared to exchanges between friends. Perceived overpayment inequity may be more likely when friends are involved. Thus, individuals will probably react to overpayment inequity only when they believe their actions have led to a friend's being treated unfairly. The individual receives few signals from the organization that it (the organization) is being treated unfairly.[40]

Despite limitations, the equity theory provides a relatively insightful model to help explain and predict employee attitudes about pay. The theory has also emphasized the importance of comparisons in the work situation. The identification of comparison persons seems to have some potential value when attempting to restructure a reward program. The theory also raises the issue of methods for inequity resolution. An inequitable situation can cause morale, turnover, and absenteeism problems.

---

[39] Edwin A. Locke, "The Nature and Causes of Job Satisfaction," in *Handbook of Industrial and Organizational Psychology*, ed. M. Dunnette (Chicago: Rand McNally, 1976), pp. 1297–1349.

[40] Campbell and Pritchard, "Motivation Theory," pp. 63–130.

Reinforcement Theory

In Chapter 3 operant conditioning was presented as an important approach for understanding how individuals learn. It relies on the use of reinforcement to improve learning. Reinforcement theory and operant principles also can be used to explain, analyze, and implement motivation programs in organizations.

The *principles* of operant conditioning describe the relationship between behavior and various environmental events (recall from Chapter 3, Antecedents—Behavior—Consequence or A—B—C). Although both antecedents (e.g., a supervisor's request) and a consequence (e.g., a merit pay increase) can alter behavior, most applications of operant conditioning principles emphasize the consequences that follow behavior (e.g., completing a job). Behavior change is assumed to occur whenever certain consequences are *contingent* upon performance. A consequence is thought to be contingent when it is delivered *only* after the target behavior is adequately performed.

In organizations, many consequences are contingent upon behavior. For example, promotions are contingent upon sustained performance and a group bonus is contingent upon the group's production level. A *contingency* refers to the relationship between a behavior and the events that follow the behavior. The notion of contingency is important in applying operant conditioning in the form of behavior modification. The use of behavior modification programs will be discussed in more detail in the next chapter.

The major principles of operant conditioning were covered in Chapter 3. Thus, Figure 4–9 is presented to refresh the reader's memory of the main principles. As noted *positive reinforcement,* an increase in the frequency of behavior, occurs when a positive reinforcer is contingently applied. *Negative reinforcement,* also an increase in the frequency of a behavior, occurs when a negative reinforcer is contingently removed. Thus, the principle of reinforcement always refers to an increase in the frequency of a response when it is followed by a contingent stimulus.

Likewise, the principle of *punishment* always refers to a decrease in the frequency of a response when it is followed by a contingent stimulus. Note the two types of punishment. Punishment by *removal* occurs when a posi-

FIGURE 4–9
Principles of Operant Conditioning

	Applied	Removed
Positive Reinforcer	Positive Reinforcement	Punishment by Removal
Negative Reinforcer	Punishment by Application	Negative Reinforcement

tive reinforcer is contingently removed (e.g., an individual's tardiness results in his losing some money from his paycheck). Punishment by *application* occurs when a negative reinforcer is contingently applied (e.g., being reprimanded by a boss for doing a poor job).[41]

Reinforcement Schedules. The nature of rewards or punishment and how they are employed significantly influence employee behavior. It is extremely important to properly time the rewards or punishments used in an organization. The timing of these outcomes is called *reinforcement scheduling*. In the simplest schedule the response is reinforced each time it occurs. This is called *continuous reinforcement*. If reinforcement occurs only after some instances of a response and not after each response, an *intermittent reinforcement* schedule is being used.

Continuous and intermittent reinforcement schedules produce important differences in performance. First, during the initial development of a response (e.g., learning and applying a new job skill), continuous reinforcement is preferred because it accelerates early performance. Second, when trying to sustain a response, (e.g., good performance) intermittent schedules are more effective.

Examples of relatively continuous reinforcement might be receiving praise after every unit is produced, or being greeted warmly everyday by the supervisor. Examples of intermittent reinforcement include preparing a report for the boss (only occasionally will he or she compliment you) or running for an elected union position (you only occasionally win these elections).

Types of Intermittent Schedules. Intermittent reinforcement can be scheduled a number of ways. Reinforcers can be delivered by a manager on the basis of a time interval. This is referred to as an *interval schedule*, meaning that the response will be reinforced after a specified time interval. Reinforcers can also be delivered after a certain number of responses. This is referred to as a *ratio schedule*, because the schedule specifies the number of responses required for each reinforcement.

Interval schedules can be either *fixed* or *variable*. A fixed interval schedule requires that an unvarying time interval must pass before the reinforcer is available. Figure 4–10 highlights the types of intermittent schedules managers can use. The *fixed interval schedule* illustrates an employee receiving a bimonthly paycheck. Every two weeks the individual is paid (reinforced). A *variable interval schedule* uses an interval that varies around an average. For example, reinforcers come available after 2, 6, 10, 18, 22, and 26 days. This averages to a reinforcer every 14 days.

A *fixed ratio* reinforcement schedule involves issuing a reinforcer after a fixed number of responses have occurred. For example, every fifth response or unit of output is reinforced. A *variable ratio* schedule also requires that a certain number of responses occur before the manager delivers

---

[41]W. E. Craighead, A. E. Kazdin, and M. J. Mahoney, *Behavior Modification* (Boston: Houghton Mifflin, 1976), pp. 111–20.

FIGURE 4–10
Intermittent Schedules of Reinforcement Used by Managers

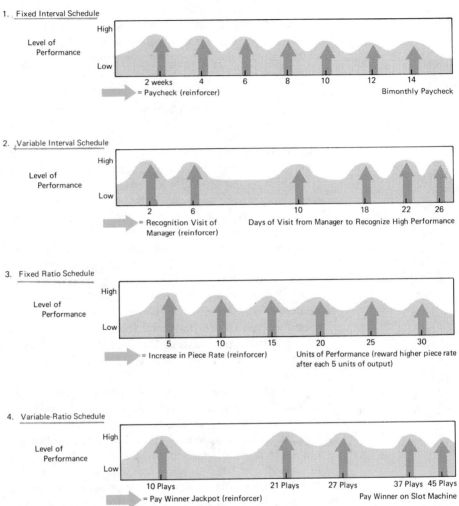

Source: Based on C. W. Hamner and D. W. Organ, *Organizational Behavior* (Plano, Tex.: Business Publications, 1978), pp. 55 (Figure 3–2).

a reinforcer. However, the number varies around an average. The example in Figure 4–10 shows that over the 140 trials the average reinforcements occurs every 28 plays; 10, 21, 27, 37, 45, or 140 divided by five reinforcements.

Research has shown that higher rates of response usually are achieved with ratio rather than interval schedules. This finding is understandable since high response rates do not necessarily speed up the delivery of a reinforcer in an interval schedule as they do with ratio schedules. A summary of the effects that the various reinforcement schedules have on behavior are presented in Table 4–1.

Research on Reinforcement Theory. The application of operant conditioning in organizations has initiated a limited number of field research studies. The popular terms used to explain operant conditioning applied to organizations include *behavior modification* or *organizational behavior modification.*

The available research on reinforcement theory applications are often limited to small samples, single organizations, and limited periods of time. Furthermore, it has on a number of occasions resulted in unexpected findings. For example, one study compared the effect of continuous and variable ratio piece-rate bonus pay plans. Contrary to predictions, the continuous schedule yielded the highest level of performance. One reason cited for less than expected effectiveness of the variable ratio schedules was that some employees working on these schedules were opposed to the pay plan. They perceived the plan as a form of gambling and this was not acceptable to them.[42]

Critics of organizational behavior modification have attacked it on a number of grounds. A frequent concern with using reinforcers is that there is no "real" change in behavior. The person is just being "bribed" to perform. Bribery refers to the illicit use of rewards to corrupt the conduct of someone. This is not really what is meant by reinforcement. In reinforcement, outcomes are delivered for behaviors that are generally agreed upon to benefit the person and the organization. Thus, this criticism is logical but really not that accurate for the type of reinforcers usually used in organizations.

One critic believes that the view that reinforcements modify responses automatically, independent of a person's beliefs, values, or mental processes is simply a wrong way to view human behavior. Locke claims that this theory is simple and appealing but that the facts do not support it. He claims that people can learn by seeing others get reinforcement. People can also learn by imitating others who are not reinforced. There is also self-reinforcement that is ignored by operant conditioning theorists.[43]

Another criticism focuses on the point that individuals can become too dependent on extrinsic reinforcers (e.g., pay). Thus, behavior may become dependent upon the reinforcer and never performed without the promise

---

[42]G. Yukl, K. N. Wexley, and J. E. Seymore, "Effectiveness of Pay Incentives under Variable Ratio and Continuous Reinforcement Schedules," *Journal of Applied Psychology*, February 1972, pp. 19–23.

[43]Edwin A. Locke, "The Myths of Behavior Mod in Organizations," *Academy of Management Review*, October 1977, pp. 543–53. In addition to Locke's critique of operant conditioning, also see Jerry L. Gray "The Myths of the Myths about Behavior Mod in Organizations: A Reply to Locke's Criticisms of Behavior Modification," *Academy of Management Review*, January 1979, pp. 121–29 and Marcia Parmerlee and Charles Schwenk, "Radical Behaviorism: Misconceptions in the Locke-Gray Debate," *Academy of Management Review*, October 1979, pp. 601–7.

TABLE 4–1
Reinforcement Schedules and Effects on Behavior

Schedule	Description	When Applied to Individual	When Removed by Manager	Organizational Example
Continuous	Reinforcer follows every response	Fastest method for establishing new behavior	Fastest method to cause extinction of new behavior	Praise after every response, immediate recognition of every response
Fixed interval	Response after specific time period is reinforced	Some inconsistency in response frequencies	Faster extinction of motivated behavior than variable schedules	Weekly, bimonthly, monthly paycheck
Variable interval	Response after varying period of time (an average) is reinforced	Produces high rate of steady responses	Slower extinction of motivated behavior than fixed schedules	Transfers, promotions, recognition
Fixed ratio	Fixed number of responses must occur before reinforcement	Some inconsistency in response frequencies	Faster extinction of motivated behavior than variable schedule	Piece Rate, commission on units sold
Variable ratio	A varying number (average) of responses must occur before reinforcement	Can produce high rate of response that is steady and resists extinction	Slower extinction of motivated behavior than fixed schedules	Bonus, award, time off

Source: Adapted from O. Behling, C. Schriesheim, and J. Tolliver, "Present Theories and New Directions in Theories of Work Effort," *Journal of Supplement Abstract Service of the American Psychological Association*, 1974, p. 57.

of the reinforcer. There is the point that when reinforcement is no longer provided, the behavior will eventually become extinct. There is some research available that discounts this criticism which shows that when reinforcers are terminated extinction does not always occur.[44] Unfortunately, these studies for the most part involve children and mental patients. Whether these same results can be expected of normal adults has not been adequately tested.

The following close-up points out that each of the motivation theories discussed to this point have value if they are used correctly. The psychologists and social psychologists who proposed them were experts in explaining needs, motives, and values, but really were not so astute at explaining what managers could do to motivate employees.

ORGANIZATIONS: CLOSE-UP

Should Managers Be Psychologists? NO!

Do you have to be a psychologist to understand and use the motivation theories presented in this chapter? We hope not. The theories point out that managers are not able to know with certainty what goes on inside the person's head. Motivation is merely an abstract concept invented from evidence taken from observed behavior, which supposedly explains that behavior. Yes, motivation is something that comes from within, but managers still do not know exactly what goes on inside.

Some believe that it's up to the manager and the company to set the stage, create the atmosphere to allow the employee's internal motivation to appear. To do so, managers need to tailor rewards to individual motivation. The manager has to search and find out what makes an individual tick. That is, what triggers the internal state that is eventually observed by managers as higher performance or less absenteeism.

The details, complexities, and problems associated with needs, motives, values, and physical responses to work are not really in the domain of managers. The manager is an amateur in this arena. This arena is really better suited for the professional psychologist. Likewise, the psychologist is an amateur when it comes to the day-to-day operations of managing people and creating stimulating work environments.

Thus, the psychologist is the expert who is best prepared to discuss, analyze, and interpret needs, drives, and values. On the other hand, the manager is the expert when it comes to creating the appropriate atmosphere for an employee's internal motivation to grow and be sustained. Experts in one area can look rather foolish and even be dangerous in another area. Managers need to beware and use their expertise where they are experts.

---

[44] See G. L. Paul and R. J. Lentz, *Psychosocial Treatment of Chronic Mental Patients: Milieu versus Social Learning Programs* (Cambridge, Mass.: Harvard University Press, 1977), and D. C. Russo and R. L. Koegel, "A Method for Integrating an Autistic Child into a Normal Public School Classroom," *Journal of Applied Behavior Analysis*, October 1977, pp. 579–90.

MAJOR MANAGERIAL ISSUES

A. Any attempt to improve job performance of individuals must invariably utilize motivation theories. This results from the fact that motivation is concerned with behavior, or, more specifically, goal-directed behavior.

B. A major reason why behaviors of employees differ is that needs and goals of people vary. Social, cultural, hereditary, and job factors are forces that influence behaviors. In order to understand the circular nature of motivation, the manager must learn about the needs of subordinates.

C. The theories of motivation can be classified as being either content or process. Each theory in both categories emphasizes a "particular" orientation. Some of course are more explicit but each illustrates that employees desire some goal(s) in performing their jobs. The manager should try to determine the various goals desired by subordinates.

D. The Maslow theory assumes that people have a need to grow and develop. The implication is that motivational programs will have a higher probability of success if the upper level need deficiencies are reduced. Although Maslow's need hierarchy has not met most of the standards of scientific testing, it appears that an adequately fulfilled need does not provide a good target for managers in building motivators that can influence performance.

E. Herzberg's two-factor theory of motivation identifies two types of factors in the workplace, satisfiers and dissatisfiers. One apparent weakness of the theory is that its findings have not been replicated by other researchers. Despite this and other shortcomings it focuses on job-related factors in managerial terminology.

F. McClelland has proposed a theory of learned needs. The behavior associated with the needs for achievement, affiliation, and power is instrumental in the job performance of an individual. A manager should attempt to acquire an understanding of these needs.

G. Expectancy theory of motivation is concerned with the expectations of a person and how they influence behavior. One value of this theory is that it can provide a manager with a means for pinpointing desirable and undesirable outcomes associated with task performance.

H. Equity theory focuses on comparisons, tension, and tension reduction. Most of the research work to date has involved pay. Equity theory is a more straightforward and understandable explanation of employee attitudes about pay than expectancy theory. The manager should be aware of the fact that people compare their rewards, punishments, job tasks, and other job-related dimensions to those of others.

I. Reinforcement theory relies on applying the principles of operant conditioning to motivate people. The major feature of this theory emphasizes the use of positive reinforcement and reinforcement schedules.

DISCUSSION AND REVIEW QUESTIONS

1. Vroom's expectancy model includes the concepts of valence, expectancy, and instrumentality. What are the meanings of these concepts, and how could a manager determine these concepts as they apply to his or her subordinates?

2. Could a manager who understands equity theory utilize this knowledge in developing pay programs? How?

3. What is the stigma associated with behavior modification? What do you think is necessary to reduce some of the managerial resistance to this approach?

4. Some people believe that pay satisfaction is a factor which reduces need deficiencies at upper and lower need levels. What is the logic of those who assume that pay satisfaction permeates the entire need hierarchy?

5. Why is it difficult to conclude that measurement of n Ach is scientifically based?

6. What type of schedules of reinforcement can be used by managers? Explain.

7. What is the difference between motivation and satisfaction? Can an employee be motivated and still indicate low job satisfaction? Explain.

8. Would environmental conditions such as double-digit or runaway inflation influence the need deficiencies that an employee experiences on the job? How?

9. Would moderate or difficult goals be preferred by the high n Ach individual? Explain.

10. How do learning principles and positive reinforcement influence needs such as those discussed by McClelland? How can a company utilize the McClelland theory of motivation in personnel selection and placement programs?

ADDITIONAL REFERENCES

Adams, J. S., and S. Freedman. "Equity Theory Revisited: Comments and Annotated Bibliography." In *Advances in Experimental Social Psychology*, edited by L. Berkowitz. New York: Academic Press, 1976, vol. 8.

Behling, O.; C. Schriesheim; and J. Tolliver. "Alternatives to Expectancy Theories of Work Motivation." *Decision Sciences*, 1975, pp. 449–61.

Carrell, M. R. "A Longitudinal Field Assessment of Employee Perceptions of Equitable Treatment." *Organizational Behavior and Human Performance*, 1978, pp. 108–18.

Carrell, M. R., and J. Dittrich. "Equity Theory: The Recent Literature, Methodological Considerations, and New Directions." *Academy of Management Review*, 1978, pp. 202–10.

Honig, W. K., and J. E. R. Staddon, eds. *Handbook of Operant Behavior*. Englewood Cliffs, N.J.: Prentice-Hall, 1977.

Ivancevich, J. M., and J. T. McMahon. "Black-White Differences in a Goal-Setting Program." *Organizational Behavior and Human Performance*, 1977, pp. 337–52.

Komaki, J.; W. M. Wadell; and M. G. Pearce. "The Applied Behavior Analysis Approach and Individual Employees: Improving Performance in Two Small Businesses." *Organizational Behavior and Human Performance*, 1977, pp. 337–52.

Nord, W. R. "Job Satisfaction Reconsidered." *American Psychologist*, 1977, pp. 1026–35.

Scott, W. E., Jr. "Expectancy Postulates in Leadership." In *Point and Counterpoint in Organizational Behavior*, edited by B. Karmel. Philadelphia: W. B. Saunders, 1979.

Skinner, B. F. *Contingencies of Reinforcement*. New York: Appleton-Century-Crofts, 1969.

Staw, B. M. "Motivation in Organizations: Toward Synthesis and Redirection." In *New Directions in Organizational Behavior*, edited by B. M. Staw and G. R. Salancik. Chicago: St. Clair, 1977, pp. 55–96.

Yukl, G. A.; G. P. Latham; and E. L. Pursell. "The Effectiveness of Performance Incentives under Continuous and Variable Ratio Schedules of Reinforcement." *Personnel Psychology*, 1976, pp. 221–31.

A MOTIVATOR OF PEOPLE MUST BE REPLACED: THE AFTERMATH

The McLaughlin Engineering Corporation employs approximately, 1,200 operating employees. The plant is old, but is kept reasonably clean and is known as one of the better production facilities in the area. The plant has a research and development department, an industrial relations department, an accounting and financial control department, a distribution department, and four operating departments that produce valves, metal brackets, metal shelves, and pistons. Exhibit 1 is an organizational chart of a typical operating department.

EXHIBIT 1

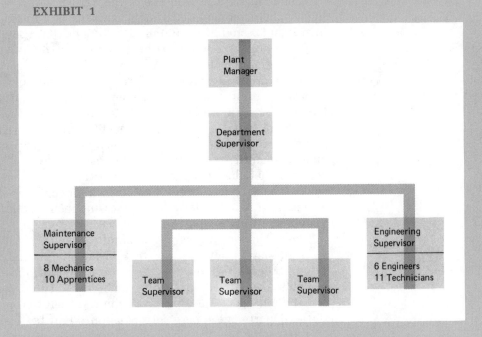

The plant manager, Joe Ruggio, was responsible for all production, maintenance, and engineering work performed in the departments. The department supervisor of the unit represented above was Clyde Campbell. He reported directly to Joe and had two support units—maintenance and engineering. Clyde also had three team supervisors reporting directly to him. These men were each responsible for one of the three shifts—days (8–4), afternoons (4–12), nights (12–8).

The maintenance team consisted of 8 mechanics and 10 apprentice mechanics who worked on maintaining the machinery. They worked closely with the engineering team who worked primarily on experimenting with new equipment, new plant layouts, and other problems of technological change. Although the engineers were college graduates they worked extremely well with the mechanics and respected their technical knowledge.

The mechanics and engineers also respected the team supervisors who worked hard and were interested in task accomplishment and people problems. The smooth coordination and mutual respect among the managerial and operating employees were certainly trademarks of McLaughlin. At the annual supervisory conference, the founder Tommy McLaughlin, even at age 62, would mention the importance of respect, trust, and confidence. This message was continaully presented in the company newspaper and at almost every annual award dinner.

Clyde had worked with McLaughlin for 18 years and had a reputation of being a technical expert in every phase of production. In fact, all of the four operating department supervisors were known throughout the organization for their technical and engineering skills.

The company has been one of the most popular within the community. In fact, the personnel department typically has an employment waiting list of at least 50 engineers, 100 mechanics, and 300 operating employees. Generally, about 80 percent of these people are qualified, but turnover is so low that there has been little hiring in the past three years.

The engineering group had no desire to unionize, and the mechanics who were unionized did not become involved in union politics. The plant has never had a strike, although other plants in the area are continually striking for better wages, fringe benefits, and other related matters.

The performance of the plant had been improving in every area—in quality, quantity, and costs—for the past 10 years. The operating employees said that they respected the company and the management team because the managers knew what the employees' problems were all about. The managers were viewed as possessing technical knowledge and not just "paper shuffling" expertise.

Clyde became seriously ill around Christmas. He tried to come back to work in March, but was too weak physically and eventually had to take a disability leave in June. The three team supervisors were all considered for promotion to Clyde's position, but it was felt that they lacked experience to handle the job. The selection committee felt that promoting an engineer to the department supervisory position might be interpreted as favoritism by the mechanics. Thus Nelson Morley, a 43-year-old engineer from Staley Engineering Corporation was hired to replace Clyde.

Nelson changed a few of Clyde's operating procedures concerning the reporting of productivity. The performance report procedure was one major change that many people disliked. Nelson would meet with the team supervisors once a month to go over reports on performance of the three shifts. Clyde had met with the managers only as a team and did not meet separately with supervisors, engineers, and mechanics. There had been no regularity in Clyde's arrangement; the teams might meet once a week, twice a month, or once every six months.

Even before Nelson joined the company a number of mechanics, engineers, and operating employees had said that they would leave if Clyde did not return. They believed that they performed well because of him. He was what they described as a "motivator of men."

Nelson was called an "outside renegade" behind his back. The quality of work and timeliness in filling orders suffered significantly after Nelson took over. The total team had been split because of his practice of only meeting with team supervisors. The engineers and mechanics began to quarrel with the supervisors about standards and procedures. These disagreements seemed to be most intense immediately after the monthly meetings between Nelson and the team supervisors.

One supervisor said, "Nelson is now the boss and we must get into step and follow his procedures." This feeling was not shared by a single mechanic or engineer. It appeared to them that the team supervisors were joining up with Nelson.

Joe was very concerned with the turn of events in the department and asked Nelson to visit with him. The objective of the meeting was to work out a plan so that performance and satisfaction would return to more acceptable levels.

Questions for Consideration

1. What type of plan could Joe and Nelson develop to correct the situation described?
2. Will Nelson be viewed as the "motivator of men" in this situation? Explain your answer in terms of a need satisfaction model.

EXPERIENTIAL EXERCISE

APPLYING MOTIVATION THEORY

Objectives

1. To evaluate the merits of different motivation theories.
2. To emphasize the decisions that must be made by managers in motivating people.
3. To apply motivation principles.

Related Topics

The manager must make decisions to succeed.
The difficulty of diagnosing situations.

Starting the Exercise

Set up groups of five to eight students to read the facts and the situation facing Margo Williams.

The Facts

In the chapter a number of popular content and process theories were discussed. Some of the major points raised were the following:

Maslow—Motivation involves satisfying needs in a hierarchical order.

Herzberg—Some job factors are intrinsically satisfying and motivate individuals.

McClelland—Motives are acquired from a person's culture.

Expectancy Theory—Motivation is a function of (a) expectancy; (b) valence; and (c) instrumentality.

Equity Theory—Individuals are motivated to achieve equity between their inputs/outputs in comparison to the inputs/outputs of a comparison person(s).

Reinforcement Theory—Positive reinforcers can be applied to motivate behavior.

With these six theories in mind, review the work situation that is currently facing Margo Williams.

Margo Williams is a project engineer director in a large construction company. She is responsible for scheduling projects, meeting customers, reporting progress on projects, costs, and subordinate development. A total of 20 men and 8 women report to Margo. All of them are college graduates and have at least eight years of job experience. Margo is a Ph.D. engineer, but only has four years of project engineering experience.

The biggest problems facing Margo involve the lack of respect and response she receives from her subordinates. These problems have been considered by Margo's supervisor and it is assumed that her moderate record of success could be improved if she could correct the situation. Margo is now considering a course of action that could motivate her subordinates to show more respect and respond more favorably to her requests.

Exercise Procedures

1. Set up small discussion groups of five to eight students to develop a motivation plan for Margo. The group should work on developing a plan that uses the motivation principles discussed in the chapter.

2. After working as a group for approximately 30 minutes, a group leader should present the plan to the class.

3. Discuss each group's plan for the remainder of the class period.

Chapter 5 ——————

Motivation: Applications in Organizations

AN ORGANIZATIONAL ISSUE FOR DEBATE
Participation Is for Everyone

ARGUMENT FOR

Some argue that there are moral reasons why employees should be permitted to participate in management decisions. The impetus for this argument evolves from those who support participative practices in all phases of life.

The advocates of participative practices (e.g., allowing workers to make decisions about the kind of work they do, how they are to do their job, and with what resources) have in various sources accused those who are skeptical of using participation as being "exploitive," "dictatorial," "autocratic," and even "suppressive."

The negative view of nonparticipation is concisely captured in a poem found in a paper supporting participation. The poem read:

> Sweet Mary your production's poor,
> Just dry your tears and go,
> For speed and greed are rated high,
> But love for others no.

———————

This debate was developed from Edwin A. Locke and David M. Schweiger, "Participation in Decision Making," in *Research in Organizational Behavior*, ed. B. Staw (Greenwich: JAI Press, 1979), pp. 266–68. The poem in the debate is found in J. Gillespie, "Toward Freedom in Work," in *The Case for Participatory Democracy: Some Prospects for a Radical Society*, ed. C. G. Benello and D. Ronseopoulos (New York: Grossman, 1971), p. 74.

ARGUMENT AGAINST

Participative management for everyone is a claim made by advocates of this psuedohumanistic approach to motivation. Certainly not all employees want to participate in the least bit with any decisions related to their jobs. Some prefer to work hard, keep a low profile, be pleasant with co-workers, and earn a comfortable living. It is this "silent majority" that do not want someone or some group to force participation on them. They take pride in what they do, like what they do, and simply prefer to not participate in decisions. Who has the moral right in the first place to tell someone that he or she "must," "should," "will," or "needs" to participate?

The advocates of participation often point to research supporting their approach. A careful review of the research indicates biased interpretation and reporting of results. For example, some studies involve a number of changes in such areas as policies, procedures, degree of participation permitted, and incentives. The pro-participation interpretation attributes successes or improvements to participative management. Another example is the description of the participative leader in studies as considerate, warm, supportive, respectful, rational, and astute. On the other hand, the authoritarian leader is described as cold, arbitrary, production-oriented, harsh, and

ARGUMENT FOR (continued)

Today there are even some behavioral scientists who suggest that government legislation be used to force organizations to improve the "quality of work life." It is their position that organizations have a responsibility to take care of people, to support their personal development, and to permit such practices as participation.

People are assumed to want to participate and to be involved. It is the cold realities of profit-orientation that have literally forced organizations to be more concerned about nonparticipation than about participation. A reorientation in such thinking is needed to correct the mistakes of nonparticipation. What is also needed is an awareness of the benefits of participation. If only managers could be made aware of the positive results associated with participation such as improved morale, increased job satisfaction, and increased performance.

As members of society become more educated there must be a shift in organizations toward more participative management. The educated man or woman wants more say in how he or she will do a job. This is what educated people demand and seek—autonomy, self-actualization, and the right to make decisions.

The pro-participation arguments are supported by not only research in the United States but also studies being conducted in other countries. Research from Germany, France, Sweden, and even Yugoslavia present compelling evidence on the value of participation.

ARGUMENT AGAINST (continued)

impersonal. Are there no authoritarian leaders who are firm, definite, considerate, knowledgeable, and respected or participative leaders who are weak, poorly prepared, ignorant, and unassertive? Yes, there are these kind of leaders. And yes they are never mentioned by the pro-participative writers, scholars, and intellects. Why?

If and where participative management is used the choice should be carefully made. There is no guarantee that it will always work. This type of careful consideration and questioning of where it should be applied is healthier than forcing it into imperfect, unsuitable situations. What would be more helpful to practicing managers is a softening of the pro-participative bias in theory, research, and application claims.

The evidence is not available that participation is the best method to use. Furthermore, the interpretation bias is too blatant to ignore or to not attack as a poor use of scientific principles. In addition, the moral argument is hollow since managers have no right to force any system of management or technique on others. The most nonparticipative practice of all is actually displayed by advocates of participation when they force others to participate.

The previous chapter was devoted to a number of popular motivational theories discussed in the organizational behavior literature. In this chapter four applied areas of motivation used by managers are examined: goal setting, behavior modification, participative management, and the modified or compressed workweeks. In recent years, the application of these four approaches has become more prominent and widespread.

The purpose of this chapter is to (1) describe the application, (2) report on some of the available research, (3) review at least one application in an organization, and (4) critique the application in managerial terms. One thing that each of these applied areas have in common is that practicing managers are using them in work organizations. They are being tried, modified, and even discarded by managers who are concerned about motivating subordinates.

GOAL SETTING

■ There has been considerable and growing interest in applying goal setting to organizational problems and issues since Locke presented what is now considered a classic paper in 1968.[1] He proposed that goal setting is a cognitive process that has some practical utility.

Descriptions of Goal Setting

A goal is what an individual is trying to achieve, it is the object of an action. For example, attempting to produce four units on a production line, or to cut direct costs by $3,000, or to decrease absenteeism in a department by 12 percent are goals. Frederick W. Taylor has had a direct influence on the current thinking about goals and goal-setting practices.

Locke proposes that Taylor used assigned goals as one of his key techniques of Scientific Management. Each employee was assigned a challenging but attainable goal based on the results of motion and time study. The methods by which the individual achieved the assigned goals (e.g., tools used, work procedures followed, pacing needed to do the job) were spelled out in detail.[2]

Thus, to Locke's credit he points out the significant influence of Taylor in his formulation of goal setting. He also carefully describes the attributes of the mental (cognitive) processes of goal setting. The attributes he specifically highlights are goal specificity, goal difficulty, and goal intensity.

Goal specificity is the degree of quantitative precision (clarity) of the goal. *Goal difficulty* is the degree of proficiency or level of performance sought. *Goal intensity* pertains to the process of setting the goal or the process of determining how to reach it.[3] To date goal intensity has not been widely studied, although a related concept *goal commitment* has been con-

---

[1] Edwin A. Locke, "Toward a Theory of Task Motivation and Incentives," *Organizational Behavior and Performance*, May 1968, pp. 157–89.

[2] Frederick W. Taylor, *The Principles of Scientific Management* (New York: W. W. Norton, 1947).

[3] Edwin A. Locke, Karyll N. Shaw, Lise M. Saari, and Gary P. Latham, "Goal Setting and Task Performance: 1969–1980," Technical Report GS–1, Office of Naval Research, June 1980, p. 6.

FIGURE 5–1
Goal Setting Applied to Organizations

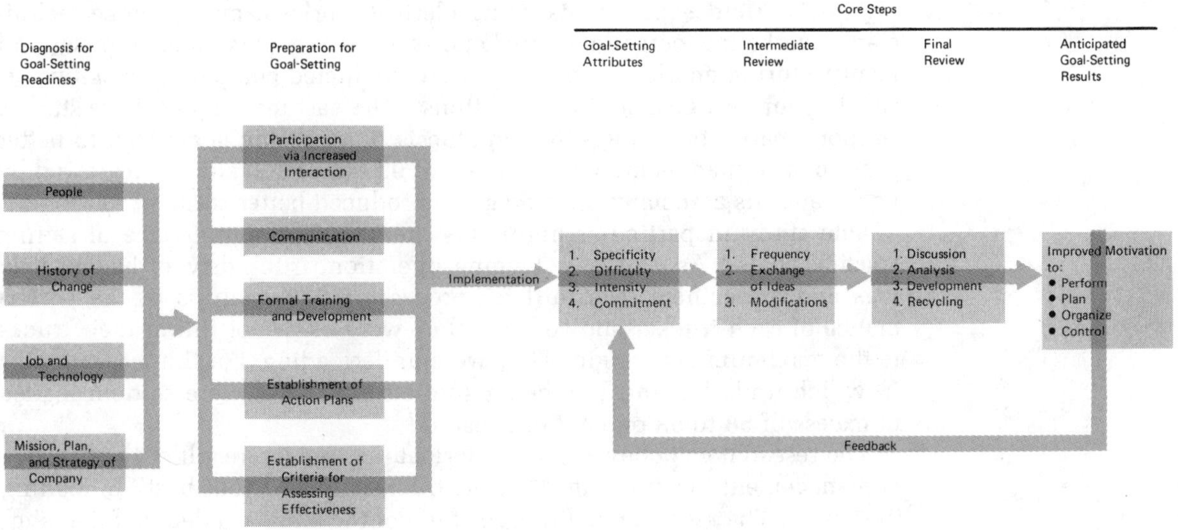

Diagnosis for Goal-Setting Readiness	Preparation for Goal-Setting	Core Steps			
		Goal-Setting Attributes	Intermediate Review	Final Review	Anticipated Goal-Setting Results

People

History of Change

Job and Technology

Mission, Plan, and Strategy of Company

Participation via Increased Interaction

Communication

Formal Training and Development

Establishment of Action Plans

Establishment of Criteria for Assessing Effectiveness

Implementation

1. Specificity
2. Difficulty
3. Intensity
4. Commitment

1. Frequency
2. Exchange of Ideas
3. Modifications

1. Discussion
2. Analysis
3. Development
4. Recycling

Improved Motivation to:
• Perform
• Plan
• Organize
• Control

Feedback

sidered in a number of studies. *Goal commitment* is the amount of effort used to achieve a goal.

Figure 5–1 portrays applied goal setting from a managerial perspective and the sequence of events for such a program. The key steps in applying goal setting are (1) *diagnosis* for readiness—determining if the people, the organization, and the technology are suited for goal setting, (2) *preparing* employees via increased interpersonal interaction, communication, training, and action plans for goal setting, (3) *emphasizing* the attributes in goals that should be understood by a manager and subordinates, (4) *conducting* intermediate reviews to make necessary adjustments in established goals, and (5) performing the final review to check goals set, modified, and accomplished. Each of these steps needs to be carefully planned and implemented if goal setting is to be an effective motivational technique. In too many applications of goal-setting, steps outlined in or issues suggested by Figure 5–1 are ignored.

Goal-Setting Research

The amount of research on goal setting between 1968 and 1980 has increased considerably. Locke's 1968 paper on goal setting certainly contributed to the increase in laboratory and field research on goal setting. Another force behind the increase in interest and research is that managers wanted practical and specific techniques to apply in their organizations. Goal setting offered such a technique for some managers.[4]

Specific Goals versus Vague Goals. Research has found that specific

---

[4]Edwin A Locke, "The Ubiquity of the Technique of Goal Setting in Theories of and Approaches to Employee Motivation," *Academy of Management Review*, July 1978, p. 600.

goals lead to higher output than vague goals such as do your best.[5] The do-your-best groups in research studies are considered equivalent to not having goals. Field experiments using clerical workers, maintenance technicians, marketing personnel, truckers, engineering personnel, typists, and manufacturing employees have all been conducted comparing specific versus do-your-best goal-setting conditions.[6] The vast majority of these studies supports partly or in total the hypothesis that specific goals lead to better performance than vague goals. In fact of 99 out of 110 studies reviewed by Locke and his associates specific goals produced better results.[7]

One study in particular highlights the practical significance of setting specific goals.[8] As part of a logging operation, truck drivers had to load logs and drive them to a mill for processing. An analysis of the performance of each trucker showed that they were often not filling their trucks to the maximum net weight. They were underloading. For the three months in which underloading was being studied the trucks were seldom loaded in excess of 58 to 63 percent of capacity.

The researchers believed that underloading was the result of the practice of management to simply instruct the truckers to "do your best" in loading the trucks. The researchers through study of the situation decided that simply setting a specific goal could be the motivational impetus to improve the situation. The researchers decided that a specific goal of 94 percent of capacity would be assigned to the drivers. It was agreed that no driver would be disciplined for failing to reach the assigned goal. No monetary rewards or fringe benefits other than praise from the supervisor were given for improving upon the performance. No specific training or instruction was given to the managers or the drivers.

Within the first month after assigning the goal, performance increased to 80 percent of the truck's limit. After the second month, however, performance decreased to 70 percent. Interviews with the drivers indicated that they were testing management's promise not to take disciplinary action if goals were not met. After the third month performance exceeded 90 percent of the truck's limit. This performance has been maintained for seven years after the original research.

This field experiment and the results are impressive. It suggests that setting specific goals can be a powerful force. The value of goal-setting is reflected in a statement of the researchers:

> The setting of a goal that is both specific and challenging leads to an increase in performance because it makes it clearer to the individual what he is supposed to do. This in turn may provide the worker with a sense of achievement, recognition, and commitment, in that he can compare how well he is

---

[5] Locke, "Task Motivation and Incentives."

[6] For a complete analysis, see Locke et al., "Goal Setting."

[7] Ibid.

[8] Gary Latham and J. James Baldes, "The Practical Significance of Locke's Theory of Goal Setting," *Journal of Applied Psychology*, February, 1975, pp. 122–24.

doing now versus how well he has done in the past and in some instances, how well he is doing in comparison to others.[9]

Goal Difficulty.   It is generally agreed that the more difficult the goal, the higher the level of performance. The important point, however, is that it works this way if the goals are accepted. A point of diminishing returns appears to be a real issue concerning goal difficulty. Although laboratory and field studies find that people with high (difficult) goals consistently perform better there is a critical point.[10] If and when a goal is perceived as so difficult that it is virtually impossible to attain, the result is often frustration rather than achievement.

The difficulty of fund raising goals of the United Fund point up the issue of frustration.[11] The more difficult the goal, the more money raised. This was true only when the goals were seen as achievable. When they were not viewed as attainable the morale of fund raisers suffered.

Individual Differences.   Scattered throughout the goal-setting literature are studies that examine the effects of individual difference on goal setting. Most have dealt with the effects of education, race, and job tenure on the goal-setting process. In one study involving electronics technicians it was found that goal difficulty (challenge) was significantly related to performance only for those technicians with 12 or more years of education. The technicians with less education reported that goal clarity (e.g., having a clear understanding of the goal) and goal feedback (e.g., receiving feedback on how results match the goal) were significantly related to performance.[12]

In a field experiment loggers working under assigned, participative, and do your best conditions were compared. It was found that participative goal setting affected the performance of the less educated loggers but did not affect the performance of the more educated loggers.[13]

One study examined race as a goal-setting variable. Goal clarity and goal feedback were related to performance for blacks only.[14] On the other hand, goal difficulty (challenge) was found to be related to performance for whites only. It was proposed by the researchers that perhaps clarity and feedback affected the black goal setters because blacks have a higher need for security. One way to derive more security is to have goal clarity and receive quality feedback.

In general individual difference studies on goal setting are inconclusive.

---

[9]Ibid., p. 124.

[10]Locke, et al., "Goal Setting."

[11]A Zander and T. T. Newcomb, Jr., "Goal Levels of Aspirations in United Fund Campaigns," *Journal of Personality and Social Psychology*, June 1967, pp. 157–62.

[12]John M. Ivancevich and J. Timothy McMahon, "Education as a Moderator of Goal-Setting Effectiveness," *Journal of Vocational Behavior*, August 1977, pp. 83–94.

[13]Gary P. Latham and Gary A. Yukl, "Assigned versus Participative Goal Setting with Educated and Uneducated Wood Workers," *Journal of Applied Psychology*, June 1975, pp. 299–302.

[14]John M. Ivancevich and J. Timothy McMahon, "Black-White Differences in a Goal Setting Program," *Organizational Behavior and Human Performance*, December 1977, pp. 287–300.

There is no clear pattern that education, race, tenure, sex, age, need for achievement, self-esteem, or any of the variables studied are significant.

Goal Setting: An Application at Tenneco

Tenneco is a large, diversified, multiindustry company operating in eight major industries.[15] Some of the Tenneco companies include J. I. Case, manufacturer and marketer of farm and construction equipment; Packaging Corporation of America, a vertically integrated supplier of paperboard, folding cartons, and corrugated containers. Unlike most users of goal setting Tenneco decided to emphasize not only performance goals but also personal development goals in their program.

The chairman of the board at Tenneco issued statements, memos, and guidelines for the goal-setting effort. The emphasis on personal development was to be accomplished through a program that required setting goals that focused on performance and development criteria of success for managers. The program was designed by a task force representing each of Tenneco's companies.

One phase that was especially stressed in Tenneco was formally training the goal-setting participants (managers) in "how to do it." A corporate level training package was prepared. However, each company altered, added to, or subtracted from the corporate training package. The training package presented what goal setting was, how it was to be used, and the skills needed to be effective in goal setting.

Reexamine Figure 5–1 since this is basically the sequence of events and framework followed in Tenneco's goal-setting program. Management systematically diagnosed, prepared for goal setting, and implemented each of the core steps—goal setting, intermediate reviews, and a final review. The evaluations of the Tenneco goal-setting program suggest:

1. Improved morale after the program was implemented.
2. A more relaxed (less job tension) work environment for users of the goal-setting program.
3. More success in those Tenneco units in which management (supervisors) actively participate in and support goal setting.
4. The necessity to spend time in diagnosis, training, and evaluation so that proper alterations in procedures and types of goals set can be made.
5. That many individuals have difficulty in establishing personal development goals. This difficulty may be caused by the overemphasis on performance. Many individuals have not had to think in terms of their own personal development. Thus, there is some initial difficulty in setting personal development goals.

---

[15] Based on the detailed study as presented in unpublished reports, executive summaries, and in John M. Ivancevich, J. Timothy McMahon, J. William Streidl, and Andrew D. Szilagyi, Jr., "Goal Setting: The Tenneco Approach to Personnel Development and Management Effectiveness," *Organizational Dynamics*, Winter 1978, pp. 58–80.

6. Patience is needed before declaring an applied goal-setting program like Tenneco's a success or a failure. Those using goal setting should use time periods of longer than six months or even a year before reaching any conclusions. At Tenneco numerous improvements and some negative results (irritation with paperwork, not being trained properly or long enough to do the goal setting) did not show up until one to two years after the program was initiated.

Tenneco is not presented as either a success or a failure case of applied goal setting. Instead it is a view of the complexities, details, and hard work associated with goal setting. There is no easy or ideal way to apply goal setting. Instead advanced preparation for successes, failure, and changes along the way seems to be the best way to approach goal setting in work organizations.

A Brief Critique of Goal Setting

Unfortunately there are some arguments against using or becoming too enthusiastic about goal setting. Some managers and researchers have found that:

Goal setting is rather *complex* and *difficult* to *sustain*. The Tenneco case displayed how difficulties across divisions became somewhat disruptive when use of a corporate set of guidelines for action was implemented.

Goal setting works well for simple jobs—clerical, typists, loggers, and technicians but not for complex jobs. Goal setting with jobs in which quantitative goals are not easily measured (e.g., teaching, nursing, engineering, accounting) have posed some problems.

Goal setting encourages game playing. Set low goals to look good later is one tactic or game played by subordinates who do not want to be caught short. Managers play games by setting an initial goal that is generally not achievable and then finding out how subordinates react.

Goal accomplishment can become an obsession. In some situations goal setters have become so obsessed with achieving their goals that they neglect other important areas of their jobs.

Goal setting is used as another check on employees. Actually it is a control device to monitor performance.

Goal setting can be a very powerful technique for motivating employees. When used correctly, carefully monitored, and actively supported by managers, goal setting can improve performance. However, using goal setting or any technique to correct every problem is not feasible. This unfortunately is what some enthusiastic advocates have turned goal setting into— a panacea for everything. No applied approach can be *the* technique to solve all performance problems.

BEHAVIOR MODIFICATION

■ The use of behavior modification (a term that is used synonymously with organizational behavior modification (O B Mod) and operant conditioning) has become widely applied in work organizations. In Chapter 3 the work of B. F. Skinner upon which behavior modification is largely based was developed.

Description of Behavior Modification

Recall that Skinner believes that: (1) behavior which appears to lead to a positive consequence (e.g., a reward) tends to be repeated, while behavior that leads to a negative consequence tends not to be repeated; and (2) therefore, by providing properly scheduled rewards, it is possible to influence behavior.

Behavior modification assumes that behavior is more important than its "psychological causes" such as the needs, motives, and values held by individuals. Thus, the behaviorist focuses on specific behaviors and not on intangibles such as esteem needs or personality structure. For example, if a behaviorist is told that an employee is not performing well, he or she would probably ask, "what specific behavior led to reaching this conclusion?" The behaviors that are discrete and distinguishable are the most important in developing any behavior modification plan to correct a performance problem.

In addition to the attention devoted to discrete and distinguishable behaviors there is an emphasis on the consequences of behavior. For example, suppose that all new management trainees are given a two-day training program on preparing budget reports. However it is noticed shortly after the training sessions are completed that few reports are prepared correctly. One explanation may be that the training program was ineffective. This may be the problem.

However, the behaviorist might approach the problem from a different direction. First, he or she could determine if the trainees understand the importance of correct reports. He or she may then find out who is turning in correct reports and find out the consequences incurred by these trainees. It could be that turning in correct reports results in nothing, there is no observable consequence. In the same manner submitting an incorrect report also results in no consequence, positive or negative. This finding may result in developing a program of positive and negative consequences (e.g., recognition, praise, a meeting with the boss to go over mistakes). The behaviorist believes that people tend to repeat behaviors that lead to positive consequences. This principle could serve as a cornerstone in improving report accuracy of trainees.

The proposed application of behavior modification in organizations follows a problem-solving process.[16] Figure 5–2 shows a problem-solving model that emphasizes five major points. First, the manager must identify

---

[16]Two excellent behavior modification problem solving processes, that are very similar, are found in Lawrence M. Miller, *Behavior Management* (New York: John Wiley & Sons, 1978), pp. 64–66; and Fred Luthans, *Organizational Behavior* (New York: McGraw-Hill, 1981), pp. 270–89.

FIGURE 5–2
Applied Behavior Modification:
A Manager's Step-by-Step Procedure

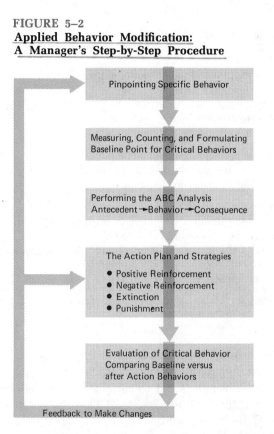

Pinpointing Specific Behavior

Measuring, Counting, and Formulating
Baseline Point for Critical Behaviors

Performing the ABC Analysis
Antecedent →Behavior →Consequence

The Action Plan and Strategies
• Positive Reinforcement
• Negative Reinforcement
• Extinction
• Punishment

Evaluation of Critical Behavior
Comparing Baseline versus
after Action Behaviors

Feedback to Make Changes

and define the specific behavior. A behavior is pinpointed when it can be accurately and reliably observed and recorded. To be pinpointed as an important behavior there must be positive answers to the questions: (1) Can it be seen? and (2) Can it be measured?[17]

Second, the manager must measure or count the occurrences of the pinpointed behavior. This count provides the manager with a clear perspective of the strength of the behavior under the present or before change situation. The count serves as the means of evaluating any changes in behavior that may occur later on. Many managers graph these data to determine whether the behavior is increasing, decreasing, or remaining the same.

Third, the manager conducts an analysis of the ABCs of the behavior.[18] This is also called functionally analyzing the behavior.[19] The A designates analyzing the antecedents of the actual behavior B. The B designates the

---

[17]Discussed by Luthans, *Organizational Behavior,* and Fred Luthans and Jason Schweizer, "How Behavior Modification Techniques Can Improve Total Organizational Performance," *Management Review,* September 1979, pp. 43–50.

[18]Thomas K. Connellan, *How to Improve Human Performance: Behaviorism in Business and Industry* (New York: Harper & Row, 1978), pp. 48–75.

[19]Luthans, *Organizational Behavior,* p. 276.

TABLE 5–1
Performance Analysis Questions

Antecedent
1. Does the employee know what is expected?
    Are the standards clear?
    Have they been communicated?
    Are they realistic?

Behavior
2. Can the behavior be performed?
    Could the employee do it if his or her life depended upon it?
    Does something prevent its occurrence?

Consequence
3. Are the consequences weighted in favor of performance?
4. Are improvements being reinforced?
    Do we note improvements even though the improvement may still leave the
    employee below company standards?
    Is reinforcement specific?

Source: Thomas K. Connellan, *How to Improve Human Performance: Behaviorism in Business* (New York: Harper & Row, 1978), p. 51.

pinpointed critical behaviors. Finally C indicates the contingent consequence. Specific analyses of the ABCs is attempting to determine where the problems lie. Connellan has developed a set of performance analysis questions to get at the problem source.[20] These are presented in Table 5–1.

The ABC analysis permits the manager to consider performance analysis questions that are important in formulating any specific program. For example, in analyzing absenteeism the manager using a question format and the type of framework displayed in Table 5–2 is systematically viewing the problem of absenteeism in terms of antecedents, behaviors, and consequences.

Fourth, the first three steps in an applied behavior modification program set the stage for the actual action step. The goal of operant conditioning is to strengthen desirable and observable critical performance behaviors and/or weaken undesirable behaviors. The strategies for accomplishing these goals were discussed in the previous chapter under the heading of reinforcement theory. Included as strategies are positive reinforcers, negative reinforcers, punishment, and extinction. The application of these four strategies are presented in terms of the ABCs in Figure 5–3.

Positive reinforcement is the preferred strategy in most applied behavior modification programs. However it is not always easy to identify positive reinforcers. The most obvious approach is to ask subordinates what is rewarding. It is often found that the person answering will not tell the truth.

---

[20] Connellan, *How to Improve Human Performance*, p. 51.

TABLE 5–2
Using the ABCs Analysis: An Absenteeism Problem

A Antecedent(s)	B Behavior(s)	C Consequence(s)
Family problems: wife, children	Staying home	Public reprimand
Personal health	Shopping	Private reprimand
Illness	Overslept	Written record
Jury duty	Getting up late	and reprimand
No transportation	Attending sporting	Reduction in pay
Company policies	event	Suspension
Group norm	Working at home	Fired
Friends visiting	Visiting	Social isolation
Injured on way to work	Served on jury	from group
Hangover	In emergency room	
No child care facilities	at hospital	
Do not have proper tools	At doctor's office	
or clothing		

Source: Adapted from Fred Luthans and Mark Martinko, "An Organizational Behavior Modification Analysis of Absenteeism," *Human Resources Management*, Fall 1976.

FIGURE 5–3
Reinforcement Strategies Applying the ABCs

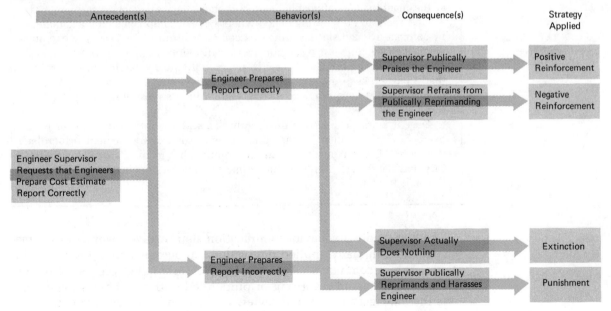

Another identification method is to use attitude surveys asking about job reward preferences.

An example of applying reinforcers is found in the gambling casinos of Atlantic City and Las Vegas. The owners may not be at all familiar with the details of reinforcement but they sure can apply them in the casinos. The following close-up shows how reinforcers encourage gamblers to keep playing.

ORGANIZATIONS: CLOSE-UP

The Use of Behavior Modification in Atlantic City and Las Vegas

There seems to be some knowledge about how reinforcement works among casino owners in Atlantic City and Las Vegas. These owners seem to know how people (the visitors, compulsive gamblers, the amateurs) react to reinforcement (a jackpot).

Most players of slot machines assume that jackpots occur according to some random reinforcement schedule. If the casino owners set the machines to pay off on a fixed ratio schedule, then counting the number of pulls between each jackpot would be a successful technique. If the slot was on a fixed interval schedule, then all the player would have to do is watch the clock and time the occurrence of jackpots. The casino owners know that staying with the machine and feeding in coins is more likely to occur if there is a random reinforcement schedule. Then the player has no idea when he or she will strike it rich. They must keep playing to win, even once or twice. Thus, what we find in Atlantic City and Las Vegas is a program of random reinforcement.

The casino owners also know the value of atmosphere in keeping players at the machine. An atmosphere of excitement is created because people all around seem to be winning. The owners have accomplished this excitement by connecting each slot machine to a central control. Why? So that when any single slot machine hits a jackpot sirens wail, lights flash, bells sound off, and screams of joy are heard and seen by everyone. This display informs everyone that it pays to keep playing. Keep inserting those coins. The payoff is money. If you want to be a winner and there are winners all around, keep feeding those coins.

Does it work? The casino owners think so. Many of them may never have heard of B. F. Skinner, but he sure provided some reinforcement principles that work. The slot machines are so popular that many visitors to Atlantic City and Las Vegas spend all their time feeding those coins and waiting for the bells to go off.

The final applied behavior modification step involves evaluation. A major weakness in many applied motivational programs is that formal evaluations are not conducted. The evaluation of an applied program involves the continuation and recording of pinpointed critical behaviors. This permits the manager to trace and review changes in behavior before and after the implementation of an action program. The use of evaluation permits managers to measure performance on an ongoing basis. Furthermore, evaluation can provide feedback to the manager on the behaviors being exhibited. This feedback can serve to make necessary and timely corrections in the program.

Behavior Modification Research

A characteristic of behavior modification research is its emphasis on use of the scientific approach. Researchers in this area take extreme care with clearly defining concepts, carefully classifying variables, and presenting results so that the data trends and changes can be easily distinguished. An example of these features is found in the reports of behavior modification research in a manufacturing plant.[21]

Two groups of production supervisors were used in the study (placed into either an experimental or control condition). The experimental group received training in how to conduct an applied behavior modification program with subordinates. The training emphasized the type of steps spelled out in Figure 5–2. The departments of the trained managers appeared to improve behaviors related to effectiveness. Their performance after the supervisors returned from training revealed fewer complaints, lower group scrap rate, and fewer rejects. Figure 5–4 shows these results.

FIGURE 5–4
Impact of Behavior Modification Training

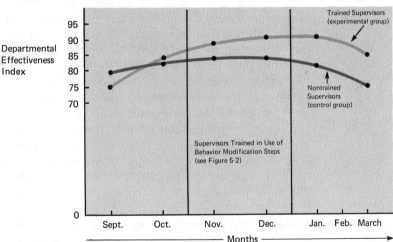

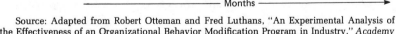

Source: Adapted from Robert Otteman and Fred Luthans, "An Experimental Analysis of the Effectiveness of an Organizational Behavior Modification Program in Industry," *Academy of Management,* Proceedings, 1975, p. 141.

[21]Robert Otteman and Fred Luthans, "An Experimental Analysis of the Effectiveness of an Organizational Behavior Modification Program in Industry," *Academy of Management,* Proceedings, 1975, pp. 140–42. For a more complete discussion, see Fred Luthans and Robert Kreitner, *Organizational Behavior Modification* (Glenview, Ill.: Scott, Foresman, 1975), pp. 150–59.

Unfortunately this well-documented study (1) was conducted in a single firm—can results be replicated in other firms? (2) only used two groups of nine production supervisors—is it manageable with larger groups? (3) covered only a seven-month period as presented—do the results hold or sustain themselves for longer periods of time? and (4) fails to discuss the costs and benefits of the training in terms of economics—it is assumed that improvement saved money, but what did the training and research cost? [22]

Behavior Modification: An Application at Emery Air Freight

In the past decade there have been numerous attempts to apply behavior modification principles in organizations. The list of users includes Michigan Bell Telephone, Ford Motor Company, American Can, United Air Lines, Warner-Lambert, Chase Manhattan Bank, Procter & Gamble, Standard Oil of Ohio. The results of some of these applications of behavior modification principles are summarized in Table 5–3.

A review of the results summarized in Table 5–3 points out some noticable features of most applied behavior modification programs. First, for the most part the programs are applied at the operating employee level (e.g., mechanics, maintenance employees, clerks). The tasks of operating employees are more compatible with the features of behavior modification— identifying critical behaviors, performance of the ABC analysis, and evaluation of changes in behavior. Second, each of the programs have specified goals. Goal setting is extremely important in behavior modification. Third, most programs focus on absenteeism and performance. Fourth, the feedback cycle is usually short—daily or weekly. Again pointing out that behavior modification may be more suited at operating levels where short-run criteria are typically used to evaluate performance. Feedback for middle and upper level managerial employees is not on such a short cycle.

Fifth, the popular set of positive reinforcers used in applied programs centers on praise, recognition, and self-feedback. Money is not that widely used in applied behavior modification programs. Finally, most reports of applied behavior modification (especially when a company is identified) present successful results. It is interesting and rare to find a reported result such as that found at the Connecticut General Life Insurance Co.

Of the many reported applications of behavior modification principles the most publicized is the program implemented at Emery Air Freight Company under the direction of Edward Feeney, a company executive. [23] The approach he used was to (1) regularly inform employees how well they were meeting specific goals and then (2) reward improvement with praise and recognition.

Feeney closely examined air freight operations at Emery (the processing

---

[22]These comments do not only apply to behavior modification research. A significant amount of organizational behavior research could be reviewed in this same manner. However, since the vast majority of research in this applied area has these characteristics they are mentioned and raised at this point.

[23]"At Emery Air Freight: Positive Reinforcement Boosts," *Organizational Dynamics,* Winter 1973, pp. 43.

TABLE 5–3
Results of Applying Behavior Modification Programs in Organizations: A Summary

The Organization	Type of Employees	Goals of Program	Frequency of Feedback	Positive Reinforcers Applied	Results
Michigan Bell	Operating level (e.g., mechanics, maintenance workers)	a. Decrease turnover and absenteeism b. Increase productivity c. Improve union-management relations	a. Lower level— daily and weekly b. Higher level— monthly and quarterly	a. Praise and recognition b. Opportunity to see onself improve	a. Attendance performance im-proved by 50 percent b. Productivity and efficiency has con-tinued to be above standard where pos-itive reinforcement is being used
Connecticut General Life Insurance Co.	Clerical and first-line supervisors	a. Decrease absenteeism b. Decrease lateness	Immediate	a. Self-feedback b. System feedback c. Earned time off	a. Chronic absenteeism and lateness has been drastically reduced b. Some divisions refused using posi-tive reinforcement because it was "outdated"
General Electric	Employees at all levels	a. Meet EEO objectives b. Decrease absenteeism and turnover c. Improve training d. Increase productivity	Immediate—uses modeling and role play as training tools to teach users	a. Praise b. Rewards c. Constructive feedback	a. Cost savings b. Increased pro-ductivity c. Increased self-esteem in minor-ity groups d. Direct labor cost decreased
B. F. Goodrich Chemical Co.	Manufacturing employees at all levels	a. Better meeting of schedules b. Increased productivity	Weekly	a. Praise b. Recognition c. Freedom to choose one's own activity	Production increases of over 300 percent

Source: Adapted from W. Clay Hamner and Ellen P. Hamner, "Behavior Modification on the Botton Line," *Organizational Dynamics*, Spring 1976, pp. 12–14.

of parcels) and found discrepancies between what should be done and what was being done. For example, in the air freight business small shipments intended for the same destinations fly at lower shipping rates when shipped together in containers (rather than as a single parcel). Thus, by encouraging employees to accumulate their shipments and use containers, the firm could ship at lower rates.

A "performance audit" showed that workers only used containers (the lower cost of shipping) about 45 percent of the time, although they thought they were using them about 90 percent of the time. Over half the containers were being shipped significantly below capacity. Management's goal was to increase container usage to 90 to 95 percent. A reinforcement program was established complete with a workbook for managers that specified how to provide praise, rewards, and feedback to their subordinates.

The results of the program were impressive. In 80 percent of the situations where it was applied, container usage increased from 45 percent to 95 percent. Savings from container usage alone amounted to over $500,000 a year and increased to $2 million during the first three years. As a result of these findings Emery began using a similar system for handling customer problems on the telephone and for estimating the container sizes needed for shipment of lightweight packages.

While the use of praise, recognition, and feedback was initially successful at Emery, these effects diminished over time. Their use became too routine. As a result, Emery had to introduce other reinforcers. These included invitations to business luncheons, public recognition for good performance such as a letter sent home or placed on the bulletin board, being assigned more desirable jobs after completing a less desirable one, and receiving special time off from the job. Again like other applied motivation programs managers had to be creative enough to introduce new reinforcers or techniques to keep the program fresh and meaningful.

A Brief Critique of Behavior Modification

Criticism of reinforcement theory covered in the previous chapter apply here. Recall that behavior modification has been criticized because it is considered to be:

Bribery.

Inaccurate and misleading because it disregards beliefs, values, mental processes—the cognitive processes of people.

Manipulative.

Based on animal studies conducted in laboratories.

Another popular criticism is that behavior modification is not a new technique for motivating employees. In discussing Feeney's Emery Air Freight application it was noted: "There is little difference between Feeney's ideas and some key elements of Scientific Management presented more than 60 years ago by Taylor."[24] The practicing manager might ask, "Why should we be concerned about whether something is new, old, or somewhere in between? Does it work?"

In reality goal setting and behavior modification share much in common. It would seem that efforts to spell out how these applications work and what problems they each solve best could benefit managers. Certainly behavior modification is different than goal setting. However, they are complementary techniques. Both orientations focus on goal accomplishment and both are performance-oriented approaches. Instead of stating that one application is better than another and assuming that over time one approach will fade from popularity, linking the approaches and pointing out each of their strengths, weaknesses, and problems seem to be a more valuable endeavor.[25]

The criticisms of behavior modification should always be considered by practicing managers. However, it should be noted that for the most part the same charge could be made about other approaches—goal setting, job enrichment, performance appraisal, and restructuring an organization. Behavior modification is probably going to continue to be applied in organizations despite the attacks of critics.

PARTICIPATIVE MANAGEMENT

■ Participative management has created much interest among managers. Participative management is not a specific technique but is rather a concept of applied management that involves employee participation in developing and implementing decisions that directly affect their jobs. The use of participation as part of a motivation program stems from the philosophy and assumptions offered by human relations advocates. Its use is based on trust, respect, and supportiveness between managers and subordinates, as noted in the following close-up.

ORGANIZATIONS: CLOSE-UP

Participative Management at Donnelley Mirrors, Inc.

An example of participative management is reported by Donnelley Mirrors, Inc. (DMI), located in Holland, Michigan. DMI has about 70 percent of the domestic market in automobile mirrors and is a major manufacturer of other glass products.

DMI began a participative program by applying interlocking work teams.

---

[24]Edwin A. Locke, "The Myths of Behavior Mod in Organizations," *Academy of Management Review*, October 1977, p. 549.

[25]Donald B. Fedor and George R. Ferris, "Integrating OB Mod with Cognitive Approaches to Motivation," *Academy of Management Review*, January 1981, pp. 115–25.

ORGANIZATIONS: CLOSE-UP (continued)

The president, John F. Donnelley, explained his participative management program this way:

> . . . the concept of interlocking work teams. It has been very useful. To show you how the teams work, let's first contrast them with the usual organization set up. . . . the one-to-one lines of reporting are gone. If the peer members of the team support one another, they can deal more realistically with the boss. He can, in fact, must, become a leader to remain effective.
>
> The key to communication of ideas between work teams is the linking pin person. His presence and influence on the "home team" and in the team at the next level provide a steady flow of information and understanding of people's needs and of company policies in both directions. The concept is one of participation. Each person manages his own task with participation in the entire company's concerns through his linking pin.
>
> With this approach, we try to achieve consensus among team members, and very often we do. When a team cannot decide an issue, the team leader, using the member's input, makes the decision. Thus there is no abdication of management responsibility, while there is a maximum of participation by those the decision affects.

Donnelley not only believes in participative management, but he encourages its use at the operating level.

Source: John F. Donnelley, "Participative Management at Work," *Harvard Business Review*, January–February 1977, pp. 117–27.

Description of Participative Management

There are many descriptions of what constitutes participative management. One study found that despite differing opinions about what constitutes participation, managers generally have a high level of agreement about participative characteristics. Table 5–4 presents a summary of how 318 managers view participation.[26] A 1 (low participation) to 7 (high participation) rating scale was used to determine the rank order positions. Giving subordinates a share in decision making was considered the most common characteristic of participative management. In general the results of the survey suggested that participation means more subordinate involvement.

Participative management varies on a number of dimensions.[27] Participation can be forced or voluntary. In some countries workers are forced by law or government decree to participate in job-related decisions. Voluntary participation occurs when management initiates the idea and employees agree to participate.

---

[26]Larry E. Greiner, "What Managers Think of Participative Leadership," *Harvard Business Review* (March–April 1973), pp. 114.

[27]For an excellent comprehensive and insightful discussion of participation, see Edwin A. Locke and David M. Schweiger, "Participation in Decision Making: One More Look," in *Research in Organizational Behavior*, ed. B. M. Staw (Greenwich, Conn.: JAI Press, 1979).

TABLE 5–4
Managers' Views of Participation

Rank		Average Scale Rating
1.	Gives subordinates a share in decision making	6.08
2.	Keeps subordinates informed of the true situation, good or bad, under all circumstances	5.69
3.	Stays aware of the state of the organization's morale and does everything possible to make it high	5.45
4.	Is easily approachable	5.38
5.	Counsels, trains, and develops subordinates	5.34
6.	Communicates effectively with subordinates	5.22
7.	Shows thoughfulness and consideration of others	5.19
8.	Is willing to make changes in ways of doing thing	4.96
9.	Is willing to support subordinates even when they make mistakes	4.92
10.	Expresses appreciation when a subordinate does a good job	4.80

Source: Larry E. Greiner, "What Managers Think of Participative Leadership," *Harvard Business Review*, March–April 1973, pp. 114.

Second, participation can be *formal* or *informal*. In formal participative management there is usually the creation of a formal decision-making unit or mechanism (e.g., a union, a board). In informal participation there would be a verbal agreement between each supervisor and subordinate about the domain of participation.

Third, participation may be *direct or indirect*. Direct participation occurs when each person can present a view, discuss a point, object to what others want or are saying. In indirect participation an elected representative speaks for employees to a higher level group.

Participation can vary in degree. There can be a condition of *no participation* where the supervisor directs and specifies exactly what is to be done. There can also be various degrees of *consultation* whereby the supervisor consults with subordinates before or after making a decision. Finally, there can be a state of *full participation* in which supervisors and subordinates are equals in reaching final decisions.

Four broad categories of decisions seem to be compatible with participative management.[28] They are:

1. *Routine Personnel Matters*. Hiring, discipline, training, and method of payment to be used
2. *Job Itself*. Work methods, job design, goal setting, speed of work.
3. *Working Conditions*. Rest pauses, hours of work, plant or office layout, interior decorating.
4. *Company Policies*. Layoffs, profit sharing, fringe benefit package, capital investment, dividends.

[28] Ibid., p. 276.

There is among participative management advocates a steady stream of claims about its positive impact on employees. It is assumed that through participation employees will be able to pool information, knowledge, energy, and creativity to solve problems. The increased flow of communication in a participative situation is assumed to be valuable. It is therapeutic and supportive because people feel like they are involved and important.

In motivational terms participation is discussed as a mechanism for reducing resistance to change. Through participation employees are assumed to increase their trust, respect, and understanding of others which results in smoother changes.[29] Furthermore, the employee who participates in decision making is viewed as becoming "ego-involved," emotionally and cognitively committed to the decision. There is a sense of ownership.[30]

Participative Management Research

The general theme found in research studies of participative management indicates that:

Participation can facilitate organizational changes through increased employee commitment.

Employees who participate in setting their own goals tend to be more committed than employees who do not participate.

For the most part, but by no means in all cases, employees who participate are more satisfied with their job.

Motivation factors may affect the success of participative management. Some theorists suggest that participation is not very effective among the generally unmotivated employees; e.g., those with low need for achievement or low job involvement.[31] On the other hand, research indicates that participative management has enhanced motivation among this type of employee.[32] One explanation for this finding is that perhaps employees with low motivation feel powerless. Participative management would give them a feeling of control which manifests itself as more commitment, greater job involvement, and the setting of challenging goals.[33]

Participation does not always lead to better performance. For many employees and jobs, participation is just not appropriate. The use of participative management depends on the (1) time available—participation takes more time; (2) the employees desire to participate—not everyone wants to participate; (3) reward system—participation will

---

[29] J. R. P. French, J. Israel, and D. As, "An Experiment in a Norwegian Factory: Interpersonal Dimensions in Decision Making," *Human Relations*, February 1960, pp. 3–19.

[30] M. Sorcher, "Motivation, Participation, and Myth," *Personnel Administration*, September/October 1971, pp. 20–24.

[31] M. Fein, "Improving Productivity by Improved Productivity Sharing," *Conference Board Record*, July 1976, pp. 44–49.

[32] R. M. Steers, "Task-goal Attributes, n Achievement, and Supervisory Performance," *Organizational Behavior and Human Performance*, June 1975, pp. 392–403.

[33] Locke and Schweiger, "Participation," p. 320.

not be so important if pay is inequitable or promotions are unfair; and (4) nature of the task—if employees can't control the task, participation will be difficult to use.

Participative Management: An Application at World Bank

Robert McNamara, as president of the World Bank, announced that the bank was going to reorient its lending program. The program was to shift from mainly helping the rich in developing countries to mainly helping the poor.[34] To accomplish this change there had to be (1) active participation of the poor people (grass roots) in planning and managing the new projects started in their country each year and (2) more involvement of the Bank's employees in making decisions that affected them at the Washington, D.C., headquarters where 95 percent of the staff work took place.

These two changes have resulted in significant increases in participation of local (in the poor countries) leadership. Also more than 20 work units at headquarters have initiated efforts to increase the role of staff in decision making. The staff is now making decisions that previously were made by senior executives.

In examining the move to participative management one might ask why should it work in such a powerful prestigious, and highly publicized organization like the World Bank. In brief, a detailed analysis conducted by McNamara showed that the staff and local people in countries where the bank's money was being used to build roads, dams, and utility plants was not being properly managed. As a result staff morale was declining and local citizens were apathetic. The Staff Association—an internal union of bank employees became more militant about the situation at the bank.

The initial effort to become more participative began as an informal group which met to discuss its concerns over lunch. These discussions led to a work-improvement experiment in one unit—that is, more staff participation in decision making. It seemed to be successful. Next a participation advisory committee (PARTAC) was formed. It was created by 78 union delegates to study participative management. This committee met and discussed, analyzed, and studied participative management and World Bank problems.

The committee was divided into subgroups to study different problems. Each group wrote a description of a problem and a recommended solution. These were reviewed, rewritten, and circulated to all members. Then they were discussed by the full committee.

After much work by PARTAC, a number of work-improvement projects were developed that encouraged the increased use of participative management at World Bank. Others in the bank not on the committee began to take notice of PARTAC's recommendations. Then a number of units took the recommendations of PARTAC and implemented more participative management practices.

---

[34]John Simmons, "Participatory Management at the World Bank," *Training and Development Journal*, March 1980, pp. 50–54.

The lessons offered by the World Bank shift to participative management indicate that a change like this requires careful planning, a substantial effort of committed people inside the organization, and top-management support. The words of the president at World Bank to increase participation at the grass roots and the staff levels certainly helped others to look more seriously at participative management. In the 1980s it is too early to tell if the move toward increased participation will have positive organizational and personal affects.

A Brief Critique
of Participative
Management

Participative management has a humanistic appeal and is a popular procedure among a number of behavioral scientists. Unfortunately like all the applications covered in this chapter it is not always successful or even well understood by practitioners. The research evidence offers support that participative management practices with some groups, in the right setting, and using the optimal degree of participation can increase satisfaction.

There appears to be an assumption made by participative management advocates that all individuals want to or prefer participation. This assumption unfortunately is not usually supported by a diagnostic study or inquiry that identifies these preferences, but is instead the opinion held by advocates.

There are also statements that increased participation leads to better performance. Again research results do not totally support this view. Sometimes, a nonparticipative situation, with an autocratic leader who is very directive yields the highest performance group. Whether this type of situation and leadership style can generate high performance over time is an important issue. There are some who believe that eventually having no say in decisions and being closely supervised will result in a backlash.[35] The results of this backlash will be lower morale and poorer performance.

THE MODIFIED OR
COMPRESSED
WORKWEEK

■ In recent years there have been three related, but unique, themes in work scheduling applied in organizations. First, there has been a move to shorten the workweek (i.e., fewer days per week and/or fewer hours per day). This is called the modified or compressed workweek. The most common modified schedule is a 10-hour day, often designated as the 4/40.

A second modification or theme in scheduling is discretionary working time or staggered or flexible working hours. *Flexitime* also known as gliding time is extremely popular. It allows employees to choose when they come to work and leave work, within constraints set by management. Flexitime schedules attempt to shift some control over working time to the employee. It gives some autonomy, self-management, and decision making to employees.

The third recent theme in work scheduling relates to part-time employment. A part-time system is characterized by jobs with a content that does

---

[35] Rensis Likert, *New Patterns of Management* (New York: McGraw-Hill, 1961).

not qualify them as whole-day jobs. For employees, part-time employment is a solution to the problem of doing two things at once. For example, it permits a homemaker to perform home and family roles while pursuing a career. It would also let students acquire new knowledge while they still earn some income. For organizations part-time employment lets managers tailor the size of their work force to the size of the work load.[36]

In this discussion of applied motivation programs each of these three themes could be developed. They each have powerful motivational potential. However, the modified workweek will be covered as simply one example of this motivational technique.

Description of the Modified Workweek

The four-day week or 4/40 (e.g., there is also the 3/36 and 4/32) means that a regular full-time workweek of 40 hours is worked in four 10-hour days instead of five 8-hour days. Four-day and other compressed workweeks started in the United States about 1970.

The 4/40 plan provides the employee with long weekends throughout the year. The incentive for the 4/40 is the belief that the system will lead to increased productivity. The employee will benefit from increased leisure time and more freedom to conduct personal business, a family life, and educational objectives.

Modified workweeks are suitable for some situations. They can help businesses that have costly start-ups and shutdowns, unutilized capital equipment, and long travel time to job sites. For example, police departments can use three 10-hour shifts per day to get 6 hours of double staffing during high-crime night hours. Road construction crews can go out for four days for 10 hours at a time to cut down the number of trips made to work sites. Computer installations can use two 12-hour shifts, each working three consecutive days to get round-the-clock utilization on Monday–Saturday.

Modified Workweek Research

A recent review of the research on the modified workweek indicates that 14 studies can be consulted to examine the impact of such a scheduling plan.[37] Nine studies investigated some aspect of job satisfaction. Five of these studies found that satisfaction with the job improved after the modified workweek was installed.

Of the nine studies measuring the effects of age, five reported that younger workers were more favorable than older workers; the remainder reported no differences. Eight studies investigated the role of sex. Two found that men were more favorable than women; the remainder indicated

---

[36] Stanley D. Nollen, "What Is Happening to Flexitime, Flexihour, Gliding Time, the Variable Day? and Permanent Part-Time Employment? and the Four-Day Work Week?" *Across the Board*, April 1980, pp. 6–21.

[37] Sincha Ronen and Sophia B. Primps, "The Compressed Work Week as Organizational Change: Behavioral and Attitudinal Outcomes," *Academy of Management Review*, January 1981, pp. 61–74.

no difference. Of the six studies investigating the effect of the modified workweek on home and personal life, four reported a positive effect.

Six studies surveyed changes in leisure and recreational activities after installation of modified workweeks. All reported positive results. Of the five studies reporting the effects of the modified workweek on fatigue, all reported that fatigue had increased. This is consistent with expectations that working a longer day will be more tiring.

The research for the most part suggests that the modified workweek has in some situations a positive impact on job satisfaction, home/personal life satisfaction, and leisure/recreation satisfaction. It also, however, can increase employee fatigue which could be a problem in jobs where alertness (e.g., air traffic controller, police officer) are important. The evidence is not unanimous, nor is it usually based on rigorous research.

The Modified Workweek: An Application in a Manufacturing Company

An experimental-control group design and test of the 4/40 work week was studied at a medium-sized manufacturing plant in the Midwest.[38] The company executive committee decided to establish two divisions as 4/40 units and two divisions at 5/40 units. It was expected that the 4/40 unit would show increased satisfaction, lower job anxiety-stress, decreased absenteeism, and increased job performance.

To follow the impact of the application of the 4/40 versus the 5/40 units data were collected and analyzed before the change to the modified workweek, 3 months after the change, 12 months after the change, and 24 months after the change.

Approximately 12 months after the 4/40 changes occurred there was improvement in autonomy, personal worth, security, and pay satisfaction in the modified workweek units. There was also a reduction in the anxiety-stress in these units. However, these improvements were not sustained over time. Apparently, in this application of the modified workweek there was only a pronounced short-run satisfaction improvement. The long-run, 24 months after the application of the 4/40, results indicated very little differences between the units. This application suggests that the effects of the 4/40 can wear off. If satisfaction, anxiety-stress, and absenteeism improvements are to be sustained more managerial work than simply applying a 4/40 schedule appears to be needed.

A Brief Critique of the Modified Workweek

For workers the four-day workweek yields two clear advantages: a three-day weekend and one less commuting trip per week. There are problems of providing customer service and covering necessary duties on the fifth day that make 4/40 applications limited to only some jobs. There are also problems associated with a longer day—fatigue, higher accident proneness, less time for evening meetings during the week

---

[38] John M. Ivancevich, "Effects of the Shorter Work Week on Selected Satisfaction and Performance Measures," *Journal of Applied Psychology*, December 1974, pp. 717–21; and John M. Ivancevich and Herbert L. Lyon, "The Shortened Work Week: A Field Experiment," *Journal of Applied Psychology*, February 1977, pp. 34–37.

The results of research on the modified workweek are mixed. There seems to be short-run improvements in satisfaction and absenteeism. These of course are welcomed by any organization. However, are these enough to change a system from a 5/40 to a 4/40? Each organization must answer this question for themselves.

Despite the mixed research results on the 4/40, a renewed energy crunch, or a stronger move to energy conservation may make the modified workweek more popular in the 1980s. In addition, if laws are eventually passed that do not force an employer to pay employees an overtime premium for all hours worked beyond eight in a day, the 4/40 may be used in more organizations.

APPLICATIONS: A FINAL WORD

■ Managers continue to search and experiment with programs and techniques to motivate employees. The search and experimentation efforts have led to the use of many popular techniques including goal setting, behavior modification, participative management, and modified workweeks. Each of these techniques has been applied with varying degrees of success. None of them have been successful in every situation or with all people. There simply is no perfect or ideal motivational technique that will always work. Table 5–5 summarizes the record of these four applied motivational practices. It is provided to present in one place the main characteristics and features of each practice.

MAJOR MANAGERIAL ISSUES

A. Goal setting actually was first discussed and used by F. W. Taylor in his Scientific Management practices.

B. The attributes of a goal that are important to understanding goal setting are goal specificity (the degree of precision), goal difficulty (the proficiency needed to accomplish the goal), and goal commitment (the effort used to accomplish the goal).

C. There are numerous laboratory and field studies available that indicate that goal setting can and does have some motivational value in work organizations.

D. Behavior modification focusses on behavior and consequences. Little attention is paid to the psychological causes of behavior.

E. The application of behavior modification requires (1) the pinpointing of specific behavior, (2) measuring, counting, and formulating a baseline point of behaviors, (3) the use of the ABC—antecedent-behavior-consequence—analysis, (4) an action plan, and (5) an evaluation program.

F. Participative management is more than a technique, it is a philosophy of management that encourages employee involvement in relevant and important decision making.

TABLE 5–5
Four Application Approachs with Motivating Potential: A Summary Review

Approach or Technique	Research Evidence Supporting Its Application	Primary Use in Organizations	Popularity in the 1980s	Degree of Complexity Involved in Application	Major Weakness
Goal setting	Laboratory and field studies supporting its practical utility	At operating level and first-line supervisory level	Growing	Can range from simple to complex depending on where it is used	Little research done on improving or training in the goal-setting process itself
Behavior modification	Field studies increasing in past 10 years; has appeal to managers who can identify critical behaviors	At operating level	Increasing	Can be simple to moderately complex	Very controversial and few long-range studies testing its long-term effects
Participative management	Laboratory and field studies with very mixed results	At operating and managerial level	Some increase	Can be extremely complex	Applied on the basis of morality instead of whether people want to participate
Modified workweek	Limited number of field studies with mixed results	At operating level	Status quo—not increasing	Simple if the job fits the technique and vice versa	Can disrupt operations and has shown only short-term effects to date

> **MAJOR MANAGERIAL ISSUES** (continued)
>
> G. There is some research available that indicates that participation can facilitate organizational changes through increased employee commitment and that employees who participate are more satisfied with their jobs.
>
> H. Modified or compressed workweeks are used to increase production and as a recruitment attraction. Research, however, does not always clearly support these anticipated objectives.
>
> I. Managers in using the modified workweek must first determine if it fits the situation—customer service requirements, hours of operation, equipment usage. Forcing it into an unsuited situation will often lead to more motivational problems then it solves.
>
> J. Each of the applications discussed—goal setting, behavior modification, participative management; and modified workweeks—has significant practical utility. If properly used, understood, and monitored each can generate positive organizational and personal results.

DISCUSSION AND REVIEW QUESTIONS

1. What is meant by the cognitive approach to motivation?

2. Why would someone refer to applied behavior modification as a form of bribery?

3. Would a modified workweek be suitable for scheduling the work of nurses in an operating room? Why?

4. Why should research studies be consulted by a manager before he or she implements any of the approaches discussed in this chapter?

5. What would be some of the problems of forcing participation on an individual? That is, informing an employee that participation in important decisions is now a requirement of the job.

6. Why is it important to pinpoint critical behaviors in any behavior modification application?

7. Someone stated that, "goal setting is as common off the job as on the job?" Do you agree? Why?

8. Compare the research results on behavior modification and on the modified workweek? Are there differences in the kind of research being conducted on these two applications?

9. Is goal setting an approach that should be implemented in all organizations? Why?

10. Under what type of work situations do you believe participative management would work best? Explain.

ADDITIONAL REFERENCES

Cohen, A. R., and H. Gadon. *Alternative Work Schedules: Integrating Industrial and Organizational Needs.* Reading, Mass.: Addison-Wesley Publishing, 1978.

Foster, L. W.; J. C. Latack; and L. J. Reindl. "Effects and Promises of the Shortened Workweek." Paper presented at the 39th Annual Meeting of the Academy of Management, Atlanta, Georgia, 1979.

Latham, G. P., and E. A. Locke. "Goal Setting—A Motivational Technique that Works." *Organizational Dynamics,* 1979, pp. 68–80.

Latham, G. P., and L. M. Saari. "The Effects of Holding Goal Difficulty Constant on Assigned and Participatively Set Goals." *Academy of Management Journal,* 1979, pp. 163–168.

Locke, E. A. "The Ubiquity of the Technique of Goal Setting in Theories of and Approaches to Motivation." *Academy of Management Review,* 1978, pp. 594–601.

———; D. B. Feren; V. M. McCaleb; K. N. Shaw; and A. T. Denny. "The Relative Effectiveness of Four Methods of Motivating Employee Performance." Paper presented at the American Psychological Association Meeting, New York, September 1979, pp. 1–41.

Maklan, P. M. *The Four-Day Workweek: Blue-Collar Adjustment to a Nonconventional Arrangement of Work and Leisure Time.* New York: Praeger Publishers, 1977.

McGee, W., and W. L. Tullar. "A Note on Evaluating Behavior Modification and Behavior Modeling as Industrial Training Techniques." *Personnel Psychology,* 1978, pp. 477–84.

Mitchell, T. R. "Motivation and Participation: An Integration." *Academy of Management Journal,* 1973, pp. 670–79.

Pedalino, E., and V. V. Gamboa. "Behavior Modification and Absenteeism: Intervention in One Industrial Setting." *Journal of Applied Psychology,* 1974, pp. 694–98.

"Productivity Gains from a Pat on the Back." *Business Week,* 1978, pp. 56–62.

Quick, J. C. "Dyadic Goal Setting within Organizations' Role Making and Motivational Considerations." *Academy of Management Review,* 1979, pp. 369–80.

Terborg, J. "The Motivational Components of Goal Setting." *Journal of Applied Psychology,* 1976, pp. 613–21.

Tuney, J. R., and S. L. Cohen. "Participative Management: What Is the Right Level?" *Management Review,* 1980, pp. 66–69.

CASE FOR ANALYSIS

Brown and Ferris Insurance Company was faced with a pressing absenteeism problem among clerical workers. On Mondays and Fridays approximately 26 percent of the clerical personnel were absent from their jobs. Through discussions with clerical supervisors management determined that absenteeism was now a part of the accepted norm. The employees simply wanted some time off, regardless of losing a day's pay. They liked to be able to choose for themselves when they would be absent.

The three-day weekend gave the employees some time to attend to personal business. Tom Amoss, the director of human resources at Brown and Ferris, had just attended an executive development program at the local university. One idea that really caught his attention was applied behavior modification. Brown and Ferris's estimated costs of absenteeism were running about $8,000 per week. So Tom felt that maybe behavior modification could reduce some of this expense.

Tom presented his plan to combat absenteeism to Randy Pandlers, the vice president of administrative services. Randy thought that Tom really had gone off the deep end. Tom's plan went like this. Each Friday at 3:00 P.M. a weekly lottery drawing would be held. The time cards of all clerical employees who had worked every day that week would be placed in a drum and five winners drawn at random. The five winners would receive prizes such as certificates for $150 of groceries, cameras, and a television set. At the end of a month, a monthly lottery would be held. Employees eligible had to have one month of perfect attendance. There would be one card drawn, and the winner would receive a prize of $1,000 cash. A six-month lottery (an all-expenses-paid, one-week vacation for two at a famous resort hotel) and an annual lottery (a $4,000 prize) were also included in the plan.

Randy after listening to Tom and doing some fast calculations agreed to go ahead with the plan. He felt that it just might work. The plan has been in effect for four months, and absenteeism on Monday and Friday are now averaging about 6 percent on each day. However, one problem has emerged. Some employees are coming to work when they are really sick. Some actually drag themselves out of sick beds to get to work and remain eligible for the lottery. They just are not able to do the work, and they are actually presenting a health hazard to other employees.

Questions for Consideration

1. Why do you think this behavior modification plan has had some success?
2. Do you believe that the success can be continued over a long period of time—a year? Why?
3. What about the issue of ill employees coming to work? What would you do to correct this problem?
4. Is this lottery plan a form of bribery? Explain.

EXPERIENTIAL EXERCISE

**GOAL SETTING:
HOW TO DO IT
AND A CRITIQUE**

Objectives

1. To present what is meant by the term *goal*.
2. To illustrate guidelines for preparing goals.
3. To involve the reader with some hints to evaluate the quality of a goal.

Related Topics

Goals are statements of measurable results that a person is attempting to accomplish. They help a person develop a plan to turn expectations and wishes into reality. Goals are found in most motivation applications in organizations. For example, in behavior modification programs, goals are the targets of behavior changes.

**Starting the
Exercise**

Each person is to work alone for at least 30 minutes with this exercise. After sufficient time has elapsed for each reader to work through the exercise the instructor will go over each goal and ask for comments from the class or group. The discussion should display the understanding of goals that each participant has and what will be needed to improve his or her goal writing skills.

The Facts

Writing and evaluating goals seems simple but is often not well done in organizations. The press of time, previous habits, and little concern about the attributes of a goal statement are reasons why goals are often poorly constructed.* Actually a number of guidelines should be followed in preparing goals. Remember these points:

1. A well-presented goal statement contains four elements:
   a. An action or accomplishment verb.
   b. A single and measurable result.
   c. A date of completion.
   d. A cost in terms of effort, resources, or money or some combination of these factors.
2. A well-presented goal statement is short; it is not a paragraph. It should be presented in a sentence.
3. A well-presented goal specifies only the what and when and doesn't get into how or why.
4. A well-presented goal statement is challenging and attainable. It should cause the person to stretch his or her skills, abilities, and effort.
5. A well-presented goal statement is meaningful and important. It should be a priority item.

---

*For a discussion of how to set goals, see George Morrisey, *Getting Your Act Together* (New York: John Wiley & Sons, 1980); especially see chap. 7.

6. A well-presented goal statement must be acceptable to you so that you will try hard to accomplish it.

The goal statement model should be:

To (action or accomplishment verb) (single result) by (a date—keep it realistic) at (effort, use of what resource, cost).

An example for a production operation:

To reduce the production cost per unit of Mint toothpaste by at least 3 percent by March 1, at a changeover of equipment expense not to exceed $45,000.

Examine the next four statements that are presented as goal statements. Below each goal write a critique of the statement. Is it a good goal statement? Why? Discuss your viewpoints in the class/group discussion.

To reduce my blood pressure to an acceptable level.

_____

_____

_____

To make financial investments with a guaranteed minimum return of at least 16 percent.

_____

_____

_____

To spend a minimum of 45 minutes a day on a doctor approved exercise plan, starting Monday, lasting for six months, at no expense.

_____

_____

_____

To spend more time reading nonwork related novels and books during the next year.

_____

_____

_____

Chapter 6

Stress and the Individual

AN ORGANIZATIONAL ISSUE FOR DEBATE
Avoiding Stress and Remaining Healthy

ARGUMENT FOR

It has long been a common opinion that prolonged strain resulting from job stress can make individuals sick. Medical researchers have collected some evidence that job-related stress can be and is a contributor to chronic illnesses such as heart disease and peptic ulcers. Managers being bombarded by stress-producing job demands, and nonmanagers being prodded by restrictive managers, may eventually become statistics in reports on coronary heart disease or other illnesses. Thus, some advice being offered is that stressful jobs or hard-charging lifestyles should be avoided.

The hard driving, competitive perfectionist who is valued by organizations is considered a prime candidate for an early coronary. If not a coronary, it may be migraines, ulcers, asthma, ulcerative colitis, or even adult acne. The hard-charger has been called a Type A behavior pattern (TABP). He (a male in most cases but women in growing numbers are beginning to fit the TABP classification) marches to a "drummer" who requires winning at all costs. The Type A style is to wade in, do the job, enjoy the taste of success, and move on to the next challenge. This "racehorse" style will mean that the TABP person has a one in five chance of having a heart attack before reach-

ARGUMENT AGAINST

Unfortunately, there is a great deal of confusion about what stress is and how individuals deal with it. We hear a great deal about the dangers of TABP. However, others claim that the "racehorse" can't be a "turtle" without suffering anxiety and stress. Individual differences must be considered when discussing stress and how people react to it. It would be far more stressful for many Type A's to change their style than to continue being a hard-charger.

There is also some concern over the practice of classifying individuals. Can we be sure that the measurements being used are accurate? Hans Selye, a leading medical authority on stress, believes that all the stress inventories used to classify respondents are flawed because they fail to give enough weight to individual differences.* He states that each individual is really the best judge of his/her stress threshold. Instead of using an inventory to detect stress tolerance or conditions, each person should be the judge. Self-awareness is the best way to deal with stress conditions. The Type A may know without a doubt that he/she is a hard-charger, competitive, and a

---
*Hans Selye, "On the Benefits of Eustress," *Psychology Today*, March 1978, p. 63.

ing his 60th birthday. The message here is that avoiding stress means that life can be prolonged.

perfectionist. This person may also know how healthy he or she feels physically and psychologically. There are just some individuals who need stress, long hours, and a lot of work pressure. Instead of stating that TABP is bad, it is more accurate to state that some people are not suited to be Type As.

Interest in stress has become widespread in recent years. However, the experience of stress is not new; our cave-dwelling ancestors experienced it every time they left their caves and encountered their enemy, the sabre-toothed tigers. The tigers of yesteryear are gone but have been replaced by other forms of predators—work overload, a nagging boss, time deadlines, excessive inflation, poorly designed jobs, marital disharmony, the drive to keep up with the Joneses. These work and nonwork predators interact and create stress for individuals on and off the job. This chapter will focus primarily on the individual at work in organizations and the stress created in this setting. Much of the stress experienced by people in our industrialized society originates in our organizations; much of that which does not affects our behavior and performance in these same organizations.

WHAT IS STRESS?   ■ Stress means an incredibly different array of things to different people. In an uncomplicated way it is best to consider stress as something that involves the interaction of the individual with the environment.[1] Most definitions of stress recognize the individual and the environment in terms of a stimulus interaction, response interaction, or stimulus-response interaction.

Stimulus Definition   A stimulus definition of stress would be the following: *Stress* is the force or stimulus acting upon the individual that results in a response of strain, where strain is pressure or, in a physical sense, deformation. One problem with this definition is that it fails to recognize that two people subjected to the same level of stress may show far different levels of strain.

Response Definition   A response definition of stress would be the following: *Stress* is the physiological or psychological response of an individual to an environmental stressor, where a *stressor* is an external event or situation which is potentially harmful. In the stimulus definition stress is an external event; here it is an internal response. This definition fails to enable anyone to predict the nature of the stress response or even whether there will be a stress response.

Stimulus-Response Definition   An example of a stimulus-response definition would be that *stress* is the consequence of the *interaction* between an environmental stimulus and the response of the individual. Stress is viewed as more than either a stimulus or a response; it is the result of a unique interaction between stimulus conditions in the environment and the individual's predisposition to respond in a certain way.

---

[1]John M. Ivancevich and Michael T. Matteson, *Stress at Work: A Managerial Perspective* (Glenview, Ill.: Scott, Foresman, 1980), p. 6.

**A Working
Definition**

Each of the three definitions offers important insights into what constitutes stress. Each is used to develop a working definition for this chapter. We define stress as

> an adaptive response, mediated by individual differences and/or psychological processes, that is, a consequence of any external [environmental] action, situation, or event that places excessive psychological and/or physical demands upon a person.

This working definition portrays stress in a more negative light than most definitions. That is, stress is a neutral word in most discussions. We have, however, included the term *excessive* in our definition. Certainly, not all stress is negative. The positive stress that is referred to as *eustress* (from the Greek *eu*, meaning good, as in euphoria) by Dr. Hans Seyle is stimulating in a positive sense. Eustress is necessary in our lives. However, because of space constraints we are not able to develop our discussion of eustress in this chapter.

The above working definition allows us to focus attention on specific environmental conditions that are potential sources of stress, called *stressors*. Whether stress is felt or experienced by a particular individual will depend on the unique characteristics of that individual. Furthermore, the definition emphasizes an *adaptive response*. The vast majority of our responses to work environment stimuli do not require adaptation and thus are not really potential sources of stress.

**THE PSYCHO-
PHYSIOLOGY
OF STRESS**

■ If for some reason you happened to place your hand on a hot stove, a number of predictable events would occur. There would be pain. There would also be tissue damage as successive layers of skin were exposed to the stove. Depending on your reaction time, the hand would be pulled from the stove. You might even give off a few choice words.

This event displays an interaction between you and the environment. It is an event that would result in physical and psychological consequences. It is also an event that magnifies what is stress and how we respond to it—physically and psychologically.

**The General
Adaptation
Syndrome**

Dr. Hans Selye, the pioneer of stress research, conceptualized the psychophysiological responses to stress.[2] Selye considered stress a nonspecific response to any demand made upon an organism. He labeled the three phases of the defense reaction a person establishes when stressed as the General Adaptation Syndrome (GAS). Selye called it *general* because the consequence of stressors had effects upon several areas of the body; *adaptation* refers to its stimulation of defenses designed to help the body adjust

---

[2]Hans Selye, *The Stress of Life* (New York: McGraw-Hill, 1976); and Hans Selye, *Stress without Distress* (New York: J. B. Lippincott, 1974).

or deal with the stressors; and *syndrome* indicates that individual pieces of the reaction occur more or less together. The three distinct phases are called *alarm, resistance,* and *exhaustion.*

The *alarm stage* is the initial mobilization by which the body meets the challenge posed by the stressor. When a stressor is recognized, the brain sends forth a biochemical message to all the body's systems. Respiration increases, blood pressure rises, pupil's dilate, muscles tense up, and so forth.

If the stressor continues, the GAS proceeds to the *resistance stage.* Signs of being in the resistance stage include fatigue, anxiety, and tension. The person is now fighting the stressor. While resistance to a particular stressor may be high during this stage, resistance to other stressors may be low. A person has only finite sources of energy, concentration, and ability to resist stressors. Individuals are often more illness-prone during periods of stress than at other times.[3]

The final GAS stage is *exhaustion.* Prolonged and continual exposure to

FIGURE 6–1
Selye's General Adaptation Syndrome (GAS)

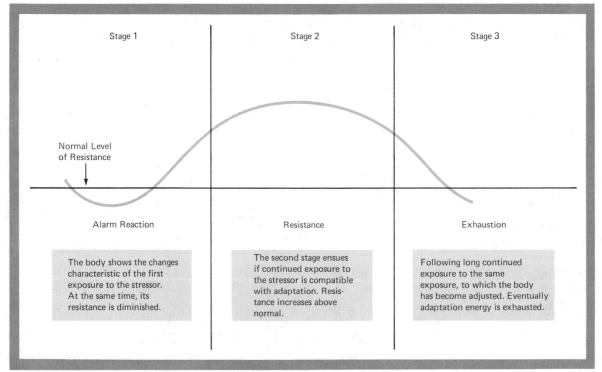

[3] Selye, *Stress without Distress,* p. 5.

the same stressor may eventually use up the adaptive energy available, and the system fighting the stressor becomes exhausted. The three stages of the GAS are presented in Figure 6–1.

It is important to keep in mind that the activation of the GAS places extraordinary demands upon the body. Clearly, the more frequently the GAS is activated and the longer it remains in operation, the more wear and tear on the psychophysiological mechanisms occur. The body and mind have limits. The more frequently an individual is alarmed, resists, and becomes exhausted by work, nonwork, or the interaction of these activities, the more susceptible the person is to fatigue, disease, aging, and other negative consequences.

Consequences of Stress

The mobilization of the body's defense mechanisms are not the only potential consequences of contact with a stressor(s). The effects of stress are many and varied. Some, of course, are positive, such as self-motivation, stimulation to work harder, or increased inspiration to live a better life. However, many are disruptive and potentially dangerous. Cox has identified five types of potential consequences or effects of stress.[4] His categories include:

Subjective Effects. Anxiety, aggression, apathy, boredom, depression, fatigue, frustration, loss of temper, low self-esteem, nervousness, feeling alone.

Behavioral Effects. Accident proneness, drug abuse, emotional outbursts, excessive eating, excessive drinking or smoking, impulsive behavior, nervous laughter.

Cognitive Effects. Inability to make sound decisions, poor concentration, short attention span, hypersensitivity to criticism, and mental blocks.

Physiological Effects. Increased blood glucose levels, increased heart rate and blood pressure, dryness of the mouth, sweating, dilation of pupils, hot and cold flashes.

Organizational Effects. Absenteeism lower productivity, alienation with co-workers, job dissatisfaction, reduced organizational commitment and loyalty.

These five types are not all-inclusive; nor are they limited to only those effects over which there is universal agreement and clear scientific evidence. They represent, however, some of the potential effects that are frequently associated with stress. The types are not intended as a way of infering that stress always causes the effects listed above. Clearly job dissatisfaction, increased heart rate, or excessive alcohol intake may be to-

---

[4]T. Cox, 5tress (Baltimore: University Park Press, 1978), p. 92.

tally unrelated to stress. However, the possibility that stress may either be a primary or contributing cause of these effects cannot be ignored.

Physical and Mental Health

Of the potential consequences of stress, those classified as health effects are perhaps the most controversial and organizationally dysfunctional. Those who hypothesize a link between stress and physical health problems are, in effect, suggesting that an emotional response is responsible for producing a physical change in an individual.[5] In fact most medical textbooks attribute between 50 and 75 percent of illness to stress-related origins.[6]

Perhaps the most significant of the potential stress-physical illness relationships is that of coronary heart disease (CHD). Although virtually unknown in the industrialized world 60 years ago, CHD accounts for half of all deaths in the United States annually. The disease is so pervasive that American males who are now between the ages of 45 and 55 have one chance in four of dying from a heart attack in the next 10 years.

Traditional risk factors such as obesity, smoking, heredity, high cholesterol, and high blood pressure can account for no more than about 25 percent of the incidence of coronary heart disease. There is growing medical opinion that job and life stress may be a major contributor in the remaining 75 percent.[7]

Even this brief overview of health consequences of stress would be incomplete without some mention of mental health effects. Kornhauser studied extensively the mental health of industrial workers.[8] He did not find a relationship between mental health and such factors as salary, job security, and working conditions. Instead, clear associations between mental health and job satisfaction emerged. Poor mental health was associated with frustration growing out of not having a satisfying job.

In addition to frustration, the anxiety and depression that may be experienced by individuals under a great deal of stress may manifest itself in the form of alcoholism (about 15 percent of the adult population are problem drinkers), drug dependency (over 150 million tranquilizer prescriptions are written in the United States annually), hospitalization (over 25 percent of occupied hospital beds have people with psychological problems), and, in extreme cases, in suicide. Even the relatively minor mental disruptions produced by stress, such as the inability to concentrate or reduced problem-solving capabilities, may prove very costly to an organization.

---

[5]P. Astrand and K. Rodahl, *Textbook of Work Physiology* (New York: McGraw-Hill, 1970).

[6]M. H. Brenner, "The Stressful Price of Prosperity," *Science News*, March 18, 1978, p. 166.

[7]David C. Glass, *Behavior Patterns, Stress and Coronary Disease* (Hillsdale, N.J.: Erlbaum Associates, 1977), pp. 5–6.

[8]A. Kornhauser, *Mental Health of the Industrial Worker* (New York: John Wiley & Sons, 1965).

STRESS AND WORK: A MODEL

■ For most employed individuals, work is more than a 40-hour-a-week commitment. Even if the actual work time is 40 hours, by the time work-related activities such as travel time, preparation for work, and lunch time are added in, most individuals spend 10 or more hours a day on work-related activities.

Not only is a lot of time spent on work-related activities, but many individuals find a substantial portion of their satisfaction and identity in their work. Consequently, work and nonwork activities are interdependent. The distinction between stress at work and stress at home is an artificial one at best. Sources of stress at work spill over into a person's nonwork activities. As a consequence of stressors experienced at work, the individual may come home irritable, short-tempered, and fatigued. This may result in arguments with the spouse. This marital conflict may be a source of subsequent stress that in turn negatively affects job performance. Thus, stress at work and stress away from work are often interrelated. However, our main concern here is with stressors at work.

In order to better understand the link between stressors, stress, and consequences, we have developed an integrative model of stress and work. A managerial perspective is used to develop the parts of the model shown in Figure 6–2. The model divides stressors at work into four categories: phys-

FIGURE 6–2
Stress and Work: A Working Model

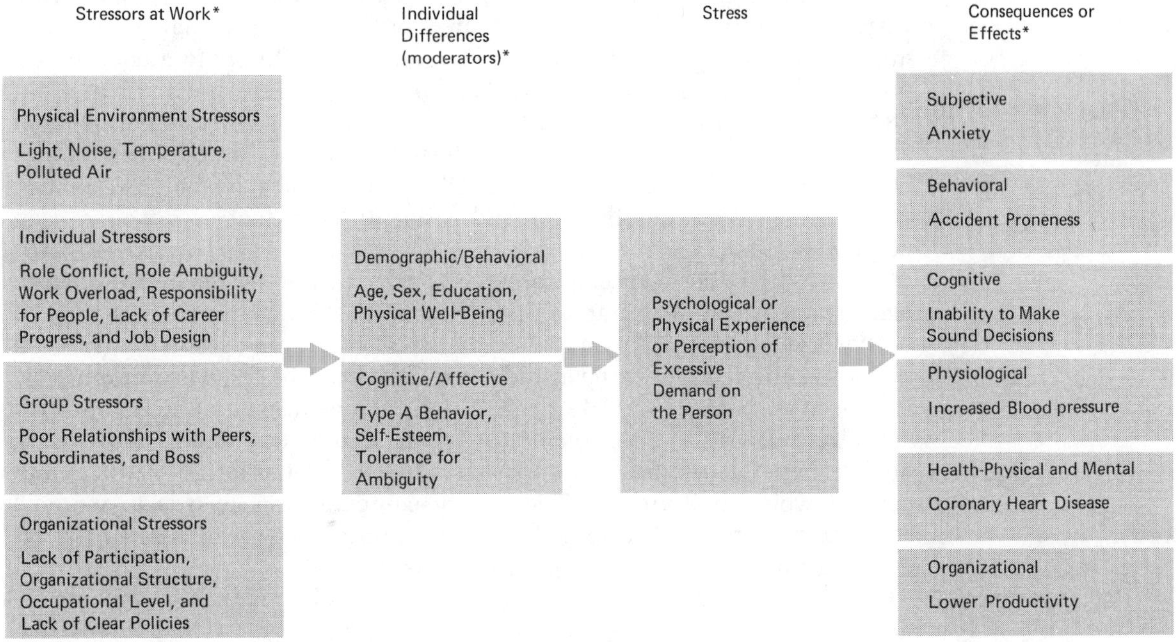

Stressors at Work*	Individual Differences (moderators)*	Stress	Consequences or Effects*
Physical Environment Stressors Light, Noise, Temperature, Polluted Air			**Subjective** Anxiety
			Behavioral Accident Proneness
Individual Stressors Role Conflict, Role Ambiguity, Work Overload, Responsibility for People, Lack of Career Progress, and Job Design	**Demographic/Behavioral** Age, Sex, Education, Physical Well-Being	**Psychological or Physical Experience or Perception of Excessive Demand on the Person**	**Cognitive** Inability to Make Sound Decisions
Group Stressors Poor Relationships with Peers, Subordinates, and Boss	**Cognitive/Affective** Type A Behavior, Self-Esteem, Tolerance for Ambiguity		**Physiological** Increased Blood pressure
			Health-Physical and Mental Coronary Heart Disease
Organizational Stressors Lack of Participation, Organizational Structure, Occupational Level, and Lack of Clear Policies			**Organizational** Lower Productivity

*Only some of these variables will be discussed in the chapter. For a more complete discussion of these stressors and moderators, see John M. Ivancevich and Michael T. Matteson, *Stress and Work: A Managerial Perspective* (Glenview, Ill.: Scott, Foresman, 1980).

ical, individual, group, and organizational. As already discussed the model presents four potential effects of stress. In this book we are more concerned with the effects that influence job performance.

The model introduces individual differences by giving attention to cognitive/affective and demographic/behavioral factors. Only a few of the many possible individual differences are presented. These differences are presented as possible moderators of the stressor-stress as well as the stress-effects linkages.

Before examining parts of the model in more detail, several caveats are in order. This model, or any model, attempting to integrate stress and work phenomena is not totally complete. There are so many important variables to include that a complete treatment would require much more space. Furthermore, the variables illustrated are offered only as ones that provide managerial perspective of stress. They are certainly not the only appropriate variables to consider. Finally, accurate and reliable measurement is extremely important because management initiated programs to manage stress at optimal levels will depend on how well these and other variables are measured.

Physical Environmental Stressors

Physical environment stressors are often termed *blue-collar stressors* because they are more a problem in blue-collar occupations.[9] Over 14,000 workers die annually in industrial accidents (nearly 55 a day, or 7 people every working hour), over 100,000 workers are permanently disabled every year, and employees report more than 5 million occupational injuries annually.[10] Stress is caused by the risks associated with being a coal miner, police officer, fire fighter, ironworker, foundry worker, or chemical plant employee. New estimates of the toll of workplace chemicals, radiation, heat stress, pesticides, and other toxic materials leads the National Institute of Occupational Safety and Health (NIOSH) to estimate that about 100,000 workers may die annually from industrial diseases that could have been prevented.

Many blue-collar workers are nervous and stressed by the alleged health consequences from working in their present jobs. Since the passage in 1970 of the Occupational Safety and Health Act (OSHA) some of the experienced stress in individuals has been reduced. Gains can be traced to employers' increased acceptance of OHSA regulations. As well, many unions enthusiastically support the act. Problems still exist and management is now being held responsible by the courts for stress that is related to the physical and general work environment. Today jury compensation awards to workers are becoming more widespread. The following close-up illustrates the increasing role of the courts in job stress cases.

---

[9]E. C. Poulton, "Blue-Collar Stressors," in *Stress at Work*, ed. C. L. Cooper and R. Payne (New York: John Wiley & Sons, 1978), pp. 51–80.

[10]Arthur B. Shostak, *Blue-Collar Stressors* (Reading, Mass.: Addison-Wesley Publishing, 1980), p. 19.

ORGANIZATIONS: CLOSE-UP

Job Stress Is Now a Legal Issue

Feeling stress on the job? File a claim!

Many workers are, and they're winning workers' compensation payments for emotional illness traced to the pressures of their jobs.

"It's a major concern for employers and insurance companies," says Andre Maisonpierre, vice president of the Alliance of American Insurers, a trade group. He warns that psychiatric-injury awards "could have some major cost implications."

Following court decisions, about 15 states now make disability payments in cases where severe anxiety, depression or other mental problems have been caused by work stress. The most common, clear-cut case is compensation for the shock suffered when a worker sees a co-worker fall to his or her death.

In one significant case, the Michigan Supreme Court recently granted lifetime workers' compensation to a General Motors Corp. parts inspector who was considered to be a "compulsive perfectionist." He suffered mental strain when assembly-line workers insisted on installing parts he had labeled defective.

Are stress claims valid? Answers vary. Consider some cases in which workers won compensation.

A Burroughs Corp. secretary become hysterical when her boss constantly criticized her for going to the bathroom too often. She said he also asked prying questions about her new husband's family. The state workers' disability compensation bureau awarded her $7,000. Her attorney hopes to get a larger settlement from an appeal board.

After working with radioactive materials for 30 years and developing cancer in one eye, a Los Alamos Scientific Laboratory technician feared he would die from the exposure. The New Mexico Supreme Court decided his anxiety neurosis had totally disabled him; he received $75,000.

A Maine state trooper's duties involved cruising around a quiet, rural area. But he became severely depressed because he was on call 24 hours a day. He claimed his sex life deteriorated because he never knew when the phone would ring. The state supreme court approved the officer's claim for total, permanent disability, but the attorney general asked the court to reconsider—and then settled out of court for $5,000.

Source: Joann S. Lublin, "On-the-Job Stress Leads Many Workers to File—and Win—Compensation Awards," *The Wall Street Journal*, September 17, 1980.

Individual Stressors

Stressors at the individual level have been studied more than any other category presented in Figure 6–2. Role conflict is perhaps the most widely studied individual level stressor.[11] *Role conflict* is present whenever com-

---

[11]John R. P. French and Robert D. Caplan, "Organizational Stress and Individual Strain," in *The Failure of Success*, ed. J. Marrow (New York: AMACOM, 1973), pp. 30–66.

pliance by an individual to one set of expectations about the job are in conflict with another set of expectations. Being torn by conflicting demands from a supervisor about the job, and being pressured to get along well with people you are not compatible with are facets of role conflict. Regardless of whether the role conflict results from organization policies or from another person it can be a significant stressor for some individuals.

Kahn et al. report on an interview survey of a national sample of male wage and salary employees that revealed that 48 percent of the participants experienced role conflict.[12] In a study at Goddard Space Flight Center it was determined that about 67 percent of the employees reported some role conflict. The study also found that workers who suffered more role conflict had lower job satisfaction and higher job-related tension.[13] It is interesting to note that the researchers also found that the greater the power or authority of the people sending the conflicting role messages, the more job dissatisfaction produced by role conflict. A larger and more medically oriented study found that for white-collar workers role conflict was related to abnormal electrocardiographic readings.[14] Later in Chapter 7, "Group Behavior," we shall see that role conflict is also important in the conflict which occurs within the organization groups.

In order for employees to perform their jobs well they need certain information regarding what they are expected to do and not to do. Employees need to know their rights, privileges, and obligations. *Role ambiguity* is a lack of understanding about the rights, privileges, and obligations a person has for doing the job. Studies have addressed the question of role ambiguity. In the study at Goddard Space Flight Center administrators, engineers, and scientists completed a role ambiguity stress scale. Blood samples, blood pressure, and pulse rate readings were also obtained.[15] It was found that role ambiguity was significantly related to low job satisfaction and to feelings of job-related threat to one's mental and physical well-being. Furthermore, the more ambiguity the person reported, the lower was the individual's utilization of intellectual skills, knowledge, and leadership skills.

Everyone has experienced *work overload* at one time or another. Overload may be of two different types: quantitative or qualitative. Having too many things to do or insufficient time to complete a job is *quantitative* overload. *Qualitative* overload, on the other hand occurs when individuals feel that they lack ability to complete their jobs or that performance standards are too high.

From a health standpoint studies as far back as 1958 established that quantitative overload may cause biochemical changes, specifically, eleva-

[12] R. L. Kahn, D. M. Wolfe, R. P. Quinn, J. D. Snoek, and R. A. Rosenthal, *Organizational Stress: Studies in Role Conflict and Ambiguity* (New York: John Wiley & Sons, 1964), p. 94.

[13] Ibid.

[14] John R. P. French and Robert D. Caplan, "Psychosocial Factors in Coronary Heart Disease," *Industrial Medicine*, September 1970, pp. 383–97.

[15] Kahn et al., *Organizational Stress*.

FIGURE 6–3
The Underload/Overload Continuum

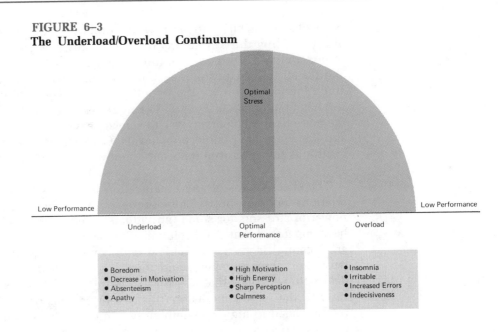

tions in blood cholesterol levels.[16] It has also been suggested that overload is most harmful to those who experience the lowest job satisfaction.[17] Still another study found overload to be associated with lowered confidence, decreased work motivation and increased absenteeism. It may also be indirectly responsible for decreases in decision-making quality, deteriorating interpersonal relations, and increases in accidents.[18]

One study examined the relationship of overload, underload, and stress among 1,540 executives of a major corporation. Those executives in the low and high ends of the stress ranges reported and had more significant medical problems. This study suggests that the relationship between stressors, stress, and disease may be curvilinear. That is, those who are underloaded and those who are overloaded represent two ends of a continuum, each with significantly elevated number of medical problems.[19] The underload/overload continuum is presented in Figure 6–3. Ideally the optimal stress level provides the best balance of challenge, responsibility, and reward.

Any type of *responsibility* can be a burden for some people. Different

[16]B. L. Margolis, W. M. Kroes, and R. P. Quinn, "Job Stress: An Untested Occupational Hazard," *Journal of Occupational Medicine*, October 1974, pp. 659–61.

[17]Stephen M. Sales, "Organizational Role as a Risk Factor in Coronary Disease," *Administration Science Quarterly*, September 1969, pp. 325–36.

[18]S. Kasl, "Work and Mental Health," in *Work and the Quality of Life*, ed. James O'Toole (Cambridge, Mass.: MIT Press, 1974), pp. 171–96.

[19]Clinton Weiman, "A Study of Occupational Stressors and the Incidence of Disease/Risk," *Journal of Occupational Medicine*, February 1977, pp. 119–22.

types of responsibility apparently function differently as stressors. One way of categorizing this variable is in terms of responsibility for people versus responsibility for things. The intensive care unit nurse, the neurosurgeon, and the air traffic controller each have a high responsibility for people. One study found support for the hypothesis that responsibility for people contributes to job-related stress.[20] The more responsibility for people reported, the more likely the person was to smoke heavily, have high blood pressure, and show elevated cholesterol levels. Conversely, the more responsibility for things the employee reported, the lower these indicators.

Group Stressors

The effectiveness of any organization is influenced by the nature of the relations among groups. There are many group characteristics that can be powerful stressors for some individuals. A number of behavioral scientists have suggested that good relationships between members of a work group are a central factor in individual well-being.[21] Poor relations include low trust, low supportiveness, and low interest in listening to and trying to deal with problems that confront an employee.[22] Studies in this area have reached the same conclusion: mistrust of persons one works with is positively related to high role ambiguity, which leads to inadequate communications between people and low job satisfaction.

Organizational Stressors

A problem with studying organizational stressors is identifying which are the most important ones. Participation in decision making is considered to be an important part of working within organizations for some individuals. *Participation* refers to the extent that a person's knowledge, opinions, and ideas are included in the decision process. Participation, however, can also contribute to stress. Some people may be frustrated by the delays often associated with participative decision making. Others may view shared decision making as a threat to the traditional right of a supervisor or manager to have the final say.

Organizational structure and its impact on stress and behavior is another stressor that has rarely been studied. One available study of trade salespersons examined the relationships between tall (bureaucratically structured), medium, and flat (less rigidly structured) structures on job satisfaction, stress, and performance. It was determined that salespersons in the flatter, less bureaucratically structured arrangement experienced less stress, more job satisfaction, and performed more effectively than salespersons in the medium and tall structures.[23]

---

[20]French and Caplan, "Psychosocial Factors," p. 387.

[21]Chris Argyris, *Integrating the Individual and the Organization* (New York: John Wiley & Sons, 1964); and Cary L. Cooper, *Group Training and Organizational Development* (Basel, Switzerland: Karger, 1973).

[22]French and Caplan, "Psychosocial Factors."

[23]John M. Ivancevich and James H. Donnelly, "Relation of Organizational Structure to Job Satisfaction, Anxiety-Stress, and Performance," *Administrative Science Quarterly*, June 1975, pp. 272–80.

There are a number of studies which examine the relationship of organizational level to health effects. The majority of these studies suggest the notion that risk of health problems such as contracting coronary heart disease increases with organizational level.[24] Not all researchers, however, support the notion that the higher one is in an organization hierarchy the greater the health risk. A study of Du Pont employees found the incidence of heart disease was inversely related to salary level.[25]

The nature of the classifications used in these studies has contributed to the confusion of results.[26] The trend now is to look in more detail at significant job components, as a way of explaining the effects of stress. Several studies, for example, have tried to assess whether inactivity or increased intellectual and emotional job demands contribute most to the increased risk of coronary heart disease. One early study contributes to this form of analysis in that it found that downtown bus drivers (sedentary jobs) and conductors (active jobs) had higher coronary heart disease than their suburban counterparts.[27] More research is needed to determine if emotional job demands are more powerful than inactivity in explaining the incidence of health problems.

This is only a very small sample of the tremendous amount of behavioral and medical research available on stressor, stress, and effects linkages. The information available like other organizational research is contradictory in some cases. However, what is available implies a number of important points. These points are:

1. There is a relationship between stressors at work and physical, psychological, and emotional changes in individuals.
2. The adaptive responses to stressors at work have been measured by self-rating, performance appraisals, and biochemical tests. Much more work must be done in properly measuring stress at work.
3. There is no universally acceptable list of stressors. Each organization has its own unique set that should be examined.
4. Individual differences explain why a stressor to one person is disruptive and unsettling while the same stressor is challenging to another person.

INDIVIDUAL DIFFERENCES

■ Stressors evoke different responses from different people. Some individuals are better able to cope with a stressor than others; they can adapt their

[24] R. V. Marks, "Social Stress and Cardiovascular Disease," *The Milbank Memorial Fund Quarterly,* April 1967, pp. 51–107.

[25] S. Pell and C. A. D'Alonzo, "Myocardial Infarction in a One Year Industrial Study," *Journal of American Medical Association,* June 1958, pp. 332–37.

[26] Cary L. Cooper and Judi Marshall, "Occupational Sources of Stress: A Review of the Literature Relating to Coronary Heart Disease and Mental Ill Health," *Journal of Occupational Psychology,* March 1976, pp. 11–28.

[27] J. N. Morris et al., "Coronary Heart Disease and Physical Activity at Work: "Coronary Heart Disease in Different Occupations," *The Lancet,* October 1953, pp. 1053–57.

behavior in such a way that meets the stressor head on. On the other hand some individuals are more predisposed to stress; that is, they are not able to adapt to the stressor.

The model presented in Figure 6–2 suggests that individual differences moderate the relationship between stressors and stress. A *moderator* is a condition, behavior, or characteristic that qualifies the relationship between two variables. The effect may be to intensify or weaken the relationship. The relationship between the number of gallons of gasoline used and total miles driven, for example, is affected by the variable, speed (moderator). Likewise, an individual's personality may moderate or affect the extent to which that individual experiences stress as a consequence of being in contact with a particular stressor.

Sex

The stress research literature suggests that women have neither experienced the stress levels encountered by men, nor have they shown the negative effects of stress nearly to the extent men have. Women have a longer life expectancy than men. According to projections made by the National Center for Health Statistics the American man can expect to die about eight years sooner than the average American woman. At certain ages, compared to women, men are four times more likely to die of coronary heart disease, five times more likely to die from alcohol-related disease, and seven times more likely to commit suicide.[28]

Why do these difference exist? There are two feasible answers to that question. First, there are biological differences between the sexes that predispose men to disease and death (or conversely, protect women). Second, the differences are not true sex differences, but arise because of the differences in the roles played by members of the two sexes.

It seems unlikely that biological differences have a great deal to do with it. The difference in life expectancy from 1900 to 1980 (1900—men, 46.3; women, 48.3—1980—men, 70.0; women, 77.7) has widened. Biological differences simply are not altered in such a short period of time. This is not to imply that there may not be some built-in differences. Women, for example, tend to react better physiologically than men while under stress.[29]

The better explanation would seem to be based on role differences. While there are obviously a growing number of exceptions today, throughout much of history men and women have played different roles in society. The man went to work while the woman worked at home. He provided the economic base and she provided the supportive, nurturing base.

What is indicated here is based on historical facts and the role differences that have existed for men and women. Today, there are signs that roles of men and women are slowly changing and differences are being redefined. More and more women are moving into the mainstream of or-

---

[28] Ivancevich and Matteson, *Stress at Work*, p. 173.

[29] Walter McQuade and Ann Aikman, *Stress* (New York: Bantam Books, 1975); and Walter McQuade and Ann Aikman, *The Longevity Factor* (New York; Simon & Schuster, 1979).

ganizational life. Consequently, they are experiencing the type of stressors displayed in Figure 6–2 in greater numbers and to a greater degree.

While it is too soon to make any definitive conclusions, indications are that as differences between male and female roles narrows, so also will the differences with regard to stress response. For example, coronary disease among females below age 45 is increasing.[30] Incidence of peptic ulcers among females is also increasing. The upward mobile, career-oriented woman is subjected to all the stressors shown in Figure 6–2.

Self-Esteem

The old maxim that individuals who feel good about themselves are happy people has a certain amount of validity. Posession of some minimum level of self-esteem is beneficial to effective functioning in various situations. For example, research indicates that the critical difference between those who survive a wartime prison camp experience and those who do not is self-esteem. Those who survive are able to muster forces to support their self-esteem and consequently endure the stress of captivity.[31] Higher levels of self-esteem appear to be associated with greater confidence in one's ability to deal successfully with stressors. A direct indication that this is the case has been found in the research literature. It has been found that negative relationships existed between qualitative role overload and self-esteem. In one study employees who reported being dissatisfied with themselves, their skills and abilities (low self-esteem), also reported high qualitative overload stress.[32]

Self-esteem has also been linked to stress-related health changes. Several studies have identified a significant negative relationship between self-esteem and coronary heart disease risk factors.[33] The available research suggests that self-esteem, an individual difference, can either hinder or facilitate the stress response.

Type A Behavior Pattern (TABP)

In the 1950s two medical practitioners and researchers, Meyer Friedman and Ray Rosenman, discovered what they called the Type A Behavior Pattern (TABP).[34] They searched the medical literature and found that traditional coronary risk factors such as dietary cholesterol, blood pressure, and heredity could not totally explain or predict coronary heart disease. Other factors seemed to them to be playing a major role in coronary heart disease (CHD). Through interviews with and, observation of patients they began to

---

[30] N. Kinzer, *Stress and the American Woman* (New York: Doubleday, 1979).

[31] B. Bettelheim, "Individual and Mass Behavior in Extreme Situations," in *Readings in Social Psychology*, ed. E. E. Maccoby (New York: Holt, Rinehart & Winston, 1958).

[32] E. F. Mueller, "Psychological and Physiological Correlates of Work Overload among University Professors " (Ph.D. diss., University of Michigan, 1965).

[33] S. Kasl and S. Cobb, "Blood Pressure Changes in Men Undergoing Job Loss: A Preliminary Report," *Psychosomatic Medicine*, January–February 1970, pp. 19–38.

[34] Meyer Friedman and Ray H. Rosenman, *Type A Behavior and Your Heart* (New York: Alfred A. Knopf, 1974).

uncover a pattern of behavior or traits. They eventually called this behavior the Type A Behavior Pattern (TABP).

The person with TABP has these characteristics:

Chronically struggles to get as many things done as possible in the shortest time period.

Aggressive, ambitious, competitive, and forceful.

Speaks explosively, rushes others to finish what they are saying.

Impatient, hates to wait, considers waiting a waste of precious time.

Preoccupied with deadlines and is work oriented.

Always in a struggle, with people, things, events.

The converse Type B individual is mainly free of the TABP characteristics and generally feels no pressing conflict with either time or persons. The Type B may have considerable drive, want to accomplish things, and works hard. The Type B has a confident style that allows him or her to work at a steady pace and not to race against the clock. On the other hand the Type A is in a constant race. The difference has been likened to a racehorse for Type A and a turtle for Type B.

As cardiologists Friedman and Roseman observed numerous coronary patients, most of whom were Type As. One incident highlighted to them what individuals with TABP were like. They called an upholsterer to fix the seats and chairs in their reception room. After inspecting the chairs the man asked what sort of physicians they were. They informed him, cardiologists. He then told them that he noticed a peculiar thing about the wear and tear on the office furniture. Only the front edge of each seat was worn out. Friedman and Rosenman interpreted this to indicate the impatience of their patients sitting on the edge of their seats to see the doctor. Type As would tend to do such things while waiting impatiently in an office.

Since the early work of Friedman and Rosenman on TABP, a number of studies have found it to be a significant predictor of premature CHD.[35] In fact recent investigations strongly suggest that TABP individuals have approximately twice the risk of developing CHD as Type B individuals.[36] Furthermore, this doubled CHD risk factor for TABP persons is independent of the influence of the traditional coronary risk factors.

Western Collaborative Group Study. A longitudinal study called the Western Collaborative Study was initiated in the early 1960s. This study used over 3,000 employees from 11 different corporations. It is an excellent example of some of the research that has been done to study TABP. The subjects (all male, ages 39 to 59) were free of coronary disease at the start of the study. Each year they underwent a physical exam and their behavior patterns were assessed.

---

[35] For a thorough review and appraisal, see Michael T. Matteson and John M. Ivancevich, "The Coronary-Prone Behavior Pattern: A Review and Appraisal," *Social Science and Medicine,* July 1980, pp. 337–51.

[36] Ibid., p. 343.

The first follow-up data were reported after two and a half years.[37] Of the original sample, 70 participants had heart disease and 77 percent of these were Type As (compared with 50 percent for the entire sample). The TABP was particularly predictive for the younger subjects; in the 39- to 49-year group, Type A men experienced six and a half times the incidence of heart disease than Type Bs did.

Data after four and a half years of follow-up included 133 participants with heart disease.[38] The predictive line between coronary problems and Type A behavior was still present. It was also found at the eight-year-data point that Type A men had more than twice the rate of coronary disease than Type B men.

Type A Measurement. Several methods have been developed for assessing TABP. Self-report scales and structured interview procedures are the most popular.[39] Friedman and Rosenman strongly urge the use of their structured interview. The structured interview places an individual in a challenging situation, in which TABP is assessed on the basis of voice stylistics, nonverbal mannerisms, and verbal content.

Susceptible Type A Individuals. Research is being conducted to determine which individual differences are associated with Type A tendencies. There are some indications that TABP is associated with age. In one study of males and females it was found that the older half of the sample had lower mean Type A scores.[40] In a similar study the 36- to 55-year-old group had the strongest Type A tendencies.[41]

Some research has found that TABP is more prevalent in males than in females.[42] However, as more women enter the work force and move into different roles it is expected that TABP will become increasingly common. Even today studies show that there is a strong association between TABP in women and the outset of coronary heart disease.[43] Interestingly, one study revealed that, unlike men, working women showed maximum Type A scores between the ages of 30 to 35 years.[44] These researchers advocated

---

[37] R. H. Rosenman, M. Friedman, W. Straus, M. Wurm, R. Kositchek, W. Hahn, and N. T. Werthessen, "A Predictive Study of Coronary Heart Disease," *Journal of American Medical Association,* February 1964, pp. 15–22.

[38] R. Rosenman et al., "Coronary Heart Disease in the Western Collaborative Group Study: A Follow-Up Experience of 4½ Years," *Journal of Chronic Diseases,* April 1970, pp. 173–90.

[39] James M. MacDougall, Theorore M. Dembroski, and Linda Musante, "The Structured Interview and Questionnaire Methods of Assessing Coronary-Prone Behavior in Male and Female College Students," *Journal of Behavioral Medicine,* March 1979, pp. 71–84.

[40] M. A. Chesney and R. H. Rosenman, "Type A Behavior in the Work Setting," in *Current Concerns in Occupational Stress,* ed. C. Cooper and R. Payne (New York: John Wiley & Sons, 1980), pp. 187–212.

[41] J. H. Howard, D. A. Cunningham, and P. A. Rechnitzer, "Work Patterns Associated with Type A Behavior: A Managerial Population," *Human Relations,* September 1977, pp. 825–36.

[42] I. Waldrow, "The Coronary-Prone Behavior Pattern, Blood Pressure, and Socio-Economic Studies in Women," *Journal of Psychosomatic Research,* March 1978, pp. 79–87.

[43] Chesney and Rosenman, "Type A Behavior."

[44] I. Waldrow, S. Zyzanski, R. B. Shekelle et al. "The Coronary Prone Behavior Pattern in Employed Men and Women," *Journal of Human Stress,* 1977, pp. 2–18.

that this "age peak" was due to the fact that more Type B females tend to leave their jobs when having children before the age of 30. Therefore, it is the Type A women who tend to continue with their careers.

For the most part the research to date on TABP has shown association with but not a cause and effect relationship with CHD. Thus, specific predictions are not advised at this time. Furthermore, few studies have thus far focused on women, and virtually none has examined the extent to which Type A behavior constitutes a risk factor among black, Mexican-Americans, and other minority populations. There are also critics of the methods used for classifying people as A or B. They claim that the classification system is based on faulty measurement and subjective conclusions.[45]

The accumulated evidence at this point strongly suggests that managers attempting to manage stress should include TABP in their assessments. Failure to include TABP would ignore some of the better interdisciplinary-behavioral and medical research that has been conducted over the past 25 years. Of all the moderators that could or should be included in a stress model TABP seems one the the most promising for additional consideration.

ORGANIZATIONAL PROGRAMS TO MANAGE STRESS

■ An astute manager never ignores a turnover or absenteeism problem, a decline in previously acceptable levels of performance, reduced quality in production, or any other sign that the organization's performance goals are not being met. The effective manager, in fact, views these occurrences as symptoms and looks beyond them to identify and correct the underlying causes. Yet most managers today are likely to search for traditional causes such as poor training, defective equipment, or inadequate instructions on what needs to be done. In all likelihood stress is not on the list of possible problems. Thus, the very first step in any program to manage stress within tolerable amounts is recognition that it exists. Any intervention program to manage stress must first determine if stress exists and what is contributing to its existence. A few specific organizational programs will be presented in this section.

Role Analysis and Clarification

In the model presented in Figure 6–2 the importance of how the employee sees the job is highlighted. Is it clear? What is expected of me? Can I do a good job with these expectations? These and other similar questions emphasize the role a person is expected to perform. It has been suggested that when stress is found in a role, adaptive responses can be initiated by management. Three such responses are to: redefine the person's role, reduce role overload by redistributing the work, and implement procedures for reducing stress when it occurs (e.g., allow the employee to have a meet-

---

[45] J. J. Ray and R. Bozek, "Dissecting the A-B Personality Type," *British Journal of Medical Psychology,* June 1980, pp. 181–86.

ing with those who are causing problems so that a solution can be worked out).[46]

Each of these methods attempts to improve the fit between the person in a particular role and the job or organizational environment. This same logic is used in job enrichment programs. Job enrichment involves redefining and restructuring a job to make it more meaningful, challenging, and intrinsically rewarding (see Chapter 12). In the context of job stress, the impact of job enrichment is on making the job more stimulating and challenging. Therefore, the jobholder would be assigned tasks that are intrinsically rewarding. Consequently, a fit between the person and the job would result.

Companywide Programs

Stress-management programs can be offered on a companywide basis. Some programs indicate the specific problem on which they are focused: alcohol or drug abuse program, job relocation program, career counseling program, and so forth. Others are more general: the Emotional Health Program of Equitable Life, the Employee Assistance Center at B. F. Goodrich, the Illinois Bell Health Evaluation Program, and the Caterpillar Tractor Special Health Services.[47]

Originally, labels such as mental health were used. However, to get away from the connotation of serious psychiatric disease, companies have changed the names of their programs. Today a popular name is stress-management. There appear to be two prototype stress-management programs used: a clinical and an organizational. The former is initiated by the firm and focuses on individual problems. The latter deals with units or groups in the work force and works on problems of the group or the total organization.

Clinical Programs. These programs are based on the traditional medical approach to treatment. Some of the elements in the program include:

Diagnosis. Person with problem asks for help. People or person in employee health unit attempts to diagnose problem.

Treatment. Counseling or supportive therapy are provided. If staff within company can't help, employee is referred to professionals in community.

Screening. Periodic examination of individuals in highly stressful jobs are provided to detect early indications of problems.

Prevention. Educating and persuading employees at high risk that something must be done to help them cope with stress.

Clinical programs must be staffed by competent personnel if they are to provide benefits. The trust and respect of users must be earned. This is

---

[46] French and Caplan, "Organizational Stress."

[47] Leon J. Warshaw, *Managing Stress* (Reading, Mass.: Addison-Wesley Publishing, 1979), p. 31.

possible if a qualified staff exists to provide for diagnosis, treatment, screening, and prevention. An example of one organization's stress-management program is outlined in the following close-up.

ORGANIZATIONS: CLOSE-UP

Kaiser-Permanente's Management of Stress Program

Kaiser-Permanente, a health maintenance organization (HMO) is using a clinical/organization hybrid type of stress preventive program for staff personnel at its Los Angeles Medical Center. The original program was developed by a physician, private therapist, nurse, and psychiatric personnel. So far it has been available for nursing directors and supervisors, middle-level managers, and a group of physicians and nurses.

The program takes place over four consecutive days (eight hours twice and four hours twice) and combines educational and experiential components. Two principal sources of stress are emphasized—intrapersonal (from within individual employees) and interpersonal.

In lectures and seminars, participants are given a basic understanding of the mechanics of stress, its sources, and its consequences. Principles of illness prevention are discussed, and the group is taught relaxation and breathing techniques to lower the "stress response threshold." In addition participants engage in role playing, psychodrama, and assertiveness training.

Each participant is given cassette tapes with relaxation instructions, a Stress Symptom Checklist, and materials for constructing their own stress profiles. Participants are instructed and asked to keep daily stress journals, recording situations (stressors) that arouse stress, the symptoms invoked, and other factors.

These diaries are kept for four weeks following the workshops; then the group meets in a follow-up session to review what was learned, how they coped, and what they will do next.

Source: Philip Goldberg, *Executive Health* (New York: McGraw-Hill, 1978), p. 240.

Organizational Programs. Organizational programs are aimed more broadly at an entire employee population. They are sometimes extensions of the clinical program. Often they are stimulated by problems identified in a group or a unit or by some impending change such as relocation of a plant, closing of a plant, or the installation of new equipment. Such programs are found in IBM, Dow Chemical, and Equitable Life.

A variety of managerial actions and programs can be used to manage work stress. Included in a list of such organizational programs would be management by objectives, organizational development programs, redesigning the structure of the organization, job enrichment, establishing autonomous work groups, establishing variable work schedules, and providing employee health facilities. For example, companies like Xerox, Rockwell International, Weyerhaeuser, and Pepsi-Cola are spending thousands of dollars for gyms equipped with treadmills, exercycles, jogging tracks, and full-time physical educational and health care staffs. One of the more impressive is found at Kimberly-Clark, where $2.5 million has been invested in a 7,000-square-foot health testing facility and a 32,000-square-foot physical fitness facility staffed by 15 full-time health care personnel.[48]

INDIVIDUAL APPROACHES TO MANAGE STRESS

■ There are also a vast variety of individual approaches to managing stress. All one has to do is visit any bookstore and look at the self-improvement section. It is stocked with numerous "how to do it" books for reducing stress. We have selected only a few of the more popularly cited methods for individually managing stress. They have been selected because (1) some research is available on their impact, (2) they are widely cited in the scientific, as well as the popular press, and (3) sophisticated evaluations of their effectiveness are under way.

Relaxation

Just as stress is an adaptive response of the body, there is growing evidence that there is an anti-stress response, "a relaxation response."[49] Benson reports that in this response muscle tension decreases, heart rate and blood pressure decrease, and breathing slows.[50] The stimuli necessary to produce relaxation include: (*a*) a quiet environment, (*b*) closed eyes, (*c*) a comfortable position, and (*d*) a repetitive mental device.

Meditation

A form of meditation that has attracted many individuals is called transcendental meditation, or TM. Its originator, Maharishi Mahesh Yogi, defines it as turning the attention toward the subtler levels of thought until the mind transcends the experience of the subtlest state of thought and arrives at the source of thought.[51]

The basic procedure used by TM is simple, but the effects claimed for it are extensive. One simply sits comfortably with closed eyes, and engages in the repetition of a special sound (a mantra) for about 20 minutes twice a day. Studies are available that indicate that TM practices are associated with reduced heart rate, lowered oxygen consumption, and decreased blood pressure.[52]

Biofeedback

Individuals can be taught to control a variety of internal body processes by a technique called biofeedback. In biofeedback, small changes occurring in the body or brain are detected, amplified, and displayed to the person. Sophisticated recording and computer technology make it possible for a

---

[48] Ivancevich and Matteson, *Stress at Work*, p. 215.

[49] Herbert Benson, *The Relaxation Response* (New York: William Morrow, 1975).

[50] Herbert Benson and Robert L. Allen, "How Much Stress Is Too Much?" *Harvard Business Review*, September–October 1980, p. 88.

[51] P. Carrington, *Freedom in Meditation* (New York: Anchor Press, 1978).

[52] D. Kuna, "Meditation and Work," *Vocational Guidance Quarterly*, June 1975, pp. 342–46.

person to attend to subtle changes in heart rate, blood pressure, temperature, and brain-wave patterns that would normally be unobservable.[53] Most of these processes are affected by stress.

The ongoing biological processes are made available to the individual by the feedback he or she receives. The person is able to monitor what is biologically occurring. The ability to gain insight and eventual control over one's bodily processes can lead to significant changes.

Despite the results of some generally well-designed research studies, individuals using biofeedback devices must remain cautious. It is unlikely that the average employee could alter any biological process without proper training.

MAJOR MANAGERIAL ISSUES

A. As individuals we establish a defense reaction to stress. It has been called the General Adaptation Syndrome (G.A.S.). The three phases of G.A.S. are called alarm, resistance, and exhaustion.

B. The consequences of stress are numerous, and can be classified as: subjective, behavioral, cognitive, physiological, health, and organizational.

C. Stress at work influences a person's nonwork activities. The interrelatedness of work and nonwork stress must be considered when attempting to explain and understand employee behavior and performance.

D. Stressors are external events which are potentially, but not necessarily harmful to individuals. One way to classify stressors at work is on the basis of physical environment, individual level, group level, and organizational level.

E. Stressors at work evoke different responses from different people. Individual differences are considered to be moderators of the stressor-stress and stress-effects relationships shown in Figure 6–2.

F. Some interesting and challenging moderators that have been identified include sex, self-esteem, and the Type A Behavior Pattern (TABP).

G. Some research suggests that TABP is associated with coronary heart disease.

H. There are numerous organizational sponsored and initiated programs available for managing work stress. Some of the most popular include role analysis and clarification practices, companywide clinical programs, and providing physical health facilities for employees.

I. Individual interventions for managing stress are numerous. Some of the more promising individual programs include relaxation, meditation, and biofeedback.

---

[53] Philip G. Zimbardo, *Psychology and Life* (Glenview, Ill.: Scott, Foresman, 1979), p. 551.

DISCUSSION AND REVIEW QUESTIONS

1. Why would a manager have to consider individual differences when investigating what is assumed to be job stress?

2. Would it be difficult to change or modify an individual's style from a Type A Behavior Pattern to a Type B Behavior Pattern? Why?

3. What role would self-motivation play in any individually based program to manage stress?

4. Why would the goal of eliminating *all* stress in the workplace be contrary to organizational effectiveness?

5. Should managers be concerned about the potential health effects of job stress? Why?

6. In what occupations, other than those discussed in this chapter, would the responsibility for people variable be stressful for many job occupants?

7. What principles of operant conditioning are used in the biofeedback approach to managing individual stress?

8. What are some of the potential organizational costs of excessive stress?

9. What is the role differences explanation of why men and women respond differently to stress?

10. Someone was heard stating that "the way to reduce stress is to allow employees to participate in decision making." Comment on the accuracy of such a statement.

ADDITIONAL REFERENCES

Baumgarten, M., and R. Oseashon. "Studies on Occupational Health: A Critique." *Journal of Occupational Medicine*, 1980, pp. 171–76.

Birk, L., ed. *Biofeedback: Behavioral Medicine.* New York: Grune & Straton, 1973.

Brown, B. *Stress and the Art of Biofeedback.* New York: Harper & Row, 1977.

Campbell, A. "Subjective Measures of Well-Being." *American Psychologist*, 1976, pp. 117–24.

Cousins, N. "The Mysterious Placebo: How Mind Helps Medicine Work." *Saturday Review*, 1977, pp. 8–12.

Dohrenwend, B. S., and B. P. Dohrenwend, eds. *Stressful Life Events—Their Nature and Effects.* New York: John Wiley & Sons, 1974.

Freudenbeyer, H. J. *Burn-Out.* New York: Anchor Press, 1980.

Gotteshalk, L. A. "Psychosomatic Medicine Today: An Overview." *Psychosomatics*, 1978, pp. 89–93.

Greenberg, J. "The Stress-Illness Link: Not If, But How." *Science News*, 1977, pp. 394–98.

Hagen, D. Q. "The Executive under Stress." *Psychiatric Annals*, 1978, pp. 49–51.

Ivancevich, J. M., and M. T. Matteson. "Optimizing Human Resources: A Case for Preventive Health and Stress Management." *Organizational Dynamics*, Autumn 1980, pp. 5–23.

Lazarus, R. S. "Positive Denial: The Case for Not Facing Reality." *Psychology Today*, 1979, pp. 44, 47–48, 51–52, 57, 60.

Matteson, M., and J. Ivancevich. *Job Stress and Health.* New York: Free Press, 1982.

Organ, D. W. "The Meaning of Stress." *Business Horizons*, 1979, pp. 32–40.

Pelletier, K. R. *Mind as Healer, Mind as Slayer.* New York: Delacorte Press, 1977.

———. *Holistic Medicine.* New York: Delacorte Press, 1979.

CASE FOR ANALYSIS

AM I A SUCCESS OR FAILURE?

At age 46, Jim Roswell is a self-made man. Although he never graduated from college, Jim was recently promoted to vice president of operations of a $80 million annual sales manufacturing firm. He is known around the firm as a take-charge, no-nonsense man who likes people and children. Jim is very active in Boy Scouts, managing Little League baseball, and local business groups. He is married, has a son who is in college, and a daughter who is a senior in high school.

Recently Jim has experienced what he calls a midlife breakdown in health. He has complained about breathing difficulties, lower back pain, insomnia, and recurring and intense headaches. His physician has found no physiological basis for the problems and is considering asking Jim to see a psychiatrist.

Jim has worked his way up the ranks. He started with the company 23 years ago as an assembler. Through hard work, his ability to work with people, and his thorough way of doing things he received one promotion after another. His last two promotions required him to move first from Miami to Atlanta and then to Colorado Springs. His wife who was very active in the Miami community became very upset with the move to Atlanta.

As Jim's responsibilities grew, he found that he had to delegate more and more authority. Since some of his subordinates were not well trained he worked hard helping them do their jobs. This extra work took him away from his family. His wife began to experience frequent bouts of depression. Finally, under a physician's care she began to take antidepressant medication. One of the side effects of the medication was that she was always fatigued.

Jim feels like his world is caving in around him. Now his son recently informed him that he was getting married and thinking about dropping out of school for a few years. His daughter has become very antagonistic about life in general, and her grades have slipped badly this year.

The situation facing Jim seems very bleak to him. He is really having difficulty justifying all the hard work he put in trying to be successful. In the organizational world he thinks he has been successful; at home he is at a loss to explain what went wrong. He really is fighting against becoming a regular visitor to a psychiatrist. He feels that all his life he made adjustments and is puzzled about his current inability to cope with his problems.

Questions for Consideration

1. What stressors in Jim's life are having an effect on his thinking, behavior, and performance?

2. Explain how work and nonwork stressors are influencing Jim's view of the world?

3. Is Jim going to be able to solve his problems on his own? Why?

EXPERIENTIAL EXERCISE I

**ANALYSIS OF
YOUR TYPE A
TENDENCIES**

Objectives

1. To provide each student with a view of their Type A Behavior Pattern.
2. To enable students to compare TABP scores with others in the class.

Related Topics

TABP has been associated with various behavioral characteristics such as impatience, time urgency, competitiveness, and hard driving. It has also been associated with coronary heart disease. Those with more pronounced TABP appear to have a greater chance of contracting coronary heart disease.

**Starting the
Exercise**

Each student should complete the behavior activity profile. The instructor has the scoring and some norms for the student to use.

Exercise Procedures

Phase I: 15 minutes
1. Individually complete and score the behavior activity profile.

Phase II: 20 or more minutes
1. Meet in small groups (four to six people) and discuss the behavior activity profile—yours and those of other members of the group.

BEHAVIOR ACTIVITY PROFILE

Because we are all unique individuals we have different ways of behaving and acting, as well as different values, thought patterns, approaches to relationships, even ways of moving. The Behavior Activity Profile is designed to assess the characteristic style or approach you exhibit in a number of situations. There are no "right" or "wrong" answers. The best answer to each item is the response that most nearly describes the way you really feel, behave, or think.

Instruction. For each item in the profile you will be presented with two alternatives. You are asked to indicate which of the two alternatives is more descriptive of you. In some items you may feel that the two alternatives are equally descriptive; for other items you may feel that neither alternative is descriptive. Nonetheless, try to determine which alternative is relatively more descriptive. For each item you have five points which you may distribute between the two alternatives in any of the following ways:

If X is totally descriptive of you and Y is not at all descriptive, place a 5 in the X box and a 0 in the Y box.

X	Y
5	0

If X is mostly descriptive of you and Y is somewhat or reasonably descriptive, place a 4 in the X box and a 1 in the Y box.

X	Y
4	1

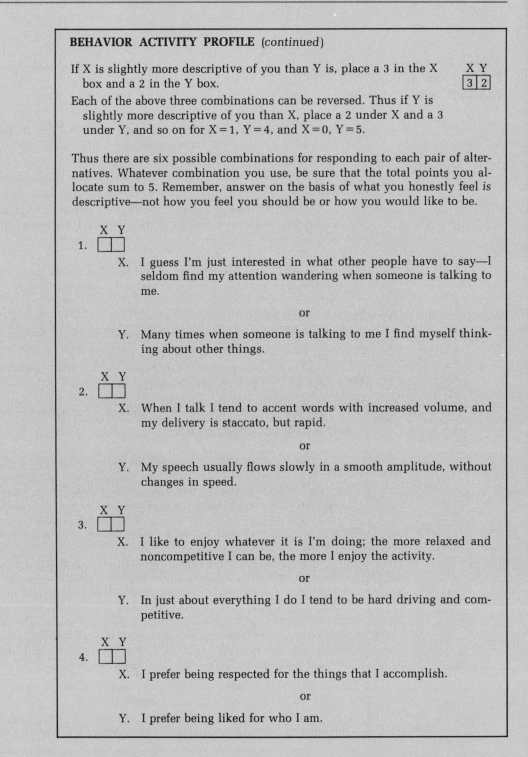

BEHAVIOR ACTIVITY PROFILE (continued)

If X is slightly more descriptive of you than Y is, place a 3 in the X box and a 2 in the Y box.

X	Y
3	2

Each of the above three combinations can be reversed. Thus if Y is slightly more descriptive of you than X, place a 2 under X and a 3 under Y, and so on for X = 1, Y = 4, and X = 0, Y = 5.

Thus there are six possible combinations for responding to each pair of alternatives. Whatever combination you use, be sure that the total points you allocate sum to 5. Remember, answer on the basis of what you honestly feel is descriptive—not how you feel you should be or how you would like to be.

1.

X	Y

    X. I guess I'm just interested in what other people have to say—I seldom find my attention wandering when someone is talking to me.

or

    Y. Many times when someone is talking to me I find myself thinking about other things.

2.

X	Y

    X. When I talk I tend to accent words with increased volume, and my delivery is staccato, but rapid.

or

    Y. My speech usually flows slowly in a smooth amplitude, without changes in speed.

3.

X	Y

    X. I like to enjoy whatever it is I'm doing; the more relaxed and noncompetitive I can be, the more I enjoy the activity.

or

    Y. In just about everything I do I tend to be hard driving and competitive.

4.

X	Y

    X. I prefer being respected for the things that I accomplish.

or

    Y. I prefer being liked for who I am.

BEHAVIOR ACTIVITY PROFILE (continued)

X Y

5. ☐☐

　X. I let people finish what they are doing or saying before I respond in any way—no use in jumping the gun and making a mistake.

　　or

　Y. I usually anticipate what a person will do or say next; for example, I'll start answering a question before it has been completely asked.

X Y

6. ☐☐

　X. Probably my behavior is seldom or never governed by a desire for recognition and influence.

　　or

　Y. If I were really honest about it, I'd have to admit that a great deal of what I do is designed to bring me recognition and influence.

X Y

7. ☐☐

　X. Frankly, I frequently get upset or angry with people even though I may not show it.

　　or

　Y. I rarely get upset with people; most things simply aren't worth getting angry about.

X Y

8. ☐☐

　X. Quite candidly, I frequently feel impatient toward others either for their slowness or for the poor quality of their work.

　　or

　Y. While I may be disappointed in the work of others, I just don't let it frustrate me.

X Y

9. ☐☐

　X. My job provides me with my primary source of satisfaction; I don't find other activities nearly as gratifying.

　　or

　Y. While I like my job, I regularly find satisfaction in numerous pursuits such as spectator sports, hobbies, friends, and family.

BEHAVIOR ACTIVITY PROFILE (continued)

10. X Y
     ☐ ☐

    X. If I had to identify one thing that really frustrates me, it would be having to stand in line.

                  or

    Y. Quite honestly, I find it kind of amusing the way some people get upset about waiting in line.

11. X Y
     ☐ ☐

    X. I don't have to control my temper; it's just not a problem for me.

                  or

    Y. Quite frankly, I frequently find it hard to control my temper, although I usually manage to do so.

12. X Y
     ☐ ☐

    X. I work hard at my job because I have a very strong desire to get ahead.

                  or

    Y. I work hard at my job because I owe it to my employer, who pays my salary.

13. X Y
     ☐ ☐

    X. It's very unusual for me to have difficulty getting to sleep because I'm excited, keyed up, or worried about something.

                  or

    Y. Many times I'm so keyed up that I have difficulty getting to sleep.

14. X Y
     ☐ ☐

    X. I may not be setting the world on fire, but I don't really want to either.

                  or

    Y. I often feel uncomfortable or dissatisfied with how well I am doing in my job or career.

15. X Y
     ☐ ☐

    X. It really bothers me when for some reason plans I've made can't be executed.

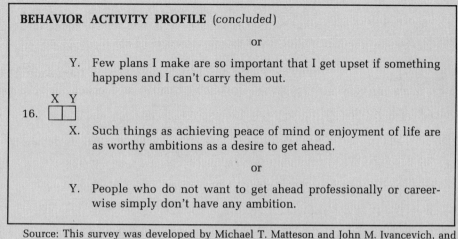

BEHAVIOR ACTIVITY PROFILE (concluded)

or

Y. Few plans I make are so important that I get upset if something happens and I can't carry them out.

X Y

16. ☐☐

X. Such things as achieving peace of mind or enjoyment of life are as worthy ambitions as a desire to get ahead.

or

Y. People who do not want to get ahead professionally or career-wise simply don't have any ambition.

Source: This survey was developed by Michael T. Matteson and John M. Ivancevich, and it is copyrighted by STress RESearch Systems, P.O. Box 883, Spring, Texas 77373.

EXPERIENTIAL EXERCISE II

ANALYSIS OF JOB-RELATED STRESS

Objectives

1. To illustrate that individuals view job-related stress factors differently.
2. To display how groups can reach different conclusions than individuals about job-related stress.
3. To emphasize how positive job-related factors can initiate some amount of stress within individuals.

Related Topics

Life event changes influence the behavior and performance of employees. They are important and vary in the amount of influence that they exert physiologically.

Starting the Exercise

Allow individuals to complete Phase I of the exercise without any consultation between each other. Then set up small groups to complete Phase II. In Phase III individuals will be involved in reviewing the work of the groups.

The Facts

Thomas Holmes and other researchers at the University of Washington School of Medicine have developed a stress scaling system that can be used to address the issue of life-change stressors. Table A shows the relative impact of different life changes, with the most stressful life event—death of a spouse—given a scale value of 100 points. Some of the events listed are generally considered to positive life events—outstanding personal achievement (28), gain of a new family member (39), and marital reconciliation (45). Even these positive events generate stress because of new roles, expectations, and activities that go along with the changes. Holmes has found through empirical analysis that the accumulation of more than 200 scale points in a year results in a better than 50 percent chance that the

TABLE A
Scaling of Life Change Units for Various Experiences

Life Event	Scale Value
Death of spouse	100
Divorce	73
Marital separation	65
Jail term	63
Death of a close family member	63
Major personal injury or illness	53
Marriage	50
Fired from work	47
Marital reconciliation	45
Retirement	45
Major change in health of family member	44
Pregnancy	40
Sex difficulties	39
Gain of a new family member	39
Business readjustment	39
Change in financial state	38
Death of a close friend	37
Change to a different line of work	36
Change in number of arguments with spouse	35
Mortgage over $10,000	31
Foreclosure of mortgage or loan	30
Change in responsibilities at work	29
Son or daughter leaving home	29
Trouble with in-laws	29
Outstanding personal achievement	28
Wife begins or stops work	26
Begin or end school	26
Change in living conditions	25
Revision of personal habits	24
Trouble with boss	23
Change in work hours or conditions	20
Change in residence	20
Change in schools	20
Change in recreation	19
Change in church activities	19
Change in social activities	18
Mortgage or loan less than $10,000	17
Change in sleeping habits	16
Change in number of family get-togethers	15
Change in eating habits	15
Vacation	13
Christmas	12
Minor violations of the law	11

Source: From L. O. Ruch and T. H. Holmes, "Scaling of Life Change: Comparison of Direct and Indirect Methods," *Journal of Psychosomatic Research*, 15 (1971): 224.

individual will sustain some type of major illness in the following year. The assumption offered is that when a person's endocrine system is overburdened with stressful events, the body cannot perform its normal function of fighting of diseases.

Perhaps an accumulation of job-related stresses could also result in overburdening the body's disease resistant mechanisms. Listed in Table B are some job factors that could cause stress. The three sets of factors are supervisor, individual, and peer initiated. Assume that these factors apply to an individual working in a typical organization. Also assume that the individual is relatively young and has about six years' experience in the organization.

TABLE B
A List of Job Factors

Supervisor Initiated	Individually Initiated	Peer Initiated
Demotion	Challenging production goals	Production norms
Criticism	Challenging career goals	Praise
Suspension	High effort	Acceptance
Probation	Poor attitudes	Cohesiveness
Praise	Personal development	Reprimand
Recognition	Self-assessment	Improved status
A bonus	Request for pay raise	
Promotion		
Positive performance		
Positive performance evaluation session		
Negative performance evaluation session		

Exercise Procedures

Phase 1: 20 minutes

1. Individually place scale values on each of the job factors listed in Table B. Place 100 points on the factors you consider to be the most potentially stressful.
2. Record your individual evaluations on a separate sheet of paper.

Phase II: 40 minutes

1. Set up groups of five to six people and discuss the individual assignments of scale points made by members.
2. Reach some type of group consensus on what is a reasonable value for each of the items.

Phase III: 30 minutes

1. Each group places the group consensus for the scale values on the board or a chart for each class member to review.
2. Discuss the different values developed by each of the groups.

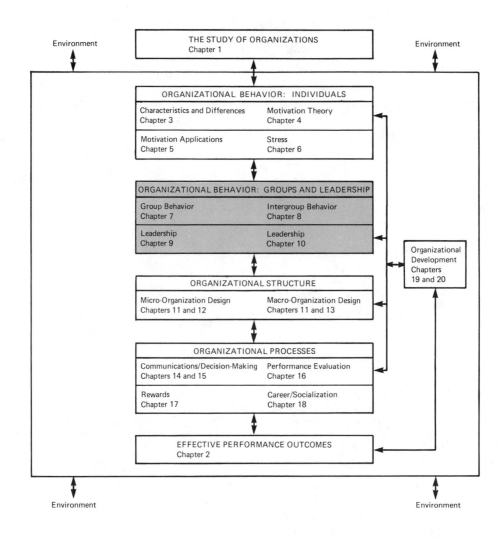

Part Three

BEHAVIOR WITHIN ORGANIZATIONS: GROUPS AND INTERPERSONAL INFLUENCE

Chapter 7

Group Behavior

AN ORGANIZATIONAL ISSUE FOR DEBATE
Does Allowing Work Groups More Freedom Improve Group Performance?

ARGUMENT FOR

Supported in a Paper Mill

The belief here was that autonomous work groups are a better way to utilize human resources and increase member satisfaction. The idea was to break away from the one-man–one-machine organization and have a small group monitor several machines. The experiment began in the chemical pulp department, with division of 35 workers into four continuous shift groups of 8 to 9 workers. Foremen were eliminated, and the number of supervisors cut in half. Workers were trained in quality control and information handling.

The experiment worked. In six years it spread virtually throughout the plant, and reduced turnover from 25 to 6 percent a year while doubling productivity. It gave management much more flexibility in scheduling work and enabled the plant to stay open through holiday periods.

Source: *Behavioral Sciences Newsletter*, August 8, 1977, p. 1.

ARGUMENT AGAINST

Not Supported in a Steel Fabricating Plant

Here the belief was also that autonomous work groups would improve performance. Attempts were made to break away from the one-man–one-machine organization. Workers were allowed to move among the various machines, and also be responsible for some equipment maintenance.

This experiment did not work. Both workers and middle managers were hostile to the idea. In one instance one of five workers was ill for two weeks. The remaining workers handled the five machines and, in addition, produced more than all five workers had previously done. Unfortunately, the experiment was halted because both workers and middle management were unwilling to alter the basic work patterns or wage structure.

In this chapter we shall examine groups in organizations. While the existence of groups in organizations probably does not alter the individual's motivations or needs, the group does influence the behavior of individuals in an organizational setting. In other words, organizational behavior is more than the logical composite of individuals' behavior. It is not their sum or product but rather a much more complex phenomenon, a very important part of which is the group. This chapter wil provide the reader with a model for understanding the nature of groups in organizations. It will include the various types of groups, reasons for the formation of groups, the characteristics of groups, and some end results of group membership.

No generally accepted definition of a group exists. Instead of immediately offering a definition, it seems more appropriate to present a range of definitions and then to synthesize these to develop a broad definition of a group. There is certainly much overlap in these definitions, and it is evident that the originators were looking at different aspects of groups.

A GROUP IN TERMS OF PERCEPTION

■ One definition is based on the perceptions of group members. It is proposed that members must perceive their relationships to others to be considered a group. An example of this type of definition is as follows:

> A small group is defined as any number of persons engaged in interaction with one another in a single face-to-face meeting or series of such meetings, in which each member receives some impression or perception of each other member distinct enough so that he can, either at the time or in later questioning, give some reaction to each of the others as an individual person, even though it may be only to recall that the other was present.[1]

This definition points out that members of the group must perceive the existence of each member as well as the existence of a group.

A GROUP IN TERMS OF ORGANIZATION

■ Sociologists view the group primarily in terms of organizational characteristics. One such definition follows:

> . . . an organized system of two or more individuals who are interrelated so that the system performs some function, has a standard set of role relationships among its members, and has a set of norms that regulate the function of the group and each of its members.[2]

This definition emphasizes some of the important characteristics of groups, such as roles and norms, which will be discussed later in this chapter.

---

[1]R. F. Bales, *Interaction Process Analysis: A Method for the Study of Small Groups* (Reading, Mass.: Addison-Wesley Publishing, 1950), p. 33.

[2]J. W. McDavid and M. Harari, *Social Psychology: Individuals, Groups, Societies* (New York: Harper & Row, 1968), p. 237.

A GROUP IN TERMS OF MOTIVATION

■ A group that fails to aid its members in satisfying their needs will have a difficult time remaining a viable group. Employees who are not satisfying their needs in a particular group will search for other groups to aid in important need satisfactions. This motivational interpretation defines a group as:

> . . . a collection of individuals whose existence as a collection is rewarding to the individuals.[3]

As pointed out in the previous chapter, it is difficult to ascertain clearly what facets of the work organization are rewarding to individuals. The problems of identifying and verifying a need hierarchy point out the shortcomings of defining a group in terms of motivation.

A GROUP IN TERMS OF INTERACTION

■ Some theorists assume that interaction in the form of interdependence is the core of "groupness." A definition which stresses interpersonal interactions is the following:

> We mean by a group a number of persons who communicate with one another often over a span of time, and who are few enough so that each person is able to communicate with all the others, not at secondhand, through other people, but face-to-face.[4]

In our view, each of these definitions is correct, since they point to important features of groups. Furthermore, we assume that if a group exists in an organization, then its members:

1. Are motivated to join.
2. Perceive the group as a unified unit of interacting people.
3. Contribute in various amounts to the group processes (i.e., some people contribute more time or energy to the group).
4. Reach agreements and have disagreements through various forms of interaction.

Therefore, for our purposes in this book, a group is defined as:

> Two or more employees who interact with each other in such a manner that the behavior and/or performance of a member is influenced by the behavior and/or performance of other members.[5]

TYPES OF GROUPS

■ An organization has technical requirements which arise from its stated goals. The accomplishment of these goals requires certain tasks to be per-

---

[3] Bernard M. Bass, *Leadership, Psychology, and Organizational Behavior* (New York: Harper & Row, 1960), p. 39.

[4] G. C. Homans, *The Human Group* (New York: Harcourt Brace Jovanovich, 1950), p. 1.

[5] See M. E. Shaw, *Group Dynamics: The Psychology of Small Group Behavior*, 2d ed. (New York: McGraw-Hill, 1976).

formed and employees are assigned to perform these tasks. Thus, as a result, most employees will be members of a group based on their position in the organization. These groups we shall label as *formal groups*. On the other hand whenever individuals associate on a fairly continuous basis there is a tendency for groups to form whose activities may be different from those required by the organization. These groups we shall label as *informal groups*. While this distinction is convenient for our discussion of the types of groups in organizations, both types of groups exhibit the same general characteristics.

Formal Groups

The demands and processes of the organization lead to the formation of different types of groups. Specifically, two types of formal groups exist.

Command Group. The command group is specified by the organization chart. The group is comprised of the subordinates who report directly to a given supervisor. The authority relationship between a department manager and the supervisors, or between a senior nurse and her subordinates, constitutes a command group.

Task Group. A task group is comprised of the employees who work together to complete a particular task or project. For example, the activities of clerks in an insurance company when an accident claim is filed are required tasks. These activities create a situation in which several clerks must communicate and coordinate with each other if the claim is to be handled properly. These required tasks and interactions facilitate the formation of a task group. The nurses assigned to duty in the emergency room of a hospital usually constitute a task group, since certain activities are required when a patient is treated.

Informal Groups

Informal groups are natural groupings of people in the work situation in response to social needs. In other words, they do not arise as a result of deliberate design but rather evolve naturally. Two specific informal groups are identified.

Interest Group. Individuals who may not be members of the same command or task group may affiliate to achieve some mutual objective. Employees grouping together to present a unified front to management for more benefits and waitresses "pooling" their tips are examples of interest groups. Also, note that the objectives of such groups are not related to those of the organization but are specific to each group.

Friendship Group. Many groups form because the members have something in common such as age, political beliefs, or ethnic background. These friendship groups often extend their interaction and communication to off-job activities.

If employees' affiliation patterns were documented, it would become readily apparent that they belong to numerous and often overlapping groups. A distinction has been made between two broad classifications of groups: formal and informal. The major difference between them is that formal groups (command and task) are designated by the formal organization and are a means to an end while informal groups (interest and friendship) are important for their own sake (that is, they satisfy a basic need for association).

WHY PEOPLE FORM GROUPS

■ Formal and informal groups form because of various reasons. Some of the reasons concern needs, proximity, attraction, goals, and economics.

The Satisfaction of Needs

The desire for need satisfaction can be a strong motivating force leading to group formation.[6] Specifically, the security, social, esteem, and self-actualization needs of some employees can be satisfied to a degree by affiliating in groups.

Security.   Without the group to lean on when various management demands are made, certain employees may assume they are standing alone facing management and the entire organization system. This "aloneness" leads to a degree of insecurity. By being a member of a group, the employee can become involved in group activities and discuss management demands with other members who hold supportive views. The interactions and communications existing between members of the group serve as a buffer to management demands. This may be especially true in the case of a new employee. The new employee may depend heavily on the group for aid in correctly performing the job. This reliance can certainly be interpreted as providing the new employee with a form of security need satisfaction.

Social.   The gregarious nature of people often results in the need for affiliation. This desire to belong and to be a part of a group points up the intensity of the social needs of American people. This is true not only on the job but also away from the workplace as evidenced by the numerous social, political, civic, and fraternal organizations that exist.

Esteem.   In a particular work environment, a certain group may be viewed by employees as being a high-prestige group for a variety of reasons (for example, technical competence, outside activities, and so on). Consequently, membership in this group carries with it a certain prestige which is not enjoyed by nonmembers. For employees with high esteem needs, membership in such a group can provide much need satisfaction.

Proximity and Attraction

Interpersonal interaction can result in group formation. Two important facets of interpersonal interaction are proximity and attraction. By *proximity* we mean the physical distance between employees performing a job. The term *attraction* designates the attraction of people to each other because of perceptual, attitudinal, performance, or motivational similarity.

Individuals who work in close proximity have numerous opportunities

---

[6] For a discussion of the group as an instrument for satisfaction of individual needs, see C. Gratton Kemp, *Perspectives on Group Processes* (Boston: Houghton Mifflin, 1970), pp. 26–29. Also see Linda N. Jewell and H. Joseph Reitz, *Group Effectiveness in Organizations* (Glenview, Ill.: Scott, Foresman, 1981). This is an excellent comprehensive work devoted entirely to the subject of groups in organizational settings.

to exchange ideas, thoughts, and attitudes about various on- and off-the-job activities. These exchanges often result in some type of group formation. This proximity makes it possible for individuals to learn about the characteristics of other people. To sustain the interaction and interest, a group often is formed.

<u>Group Goals</u>

The group's goals, if clearly understood, can be a reason why an individual is attracted to a group. For example, an individual may join a group that meets after work to become familiar with the metric measuring system. Assume that this system is to be implemented in the work organization over the next two years. The person who joins voluntarily the after-hours group believes that learning the new system is a necessary and important goal for employees.

It is not always possible to identify group goals. The assumption that formal organizational groups have clear goals must be tempered by the understanding that perception, attitudes, personality, and learning can distort goals. The same can be said about informal group goals.

<u>Economic Reasons</u>

In many cases groups form because individuals believe that they can derive greater economic benefits from their jobs if they form into groups. For example, individuals working at different points on an assembly line may be paid on a group incentive basis where the production of the group determines the wages of each member. By working and cooperating as a group, the individual may actually obtain higher economic benefits.

There are numerous other instances where economic motives result in group formation: workers in nonunion organizations form a group to exert pressure on top management for more benefits, waitresses in a restaurant "pool" their tips and share equally. Whatever the circumstances, the group members have a common interest—increased economic benefits—which leads to group affiliation.

These are only some of the numerous reasons why people join groups. It appears that people join groups because they are perceived as a means of satisfying needs. It is also obvious that the activities and goals of a group are factors in attracting members. Another important facet of group formation involves the proximity of people to each other, which is a reason for interaction and the discovery of similar characteristics.

STAGES OF GROUP DEVELOPMENT

■ Like individuals, groups learn. The performance of a group depends on both individual learning and how well the members learn to work with each other. In this section we will describe some general stages through which groups develop. Our purpose here is to point out that some kind of sequential developmental process is involved. Basically, group members progress from concern about trusting each other to concern about communication and finally maintaining controls.[7]

One model of group development assumes that groups proceed through four stages of development: (1) mutual acceptance; (2) communication and decision making; (3) motivation and productivity; and (4) control and organization.[8]

Mutual Acceptance

In the early stages of group formation, members are generally reluctant to communicate with each other. Members typically are not willing to express opinions, attitudes, and beliefs. This is similar to the situation facing a faculty member at the start of a new semester. Assume that the class objective is to develop and offer to the city government a plan for traffic control. The class response to the instructor's questions of any form is disappointing and in many cases nonexistent.

Communication and Decision Making

After a group reaches the point of mutual acceptance, the members begin to communicate openly with each other. This communication results in increased confidence and even more interaction within the group. The discussions begin to focus more specifically on problem-solving tasks and the development of alternative strategies to accomplish the tasks.

Motivation and Productivity

This is the stage of development in which effort is expended to accomplish the group's goals. The group is working as a cooperative unit and not a competitive unit.

Control and Organization

This is the stage in which group affiliation is valued and members are regulated by group norms. The group goals take precedence over individual goals, and the norms are complied with or sanctions are exercised. The ultimate sanction is ostracism for not complying with the group goals or norms. Other forms of control are temporary isolation or harassment.

CHARACTERISTICS OF GROUPS

■ As groups evolve through their various stages of development they begin to exhibit certain characteristics. To understand group behavior it is necessary to be aware of these general characteristics.

Structure

Within any group, some type of structure evolves over a period of time. The group members are differentiated on the basis of such factors as expertise, aggressiveness, power, and status. Each member occupies a *position* in the group. The pattern of relationships among the positions constitutes a *group structure*.

---

[7]For a recent study of group development, see J. M. Ivancevich and J. T. McMahon, "Group Development, Trainer Style and Carry-Over Job Satisfaction and Performance," *Academy of Management Journal*, September 1976, pp. 395–412.

[8]Bernard Bass, *Organizational Psychology* (Boston: Allyn & Bacon, 1965), pp. 197–98.

Members of the group evaluate each position in terms of its prestige, status, and importance to the group. In most cases there is some type of status difference among positions such that the group structure is hierarchical. The occupant of each position is expected by the members to enact certain behaviors during group interaction. The set of expected behaviors associated with a position in the structure constitutes the role of the occupant of that position.

Status Hierarchy

Status and position are so similar that the terms are often used interchangeably. The status *assigned* to a particular position is typically a consequence of certain characteristics which differentiate one position from the other. In some cases, a person is *ascribed* status because of such factors as job seniority, age, or assignment. The oldest worker may be perceived as being more technically proficient and is ascribed status by a group of technicians.

Status differences exert a powerful influence upon the pattern and content of communications in a group. For example, more communications tend to be directed toward high-status group members and the content of such messages tends to be more positive than messages initiated from a high-status person to lower status individuals.[9]

Roles

Each position in the group structure has an associated role which consists of the expected behaviors of the occupant of that position. The director of nursing services in a hospital is expected to organize and control the department of nursing. The director is also expected to assist in preparing and administering the budget for the department. A nursing supervisor, on the other hand, is expected to supervise the activities of nursing personnel engaged in specific nursing services, such as obstetrics, pediatrics, and surgery. These expected behaviors are generally agreed upon not only by the occupants, the director of nursing and the nursing supervisor, but also by other members of the nursing group and by other hospital personnel.[10]

The *expected role* is only one type of role. There are also a "perceived role" and an "enacted role." The *perceived role* is the set of behaviors which a person in a position believes he or she should enact. In some cases, the perceived role may correspond to the expected role. As discussed in Chapter 3, perception can, in some instances, be distorted or inaccurate. The *enacted role* is the behavior that a person actually carries out. Thus three possible role behaviors can result. There is then a possibility of conflict and frustration resulting from differences in these three role types. In fairly stable or permanent groups, there is typically good agreement be-

---

[9] For a recent relevant study, see L. A. Nikolai and J. D. Bazley, "An Analysis of the Organizational Interaction of Accounting Departments," *Academy of Management Journal*, December 1977, pp. 608–21.

[10] For example, see C. E. Schneier and P. W. Beatty, "The Influence of Role Prescriptions on the Performance Appraisal Process," *Academy of Management Journal*, March 1978, pp. 129–34.

tween expected and perceived roles. When the enacted role deviates too much from the expected role, the person can either become more like the expected role or leave the group.

Individuals, because of membership in different groups, perform multiple roles. These multiple roles result in a number of expected role behaviors. In many instances, the behaviors specified by the different roles are compatible. However, in many circumstances, they are not. When this occurs, the individual experiences role conflict. There are several types of role conflict and some important consequences. Role conflict will be discussed later in the chapter.

Norms

Norms are the standards that are shared by members of the group. Norms have certain characteristics that are important to group members. First, norms are only formed with respect to things that have significance for the group. If production is important, then a norm will evolve. If helping other group members complete a task is important, then a norm will develop.[11] Second, norms are accepted in various degrees by group members. Some norms are accepted by all members completely, while other norms are only partially accepted. Third, norms may apply to every member, or they may apply to only some group members. Every member is expected to comply with the production norm, while only group leaders are expected to disagree verbally with a management directive.

Norm Conformity. An issue of concern to managers is why employees conform to group norms. This is especially important when a person with skill and capability is performing significantly below his or her capacity so that group norms are not violated. Four general classes of variables influence conformity to group norms.

1. Personality of group members.
2. The stimuli which evoke the response.
3. Situational factors.
4. Intragroup relationships.[12]

Personality is the relatively stable set of characteristics, tendencies, and temperaments that have been formed by inheritance and by social, cultural, and environmental factors. Research on personality characteristics suggests that the more intelligent are less likely to conform than the less intelligent,[13] and that authoritarians conform more than nonauthoritarians.[14]

---

[11] For an example, see R. J. Burke, T. Weir, and G. Duncan, "Informal Helping Relationships in Work Organizations," *Academy of Management Journal*, September 1976, pp. 370–77.

[12] H. T. Reitan and M. E. Shaw, "Group Membership, Sex-Composition of the Group, and Conformity Behavior," *Journal of Social Psychology*, October 1964, pp. 45–51.

[13] Bernard M. Bass, C. R. McGehee, W. C. Hawkins, P. C. Young, and A. S. Gebel, "Personality Variables Related to Leaderless Group Discussion," *Journal of Abnormal and Social Psychology*, January 1953, pp. 120–28.

[14] E. B. Nalder, "Yielding, Authoritarianism, and Authoritarian Ideology Regarding Groups," *Journal of Abnormal and Social Psychology*, May 1959, pp. 408–10.

Stimulus factors include all the stimuli that are related to the norm to which the group member is conforming. The more ambiguous the stimulus, the greater will be the conformity to group norms. For example, suppose that top management adopts a specific type of performance appraisal interview. The group of managers who are to conduct the interviews may be initially unsure of the process because of its newness and complexity. The lack of clarity generally results in the group performing closer to the old group performance appraisal procedures than to the new ones as outlined by top management. The managers conform to a group-imposed norm until the interview process is clarified and key group members begin to utilize the procedure.

The *situational factors* pertain to variables such as the size and structure of the group. Asch found that conformity increased with group size up to four and was constant thereafter.[15] He also found that conformity was greater when there is unanimity.

The term *intragroup relationship* includes such variables as the kind of group pressure exerted, how successful the group has been in achieving desired goals, and the degree to which a member identifies with the group.

Potential Consequences of Conforming to Group Norms.   The research on conformity distinctly implies that conformity is a requirement of sustained group membership. The member who does not conform to important norms is often punished by a group. One form of punishment is to isolate or ignore the presence of the deviant. There are some potential consequences, negative and positive, of conformity. Conformity can result in a loss of individuality and the establishment of only moderate levels of performance. This type of behavior can certainly be costly to an organization which needs above-average levels of performance to remain competitive.

There are, of course, potential positive consequences of conforming to group norms. If no conformity existed, a manager would have an extremely difficult, if not impossible, time in predicting the group's behavior patterns. This inability to estimate behavior could result in unsuccessful managerial attempts to channel the group's effort toward the accomplishment of organizational goals. This, of course, is a problem facing managers of formal groups. They have no systematic way to predict behavior, such as a group's response to a new computer system or a new performance appraisal system, if there is a lack of conformity to group norms.

Leadership

The leadership role in groups is an extremely crucial group characteristic. The leader of a group exerts some influence over the members of the group. In the formal group, the leader can exercise legitimately sanctioned

[15] S. E. Asch, "Effects of Group Pressure upon the Modification and Distortion of Judgments," in *Groups, Leadership and Men,* ed. H. Guetzkow (Pittsburg: Carnegie Press, 1951), pp. 177–90.

power. That is, the leader can reward or punish members who do not comply with the directives, orders, or rules.

The leadership role is also a significant factor in an informal group. The person who becomes an informal group leader is generally viewed as a respected and prestigious member who:

1. Aids the group in accomplishing its goals.
2. Enables members to satisfy needs.
3. Embodies the values of the group. The leader in essence is a personification of the values, motives, and aspirations of the membership.
4. Is the choice of the group members to represent their viewpoint when interacting with other group leaders.
5. Is a facilitator of group conflict, an initiator of group actions, and is concerned with maintaining the group as a functioning unit.

The informal leader can, and often does, change because of the situation and various conditions which exist at a particular moment. A leader who is not able to maintain the respect and prestige as perceived by members can be replaced by another leader thought to be more prestigious and worthy of the respect of the membership. To remain a leader in any type of group a person must have the necessary knowledge and skills needed to aid and guide the group toward task accomplishment.

Cohesiveness

Formal and informal groups seem to possess a closeness or commonness of attitude, behavior, and performance. This closeness has been referred to as cohesiveness. It is generally regarded as a force acting on the members to remain in a group that is greater than the forces pulling the member away from the group.[16] A cohesive group, then, involves individuals who are attracted to each other. The group that is low in cohesiveness does not possess interpersonal attractiveness for the members.

There are, of course, numerous sources of attraction to a group. A group may be attractive because:

1. The goals of the group and the members are compatible and clearly specified.
2. The group has a charismatic leader.
3. The reputation of the group indicates that the group successfully accomplishes its tasks.
4. The group is small enough to permit members to have their opinions heard and evaluated by others.
5. The members are attractive in that they support each other and help

---

[16]James H. Davis, *Group Performance* (Reading, Mass.: Addison-Wesley Publishing, 1969), p. 78.

each other overcome obstacles and barriers to personal growth and development.[17]

These five factors are related to need satisfaction. As discussed earlier, one of the reasons for group formation is to satisfy needs. If an individual is able to join a cohesive group then there should be an increase in the satisfaction of needs through this group affiliation.

Since highly cohesive groups are composed of individuals motivated to be together, there is a tendency to expect effective group performance. This logic is not conclusively supported by research evidence. In general, as the cohesiveness of a work group increases, the level of conformity to group norms also increases and these norms may be inconsistent with those of the organization. The group pressures to conform are more intense in the cohesive group. A member who attempts to defy the group jeopardizes his or her position and status in the cohesive unit.[18]

The importance of group cohesiveness was indicated in a study conducted by the Tavistock Institute in Great Britain.[19] The coal mining industry in England following World War II introduced a number of changes in mining equipment and procedures. Prior to this new technology, miners worked together as teams. The group of miners dug out the coal, loaded it into cars, and moved it to a station where it was taken from the mine. The tasks, physical proximity, and dangers of mining were forces that resulted in the development of cohesive teams. The teams provided the members with opportunities to interact. Thus, highly cohesive groups had developed prior to the introduction of the new equipment.

The new technology disrupted the groups. The machinery did some of the tasks previously accomplished by the miners. It also destroyed many of the opportunities for miners to socialize. Without the support of the highly cohesive groups, and with an increase in physical distance between miners, the coal miners began to slow down their production. Other groups or teams formed, but they were not as attractive to the miners as the traditional teams that worked close to each other.

The recognition of the impact of groups on performance is a vital one for managers. The following close-up outlines the productive utilization of work groups in the banking industry.

------

[17]D. Cartwright and A. Zander, *Group Dynamics: Research and Theory* (New York: Harper & Row, 1968).

[18]A. J. Lott and B. E. Lott, "Group Cohesiveness as Interpersonal Attraction: A Review of Relationships with Antecedent and Consequent Variables." *Psychological Bulletin*, October 1965, pp. 259–309.

[19]E. L. Trist and K. W. Bamforth, "Some Social and Psychological Consequences of the Longwall Method of Coal Getting," *Human Relations*, February 1951, pp. 3–38. For other important research on group cohesiveness, see S. E. Seashore, *Group Cohesiveness in the Industrial Work Group* (Ann Arbor: Institute for Social Research, University of Michigan, 1954), and S. M. Klein, *Workers under Stress: The Impact of Work Pressure on Group Cohesion* (Lexington: The University of Kentucky Press, 1971).

ORGANIZATIONS: CLOSE-UP

Quality Circles in the Banking Industry

Each month the manager of the research and adjustment unit at the Central Bank of Birmingham gathers his group of seven clerks and assistant supervisors around an oval conference table so they can tell him what many managers don't like to hear: the problems they face in performing their day-to-day work in the unit.

Operating on the principle that no one knows a job better than the people who perform it, "quality circles" as they are called, attempt to utilize this expertise to solve work problems and improve organizational performance. It is estimated that some 500 U.S. corporations utilize this approach. Most are manufacturers and only lately have they been attempted in service industries such as banking.

In addition to Central Bank, Irving Trust in New York, First Tennessee Bank in Memphis, United California Bank, Bank of America, and the Federal Reserve Bank of Atlanta are conducting similar meetings. Others will begin using the approach this year.

The process consists of five key stages: problem identification, problem selection, analysis, discussion of alternative solutions, and presentation to management. Only after a problem has been defined and analyzed do circle members attempt to devise solutions.

Source: Phillip L. Zweig, "Quality Circles Helping Banks Solve Problems, Improve Performance," *American Banker*, January 19, 1981, pp. 1, 12, 14.

Cohesiveness and Performance. The concept of cohesiveness is an important one for the understanding of groups in organizations. The degree of cohesiveness in a group can have positive or negative effects depending upon how congruent group goals are with those of the formal organization. In fact, four distinct possibilities exist as illustrated in Figure 7–1.

Figure 7–1 indicates that if cohesiveness is high and the group accepts and agrees with formal organization goals then group behavior will likely be positive from the formal organization standpoint. However, if the group is highly cohesive but with goals which are not congruent with the formal organization, then group behavior will likely be negative from the formal organization standpoint.

Figure 7–1 also indicates that if a group is low in cohesiveness and the members have goals not in agreement with those of management, then the results will probably be negative from the standpoint of the formal organization although the behavior will be more on an individual basis than on a group basis because of the low cohesiveness. On the other hand it is possible to have a group low in cohesiveness where the members' goals agree with those of the formal organization. Here the results will probably

FIGURE 7–1

The Relationship between Group Cohesiveness and Agreement with Organizational Goals and Group Performance

		Agreement with Organizational goals	
		Low	High
Degree of Group Cohesiveness	Low	Performance oriented away from formal organizational goals.	Performance probably oriented toward achievement of formal organizational goals.
	High	Performance probably oriented away from formal organizational goals.	Performance oriented toward achievement of formal organizational goals.

be positive although again more on an individual basis than a group basis.[20]

When the goals of a cohesive group conflict with those of management, some form of managerial intervention is usually necessary. These intervention techniques will be discussed in detail in the next chapter.

Groupthink.   We have suggested that highly cohesive groups are very important forces in organizational behavior. Suppose that a manager were able to produce a highly cohesive group. In other words, place similar people in an isolated setting with a common goal and reward them for performance. Would this be good? On the surface, it may look like a good idea. One author has provided a very provocative account about such groups.[21] In his book, Irving Janis analyzes the foreign-policy decisions made by the presidential administrations and comes to the conclusion that these groups were highly cohesive, close-knit groups. He labeled their decision-making process as groupthink which has the following characteristics:

Illusion of Invulnerability.   Members of the group believed they were invincible. For example, on the eve of the disastrous attempt to invade Cuba in April 1961 (the Bay of Pigs invasion), Robert Kennedy stated that with the talent in the group, they could overcome whatever challenged them with "common sense and hard work" and "bold new ideas."

Tendency to Moralize.   The groups had a general tendency to view the United States as the leader of the free world. Any opposition was characterized as weak, evil, or unintelligent.

---

[20] The general idea for the figure came from F. E. Kast and J. E. Rosenzweig, *Organization and Management* (New York: McGraw-Hill, 1970), p. 284.

[21] Irving Janis, *Victims of Groupthink: A Psychological Study of Foreign Policy Decisions and Fiascos* (Boston: Houghton Mifflin, 1973).

Feeling of Unanimity.   The group reports that each member of the Executive Committee supports the president's decisions. Later on, however, members indicate that they had serious doubts at the time the decisions were being made. For example, Arthur Schlesinger and Theodore Sorenson both reported they had reservations about the decisions being made with respect to Southeast Asia during the Kennedy years. Both men admitted regretting their hesitancy to let their views be known at the time. However, at the time they believed that everyone else was in total agreement and that they were the only differing view. Rather than appear weak or soft, each kept his view to himself.

Pressure to Conform.   Occasionally, President Kennedy would bring in an expert to respond to questions which members of the group might have. The purpose was to have the expert in effect silence the critic instead of actively encouraging discussion of divergent views. Other forms of informal pressures to conform were also used on cabinet and staff members. In one instance, Arthur Schlesinger reported that Robert Kennedy mentioned informally to him that while he could see some problems associated with a particular decision, the President needed unanimous support on the issue. There was a strong preceived need for group solidarity.

Opposing Ideas Were Dismissed.   Any individual or group outside who criticized or opposed a decision or policy received little or no attention from the group. Even ideas and arguments that appeared valid or relevant were often dismissed prematurely. Janis notes that much evidence that indicated strongly that the invasion of Cuba would fail was given little consideration.

Certainly, some level of group cohesiveness is necessary for a group to tackle a problem at all. If seven individuals from seven different organizational units are assigned a task, the task may never be completed effectively. The point is that more cohesiveness may not necessarily be better. While members of task groups may redefine solving a problem to mean reaching agreement rather than making the best decision, members of cohesive groups may redefine it to mean preserving relations among group members and preserving the image of the group. The invasion of Cuba decision described by Janis is an example of the negative impact of group pressures on the quality of decision made by the group. He specifically describes groupthink as the "deterioration of mental efficiency, reality testing, and moral judgment" in the interest of group solidarity.[22]

In Chapter 15 on decision making, group decisions will be examined in greater detail. Our discussion of groupthink at this point is to illustrate the impact of group dynamics and cohesiveness on group performance. As a summary, the sometimes negative impact of these phenomena is illustrated in another setting in the following close-up.

---

[22]Janis, *Victims of Groupthink,* p. 9.

ORGANIZATIONS: CLOSE-UP

A Negative Impact of Group Pressure

Research has indicated that corporations may pass through a similar process which eventually leads them to criminal activities such as price fixing and bribery. The first step toward such behavior appears to come amid an atmosphere of intense competition or trying financial times. At this point when the chief executive officer should be exhibiting high ethical standards, a lowered moral tone may appear and begin to permeate the entire organization. Performance pressures on managers are intense and this combination of factors may lead to an atmosphere that rewards illegitimate means of attaining corporate goals.

Finally, a member of top management begins engaging in specific illegal activities. Other key people become involved and most others tend to go along with the situation and do what is asked of them. Anyone in management who objects is merely excluded.

Source: David Ermann, "Corporate and Governmental Deviance," *International Management*, August 1978.

Intergroup Conflict

We have discussed the ways and means utilized by groups in handing conflict between members of the group. However, an important characteristic of groups is that they also conflict with other groups in the organization. There are many reasons why groups often conflict with one another. Many times the consequences of this conflict may be good for the organization while at other times they may be extremely negative.

This chapter is concerned mainly with what happens *within* groups: the types, development, and characteristics. The subject of what happens *between* groups (intergroup behavior) is also important. So much, in fact, that the next chapter is devoted entirely to the subject of intergroup behavior and conflict. At this point it is sufficient to note that intergroup conflict is an important characteristic of group behavior.

This concludes our section on the characteristics of groups. While others could undoubtedly be discussed, we have identified structure, status hierarchy, roles, (expected, perceived, and enacted), norms, leadership, cohesiveness and intergroup conflict as important characteristics of groups in organizations.

THE CONCEPT OF ROLE

■ Throughout this chapter, as well as the remainder of the book, the concept of role is very important to the understanding of organizational behavior. We use the term *role* to refer to the expected behavior patterns attributed to a particular position.

To communicate the importance of the concept of role, let us leave the organizational setting for a moment. The role of wife and husband is familiar to to everyone. The role of a wife or husband is the culturally defined expectations associated with that particular position. It may include attitudes and values as well as specific kinds of behavior. It is what the individuals must do in order to validate their occupancy of the particular positions.[23] In other words, what kind of a husband or wife an individual is depends a great deal on how he or she performs the culturally defined roles associated with the positions. For example, consider your own perceptions of the roles associated with physicians, law enforcement officers, military officers, politicians, college professors, or business executives.

Certain activities are expected of all positions in the formal organization. These activities constitute the role for that position from the standpoint of the formal organization. The formal organization develops job descriptions which define the activities of a particular position and how it relates to other positions in the organization. However, roles may not be set forth explicitly by the formal organization and yet be clearly understood by group members. This is true for both formal (task and command) groups as well as informal (interest and friendship) groups. Thus, whether they are formally or informally established, status hierarchies and accompanying roles are integral parts of every organization.

Multiple Roles and Role Sets

Most individuals play many roles simultaneously. This is because we occupy many different positions in a variety of organizations—home, work organization, church, civic organization, and so forth. Within each of these organizations we occupy and perform certain roles. Thus, most individuals perform *multiple roles.* Also, for each position there may be different role relationships. For example, the position of college professor not only involves the role of teacher in relation to students, but also numerous other roles relating the position to administrators, peers, the community, and alumni. Each group may expect different things. This we term the *role set*. It refers to those individuals who have expectations for the behavior of the individual in the particular role. The more expectations the more complex the role set. A college professor likely has a more complex role set than a forest ranger and less than a politician.

Thus, multiple roles refers to different roles while role sets refers to the different expectations associated with one role. Therefore, an individual involved in many different roles, each with a complex role set faces the ultimate in complexity of individual behavior. The concepts of multiple roles and role sets are important because there may be complications which often make it extremely difficult to define specific roles especially in organizational settings.[24] This can often result in *role conflict* for the individual.

---

[23] See two classic discussions of these concepts in Robert K. Merton, *Social Theory and Social Structure* (New York: Free Press, 1957): and Ralph Linton, "Concepts of Role and Status," in *Readings in Social Psychology*, eds. Theodore E. Newcomb and Eugene L. Hartley, (New York: Holt, Rinehart & Winston, 1947).

[24] An important work in this field is R. L. Kahn, D. M. Wolfe, R. P. Quinn, and J. D. Snoek, *Organizational Stress: Studies in Role Conflict and Ambiguity* (New York: John Wiley & Sons, 1964), pp. 12–26.

Role Perception

The reader can readily imagine that different individuals can have different perceptions of the behavior associated with a given role. In an organizational setting accuracy in role perception can have a definite impact on performance.[25] This matter is further complicated in an organization because there may be three different perceptions of the same role: that of the formal organization, the group, and the individual. This increases even further the possibility of role conflict.

The Organization. The positions which individuals occupy in an organization are the sum total of their organizationally defined roles. This would include the position in the chain of command, the amount of authority associated with the position, and the functions and duties of the position. These roles are defined by the organization and relate to the position and not a particular individual.

The Group. Role relationships develop which relate individuals to the various groups to which they belong. These may be formal and informal groups and the expectations evolve over time and may or may not be congruent with the organization's perception of the role. In this respect they are similar to group norms.

The Individual. Every individual who occupies a position in an organization or group has a clearly defined perceptionof his or her role. This perception will be greatly influenced by background and social class, since they affect the individual's basic values and attitudes. These are brought to the organization and will affect the individuals' perception of their roles.

Role Conflict

With an understanding of the concept of role and its many complexities let us now consider the idea of *role conflict*. Because of the multiplicity of roles and role sets, it is possible for an individual to face a situation of the simultaneous occurrence of two or more role requirements for which the performance of one precludes the performance of the other. When this occurs, the individual faces a situation of role conflict. We shall examine several forms of role conflict which can occur in organizations.[26]

Person-Role Conflict. This conflict occurs when role requirements violate the basic values, attitudes, and needs of the individual occupying the position. A supervisor who finds it difficult to dismiss a subordinate with a family, or an executive who resigns rather than engage in some unethical activity are examples of this type of role conflict.[27]

---

[25] For a relevant study, see A. D. Szilagyi, "An Empirical Test of Causal Inference between Role Perceptions, Satisfaction with Work, and Organizational Level," *Personnel Psychology*, Autumn 1977, pp. 375–88.

[26] R. Tagiuri, P. R. Lawrence, R. Barnett, and D. C. Dumphy, *Behavioral Science Concepts in Case Analysis* (Boston: Division of Research, Graduate School of Business Administration, Harvard University, 1968), pp. 106–10.

[27] For example, see N. Keeley, "Subjective Performance Evaluation and Person-Role Conflict under Conditions of Uncertainty," *Academy of Management Journal*, June 1977, pp. 301–14. For an analysis of some of the organizational implications of this type of conflict, see L. Roos and F. Starke, "Roles in Organizations," in *Handbook of Organizational Design*, ed. W. Starbuck and P. Nystrom (Oxford, England: Oxford University Press, 1980).

Intrarole Conflict. This occurs when different individuals define a role according to different sets of expectations, making it impossible for the person occupying the role to satisfy all. This is more likely to occur when a given role has a complex role set (many different role relationships). The foreman in an industrial situation has a rather complex role set and thus may face this type of conflict. On one hand, top management has a set of expectations which stress the foreman's role in the management hierarchy. However, being a first-line supervisor the foreman may have close friendship ties with members of the command group who may possibly be former working peers. This is why foremen and first-line supervisors are often described as being "in the middle."[28]

Interrole Conflict. This type of conflict is the result of facing multiple roles. It occurs because individuals simultaneously perform many roles, some of which have conflicting expectations. A scientist in a chemical plant who is also a member of an administrative group might experience role conflict of this kind. In such a situation the scientist may be expected to behave in accordance with the expectations of management as well as the expectations of professional chemists. A physician placed in the role of hospital administrator might also experience this type of role conflict. In the next chapter we shall see that this type of role conflict is often the cause of conflict between groups in many organizations.

The Results of Role Conflict

Behavioral scientists agree that an individual confronted with role conflict will experience psychological stress which may result in emotional problems and indecision. While there are certain kinds of role conflict which managers can do little to avoid, there are certain types which can be minimized. For example, some types of role conflict (especially intrarole conflict) can be the result of violations in the classical principles of chain of command and unity of command. The rationale of the early management writers for these two principles was that violation would likely cause conflicting pressures on the individual. In other words, when individuals are faced with conflicting expectations or demands from two or more sources the likely end result will be a decline in performance.[29]

In addition, interrole conflict can result from conflicting expectations of formal or informal groups with the results being similar to those of intrarole conflict. Thus, a highly cohesive group with goals not congruent with those of the formal organization can cause a great deal of interrole conflict for its membership.

One final point must be made concerning role conflict. Research has

---

[28] For excellent discussions of the conflict-laden position of foremen, see F. J. Roethlisberger, "The Foreman: Master and Victim of Double Talk," *Harvard Business Review*, September–October 1965, pp. 23 ff.; and F. C. Mann and J. K. Dent, "The Supervisor: Member of Two Organizational Families," *Harvard Business Review*, November–December 1954; pp. 103–12.

[29] For the view of an early writer on the behavioral end-results of violations in the principles of chain of command and unity of command, see Chester I. Barnard, *The Functions of the Executive* (Cambridge, Mass.: Harvard University Press, 1938), p. 277.

shown that role conflict does occur frequently and with negative effects on performance over a wide spectrum of occupations.[30] For example, unskilled employees, salespersons, school administrators, teachers, scientists, military chaplains, nurses, and managers have all been studied under various role conflict conditions.

AN INTEGRATED MODEL OF GROUP FORMATION AND DEVELOPMENT

■ Figure 7–2 summarizes what has been discussed to this point. It indicates the potential end results from group behavior: individual performances, group performances and overall organizational effectiveness and performance. The model also includes feedback from the potential behavioral consequences and each of the other elements in the model. Each segment can influence each of the other segments.

FIGURE 7–2
A Model of Group Formation and Development

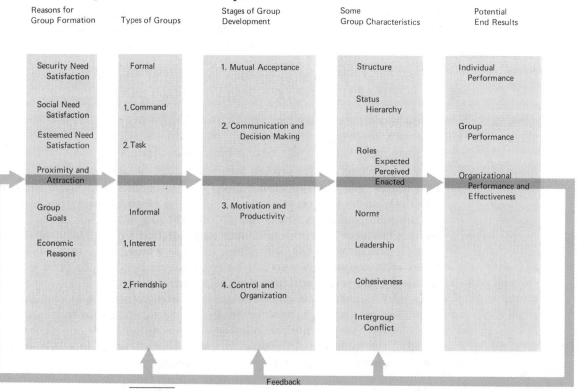

[30]For representative examples, see A. Etzioni, "Authority Structure and Organizational Effectiveness," *Administrative Science Quarterly*, June 1959, pp. 43–67; N. Kaplan, "The Role of the Research Administrator," *Administrative Science Quarterly*, June 1959, pp. 20–41; W. A. Evans, "Role Strain and the Norm of Reciprocity in Research Organizations," *American Journal of Sociology*, November 1964, pp. 346–54; R. G. Corwin, "The Professional Employee: A Study of Conflict in Nursing Roles," *American Journal of Sociology*, May 1961, pp. 604–15; J. M. Ivancevich and J. H. Donnelly, Jr., "A Study of Role Clarity and Need for Clarity for Three Occupational Groups," *Academy of Management Journal*, March 1974, pp. 28–36; and R. H. Miles, "A Comparison of the Relative Impacts of Role Perceptions of Ambiguity and Conflict by Role," *Academy of Management Journal*, March 1976, pp. 25–34.

MAJOR MANAGERIAL ISSUES

A. A group can be defined in terms of perception, organization, motivation, or interaction. We recommend thinking about a group as employees who interact in such a manner that the behavior and/or performance of a member is influenced by the behavior and/or performance of other members.

B. Managers, by being aware of group characteristics and behaviors, can be prepared for the potential positive and negative end results of group activities. In a proactive sense, the manager could intervene to modify the perceptions, attitudes, and motivations which precede the end results.

C. People are attracted to groups because of the potential for satisfying needs, physical proximity and attraction, and the appeal of group goals and activities. In essence, people are attracted to each other; this is a natural process. The manager can structure a work area to minimize interaction, but no manager can or should eliminate interaction. Consequently, since interaction is inevitable, informal group formation is also certain to occur. The manager who perceives the interactions as potential dangers will have difficulty reacting constructively to inevitable group formation.

D. Groups develop at different rates and with unique patterns depending on the task, the setting, the membership's individual characteristics and behavioral patterns, and the manager's style of managing.

E. Some characteristics of groups are:

    1. Structure.
    2. Status hierarchy.
    3. Roles.
    4. Norms.
    5. Leadership.
    6. Cohesiveness.
    7. Intergroup conflict.

These characteristics pervade all groups and should be considered important. In an informal group, these characteristics emerge from within the unit, while in a formal group they are established by the managerial process. They provide a degree of predictability for the membership behavior patterns that is important to the group and to outsiders (e.g., management, other groups). A group that is unstable or unpredictable is a problem for members and others who interact with it.

F. Each group possesses some degree of cohesiveness. This attractiveness of the group can be a powerful force in influencing individual behavior and performance.

G. Research studies indicate that cohesive groups can formulate goals and norms which can be either congruent or incongruent with those of management. When these goals and norms are incongruent some form of managerial intervention is necessary.

MAJOR MANAGERIAL ISSUES (continued)

H. The concept of role is important for an understanding of group behavior. These are the expected behavior patterns attributed to a particular position. Most individuals perform multiple roles each with its own role set (expectations of others for the role). An individual involved in many different roles, each with a complex role set, faces the ultimate in complexity of individual behavior.

I. In organizations there may be as many as three perceptions of the same role; the organization's, the group's, and the individual's. When an individual faces a situation of the simultaneous occurrence of two or more role requirements for which the performance of one precludes the performance of the other, the individual experiences role conflict. Three different types of role conflict: person-role conflict, intrarole conflict, and interrole conflict can occur in organizational settings. Each is important since research has shown that the consequences to the individual are increased psychological stress and other emotional reactions. Management can minimize certain types and should continually be aware that the consequences of role conflict to the organization is ineffective performance of individuals and groups.

DISCUSSION AND REVIEW QUESTIONS

1. Think of an informal group to which you belong. Does a status hierarchy exist in the group? What is it based upon?

2. For the group you have selected above, can you describe any evolution or developmental process such as described in the chapter? Discuss.

3. What are some of the attitudes, beliefs, etc., you held when you first joined the class in which you are using this book? Describe them and then indicate if you believe they have had any impact on your behavior and performance in the class.

4. Are there any cohesive subgroups in your class?

How do you know? Do you think it has influenced their behavior or performance in the class?

5. Describe some sources of person-role conflict, intrarole conflict, and interrole conflict that you have either experienced personally or have watched others experience.

6. Why is it important for a manager to be familiar with concepts of group behavior?

7. Why is cohesiveness an important concept in managing group behavior?

ADDITIONAL REFERENCES

Alderfer, C. P.   "Effect of Individual, Group, and Intergroup Relations on Attitudes toward a Management Development Program." *Journal of Applied Psychology*, 1971, pp. 302–11.

Cobb, A. T.   "Informal Influence in the Formal Organization: Perceived Sources of Power among Work Unit Peers." *Academy of Management Journal*, 1980, pp. 155–60.

Cohen, A. R.; S. L. Fink; H. Gadon; and R. D. Willits. *Effective Behavior in Organizations.* Homewood, Ill.: Richard D. Irwin, 1980.

Delbecq, A. L., and A. VandeVen. "A Group Process Model for Problem Identification and Program Planning." *Journal of Applied Behavioral Science,* 1971, pp. 466–92.

Gandy, J., and V. V. Murry, "The Experience of Workplace Politics." *Academy of Management Journal,* 1980, pp. 237–51.

Graham, G. H. "Interpersonal Attraction as a Basis of Informal Organization." *Academy of Management Journal,* 1971, pp. 483–95.

Green, Thad B. "An Empirical Analysis of Nominal and Interacting Groups." *Academy of Management Journal,* 1975, pp. 63–73.

Hackman, J. R. "Group Influences on Individuals." In *Handbook of Industrial and Organizational Psychology,* edited by M. D. Dunnette. Chicago: Rand McNally, 1976.

Lewis, G. H. "Role Differentiation." *American Sociological Review,* 1972, p. 424–34.

Liddell, W. W., and J. W. Slocum, Jr. "The Effects of Individual-Role Compatibility upon Group Performance: An Extension of Schutz's FIRO Theory." *Academy of Management Journal,* 1976, pp. 413–26.

Malcolm, A. *The Tyranny of the Group.* Totowa, N.J.: Littlefield, Adams, 1975.

Mazar, A. "A Cross-Species Comparison of Status in Small Established Groups." *American Sociological Review,* 1973, pp. 513–30.

Reif, W. F.; R. M. Monczka; and J. W. Newstrom. "Perceptions of Formal and Informal Organizations: Objective Management through the Semantic Differential Technique." *Academy of Management Journal,* 1973, pp. 389–403.

Sims, H. P., Jr., and A. D. Szilagyi. "Leader Structure and Subordinate Satisfaction for Two Hospital Administrative Levels: A Path Analysis Approach." *Journal of Applied Psychology,* 1975, pp. 194–97.

Smith, P. B. *Groups within Organizations.* New York: Harper & Row, 1973.

Steiner, I. D. *Group Processes and Productivity.* New York: Academic Press, 1972.

Turner, A. N. "A Conceptual Scheme for Describing Work Group Behavior." In *Organizational Behavior and Administration,* edited by P. R. Lawrence et al. Homewood, Ill.: Richard D. Irwin, 1961, pp. 213–23.

Jim Lyons had just completed his second month as manager of an important office of a nationwide sales organization. He believed that he had made the right choice in leaving his old company. This new position offered a great challenge, excellent pay and benefits, and tremendous opportunity for advancement. In addition, his family seemed to be adjusting well to the new community. However, in Jim's mind there was one very serious problem which he believed must be confronted immediately or it could threaten his satisfaction in the long run.

Since taking the job, Jim had found out that the man he replaced had made an institution of the hard-drinking business lunch. He and a group of other key executives had virtually a standing appointment at varous local restaurants. Even when clients were not present, they would have several drinks before ordering their lunches. When they returned it was usually well into the afternoon and they were in no condition to make the decisions or take the actions that were often the pretext of the lunch in the first place. This practice had also spread to the subordinates of the various executives and it was not uncommon to see various groups of salespersons doing the same thing a few days each week. Jim decided that he wanted to end the practice, at least for himself and members of his group.

Jim knew this was not going to be an easy problem to solve. The drinking had become institutionalized with a great deal of psychological pressure from a central figure—in this case, the man he replaced. He decided to plan the approach he would take and then discuss the problem and his approach for solving it with his superior, Norm Landy.

The following week Jim made an appointment with Norm to discuss the situation. Norm listened intently as Jim explained the drinking problem but did not show any surprise at learning about it. Jim then explained what he planned to do.

"Norm, I'm making two assumptions on the front end. First, I don't believe it would do any good to state strong new policies about drinking at lunch, or lecturing my people about the evils of the liquid lunch. About all I'd accomplish there would be to raise a lot of latent guilt which would only result in resentment and resistance. Second, I am assuming that the boss is often a role model for his subordinates. Unfortunately, the man I replaced made a practice of the drinking lunch. The subordinates close to him then conform to his drinking habits and exert pressure on other members of the group. Before you know it everyone is a drinking buddy and the practice becomes institutionalized even when one member is no longer there.

"Here is what I intend to do about it. First, when I go to lunch with the other managers, I will do no drinking. More importantly, however, for the members of my group I am going to establish a new role model. For example, at least once a week we have a legitimate reason to work through lunch. In the past everyone has gone out anyway. I intend to hold a business lunch and have sandwiches and soft drinks sent in. In addition, I intend to make it a regular practice to take different groups of my people to lunch at a no-alcohol coffee shop.

"My goal, Norm, is simply to let my subordinates know that alcohol is not a necessary part of the workday, and that drinking will not win my approval. By not drinking with the other managers, I figure that sooner or later they too will get the point. As you can see I intend to get the message across by my behavior. There will be no words of censure. What do you think Norm?"

Norm Landy pushed himself away from his desk and came around and seated himself beside Jim. He then looked at Jim and whispered, "Are you crazy? I guarantee you, Jim, that you are going to accomplish nothing but cause a lot of trouble. Trouble between your group and other groups if you succeed, trouble between you and your group, and trouble between you and the other managers. Believe me, Jim, I see the problem, and I agree with you that it is a problem. But the cure might kill the patient. Will all that conflict and trouble be worth it?"

Jim thought for a moment and said "I think it will be good for the organization in the long run."

Questions for Consideration

1. Do you agree with Norm Landy or Jim Lyons? Why?
2. Do you think anything can be done about this situation? Why? What is your opinion of Jim's plan?
3. What would you do in Jim's situation? Be specific.

Chapter 8

Intergroup Behavior and Managing Conflict

AN ORGANIZATIONAL ISSUE FOR DEBATE
Should Management Seek To Eliminate Conflict?*

ARGUMENT FOR

Many practicing managers view group conflict negatively and thus seek to resolve or eliminate all types of conflict. These managers adhere to the beliefs of classical organization theorists that conflict disrupts the organization and prevents optimal performance. As such it is a clear indication that something is wrong with the organization and that sound management principles are not being applied in directing the activities of the organization.

Since their desire was to eliminate conflict, early writers based their approaches on principles of authority, delegation of authority, and unity of command. They believed that conflict could be eliminated or avoided by recruiting the right people, carefully specifying job descriptions, structuring the organization in such a way as to establish a clear chain of command, and establishing clear rules and procedures to meet various contingencies.

Many writers believe that this view is held today by the majority of practicing managers. They view all conflict as disruptive; their task is to eliminate it by more effective management and organizational structure.

* The first view is discussed in detail in C. B. Derr, *A Historical Review of Management Organization Conflict* (Boston: Graduate School of Education, Harvard University, 1972), pp. 1–22. The opposing view is discussed in detail in M. Olson, *The Logic of Collective Action* (Cambridge, Mass.: Harvard University Press, 1965).

ARGUMENT AGAINST

Many theorists and some managers believe that a more realistic view of conflict is that it cannot be avoided. They believe it is inevitable and can result from numerous factors including the structure of the organization itself, the performance evaluation system, and even something as seemingly unimportant as the physical design of an office and its furnishings.

In fact, these individuals believe that a certain amount of conflict is not only useful but that optimal organizational performance requires a moderate level. Without it, there will be no felt need to change and attention will not be called to problem areas.

Obviously, these individuals realize that too much conflict is undesirable. Thus, they believe that conflict may either "add to" or "detract from" organizational performance in varying degrees. In other words, conflict can be functional or dysfunctional for the organization depending on the amount and kind. Under this viewpoint, management's task becomes one of managing the level of conflict in order to achieve optimal performance.

For any organization to perform effectively, interdependent individuals and groups must work out their relations across organizational boundaries, between individuals, and among groups. Each individual or group depends on another. It may be for information, assistance, or coordinated action. But the fact is, they are interdependent. Such interdependence may foster cooperation or conflict.

For example, the entire faculty of a college may meet to discuss ways to convince the university administration that the annual budget for the college must be increased. Such a meeting may be reasonably free of conflict. Decisions get made, strategies are developed and faculty return to their duties. This is intergroup cooperation to achieve a common goal. However, this may not be the case if a budget increase is granted. Individual departments in the college have their own goals and conflict is likely to result at this point because of conflicting departmental goals and competition for resources (new faculty, secretarial assistance). This example illustrates that quite a range can exist between cooperation and conflict and that groups can cooperate on one point and at the same time conflict on another.

This chapter focuses on conflict that occurs between groups in organizations. This is certainly not the only type of conflict that can exist in organizations. Conflict between individuals, however, can usually be more easily resolved through existing mechanisms such as terminations, transfers, or changes in work schedules. Conflict between groups is likely to be the most disruptive to the organization.

We shall begin the chapter by examining attitudes toward conflict. Reasons for the existence of intergroup conflict and its consequences are then presented. Finally, we shall outline various techniques used to successfully manage conflict.

A REALISTIC VIEW OF INTERGROUP CONFLICT

■ Recognizing the reality that conflict is inevitable in organizations, the authors take the view that intergroup conflict can be both positive and negative. How positive or negative it is depends upon the impact the conflict has on the organization's goal achievement. Conflict may be beneficial if it is used as an instrument for change or innovation and results in better problem solving. However, too much conflict is likely to result in chaos. We saw in an earlier chapter that individuals have differing abilities to withstand stress. Thus, it appears that the critical issue is not conflict itself but rather how it is managed. Using this approach we can define conflict in terms of the *effect it has on the organization*. In this respect we shall discuss both *functional* and *dysfunctional* conflict.[1]

---

[1]This view reflects current thinking among management theorists and a growing number of practitioners. It has been labeled the *interactionist* view. For a major work devoted entirely to the subject of organizational conflict which discusses this and other views, see Stephen P. Robbins, *Managing Organizational Conflict* (Englewood Cliffs, N.J.: Prentice-Hall, 1974). Also see Stephen P. Robbins, *Organizational Behavior* (Englewood Cliffs, N.J.: Prentice-Hall, 1979).

Functional Conflict

Functional conflict represents a confrontation between groups that enhances and benefits the organization's performance. Two departments in a hospital may be in conflict concerning the most efficient and adaptive method of delivering health care to low-income rural families. The conflict supports the organization's performance and each group agrees on the goal but not on the means to achieve the goal. Whatever the outcome, low-income rural families will likely end up with better medical care. Without this type of conflict in organizations, there would be little commitment to change and most groups would likely become stagnant.

Dysfunctional Conflict

Any confrontation or interaction between groups that hinders the achievement of organizational goals can be considered dysfunctional. Management must seek to eliminate this type of conflict. The point at which functional conflict becomes dysfunctional is, in most cases, impossible to identify precisely. Because of such factors as tolerance for stress and conflict, a level that creates healthy and positive movement toward one group's goals, may, in another group (or at a different time for the same group), be extremely disruptive and dysfunctional.[2] Another contingency would be the type of organization. Routine manufacturing organizations, professional sports teams, and crises organizations such as police and fire departments would have different points where functional conflict becomes dysfunctional than would organizations such as universities, research and development firms, and motion picture production firms.

Dysfunctional conflict can negatively impact individual, group, and organizational performance. Such a situation is illustrated vividly in the following close-up.

ORGANIZATIONS: CLOSE-UP

Negative Conflict at Bendix

During 1980 Mary Cunningham became very well known. Her promotion to the very important position of vice president for strategic planning at Bendix Corporation was accompanied by rumors that it was the result of her personal relationship with Chairman William Agee. With pressure from various groups and individuals mounting, she decided that her effectiveness was being impaired, and resigned. She stated "Anyone in the executive-assistant role is blessed by tremendous opportunities to learn, but cursed by the danger of being so close to the seat of power." In large part, she blames her trouble at Bendix on the fear and jealousy of other individuals and groups who perceived their security threatened by divestiture decisions she made in the course of her job. "The ultimate cause," she states, "is that you didn't have the people surrounding the chairman that you really needed—except me."

Source: *Newsweek*, December 15, 1980, p. 84.

---

[2]Ibid., p. 24.

Conflict and Organizational Performance

Thus far we have said that conflict may either have a positive or negative impact on organizational performance depending on how it is managed. For every organization there is an optimal level of conflict which can be considered highly functional and which positively influences performance. If the conflict level is too low, performance suffers. Innovation and change are difficult and the organization has difficulty adapting to change in its environment. If this low conflict level continues, the very survival of the organization can be threatened.[3] On the other hand if the level of conflict is too high, the resulting chaos can also threaten the organization's survival.[4] This proposed relationship is presented in Figure 8–1 and explained for three hypothetical situations.

The question we must ask at this point is, "Does research support this view of conflict?" Is evidence available which supports the relationship between level of conflict and performance? Such a relationship would be difficult to determine in a large-scale organization such as a business firm. There is, however, a growing body of research conducted in smaller field experiments using problem-solving groups, research teams, and work groups, and in laboratory experiments which do support this relationship.

One study found that performance definitely improved when there was conflict in the group than when little or no conflict was present. In fact, when each group reviewed decisions that had been reached by individual members, the average improvement for the conflict groups was significantly higher than the improvement of the groups with little or no conflict.[5] Related research has also found that the more diverse a group's membership is with respect to such factors as personality, backgrounds, and attitudes, the more likely the group will be superior in performance. In addition, high incompatibility *between* groups has been found to be related to high performance.[6]

---

[3] At this point it is interesting to speculate on the relationship (if any) between conflict and organizational performance in organizations such as Xerox, McDonald's, and Sears. These organizations were "high" performers during the last decade. Consider the same relationship in such "low" performers as A&P, Hersheys, and Montgomery Ward. Such a study, if it were possible to conduct, would certainly have been interesting.

[4] An example familiar to the reader is the popular press coverage of the results of "dissension" on professional sports teams and its impact on performance. When performance suffers, the conflict is usually blamed on the coach or manager who is held responsible by the press.

[5] J. Hall and M. S. Williams, "A Comparison of Decision-Making Performance in Established and Ad Hoc Groups," *Journal of Personality and Social Psychology*, February 1966, pp. 217–22.

[6] See L. R. Hoffman and N. R. F. Maier, "Quality and Acceptance of Problem Solutions by Members of Homogeneous and Heterogeneous Groups," *Journal of Abnormal and Social Psychology*, April 1961, pp. 401–7; C. G. Smith, "Scientific Performance and the Composition of Research Teams," *Administrative Science Quarterly*, December 1971, pp. 486–95; W. J. Underwood and L. J. Krafft, "Interpersonal Compatibility and Managerial Work Effectiveness: A Test of the Fundamental Interpersonal Relations Orientation Theory," *Journal of Applied Psychology*, October 1973, pp. 89–94; and Raymond E. Hill, "Interpersonal Compatibility and Work Group Performance among Systems Analysts: An Empirical Study," *Proceedings of the 17th Annual Midwest Academy of Management Conference*, Kent, Ohio, April 1974, pp. 97–110.

FIGURE 8–1

Proposed Relationship between Intergroup Conflict and Organizational Performance

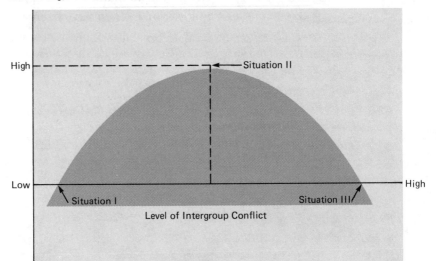

	Level of Intergroup Conflict	Probable Impact on Organization	Organization Characterized by	Level of Organizational Performance
Situation I	Low or none	Dysfunctional	Slow adaptation to environmental changes Few challenges Little stimulation of ideas Apathy Stagnation	Low
Situation II	Optimal	Functional	Positive movement toward goals Innovation and change Search for problem solutions Creativity and quick adaptation to environmental changes	High
Situation III	High	Dysfunctional	Disruption Interference with activities Coordination difficult Chaos	Low

Views toward Intergroup Conflict in Practice

Though evidence exists which supports the view that dysfunctional conflict should be eliminated and functional conflict encouraged, what actually happens in most organizations?[7] In practice, most managers attempt to eliminate all types of conflict, whether dysfunctional or functional. Why is this the case? Some reasons which have been advanced are:

1. Anticonflict values have historically been reinforced in the home, school, and church. Conflict between children and/or children and parents has for the most part been discouraged. In school systems conflict has traditionally been discouraged. Teachers had the answers and both teachers and children were rewarded for orderly classrooms. Finally, most religious doctrines stress peace and tranquility, and acceptance without questioning.
2. Managers are often evaluated and rewarded for the lack of conflict in their areas of responsibility. Anticonflict values, in fact, become part of the "culture" of the organization. Harmony and satisfaction are viewed positively while conflicts and dissatisfaction are viewed negatively. Under such conditions, the obvious result is that managers seek to avoid conflict which could disturb the status quo.[8]

WHY INTERGROUP CONFLICT OCCURS

■ It has been suggested that every group is in at least partial conflict with every other group it interacts with.[9] Whether or not this is an exaggeration is not important. The important point is that intergroup conflict is very common. In this section we shall examine why such conflicts are so common.

Interdependence

Work interdependence occurs when two or more groups must depend on each other to complete their tasks. The conflict potential in such situations is high. Three distinct types of interdependence among groups have been identified.[10]

Pooled Interdependence. Pooled interdependence occurs when it is not necessary for the groups to interact except through the total organization which supports them. For example, an IBM sales office in one region may have no interaction with their peers in another region. Similarly, two bank branches will have little or no interaction. However, in both cases the groups are interdependent because the performance of each must be adequate if the total organization is to thrive. The conflict potential in pooled interdependence is relatively low and management can rely more on standard rules and procedures developed at the main office for coordination.

---

[7]This section is based on Stephen P. Robbins, *Managing Organizational Conflict,* and Stephen P. Robbins, *The Administrative Process: Integrating Theory and Practice* (Englewood Cliffs, N.J.: Prentice-Hall, 1976), chap. 7.

[8]Ibid.

[9]This has been referred to as the "law of interorganizational conflict." See Anthony Downs, *Inside Bureaucracy* (Boston: Little, Brown, 1968).

[10]J. Thompson, *Organizations in Action* (New York: McGraw-Hill, 1967).

Sequential Interdependence. Sequential interdependence occurs when one group must complete its task before another group can complete its task. For example, in a manufacturing plant the product must be assembled before it can be painted. Thus the assembling department must complete its task before the finishing department can begin theirs.

Under these circumstances, since the output of one group serves as the input for another, conflict between the groups is more likely to occur. Coordinating this type of interdependence involves effective use of the management function of planning.

Reciprocal Interdependence. In this situation the output of each group serves as input to other groups in the organization. Consider the relationship which exists between the anesthesiology staff, nursing staff, technician staff, and surgeons in a hospital operating room. This is reciprocal interdependence of a high degree. The same interdependence exists among groups involved in space launchings and between airport control towers, flight crews, ground operations, and maintenance crews. Clearly, the potential for conflict is greater in this situation and effective coordination involves management's effective use of the organizational processes of communication and decision making.

Thus, all organizations have pooled interdependence among groups. More complex organizations have sequential interdependence while the most complex organizations will have pooled, sequential, and reciprocal interdependence among groups. The more complex the organization the greater potential for conflict and the more difficult the task facing management.

Differences in Goals

Often, various groups in an organization have goals that cannot be achieved simultaneously. As the subunits of an organization becomes specialized. they often develop dissimilar goals. This differentiation among the various functions of the organization can lead to different expectations in many areas. For example, a group of assembly-line workers may expect close supervision while a group of research scientists may expect a great deal of participation in decision making. The more complex the organization, the greater the differentiation of functions is likely to be and, therefore, the greater potential for conflict. Examples of such conflict are the age-old conflicts between production departments and marketing departments, and marketing departments and credit departments. Production departments can best achieve their goal of low production costs with long production runs. This means fewer models, colors, and so forth, which conflicts with marketing's goal of broad product lines, many models, colors, and so on, for greater customer satisfaction. Finally, marketing departments usually seek to maximize gross income, while the credit department seeks to minimize credit losses. Depending upon which goal is used, different customers might be selected. There are certain conditions which foster this type of conflict.

Limited Resources. If money, space, labor force, materials, and so forth, were unlimited, each group could pursue, at least to a relative degree, its own goals. Unfortunately, this is not the case and resources must be shared or allocated. When resources are limited and must be allocated, mutual dependence increases and any differences in group goals become more apparent. What often occurs is a win-lose competition which can easily result in dysfunctional conflict.

Reward Structures. Intergroup conflict is more likely to occur when the reward system is related to individual group performance rather than to overall organizational performance. Under such circumstances performance is, in fact, viewed as an independent variable although the performance of the group is in reality very interdependent. Suppose that in the example provided above, the marketing group is rewarded for sales produced and the credit group on the amount of credit losses. In such a situation, competition will be directly reinforced and dysfunctional conflict will be inadvertently rewarded.

Intergroup conflict arising from differences in goals can be dysfunctional to the organization as in the examples provided above. It is important to note, however, that depending on the type of organization, it can also be dysfunctional to third-party groups—usually the clients the organization serves. The present controversy over the conflict between the goals of quality health care for patients and teaching needs of future physicians is an example.

Differences in Perceptions

The differences that groups may have in goals may also be accompanied by different perceptions of reality. Differing perceptions of what constitutes reality is likely to lead to conflict. A problem in a hospital may be viewed in one way by the administrative staff and in another way by the medical staff. Alumni and faculty may have different perceptions concerning the importance of a winning football program. Later in the book we shall see that differing perceptions are leading causes of breakdowns in communication. There are many factors which cause groups in organizations to form differing perceptions.

Different Goals. Differences in group goals is an obvious contribution to differing perceptions. It marketing's goal is to maximize sales they will certainly view a major breakdown in production differently than the production department whose goal is to minimize production costs.

Different Time Horizons. How a group perceives reality is influenced by the time perspective it has. This will influence the priorities and importance they assign to different activities. The research scientists working for a chemical manufacturer may have a time perspective of several years while the manufacturing engineers one of less than a year. A bank president might focus on 5- and 10-year time spans while middle managers probably think in much shorter spans. With such differences in time horizons it is easy to see that problems and issues deemed critical by one group may be dismissed as not important by the other.

Status Incongruency. Conflicts concerning the relative status of different groups are common and influence perceptions. Usually, many different standards are utilized (rather than an absolute one) the result being that there are many status hierarchies, depending upon which standard is used. For example, conflict often occurs because of work patterns—which group initiates work and which responds. One group may perceive a status difference because they must accept the salesperson's initiation of work, a status difference the salesperson may reinforce. Academic snobbery is popular in many colleges and universities where members of a particular academic discipline perceive themselves as having higher status than others for one reason or another.

Inaccurate Perceptions. Inaccurate perceptions often result in developing stereotypes of the other group. While differences between the groups may certainly exist, each group exaggerates them when the actual differences may be small. Thus we hear that "all women executives are a certain way" or "all bank trust officers behave in a certain manner." Since the differences between the groups are emphasized the stereotypes are reinforced, relations deteriorate, and conflict develops.

The Increased Demand for Specialists

Early in management history conflicts were recorded between staff specialists and line generalists. Today line/staff differences are probably the most common type of intergroup conflict.[11] With the growing necessity for technical expertise in all areas in organizations the role of staff can be expected to expand and with it, line and staff conflict. As a result we are including the expected increase in the use of specialists as an additional source of intergroup conflict.

The major cause of line/staff conflict has been mentioned above. Line and staff persons simply view each other and their role in the organization from different perspectives.[12] They have all the problems we have discussed: different goals, time horizons, and status perceptions. Table 8–1 summarizes some additional causes of conflict between staff specialists and line generalists.[13] With the growth of sophistication, specialization, and

---

[11] For research see J. A. Belasco and J. A. Alutto, "Line and Staff Conflicts: Some Empirical Insights," *Academy of Management Journal*, March 1969, pp. 469–77.

[12] For a classic discussion, see L. A. Allen, "The Line-Staff Relationship," *Management Record*, September 1955, pp. 346–49.

[13] See M. Dalton, "Conflicts between Staff and Line Managerial Officers," *American Sociological Review*, June 1950, pp. 342–51; A. W. Gouldner, "Cosmopolitans and Locals: Toward an Analysis of Latent Social Roles," *Administrative Science Quarterly*, December 1957, pp. 281–306; A. Etzioni, ed., *Complex Organizations*, (New York: Holt, Rinehart & Winston, 1961); A. Etzioni, *Modern Organization* (Englewood Cliffs, N.J.: Prentice-Hall, 1964); R. W. Scott, "Professionals in Bureaucracies: Areas of Conflict," in *Professionals*, ed. H. M. Vollmer and D. L. Mills (Englewood Cliffs, N.J.: Prentice-Hall, 1966); P. R. Lawrence and J. W. Lorsch, *Organization and Environment: Managing Differentiation and Integration* (Boston: Graduate School of Business Administration, Harvard University, 1967); E. Rhenman, *Conflict and Cooperation in Business* (New York: John Wiley & Sons, 1970); P. K. Berger and A. J. Grimes, "Cosmopolitan-Local: A Factor Analysis of the Construct," *Administrative Science Quarterly*, June 1973, pp. 223–35; and J. E. Sorensen and T. L. Sorensen, "The Conflict of Professionals in Bureaucratic Organizations," *Administrative Science Quarterly*, March 1974, pp. 98–106.

TABLE 8–1
Common Causes of Line/Staff Conflict

Perceived Diminishing of Line Authority. Line managers perceive that the specialist will encroach on their job thereby diminishing their authority and power. As a result, often-heard complaints by specialists are that line executives do not make proper use of staff specialists and do not give staff members sufficient authority. This complaint is voiced by staff specialists in consumer products firms, banks, hospitals, and government agencies.

Social and Physical Differences. Often major differences exist between line managers and staff specialists with respect to age, education, dress, and attitudes. In many cases staff specialists are younger, with higher educational levels or training in a specialized field.

Line Dependence on Staff Knowledge. Since line generalists often do not have the technical knowledge necessary to manage their departments, they realize they are dependent on the specialist. This gap between knowledge and authority may be even greater when the staff specialist is lower in the organizational hierarchy than the manager, which is often the case. As a result staff members often complain that line managers resist new ideas.

Different Loyalties. Often, divided loyalties exist between line managers and staff specialists. The staff specialist may be loyal to a discipline while the line manager is loyal to the organization. The member of the product development group may be a chemist first and a member of the organization second. The production manager's first loyalty, however, may be to the organization.

complexity in most organizations, line/staff conflict will continue to be a major concern in the management of organizational behavior.

THE CONSEQUENCES OF DYSFUNCTIONAL INTERGROUP CONFLICT

■ Behavioral scientists have spent a great deal of effort analyzing how dysfunctional intergroup conflict affects groups experiencing it.[14] Over two decades of research on this topic enable us to state that groups that have been placed in a conflict situation will react in fairly predictable ways. We shall examine changes which occur within the groups and then changes which occur between the groups.

Changes within Groups

The following are changes which are likely to occur *within* the groups involved in intergroup conflict.

Increased Group Cohesiveness. Competition, conflict, or external threat usually result in group members putting aside individual differences and closing ranks. Members become more loyal to the group and group membership becomes more attractive.

---

[14]The classic work is M. Sherif and C. Sherif, *Groups in Harmony and Tension* (New York: Harper & Row, 1953). Their study was conducted among groups in a boys' camp. They stimulated conflict between the groups and observed the changes which occurred in group behavior. Also see their "Experiments in Group Conflict," *Scientific American*, March 1956, pp. 54–58.

Rise in Autocratic Leadership. In extreme conflict situations where threats are perceived, democratic methods of leadership are likely to become less popular. Members want strong leadership. Thus, the leadership is likely to become more autocratic.

Focus on Activity. The emphasis is on doing what the group does and doing it very well. Tolerance for members who "goof off" is low and there is less concern for individual member satisfaction. The emphasis is on accomplishing the group's task and defeating the "enemy."

Emphasis on Loyalty. Conformity to group norms becomes even more important in conflict situations. Group goals take precedence over individual satisfaction as members are expected to demonstrate their loyalty. In extreme conflict situations, interaction with members of the "other group" may be outlawed.

Changes between Groups

In conflict situations certain changes are likely to occur *between* the groups involved.

Distorted Perceptions. The perceptions of the group by its members becomes distorted as well as their perceptions of the other group. Obviously, the members' perception of the importance of their group becomes distorted. They are superior in performance to the other and more important to the survival of the organization. The other group, of course, is not as important. For example, nurses might conclude that they are more important to a patient than physicians, while the physicians might consider themselves more important than the hospital administrators in a conflict situation. The marketing group in a business organization might think "without us selling the product there would be no money to pay anyone else's salary." The production group might say, "If we don't make the product, there is nothing to sell." The point, of course, is that no one group is more important but that conflict can cause these gross misperceptions of reality.

Negative Stereotyping. As the conflict increases and perceptions become more distorted, all the negative stereotypes previously developed are reinforced. A management representative may say, "I've always said these union guys are just plain greedy. Now they've proved it." The head of a local teacher's union might say, "Now we know that all politicians are interested in is getting reelected, certainly not the quality of secondary education." As a result of the conflict, the members of the group see less differences *within* their group than actually exist and greater differences *between* the groups than actually exist.

Decreased Communication. In conflict situations, communication between the groups involved usually breaks down. This can be extremely dysfunctional especially in situations where a sequential interdependence or reciprocal interdependence relationship exists between the groups. The decision-making process can be adversely affected, and the groups the organization serves can be hurt. Consider the possible consequences to patients if a conflict between hospital technicians and nurses reached the point where the quality of health care provided was negatively influenced. While this is an extreme situation the point should be clear.

While these are not only dysfunctional consequences of intergroup conflict, they are the most common and have been well documented in the research literature. Others such as violence and aggression are certainly possible and have occurred. The dysfunctional consequences of intergroup conflict discussed here are, however, the most typical which occur within and between groups in conflict.[15] When such situations occur, some form of managerial intervention is necessary. This is the subject of the following section.[16]

MANAGING INTERGROUP CONFLICT THROUGH RESOLUTION

■ Since managers of organizational behavior must live with intergroup conflict, they must confront the problem of managing it. In this section we shall examine techniques which have been used successfully in resolving intergroup conflict when it has reached a level that is dysfunctional to the organization.[17]

Problem Solving

Problem solving is also referred to as the confrontation method since it seeks to reduce the conflict through face-to-face meetings of the conflicting groups. The purpose of the meeting is to identify and solve the problem. The conflicting groups openly debate the issue bringing together all relevant information until a decision is reached. For conflicts resulting from misunderstandings or language barriers this method has been effective. For solving more complex problems (e.g., where the groups have different value systems) this method will usually not work.

Superordinate Goals

Superordinate goals involves developing a common set of goals and objectives. These goals and objectives cannot be attained without the cooperation of the groups involved. In fact, they are unattainable by one group singly and supersede all other goals of any of the groups involved in the conflict.[18] For example, several unions in the automobile industry have, in recent years, agreed to no pay increases and in some cases to pay reduc-

---

[15] For additional discussion, see J. Litterer, "Conflict in Organization: A Re-Examination," *Academy of Management Journal*, September 1966, pp. 178–86; J. W. Lorsch and J. J. Morse, *Organizations and Their Members: A Contingency Approach* (New York: Harper & Row, 1974); and E. Schein, "Intergroup Problems in Organizations," in *Organization Development: Theory, Practice, and Research*, ed. W. French, C. Bell, and R. Zawacki (Plano, Tex.: Business Publications, 1978), pp. 80–84.

[16] Also see David M. Herold, "Improving the Performance Effectiveness of Groups through a Task-Contingent Selection of Intervention Strategies," *Academy of Management Review*, April 1978, pp. 315–51.

[17] Based on Robbins, *Managing Organizational Conflict*, pp. 67–77.

[18] See M. Sherif and C. Sherif, *Social Psychology* (New York: Harper & Row, 1969), pp. 228–62, for a detailed discussion of this method. Also see J. D. Hunger and L. W. Stern, "An Assessment of the Functionality of the Superordinate Goal in Reducing Conflict," *Academy of Management Journal*, December 1976, pp. 591–605.

tions because the survival of the industry was threatened. When the crisis is over, demands for higher wages will undoubtedly return.

Expansion of Resources

As we have noted earlier, a major cause of intergroup conflict is limited resources. Whatever one group succeeds in obtaining is at the expense of the other. The scarce resource may be a particular position (e.g., president of the firm), money, space, and so forth. For example, one major publishing firm decided to expand by establishing a subsidiary firm. Most observers believed the major reason was to become involved in other segments of the market. While this is partially correct, one real reason was to enable the firm to keep valued personnel who previously had left the firm. By establishing the subsidiary they practically doubled their executive positions since each had a president, various vice presidents, and other executives. Obviously, this technique is very successful in most cases since everyone is satisfied. In reality, however, resources do not usually exist in such amounts that they can be so easily expanded.

Avoidance

Like most other unpleasant realities, some way can usually be found to avoid conflict. While it may not bring any long-run benefits, it certainly works in the short run. As a result the conflict is not effectively resolved, nor is it eliminated. The limitations of avoiding conflict are obvious but it is an alternative and in some circumstances may be the best short-run alternative.

Smoothing

Here the emphasis is on the common interests of the conflicting groups and a de-emphasis of their differences. The basic belief is that by stressing the shared viewpoints on certain issues, movement toward a common goal is facilitated. If the differences between the groups are serious, smoothing—like avoidance—is at best a temporary short-run solution.

Compromise

Compromise is a traditional method used to resolve conflicts. Hopefully, there is no distinct winner or loser because the decision reached is probably not ideal for either group. Compromise can be used very effectively when the sought after goal (e.g., money) can be divided. If this is not possible, one group gives up something of value for a concession. Compromise may involve third-party interventions as well as total group or representative negotiating and voting.[19]

Authoritative Command

As we noted at the opening of the chapter, the use of the formal authority hierarchy may be the oldest and most frequently used method for resolving intergroup conflict. Subordinates will usually abide by a superior's decision whether or not they agree. Thus, it usually works in the short run.

---

[19] For a discussion of the problems associated with compromise, see W. Notz and F. Starke, "Final Offer vs. Conventional Arbitration as Means of Conflict Management," *Administrative Science Quarterly*, June 1978, pp. 189–203.

As with avoidance, smoothing, and compromise, however, it does not focus on the cause of the conflict but rather on the results of it.

Altering the Human Variable

Altering the human variable involves changing the behavior of the members of the groups involved. While certainly difficult, this method does center on the cause of the conflict. Part Six of this book focuses specifically on this topic with two chapters concerned solely with changing organizational behavior. At that time we shall see that while the method is slower and often costly, the results can be significant in the long run.

Altering the Structural Variables

Altering the structural variables involves changing the formal structure of the organization. Structure refers to the fixed relationships among the jobs of the organization and includes the design of jobs and departments. How organizations are structured is the subject of the next part of the book. At this point let us say that altering the structure of the organization as a means of resolving intergroup conflict would involve such things as transferring, exchanging, or rotating members of the groups, or creating a position to serve as a coordinator or "go-between."

Identifying a Common Enemy

In some respects identifying a common enemy is the negative side of superordinate goals. Groups in conflict may temporarily resolve their differences to combat a common enemy. The common enemy may be a competitor who has just introduced a clearly superior product. Conflicting groups in a bank may work in close harmony when the government bank examiners make a visit. This phenomenon is very evident in domestic conflicts. Most police officers prefer not to become involved in heated domestic conflicts because, in far too many cases, the combatants "close ranks" and turn on the police officer.

Whatever the techniques utilized to deal with intergroup conflict (and there are undoubltedly others), the important point is that managers must not only recognize its existence and understand its causes, but also develop skills to deal with it. Just such a program is discussed in the following close-up.

ORGANIZATIONS: CLOSE-UP

Conflict Management at Union Carbide

Union Carbide is an organization concerned with how its managers manage conflict. Recently, it sent 200 managers to a three-day workshop to help them develop such skills. One of the techniques used for learning how to deal with conflict in organizational settings is known as the egg drop exercise.

As part of this exercise, managers are divided into teams, racing against a

> **ORGANIZATIONS: CLOSE-UP** (continued)
>
> clock as well as other teams. They are instructed to build a device out of material that will catch eggs gently enough to keep them from breaking. They acquire the needed building materials from an auctioneer who "sells" such items as metal strips and pieces of string, for which the teams bid. Each team is allocated funds to bid for auctioned items. A videotape machine records the bidding, discussion, and construction of the device.
>
> At the completion of the exercise, the managers view a replay. What they often see is bickering, arguing, mocking each other, hostility, impatience, and relying on authoritarian orders. While the objective of the exercise is to beat the other teams, the managers often discover that most of their conflicts were with persons on their own team.
>
> Source: "Teaching How to Cope with Workplace Conflicts," *Business Week*, February 18, 1980, pp. 136, 139.

We have provided brief discussions of some of the most commonly used methods for managing intergroup conflict. Note that each has strengths and weaknesses and is successful under different conditions and in different situations. At this point it would be useful to summarize what we have said thus far about intergroup conflict. This summary is presented as Figure 8–2. It indicates the relationship between causes and types of intergroup conflict, the consequences of intergroup conflict, and techniques for resolving it.

MANAGING INTERGROUP CONFLICT THROUGH STIMULATION

■ The previous section centered entirely on conflict management techniques designed to *resolve* intergroup conflict. We have throughout the chapter, however, stressed the fact that some conflict is beneficial. This is even noted in Figure 8–2 which indicates some of the functional consequences of intergroup conflict. It indicates that change can develop out of conflict, from an awareness of problems, and from creative search for alternative solutions. We have already examined the situation where conflict is dysfunctional because it is too high and requires resolution. Following our logic, therefore, it is also possible that intergroup conflict may be too low and requires stimulation.[20] In this section we shall examine techniques that have been used successfully to stimulate conflict to a functional level.[21]

Communication

By intelligent use of the organization's communication channels, a manager can stimulate conflict. Information can be carefully placed into formal channels to create ambiguity, reevaluation, or confrontation. Information

---

[20]This view is consistent with the *interactionist* view of conflict management.

[21]See Robbins, *Managing Organizational Conflict*, chap. 9.

FIGURE 8–2
An Overview of Intergroup Conflict

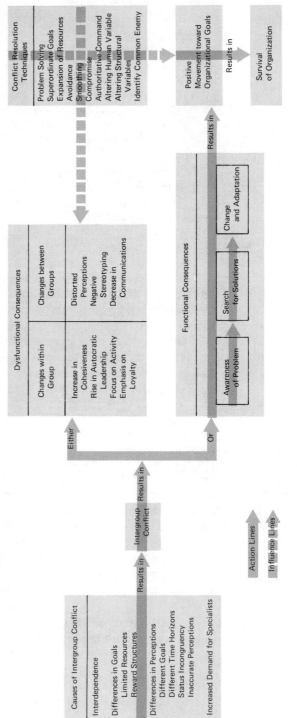

which is threatening (e.g., a proposed budget cut) can stimulate functional conflict and improved performance. Carefully planted rumors in the grapevine can also serve a useful purpose. For example, a hospital administrator started a rumor concerning a proposed reorganization of the hospital. His purpose was to stimulate new ideas on how to more effectively carry out the mission of the hospital as well as reduce apathy among the staff.

Bringing Outside Individuals into the Group

A widely used technique to "bring back to life" a stagnant organization or subunit of an organization is to bring in (hire or transfer) individuals whose attitudes, values, and backgrounds differ from present members. Many college faculties consciously seek new members with different backgrounds and often discourage the hiring of graduates of their own programs. This is to ensure a diversity of viewpoints on the faculty. This technique is also widely used in government and business. Recently a bank president decided not to promote from within for a newly created position of marketing vice president. Instead he hired a highly successful executive from the very competitive consumer products field. He felt that while she knew little about marketing services, her approach to, and knowledge of, marketing was what the bank needed to become a strong marketer.

Altering the Organization Structure,

In the last section we saw that changing the structure of the organization can be a useful technique for resolving intergroup conflict. It also is excellent for creating conflict. For example, a school of business has several departments. One department is entitled the Department of Business Administration and includes all the faculty which teach courses in management, marketing, finance, production management, and so forth. Accordingly, the department is rather large with 32 members under one department chair who reports to the dean. A new dean was recently hired and he is considering dividing the department into several separate departments (e.g., departments of marketing, finance, management), each with five or six members and a chairperson. The reasoning is that reorganizing in this manner will create competition among the groups for resources, students, faculty, and so forth, where none existed before because they were all in the same group. Whether this change will improve performance remains to be seen.

Stimulating Competition

The use of various incentives such as awards and bonuses for outstanding performance is likely to stimulate competition. If properly utilized such incentives may maintain a healthy atmosphere of competition which may result in a functional level of conflict. Incentives can be given for least defective parts, highest sales, best teacher, greatest number of new customers, or in any area where increased conflict will likely lead to more effective performance.

MAJOR MANAGERIAL ISSUES

A. Conflict between groups is inevitable in organizations. This conflict may be positive or negative depending upon its impact on the organization's goal achievement.

B. Functional conflict represents a confrontation between groups that enhances and benefits the organization's performance.

C. Dysfunctional conflict results from a confrontation or interaction between groups that hinders the achievement of organizational goals.

D. While most managers try to eliminate conflict, evidence exists which indicates that for most organizations an optimal level of conflict can positively influence organizational performance.

E. Intergroup conflict results from such factors as work interdependence, differences in goals, differences in perceptions, and the increasing demand for specialists.

F. Dysfunctional conflict results in changes taking place within and between the groups involved. Within the group there may be an increase in group cohesiveness, a rise in autocratic leadership, a focus on the task, and an emphasis on loyalty. Changes occuring between the groups include distorted perceptions, negative stereotyping, and a decrease in communication.

G. One of the difficult tasks a manager must confront is diagnosing and managing intergroup conflict. Some useful techniques for resolving intergroup conflict include problem solving, superordinate goals, expansion of resources, avoidance, smoothing, compromise, authority, and changing either the people or the organization's structure. Each is useful in specific situations and circumstances.

H. Conflict management techniques also exist for those situations where the manager diagnoses a level of conflict that is dysfunctional because it is too low. Conflict stimulation techniques include using the communication channels, hiring or transferring-in outside individuals, and changing the organization's structure. The important point is that effective conflict management involves both resolution and stimulation.

DISCUSSION AND REVIEW QUESTIONS

1. From your personal experiences, describe situations where conflict was functional and where it was dysfunctional.

2. Is the competition for grades among students functional or dysfunctional? Why?

3. Some individuals believe that conflict is necessary for change to take place. Comment.

4. Why is union-management conflict often so dysfunctional?

5. Identify an intergroup conflict situation at your school. Is it functional or dysfunctional? Why? If dysfunctional, what conflict management technique would you recommend to either resolve it or stimulate it?

6. Assume that you were chosen by the president of your school to recommend strategies for eliminating student apathy. What would your recommendation be?

7. What is meant when it is said that a manager must be able to diagnose intergroup conflict situations? How can a manager obtain these diagnostic skills?

8. Discuss your personal view toward intergroup conflict in organizations.

ADDITIONAL REFERENCES

Aldrich, H. "Organizational Boundaries and Interorganizational Conflict." *Human Relations,* 1971, pp. 279–93.

Boulding, E. "Further Reflections on Conflict Management." In *Power and Conflict in Organizations,* edited by R. Kahn and E. Boulding. New York: Basic Books, 1964, pp. 146–50.

Campbell, D. R. "Stereotypes and the Perception of Group Differences." *American Psychologist,* 1967, pp. 817–29.

Cherington, D. J. "Satisfaction in Competitive Behavior." *Organizational Behavior and Human Performance,* 1973, pp. 47–71.

Doob, L. W., and W. J. Foltz. "The Belfast Workshop: An Application of Group Techniques to a Destructive Conflict." *Journal of Conflict Resolution,* 1973, pp. 489–512.

Dutton, J. M., and R. E. Walton. "Interdepartmental Conflict and Cooperation: Two Contrasting Studies." *Human Organization,* 1966, pp. 207–20.

Filley, A. C. *Interpersonal Conflict Resolution.* Glenview, Ill.: Scott, Foresman, 1975.

French, W. L.; C. H. Bell; and R. A. Zawacki. *Organizational Development: Theory, Practice, Research.* Plano, Tex.: Business Publications, 1982.

Kelly, J. "Make Conflict Work for You." *Harvard Business Review,* 1970, pp. 103–13.

Kilmann, R. H., and K. W. Thomas. "Four Perspectives on Conflict Management: An Attributional Framework for Organizing Descriptive and Normative Theory." *Academy of Management Journal,* 1978, pp. 59–68.

Latack, J. C. "Person/Role Conflict: Holland's Model Extended to Role-Stress Research, Stress Management, and Career Development." *Academy of Management Review,* 1981, pp. 89–104.

Likert, R., and J. G. Likert. *New Ways of Managing Conflict.* New York: McGraw-Hill, 1976.

Mead, M. *Cooperation and Competition among Primitive Peoples.* New York: McGraw-Hill, 1961.

Pondy, L. "Organizational Conflict: Concepts and Models." *Administrative Science Quarterly,* 1967, pp. 296–320.

Robbins, S. P. "Conflict Management and Conflict Resolution Are Not Synonymous Terms." In *The Dynamics of Organizational Theory: Gaining a Macro Perspective,* edited by J. F. Veiga, and J. N. Yanouzas. St. Paul, Minn.: West Publishing, 1979, pp. 299–306.

Schmidt, S. M., and T. A. Kochan. "Conflict: Toward Conceptual Understanding." *Administrative Science Quarterly,* 1972, pp. 359–70.

Twomey, D. F. "The Effects of Power Properties on Conflict Resolution." *Academy of Management Review,* 1978, pp. 144–50.

Underwood, W. J., and L. J. Krafft. "Interpersonal Compatibility and Managerial Work Effectiveness: A Test of the Fundamental Interpersonal Relations Orientation Theory." *Journal of Applied Psychology,* 1973, pp. 89–94.

Zechmeister, K., and D. Druckman. "Determinants of Resolving a Conflict of Interest." *Journal of Conflict Resolution,* 1973, pp. 63–68.

CASE FOR ANALYSIS

**WE'LL JUST LET
THEM SHOW
THEIR STUFF**

Seven months ago Captain John Shea announced that he would retire as police chief of Bay Ridge in one year. This was to allow Mayor Foster Taff and the city commissioners one year to initiate the search and selection process for his replacement. Captain Shea had come to Bay Ridge from a much larger city in Florida six years ago. He had served as assistant police chief in that city for five years.

During his term as chief, Shea had initiated many changes in the department. For the most part the changes had been accepted and nearly everyone agreed that Shea had done a fine job. The crime rate was presently below the national average, citizen/police relations appeared good and morale of the police officers also seemed very good. The Bay Ridge Police Association (BRPA), the organization which represented the police officers, occasionally had minor disagreements with the chief and the city administration. However, these conflicts were small compared to the conflicts taking place in other cities. During the last five years, salaries for foot patrol officers had surpassed the national average for cities the size of Bay Ridge.

Many individuals were quite surprised at the relative success of Shea. He had been the "outside candidate" for the job and was selected over two veteran members of the force. The two inside candidates had engaged in a bitter in-fight which had divided the department at that time. One of the men has subsequently taken a chief's position elsewhere. One city commissioner had recently stated off the record, "I don't know how Shea did it. I didn't give him a snowball's chance six years ago. I thought he was crazy for taking the job and jumping in that hornet's nest. I guess being 1,000 miles away he may not have known what he was getting into. But he sure has done one helluva job."

During the last seven months an intensive search had been conducted. Applications had been received from all over the country. In addition to the search committee made up of city officials, three professors from the management department of a local university were hired as consultants to serve as an advisory committee to the search committee.

A total of 12 candidates were invited to personally interview for the job. Each candidate was interviewed intensively by both committees. Surprisingly, both committees agreed on the top three choices although not in the same order. They were:

> Phillip Kinney—23 years on the Bay Ridge Police Force. Holds the rank of captain and has been the head of the Robbery Division for three years. Excellent record in the Robbery Division. Holds every departmental commendation. He is 51 years old, married with three grown children. He is a graduate of Bay Ridge High School and was one of the final two inside candidates in the search seven years ago. According to inside sources he barely missed getting appointed.

Anthony Jackson—presently holds the rank of lieutenant in the Narcotics Division. He has an outstanding record of accomplishment since becoming the first black person on the police force 15 years ago. He is extremely popular in the black community and has been credited by the press with being instrumental in improving relations between the department and the black community. In fact, many black civic leaders have encouraged him to take a leave of absence to run for political office. He is 39 years old, married with two young children, and holds a B.S. degree in law enforcement. He ran unsuccessfully for president of the BRPA in the last election.

Paul Stephens—20 years in the department. Presently holds the rank of captain in the Homicide Division. He is considered to be one of the top homicide detectives in this region of the country, often serving as a consultant to police departments in other cities on difficult cases. Holds every department commendation. He is presently single and has one child by an earlier marriage. He holds a B.S. degree in law enforcement and is president of the BRPA.

The recommendations were presented to Mayor Taff by City Manager Bill Joslin with the recommendation that he select one of the three to replace Shea. His first comment to Taff was "Shea must have also developed some good people while he was here. None of the outside candidates made the cut."

"Who does Shea like?" the mayor asked. "He's not saying," Joslin replied. He said since he won't have to work for the guy, he shouldn't influence the selection. That's also why he declined to serve on the search committee. He has also told that to the press this morning. Apparently, someone leaked the names of the three finalists to a TV station and they cornered Shea on the way out of his house this morning.

"Which one do you like?" asked Joslin adding "I think you should announce your choice as soon as you've made it."

"No" said the mayor. "I think I'll wait. We've got about five months." "Why wait?" asked Joslin. There was a short silence and the mayor replied, "We'll just let them show their stuff."

Questions for Consideration

1. What do you think of the mayor's decision to wait? Why?
2. What are the advantages of waiting? The disadvantages?
3. Could the mayor's decision have any positive or negative impact outside the department? Discuss.

EXPERIENTIAL EXERCISE

**LOST ON THE
MOON: A GROUP
DECISION
EXERCISE**

Objective

After reading the "Situation" below, you will first individually, and then as a member of a team, rank in importance a number of items available for carrying out your mission. Your objective is to come as close as possible to the "best solution" as determined by experts of the National Aeronautics and Space Administration.

Instructions

PHASE I: Read the "Situation" below and the directions which follow it. Then, in column 2 ("Your Ranks") of the work sheet, assign priorities to the 15 items listed. Use a pencil since you may wish to change your rankings. Somewhere on the sheet it may be useful to note your logic for each ranking.
TIME: 15 minutes

PHASE II: Your instructor will assign you to a team. Your task is to arrive at a consensus on your rankings. Share your individual solutions and reach a consensus—one ranking for each of the 15 items that best satisfies all the team members. Thus, by the end of Phase II, all members of the team should have the same set of rankings in column 4 ("Group Ranks"). Do not change your individual rankings in column 2.
TIME: 25 minutes.

PHASE III: Your instructor will provide you with the "best solution" to the problem, that is, the set of rankings determined by the NASA experts, along with their reasoning. Each person should note this set of rankings in column 1 ("NASA's Ranks"). (Note: While it is fun to debate the experts' rankings and their reasoning, don't forget that the objective of the game it to learn more about decision making, not how to survive on the moon!)

Evaluation

It is time now to see how well you did, individually and as a team. First, find your individual score by taking the absolute difference between Your Rank (column 2) and NASA's Rank (column 1), and writing it in the first Error Points column (column 3). (Thus, for "Box of Matches," if you ranked it 3 and NASA's rank were 8, you would put a 5 in column 3 next to "Box of Matches." Then total the error points in column 3, and write the total in the space at the bottom of the column.

"LOST ON THE MOON"

The Situation

Your spaceship has just crash-landed on the moon. You were scheduled to rendezvous with a mother ship 200 miles away on the lighted surface of the moon, but the rough landing has ruined your ship and destroyed all the equipment aboard, except for 15 items listed below.

Your crew's survival depends on reaching the mother ship, so you must choose the most critical items available for the 200-mile trip. Your task is to rank the 15 items in terms of their importance for survival. Place number one by the most important item, number two by the second most important, and so on through number 15, the least important.

Work Sheet Items	1 NASA's Ranks	2 Your Ranks	3 Error Points	4 Group Ranks	5 Error Points
Box of matches	___	___	___	___	___
Food concentrate	___	___	___	___	___
50 ft. of nylon rope	___	___	___	___	___
Parachute silk	___	___	___	___	___
Solar-powered portable heating unit	___	___	___	___	___
Two .45 caliber pistols	___	___	___	___	___
One case of dehydrated pet milk	___	___	___	___	___
Two 100-pound tanks of oxygen	___	___	___	___	___
Stellar map (of the moon's constellation)	___	___	___	___	___
Self-inflating life raft	___	___	___	___	___
Magnetic compass	___	___	___	___	___
Five gallons of water	___	___	___	___	___
Signal flares	___	___	___	___	___
First-aid kit containing injection needles	___	___	___	___	___
Solar-powered FM receiver-transmitter	___	___	___	___	___
Total error points		Individual___		Group___	

Next score your group performance in the same way, this time taking the absolute differences between Group Ranks (column 4) and NASA's ranks (column 1), and writing them in the second Error Points column (column 5). Total the group error points. (Note that all members of the team will have the same Group Error Points.)

Finally, prepare three pieces of information to be submitted to your instructor when he calls on your team:

1. Average Individual Error Points (the average of the points in the last space in column 3. One team member should add these figures and divide by the number of team members to get the average).
2. Group Error Points (the figure at the bottom of column 5).
3. Number of team members who had fewer Individual Error Points than the Group Error Points.

Using this information, your instructor will evaluate the results of the exercise and discuss your performance with you. Together, you will then explore the implications of this exercise for the group decision-making process.

Chapter 9

Leadership: Trait, Personal-Behavioral, and Attribution Approaches

AN ORGANIZATIONAL ISSUE FOR DEBATE
A General Description of Leadership

ARGUMENT FOR

There are writers who believe that a new type of person is taking over leadership of the most technically advanced companies in the United States. In contrast to the "jungle fighter" industrialists of the past, the new leader is driven not to build or to preside over a large empire, but to plan, organize, and control winning teams. Unlike the security-seeking organization man of William F. Whyte, the new kind of leader is excited by the chance to cut deals and to gamble. The new leader is called a *gamesman*.

The most dynamic companies with these innovative leaders are able to create their own markets. Companies like IBM, Xerox, Dow Chemical, and TRW Systems have many of these gamesmen types. These companies are able to face tough competition and develop new products and technology.

Some of the different types of leaders who manage in organizations are described using some catchy terminology.

1. *The Craftsman*—This is the type of individual who is production oriented, concerned with quality, and interested in building a sound record.

Source: Based on Michael Maccoby, *The Gamesman* (New York Simon & Schuster, 1976)

ARGUMENT AGAINST

Although books like *The Gamesman* become bestsellers, they really do not improve our understanding of what is effective leadership in organizations around the world. They are imaginative but not very explanatory, scientifically based, or accurate. In fact, it is even dangerous to reach any conclusions on the basis of interviews conducted with only 250 managers. This is what the author of *The Gamesman*, Michael Maccoby, did to develop his conclusions about the *Craftsman*, the *Jungle Fighter*, the *Company Man*, and the *Gamesman*.

It may be true that some effective executives in organizations are *gamesmen*, but to suggest that this or any similarly developed framework adds to our knowledge is disappointing because the study of organizational leadership has advanced past the practice of listing descriptions of types of individuals. It has become rather clear that effective leadership is contingent upon having the right person for the situation at hand and a particular group of subordinates. Leader behavior characteristics, subordinate characteristics, organizational climate, and goals must be considered. These situational variables are not investigated scientifically by Maccoby.

The failure to scientifically study situational variables results in just another list of descrip-

2. *The Jungle Fighter*—This type individual is interested in gaining power. Life and work are viewed as a jungle. Peers are viewed as accomplices or enemies. Two types of jungle fighters are the *lions*, who conquer and build, and *foxes*, who move ahead by politicking.
3. *The Company Man*—This individual is interested in cooperation, commitment, and security.
4. *Gamesman*—This is the new type of leader. This person thrives on challenge, competitive activity, and new and fresh approaches. The main goal of this type of person is to be a winner. This person is interested in developing the tactics and strategies needed to be a winner.

tions of types of leaders. What is needed and is more appropriate is a careful analysis of what leaders do and what the results of this behavior is in terms of performance.

Leadership has long been a focus of theorists, researchers, and practitioners. Nevertheless, it appears that despite numerous theories and research studies of leadership, there is no universally accepted approach. Some of the highlights of leadership research will be covered in this and the next chapter.[1] The reader is asked to give special attention to the common themes. It will also become apparent that effective leadership is necessary for organizational effectiveness and that the performance of employees is typically poorer when it is absent.

LEADERSHIP

■ The idea that leadership is a synonym for management is not completely valid. Leadership is a narrower concept than management. A manager in a formal organization is responsible and entrusted to perform such functions as planning, organizing, and controlling. However, leaders also exist in informal groups. Informal leaders are not always formal managers performing managerial functions which are required by the organization. Consequently, leaders are only in some instances actually managers.

The concept of role was clarified in Chapter 7 dealing with group behavior. In the formal organization, roles often have specific responsibilities associated with them. For example, the first-line supervisory role may be one in which the role occupant is responsible for the level and quality of production generated by a particular group of employees. Exactly how the supervisor fulfills the responsibility involves the occupant's style. Some first-line supervisors rely on the *authority* of the position to secure compliance with performance standards, while others use a more *participative* approach which involves joint decision making on the part of the leader (manager) and followers (subordinates).

A hierarchy of roles also exists in informal groups. The informal leader is accepted as the person to carry out the duties of the position. Once again, how the leader brings about compliance from followers will largely depend on the leadership style used. What is effective for one leader may not be for another. This, in essence, is the crux of the leadership issue: what makes for effective leadership? As indicated earlier, there is no simple or single answer to this important question. Two important considerations involve power and acceptance by followers.

SOME SOURCES AND BASES OF POWER

■ Generally, power includes the personal and positional attributes that are the basis for a leader's ability to influence others. In managerial terms, power involves the ability to mobilize resources, to get and use whatever it is that people need for the goals that they are attempting to accomplish.[2]

[1]For a thorough compilation of leadership theory and research, see Ralph M. Stogdill, *Handbook of Leadership* (New York: Free Press, 1974).

[2]Rosabeth M. Kanter, *Men and Women of the Corporation* (New York: Basic Books, 1977), pp. 166.

Note that power involves personal and positional attributes to influence roles, processes, and/or things, while the concept of *authority* involves the use primarily of position-related power. It is the formal power granted to a person by the organization. For example, a first-line supervisory position has authority because of hierarchy rank—not because of personal characteristics, such as the charisma of a supervisor.

Power in an organization is largely a function of being in the right place, at the right time, with the right resources, and working efficiently.[3] Position in the organization, work flow, or communication network all involve the notion of place. One example of being in the right place is illustrated by the statement:

> Those subunits most able to cope with the organization's critical problems and uncertainties acquire power. In its simplest form, the strategic-contingencies theory implies that when an organization faces a number of lawsuits that threaten its existence, the legal department will gain power and influence over organizational decisions.[4]

This statement indicates that a unit or person, by virtue of being faced with strategic and critical contingencies, is in a position to gain power.

It follows that the right place is intimately linked with proper timing activities. Opportunities to handle emergencies and nonroutine situations and to provide technical, administrative, or behavior expertise are related to time. Timing is important because the opportunity to deal with an issue (e.g., discipline or performance problem) will depend on being in position to do something when it happens.

Control of resources is also an important factor in understanding the sources of power. The control of resources is determined by such factors as position in the hierarchy, location in the work flow, and the access to information. For example, a top-level executive has more control of people, money, and equipment than a first-line supervisor. Those units or people in the work flow (e.g., the office, the assembly line) who have access to scarce resources have greater potential power. In the days of the manual switchboard, the operator was in a position of controlling access to information. Today information gatekeepers are also able to gain power. For example, the salesperson who has direct contact with major clients may have information which grants power well beyond the hierarchical level associated with his or her sales job.[5]

If a person or unit is able to accomplish its goals, then, by definition, power is granted. That is, working efficiently and accomplishing something means that the unit or person has power. It is the successful (efficient) unit or person that is granted more power (e.g., given more re-

[3] Morgan W. McCall, Jr., "Power, Authority, and Influence," in *Organizational Behavior*, ed. S. Kerr (Columbus, Ohio: Grid, 1979), p. 189.

[4] G. R. Salancik and J. Pfeffer, "Who Gets Power—And How They Hold on to It: A Strategic-Contingency Model of Power," *Organizational Dynamics*, Winter 1977, pp. 4–5.

[5] McCall, "Power, Authority, and Influence," pp. 190–93.

sources, respected, listened to). The efficient unit or person is provided what is needed to build an even greater degree of power.

In work organizations, the ability to influence, persuade, and motivate followers, in addition to place, timing, information access, and efficiency, is also based upon the perceived power of the leader. French and Raven identify forms of perceived power a leader may possess as follows:

Coercive—power based upon fear. A follower perceives that failing to comply with the request initiated by a leader could result in some form of punishment: a reprimand or social ostracism from a group.

Reward—power based upon the expectation of receiving praise, recognition, or income for compliance with a leader's request.

Legitimate—power derived from an individual's position in the group or organizational hierarchy. In a formal organization, the first-line supervisor is perceived to have more power than operating employees. In the informal group, the leader is recognized by the members as having legitimate power.

Expert—power based upon a special skill, expertise, or knowledge. The followers perceive the person as having relevant expertise and believe that it exceeds their own.

Referent—power based on attractiveness and appeal. A leader who is admired because of certain traits possesses referent power. This form of power is popularly referred to as charisma. The person is said to have charisma to inspire and attract followers.[6]

The following close-up illustrates how Vince Lombardi, a football coach, was able to use the types of power discussed by French and Raven.

ORGANIZATIONS: CLOSE-UP

Vince Lombardi's Ability to Influence

Vince Lombardi is recognized as one of the most effective coaches in professional football history. He used his legitimate, expert, coercive, reward, and referent power to influence football players in many different ways. With one player he would use harsh criticism, verbal abuse, and threats. However, with another player he would cajole, stroke, and softly encourage. His ability to use his power is legendary and is an example of how one person can use a full range of power to influence followers.

Here are some brief comments that indicate how various players viewed Coach Lombardi's use of power:

Jerry Kramer (lineman): To be honest, very few of the guys liked him at first. For one thing, he had us running like we had never run before. But the main thing was that we resented a guy coming in from college and telling us what to do. However, before long his enthusiasm, his spirit was infectious.

---

[6]This typology was developed by John R. P. French and Bertram Raven, "The Bases of Social Power," in *Group Dynamics*, ed. Darwin Cartwright and A. F. Zander, 2d ed. (Evanston, Ill.: Row, Peterson, 1960), pp. 607–23.

> **ORGANIZATIONS: CLOSE-UP** (continued)
>
> He was always a great psychologist, great at analyzing individuals, knowing which players needed to be driven and which ones needed a friendly pat on the fanny.
>
> Kyle Rote (running back and flanker): You may find this hard to believe, but Vince Lombardi impressed me as a shy person . . . Vinny was also a perfectionist.
>
> Willie Davis (defensive end): In the first place, he worked so hard that I always felt the old man was really putting more into the game on a day-to-day basis than I was. I felt obligated to put something extra into it on Sunday. I had to, just to be even with him.
>
> Yes, Vince Lombardi was tough, worked hard, could motivate by example, and used all his power to do the job.
>
> Source: Jerry Kramer, *Winning Is the Only Thing* (New York: Thomas Y. Crowell, 1976).

The Two-Way Power Flow

Power in organizations is a two-way phenomenon, flowing from one individual (leader) to other people (subordinates) and back. A supervisor may control the amount of salary increment a subordinate receives, but subordinates have some say in what the supervisor will receive as a raise. If subordinates perform well, the evaluation of their outputs and effort can help the supervisor receive a high rating. However, if subordinates create production problems, restrict and disrupt output, and are generally not cooperative, they can negatively influence the performance evaluation of the supervisor. In fact, it is very likely the negative subordinate behavior will be the main contributor to a poor performance rating for the supervisor. Therefore, it is best to consider power as a two-way flow between the leader and subordinates.

Power and Politics

Political maneuvering involves acquiring power within the organization. People try to achieve goals that are important to them. One means of achieving these goals is to gain as much power as possible. Only so much position power is available within any organization. As we move down the management hierarchy, each successive level of people has less position power than the one above.[7]

Zaleznik, a consultant and organizational researcher, assumes that power is inevitable in organizations. He states:

> Whatever else organizations may be . . . they are political structures. This means that organizations operate by distributing authority and setting a stage for the exercise of power. It is no wonder, therefore, that individuals who are

---

[7] Andrew J. DuBrin, *Human Relations: A Job Oriented Approach* (Reston, Va.: Reston Publishing, 1981), p. 117.

highly motivated to secure and use power find a familiar and hospitable environment in business.[8]

Since power and politics are used in organizations, it is important for managers to understand the manner in which both are applied. Individuals do not like to have power used on them. The use of expert and referent power is not usually resisted by subordinates or followers. However, when coercive power is used, there is often some resistance. Furthermore, it is important to understand that people seek power through such political maneuverings as joining ranks with individuals with power, developing expertise in an important field or area, controlling crucial information, displaying loyalty and commitment, and making the immediate superior look good.

LEADERSHIP DEFINED

■ The five bases of power suggest that power can be defined as the ability to influence another person's behavior. Where one individual attempts to affect the behavior of a group, we describe the effort as leadership. More specifically "Leadership is an attempt at interpersonal influence, directed through the communication process, toward the attainment of some goal or goals."[9] This definition implies that leadership involves the use of influence and that all interpersonal relationships can involve leadership. A second element in the definition involves the importance of communication. The clarity and accuracy of communication affect the behavior and performance of followers.

Another element of the definition focuses on the accomplishment of goals. The effective leader may have to deal with individual, group, and organizational goals. Leader effectiveness is typically considered in terms of the degree of accomplishment of one or a combination of these goals. Individuals may view the leader as effective or ineffective in terms of their satisfactions derived from the total work experience. In fact, acceptance of a leader's directives or requests rests largely on the followers' expectations that a favorable response will lead to an attractive outcome.

Coercive, reward, and legitimate power are primarily specified by an individual's role in a hierarchy. This role can, of course, be in a formal or an informal group. The degree and scope of a leader's expert and referent power are dictated primarily by personal attributes. Some leaders, because of personality or communication difficulties, cannot influence others through expert or referent power.

Figure 9–1 summarizes the key sources and perceived bases of power. It also presents some of the possible moderating factors between the sources and perceived bases of power and outcomes (goals). The model suggests that (1) a successful leader is one who is aware of sources of power and the

---

[8] Abraham Zaleznik, "Power and Politics in Organizational Life," *Harvard Business Review*, May–June 1970, p. 47.

[9] Edwin A. Fleishman, "Twenty Years of Consideration and Structure," in *Current Developments in the Study of Leadership*, eds. Edwin A. Fleishman and James G. Hunt (Carbondale: Southern Illinois University, 1973), p. 3.

FIGURE 9–1
A Leadership Model Emphasizing the Role of Power

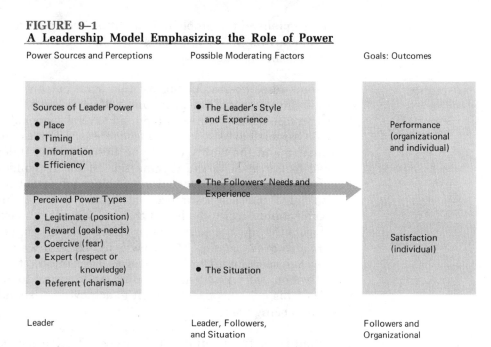

Power Sources and Perceptions	Possible Moderating Factors	Goals: Outcomes

Sources of Leader Power
- Place
- Timing
- Information
- Efficiency

Perceived Power Types
- Legitimate (position)
- Reward (goals-needs)
- Coercive (fear)
- Expert (respect or knowledge)
- Referent (charisma)

- The Leader's Style and Experience
- The Followers' Needs and Experience
- The Situation

Performance (organizational and individual)

Satisfaction (individual)

Leader   Leader, Followers, and Situation   Followers and Organizational

importance of perceived power and (2) the accomplishment of goals will depend not only on power sources and perceptions but also on follower needs, the situation, and experience of the leader.

TRAIT THEORIES

■ Much of the early work on leadership focused on identifying the traits of effective leaders. This approach was based on the assumption that a finite number of individual traits of effective leaders could be found. Thus, most research was designed to identify intellectual, emotional, physical, and other personal characteristics of successful leaders. The personnel testing component of scientific management supported to a significant extent the trait theory of leadership[10] Besides personnel testing, the traits of leaders have been studied by observing behavior in group situations, choice of associates (voting), by nomination of rating by observers, and by analysis of biographical data.

Intelligence

In a review of 33 studies, Stogdill found that there is a general trend which indicates that leaders are more intelligent than followers.[11] One of the most significant findings is that extreme intelligence differences between leaders and followers may be dysfunctional. For example, a leader with a relatively high IQ who is attempting to influence a group with members with average IQ's may be unable to understand why the members do

---

[10]Ralph M. Stogdill, "Historical Trends in Leadership Theory and Research," *Journal of Contemporary Business*, Autumn 1974, p. 4.

[11]Stogdill, *Handbook of Leadership*, pp. 43–44.

not comprehend the problem. In addition such a leader may have difficulty communicating ideas and policies. Being too intelligent would be a problem in some situations.

Personality

Some research results suggest that such personality traits as alertness, originality, personal integrity, and self-confidence are associated with effective leadership.[12] Ghiselli reported several personality traits which tend to be associated with leader effectiveness.[13] For example, he found that initiative and the ability to act and initiate action independently were related to the level in the organization of the respondent. The higher the person went in the organization the more important this trait became. He also found that self-assurance was related to hierarchical position in the organization. Finally, he found that individuals who exhibited individuality were the most effective leaders. Some writers argue that personality is unrelated to leadership. This view is too harsh if we consider how personality has been found to be related to perception, attitudes, learning, and motivation. The problem is finding valid ways to measure personality traits. This goal has been difficult to achieve, but some progress, although slow, is being made.[14]

Physical Characteristics

Studies of the relationship between effective leadership and physical characteristics such as age, height, weight, and appearance provide contradictory results. Being taller and heavier than the average of a group is certainly not advantageous for achieving a leader position.[15] However, many organizations believe that it requires a physically large person to secure compliance from followers. This notion relies heavily on the coercive or fear basis of power. On the other hand, Truman, Gandhi, Napoleon, and Stalin are examples of individuals of small stature who rose to positions of leadership.

Supervisory Ability

Using the leaders' performance ratings, Ghiselli found a positive relationship between a person's supervisory ability and level in the organizational hierarchy. The supervisor's ability is defined as the "effective utilization of whatever supervisory practices are indicated by the particular requirements of the situation."[16] Once again, a measurement of the concept is needed and this is a difficult problem to resolve.

---

[12] For example, see Chris Argyris, "Some Characteristics of Successful Executives," *Personnel Journal*, June 1955, pp. 50–63; and J. A. Hornaday and C. J. Bunker, "The Nature of the Entrepreneur," *Personnel Psychology*, Spring 1970, pp. 47–54.

[13] Edwin E. Ghiselli, "The Validity of Management Traits in Relation to Occupational Level," *Personnel Psychology*, Summer 1963, pp. 109–13.

[14] For example, see Robert W. Lundin, *Personality* (New York: Macmillan, 1974); and Leonard Krasner and Leonard P. Ullman, *Behavior Influence and Personality* (New York: Holt, Rinehart & Winston, 1973).

[15] Ralph M. Stogdill, "Personal Factors Associated with Leadership," *Journal of Applied Psychology*, January 1948, pp. 35–71.

[16] Edwin E. Ghiselli, *Exploration in Managerial Talent* (Santa Monica, Calif.: Goodyear Publishing, 1971).

Although some traits appear to differentiate effective and ineffective leaders, there still exist many contradictory research findings. There are a number of possible reasons for the disappointing results. First, the list of potentially important traits is endless. Every year new traits, such as the sign under which a person is born, handwriting style, and order of birth are added to personality, physical characteristics, and intelligence. This continual "adding on" results in more confusion among those interested in identifying leadership traits. Second, trait test scores are not consistently predictive of leader effectiveness. Traits do not operate singly, but in combination, to influence followers. This interaction influences the leader-follower relationship. Third, the patterns of effective behavior depend largely on the situation. The leadership behavior which is effective in a bank may be ineffective in a laboratory. Finally, the trait approach does not provide insight into what the effective leader does on the job. Observations are needed that describe the behavior of effective and ineffective leaders.

Despite these shortcomings the trait approach is not completely invalid. Stogdill concisely captures the value of the trait approach in the following statement:

> . . . the view that leadership is entirely situational in origin and that no personal characteristics are predictive of leadership . . . seems to overemphasize the situational and underemphasize the personal nature of leadership.[17]

The following close-up presents the results of a survey of views on leadership.

ORGANIZATIONS: CLOSE-UP

Morality, Courage, Common Sense—Some Key Leadership Traits

A survey on American leadership asked people to name three attributes or traits they believe are most needed in today's leaders. Ratings of attributes, as measured by percentages of the responses are as follows:

	Percent
Moral integrity	76.1%
Courage	55.2
Common sense	52.9
Grasp of economics	29.1
Intellectual excellence	28.6
Social concern	22.0
Political ability	15.7
Foreign-affairs expertise	8.2
Charisma	5.5
Others	6.4

---

[17] Stodgill, "Personal Factors," p. 72.

ORGANIZATIONS: CLOSE-UP (continued)

Typical of individual comments were these:

William Pincus, president of the Council on Legal Education for Professional Responsibility in New York: "We need persons who can act and take the consequences, overcoming the all-too-prevalent timidity about using power and the fear of being held responsible."

Rabbi Israel Klavan, head of the Rabbinical Council of America in New York: "Charisma is essential to effective leadership of mass movements. Moral integrity prevents the charismatic figure from becoming a demagogue."

Jerry Hammond, a black city councilman in Columbus, Ohio: "The situation has been such that two of the qualities that I rank lowest—charisma and political ability—have been the major attributes of so many of our leaders."

Maurice B. Mitchell, chancellor of the University of Denver: "The dependence on charm and charisma have led, in some measure, to the substitution of glibness for responsible action and words."

William J. Campbell, a U.S. district judge in Chicago: "The most uncommon virtue is still common sense. To lead, one must also possess the courage and moral integrity to use it."

PERSONAL-BEHAVIORAL THEORIES

■ A number of theorists argue for the use of a particular style to bring about high performance levels in areas such as production and satisfaction. The style, or personal-behavioral leadership approaches that have been the most widely used in practice are based on research conducted at the University of Michigan, the Ohio State, and by Blake and Mouton. These approaches have been widely publicized, researched, and applied in organizational settings. Each of the approaches attempts to identify what leaders do when leading.[18]

The University of Michigan Studies: Job-Centered and Employee-Centered

Since 1947, Likert has been studying how best to manage the efforts of individuals to achieve desired performance and satisfaction objectives.[19] The purpose of most of the leadership research from the University of Michigan has been to discover the principles and methods of effective leadership. The effectiveness criteria used in many of the studies include:

Productivity per work hour or other similar measures of the organization's success in achieving its production goals.

Job satisfaction of members of the organization.

---

[18]Jeffrey C. Barrow, "The Variables of Leadership: A Review and Conceptual Framework," *Academy of Management Review*, April 1977, pp. 231–51.

[19]For a review of this work, see Rensis Likert, *New Patterns of Management* (New York: McGraw-Hill, 1961); and Rensis Likert, *The Human Organization* (New York: McGraw-Hill, 1967).

Turnover, absenteeism, and grievance rates.

Costs.

Scrap loss.

Employee and managerial motivation.

Studies have been conducted in a wide variety of industries: chemical, electronics, food, heavy machinery, insurance, petroleum, public utilities, hospitals, banks, and government agencies. Data have been obtained from thousands of employees doing different job tasks, ranging from unskilled work to highly skilled research and development work.

Through interviewing leaders and followers, the researchers identified two distinct styles of leadership which are referred to as *job-centered* and *employee-centered.* The job-centered leader practices close supervision so that subordinates perform their tasks using specified procedures. This type of leader relies on coercion, reward, and legitimate power to influence the behavior and performance of followers. The concern for people is viewed as important, but is a luxury that cannot always be practiced by a leader.

The *employee-centered* leader believes in delegating decision making and aiding followers in satisfying their needs by creating a supportive work environment. The employee-centered leader is concerned with followers' personal advancement, growth, and achievement. These actions are assumed to be conducive for the support of group formation and development.

The potential effect of these two personal-behavioral styles was tested in an experimental study.[20] This study included 500 clerical employees in four divisions which were organized in the same way, used the same technology, did the same kind of work, and employed individuals of comparable aptitudes.

The work load of the divisions varied and peaked from time to time. At any one time a given amount of work had to be processed. The volume was impossible to change and the only way to increase production was to increase the size of the group.

The experiment with these four divisions lasted for one year. There was a training period for supervisory and managerial staffs lasting approximately six months. Production was measured continuously and computed weekly. Employee and supervisory attitudes, perceptions, motivations, and related variables were measured just before and just after the experimental year.

In two of the four divisions, an attempt was made to make the decision-making process more participative. More general supervision was introduced. In addition, the formal leaders were given training in participative leadership. In the other two divisions which were called the hierarchically controlled divisions, there was an effort to increase the closeness of super-

---

[20]Nancy C. Morse and E. Reimer, "The Experimental Change of a Major Organizational Variable," *Journal of Abnormal and Social Psychology,* January 1956, pp. 120–29.

vision and to centralize decision making. The formal leaders in these divisions were trained for the same length of time as their counterparts in the participative divisions, but the training focused on company policies, rules, and procedures.

Production increased under both systems, with the increase being 25 percent in the hierarchically controlled and 20 percent in the participative. These increases were achieved by different procedures in the two systems. In the hierarchically controlled divisions, direct pressure and the job-centered behavior of the leaders were assumed to be the reasons for the increase. However, in the participative divisions the clerks themselves reduced the size of the work force and developed a number of procedural changes. It was also believed that production in the participative divisions increased because of the more cohesive effort of the groups and less absenteeism. The indicators of employee satisfaction included absenteeism, turnover, and attitudes. The findings revealed that these indicators improved in the participative divisions and deteriorated in the hierarchically controlled divisions.

The researchers believe that these results suggest that similar organizations typically focus on short-run effectiveness measures. The reward and promotion systems are integrated with production results. In addition, managers are transferred often and are forced to generate short-run results. Thus, if we only look at production the hierarchically controlled divisions are more effective. However, if the satisfaction indicators are considered, the acceptance of the superiority of the job-centered style becomes tenuous and questionable. Likert believes that the short-run increases are gained at a cost of negative attitudes and increased absenteeism and turnover. The conclusions reached by Likert and other supporters of this leadership approach suggest that employee-centered leadership behaviors are more effective.

The Michigan studies do not clearly show that one particular style of leadership is always the most effective. Furthermore, it fails to predict which style will be the most effective. Finally, it only examines two aspects of leadership—task and people behavior.

The Ohio State Studies: Initiating Structure and Consideration

Among the several large research programs on leadership that developed after World War II, one of the most significant was Ohio State's, which resulted in a two-factor theory of leadership.[21] These studies isolated two leadership factors referred to as *initiating structure and consideration*. The definitions of these factors are as follows: *Initiating structure involves behavior in which the leader organizes and defines the relationships in the*

[21]For a review of the studies see Stogdill, *Handbook of Leadership*, chap. 11. Also see Edwin A. Fleishman, "The Measurement of Leadership Attitudes in Industry," *Journal of Applied Psychology*, June 1953, pp. 153–58; C. L. Shartle, *Executive Performance and Leadership* (Englewood Cliffs, N.J.: Prentice-Hall, 1956); Edwin A. Fleishman, E. F. Harris, and H. E. Burtt, *Leadership and Supervision in Industry* (Columbus: Bureau of Educational Research, Ohio State University, 1955); and Edwin A. Fleishman, "Twenty Years of Consideration and Structure," in *Current Developments in the Study of Leadership*, eds. Edwin A. Fleishman and James G. Hunt (Carbondale: Southern Illinois University, 1973), pp. 1–37.

FIGURE 9–2
The Scores of Five Leaders: Initiating Structure and Consideration

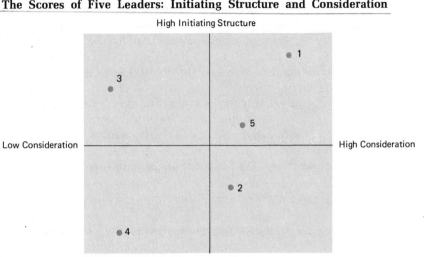

group, tends to establish well-defined patterns and channels of communication, and spells out ways of getting the job done. *Consideration* involves behavior indicating friendship, mutual trust, respect, warmth, and rapport between the leader and followers.

These dimensions are measured by two separate questionnaires. The Leadership Opinion Questionnaire (LOQ) attempts to assess how leaders think they behave in leadership roles. The Leader Behavior Description Questionnaire (LBDQ) measures the perceptions of subordinates, peers, or superiors.

The initiating structure and consideration scores derived from the responses to the questionnaires provide a way to measure leadership style. Figure 9–2 provides a hypothetical view of the behaviors of five different leaders. These hypothetical points indicate that leaders have scores on both dimensions. Individual 1 is high on both initiating structure and consideration; individual 4 is low on both dimensions.

Since the original research undertaken to develop the questionnaire, there have been numerous studies of the relationship of these two leadership dimensions and various effectiveness criteria. Many of the early results stimulated the generalization that leaders above average in both consideration and initiating structure were more effective. In a study at International Harvester, however, the researchers began to find some more complicated interpretations of the two dimensions. In a study of supervisors, it was found that those scoring higher on structure had higher proficiency ratings (ratings received from superiors), but also had more employee grievances. The higher consideration score was related to lower proficiency ratings and lower absences.[22]

---

[22]Fleishman, Harris, and Burtt, *Leadership and Supervision.*

A study of research and development departments introduced the issue of organizational climate to the leadership-effectiveness question.[23] The focus of this study was research, development, and engineering personnel in three large organizations: a petroleum refinery, a business machine manufacturer, and an air frame manufacturer. The results indicated that leadership behavior had differential effects on employee satisfaction depending upon different organizational climates. For example, the climate of the air frame company was rigidly structured and formalized. In this type of climate, the opportunity for a leader to be instrumental in aiding the followers in satisfying pay, security, social, and advancement needs may be limited. Thus, organizational climate appears to affect the relationship between the leader's consideration behavior and the follower's satisfaction.

This study also found positive relationships between initiating structure and satisfaction. These relationships were weakest in the highly structured air frame company. Perhaps these results are explained by the fact that the air frame company is already highly structured and the leader initiating more structure is engaging in an effort which is not required.

The Ohio State personal-behavioral theory has been criticized because of simplicity, lack of generalizability, and reliance on questionnaire responses to measure leadership effectiveness. The critique of Korman is perhaps the most publicized.[24] He has criticized the Ohio State research on leadership in the following manner.

1. The researchers have made little attempt to conceptualize situational variables and their influence on leadership behavior.
2. Most of the research studies yield generally insignificant correlations between leader behavior measures and effectiveness criteria.
3. The theory has not provided any answer to the question of causality.

Some of the problems have been partially corrected.[25] For example, it has been pointed out in more recent research that many variables affect the relationship between leadership behavior and organizational effectiveness. Some of these include employee experience, competence, job knowledge, expectations for leader behavior, the upward influence of leaders, the degree of autonomy, role clarity, and urgency of time.[26]

---

[23] Robert J. House, Alan C. Filley, and Steven Kerr, "Relation of Leader Consideration and Initiating Structure to R and D Subordinates' Satisfaction," *Administrative Science Quarterly*, March 1971, pp. 19–30.

[24] Abraham K. Korman, "Consideration, Initiating Structure, and Organizational Criteria— A Review," *Personnel Psychology*, Winter 1966, pp. 349–61.

[25] Steven Kerr and Chester Schriescheim, "Consideration, Initiating Structure, and Organizational Criteria—An Update of Korman's 1966 Review," *Personnel Psychology*, Winter 1974, pp. 555–68.

[26] R. C. Cummins, "Leader-Member Relations as a Moderator of the Effects of Leader Behavior and Attitude," *Personnel Psychology*, Winter 1972, pp. 655–60, and James G. Hunt and V. K. C. Liebscher, "Leadership Preference, Leadership Behavior, and Employee Satisfaction," *Organizational Behavior and Human Performance*, February 1973, pp. 59–77.

**Managerial Grid®:
Concern for People
and Concern for
Production**

The conceptual framework for the managerial grid assumes that there is an unnecessary dichotomy in the minds of most leaders about the concern for people and concern for production. It is Blake and Mouton's assumption that people and production concerns are complementary, rather than mutually exclusive.[27] They further believe that leaders must integrate these concerns to achieve effective performance results.

FIGURE 9–3
Managerial Grid®

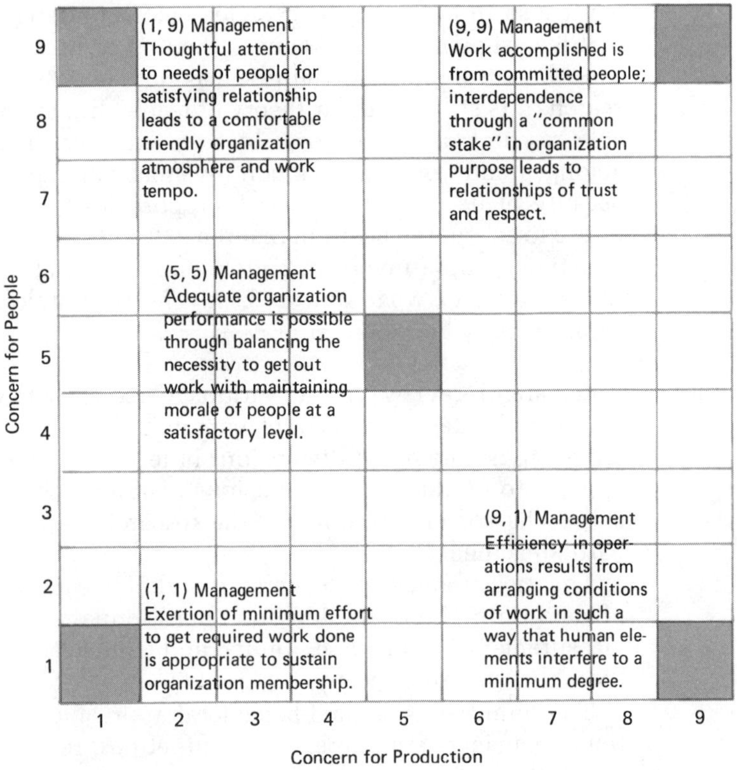

Concern for People (vertical axis, 1–9)
Concern for Production (horizontal axis, 1–9)

(1, 9) Management
Thoughtful attention to needs of people for satisfying relationship leads to a comfortable friendly organization atmosphere and work tempo.

(9, 9) Management
Work accomplished is from committed people; interdependence through a "common stake" in organization purpose leads to relationships of trust and respect.

(5, 5) Management
Adequate organization performance is possible through balancing the necessity to get out work with maintaining morale of people at a satisfactory level.

(1, 1) Management
Exertion of minimum effort to get required work done is appropriate to sustain organization membership.

(9, 1) Management
Efficiency in operations results from arranging conditions of work in such a way that human elements interfere to a minimum degree.

Source: Robert R. Blake and Jane S. Mouton, *The Managerial Grid* (Houston: Gulf Publishing, 1964), p. 10.

The thoughts of Blake and Mouton resulted in development of the grid chart. An example of the managerial grid is provided in Figure 9–3. Theoretically, there are 81 possible positions on the grid, representing as many leadership styles, but the focus usually centers around five styles: 1, 1; 1, 9; 9, 1; 5, 5; and 9, 9.

The 9, 1 leader is primarily concerned with production task accomplish-

[27] Robert R. Blake and Jane S. Mouton, *The New Managerial Grid* (Houston: Gulf Publishing, 1978), and Robert R. Blake and Jane S. Mouton, *The Versatile Manager: A Grid Profile* (Homewood, Ill.: Dow Jones-Irwin, 1981).

ment and has little, if any, concern for people. This person wants to meet schedules and get the job done at all costs. The 1, 9 style reflects a minimal concern for production coupled with a maximal concern for people; the 1, 1 style reflects minimal concern for both people and production; and the 5, 5 style reflects a moderate concern for both. The 9, 9 style is viewed as the ideal approach for integrating a maximum concern for production with a maximum concern for people.

According to Blake and Mouton, the grid enables leaders to identify their own leadership styles. Furthermore, it serves as a framework for leaders to use in assessing their styles before undertaking a training program that is designed to move them to the 9, 9 style.

Although the managerial grid has not been thoroughly supported by research, it is still a popular theory of leadership among managers. The available research is in the form of case analyses. Thus, the grid is popular among practitioners and is controversial among theorists and researchers because of its lack of empirical support. Many managers and researchers refuse to accept the position that the 9, 9 style is superior to other styles. The situation, people involved, and resources available need to be placed into any analysis of what style is best. The 9, 9 style in some circumstances would simply be a total failure.

A Synopsis of the Personal-Behavioral Theories

A careful review of the various personal-behavioral theories and research indicates a number of common threads. Each of the theories attempts to isolate broad dimensions of leadership behavior. The logic of this appears to be that multidimensions confound the interpretation of leadership behavior and complicate the research designs developed to test the particular theory.

The measurement of leadership style for each of the theories is accomplished through paper-and-pencil questionnaire responses. This method of measurement is, of course, limited and controversial. The common bases of these theories are presented in Table 9–1.

The numerous personal-behavioral approaches are impressive, but practicing managers are interested in guidelines, results, and procedures to improve their styles. Each of the approaches is associated with highly respected theorists, researchers, or consultants, and each has been studied in different organizational settings. Yet, the linkage between leadership and such important performance indicators as production, efficiency, and satisfaction is not conclusively resolved by any of the three personal-behavioral theories.

ATTRIBUTION THEORY OF LEADERSHIP

■ Attribution theory suggests that understanding and predicting how people will react to events around them is enhanced by knowing what their causal explanation for those events are. Kelley stresses that it is mainly concerned with the cognitive processes by which a person interprets behavior as being caused by (or attributed to) certain cues in the relevant

TABLE 9–1
A Review of the Predominant Personal-Behavioral Approaches

Leadership Factors	Prime Initiator(s) of the Theory	How Behavior Is Measured	Subjects Researched	Principal Conclusions
Employee-centered and job-centered	Likert	Through interview and questionnaire responses of groups of followers.	Formal leaders and followers in public utilities, banks, hospitals, manufacturing, food, government agencies.	Employee-centered and job-centered styles result in production improvements. However, after a brief period of time the job-centered style creates pressure that is resisted through absenteeism, turnover, grievance, and poor attitudes. The best style is employee-centered.
Initiating structure and consideration	Fleishman, Stogdill, and Shartle	Through questionnaire responses of groups of followers, peers, the immediate superior, and the leader.	Formal leaders and followers in military, education, public utilities, manufacturing, and government agencies.	The combination of initiating structure and consideration behavior which achieves individual, group, and organizational effectiveness depends largely on the situation.
Concern for production and concern for people	Blake and Mouton	Through interviews and questionnaire responses of groups of followers and the leader.	Formal leaders in electronics and petroleum companies.	The 9, 9 style is related to improvements in productivity, cost, and timeliness of output. Organizations should attempt to stimulate leaders to adopt the 9, 9 style.

environment.[28] The emphasis of attribution leadership theory is on "why" some behavior has occurred. Most causes of subordinate or follower behaviors are not directly observable, therefore to determine causes requires reliance on perception. In attribution theory individuals are assumed to be rational and concerned about the causal linkages in their environments.

The attributional approach starts with the position that the leader is essentially an *information processor*.[29] In other words the leader is searching for informational cues that explain "why" something is happening. From these cues leaders attempt to construct causal explanations that guide his or her leadership behavior. The process in simple terms appears to be follower behavior ⟶ leader attributions ⟶ leader behavior.

The Leader's Attributions

Kelley suggests that the primary attributional task of the leader is to categorize the causes of follower or subordinate behavior into three source dimensions: person, entity, or context. That is, for any given behavior, such as poor quality of productive output, the leader's job is to determine if the poor quality was caused by the person (e.g., inadequate ability), the task (entity), or some unique set of circumstances surrounding the event (context).

The leader seeks three types of information when forming attributions about a follower's behavior-distinctiveness, consistency, and consensus. For any behavior the leader first attempts to determine if the behavior was *distinctive* in response to a task; that is, did the behavior occur on this task but not on other tasks. Next, the leader is concerned about *consistency*, how frequent does this behavior occur. Finally, the leader estimates the extent to which others also behave the same way; if the behavior is unique to one person it is said to have *low consensus*; if it is common to other members this reflects *high consensus*.

Leader's Perception of Responsibility

The judgment of responsibility is considered to moderate the leader's response to an attribution. Clearly, the more a behavior is seen as caused by some characteristic of the follower (i.e., an internal cause) and the follower is judged to be responsible for the behavior, the more likely the leader is to take some action toward the follower. For example, it is possible to attribute an outcome (e.g., poor performance) to factors outside the control of a person, such as not having the tools to do the job well, or to internal causes, such as a lack of effort. When the performance failure is caused by internal forces it could be expected that leader-initiated punishment could be severe.

---

[28] H. H. Kelley, "Attribution Theory in Social Psychology," *Nebraska Symposium on Motivation*, ed. D. Levine (Lincoln: University of Nebraska Press, 1967), p. 193.

[29] Stephen G. Green and Terence R. Mitchell, "Attributional Processes of Leaders in Leader-Member Interactions," *Organizational Behavior and Human Performance*, June 1979, pp. 429–58.

**An Attributional
Leadership Model**

Attribution theory appears to offer a framework for explaining leader behavior in more insightful terms than either the trait or personal-behavioral theories. It attempts to explain *why* behaviors are happening. The trait and personal-behavioral theories are more descriptive and do not focus on the why issue. Furthermore, attributional theory can offer some predictions about a leader's response to a follower's behavior. In Figure 9–4 an attributional leadership model is presented.

Two important linkages are emphasized in Figure 9–4. At the first linkage point the leader attempts to make an attribution about poor quality performance. These attributions are moderated by the three information sources—distinctiveness, consistency, and consensus. The second linkage point suggests that the leader's behavior or response is determined by the type of attributions he or she makes. This relationship between attribution and leader behavior is moderated by the leader's perception of responsibility. Is the responsibility internal or external?

An empirical test of attribution leadership theory examined nursing supervisors who were also considered leaders. Distinctiveness, consistency, and consensus did influence the leader's attributions; leaders who made internal cause attributions (e.g., lack of effort) tended to use more punitive behaviors; and leaders tended to make more internal attributions and to respond more harshly when the problems were serious.[30]

**FIGURE 9–4
An Attribution Model of Leadership**

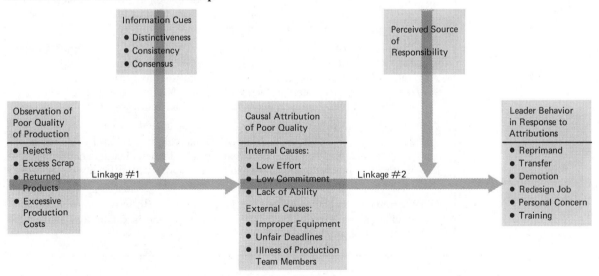

Source: Adapted from Terence R. Mitchell and Robert E. Wood, "An Empirical Test of an Attributional Model of Leaders Responses to Poor Performance," in Richard C. Huseman, ed., *Academy of Management Proceedings*, 1979, p. 94.

---

[30] Terence R. Mitchell and Robert E. Wood, "An Empirical Test of an Attributional Model of Leader's Responses to Poor Performance," in Richard C. Huseman, ed., *Academy of Management Proceedings*, 1979, pp. 94–98.

Currently, the research support for the attributional theory of leadership is limited. There is a need to test the theory in more organizational settings. Understanding the causes of leader behavior or at least searching for these causes seems more promising for managerial use than simply adding another trait or descriptive theory to the leadership literature.

MAJOR MANAGERIAL ISSUES

A. Leadership is the ability to influence followers which involves the use of power and the acceptance of the leader by the followers. The ability to influence is related to the followers' need satisfaction.

B. Sources of power exist because of place, timing, access to information, efficiency, and perceptions.

C. Power flows from the leader to subordinates and from subordinates to the leader. This mutual influence can affect the rewards and punishments received by both parties.

D. The trait approach has resulted in attempts to predict leadership effectiveness from physical, sociological, and psychological traits. The search for traits has led to studies involving effectiveness and such factors as height, weight, intelligence, and personality.

E. There continues to be a great deal of semantic confusion and overlap regarding the definition of leadership behavior. Such terms as *employee-centered, job-centered, initiating structure, consideration, concern for production* and *concern for people,* are classified as personal-behavioral descriptions of what the leader does.

F. Research studies have resulted in generally inconclusive findings about the relation of leader behavior to follower effectiveness. The evidence to date is in some cases suggestive. For example, most studies indicate that leaders who are considerate (employee-centered, concerned for people, supportive) will generally have more satisfied followers.

G. The personal-behavioral approaches suggest that situational variables such as the follower's expectations, skills, role clarity, and previous experiences should be seriously considered by leaders. Leaders can do little to improve effectiveness unless they can properly modify these variables or change their style of leadership.

H. Attribution theory of leadership is concerned with why a particular behavior has occurred. The leader in this approach is considered to be an information processor.

DISCUSSION AND REVIEW QUESTIONS

1. Some view organizations as political systems. Do you believe that politics within an organization can be used to achieve goals? Explain.

2. Is there a one best style of leadership? Why?

3. What is the major difference between attributional and personal-behavioral explanations of leader behavior?

4. Why is the Blake and Mouton managerial-grid approach attractive to many practicing managers?

5. What could be the consequences of leaders assuming that subordinates have no power to exert on them?

6. Is it possible to train, in management or organizational behavior courses, leaders in the way to lead followers? Explain.

7. Does the informal leader possess legitimate power? Explain.

8. What are the similarities between the employee-centered, consideration, and concern-for-people concepts?

9. Why would a leader be replaced in a formal organizational group and in an informal group?

ADDITIONAL REFERENCES

Bennis, W. "Leadership: A Beleaguered Species." *Organizational Dynamics,* 1976, pp. 3–16.

Blackburn, R. S. "Lower Participant Power: Toward a Conceptual Integration." *Academy of Management Review,* 1981, pp. 127–31.

Calder, B. J. "An Attribution Theory of Leadership." In *New Directions in Organizational Behavior,* edited by B. M. Staw and G. R. Salancik. Chicago: St. Clair Press, 1977.

Hollander, E. P. *Leadership Dynamics: A Practical Guide to Effective Relationship.* New York: Free Press, 1978.

Kotter, J. P. "Power, Success, and Organizational Effectiveness." *Organizational Dynamics,* 1978, pp. 26–40.

McClelland, D. C., and D. H. Burnham. "Power Is the Great Motivator." *Harvard Business Review,* 1976, pp. 100–10.

Nord, W. R. "Dreams of Humanization and the Realities of Power." *Academy of Management Review,* 1978, pp. 674–79.

Schriesheim, C. A.; R. J. House; and S. Kerr. "Leader Initiating Structure: A Reconciliation of Discrepant Research Results and Some Empirical Tests." *Organizational Behavior and Human Performance,* 1976, pp. 297–321.

Sheridan, J. E., and D. J. Vredenburgh. "Usefulness of Leadership Behavior and Social Power Variables in Predicting Tension, Performance, and Turnover of Nursing Employees." *Journal of Applied Psychology,* 1978, pp. 89–95.

Vroom, V. H. "Decision Making and Leadership." *Journal of Contemporary Business,* 1974, pp. 47–64.

THE DISMISSAL OF AN INFORMAL LEADER

The Houston Engineering Corporation was feeling the crunch of inflation and the cutback in orders from customers in the Houston, Dallas, and New Orleans regional areas. The sales personnel were primarily college educated with approximately 70 percent having B.S. degrees in engineering.

Recently, the salespeople in the Houston region have complained about such factors as pay inequities, the performance appraisal system, and restrictions placed on expense accounts. The following memo from an area manager, Tom Murphy, especially irritated a number of senior salespersons. It read as follows:

Ladies and Gentlemen:

As you know, we are currently in an extreme period of low order intake and we must cut our expense budgets lower than ever before. I must ask you to do things in line with expense account reduction that I have not requested in my ten years as area manager. Eliminate all potentially nonproductive lunches with clients and submit an accurate account for your weekly mileage. Unless we have more orders and better control of expenses, there will be a further cut in your budgets. I need your help to accomplish the corporate objective of cutting expense accounts by 18 percent.

If you require clarification, please contact me immediately.

Houston Area Manager,

Tom Murphy

Tom Murphy

Each Friday morning the Houston-area group met with Tom to map out the strategy and market coverage for the forthcoming week. These meetings also provided the salespeople with an opportunity to exchange ideas and interact informally with each other.

This memo was discussed by the salespeople after the regular meeting with Tom. The senior salespeople were upset about the content of the memo and wanted John Nester to present their complaints to Tom. There were six senior sales-people in the group, nine sales representatives, and nine sales trainees. The large number of trainees was due to the increased growth in the Houston sales area in the past 18 months. Houston was now the fifth largest city in the United States, and more corporations were moving their headquarters into the city than into any other in the country. This growth rate had resulted in hiring 11 new sales trainees, 2 of whom quit because of offers received from other organizations.

The senior sales personnel were recognized as the most prestigious and best paid of the 24 in the area. John was viewed as the informal leader who always represented the group's attitudes clearly to the area manager. He was also the best salesperson in terms of sales achieved and operating within expense account allocations. John was 38 years old, an electrical engineer and a prime candidate for taking over the slumping New Orleans sales area by the end of the year.

Before the expense account memo was circulated, the sales personnel had complained about the company's performance appraisal system. They wanted the company to grant merit increases based on specific sales objectives achieved during the year. John and two other senior salespeople, Sam Wilson and Mike Hansen, had worked up a recommendation for changing the present system. It was rejected summarily by Tom, who told them to pay more attention to selling the company's products. It was his contention that unless more orders were received there might be some cutbacks in personnel.

John visited with Tom this past Friday after the regularly scheduled meeting and discussed the memo. He explained that the sales personnel were doing the best they could, but potential clients must be cultivated carefully and this required money for lunches and dinners. Tom listened attentively and explained that this was a company policy and not his idea. The two men talked for another two hours about the direction of the company and the bright future of the Houston sales area.

On Monday at 10:30 A.M., John was called into Tom's office and informed that his services were no longer needed by the company. He was given an envelope with the current month's pay and a dismissal notification. This turn of events completely shocked him since he had believed that his future with the company was especially promising. The news of John's dismissal spread through the sales group and angered everyone.

Questions for Consideration

1. Why was John the informal leader in the sales group?
2. What type of impact do you believe John's dismissal will have on the sales group's immediate sales and level of satisfaction?
3. Why has the expense account memo caused such a problem within the sales group?
4. Do you believe that the area sales manager could have improved the procedures which expressed the organization's concern about expenses? How?

Chapter 10

Leadership: Situational Approaches

AN ORGANIZATIONAL ISSUE FOR DEBATE
Can Leaders Learn to Lead?

ARGUMENT FOR

The Vroom-Yetton model of leadership and Fiedler's contingency model are similar in that both assume that effective leadership "depends on the situation." However, one major point of departure between the two approaches to leadership involves leadership training. Fiedler is pessimistic that training managers to improve their leadership skills will ever be effective. However, Vroom's position is that managers can be trained to be flexible leaders. The Vroom leadership training method involves providing managers with a comparison of the leader's style with that of others, the situational factors that influence the leader's willingness to share power with others, and an analysis of how the leader's style compares to a normative or *how it should be* style.

As part of the leadership training program, each participant works with a set of cases describing a leader facing a realistic organizational problem. In addition, the leaders are given a lecture describing the five processes of leadership outlined in the Vroom-Yetton model and view and discuss films exhibiting different processes used by leaders to make decisions. The participant's task is to select the decision process that comes closest to depicting what he or she would actually do in a situation. Small groups are formed in

ARGUMENT AGAINST

Fiedler is a little more skeptical then Vroom about using training to improve the effectiveness of a leader. He believes that some people are helped by training, but just as many go through one program after another and perform just as badly as ever. He also suggests that many outstanding leaders have had little or no leadership training. On the average, people with much training perform about as well as people with little or no training. In fact, Fiedler cites his own research of military personnel and post office managers which found no relationship between amount of training and performance to support his negative impressions of leadership training.

It is Fiedler's contention that a number of questionable assumptions guide the development of leadership training programs. First, program developers often assume that a new training sessions telling or showing leaders how to behave and stressing that a certain style is best will result in the appropriate behavior changes. This assumption ignores the fact that leadership situations are highly emotion-charged, interpersonal relationships. It is difficult to significantly alter emotional relationships through training. Second, it is assumed that the more powerful and influential leaders will be more effective because their groups will work harder. Thus, many train-

ARGUMENT FOR (continued)

which the cases are discussed and the participants try to reach agreement on the best leadership style for each situation. The groups then analyze videotapes of group problem solving and provide each other with feedback about one another's leadership style.

Admittedly research on the effectiveness of training in the use of the Vroom-Yetton model is limited. However, the evidence available clearly indicates that trained leaders showed greater agreement with the model's prescriptions than untrained leaders and are rated by co-workers (subordinates and superiors) as more effective leaders. Perhaps training does make a difference and leaders can learn to be more effective.

ARGUMENT AGAINST (continued)

ing programs attempt to improve a leader's control and influence. Third, many training programs attempt to promote participative decision making. These programs claim that a leader who shares decision making with subordinates will be more effective.

Fiedler is opposed to devoting all of the resources and time of training efforts to change behavior. Instead he believes that organizations need to train leaders to change situations to match their needs and values. This match is easier than one that attempts to change a leader's style. Perhaps training is needed but it should focus on altering situations, not people.

The search for the "best" leadership style never discovered an effective approach for all situations. What has evolved are situation-leadership theories which suggest that leadership effectiveness depends upon the fit between personality, task, power, attitudes, and perceptions.[1] This chapter will concentrate on three situation-oriented leadership approaches: the contingency model, the Vroom-Yetton normative model, and the path-goal theory. Each of these approaches relies on a diagnosis of the situation.

THE SITUATION VARIABLE

■ The importance of the situation was studied more closely by those interested in leadership only when inconclusive and contradictory results evolved from much of the early trait and personal–behavioral research. Eventually it became known that the type of leadership behavior needed to enhance performance depends largely on the situation. What is effective leadership in one situation may be disorganized incompetence in another situation. The situational theme of leadership is appealing, but it is certainly a challenging orientation to implement. Its basic foundation suggests that an effective leader must be flexible enough to adapt to the differences among subordinates and situations.

Deciding how to lead other individuals is difficult and requires an analysis of the leader, the group, and the situation. This theme is analyzed by Tannenbaum and Schmidt in their model of leadership.[2] Managers aware of the forces they face are able to more readily modify their styles to cope with changes in the work environment. Three factors of particular importance are the forces on the managers, forces in the subordinates, and forces in the situation. Tannenbaum and Schmidt state the situational theme:

> Thus, the successful manager of men can be primarily characterized neither as a strong leader nor as a permissive one. Rather, he is one who maintains a high batting average in accurately assessing the forces that determine what his most appropriate behavior at any given time should be and in actually being able to behave accordingly.[3]

As the importance of situational factors and leader assessment of forces became more recognized, leadership research became more systematic, and contingency models of leadership began to appear in the organizational behavior and management literature. Each model has its advocates and each attempts to identify the leader behaviors most appropriate for a series of leadership situations. Each contingency model attempts to identify the leader-situation patterns that are important for effective leadership.

---

[1] Edwin A. Fleishman, "Twenty Years of Consideration and Structure," in *Current Development in the Study of Leadership*, ed. Edwin A. Fleishman and James G. Hunt (Carbondale: Southern Illinois University Press, 1973), pp. 1–37.

[2] The following discussion is based upon Robert Tannenbaum and Warren H. Schmidt, "How to Choose a Leadership Pattern," *Harvard Business Review*, May–June 1973, pp. 162–80.

[3] Ibid., p. 180.

THE CONTINGENCY LEADERSHIP MODEL

■ The contingency model of leadership effectiveness was developed by Fiedler.[4] The model postulates that performance of groups is dependent on the interaction of leadership style and situational favorableness. Leadership is viewed as a relationship based on power and influence. Thus, two important questions are considered: (1) to what degree does the situation provide the leader with the power and influence needed to be effective, or how favorable are the situational factors? and (2) to what extent can the leader predict the effects of his or her style on the behavior and performance of followers?

Some of the views of Fiedler are presented in the following close-up.

ORGANIZATIONS: CLOSE-UP

Some Thoughts of Fiedler on Leadership

Fred Fiedler is recognized by managers as an expert on leadership. He has published more than 150 articles and papers and five books on the topic of leadership and organizational behavior. Listed below are a few of Fiedler's own thoughts.

What makes an effective leader? You really can't talk about leadership like that. Leadership isn't something that you have inside you like a gall bladder or a liver. It is a relationship between a person and other individuals. General George Patton was a very effective combat tank commander, but I doubt he'd be as good as a chairman of the PTA.

So a committee chairman may not make an effective chief elected officer of an association? You really can't generalize like that. Leadership is a very complicated issue that people have been working about ever since the time of Plato. In any leadership relationship, what we are concerned with is how much control and influence the leader has in a group or an organization. Some people do well with control and others don't.

Can you give us an example of job engineering? Actually, people do this all the time. If you volunteer for things you like, you prevent other people from volunteering you for jobs you don't like. And if you like the job, chances are you are successful at it. You have engineered your job situation.
Our motto for job engineering is: If you learn to avoid situations in which you are likely to fail, you will be a success.

Source: "How to Be a Successful Leader," *The Toastmaster,* October 1980, pp. 11–14.

THE SITUATIONAL FACTORS

■ Fiedler proposes three situational factors which influence a leader's effectiveness: leader-member relations, task structure, and position power. From a theoretical as well as an intuitive point of view, interpersonal rela-

---

[4]Fred E. Fiedler, *A Theory of Leadership Effectiveness* (New York: McGraw-Hill, 1967).

tionships between leader and followers are likely to be the most important variable which determines power and influence. The leader's influence depends in part upon acceptance by the followers. If others are willing to follow because of charisma, expertise, or mutual respect, the leader has little need to rely on task structure or position power. If, however, the leader is not trusted and is viewed negatively by followers the situation is considered less favorable in Fiedler's theory.

The *leader-member* relations factor refers to the degree of confidence, trust, and respect followers have in the leader. This situational variable reflects the acceptance of the leader. It is measured in two ways. One method involves asking the followers to indicate on a sociometric preference scale whether they accept or endorse a leader. An alternative method of measurement is the "Group Atmosphere" scale. This measure consists of 10 eight-point items, answered by the followers, one of which is:

Friendly   ___: ___: ___: ___: ___: ___: ___: ___   Unfriendly
              8   7   6   5   4   3   2   1

The second most important measure of situational favorableness is referred to as *task-structure*. This dimension includes a number of components as follows:

Goal clarity—the degree to which the tasks and duties of the job are clearly stated and known to the people performing the job.

Goal-path multiplicity—the degree to which the problems encountered in the job can be solved by a variety of procedures. The assembly-line worker solves problems within a systematic framework, while a scientist has a number of different ways to solve a problem.

Decision verifiability—the degree to which the "correctness" of the solutions or decisions typically encountered in a job can be demonstrated by appeal to authority, by logical procedures, or by feedback. A quality control inspector can show defective parts and clearly indicate why a part is sent back for reworking.

Decision-specificity—the degree to which there is generally more than one correct solution. An accountant working on preparing a balance sheet has few choices, while a research scientist may have numerous potentially correct alternatives to choose from.

The most obvious way in which the leader secures power is by accepting and performing the leadership role. The leader is recognized as having the right to direct, evaluate, reward, and punish followers, though this right must be exercised within defined boundaries. *Position power* in the contingency model refers to the power inherent in the leadership position. To determine leader position power questions such as the following are asked:

Can the supervisor recommend subordinate rewards and punishments to his boss?

Can the supervisor punish or reward subordinates on his or her own?

Can the supervisor recommend promotion or demotion of subordinates.[5]

Fiedler contends that such questions provide a profile of high or low position power.

Favorableness of the Situation

The three situational factors which seem to be the most important in determining the leader's power and influence are: (1) whether leader-member relations are good or poor; (2) whether the task is relatively structured or unstructured; and (3) whether the position power is relatively strong or weak. A group can be classified as to each of these situational factors. The resulting classification is shown in Figure 10–1. It suggests that it is easier to be a leader in groups which fall into situation I in which you are liked,

FIGURE 10–1
Fiedler's Classification of Situational Favorableness

Leader-Member Relations	Good				Poor			
Task Structure	High		Low		High		Low	
Position Power	Strong	Weak	Strong	Weak	Strong	Weak	Strong	Weak
Situations	I	II	III	IV	V	VI	VII	VIII

Very Favorable ◄————————————————————► Very Unfavorable

have a structured task, and position power. The situation is more favorable for the situation I leader than the situation VIII leader.

Fiedler contends that a permissive, more lenient (relationship-oriented) style is best when the situation is moderately favorable or moderately unfavorable. Thus, if a leader were moderately liked and possessed some power, and the job tasks for subordinates were somewhat vague, the leadership style needed to achieve the best results would be relationship oriented.

In contrast, when the situation is highly favorable or highly unfavorable, a task-oriented approach generally produces the desired performance. A well-liked office manager, who has power and has clearly identified the performance goals is operating in a highly favorable situation. A project engineer, who is faced with a group of suspicious and hostile subordinates,

---

[5] Fred E. Fiedler and M. M. Chemers, *Leadership and Effective Management* (Glenview, Ill.: Scott, Foresman, 1974).

has little power, and has vague task responsibilities, needs to be task oriented in this highly unfavorable situation.

The Least Preferred Co-Worker (LPC)

A key variable in investigating leader effectiveness in the contingency model is the Least Preferred Co-Worker (LPC) score.[6] This is assumed to be an indicator of the leader's personality. The LPC score is obtained by asking the leader to think of everybody with whom he or she has ever worked and to describe the person with whom the leader could work least well, the "least preferred co-worker." A scale consisting of 16 items is used to develop the LPC score. Two of these items appear as follows:

Frustrating	__:	__:	__:	__:	__:	__:	__:	__	Helpful
	1	2	3	4	5	6	7	8	

Tense	__:	__:	__:	__:	__:	__:	__:	__	Relaxed
	1	2	3	4	5	6	7	8	

The contingency model advocates believe that the LPC is an index of behavioral preferences of the leader. A leader with a high-LPC sees good points in the least preferred co-worker and has as his or her preference the desire for strong emotional and affective ties with others. The low-LPC person, however, has different preferences and derives satisfaction from achievement.[7]

SOME RELEVANT RESEARCH

■ Over the past two decades, Fiedler and advocates of the contingency model have studied military, educational, and industrial leaders. In a summary of 63 studies based on 454 separate groups, Fiedler suggests the kind of leadership which is the most appropriate for the situational conditions.[8] Figure 10–2 summarizes his analysis.

The situational characteristics are shown at the bottom of Figure 10–2 The vertical axis indicates the correlation between a leader's LPC score and the group's performance. A median correlation above the midline shows that the relationship-oriented leaders tend to perform better than the task-oriented leaders. A median correlation below the midline indicates that the task-oriented leaders perform better than the relationship-oriented leaders.

The data presented in Figure 10–2 imply a number of things about effective leaders. First, task-oriented leaders tend to perform better than relationship-oriented leaders in situations that are very favorable (I, II, III) and in those that are unfavorable (VIII). Relationship-oriented leaders tend to perform better than task-oriented leaders in situations that are intermediate in favorableness (IV, V, and VII). These findings support the notion that both types of leaders are effective in certain situations.

---

[6] Fiedler, *A Theory of Leadership Effectiveness*, p. 41.

[7] Ibid.

[8] Fred E. Fiedler, "How Do You Make Leaders More Effective? New Answers to an Old Puzzle," *Organizational Dynamics*, Autumn 1972, pp. 3–8.

FIGURE 10–2
A Summary of Contingency Model Research

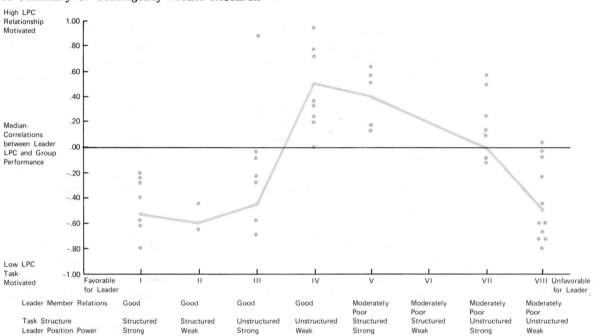

Leader Member Relations	Good	Good	Good	Good	Moderately Poor	Moderately Poor	Moderately Poor	Moderately Poor
Task Structure	Structured	Structured	Unstructured	Unstructured	Structured	Structured	Unstructured	Unstructured
Leader Position Power	Strong	Weak	Strong	Weak	Strong	Weak	Strong	Weak

Source: Fred E. Fiedler, *A Theory of Leadership Effectiveness* (New York: McGraw-Hill, 1967), p. 146.

Second, the findings indicate that the performance of a leader depends as much on the situational favorableness as it does on the individual in the leadership position. Hence, an organization can change leadership effectiveness by attempting to change the leader's behavior or by changing the leader's situation.

Can Leaders Be Trained?

Fiedler states:

> Fitting the man to the leadership job by selection and training has not been spectacularly successful. It is surely easier to change almost anything in the job situation than a man's personality and his leadership style.[9]

It is assumed that changing a leader's style through training is an extremely difficult task.

Fiedler contends that training programs and experience can improve a leader's power and influence if the situational favorableness is high. This

---

[9]Fred E. Fiedler, "Engineering the Job to Fit the Manager," *Harvard Business Review*, September–October 1965, p. 115. Also see Fred E. Fiedler, "The Effects of Leadership Training and Experience: A Contingency Model Interpretation," *Administrative Science Quarterly*, December 1972, pp. 453–70, and Walter Hill, "Leadership Style: Rigid or Flexible?" *Organizational Behavior and Human Performance*, February 1973, pp. 35–47.

means that a training program which improves a leader's power and influence may benefit the relationship-oriented person, but it could be detrimental to the task-oriented person.

Since training program stimulated changes are so elusive, the better alternative is to change the favorableness of the situation. A first step recommended by Fiedler is to determine whether leaders are task- or relationship-oriented. Next, the organization needs to diagnose and classify the situational favorableness of its leadership positions. Finally, the organization must select the best strategy to bring about improved effectiveness. If leadership training is selected as an option, then it should devote special attention to teaching participants how to modify their environments and their jobs to fit their styles of leadership. That is, leaders should be trained to change their leadership situations. Fielder's recent work indicates that when leaders can recognize the situations in which they are most successful, they can then begin to modify their own situations.[10]

A Critique of the Contingency Model

Fiedler's model and research has created a number of pointed criticisms and concerns. First, Graen and others present evidence that research support for the model is not strong especially if studies conducted by researchers not associated with Fiedler are examined.[11] The earlier support and enthusiasm for the model came from Fielder and his students who conducted numerous studies of leaders. Second, a number of researchers have called attention to the questionable measurement of the LPC. These researchers claim that the reliability and validity of the LPC questionnaire measure is low.[12] Third, the meaning of the variables presented by Fiedler is not clear. For example, what is the point at which a "structured" task becomes an "unstructured" task? Who can define or display this point? Finally, critics claim that Fiedler's theory can accommodate nonsupportive results. This point is specifically made by one critic who states:

> Fiedler has revealed his genius twice; first, in devising the model, which stands like calculus to arithmetic compared with previous leadership models, and second, in his ability to integrate new findings into his models.[13]

Despite these incisive criticisms, Fiedler's contingency model has made significant contributions to the study and application of leadership princi-

---

[10] Fred E. Fiedler, "The Leadership Game: Matching the Man to the Situation," *Organizational Dynamics*, Winter 1976, pp. 6–16.

[11] G. Graen, J. B. Orris, and K. M. Alvares, "Contingency Model of Leadership Effectiveness: Some Experimental Results," *Journal of Applied Psychology*, June 1971, pp. 196–201.

[12] C. A. Schriesheim, B. D. Bannister, and W. H. Money, "Psychometric Properties of the LPC Scale: An Extension of Rice's Review," *Academy of Management Review*, April 1979, pp. 287–90.

[13] Joe Kelly, *Organizational Behavior: Its Data, First Principles, and Applications* (Homewood, Ill.: Richard D. Irwin, 1980), p. 367. © 1980 by Richard D. Irwin, Inc.

ples. He called direct attention to the situational nature of leadership. The Fiedler view of leadership also stimulated numerous research studies and much-needed debate about the dynamics of leader behavior. Certainly Fiedler has played one of the most prominent roles in encouraging the scientific study of leadership in work settings. He pointed the way and made others uncomfortably aware of the complexities of the leadership process.

THE VROOM-YETTON MODEL OF LEADERSHIP

■ Many early attempts at explaining optimal leadership behavior had an autocratic orientation. The leader made decisions, issued orders to subordinates, monitored their performance, and made necessary adjustments. However, behavioral scientists have suggested that subordinates should participate more in the decision-making process.

The research evidence provides some, but not overwhelming, support for participative decision making (PDM). In fact, it appears that PDM, like all of the leader's behaviors and traits has consequences which vary from one situation to another. Vroom and Yetton have developed a leadership decision-making model which indicates the kinds of situations in which various degrees of PDM would be appropriate.[14]

In contrast to Fiedler, Vroom and Yetton attempt to provide a normative model that a leader can use in making decisions. Their approach assumes that there is no one ideal style appropriate for every situation. Unlike Fiedler, Vroom and Yetton assume that leaders must be flexible enough to change styles to fit situations. It was Fiedler's contention that the situation must be altered to fit the fairly rigid leadership style.

Vroom and Yetton in developing their model made a number of assumptions. These were:

a. The model should be of value to leaders or managers in determining which leadership styles they should use in various situations.
b. No single leadership style is applicable to all situations.
c. The main focus should be the problem to be solved and the situation in which the problem occurs.
d. The leadership style used in one situation should not constrain the method used in other situations.
e. There are a number of social processes that will influence the amount of participation by subordinates in problem solving.

Applying these assumptions resulted in a model that is concerned with leadership decision making.

---

[14] Victor H. Vroom and Philip Yetton, *Leadership and Decision Making* (Pittsburgh: University of Pittsburgh Press, 1973), © 1973 by the University of Pittsburgh Press.

Decision Effectiveness: Quality and Acceptance

The Vroom-Yetton model emphasizes two criteria of decision effectiveness: quality and acceptance. *Decision quality* refers to the objective aspects of a decision that influence subordinates' performance aside from any direct impact on motivation. Some job-related decisions are linked to performance, while other kinds of decisions are relatively unimportant. For example, determining work flow patterns and layout, performance goals and deadlines, or work assignments usually has an important influence on group performance. On the other hand, selecting work area location for water coolers or the type of cafeteria furniture to buy has no consequence on group performance. When decision quality is important for performance and subordinates possess the ability and information that the leader does not possess, the Vroom-Yetton model would indicate that the leader use a decision procedure that allows subordinate participation.

Decision acceptance is the degree of subordinate commitment to the decision. There are many situations in which a course of action, even if it is technically correct, can fail, because it is resisted by those who have to execute it. In judging whether a problem requires subordinate commitment, the leader needs to look for two things: (1) Are subordinates going to have to execute the decision under conditions in which initiative and judgment will be required? and (2) Are subordinates likely to "feel strongly" about the decision? If the answer to either or both of these questions is yes, then the problem possesses an acceptance requirement. When subordinates can accept a decision as theirs, they will be more inclined to implement it effectively.

Five Decision-Making Styles of Leaders

The Vroom-Yetton model designates five decision-making styles that are appropriate for decisions involving none or all of the leader's subordinates. These styles include two types of autocratic style (Al and All), two types of consultative style (Cl and Cll), and a joint or group style (Gll). The five styles are defined in Table 10–1.

The Diagnostic Procedure for Leaders

Vroom and Yetton suggest that leaders perform a diagnosis of the situation and problem by applying a number of decision rules. These rules will help determine which decision-making style of leadership is appropriate for the particular situation. By using a careful diagnosis, the leader would minimize the chances of reducing decision quality and acceptance. The diagnosis decision rules are:

1. *The Leader-Information Rule.* If the quality of the decision is important, and the leader does not possess enough information or expertise to solve the problem alone, then Al is eliminated as a possible style.
2. *The Goal Congruence Rule.* If the quality of the decision is important and subordinates are not likely to pursue the organizational goals in their efforts to solve the problem, then Gll is eliminated as a possible style.
3. *Unstructured Problem Rule.* In decisions in which the quality of the

TABLE 10–1
Five Decision Styles

Group Problems

AI. You solve the problem or make the decision yourself, using information available to you at the time.

AII. You obtain the necessary information from your subordinates, then decide the solution to the problem yourself. You may or may not tell your subordinates what the problem is in getting the information from them. The role played by your subordinates in making the decision is clearly one of providing the necessary information to you, rather than generating or evaluating alternative solutions.

CI. You share the problem with the relevant subordinates individually, getting their ideas and suggestions without bring them together as a group. Then you make the decision, which may or may not reflect your subordinates' influence.

CII. You share the problem with your subordinates as a group, obtaining their collective ideas and suggestions. Then you make the decision, which may or may not reflect your subordinates' influence.

GII. You share the problem with your subordinates as a group. Together you generate and evaluate alternatives and attempt to reach agreement (consensus) on a solution. Your role is much like that of chairman. You do not try to influence the group to adopt "your" solution, and you are willing to accept and implement any solution which has the support of the entire group

Note: A = autocratic; C = consultative; G = group.
Source: Reprinted from *Leadership and Decision-Making*, p. 13, by Victor H. Vroom and Philip W. Yetton, by permission of the University of Pittsburgh Press. © 1973 by the University of Pittsburgh Press.

decision is important, if the leader lacks the necessary information or expertise to solve the problem alone, and if the problem is unstructured, the method of solving the problem should provide for interaction among subordinates likely to possess relevant information. Thus, Al, All, and Cl are eliminated as possible styles.

4. *The Acceptance Rule.* If the acceptance of the decision by subordinates is critical to effective implementation and if it is not certain that an autocratic decision will be accepted, Al and All are eliminated as a possible styles.

5. *The Conflict Rule.* If the acceptance of the decision is critical, an autocratic decision is not certain to be accepted, and disagreement among subordinates in methods of attaining the organizational goal is likely, the methods used in solving the problem should enable those in disagreement to resolve their differences with full knowledge of the prob-

lem. Accordingly, under these conditions, AI, AII, and CI, which permit no interaction among subordinates and therefore provide no opportunity for those in conflict to resolve their differences, are eliminated as feasible styles. Their use runs the risk of leaving some of the subordinates with less than the needed commitment to the final decision.

6. *The Fairness Rule.* If the quality of the decision is unimportant but acceptance is critical and not certain to result from an autocratic decision, it is important that the decision process generate acceptance. The decision process should permit the subordinates to interact with one another and negotiate over the fair method of resolving any differences with full responsibility on them for determining what is fair and equitable. Accordingly, under these circumstances, AI, AII, CI, and CII are eliminated from the feasible alternatives.

7. *The Acceptance Priority Rule.* If acceptance is critical and not certain to result from an autocratic decision, and if subordinates are motivated to pursue the organizational goals represented in the problem, then methods that provide equal partnership in the decision-making process can provide greater acceptance without risking decision quality. Accordingly, AI, AII, CI, and CII are eliminated from the feasible set of styles.

These seven decision rules are used for determining what procedures should not be used by a leader in a given situation. The first three rules are designed to protect decision quality. The remaining four rules are designed to protect decision acceptance. The application of the seven decision rules is illustrated by use of a decision-tree chart. One such chart is shown in Figure 10–3. The chart is read from left to right. Begin by considering the situation and asking question A. If the answer is no, question D is then asked, but if the answer to A is yes, ask question B. The leader would proceed from left to right until a terminal or end point is reached. For example, the feasible solutions at point 1 are AI, AII, CI, CII, and GII. On the other hand, the feasible solution suggested at point 11 is GII. Each of the styles suggested is likely to lead to a high-quality decision acceptable to subordinates. Since this is the case, most leaders and managers believe it is wisest to choose the most autocratic of the styles. The leader can save time by doing so without risking decision quality or acceptance. The specific style of leadership attempted would be based on the time needed to make a decision, the leader's preference, and the ability, knowledge, and experience of subordinates. Vroom and Yetton have developed a time-efficient Model A version of the decision tree,[15] which would lead to the selection of the least time consuming leadership style. The decision tree used in Figure 10–3 is the Model B or group development version. It maximizes

------

[15] Victor H. Vroom, "Can Leaders Learn to Lead?" *Organizational Dynamics*, Winter 1976, pp. 17–28.

FIGURE 10–3
Decision Process Flowchart (feasible set)

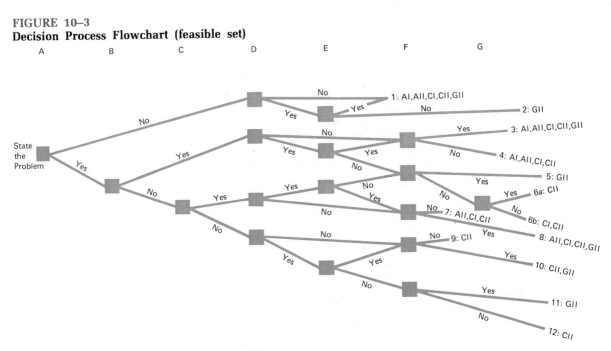

A. Does the problem possess a quality requirement?
B. Do I have sufficient information to make a high-quality decision?
C. Is the problem structured?
D. Is acceptance of the decision by subordinates important for effective implementation?
E. If I were to make the decision by myself, am I reasonably certain that it would be accepted by my subordinates?
F. Do subordinates share the organizational goals to be attained in solving this problem?
G. Is conflict among subordinates likely in preferred solutions?

the development of subordinates through increased participation in decision making when possible.

Application of the Vroom-Yetton Model

Vroom and Yetton have developed actual decision-making scenarios that portray how the model shown in Figure 10–3 can be applied. A person reading the scenarios is asked to assume the role of a leader or manager and to describe the behavior or style (e.g., AI, AII, CI, CII, or GII) that he or she would apply to the situation described. An example of a scenario is presented in Figure 10–4.

Research on the Vroom-Yetton Model

The Vroom-Yetton model is still relatively new and many research questions raised by it need to be tested. However, the research to date can be divided into two types: (1) *verification*—which is aimed at verifying the model's prescriptions, and (2) *descriptive*—which attempts to identify the determinants of actual leader or managerial behavior and the degree to which such behavior conforms to the model's prescriptions.

FIGURE 10–4
A Decision Scenario

You are supervising the work of 12 engineers. Their formal training and work experience are very similar, permitting you to use them interchangeably on projects. Yesterday, your manager informed you that a request had been received from an overseas affiliate for four engineers to go abroad on extended loan for a period of six to eight months. For a number of reasons, he argued, and you agreed, that this request should be met from your group. All of your engineers are capable of handling this assignment, and from the standpoint of present and future projects, there is no particular reason why any one should be retained over any other. The problem is somewhat complicated by the fact that the overseas assignment is in what is generally regarded in the company as an undesirable location.

Analysis (based on Figure 10–3)

Question A (Quality requirement?): NO
Question D (Subordinate acceptance critical?): YES
Question E (Is acceptance likely without participation?): NO

Feasible set of decision procedures: GII
Minimum time solution: GII

Source: Adapted from *Leadership and Decision-Making*, pp. 41–42, by Victor H. Vroom and Philip W. Yetton by permission of the University of Pittsburgh Press. © 1973 by the University of Pittsburgh Press.

Verification Research. One study examined 181 actual decision-making situations and behavior in these situations.[16] The model was then used to predict those decisions which would be effective (i.e., those in which the manager's behavior was one of the acceptable styles) and those decisions which would be ineffective (i.e., those in which the manager's behavior violated one of the seven decision rules pertaining to quality and acceptance). These predictions were then compared to the actual ratings of decision effectiveness. The results showed substantial support for the model. Of those decisions where the manager's behavior agreed with the feasible style of leadership, 68 percent were judged to have successful results. Of those decisions where the manager's behavior disagreed with the feasible style of leadership, only 22 percent had successful results.

Another test of the model was conducted in 45 retail franchises in the cleaning industry.[17] Store managers who exhibited conformity to the Vroom-Yetton leadership style prescriptions had more productive operations and more satisfied subordinates than managers exhibiting less conformity to the model.

---

[16] Victor H. Vroom and Arthur G. Jago, "On the Validity of the Vroom-Yetton Model," *Journal of Applied Psychology*, April 1978, pp. 151–62.

[17] C. Margerison and R. Glube, "Leadership Decision Making: An Empirical Test of the Vroom and Yetton Model" (Manuscript, 1978).

Descriptive Research. Descriptive research has attempted to better understand how leaders or managers *do* behave rather than how managers *should* behave. The research suggests that most managers permit a greater overall level of participative decision making than seems to be required.[18] Although the model suggests that the AI (autocratic) leadership style is appropriate for various situations, managers tend to avoid its use. On the other hand, managers seem to overuse the CI and CII styles.

Other research using the decision situation scenarios reveals that female managers are more participative than male managers,[19] and that business school students are more participative than actual managers.[20] In addition, it was found that managers higher in the managerial hierarchy are more participative than managers lower in the same hierarchy.[21]

A Critique of the Vroom-Yetton Model

The Vroom-Yetton model has been specifically criticized on a number of issues.[22] First, the reliance on self-report data is considered a major threat to the validity of the model. Leaders (managers) are asked to list the details of one successful and one unsuccessful decision-making situation they personally faced. The experience reporting occurs after the manager has studied the five decision styles and rational problem solving and practiced choosing a decision process for each of 30 decision scenarios.

It is proposed by one critic that managers report successful decisions as using a rational decision process that was appropriate to the situation, regardless of their actual behavior.[23] The self-reported behavior would tend to match the rational model, and the Vroom-Yetton model would be validated. It is noted that Jago and Vroom report that subordinates' perceptions of managerial behavior do not correlate significantly with the superior's own descriptions of the same behavior.[24] This raises another question about the validity of manager (leader) behavior self-reports.

Second, the methods just described to determine a leader's view of successful and unsuccessful behavior are also subject to experimenter and social desirability effects. Since managers have previously studied rational problem solving there may be an experimenter influence on the results. Furthermore, there may be a tendency to want to appear more participative

[18] Victor H. Vroom and Arthur G. Jago, "Decision Making as a Social Process: Normative and Descriptive Models of Leader Behavior," *Decision Sciences*, October 1974, pp. 743–69.

[19] Rick Steers, "Individual Differences in Participative Decision Making," *Human Relations*, September 1977, pp. 837–47.

[20] Arthur G. Jago and Victor H. Vroom, "Predicting Leader Behavior from a Measure of Behavioral Intent," *Academy of Management Journal* (in press).

[21] Arthur G. Jago, "Hierarchical Level Determinants of Participative Leader Behavior" (Ph.D. dissertation, Yale University, 1977).

[22] R. H. George Field, "A Critique of the Vroom-Yetton Contingency Model of Leadership Behavior," *Academy of Management Review*, April 1979, pp. 249–257.

[23] Ibid.

[24] Arthur G. Jago and Victor H. Vroom, "Perceptions of Leadership Style: Superior and Subordinate Descriptions of Decision-Making Behavior," in *Leadership Frontiers*, ed. J. G. Hunt and L. L. Larson (Carbondale: Southern Illinois University Press, 1975), pp. 103–20.

than one actually is in decision-making situations. It is socially desirable to permit followers or subordinates to participate.

Despite criticisms the Vroom-Yetton approach to leadership is an important contribution. The model was developed after thorough experimentation with similar models. In addition, tests of the model are at least as rigorous and in most cases seem more carefully planned and executed than what is being offered as tests of other leadership approaches. Also one important organizational implication of the model involves training. If current and future research support the validity of the model, more effective leadership will result if leaders are trained or instructed to use the model.[25] Training would enable leaders to choose the appropriate level of follower/subordinate participation.

PATH-GOAL MODEL

■ Like the other situational or contingency leadership approaches, the path-goal model attempts to predict leadership effectiveness in different situations. According to this model, leaders are effective because of their positive impact on followers' motivation, ability to perform, and satisfaction. The theory is designated path-goal because it focuses on how the leader influences the followers' perceptions of work goals, self-development goals, and paths to goal attainment.[26]

The foundation of path-goal theory is the expectancy motivation theory, discussed in Chapter 4. Briefly, expectancy theory states that an individual's attitudes, job satisfaction, behavior, and job effort can be predicted from: (1) the degree to which the job or behavior is seen as leading to various outcomes (expectancy) and (2) the preferences for these outcomes (valences). Thus, it is proposed that individuals are satisfied with their jobs if they believe it leads to desirable outcomes, and they work hard if they believe that this effort will result in desirable outcomes. The implication of these assumptions for leadership is that subordinates are motivated by leader style or behavior to the extent it influences expectancies (goal paths) and valences (goal attractiveness).

Some early work on the path-goal theory asserts that leaders will be effective by making rewards available to subordinates and by making these rewards contingent on the subordinates' accomplishment of specific goals.[27] It is argued that an important part of the leader's job is to clarify

---

[25] Arthur G. Jago, "Leadership Perspectives in Theory and Research," draft paper in College of Business Working Paper Series, University of Houston, 1979, p. 31.

[26] Robert J. House, "A Path-Goal Theory of Leadership Effectiveness," *Administrative Science Quarterly*, September 1971, pp. 321–39. Also see Robert J. House and Terence R. Mitchell, "Path-Goal Theory of Leadership," *Journal of Contemporary Business*, Autumn 1974, pp. 81–98, which is the basis for the following discussion.

[27] Martin G. Evans, "The Effects of Supervisory Behavior on the Path-Goal Relationship," *Organizational Behavior and Human Performance*, May 1970, pp. 277–98. Also see Martin G. Evans, "Effects of Supervisory Behavior: Extensions of Path-Goal Theory of Motivation," *Journal of Applied Psychology*, April 1974, pp. 172–78.

for subordinates the kind of behavior tht will most likely result in goal accomplishment. This activity is referred to as *path clarification*.

This early path-goal work led to the development of a complex theory involving four specific kinds of leader behavior (directive, supportive, participative, and achievement) and three types of subordinate attitudes (job satisfaction, acceptance of the leader, and expectations about effort-performance-reward relationships.)[28] The *directive leader* tends to let subordinates know what is expected of them. The *supportive leader* treats subordinates as equals. A *participative leader* consults with subordinates and uses their suggestions and ideas before reaching a decision. The *achievement-oriented* leader sets challenging goals, expects subordinates to perform at the highest level, and continually seeks improvement in performance.

Research studies suggest that these four styles can be practiced by the same leader in various situations.[29] These findings are contrary to the Fiedler notion concerning the difficulty of altering style. The path-goal approach suggests more flexibility than the Fiedler contingency model. On the other hand, the path-goal approach is similar to that of Vroom and Yetton in that it also argues for flexibility in leader behavior.

The Main Path-Goal Propositions

The path-goal theory has led to the development of two important propositions:

1. Leader behavior is acceptable and satisfying to the extent that the subordinates perceive such behavior as an immediate source of satisfaction or as instrumental to future satisfaction.
2. Leader behavior will be motivational to the extent that it makes satisfaction of subordinates' needs contingent on effective performance and it complements the environment of subordinates by providing the guidance, clarity of direction, and rewards necessary for effective performance.[30]

According to the path-goal theory leaders should increase the number and kinds of rewards available to subordinates. In addition, the leader should provide guidance and counsel to clarify the manner in which these rewards can be obtained. This means the leader should help subordinates clarify realistic expectancies and reduce the barriers to the accomplishment of valued goals. For example, counseling employees on their chances of receiving a promotion and helping them eliminate skill deficiencies so that a promotion becomes more of a reality are appropriate leadership behaviors. The leader works at making the path to goals for subordinates as clear

---

[28] Robert J. House and Gary Dessler, "The Path-Goal Theory of Leadership: Some Post Hoc and A Priori Tests," in *Contingency Approaches to Leadership*, ed. James G. Hunt (Carbondale: Southern Illinois University, 1974).

[29] House, "A Path-Goal Theory," and House and Dessler, "Path-Goal Theory."

[30] These propositions are presented by House and Mitchell, "Path-Goal Theory of Leadership," p. 84.

as possible. The style that is best suited to accomplish this is selected and applied. Thus, the path-goal approach requires flexibility from the leader to use what is appropriate in a particular situation.

The Situational Factors

Two types of situational or contingency variables are considered in the path-goal theory. The two are the *personal characteristics of subordinates* and the *environmental pressures and demands* with which subordinates must cope in order to accomplish work goals and derive satisfaction.

A personal characteristic which is important is subordinates' perception of their own ability. The higher the degree of perceived ability relative to the task demands, the less the subordinate will accept a directive leader style. This directive style of leadership would be viewed as unnecessarily close. In addition, it has been discovered that a person's *locus of control* also affects responses. Individuals who have an internal locus of control (they believe that rewards are contingent upon their efforts) are generally more satisfied with a participative style, while individuals who have an external locus of control (believe that rewards are beyond their personal control) are generally more satisfied with a directive style.[31]

The environmental variables include factors which are not within the control of the subordinate but which are important to satisfaction or to the ability to perform effectively.[32] These include the tasks, the formal authority system of the organization, and the work group. Any of these environmental factors can motivate or constrain the subordinate. The environmental forces may also serve as a reward for acceptable levels of performance. For example, the subordinate could be motivated by the work group and receive satisfaction from co-workers' acceptance for doing a job according to group norms.

The path-goal theory proposes that leader behavior will be motivational to the extent that it helps subordinates cope with environmental uncertainties. A leader who is able to reduce the uncertainties of the job is considered to be a motivator because he or she increases the subordinates' expectations that their efforts will lead to desirable rewards.

Figure 10–5 presents the features of the path-goal approach. The path-goal approach has not been subjected to a complete test. Parts of the model, however, have been examined in field settings. One study found that when task structure (the repetitiveness or routine of the job) was high, directive leader behavior was negatively related to satisfaction; when task structure was low, directive leader behavior was positively related to satisfaction. Also when task structure was high, supportive leadership was positively related to satisfaction, whereas under low task structure there was no relationship between supportive leader behavior and satisfaction.[33]

---

[31] Ibid.

[32] Ibid., p. 87.

[33] House and Dessler, "Path-Goal Theory."

FIGURE 10–5
The Path-Goal Model

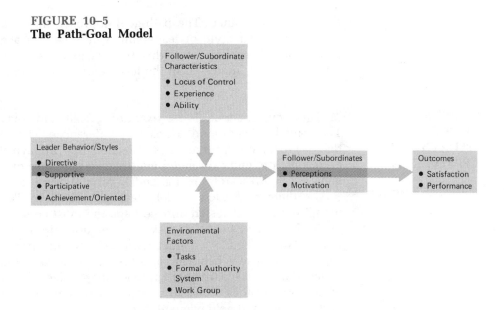

A Critique of the
Path-Goal Model

The path-goal model, like the Vroom-Yetton model, warrants further empirical attention. There is still some question about the predictive power of the path-goal model. One researcher suggested that subordinate performance may be the cause of changes in leader behavior instead of, as predicted by the model, the other way around.[34] A review of the path-goal approach suggested that the model has resulted in only a few hypotheses being developed. These reviewers also point to the record of inconsistent research results associated with the model. They note that research has consistently shown that the higher the task structure of subordinate jobs, the higher will be the relationship between supportive leader behavior and subordinate satisfaction. However, the second main hypothesis of the path-goal model has not received consistent support. This hypothesis—the higher the task structure, the lower the relationship between directive leader behavior and subordinate satisfaction—has received only some support.[35]

On the positive side one must admit that the path-goal model is an improvement over the trait and personal-behavioral theories. It attempts to indicate which factors affect the motivation to perform. In addition, the path-goal approach introduces both situational factors and individual differences when examining leader behavior and outcomes such as satisfac-

---

[34]C. Greene, "Questions of Causation in the Path-Goal Theory of Leadership," *Academy of Management Journal*, March 1979, pp. 22–41.

[35]Chester A. Schriesheim and Angelo DeNisi, "Task Dimensions as Moderators of the Effects of Instrumental Leader Behavior: A Path-Goal Approach," *Academy of Management Proceedings*, 1979, pp. 103–6.

tion and performance. The path-goal approach makes an effort to explain why a particular style of leadership works best in a given situation. As more research accumulates, this type of explanation will have practical utility for those interested in the leadership process in work settings.

COMPARISON OF THE SITUATIONAL APPROACHES

■ Three current models for examining leadership have been presented. These models have similarities and differences. They are similar in that they (1) focus on the dynamics of leadership, (2) have stimulated research on leadership, and (3) remain controversial because of measurement problems, limited research testing, and/or contradictory research results.

The themes of each model are summarized in Table 10–2. Fiedler's model is the most tested and perhaps the most controversial. His view of leader behavior centers on task- and relationship-oriented tendencies and how these tendencies interact with task and position power. Vroom and Yetton view leader behavior in terms of autocratic, consultative, or group styles. Finally, the path-goal approach emphasizes the instrumental actions of leaders and four styles to conduct these actions—directive, supportive, participative, and achievement-oriented.

The situational variables discussed in each approach differ somewhat. There is also a different view of outcome criteria for assessing how successful the leader behavior has been. Fiedler discusses leader effectiveness; Vroom and Yetton discuss the quality of a decision, follower acceptance,

TABLE 10–2
A Comparison of Three Situational Approaches to Leadership

Approach	Leader Behavior/Style	Situational Factors	Outcome Criteria
Fiedler's contingency model	Task-oriented (low LPC) Relationship-oriented (high LPC)	Task structure Leader-member relations Position power	Group's effectiveness
Vroom-Yetton	Autocratic Consultative Group	Quality of decision Information requirement Problem structure Follower's acceptance of decision Mutuality of follower and organizational goals Level of follower conflict	Quality of decision Acceptance of decision by follower's Time to make decisions
Path-goal	Directive Supportive Participative Achievement-oriented	Follower characteristics Environmental factors	Satisfaction Performance

Source: Adapted from Edwin P. Hollander, *Leadership Dynamics* (New York: Free Press, 1978).

and the timeliness of the decision; the path-goal approach focuses on satisfaction and performance.

Managers can acquire a better understanding of leadership by reviewing each of these models. Each model is more complex than any of those covered in the previous chapter, but each is able to cope more thoroughly with the complexities of leadership.

SOME REMAINING ISSUES REGARDING LEADERSHIP

■ The trait, personal-behavioral, and situational theories have advanced the understanding of leadership and have stimulated important research studies. However, there still remain a number of gaps in the current understanding of the process and outcomes of leadership in work organizations. Three particularly interesting leadership issues are (1) does leadership cause or is it more significantly affected by follower satisfaction and performance; (2) what constraints are there on leadership effectiveness; and (3) are there substitutes for leadership that affect satisfaction and performance.

Is Leader Behavior a Cause or Effect?

The discussion to this point has implied that leader behavior has an effect on the follower's performance and job satisfaction. There is, however, a sound basis from which one can argue that follower performance and satisfaction cause the leader to vary his or her leadership style. It has been argued that a person will develop positive attitudes toward objects which are instrumental to the satisfaction of his or her needs.[36] This argument can be extended to leader-follower relationships. For example, organizations reward leaders (managers) based on the performance of followers (subordinates). If this is the case it would be possible to have the leader develop positive attitudes toward high-performing followers. The expectation is that the person whose behavior causes another to be positively reinforced will in return be rewarded by the other.[37]

In a field study, data were collected from first-line managers and, for each manager, two of his first-line supervisors. The purpose of this research was to assess the direction of causal influence in relationships between leader and follower variables. The results strongly suggested that (1) leader consideration behavior caused subordinate satisfaction, (2) follower performance caused changes in the leader emphasis on both consideration and structuring behavior-performance relationship.[38]

The research available on the cause and/or effect issue is still quite limited. It is premature to conclude that all leader behavior or even a significant portion of such behavior is a response to follower behavior. However, there is a need to examine the leader-follower relationship in terms of a

---

[36]D. Katz and E. Stotland, "A Preliminary Statement to a Theory of Attitude Structure and Change," in *Psychology: A Study of Science,* ed. S. Koch (New York: McGraw-Hill, 1959).

[37]Charles N. Greene, "The Reciprocal Nature of Influence between Leader and Subordinate," *Journal of Applied Psychology,* April 1975, pp. 187–93.

[38]Greene, "Reciprocal Nature," p. 458.

reciprocal causation. That is, leader behavior causes follower behavior and that follower behavior causes leader behavior.

Constraints on Leader Behavior

Many theorists believe that appropriate leader behavior can be produced by proper training. However, external, organizational, group, and individual constraints affect leader behavior. The constraints imposed on leaders include:

External Factors.   A leader without skilled or able followers will have difficulty no matter how able he or she is. The availability of skilled and able followers is effected by the *market* (an external force). In some geographical areas there is simply a shortage of skilled people.

Organizational Policies.   The organization itself may not encourage or support a particular leadership style. For example, the Vroom-Yetton consultative style may not be permitted despite its suitability. The organization may also limit the degree of interaction between leaders and followers and the ability of leaders to reward followers. These limitations may have a negative impact on the overall effectiveness of leaders.

Group Factors.   A leader must operate within the boundaries and expectations of specific groups. The leader is expected to act and react in a particular manner. Deviation from the expected role behaviors will be challenged or ignored. Pressures to conform can emanate from co-workers, followers, or superiors. Each of these sources can constrain actual leader behavior.

Individual Skills and Abilities.   The skills and abilities of a leader are also constraints. A leader can possess only so much expertise, energy, and power. Some situations will be outside of the leader's skills and ability range. In these situations the leader's effectiveness will be seriously diminished.

These four broad categories of constraints indicate that the discretion of leaders can and often is constrained by external, organizational, group, and individual factors. Recognition of these constraints is an important step in studying, modifying, and in some cases increasing the effects of leader behavior.

Substitutes for Leadership

A wide variety of individual, task, environmental, and organizational characteristics have been identified as factors that influence relationships between leader behavior and follower satisfaction and performance. Some of these variables (e.g., follower expectations of leader behavior) appear to influence which leadership style will enable the leader to motivate and direct followers. The effects of others, however, is as a "substitute" for leadership. Substitute variables tend to negate the leader's ability to either increase or decrease follower satisfaction and/or performance.[39]

[39] Steven Kerr and John M. Jermier, "Substitutes for Leadership: Their Meaning and Measurement," *Organizational Behavior and Human Performance*, December 1978, pp. 375–403.

It is claimed that substitutes for leadership are prominent in many organizational settings. However, the dominant leadership approaches fail to include substitutes for leadership in discussing the leader behavior-follower satisfaction and performance relationship.

Table 10–3 based on previously conducted research provides substitutes for only two of the more popular leader behavior styles—relationship-ori-

TABLE 10–3
Substitutes for Leadership

	Will Tend to Neutralize	
Characteristic	Relationship- Oriented	Task-Oriented
Of the subordinate:		
1. Ability, experience, training, knowledge		X
2. Need for independence	X	X
3. "Professional" orientation	X	X
4. Indifference toward organizational rewards	X	X
Of the task:		
5. Unambiguous and routine		X
6. Methodologically invariant		X
7. Provides its own feedback concerning accomplishment		X
8. Intrinsically satisfying	X	
Of the organization:		
9. Formalization (explicit plans, goals, and areas of responsibility)		X
10. Inflexibility (rigid, unbending rules and procedures)		X
11. Highly specified and active advisory and staff functions		X
12. Closely knit, cohesive work groups	X	X
13. Organizational rewards not within the leader's control	X	X
14. Spatial distance between superior and subordinates	X	X

Source: Adapted from Steven Kerr and John M. Jermier, "Substitutes for Leadership: Their Meaning and Measurement," *Organizational Behavior and Human Performance*, December 1978, p. 378.

ented and task-oriented. For each of these leader behaviors, Kerr and Jermier present which substitutes (follower, task, or the organization) will serve to neutralize the style.[40] A substitute is considered to be a person or thing acting in place of leader behavior.

Admittedly we do not fully understand the leader-follower relationship in organizational settings. The need to continue searching for guidelines and principles is apparent. This searching now seems to be centered on more careful analysis of a situational perspective of leadership and on is-

---

[40] Ibid.

sues such as the cause-effect question, the constraints on leader behavior, and substitutes for leadership.

MAJOR MANAGERIAL ISSUES

A. The *situational approach* emphasizes the importance of forces within the leader, the subordinates, and the organization. These forces interact and must be properly diagnosed if effectiveness is to be achieved.

B. The *contingency model* proposes that the performance of groups is dependent on the interaction of leadership style and situational favorableness. The three crucial situational factors are leader-member relations, task structure, and position power.

C. The *contingency model* is not without its critics. Although weaknesses are apparent in the model, there is refinement work being done by numerous researchers. This work is not, however, providing meaningful behavioral explanations to practicing managers who are interested in how they should lead others.

D. Vroom and Yetton have developed a leadership model that can be used to select the amount of group decision-making participation needed in a variety of problem situations. The model suggests that the amount of subordinate participation depends on the leader's skill and knowledge, whether a quality decision is needed, the extent the problem is structured, and whether acceptance by subordinates is needed to implement the decision.

E. Research gathered to date on the Vroom-Yetton model has been supportive of the prescriptions offered by applying the various decision rules. In general, it appears that leaders permit a greater level of subordinate participation than seems to be required. The research also points out the need for leaders to be flexible so that high-quality decisions, that are accepted by subordinates, can be made in a reasonable amount of time.

F. The leader's role in the *path-goal theory* is to (1) increase the number and kinds of personal payoffs to subordinates and (2) provide guidance and counsel for clarifying paths and reducing problems when seeking various outcomes.

G. There is some evidence that raises the question of whether leader behavior causes follower satisfaction and/or performance or vice versa. Followers may have a significant impact on leader behavior or style.

H. Leaders are constrained by external, organizational, group, and individual factors. These constraints can limit the impact which a leader has on followers.

I. There are substitutes for leader behavior that can influence subordinates. Task, subordinate, and organizational substitutes exist. They include ability, experience, routineness of the task, and group cohesiveness.

DISCUSSION AND REVIEW QUESTIONS

1. A number of the models presented in the chapter emphasize the need for leaders to be flexible. Are there any potential problems associated with what would be classified as flexible leaders?

2. Diagnosis is mentioned as an important function of leadership. Is self-diagnosis of leadership traits, attributes, and styles difficult? Why?

3. What type of research is needed to further develop and modify the Vroom-Yetton model?

4. Select one of the situational models and develop a presentation which would clearly show why this one particular model is valuable to leaders.

5. According to the contingency theory, an alternative to modifying the style of leadership through training is changing the favorableness of the situation. What is meant by changing the favorableness of the situation?

6. What are the similarities in the contingency model and the path-goal leadership approach?

7. Why do some theorists believe that it is extremely difficult to change a leader's style?

8. Why should a leader examine the substitutes for leader behavior?

9. Why are leadership theories becoming more complex?

10. Is personality an important factor in the contingency, and path-goal theories of leadership? Explain.

ADDITIONAL REFERENCES

Argyris, C. "Leadership, Learning, and Changing the Status Quo." *Organizational Dynamics,* 1976, pp. 29–43.

Fiedler, F. E., and L. Mahar. "The Effectiveness of Contingency Model Training: A Review of the Validation of Leader Match." *Personnel Psychology,* 1979, pp. 45–62.

Fox, W. M. "Limits to the Use of Consultative-Participative Management." *California Management Review,* 1977, pp. 17–22.

Griffin, R. W. "Task Design Determinants of Effective Leader Behavior." *Academy of Management Review,* 1979, pp. 215–24.

Heller, F. A. "Leadership, Decision Making and Contingency Theory." *Industrial Relations,* 1973, pp. 183–99.

House, R. J., and M. L. Baetz. "Leadership: Some Generalizations and New Research Directions." *Research in Organizational Behavior,* edited by G. M. Straw. Greenwich, Conn.: JAI Press, 1979.

Jago, A. G. "A Test of Spuriousness in Descriptive Models of Participative Leader Behavior." *Journal of Applied Psychology,* 1978, pp. 383–87.

Janis, I., and L. Mann. *Decision Making: A Psychological Analysis of Conflict, Choice, and Commitment.* New York: Free Press, 1977.

Keller, R. T., and A. D. Szilagyi. "A Longitudinal Study of Leader Reward Behavior, Subordinate Expectancies, and Satisfaction." *Personnel Psychology,* 1978, pp. 119–29.

Lee, J. A. "Leader Power for Managing Change." *Academy of Management Review,* 1977, pp. 73–80.

Salyes, L. R. *Leadership.* New York: McGraw-Hill, 1979.

Sims, H. P. Jr., and A. D. Szilagyi. "Leader Reward Behavior and Subordinate Satisfaction and Performance." *Organizational Behavior and Human Performance,* 1975, pp. 426–38.

Yukl, G. "Toward a Behavioral Theory of Leadership." *Organizational Behavior and Human Performance,* 1971, pp. 414–40.

**A NEW
LEADERSHIP
POSITION**

The Dancey Electronics Company is located in a suburb of Dallas. Management forecasts indicated that the company would enjoy moderate growth during the next 10 years. This growth rate would require the promotion of a number of individuals to newly created positions of general manager which would, in turn, require them to spend most of their time working with departmental managers, and less time on production, output, and cost issues.

The majority of present candidates for the three new general manager positions had been with the company for at least 15 years. They were all skilled in the production aspects of operations. Don Kelly, the vice president, felt, however, that none of the candidates had the training or overall insight into company problems to move smoothly into the general manager positions. The board of directors had decided that the three new general managers would be recruited from within Dancey despite these anticipated problems.

Dancey, in attempting to find the best candidates for the new position, hired a consulting firm, Management Analysis Corporation (MAC), to perform an internal search for qualified individuals. Through interviews, testing, and a review of company records, the consulting firm generated a list of six candidates.

One of the candidates found by MAC was Joe Morris. The analysis used to assess Joe involved the study of environmental variables and his current style of leadership. Exhibit 1 presents a profile of Joe's leadership style and various environmental factors which have some impact on this style.

EXHIBIT 1
Morris Profile of Leadership

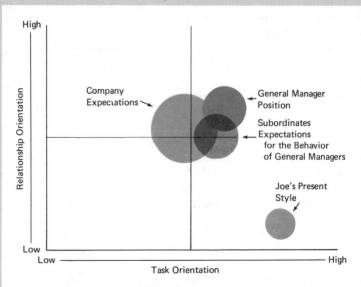

Joe's present style, which is reflected as being high in task orientation and low in relationship orientation, is similar to the style of the other five general manager candidates. The expectations of the company, the potential subordinates of the general manager, and the new position of general manager are not consistent with Joe's or any of the other candidates' present leadership styles. The shaded, intersecting area indicates where the expectations of the company, the new position, and subordinates would be consistent. This is assumed by MAC to be the ideal leadership style for candidates to use once they are promoted to the general manager position.

If Joe or any of the other candidates accepted the general manager jobs, they would have to significantly increase their relationships orientation. If they did not change their orientation there would be, according to the consulting firm, a high probability of failure.

Don Kelly was extremely adamant about not going outside of Dancey to find three potentially successful new general managers. He and the entire board of directors wanted to utilize a recruitment-from-within policy to secure the three best general managers. It was Don's belief that a leader could modify the style of leadership he or she has used to meet new situational demands. This belief, and the internal recruitment plan, led Don to call a meeting to discuss a program to improve the compatibility between the three general managers finally selected—Joe Morris, Randy Cooper, and Gregg Shumate—and the environmental factors: the company, the subordinates, and the requirements of the new position.

Questions for Consideration

1. Do you believe the diagnosis and resulting profile prepared by the Management Analysis Corporation was a necessary step in the process of finding a potentially successful group of general managers? Explain.

2. What alternatives are available to modify the potential effectiveness of Joe Morris in the new general manager position?

3. Why will it be difficult for Joe Morris to modify his style of leadership?

EXPERIENTIAL EXERCISE

**LEADERSHIP
STYLE ANALYSIS**

Objectives

1. To learn how to diagnose different leadership situations.
2. To learn how to apply a systematic procedure for analyzing situations.
3. To improve understanding of how to reach a decision.

Related Topics

Decision making and problem solving when given a number of facts about a situation.

Starting the Exercise

Review the "Decision Process Flowchart" in Figure 10–3. Also examine the Decision Scenario presented in Figure 10–4. The instructor will then form groups of four to five people to analyze each of the following three cases. Try to reach a group consensus on which decision style is best for the particular case. You are to select the best style based on use of the Vroom-Yetton model, available styles, and decision rules. Each case should take between 30 and 45 minutes to analyze as a group.

Case I

Setting: Corporate Headquarters
Your Position: Vice President

As marketing vice president, nonroutine requests from customers are frequently sent to your office. One such request, from a relatively new customer, was for extended terms on a large purchase ($2.5 million) involving several of your product lines. The request is for extremely favorable terms which you would not normally consider except for the high inventory level of most product lines at the present time due to the unanticipated slack period which the company has experienced over the last six months.

You realize that the request is probably a starting point for negotiations and you have proven your abilities to negotiate the most favorable arrangements in the past. As preparation for this negotiation, you have familiarized yourself with the financial situation of the customer using various investment reports you regularly receive.

Reporting to you are four sales managers, each of whom has responsibility for a single product line. They know of the order and, like you, believe that it is important to negotiate terms with minimum risks and maximum return to the company. They are likely to differ on what constitutes an acceptable level of risk. The two younger managers have developed a reputation of being "risk takers" whereas the two more senior managers are substantially more conservative.

Case II

Setting: Toy Manufacturer
Your Position: Vice President, Engineering and Design

You are a vice president in a large toy manufacturing company with responsibilities that include the design of new products that will meet the changing demand in this uncertain and very competitive industry. Your design teams, each under the supervision of a department head, are therefore under constant pressure to produce novel, marketable ideas.

At the opposite end of the manufacturing process is the quality control department which is under the authority of the vice president, production. When quality control has encountered a serious problem that may be due to design features, their staff has consulted with one or more of your department heads to obtain their recommendations for any changes in the production process. In the wake of consumer concern over the safety of children's toys, however, quality control responsibilities have recently been expanded to ensure not only the quality but the safety of your products. The first major problem in this area has arisen. A preliminary consumer report has "blacklisted" one of your new products without giving any specific reason or justification. This has upset you and others in the organization since it was believed that this product would be one of the most profitable items in the coming Christmas season.

The consumer group has provided your company the opportunity to respond to the report before it is made public. The head of quality control has therefore consulted with your design people, but you are told that they became somewhat defensive and dismissed the report as "overreactive fanatic nonsense." Your people told quality control that, while freak accidents are always possible, the product is certainly safe as designed. They argued that the report should simply be ignored.

Since the issue is far from routine, you have decided to give it your personal attention. Because your design teams have been intimately involved in all aspects of the development of the item, you suspect that their response is itself extreme and perhaps governed more by their emotional reaction to the report than by the facts. You are not convinced that the consumer group is totally irresponsible, and you are anxious to explore the problem in detail and recommend to quality control any changes that may be required from a design standpoint. The firm's image as a producer of high-quality toys could suffer a serious blow if the report is made public and public confidence is lost as a result.

You will have to depend heavily on the background and experience of your design departments to help you in analyzing the problem. Even though quality control will be responsible for the decision to implement any changes you may ultimately recommend, your own subordinates have the background of design experience that could help set standards for what is "safe" and to suggest any design modifications that would meet these criteria.

Case III   Setting: Corporate Headquarters
Your Position: Vice President

The sales executives in your home office spend a gret deal of time visiting regional sales offices. As marketing vice president, you are concerned that the expenses incurred on these trips are excessive—especially now when the economic outlook seems bleak and general belt tightening measures are being carried out in every department.

Having recently been promoted from the ranks of your subordinates, you are keenly aware of some cost saving measures that could be introduced. You have, in fact, asked the accounting department to review a sample of past expense reports, and they have agreed with your conclusion that several highly favored travel "luxuries" could be curtailed. Your executives, for example, could restrict first-class air travel to only those occasions when economy class is unavailable, airport limousine service to hotels could be used instead of taxis where possible, etc. Even more savings could be made if your personnel carefully planned trips such that multiple purposes could be achieved where possible.

The success of any cost saving measures, however, depends on the commitment of your subordinates. You do not have the time (nor the desire) to closely review the expense reports of these executives. You suspect, though, that they do not share your concerns over the matter. Having once been in their position, you know they feel themselves deserving of travel amenities.

The problem is to determine which changes, if any, are to be made in current travel and expense account practices in the light of the new economic conditions.

Exercise Procedures Phase I: 10–15 minutes
Individually read case and select proper decision style using Vroom-Yetton model.

Phase II: 30–45 minutes
Join group appointed by instructor and reach group consensus.

Phase III: 20 minutes
Each group spokesperson presents group's response and rationale to other groups.

These phases should be used for each of the cases.

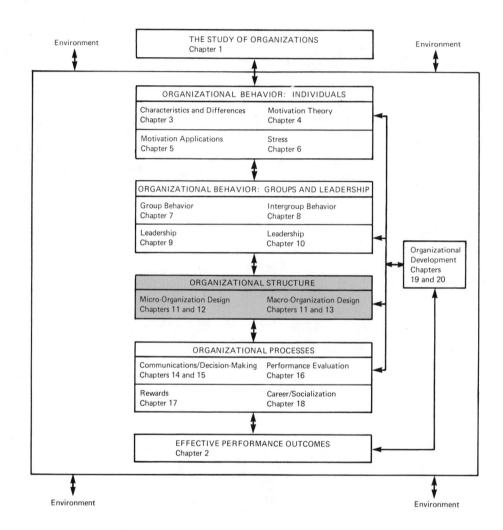

Environment

THE STUDY OF ORGANIZATIONS
Chapter 1

Environment

ORGANIZATIONAL BEHAVIOR: INDIVIDUALS

Characteristics and Differences
Chapter 3

Motivation Theory
Chapter 4

Motivation Applications
Chapter 5

Stress
Chapter 6

ORGANIZATIONAL BEHAVIOR: GROUPS AND LEADERSHIP

Group Behavior
Chapter 7

Intergroup Behavior
Chapter 8

Leadership
Chapter 9

Leadership
Chapter 10

ORGANIZATIONAL STRUCTURE

Micro-Organization Design
Chapters 11 and 12

Macro-Organization Design
Chapters 11 and 13

ORGANIZATIONAL PROCESSES

Communications/Decision-Making
Chapters 14 and 15

Performance Evaluation
Chapter 16

Rewards
Chapter 17

Career/Socialization
Chapter 18

EFFECTIVE PERFORMANCE OUTCOMES
Chapter 2

Organizational
Development
Chapters
19 and 20

Environment

Environment

Part Four

THE STRUCTURE OF ORGANIZATIONS

Chapter 11

The Anatomy of Organizations

AN ORGANIZATIONAL ISSUE FOR DEBATE
The Fixed Optimal Span of Control*

ARGUMENT FOR

The argument regarding the optimal span of control has gone on for many years. The importance of the issue warrants the attention given it. The determination of the managers' spans of control, that is, how many people will report to them, has implications for the behavior of the managers, people reporting to them, and the organization itself. Some of the most influential writers on management and organizational behavior have argued that the optimal span of control is a fixed number—5, 6, or 10 depending upon the writer.

The basis for these writers' views is that the ability of managers to supervise is finite. As more and more people are added to their units, the proportionate amount of time that managers can spend on each individual decreases. Moreover the number of possible interpersonal relationships is 50 times greater for a span of 10 than for a span of 5. Thus it was apparent to some writers that no superior can supervise directly the work of more than five or, at the most, six subordinates whose work interlocks.

*Based upon David D. VanFleet and Arthur G. Bedeian, "A History of the Span of Management," *Academy of Management Review,* July 1977, pp. 356–72.

ARGUMENT AGAINST

Those writers and practitioners who argue against the fixed optimal span of control take exception to two points. First they argue that wide spans of control and the resultant flat organizations foster greater employee participation and self-control. Managers having relatively wide spans of control are unable to direct closely the work of their subordinates; subordinates will therefore develop greater independence and learn to direct themselves. Moreover the flatter organization structure with fewer managerial levels will respond more quickly to environmental changes because information and directives will pass through fewer levels. These outcomes—greater employee initiatives and more responsive organizations—are advantages in their own right.

A second point of debate has to do with the view of contingency organization behavior theory. According to this view, the optimal span of control varies depending upon the state of numerous other variables (contingencies). Managerial ability is one such contingency, but there are others. For example, wider spans of control are possible if subordinates' jobs are highly routine, similar, formalized, and performed in one location. In such instances the amount of supervision required tends to decline because the work, in ef-

ARGUMENT FOR (continued)

The organizational design implications of the idea that the optimal span of control is a fixed number are several. Most important is that the organization would tend to have many layers of management through which information and directives would pass. Consequently the organization would be unable to respond to environmental changes as quickly as might be appropriate. Nevertheless, the disadvantages of tall, layered organizations are outweighed, according to proponents of narrow spans, by the advantages of greater supervisory control.

ARGUMENT AGAINST (continued)

fect, supervises itself. Thus for any given situation an optimal span of control may exist, but it cannot be represented by a specific number without examining the state of those variables which determine it.

Organizational *structure* affects the behavior of individuals and groups in significant ways. In fact, the effects of organizational structure on behavior are so profound as to be included in definitions of the term, for example: "Organizational structure for our purposes will be defined broadly as those features of the organization that serve to *control* or distinguish its parts."[1] Thus a purpose of organizational structure is to control behavior, to channel and direct behavior to achieve, presumably, the goals of the organization.

The statement that organizational structures facilitate the achievement of organizational goals assumes that managers know how to match organizational structures and goals and that they desire to do so. It is entirely reasonable to acknowledge that in many instances organizational structures do not contribute positively to organizational performance because managers are unable by training or intellect to design a structure which controls and channels the behavior of individuals and groups to achieve high levels of production, efficiency, satisfaction, adaptiveness, and development. It is also reasonable to acknowledge that, in some instances, organizational structures reflect and contribute to the personal goals of managers at the expense of the goals of the organization. Thus to say that organizational structures contribute positively to organizational performance requires assumptions about the abilities and motivations of those who have power to design them. In this discussion the perspective is that of a manager who desires to design an organizational structure that can make the maximum contribution to achieving organizational goals. As will be seen, the task of designing organizational structure is not an easy one. Yet a recent review of the literature examining relationships between organization structure and performance suggests that managers have considerable latitude in designing structures. That is, the difference between the effective structure and ineffective ones is so great as to provide considerable room for error.[2]

This part consists of three chapters. The present chapter examines the broad features of organizational structure. These features, or dimensions, are the result of managerial decisions which are termed *design decisions*. These decisions determine to a very great extent the job of individuals in the organization.

The behavior of individuals and groups in organizations is affected in significant ways by the *jobs* they perform. The job itself provides powerful stimuli for individual behavior. The demands on, and expectations of, in-

---

[1] Robert H. Miles, *Macro Organizational Behavior* (Santa Monica, Calif.: Goodyear Publishing, 1980), p. 18. A similar definition is "The concept of structure is usually understood to imply a configuration of activities that is characteristically enduring and persistent; the dominant feature of organizational structure is its patterned regularity." Stewart Ranson, Bob Hinings, and Royston Greenwood, *Administrative Science Quarterly*, March 1980, p. 1.

[2] Dan R. Dalton, William D. Todor, Michael J. Spendolini, Gordon J. Fielding, and Lyman W. Porter, "Organization Structure and Performance: A Critical Review, *Academy of Management Review*, January 1980, pp. 49–64.

dividuals can result in high levels of personal satisfaction or stress, anxiety, and physiological dysfunctions.[3] People's jobs require them to perform activities in combination with other people in the organization. The activities can be routine or nonroutine; they can require high or low levels of skill; they can be perceived as challenging or as trivial. The required relationships can be with other co-workers, managers, clients, suppliers, or buyers. These relationships can result in feelings of friendship, competition, cooperativeness, and satisfaction or they can be causes of stress and anxiety. The determination of required job activities and relationships is a key managerial function and is covered in Chapter 12.

The structure of an organization can be described by a number of characteristics. These characteristics not only describe the organization, but they also have implications for the behavior of individuals and groups as well as the organization itself. When the organization is the focus of attention we are concerned with its adaptiveness, flexibility, growth, and development.[4] Managers must design jobs to achieve desirable work behavior and individual motivation and satisfaction and also design a larger structure which can respond to environmental pressures. The appropriate organization design must contain characteristics which enable it to meet and respond to economic, political, and social pressures for change and development. The design of macro-organization elements is the focus of Chapter 13.

ORGANIZATION DESIGN: CONCEPTUALIZATION OF THE PROBLEM

■ Organization design refers to the process by which managers create a structure of tasks and authority. The process is decision making through which managers evaluate the relative benefits of alternative tasks and authority structures. This process may be explicit or implicit, it may be "one-shot" or developmental, it may be done by a single manager or by a team of managers. Structure refers to relatively fixed relationships that exist among the jobs in the organization. The fixed relationships result from the following decision processes:

1. The total task of the unit is broken down into successively smaller jobs. That is, the task is divided or specialized among the persons in the unit. This is the issue of *division of labor.*
2. The individual jobs are recombined and grouped together. A common basis is defined to rationalize the grouping; this is the issue of *departmentalization.*

---

[3] See, for example, Lyman W. Porter and Edward E. Lawler III, "Properties of Organization Structure in Relation to Job Attitudes and Job Behavior," *Psychological Bulletin*, July 1965, pp. 23–51; John M. Ivancevich and James H. Donnelly, Jr., "Relation of Organizational Structure to Job Satisfaction, Anxiety-Stress, and Performance," *Administrative Science Quarterly*, June 1975, pp. 272–80; and Larry L. Cummings and Chris J. Berger, "Organization Structure: How Does It Influence Attitudes and Performance?" *Organizational Dynamics*, Autumn 1976, pp. 34–49.

[4] Geoffrey Hutton, *Thinking about Organizations* (London: Tavistock Publications, 1972).

3. The appropriate size of the group reporting to one superior must be determined; this is the issue of *span of control.*
4. Authority is distributed among the jobs or groups of jobs. This is the issue of *delegation.*

The result of the process by which managers resolve these four subproblems is the structure of the organization and it can vary depending upon how each is resolved.

An organization in which there are loosely defined job descriptions, heterogeneous departments, wide spans of control, and decentralized authority differs markedly from one in which there are strictly defined jobs, homogeneous departments, narrow spans of control, and centralized authority. Consider for example only the impact of span of control. In Figure 11–1 we have a graphic comparison of two structures; each has the same total number of people to be managed, 24. In one case the maximum span of control is 12 and there are two levels of management and three managers (a president and two supervisors); in the second case, the maximum span of control is 4 and there are three levels of management and nine managers (a president, two supervisors, and six foremen).

The form and characteristics of an organizational structure vary depend-

FIGURE 11–1
Wide and Narrow Spans of Control

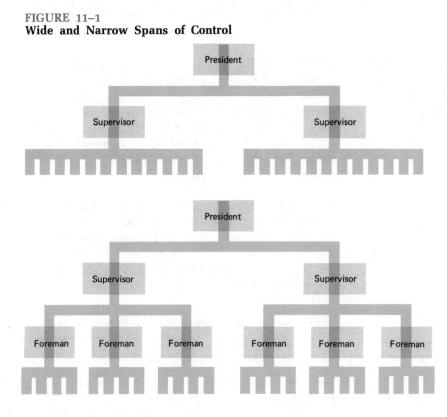

ing upon the attributes of each of the four subproblems. Conceptually, each of the four can vary along a continuum as shown:

	Specialization	
Division of Labor:		
	High	Low
	Basis	
Departmentalization:		
	Homogeneous	Heterogeneous
	Number	
Span of Control:		
	Few	Many
	Delegation	
Authority:		
	Centralized	Decentralized

Generally speaking, organizational structures will tend toward one extreme or the other along each continuum. Structures tending to the left are characterized by a number of terms including formalistic, structured, bureaucratic, System 1, and mechanistic. Structures tending to the right are termed informalistic, unstructured, nonbureaucratic, System 4, and organic. These terms are in no way precise or universally understood; this imprecision provides evidence of the relative immaturity of the state of knowledge about organization design.

DIVISION OF LABOR

■ The issues associated with division of labor are concerned with the extent to which jobs are specialized. All jobs are specialized to a degree and the ability to divide work among many jobholders is a key advantage of organizations. Rather than having a bookkeeper in a hospital performing emergency room tasks, the work is divided so that the bookkeeper concentrates on preparing bills and the emergency room clerk concentrates on admitting patients.

A major decision in developing an organizational structure is determining how much division of labor should exist. Advocates of dividing work into a small number of tasks often cite the advantages of specialization. Two of the major advantages are:

1. If a job contains few tasks it is possible to train replacements easily for personnel who are terminated, transferred, or absent. The minimum training effort results in a lower training cost.
2. When a job entails only a limited number of tasks the employee can become proficient in performing these tasks. This high level of proficiency is reflected in a better quality of output.

The benefits cited above are largely economic and technical and are usually applied to nonmanagerial jobs. However, similar benefits are applicable to specialized managerial positions.[5]

DEPARTMENTAL-IZATION

■ The process of defining the range and depth of individual jobs is analytical; that is, the total task of the organization is broken down into successively smaller tasks. But then it becomes necessary to combine the divided tasks into groups. The resultant groups are the command and task groups as discussed in an earlier chapter. The process of combining jobs into groups is termed *departmentalization,* and the managerial problem is to select a basis for combining these jobs. Numerous bases for departmentalization exist as will be demonstrated in the following discussion.

Functional Departmentalization

Jobs can be grouped according to the functions of the organization. The business firm includes functions such as production, marketing, finance, accounting, and personnel. The hospital includes such functions as surgery, psychiatry, housekeeping, pharmacy, and personnel.

The Oldsmobile Division of General Motors is structured on a functional basis. The functions are engineering, production, manufacturing, reliability, distribution, finance, and personnel as shown in Figure 11–2. The organizational structure of U.S. Ireland Army Hospital also illustrates a functional arrangement. Figure 11–3 presents the various departments and divisions in the hospital.

The functional basis is probably the most widely utilized scheme because of its commonsense appeal. That is, it seems logical to have a department which consists of experts in a particular field such as production or accounting. By having departments of specialists, management creates, theoretically, the most efficient unit possible. An accountant is generally more comfortable working with accountants and other individuals who have similar backgrounds and interests.

A major disadvantage of this departmental basis is that because specialists are working with and encouraging each other in their area of expertise and interest, the organizational goals may be sacrificed in favor of departmental goals. Accountants may see only their problems and not those of production or marketing or the total organization. In other words, the culture of, and identification with, the department are often stronger than identification with the organization and its culture.

Territorial Departmentalization

Another commonly adopted method for departmentalizing is to establish groups on the basis of geographical areas. The logic is that all activities in a given area or region should be assigned to a manager. This individual would be in charge of all operations in that particular geographical area.

---

[5]Michael Aiken, Samuel B. Bacharach, and J. Lawrence French, "Organizational Structure, Work Process, and Proposal Making in Administrative Bureaucracies," *Academy of Management Journal,* December 1980, pp. 631–52.

FIGURE 11–2
General Motors Corporation (Oldsmobile Division, Car and Truck Group)

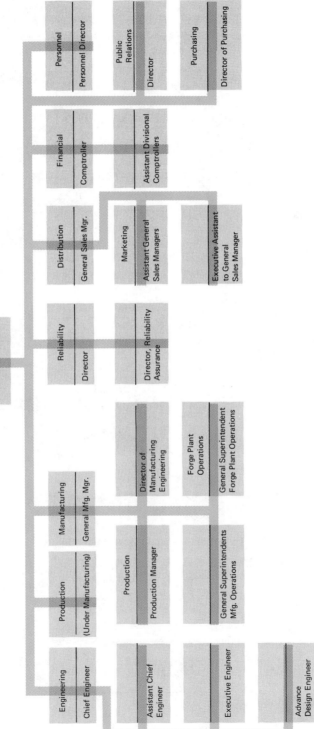

FIGURE 11-3

Organizational Structure for U.S. Ireland Army Hospital

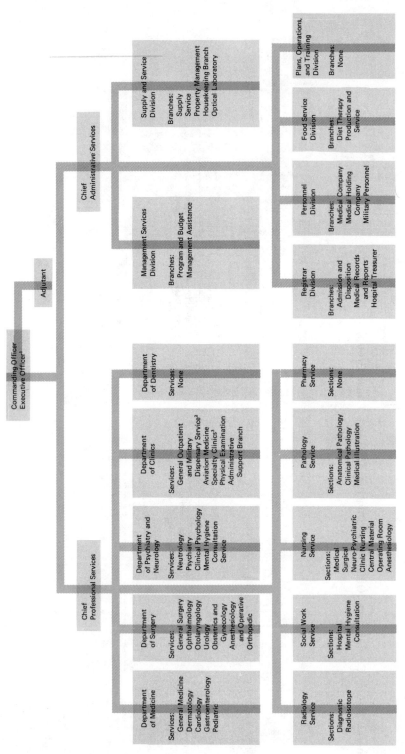

1. Also serves as Chief, Administrative Services.
2. Includes U.S. Army Dispensaries at DCSC and Lex-BG Depot.
3. Provides logistical and administrative support to Specialty Clinics.

In large organizations territorial arrangements are attractive because physical dispersion of activities makes centralized coordination difficult. For example, it is extremely difficult for someone in New York to develop routes for salespersons in Kansas City. An example of a territorial structure is presented in Figure 11–4, which illustrates the organization chart of R. H. Macy & Co., Inc.

An advantage often associated with territorial departmentalization is that it provides a training ground for managerial personnel. The company is able to place managers in territories and then assess their programs and progress in that geographical region. The experience which managers acquire in a territory away from headquarters provides valuable insights about how products and/or services are accepted in the field.

Product Departmentalization

In many large diversified companies activities and personnel are grouped on the basis of product. As a firm grows it is difficult to coordinate the various functional departments and it becomes advantageous to estab-

FIGURE 11–4
R. H. Macy & Co., Inc.

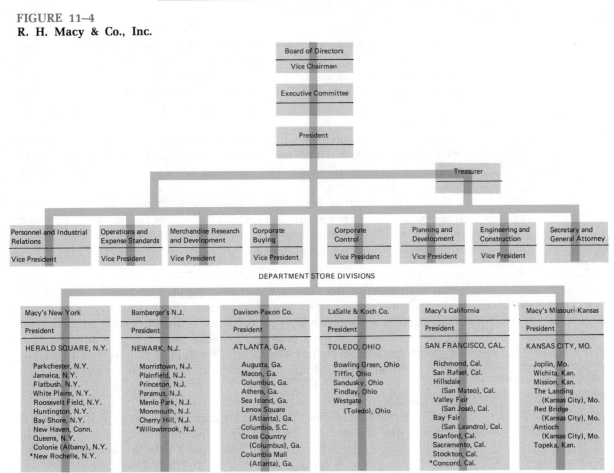

lish product units. This form of organization allows personnel to develop total expertise in researching, manufacturing, and distributing a product line. Concentration of the authority, responsibility, and accountability in a specific product department allows top management to coordinate actions. The need for coordination of production, engineering, sales, and service cannot be overestimated.

The Consumer Products Division of Kimberly-Clark specifies a product arrangement. The specific product groups shown in Figure 11–5 include feminine hygiene, household, and commercial products. Within each of these units we find production and marketing personnel. Since product managers coordinate sales, manufacturing, and distribution of a product, they become the overseers of a profit center. This is the manner in which profit responsibility is exacted from product organizational arrangements. Managers are often asked to establish profit goals at the beginning of a time period and then to compare actual profit with planned profit. This is the approach used in the Buick, Cadillac, Chevrolet, Pontiac, and Oldsmobile divisions of General Motors.

Customer Departmentalization

Examples of customer-oriented departments are the organizational structures of educational institutions. Some institutions have regular (day and night) courses and extension courses. In some instances a professor will be affiliated solely with the regular students or extension students. In fact, the title of some faculty positions often specifically mentions the extension division.

Another form of customer departmentalization is the loan department in a commercial bank. Loan officers are often associated with industrial, commercial, or agricultural loans. The customer will be served by one of these three loan officers.

Some department stores are departmentalized to some degree on a customer basis. They have groupings such as university shops, men's clothing, and boys' clothing. They have bargain floors that carry a lower quality of university, men's, and boys' clothing.

Mixed Departmentalization: Divisional Organization

An evaluation of the various forms of departmentalization suggests that each basis has its strengths and weaknesses. There is an increased desire to experiment with multiple or mixed bases within the same organization. The mixed strategies have emerged because managers are attempting to cope with growth, shifts in markets, proliferation of products and services, and government regulations. Organizations such as E. I. du Pont have structured various divisions so that a number of departmental arrangements can be utilized.

At one time, the Textile Fibers Department of E. I. du Pont included five divisions, one for each of the five fibers the department made and sold. Each division, under a division manager, had a sales division and a manufacturing division. A centralized research division also existed.

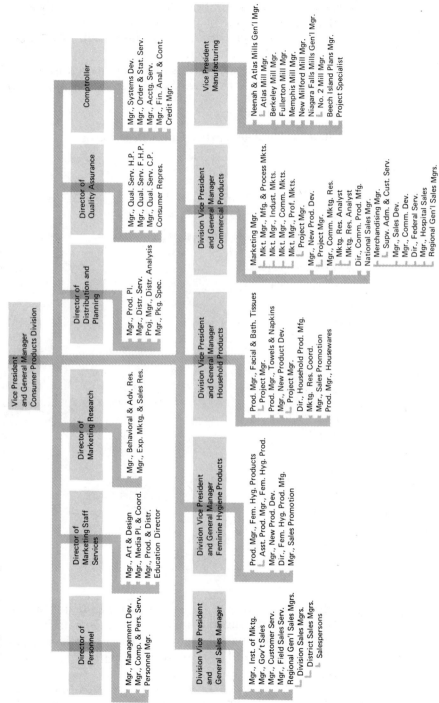

FIGURE 11-5
Kimberly-Clark Corporation (Consumer Products Division)

Vice President and General Manager Consumer Products Division

Director of Personnel
- Mgr., Management Dev.
- Mgr., Comp. & Pers. Serv.
- Personnel Mgr.

Director of Marketing Staff Services
- Mgr., Art & Design
- Mgr., Media Pl. & Coord.
- Mgr., Prod. & Distr.
- Education Director

Director of Marketing Research
- Mgr., Behavioral & Adv. Res.
- Mgr., Exp. Mktg. & Sales Res.

Director of Distribution and Planning
- Mgr., Prod. Pl.
- Mgr., Distr. Serv.
- Proj. Mgr., Distr. Analysis
- Mgr., Pkg. Spec.

Director of Quality Assurance
- Mgr., Qual. Serv. H.P.
- Mgr., Qual. Serv. F.H.P.
- Mgr., Qual. Serv. C.P.
- Consumer Repres.

Comptroller
- Mgr., Systems Dev.
- Mgr., Order & Stat. Serv.
- Mgr., Acctg. Serv.
- Mgr., Fin. Anal. & Cont.
- Credit Mgr.

Division Vice President and General Sales Manager
- Mgr., Inst. of Mktg.
- Mgr., Gov't Sales
- Mgr., Customer Serv.
- Mgr., Field Sales Serv.
- Regional Gen'l Sales Mgrs.
  - Division Sales Mgrs.
    - District Sales Mgrs.
      - Salespersons

Division Vice President and General Manager Feminine Hygiene Products
- Prod. Mgr., Fem. Hyg. Products
  - Asst. Prod. Mgr., Fem. Hyg. Prod.
- Mgr., New Prod. Dev.
- Dir., Fem. Hyg. Prod. Mfg.
- Mgr., Sales Promotion

Division Vice President and General Manager Household Products
- Prod. Mgr., Facial & Bath. Tissues
  - Project Mgr.
- Prod. Mgr., Towels & Napkins
  - Project Mgr.
- Mgr., New Product Dev.
- Dir., Household Prod. Mfg.
- Mktg. Res. Coord.
- Mgr., Sales Promotion
- Prod. Mgr., Housewares

Division Vice President and General Manager Commercial Products
- Marketing Mgr.
  - Mkt. Mgr., Mfg. & Process Mkts.
  - Mkt. Mgr., Indust. Mkts.
  - Mkt. Mgr., Comm. Mkts.
  - Mkt. Mgr., Prof. Mkts.
    - Project Mgr.
- Mgr., New Prod. Dev.
  - Project Mgr.
- Mgr., Comm. Mktg. Res.
- Mktg. Res. Analyst
- Mktg. Res. Analyst
- Dir., Comm. Prod. Mfg.
- National Sales Mgr.
  - Merchandising Mgr.
  - Supv. Adm. & Cust. Serv.
- Mgr., Sales Dev.
- Mgr., Comm. Dev.
- Dir., Federal Serv.
- Mgr., Hospital Sales
- Regional Gen'l Sales Mgrs.

Vice President Manufacturing
- Neenah & Atlas Mills Gen'l Mgr.
  - Atlas Mill Mgr.
- Berkeley Mill Mgr.
- Fullerton Mill Mgr.
- Memphis Mill Mgr.
- New Milford Mill Mgr.
- Niagara Falls Mills Gen'l Mgr.
  - No. 2 Mill Mgr.
- Beech Island Plans Mgr.
- Project Specialist

Later, the five divisions were combined so that there was just one sales division, one manufacturing division, and one research division (functional grouping). Each of these divisions was organized, however, along product lines. In the sales division there continued to be individual sales representatives for each fiber.

Eventually the structure was changed again and a merchandising division was added. There were six groups in the unit: menswear, women's

FIGURE 11–6
Organization Chart of Textile Fibers Department

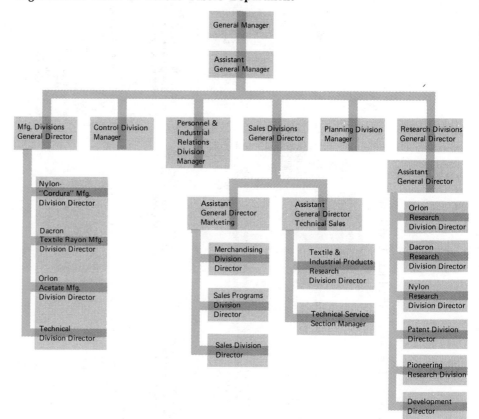

wear, home furnishings, industrial merchandising, advertising and promotion, and marketing research. The change reflects an interest in customer demands and is a form of customer departmentalization. Figure 11–6 shows the organization chart of the Textile Fibers Department after the changes.

The sales divisions of the Textile Fibers Department are shown in Figure 11–7. In this chart the various bases for departmentalization (functional, product, customer, and territorial) are illustrated.

FIGURE 11–7
Organization Chart of Sales Divisions of Textile Fibers Department

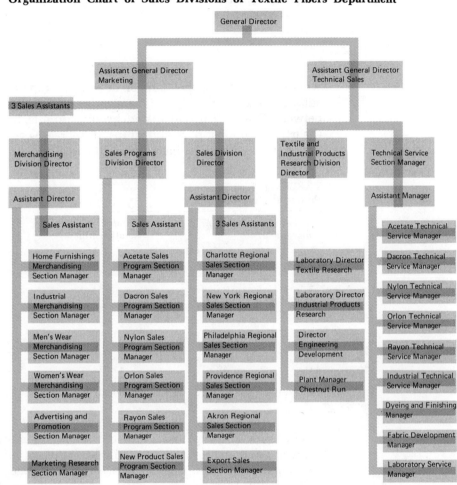

SPAN OF CONTROL

The determination of appropriate bases for departmentalization establishes the *kinds* of jobs that will be grouped together. But that determination does not establish the *number* of jobs to be included in a specific group. That determination is the issue of *span of control.* Generally the issue comes down to the decision of how many people a manager can oversee; that is, will the organization be more effective if the span of control is relatively wide or narrow? The question is basically concerned with determining the volume of interpersonal activities that the department's manager is able to handle. Moreover, as recent research has pointed out, the span of control must be defined to include not only formally assigned subordinates, but also those who have access to the manager.[6]

---

[6]William G. Ouchi and John B. Dowling, "Defining the Span of Control," *Administrative Science Quarterly,* September 1974, pp. 357–65.

The number of *potential* relationships between a manager and subordinates can be calculated by the formula:

$$R = N\left(\frac{2^N}{2} + N - 1\right)$$

where R designates the number of relationships and N is the number of subordinates assigned to the manager's command group.[7] The relationship between R and N as calculated by the formula is shown in Table 11–1. Clearly the number of relationships, R, increases geometrically as the number of subordinates, N, increase arithmetically.

TABLE 11–1
Potential Relationships

Number of Subordinates	Number of Relationships
1	1
2	6
3	18
4	44
5	100
6	222
7	490
8	1,080
9	2,376
10	5,210
11	11,374
12	24,708
18	2,359,602

The calculation assumes that the managers must contend with three types of relationships: (1) direct single, (2) direct group, and (3) cross. Direct single relationships occur between the manager and each subordinate individually. Direct group relations occur between the manager and each possible permutation of subordinates. Finally, cross relationships occur when subordinates interact with one another. These potential relationships are illustrated in Figure 11–8 for a manager (M) and two subordinates (A and B) and three subordinates (A, B, and C). Direct group relationships differ depending upon which subordinate assumes the leadership role in interaction with the manager. And depending upon the issue to be discussed or the problem to be solved, we would expect different group members to emerge as leader.

At the same time that we note the number of *potential* interactions between a manager and subordinates, we must recognize that the crucial

---

[7] A. V. Graicunas, "Relationships in Organization," in *Papers on the Science of Administration*, ed. Luther Gulick and Lyndall F. Urwick, New York: Columbia University, 1947), pp. 183–87.

FIGURE 11–8
Potential Relationships among a Manager and Two/Three Subordinates

Direct single	1. M→A	Direct single	1. M→A
	2. M→B		2. M→B
			3. M→C
Direct group	3. M→A with B	Direct group	4. M→A with B
	4. M→B with A		5. M→A with C
			6. M→B with A
			7. M→B with C
			8. M→C with A
			9. M→C with B
			10. M→A with B and C
			11. M→B with A and C
			12. M→C with A and B
Cross	5. A→B	Cross	13. A→B
	6. B→A		14. A→C
			15. B→A
			16. B→C
			17. C→A
			18. C→B

questions concern frequency and intensity. Not all interactions will occur, and those which do will vary in importance. At least three factors appear to be important in analyzing the span of control issue.

1. <u>Required Contact.</u> In research and development, medical, and production work there is a need for frequent contact and a high degree of coordination between a superior and subordinates. The use of conferences and other forms of consultation often aid in the attainment of goals within a constrained time period. For example, the research and development team leader may have to consult frequently with team members so that a project is completed within a time period that will allow the organization to place a product on the market. Thus, instead of relying upon memos and reports, it is in the best interest of the organization to have as many in-depth contacts with the team as possible. A large span of control would preclude contacting subordinates so frequently and this could have detrimental effects on completing the project.

2. <u>Level of Subordinate Education and Training.</u> The training of employees is a critical consideration in establishing the span of control at all levels of management. It is generally accepted that a manager at the lower organizational level can oversee more subordinates because work at the lower level is more specialized and less complicated than at higher levels of management.

3. <u>Ability to Communicate.</u> Instructions, guidelines, and policies must be communicated verbally to subordinates in most work situations. The need to discuss job-related factors influences the span of control. The individual who can clearly and concisely communicate with subordinates is able to manage more people than one who cannot do so.

DELEGATION OF AUTHORITY

■ The final issue which managers must consider when designing an organizational structure is that of delegation of authority. In practical terms the issue concerns the relative benefits of decentralization; that is, delegation of authority to the lowest possible level in the managerial hierarchy. The concept of decentralization does not refer to geographic dispersion of the organization's separate units; rather it refers to the delegated right of managers to make decisions without approval by higher management. In some respects the concept is related to the influence which an individual has by virtue of personal characteristics. In the context of Fiedler's theory of leadership, delegated authority is *position power*. Let us evaluate some of the arguments for decentralization.

First, some scholars assume that decentralization encourages the development of professional managers. The point is that as decision-making authority is pushed down in the organization, managers must adapt and prove themselves if they are to advance in the company. That is, they must become generalists who know something about the numerous job-related factors they must cope with in the decentralized arrangement.

Because managers in a decentralized structure often have to adapt and deal with difficult decisions, they are trained for promotion into positions of greater authority and responsibility. Managers can be readily compared with their peers on the basis of actual decision-making performance. In effect, the decentralized arrangement can lead to a more equitable performance appraisal program. This can lead to a more satisfied group of managers because they perceive themselves as being evaluated on the basis of results, not personalities.

Second, the decentralized arrangement leads to a competitive climate within the organization. The managers are motivated to contribute in this competitive atmosphere since they are compared with their peers on various performance measures.

Finally, in the decentralized pattern managers are able to exercise more autonomy, and this satisfies the desire to participate in problem solving. This freedom is assumed to lead to managerial creativity and ingenuity which contribute to the adaptiveness and development of the organization and managers.

These are only three of the advantages associated with decentralization. These advantages are not free of costs. Certainly, most advocates of decentralization are aware that certain costs may have to be incurred if an organization shifts from a centralized to a decentralized design. Some of the costs are:

1. Managers must be trained to handle decision making and this may require expensive formal training programs.
2. Since many managers have worked in centralized organizations, it is very uncomfortable for them to delegate authority in a more decentralized arrangement. These old attitudes are difficult to alter and often lead to resistance.

3. <u>To alter accounting and performance appraisal systems so they are compatible with the decentralized arrangement is costly</u>. Administrative costs are incurred because new or altered accounting and performance systems must be tested, implemented, and evaluated.

These are, of course, only some of the costs of decentralizing. Like most issues there is definitely no clear-cut answer about whether decentralization is better for an organization. It would appear that considering each organizational factor (for example, labor force, size, and control mechanisms) thoroughly is a prerequisite for reaching decisions concerning decentralization. The following close-up illustrates one firm's experience with decentralized authority.

ORGANIZATIONS: CLOSE-UP

Decentralization at Curtice–Burns, Inc.

Curtice-Burns, Inc., manages seven food manufacturing divisions with a headquarters staff of only 12 people. The headquarters staff, located in Rochester, New York, oversees the seven divisions through a decentralized organization structure. Each division is considered a profit center, and each division's chief executive is completely responsible for the division. Completely delegated authority is the rule except in the area of major capital investments. Each division chief must request funds for capital improvements to the company's board of directors. Apart from this one constraint, each division is an autonomous unit with the authority to make all the decisions necessary to run an independent business.

According to Hugh Cumming, president and CEO, "We manage by exception rather than by control. If there is a problem and the division CEO is a good manager he's already briefed corporate management that he is taking a risk and may fail. We as managers have to have failures to learn. If every time you have a failure, corporate headquarters gets into the act, nobody is going to take any chances."

In its 17 years of existence, the company has grown to sales of $260 million (as of 1978), primarily through acquisitions of other companies which subsequently became the company's divisions. In the 10 years ending in 1978 earnings per share increased from $0.62 to $3.67. Although not all of these impressive gains can be attributed to the organization structure which Curtice-Burns has adopted, Cumming believes that it has been a major contributing factor.

Source: *Management Review*, November 1979, pp. 32–33.

DIMENSIONS OF STRUCTURE

■ The four design decisions, that is, <u>division of labor, departmentalization, span of control, and delegation of authority, result in a structure, or anatomy, of organizations</u>. Researchers and practitioners of management have attempted to develop their understanding about structure in relation to performance, attitudes, satisfaction, and other variables thought to be important. The development of understanding has been hampered not only by the complexity of the relationships themselves, but also by the difficulty of defining and measuring the concept of organizational structure.

Although universal agreement on a common set of dimensions is neither possible nor desirable, some suggestions can be made. At the present time three dimensions are often used in research and practice to describe structure. They are *formalization, centralization, and complexity.*

Formalization

The dimension of formalization refers to the extent to which expectations regarding the means and ends of work are specified and written. An organization structure which is described as highly formalized would be one in which rules and procedures are available to prescribe what each individual should be doing. Such organizations would have written standard operating procedures, specified directives, and explicit policy. In terms of the four design decisions, formalization is the result of high specialization of labor and homogenous departments. The extent to which span of control and delegation of authority contribute to formalization is, at present, conjectural.[8]

Although formalization is viewed in terms of the existence of written rules and procedures, it is important to understand how they are viewed by the employees. Some organizations may have all the appearances of formalization, yet the rules and procedures are not perceived by employees as affecting their behavior. Thus even though rules and procedures exist, they must be enforced if they are to affect behavior.[9]

Centralization

Centralization refers to the location of decision-making authority in the hierarchy of the organization. More specifically, the concept refers to the dispersion of authority among the jobs in the organization. Typically, researchers and practitioners think of centralization in terms of decision making: who makes what decisions. But despite the apparent simplicity of the concept, it can be complex.

The complexity of the concept derives from three sources: First, people at the same level can have different decision-making authority. Second, not all decisions are of equal importance in organizations. For example, a typical management practice is to delegate authority to make routine operating decisions (i.e., decentralization), but to retain authority to make strategic decisions (i.e., centralization). Third, individuals may not perceive that they really have authority even though their job descriptions include it. Thus objectively they have authority, but subjectively they do not.[10]

---

[8] See Peter H. Grinyear and Masoud Yasai-Ardekani, "Dimensions of Organizational Structure: A Critical Replication," *Academy of Management Journal,* September 1980, pp. 405–21, for discussion of formalization in relation to centralization.

[9] Eric J. Walton, "The Comparison of Measures of Organization Structure," *Academy of Management Review,* January 1981, pp. 155–60.

[10] Jeffrey D. Ford, "Institutional versus Questionnaire Measures of Organizational Structure," *Academy of Management Journal,* September 1979. pp. 601–10.

Complexity

Complexity is the direct outgrowth of dividing work and creating departments. Specifically the concept refers to the number of distinctly different job titles, or occupational groupings, and the number of distinctly different units, or departments. The fundamental idea is that organizations with a great many different kinds and types of jobs and units create more complicated managerial and organizational problems than those with fewer jobs and departments.

Complexity, then, relates to *differences* among jobs and units. It, therefore, is not surprising that *differentiation* is often used synonymously with complexity. Moreover it has become standard practice to use the term *horizontal differentiation* to refer to the number of different units at the same level;[11] *vertical differentiation* refers to the number of levels in the organization. It is apparent that complexity (horizontal and vertical differentiation) is related to division of labor, departmentalization, and span of control. Refer back to Figure 11–1 and note that the degree of complexity can be increased by reducing the span of control. It can also be increased by specialization and by homogenous departmentalization.

MATRIX ORGANIZATION DESIGN

■ An emerging organization design, termed matrix organization, attempts to maximize the strengths and minimize the weaknesses of both the functional and product structures.[12] Companies such as American Cyanamid, Avco, Carborundum, Caterpillar Tractor, Hughes Aircraft, ITT, Monsanto Chemical, National Cash Register, Prudential Insurance, TWR, and Texas Instruments are only a few of the users of matrix organization. Public sector users include public health and social service agencies.[13] Although the exact meaning of matrix organization is not well established, the most typical meaning sees it as a balanced compromise between functional and product organization, between departmentalization by process and by purpose.[14]

The matrix organization form achieves the desired balance by superimposing, or overlaying, a horizontal structure of authority, influence, and communication. The arrangement can be described as in Figure 11–9, personnel assigned in each cell belong not only to the functional department, but also to a particular product or project. For example, manufacturing, marketing, engineering, and finance specialists will be assigned to work on one or more projects or products A, B, C, D, and E. As a consequence, personnel will report to two managers, one in their functional department and one in the project or product unit. The existence of a *dual authority* system is a distinguishing characteristic of matrix organization. Traditional

---

[11]Richard L. Daft and Patricia J. Bradshaw, "The Process of Horizontal Differentiation: Two Models," *Administrative Science Quarterly,* September 1980, pp. 441–56.

[12]Robert Youker, "Organization Alternatives for Project Managers," *Management Review,* November 1977, p. 48.

[13]Kenneth Knight, "Matrix Organization: A Review," *Journal of Management Studies,* May 1976, p. 111.

[14]Ibid., p. 114.

FIGURE 11–9
Matrix Organizations

Projects, Products	Functions			
	Manufacturing	Marketing	Engineering	Finance
Project or Product A				
Project or Product B				
Project or Product C				
Project or Product D				
Project or Product E				

functional and product-based organizations maintain a strict chain of command wherein each employee reports to only one superior.

Matrix structures are found in organizations which require responses to rapid change in two sectors, such as technology and markets; which face uncertainties that generate high information processing requirements; and which must deal with financial and human resources constraints.[15] Managers confronting these circumstances must obtain certain advantages which are most likely to be realized with matrix organization.[16]

Efficient Use of Resources. Matrix organization facilitates the utilization of highly specialized staff and equipment. Each project, or product, unit can share the specialized resource with other units, rather than duplicating it to provide independent coverage for each. This advantage is particularly so when projects require less than the full-time efforts of the specialist. For example, a project may require only half a computer scientist's time. Rather than having several underutilized computer scientists assigned to each project, the organization can keep fewer of them fully utilized by shifting them from project to project.

Flexibility in Conditions of Change and Uncertainty. Timely response to change requires information and communication channels which efficiently get the information to the right people at the right time. Matrix structures encourage constant interaction among project unit and functional department members. Information is channeled vertically and horizontally as people exchange technical knowledge. The result is quicker response to competitive conditions, technological breakthroughs, and other environmental conditions.

Technical Excellence. Technical specialists interact with other specialists while assigned to a project. These interactions encourage cross-fertilization of ideas such as when a computer scientist must discuss the pros

---

[15] Paul R. Lawrence, Harvey F. Kolodny, and Stanley M. Davis, "The Human Side of the Matrix," *Organizational Dynamics*, September 1977, p. 47.

[16] The following discussion is based upon Knight, "Matrix Organization."

and cons of electronic data processing with a financial accounting expert. Each specialist must be able to listen, understand, and respond to the views of the other. At the same time specialists maintain ongoing contact with members of their own discipline because they are also members of a functional department.

Freeing Top Management for Long-Range Planning. An initial stimulus for the development of matrix organizations is that top management increasingly becomes involved with day-to-day operations.[17] Environmental changes tend to create problems which cross functional and product departments and which cannot be resolved by the lower level managers. For example, when competitive conditions create the need to develop new products at faster than previous rates, the existing procedures become bogged down. Top management is then called upon to settle conflicts among the functional managers. Matrix organization makes it possible for top management to delegate ongoing decision making, thus providing more time for long-range planning.

Improving Motivation and Commitment. Project and product groups are comprised of individuals with specialized knowledge. Management assigns to them, on the basis of their expertise, responsibility for specific aspects of the work. Consequently decision making within the group tends to be more participative and democratic than in more hierarchical settings. The opportunity to participate in key decisions fosters high levels of motivation and commitment, particularly for individuals with acknowledged professional orientations.

Providing Opportunities for Personal Development. Members of matrix organizations are provided considerable opportunity to develop their skills and knowledge. They are placed in groups consisting of individuals representing diverse parts of the organization. They must, therefore, come to appreciate the different points of view expressed by these individuals; each group member becomes more aware of the total organization. Moreover they have opportunities to learn something of other specialties. Engineers develop knowledge of financial issues; accountants will learn about marketing. The experience broadens each specialist's knowledge not only of the organization, but of other scientific and technical disciplines.

At the present time the evidence to support the claims for these advantages is largely anecdotal. That is they rest on testimonials of participants in matrix organizations. One study of the experience with matrix organization structures concluded that they were relatively unsuccessful, but not because of defects in the structures. Rather it was due to faulty implementation resulting from managers' inability to adjust their traditional behavioral styles.[18] These managers were unable to cope with the stresses asso-

---

[17]Jay R. Galbraith "Matrix Organization Designs: How to Combine Functional and Project Forms," *Business Horizons*, February 1971, pp. 29–40.

[18]Chris Argyris, "Today's Problems with Tomorrow's Organizations," *Journal of Management Studies*, February 1967, pp. 31–55.

ciated with dual authority and the natural conflict that arises out of such arrangements. Despite the absence of empirical studies to support the claims of matrix organization proponents, it will not doubt become more widely used in one form or another. In practice, management can select different variations on the basic theme of matrix organization.

Different Forms of Matrix Organization

Matrix organization forms can be depicted as existing in the middle of a continuum which has functional organizations at one extreme and product organizations at the other, Figure 11–10.[19] Organizations can move from functional to matrix forms or from product to matrix forms. Ordinarily the process of moving to matrix organization is evolutionary. That is, as

FIGURE 11–10
Alternative Matrix Organization Forms

Functional	Matrix	Product
Organization	Organization	Organization

the present structure proves incapable of dealing with rapid technological and market changes, management attempts to cope by establishing procedures and positions which are outside the normal routine.

Galbraith describes this evolutionary process as moving in successive steps from task forces to product management departments. The sequence is as follows.[20]

Task Force. When a competitor develops a new product that quickly captures the market, a rapid response is necessary. Yet in a functional organization new product development is often too time-consuming because of the necessity to coordinate the various units that must be involved. A convenient approach is to create a task force of individuals from each functional department and charge it with the responsibility to expedite the process. The task force achieves its objective and dissolves, as members return to their primary assignment.

Teams. If the product or technological breakthrough generates a family of products which move through successive stages of new and improved products, the temporary task force concept is ineffective. A typical next step is to create permanent teams which consist of representatives from each functional department. The teams meet regularly to resolve interdepartmental issues and to achieve coordination. When not involved with issues associated with new product development, the team members work on their regular assignments.

Product Managers. If the technological breakthrough persists such that new product development becomes a way of life, top management will cre-

---

[19] This idea was first presented in Galbraith, "Matrix Organization." A similar presentation is in Youker, "Organization Alternatives."

[20] Based on Galbraith, "Matrix Organizations."

ate the roles of product managers. In a sense product managers chair the teams, but they now are permanent positions. Ordinarily they report to top management, but they have no formal authority over the team members. They must rely upon their expertise and interpersonal skill to influence the team members. Companies such as General Foods, Du Pont, and IBM make considerable use of the product management concept.

Product Management Departments. The final step in the evolution to matrix organization is the creation of product management departments. Figure 11–11 depicts the organization which has a product manager reporting to top management and with subproduct managers for each product line. In some instances the subproduct managers are selected from specific functional departments and would continue to report directly to their functional managers. There is considerable diversity in the application of matrix organization, yet the essential feature is the creation of overlapping authority and the existence of dual authority.

Exactly where along the continuum an organization stops in the evolution depends upon factors in the situation. Specifically and primarily important are the rates of change in technological and product developments. The resultant uncertainty and information required to deal with the uncertainty varies. Chapter 13 reviews the important aspects of technology, environmental uncertainty, and information processing. At this point matrix organization is introduced in the discussion to illustrate an alternative or-

FIGURE 11–11
Fully Evolved Matrix Organization

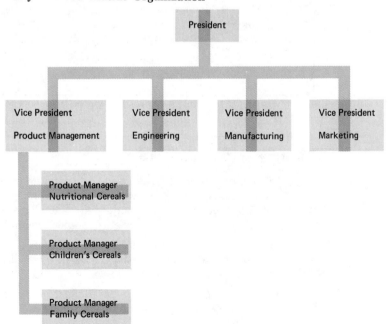

ganization design. The following close-up illustrates how one firm used a form of matrix organization.

ORGANIZATIONS: CLOSE-UP

Matrix Organization at IM&CC, Inc.

Anthony E. Cascino is vice chairman of International Minerals & Chemical Corporation. He recounts how a crisis that threatened to break down the company's decision-making processes led him to adapt matrix organization to meet the crisis. At the time of the crisis, Cascino was an executive vice president who relied upon two key managers: the vice president of marketing and the vice president of operations. Within a two-week period of time, both vice presidents left the company, and no qualified successors were available. Cascino had been removed from day-to-day operations for several years and was quite reluctant to try to do the work of the vice presidents who were no longer with the company.

The task of personally overseeing the activities of five operating divisions and five marketing divisions was impossible without some form of coordination. Cascino states that since most of the causes for adjustment generate from within the marketing divisions, he brought together the heads of the five marketing divisions and asked them to collectively assume the responsibility for coordination of their divisions. He asked them to select their own chairperson, to meet as often as necessary, and to seek his intervention only when they were unable to find solutions to their problems. The informal arrangement soon became a permanent part of the organization structure as the benefits of horizontal collaboration were recognized. The "Coordinating Committee" how includes representatives from the production divisions, and several improvements in performance criteria are traceable, according to Cascino, to this form of matrix organization as it evolved in IMCC.

Source: Anthony E. Cascino, "How One Company 'Adapted' Matrix Management in a Crisis," *Management Review*, November 1979, pp. 57–61.

MAJOR MANAGERIAL ISSUES

A. The structure, or anatomy, of an organization consists of relatively fixed and stable relationships among jobs and groups of jobs. The primary purpose of organization structure is to channel the *behavior* of individuals and groups so as to achieve effective performance.

B. Four key managerial decisions determine organization structures. These decisions are defining specialization of labor, departmentalizing, determining spans of control, and delegating authority.

C. The four key decisions are interrelated and interdependent, although each has certain specific problems which can be considered apart from the others.

MAJOR MANAGERIAL ISSUES (continued)

D. Defining the degree of specialization of labor depends initially on the technical and economic advantages of division of labor.

E. The grouping of jobs into departments requires the selection of common bases such as function, territory, product, or customer. Each basis has advantages and disadvantages which must be evaluated in terms of overall effectiveness.

F. The optimal span of control is no one specific number of subordinates. Although the number of *potential* relationships increases geometrically as the number of subordinates increases arithmetically, the important consideration is the frequency and intensity of the actual relationships.

G. The delegation of authority enables managers to make decisions without approval by higher management. Similar to other organizing issues, delegated authority is a relative, not absolute, concept. Managers by nature have some authority, the question is whether they have enough or too much.

H. In general, management must choose between two organizational types—functional or product designs. Each type has advantages and disadvantages which must be taken into account. Functional organizations tend to maximize efficiency and production performance criteria; product organizations tend to maximize adaptiveness and development criteria.

I. An emerging new design, matrix organization, tends to maximize the benefits of both functional and product organizations. Matrix organizations evolve as environmental uncertainty creates problems requiring rapid response. Through approaches such as task forces, teams, and product managers, the organization brings together resources and abilities to respond to the environmental pressure.

DISCUSSION AND REVIEW QUESTIONS

1. Describe the process of designing an organization by discussing how the manager of a retail store would analyze the four subproblems of the design decision.

2. Compare functional and product departmentalization in terms of relative efficiency, production, satisfaction, adaptiveness, and development. Consider particularly the possibility that one basis may be superior in achieving one aspect of effectiveness, yet inferior in achieving another.

3. Describe and discuss the problems which matrix organization creates for subordinates who must report to both project and functional managers.

4. Discuss the statement that in order to manage effectively a person must have the authority to hire subordinates, assign them to specific jobs, and reward them on the basis of performance. Interview any chairperson of an academic department and determine whether he or she has this authority.

5. The terms *responsibility*, *authority*, and *accountability* appear in the management and organization literature. What is your understanding of these terms? Are they different? Do they refer to fundamental questions of organizational design?

6. How can a manager know that the organizational design is ineffective? Is there any differ-

ence between *designing* and *changing* organizational structure? Explain.

7. Explain the relationships between decentralization and divisional organizational structures. Is it possible to create divisional organizations without delegating considerable authority to divisional managers? Explain.

8. Explain the process by which a product-based organization would evolve to a matrix organization.

9. Describe managerial skills and behaviors which would be required to manage effectively in a matrix organization. Are these skills and behaviors different from those required in a traditional organization? Explain.

ADDITIONAL REFERENCES

Argyris, C. *Integrating the Individual and the Organization.* New York: John Wiley & Sons, 1964.

Blau, P. M. *On the Nature of Organizations.* New York: John Wiley & Sons, 1974.

Chandler, A. D., Jr. *Strategy and Structure.* Cambridge, Mass.: MIT Press, 1962.

Davis, L. E., and J. C. Taylor, eds. *Design of Jobs.* Middlesex, England: Penguin Books, 1972.

Etzioni, A. A. *Comparative Analysis of Complex Organizations.* Glencoe, Ill.: Free Press, 1961.

Evan, W. *Organization Theory: Structures, Systems and Environments.* New York: Wiley-Interscience, 1976.

Galbraith, J. *Organization Design.* Reading, Mass.: Addison-Wesley Publishing, 1977.

Gross, E. "Universities as Organizations," in *Academic Governance,* edited by J. V. Baldridge. Berkeley, Calif.: McCutchan Publishing, 1972, pp. 22–57.

Hall, R. H. *Organizations: Structure and Process.* Englewood Cliffs, N.J.: Prentice-Hall, 1977.

Hrebiniak, L. G. *Complex Organizations.* St. Paul, Minn.: West Publishing, 1978.

Jackson, J. H., and C. Morgan. *Organization Theory.* Englewood Cliffs, N.J.: Prentice-Hall, 1978.

Kilmann, R. H.; L. R. Pondy; and D. P. Slevin, eds. *The Management of Organization Design: Strategies and Implementation, Vol. 1.* New York: Elsevier North-Holland, 1976.

Kolodny, H. F. "Evolution to a Matrix Organization." *Academy of Management Review,* 1979, pp. 543–53.

Krupp, S. *Pattern in Organization Analysis: A Critical Examination.* New York: Holt, Rinehart, & Winston, 1961.

Lawrence, P., and J. Lorsch. *Organization and Environment.* Boston: Division of Research, Harvard Business School, 1967.

McGeer, R. "The Organizational Structures of State and Local Correctional Services." *Public Administration Review,* 1971, pp. 603–16.

Meyer, M. W. *Theory of Organization Structure.* Indianapolis, Ind.: Bobbs-Merrill, 1977.

Mintzberg, H. *The Structuring of Organizations: A Synthesis of Research.* Englewood Cliffs, N.J.: Prentice-Hall, 1979.

Morris, J. H.; R. M. Steers; and J. L. Koch. "Influence of Organization Structure on Role Conflict, and Ambiguity for Three Occupational Groupings." *Academy of Management Journal,* 1979, pp. 58–71.

Sathe, V. "Institutional versus Questionnaire Measures of Organizational Structure." *Academy of Management Journal,* 1978, pp. 227–38.

Urwick, L. F. "V. A. Graicunas and the Span of Control." *Academy of Management Journal,* 1974, pp. 349–54.

Vance, S. C. *Managers in the Conglomerate Era.* New York: John Wiley & Sons, 1971.

Zey-Ferrell, M. *Dimensions of Organizations: Environment, Context, Structure, Process, and Performance.* Santa Monica, Calif.: Goodyear Publishing, 1979.

CASE FOR ANALYSIS

SELECTING BETWEEN FUNCTION AND PRODUCT AS BASIS FOR DEPARTMENTAL- IZATION

Recently, the top management of a rapidly expanding consumer products company met to consider organizational issues. The present organization structure was departmentalized according to functions as shown in Exhibit 1.

The company's product line had expanded some 10 times during the previous 16 years, and although the current economic conditions caused some concern the management believed that its products were well established. Moreover it anticipated even greater expansion during the next 20 years.

EXHIBIT 1
Consumer Products Company Partial Organization Chart

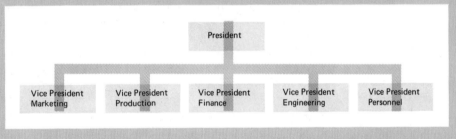

The present organization structure was the topic of discussion, because despite the growth and success of prior years management believed that in many instances the company had not been as responsive to opportunities as it might have been. Changes in consumer tastes, new manufacturing techniques, and engineering breakthroughs had not been exploited because of apparent isolation of these functions from the rest of the company. Each of the functional departments tended to emphasize its own goals and objectives; if new developments had not been included in the annually prepared operating plan, they could not be acted upon. Top management believed that it should attempt to restructure the organization to emphasize the importance of its products.

The organizational planning staff, a part of the personnel function, was instructed to prepare an analysis of alternative structures. It returned six months later with the recommendation that the company adopt a product-based structure. The structure, often termed a *divisional organization structure*, would place under the authority of a single manager all the functions necessary to produce and sell a product or line of products. The recommended structure is shown in Exhibit 2.

Reporting to each vice president would be the heads of the marketing, production, finance, engineering, and personnel departments. These function heads would carry out the necessary work to produce and sell one or more complementary products. The organizational planning staff stated

EXHIBIT 2
Consumer Products Company Partial Organization Chart, Recommended

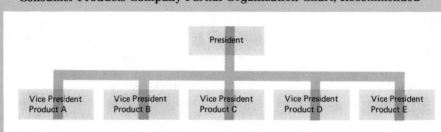

that its review of the literature on organizational structure indicated that product-based organizations were superior to function-based organizations in their ability to respond to external changes, but that they were somewhat less efficient. The impact on the profit and loss statement would be slightly higher unit costs because the size of the individual units would not be sufficient to take advantage of the economies of scale. It would also mean that the functional experts would have to be less specialized. For example, the marketing personnel would have to become involved in product development as well as selling. But the advantages of increased adaptability should offset the disadvantages of reduced efficiency.

The potential impact of the product-based organization on the satisfaction of employees was noted. According to the staff, the employees would suffer some decrease in satisfaction and increase of feelings of stress because they would have to orient their thinking toward the products and away from their specialties. The specialists would have to interact more often with other specialists in the integration of their functions. Consequently some of the bases for positive job satisfaction would be undermined. The staff could not predict how the reduction in satisfaction would affect turnover, absenteeism, or tardiness. They did state that employees should experience a greater sense of involvement in the total operations of the product departments.

Questions for Consideration

1. Has the organizational planning staff moved in the right direction in its analysis? Is its recommended structure appropriate given the nature of the company's environment?

2. How can management determine the relative advantages of the proposed organization if it cannot determine the relationship among the measures of effectiveness?

3. What differences in the two structures other than those identified by the staff would you expect?

Chapter 12

Micro-Organization Design

AN ORGANIZATIONAL ISSUE FOR DEBATE
Job Redesign: Was It Successful?*

ARGUMENT FOR

General Foods Corporation's new pet-food plant in Topeka, Kansas was designed to minimize supervision by delegating authority to workers to make job assignments, schedule coffee breaks, interview prospective employees, and decide pay raises. The system, installed in the plant by a company task force with the assistance of Richard E. Walton, Harvard University, assigns three areas of responsibility—processing, packaging and shipping, and office duties—to self-managing teams of 7 to 14 workers.

The teams, directed by a "team leader," share responsibility for a variety of tasks including those typically performed by staff personnel, for example, equipment maintenance and quality control. The team members rotate between dreary and meaningful jobs. Pay is related to the number of tasks each individual masters. The teams performed much of the work assigned to managerial and staff personnel. As stated by J. W. Bevans, Jr., manager of organizational development, the system attempted "to balance the needs of the people with the needs of the business."

The success of the program is unquestionable according to the former manager of pet-food op-

* Based upon "Stonewalling Plant Democracy," *Business Week*, March 28, 1977, pp. 78, 81–82.

ARGUMENT AGAINST

Whether General Foods' experience with job redesign was successful depends upon who you talk to. Emphatically one employee states: "The system went to hell. It didn't work." According to the critics, problems arose because the system came up against the company's bureaucracy. Lawyers, fearing reactions from the National Labor Relations Board, opposed allowing workers to vote on pay raises. Personnel managers opposed the idea of workers making hiring decisions; engineers resented workers doing engineering work. These resentments resulted in power struggles among and between corporate level staff, plant managers, and workers. Several managers, including three from the pet-food plant itself, quit General Foods.

As a consequence of the pressures, the Topeka system began to change—workers participated less, job classifications were added, and supervisors supervised. These changes were perceived as weakening of management's commitment to the philosophy underlying the system. Quality has dipped, teams have fewer team meetings, and competition among shifts has increased. A major contribution to competition was jealousy, particularly as reflected in pay decisions. Workers found it particularly difficult to discard their subjective judgments of friends when considering

ARGUMENT FOR (continued)

erations, Layman D. Ketchum: "From the standpoint of humanistic working life and economic results, you can consider it a success." As evidence of the claim, the plants' unit costs are 5 percent less than other comparable sites, amounting to an annual saving of $1 million. Employee turnover is only 8 percent and the plant went almost four years before experiencing a lost-time accident.

ARGUMENT AGAINST (continued)

their work performances. Workers at Topeka have also argued that they should share in the financial success of Topeka through the provision of bonuses tied to cost savings.

The critics observe that their negative evaluations of the Topeka system must have merit. They note as evidence, that General Foods no longer permits reporters inside the Topeka plant despite the fact that management once encouraged publicity. The critics also point out that the Topeka system has not been implemented in any other General Foods plant. One manager has predicted that "the future of that plant (Topeka) is to conform to the company norm."

The building blocks of organizational structures are the jobs which people perform. Many factors determine the level of organizational performance; a major factor is the performance of its employees. Micro-organization design refers to the process by which managers create individual job tasks and responsibilities. Apart from the very practical issues associated with job design, that is, issues which relate to effectiveness in economic, political, and monetary terms, we can appreciate the importance of work in social and psychological terms. As noted in earlier chapters the jobs we hold can be sources of psychological stress and even mental and physical impairment. On a more positive note jobs provide income, meaningful life experiences, self-esteem, esteem from others, regulation of our lives, and association with others.[1] Thus, the well-being of organizations and people depend upon how well management is able to design jobs.

QUALITY OF WORK-LIFE

■ In recent years the issue of designing jobs has gone beyond the determination of the most efficient way to perform tasks. The concept of *quality of work-life* is now widely used to refer to "the degree to which members of work organizations are able to satisfy important personal needs through their experiences in organizations."[2] The emphasis on satisfaction of personal needs does not imply de-emphasis of organizational needs. Instead contemporary managers are finding that when personal needs of employees are satisfied, the performance of the organization itself is enhanced. The concept, quality of work-life, embodies the theories and ideas of the human relations movement of the 1950s and the job enrichment efforts of the 60s and 70s.

As America moves into the 1980s, the challenge to managers is to provide for both quality of work-life and improved production and efficiency through reindustrialization. At the present time, the trade-offs between the gains in human terms from improved quality of work-life and the gains in economic terms from reindustrialization are not fully known. There are those who believe that it will be necessary to defer quality of work-life programs so as to make the American economy more productive and efficient.[3] Others would observe that reindustrialization can present opportunities to combine quality of life and reindustrialization efforts.[4]

Job design and redesign strategies, many of which are presented in this chapter, are based upon efforts (1) to identify the most important needs of employees and (2) to remove obstacles in the workplace which frustrate those needs. The hoped-for results are jobs which fulfill important needs

---

[1]David F. Smith, "The Functions of Work," *Omega*, 1975, pp. 383–93.

[2]J. Richard Hackman and J. Lloyd Suttle, eds., *Improving Life at Work* (Santa Monica, Calif.: Goodyear Publishing, 1977), p. 4.

[3]Amitai Etzioni, "Choose America Must—Between 'Reindustrialization and Quality of Life'," *Across the Board*, October 1980, pp. 43–49.

[4]Ernesto J. Poza and M. Lynne Markus, "Success Story: The Team Approach to Work Restructuring," *Organizational Dynamics*, Winter 1980, pp. 2–25.

and lead to performance outcomes such as job satisfaction, productivity, and organizational effectiveness. The remainder of this chapter reviews the important theories, research, and practices of job design. As will be seen, contemporary management has at its disposal a wide range of techniques which facilitate the achievement of personal and organizational performance.

A CONCEPTUAL MODEL OF JOB DESIGN

■ The conceptual model depicted in Figure 12–1 is based upon the extensive research literature which has appeared in the last 20 years. The model includes the various terms and concepts which appear in the current literature. When linked together these concepts describe the important determinants of job performance and organizational effectiveness. The model is far from simple to understand, much less to apply in practice. Its complex-

FIGURE 12–1
A Conceptual Framework of Job Design

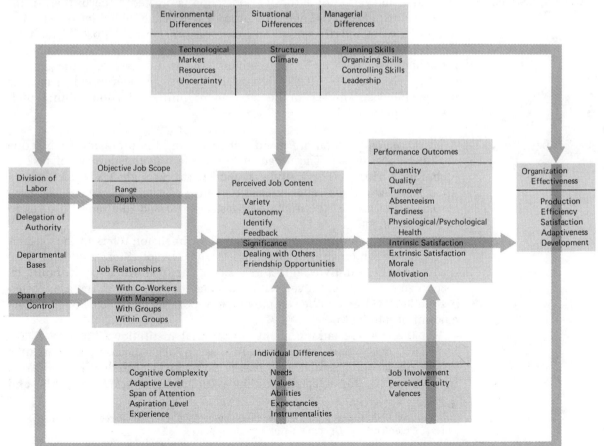

ity is due to the fact that individuals react differently to jobs. While one person may derive positive satisfaction from a job, another may not. A second difficulty is the trade-offs between organizational and individual needs. Thus, the technology of manufacturing may dictate that management adopt assembly-line mass-production methods and low-skilled jobs to achieve optimal efficiency. Such jobs, however, may result in great unrest and worker discontent. For example, General Motors' Lordstown Vega plant represented a major application of industrial engineering and job specialization. The average time per job activity was reduced to 36 seconds and each worker completed work on an assigned component at the rate of almost 100 per hour. But the plant has suffered strikes, shutdowns, and sabotage.[5] Perhaps these costs could have been avoided by a more careful balancing of organizational and individual needs.

DESIGNING JOB SCOPE AND JOB RELATIONSHIPS

■ A significant managerial decision is the determination of job scope and job relationships. Through the application of the principles of division of labor and delegation of authority, job scope is created. Each of these principles contributes to the determination of what each jobholder is expected to do and what activities, methods, and machinery will be used. The delegation of authority principle determines the degree of discretion, or choice, the jobholder has in choosing methods, and in the case of managers, assigning other people to tasks. Job relationships are determined in part by the specific basis and size of the department, unit, or division within which the job is performed.

Job Scope

Two concepts which are useful for analyzing the problem of job scope are range and depth. The *range* of a job refers to the number of tasks a jobholder performs. The individual who performs eight tasks to complete a job has a wider job range than a person performing four tasks. In most instances the greater the number of tasks performed the longer it takes to complete the job.

The second job dimension is *depth*. The dimension refers to the amount of discretion which an individual has to alter the job. Since the depth concept is related to individual factors such as personal influence, it should be recognized that an employee with the same job title and at the same organizational level as another employee may possess more, less, or the same amount of job depth.

Whether we are talking about educational institutions, business firms, hospitals, or government agencies it is essential to discuss job occupants' range and depth. The relation between job range and job depth is indicated in Figure 12–2 for selected employees of business firms, hospitals, and

---

[5] William F. Dowling, "Job Redesign on the Assembly Line: Farewell to Blue-Collar Blues?" *Organizational Dynamics*, Autumn 1973, p. 51.

FIGURE 12–2
Job Depth and Range

High Depth

BUSINESS Packaging Machine Mechanics	HOSPITAL Anesthesiologists	UNIVERSITY College Professors	BUSINESS Research Scientists	HOSPITAL Chiefs of Surgery	UNIVERSITY Presidents

Low Range ——————————————————————————————— High Range

BUSINESS AssemblyLine Workers	HOSPITAL Bookkeepers	UNIVERSITY Graduate Student Instructors	BUSINESS Maintenance Repairmen	HOSPITAL Nurses	UNIVERSITY Departmental Chairpersons

Low Depth

Range = the number of tasks a job occupant performs.
Depth = the amount of discretion to alter or influence the job.

universities. The titles placed in each cell of Figure 12–2 reflect the relative range and depth of the positions cited. For example, the chief of surgery in a hospital would possess more range and depth than the bookkeeper in the same hospital.

As indicated in Figure 12–2, research scientists, chiefs of surgery, and university presidents generally have high job range and significant depth. Research scientists perform a large number of tasks and are not closely supervised by administrators. This is interpreted to mean that the scientists possess high job range and depth.

Chiefs of surgery have significant job range in that they oversee and counsel on many diverse surgical matters. In addition they are not supervised closely and have the formal position to influence hospital surgery policies and procedures.

University presidents have a large number of tasks to perform. They must speak to alumni groups, politicians, community representatives, and students. They must develop, with the consultation of others, policies on admissions, fund raising, and adult education. They can alter the faculty recruitment philosophy and thus alter the course of the entire institution. For example, a university president may want to build an institution that is noted for high-quality classroom instruction and for providing excellent services to the community. This thrust may lead to recruiting and selecting professors who want to concentrate on these two specific goals. In contrast, another president may want to foster outstanding research and high-quality classroom instruction. Of course another president may attempt to develop an institution that is noted for instruction, research, and service. The critical point to recognize is that university presidents have sufficient depth to alter the course of a university's direction.

In the high-depth and low-range segment of Figure 12–2, we find packaging machine mechanics, anesthesiologists, and faculty members. Mechanics perform only the operations that pertain to the packaging machine.

Thus, the number of tasks they perform is limited. But they can influence how breakdowns on the packaging machine are corrected—in other words, mechanics have relatively high job depth.

Anesthesiologists perform a limited number of tasks. They are concerned with administering anesthetics to patients, a job that has low range. However, they can control the type of anesthetic administered in a particular situation. This control is indicative of high job depth.

University professors specifically engaged in classroom instruction have relatively low job range. Teaching involves comparatively more tasks than the work of the anesthesiologist, yet fewer tasks than that of the business research scientist. However, professors' job depth is greater than that of graduate student instructors. This follows from the fact that they determine how they will conduct the class, what materials will be presented, and the standards to be used in evaluating students.

Job scope, then, involves the determination of activities (range) and authority (depth). A highly specialized job is one which has few tasks to accomplish by prescribed means. Such jobs are quite routine; they also tend to be controlled by specified rules and procedures. The managerial problem is simply put, but not simply answered. It is: given the economic and technical requirements of the organization's mission, goals, and objectives, what is the optimal point along the continuum of specialization?

Job Relationships

The application of the principles of departmentalization and span of control results in groupings of jobs. These groups become the responsibility of a manager to coordinate toward organization purposes. At the same time, these principles determine the nature and extent of jobholders' interpersonal relationships, individually and within groups. As we already have seen in the discussion of groups in organizations, group performance is effected in part by group cohesiveness. And the degree of group cohesiveness depends upon the quality and kind of interpersonal relationships of jobholders assigned to a task or command group.

The wider the span of control, the larger the group and consequently the more difficult it is to establish friendship and interest relationships. Simply, people in larger groups are less likely to communicate (and interact sufficiently to form interpersonal ties) than people in smaller groups. Without the opportunity to communicate, people will be unable to establish the bases for cohesive work groups.[6] Thus an important source of satisfaction may be lost for individuals who seek to fulfill social and esteem needs through relationships with co-workers.

The basis for departmentalization which management selects also has important implications for job relationships. Functional and process bases tend to place jobs with similar depth and range in groups; while product and client bases tend to group jobs with dissimilar depth and range. Thus

---

[6] Stanley E. Seashore, *Group Cohesiveness in the Industrial Work Group* (Ann Arbor: Institute for Social Research, University of Michigan, 1954).

in functional and process departments people will be doing much the same specialty. Product and client departments, however, are comprised of jobs which are quite different and heterogeneous. Research has suggested that feelings of satisfaction, stress, and involvement are often related to the basis for departmentalization. One study suggests that jobholders in functional departments express greater satisfaction and less stress and involvement than their counterparts in product departments.[7] In part the interpretation of this finding is that people with homogeneous backgrounds, skills, and training have more common interests than those with heterogeneous ones. Thus it is easier for them to establish social relationships which are satisfying.

Scientific Management and Objective Job Scope

The major theme of scientific management is that objective analyses of facts and data collected in the workplace could provide the bases for determining the one best way to design work.[8] The essence of scientific management was stated as follows:

> First: Develop a science for each element of a man's work which replaces the old rule-of-thumb method.
> Second: Scientifically select and then train, teach, and develop the workman, whereas in the past he chose his own work and trained himself as best he could.
> Third: Heartily cooperate with the men so as to insure all of the work being done in accordance with the principles of the science which has been developed.
> Fourth: There is almost an equal division of the work and the responsibility between the management and the workmen. The management takes over all work for which they are better fitted than the workmen, while in the past, almost all of the work and the greater part of the responsibility were thrown upon the men.[9]

These four principles state and illustrate the thrust of scientific management methods: to determine a science for each job and then train people to execute the job according to the approved way (the role of management), and to remedy the difficulties created by the rule-of-thumb methods which evolved when the tasks of managers and workers were confused.

Taylor proposed that the way to improve work, that is, to make it more

---

[7] Arthur H. Walker and Jay W. Lorsch, "Organizational Choice: Product versus Function," in *Studies in Organization Design*, ed. Jay W. Lorsch and Paul R. Lawrence (Homewood, Ill.: Richard D. Irwin, 1970), pp. 48–49.

[8] The literature of scientific management is voluminous. The original works and the subsequent criticisms and interpretations would make a large volume. Of special significance are the works of the principal authors including: Frederick W. Taylor, *Principles of Scientific Management* (New York: Harper & Row, 1911); Harrington Emerson, *The Twelve Principles of Efficiency* (New York: The Engineering Magazine, 1913); Henry L. Gantt, *Industrial Leadership* (New Haven, Conn.: Yale University Press, 1916); Frank B. Gilbreth, *Motion Study* (New York: D. Van Nostrand, 1911); Lillian M. Gilbreth, *The Psychology of Management* (New York: Sturgis & Walton, 1914).

[9] Taylor, *Principles*, pp. 36–37.

efficient, is to determine (1) the "best way" to do a task (motion study), and (2) the standard time for completion of the task (time study). The improvement of work involves an analysis of the entire context and environment within which the work is done. The objective of motion study is to determine a preferable work method with consideration to raw materials, product design, order of work, tools, equipment, workplace layout, and the hand and body motions required by the workman.[10] In this context, motion and time studies are parts of the total process of work improvement.

The idea that job scope can be based solely on engineering approaches ignores the very large role played by the individual who performs the job. The conceptual framework in Figure 12–1 indicates that individual differences enter into the issue of job design at a number of points. In the following section, the issue of *job content* is examined. As we will see, the manner is which individuals react to job scope and relationships depends upon their individual perceptions.

Job Content and Individual Differences

Job content refers to aspects of a job which define its general nature as perceived by the jobholder. It is important to distinguish between the *objective* properties of a job as reflected in formal job descriptions and specifications and the *subjective* properties of a job as reflected in the perceptions of people who perform them. Scientific management techniques such as time and motion studies result in requisite activities (job range), authority (job depth), and interpersonal interactions (job relationships). However one cannot understand, much less predict, the relationship between these variables and job performance without consideration of individual differences such as cognitive complexity, adaptive level, and span of attention.[11]

If management is to understand the relationship between job content and performance, some method for measuring job content must exist. Moreover organization behavior researchers have attempted to measure job characteristics in a variety of work settings. These research efforts have accelerated in recent years as society's interest in the quality of work life has heightened. The methods which researchers use rely upon questionnaires which jobholders complete and which measure their perceptions of certain job characteristics.

An early and pioneering effort to measure job content through employee responses to a questionnaire resulted in the identification of six characteristics: variety, autonomy, required interaction, optional interaction, knowledge and skill required, and responsibility.[12] These attributes reflect the jobholder's opinion regarding necessary conditions for successful task

---

[10] Marvin E. Mundel, "Motion and Time Study," in *Handbook of Industrial Engineering and Management*, ed. William G. Ireson and Eugene L. Grant (Englewood Cliffs, N.J.: Prentice-Hall, 1955), p. 285.

[11] Donald P. Schwab and L. L. Cummings, "A Theoretical Analysis of the Impact of Task Scope on Employee Performance," *Academy of Management Review*, April 1976, p. 31–32.

[12] Arthur N. Turner and Paul R. Lawrence, *Industrial Jobs and the Worker: An Investigation of Response to Task Attributes* (Cambridge, Mass.: Harvard University Press, 1965).

completion. The consequent index of these six characteristics was termed the Requisite Task Attribute Index (RTAI). The original RTAI has been extensively reviewed and analyzed. One important development was the review by Hackman and Lawler who revised the index to include the six characteristics shown in Table 12–1.[13]

Variety, task identity, and *feedback* are perceptions of job range. *Autonomy* is the perception of job depth; and *dealing with others* and *friendship opportunities* reflect perceptions of job relationships. Thus employees sharing similar psychological perceptions *and* similar job scopes and relationships should report similar job characteristics.

TABLE 12–1
Selected Job Characteristics

Variety—The degree to which a job requires employees to perform a wide range of operations in their work and/or the degree to which employees must use a variety of equipment and procedures in their work.

Autonomy—The extent to which employees have a major say in scheduling their work, selecting the equipment they will use, and deciding on procedures to be followed.

Task Identity—The extent to which employees do an entire or whole piece of work and can clearly identify with the results of their efforts.

Feedback—The degree to which employees receive information as they are working, which reveals how well they are performing on the job.

Dealing with Others—The degree to which a job requires employees to deal with other people to complete their work.

Friendship Opportunities—The degree to which a job allows employees to talk with one another on the job and to establish informal relationships with other employees at work.

Source: Henry P. Sims, Jr., Andrew D. Szilagyi, and Robert T. Keller, "The Measurement of Job Characteristics," *Academy of Management Journal*, June 1976, p. 197.

Two approaches currently exist to measure perceived job content. The Job Characteristics Index (JCI) attempts to measure jobholders' perceptions of the six characteristics shown in Table 12–1.[14] A more widely used approach is the Job Diagnostic Survey (JDS).[15] The JDS measures variety, autonomy, task identity, feedback, and significance. Unlike the JCI which includes job relationship dimensions, the JDS attempts to measure only the "core" dimensions of job content and in doing so, includes an additional

---

[13]J. Richard Hackman and Edward W. Lawler III, "Employee Reactions to Job Characteristics," *Journal of Applied Psychology*, 1971, 259–86; and J. Richard Hackman and Greg R. Oldman, "Development of the Job Diagnostic Survey," *Journal of Applied Psychology*, 1975, 159–70.

[14]Henry P. Sims, Jr., Andrew D. Szilagyi, and Robert T. Keller, "The Measurement of Job Characteristics," *Academy of Management Journal*, June 1976, pp. 195–212.

[15]Hackman and Oldham, "Development of the Job Diagnostic Survey."

dimension, significance, which reflects the perceived importance of the work to the organization or to others. The JDS has been widely used by researchers,[16] although some evidence exists that the JCI is an alternative measure.[17] Subsequent studies will no doubt improve the measurement of job content, but it is doubtful that any perceptual measurement will ever eliminate the effects of individual differences. The effect of individual differences is to "provide filters such that different persons perceive the same objective stimuli in different manners."[18] Yet even if individuals perceive job content similarly, we cannot expect similar job performance. The link between job content and job performance is complicated not only by individual differences but also by situational differences.

PERCEIVED JOB CONTENT AND PERFORMANCE OUTCOMES

■ The relationship between job content and job performance rests almost solely on factors which are unrelated to job scope and relationships. As shown in Figure 12–1, the relationship is moderated by individual and situational differences.

Individual differences in need strength, particularly the strength of growth needs, has been shown to influence the effect of feedback on job performance. That is employees with relatively weak higher order needs are less concerned about receiving feedback than are those with relatively strong growth needs.[19] Thus managers expecting higher performance to result from increased feedback on goal attainment would be disappointed if the jobholders did not demonstrate strong growth needs. At the same time the manager must not expect continuous increases in performance to accompany larger job scope. At some point, performance turns down as individuals reach the limits imposed by their abilities. The relationship between performance and job scope even for individuals with high growth needs is likely to be curvilinear.[20]

Situational differences also affect the relationship between job content and job performance. Examples of such differences include organizational structure, climate, technology, product, and market type.[21] A special situ-

---

[16] Jon L. Pierce and Randall B. Dunham, "Task Design: A Literature Review," *Academy of Management Review,* October 1976, pp. 83–97.

[17] Jon L. Pierce and Randall B. Dunham, "The Measurement of Perceived Job Characteristics: The Job Diagnostic Survey versus the Job Characteristics Inventory," *Academy of Management Journal,* March 1978, pp. 123–28.

[18] Randall B. Dunham, Ramon J. Aldag, and Arthur P. Brief, "Dimensionality of Task Design as Measured by the Job Diagnostic Survey," *Academy of Management Journal,* June 1977, p. 222.

[19] John M. Ivancevich and J. Timothy McMahon, "A Study of Task-Goal Attributes, Higher Order Need Strength and Performance," *Academy of Management Review,* December 1977, p. 561.

[20] Joseph E. Champoux, "A Three Sample Test of Some Extensions to the Job Characteristics Model of Work Motivation," *Academy of Management Journal,* September 1980, pp. 466–78.

[21] Randall B. Dunham, "Reactions to Job Characteristics: Moderating Effects of the Organization," *Academy of Management Journal,* March 1977, p. 43.

ational variable is the social setting in which the job is performed. As has been pointed out by more than one research study, how one perceives a job is greatly affected by what other people say about it. Thus if one's friends state their jobs are boring, one is likely to state that his or her job is also boring.[22] But let us complete our discussion of the basic model by turning attention to the relationships between job performance, job outcomes, and job satisfaction.

Job Performance

Measures used to identify the performance of individuals include quantity and quality of output, absenteeism, tardiness, and turnover. These measures take on different values and for each job some implicit or explicit standard exists. Industrial engineering studies establish standards for daily quantity, and quality control specialists establish tolerance limits for acceptable quality. These aspects of job performance account for characteristics of the product, client, or service for which the jobholder is responsible. But job performance includes other aspects.

The jobholder reacts to the work itself, and reacts by either attending regularly or being absent, by staying with the job or by quitting. Moreover, physiological and health-related problems can ensue as a consequence of job performance. Stress related to job performance can contribute to physical and mental impairment; accidents and occupationally related disease can also ensue.

Job Outcomes

Job outcomes include intrinsic and extrinsic work outcomes. The distinction between intrinsic and extrinsic outcomes is important for understanding the reactions of people to their jobs.[23] In a general sense, intrinsic outcomes are objects or events which follow from the worker's own efforts, not requiring the involvement of any other person. More simply it is an outcome clearly related to action on the workers' part. Such outcomes typically are thought to be solely in the province of professional and technical jobs; yet all jobs potentially have opportunities for intrinsic outcomes. Such outcomes involve feelings of responsibility, challenge, and recognition; and result from such job characteristics as variety, autonomy, identity, and significance.

Extrinsic outcomes, however, are objects or events which follow from the workers' own efforts in conjunction with other factors or persons not directly involved in the job itself. Pay, working conditions, co-workers, and even supervision are objects in the workplace which are potentially job

---

[22] Sam E. White and Terrance E. Mitchell, "Job Enrichment versus Social Cues: A Comparison and Competitive Test," *Journal of Applied Psychology*, January 1979, pp. 1–9; Edward J. O'Connor and Gerald V. Barrett, "Informational Cues and Individual Differences as Determinants of Subjective Perceptions of Task Enrichment," *Academy of Management Journal*, December 1980, pp. 697–716.

[23] Arthur P. Brief and Ramon J. Aldag, "The Intrinsic-Extrinsic Dichotomy: Toward Conceptual Clarity," *Academy of Management Review*, July 1977, pp. 496–500.

outcomes, but which are not a fundamental part of the work. Dealing with others and friendship interactions are sources of extrinsic outcomes.

Job Satisfaction

Job satisfaction depends on the levels of intrinsic and extrinsic outcomes and how the jobholder views those outcomes. We have already noted that outcomes have different values (valences) for different people. For some people, responsible and challenging work may have neutral or even negative outcomes. For other people, such work outcomes may have high positive values. People differ in the valences they attach to job outcomes. Those differences alone would account for different levels of job satisfaction for essentially the same job tasks.

Another important individual difference is job involvement.[24] People differ in the extent (1) that work is a central life interest, (2) they actively participate in work, (3) they perceive work as central to self-esteem, and (4) they perceive work as consistent with self-concept. Persons who are uninvolved in their work cannot be expected to realize the same satisfaction as those who are. This variable accounts for the fact that two workers could report different levels of satisfaction for the same performance levels.

A final individual difference is the perceived equity of the outcome in terms of what the jobholder considers a fair reward.[25] If the outcomes are perceived to be unfair in relation to those of others in similar jobs requiring similar effort, the jobholder will experience dissatisfaction and seek means to restore the equity, either by seeking greater rewards (primarily extrinsic) or by reducing effort.

MOTIVATIONAL PROPERTIES OF JOBS

■ The interest of organization behavior researchers and managers in the motivational properties of jobs is based upon the understanding that job performance depends upon more than the ability of the jobholder. Specifically, job performance is determined by the interaction of ability and motivation as expressed by the equation:

$$\text{Job performance} = \text{Ability} \times \text{Motivation}$$

The equation reflects the fact that job performance of a person can be greater than that of a second person because of greater ability, motivation, or both. It also reflects the possibility that job performance could be zero even if the jobholder has ability; in such instances, motivation would have to be zero. Thus, it is imperative that management consider the potential impact of motivational properties of jobs. The following close-up illustrates one company's efforts to include motivational properties in employees' first jobs.

---

[24] S. D. Saleh and James Hosek, "Job Involvement: Concepts and Measurements" *Academy of Management Journal*, June 1976, pp. 213–24.

[25] J. Stacy Adams, "Toward an Understanding of Inequity," *Journal of Abnormal and Social Psychology*, November 1963, pp. 422–36.

ORGANIZATIONS: CLOSE-UP

Job Design Research at General Electric

The research carried on in General Electric under the direction of Dr. Thomas D. Hollmann, manager of personnel research, has confirmed the importance of an individual's first job. According to Hollmann, people who have experienced challenging work on their first jobs and who received good counseling tended to be productive and to stay with the company. To determine what constitutes challenging work, Hollmann and his colleagues interviewed employees with two to four year's experience with GE. These employees came from such diverse functions as engineering, manufacturing, and marketing. They were asked to describe their most and least challenging work experiences and to specify what their managers had done to encourage their career development.

The concept of challenging work that emerged from these interviews stressed the importance of job content, skill utilization, personal involvement, opportunities to interact with others, and a sense of accomplishment. With this idea of what is meant by challenging work, Hollmann was able to go to managers in GE and ask them to verify the concept and then to identify the problems associated with providing such work experiences in their units. Since the purpose of the entire effort was to *provide* challenging work to new employees rather than to *define* it, the managers were encouraged to propose solutions for the removal of barriers to such work.

Source: *Management Review*, June 1980, p. 30.

In recent years organization behavior theorists have advanced a number of suggestions for improving the motivational properties of job design. Invariably the suggestions, termed *job redesign strategies*, attempt to improve job performance and satisfaction through changes in job range and scope. In the next section the more significant of these strategies are reviewed.

REDESIGNING JOB RANGE: JOB ROTATION AND JOB ENLARGEMENT

■ The earliest attempts to redesign jobs date to the scientific management era. The efforts at that time emphasized efficiency criteria. In so doing, the individual tasks which comprise a job are limited, uniform, and repetitive.[26] This practice leads to narrow job range, and consequently, reported high levels of job discontent, turnover, absenteeism, and dissatisfaction.[27] Accordingly, strategies were devised which resulted in wider job range

---

[26]Louis E. Davis, "Job Design and Productivity: A New Approach" in *Readings in Organizational and Industrial Psychology*, ed. Gary A. Yukl and Kenneth N. Wexley (New York: Oxford University Press, 1971), p. 172.

[27]An early and classic study of the dysfunctional consequences of narrow job range and scope is Charles R. Walker and Robert H. Guest, *The Man on the Assembly Line* (Cambridge, Mass.: Harvard University Press, 1952).

through increasing the requisite activities of jobs. Two of these approaches are *job rotation* and *job enlargement*.

Job Rotation

Managers of organizations such as Western Electric, Ford, Bethlehem Steel and TRW Systems have utilized different forms of the job rotation strategy. This practice involves rotating an individual from one job to another. In so doing the individual is expected to complete more job activities since each job includes different tasks. Job rotation involves increasing the range of jobs and the perception of variety in the job content. Increasing task variety should, according to expectancy theory, increase the intrinsic valence associated with job satisfaction. However, the practice of job rotation does not change the basic characteristics of the assigned jobs and critics state that this approach involves nothing more than having people perform several boring and monotonous jobs rather than one. An alternative strategy is job enlargement.

Job Enlargement

The Walker and Guest study[28] was concerned with the social and psychological problems associated with mass production jobs in an automobile assembly plant. The researchers found that many workers disliked numerous factors associated with their specialized jobs. It was determined that mechanical pacing, repetitiveness of operations, and a lack of a sense of accomplishment were job factors which employees disliked.

Walker and Guest also found a positive relationship between the number of operations performed and the overall interest an employee had in the job. These findings are summarized in Table 12–2. The findings of this research support those motivation theories which posit that permanent increases in job variety will produce gains in performance and satisfaction. Job enlargement strategies focus upon the opposite of dividing work—they are a form of despecialization or increasing the number of tasks which an employee performs. For example, a job is structured in such a manner that instead of performing three tasks the employee performs six tasks.

Although, in many instances, an enlarged job requires a longer training

TABLE 12–2
Employee Interest and Job Variety

Number of Operations Performed	Number Reporting Work as Very or Fairly Interesting	Number Reporting Work as Not Very or Not at All Interesting	Total Employee
1	19	38	57
2–5	28	36	64
6 or more	41	18	59
Total	88	92	180

Source: Charles R. Walker and Robert H. Guest, *The Man on the Assembly Line* (Cambridge, Mass.: Harvard University Press, 1952), p. 54.

---

[28]Ibid.

period, it is assumed that satisfaction of the worker increases because boredom is reduced. The implication, of course, is that the job enlargement will lead to more productivity and improved overall efficiency.

Several studies lend support to the applicability of job enlargement. One such study involved job redesign at an IBM plant.[29] A parts manufacturing unit of the Endicott plant of IBM redesigned a number of jobs in an attempt to improve worker morale. The job of machine operator after the reorganization included setting up the job, sharpening tools, inspecting the work, and operating the equipment.

The findings of the IBM study suggest that the job enlargement strategy increased worker morale, lowered production costs, increased the interests of employees, and improved the quality of output. It was also possible to eliminate an entire level of management in the organizational structure because, under the new job enlargement program, employees had greater responsibilities and authority.

Another study which involves the effects of job enlargement is the Maytag Company study.[30] It was concerned with changing the job design on a mass-production assembly line. During different phases of the study, the job was changed. The different phases studied were as follows:

Phase I: Six operators assembled a washing machine pump on a conveyor line.

Phase II: The assembling of the pump was a four-person operation.

Phase III: The work previously done on the conveyor line was done at four individual *one-person workbenches.*

Throughout each of these changes, the time required to assemble the pump decreased. The least time-consuming design for assembling involved the one-person workbenches. This suggests that reducing assembly-line delays and enlarging the job may increase productivity in some instances.

Since these early experiences with job enlargement, the concept has become considerably more sophisticated. In recent years effective job enlargement involves more than simply increasing task variety. In addition, it is necessary to redesign certain other aspects of job range, including providing the worker a meaningful work module, performance feedback, ability utilization, and worker-paced (rather than machine-paced) control.[31] Each of these changes involves balancing the gains and losses of varying degrees of division of labor. In terms of the conceptual framework presented in Figure 12–1, variety, work modules, feedback, and worker-paced control involve questions of division of labor.

---

[29]C. R. Walker, "The Problem of the Repetitive Job," *Harvard Business Review*, May 1950, pp. 54–58.

[30]M. D. Kilbridge, "Reduced Costs through Job Enlargement: A Case," *The Journal of Business*, October 1960, pp. 357–62.

[31]Kae H. Chung and Monica F. Ross, "Differences in Motivational Properties between Job Enlargement and Job Enrichment," *Academy of Management Review*, January 1977, pp. 114–15.

The conceptual framework also indicates that psychological factors such as cognitive complexity, adaptive level, span of attention, and aspiration level intervene between job range and perceived job content. It is apparent that some employees simply cannot cope with enlarged jobs because they cannot comprehend complexity; moreover they may not have an attention span sufficiently long to stay with and complete an enlarged set of tasks. However if employees are known to be amenable to job enlargement and if they have the requisite ability, then job enlargement should increase satisfaction and product quality and decrease absenteeism and turnover.[32] These gains are not without costs, including the likelihood that employees will demand larger salaries in exchange for their performance of enlarged jobs. Yet these costs must be borne if management desires to implement the redesign strategy which enlarges job depth, *job enrichment.* Job enlargement is a necessary precondition for job enrichment.

REDESIGNING JOB DEPTH: JOB ENRICHMENT

(satisfiers & dissatisfiers)

■ The impetus for redesigning job range was provided by Herzberg's two-factor theory of motivation.[33] The basis of his idea is that factors which meet individuals' need for psychological growth, especially responsibility, job challenge, and achievement must be combined with hygiene factors to accomplish effective performance.

Herzberg points out that to achieve good performance, people with proper abilities are needed. This means that a sound selection program is needed. He also stresses the fact that motivation through job enrichment requires reinforcement. The performance appraisal system must reinforce growth behavior and provide for continued opportunities for growth.

The implementation of job enrichment is realized through direct changes in the work itself. There are a number of important ingredients that Herzberg believes will encourage the motivator factors to emerge. Some of these are:

1. *Direct feedback:* The evaluation of performance should be timely and direct.
2. *New learning:* A good job enables people to feel that they are psychologically growing. All jobs should provide an opportunity to learn something.
3. *Scheduling:* People should be able to schedule some part of their own work.
4. *Uniqueness:* Each job should have some unique qualities or features.
5. *Control over resources:* If at all possible, the workers should have control over their job tasks.
6. *Personal accountability:* People should be provided with an opportunity to be accountable for the job.

---

[32] Ibid., p. 116.

[33] Frederick Herzberg, "The Wise Old Turk," *Harvard Business Review*, September–October 1974, pp. 70–80.

A number of research studies support the assumption that job enrichment is a major determinant of better job performance and increased satisfaction. Ford states that 17 of 18 experiments at AT&T with clerical and other telephone company employees showed positive improvement after jobs were enriched.[34] A study of technicians, engineers, and sales representatives indicated that job enrichment pays off in better performance and greater satisfaction.[35]

As defined by the executive in charge of the job redesign program at Texas Instruments, job enrichment is a process for developing employees so that they think and behave like managers in managing their jobs, and a process for redefining the job and the role of the job incumbent to make such development feasible.[36] The process as implemented in TI is continuous and pervades the entire organization. Every one of the jobs in TI is viewed as subject to analysis to determine if it can be enriched to include managerial activities, and thereby made more meaningful. Moreover, as the jobs of nonmanagerial personnel are redesigned to include greater depth, the jobs of managers must be redesigned. The redesigned managerial jobs emphasize training and counseling of subordinates and de-emphasize control and direction.

An application of job enrichment in a nonmanufacturing setting is illustrated in the following close-up.

ORGANIZATIONS: CLOSE-UP

Job Enrichment at Citibank

Citibank recently undertook an extensive change in the ways its employees did their work. According to George E. Seegers, a bank vice president, a customer survey indicated that the bank scored very low on "customer service." Upon examining the causes of the problem, the bank management concluded that the reason was that its employees didn't "feel like somebody." They were dissatisfied with their rather mundane jobs created in part by the decision of the bank some time ago to introduce automatic teller machines. Building on the idea that everybody wants to feel like somebody, the bank undertook extensive changes designed to recognize the individuality of employees as well as customers.

Among the many changes implemented were the following:

Encouraging communications between the functional departments: operations, marketing, and servicing.

---

[34] Robert Ford, "Job Enrichment Lessons for AT&T," *Harvard Business Review*, January–February 1973, pp. 96–106.

[35] William J. Paul, Jr., Keith B. Robertson, and Frederick Herzberg, "Job Enrichment Pays Off," *Harvard Business Review*, March–April 1969, pp. 61–78.

[36] M. Scott Myers, *Every Employee a Manager* (New York: McGraw-Hill, 1970), p. xii.

ORGANIZATIONS: CLOSE-UP (continued)

Decentralizing operations so that one person could handle an entire transaction from the time it comes into the bank until it leaves.

Putting the employees who do the job in direct contact with the customers
and the computers.

Asking the people who do the job what is boring and/or troublesome *before*
automating.

Undertaking considerable training and education for the entire work force.

These changes in job design were done over a two-year period. The
changes were accompanied by training sessions which taught the new skills.
It was also necessary to develop new attitudes among the management personnel including the attitude that employee opinions are valuable and desirable inputs into decisions.

Source: *Management Review*, May 1980, p. 42.

As the theory and practice of job enrichment has evolved, organization
behavior theorists and managers have become aware that successful applications tap a number of motivational factors of jobs. These factors include
employee participation, goal internalization, autonomy, and group management.[37] Realizing these changes involves delegating greater authority to
workers to participate in decisions, set their own goals, and evaluate their
(and their work groups') performance; it also involves changing the nature
and style of leadership behavior. Given the ability of employees to carry
out enriched jobs and the willingness of managers to share control, gains
in performance can be expected. These positive outcomes are the result of
increasing employees' expectancies that efforts lead to performance, that
performance leads to intrinsic and extrinsic rewards, and that these rewards have power to satisfy needs.[38]

Like other approaches that have evolved from behavioral science theory,
job enrichment has its critics. Fein believes that behavioralists tend to impose their own value systems when prescribing job enrichment. He believes that when job enrichment applications and research studies are examined closely, four things are found:

1. What actually occurred was quite different from what was reported.
2. Most of the studies were conducted with employees who do not rep-
    resent a cross-section of the working population.

---

[37]Chung and Ross, "Differences in Motivational Properties," pp. 116–17.

[38]Kae H. Chung, *Motivational Theories and Practices* (Columbus, Ohio: Grid, 1977), p.
204.

3. Only a handful of job enrichment cases have been reported in the past 10 years, despite the impression that it is widespread.
4. In all instances, the experiments were initiated by management, never by workers or unions.[39]

Whether job enrichment is a powerful motivator of positive behavior is still an unanswered question because of the points raised by Fein and others. Despite these problems job enrichment is a widespread application of Herzberg's two-factor theory. It may not be scientifically pure, but it continues to be adopted.

REDESIGNING JOB RANGE AND DEPTH: COMBINED APPROACH

■ Job enrichment and job enlargement are not competing strategies. Job enlargement but not job enrichment may be compatible with the needs, values, and abilities of some individuals. Yet job enrichment, when appropriate, necessarily involves job enlargement. A promising new approach to job redesign which attempts to integrate the two approaches is the job characteristic model. Hackman, Oldham, Janson, and Purdy devised the approach and based it upon the Job Diagnostic Survey cited in an earlier section.[40]

The model attempts to account for the interrelationships among (1) certain core dimensions of jobs, (2) psychological states associated with motivation, satisfaction, and performance, (3) job outcomes, and (4) growth need strength. Figure 12–3 describes the relationships among these variables. The core dimensions of the job consist of characteristics first described by Turner and Lawrence.[41] Although variety, identity, significance, autonomy, and feedback do not completely describe job content, they, according to this model, sufficiently describe those aspects which management can manipulate to bring about gains in productivity.

The steps which management can take to increase the core dimensions include combining task elements, assigning whole pieces of work (i.e., work modules), allowing discretion in selection of work methods, permitting self-paced control. These actions increase task variety, identity, and significance; consequently the "experienced meaningfulness of work" psychological state is increased. By permitting employee participation and

[39] Mitchell Fein, "The Myth of Job Enrichment," in *Humanizing the Workplace*, ed. Roy P. Fairfield (Buffalo: Prometheus Books, 1974) pp. 71–78. For some excellent examples of job enrichment applications, see J. Richard Hackman, Greg Oldham, Robert Janson, and Kenneth Purdy, "New Strategy for Job Enrichment," *California Management Review*, Summer 1975, pp. 57–71.

[40] Hackman, Oldham, Janson, and Purdy, "A New Strategy," pp. 57–71; and J. Richard Hackman and Greg Oldham, "Development of the Job Diagnostic Survey," *Journal of Applied Psychology*, April 1975, pp. 159–70.

[41] Turner and Lawrence, *Industrial Jobs*.

FIGURE 12–3
The Job Characteristics Model

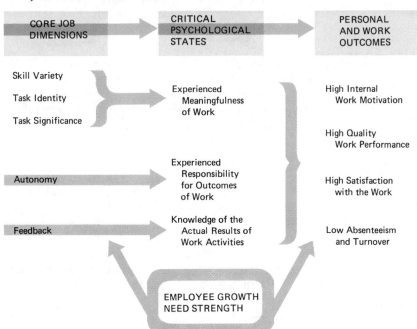

Source: J. Richard Hackman and Greg R. Oldham. "Development of the Job Diagnostic Survey," *Journal of Applied Psychology* 60 (1975): 159–70.

self-evaluation and creating autonomous work groups, the feedback and autonomy dimensions are increased along with the psychological states "experienced responsibility" and "knowledge of actual results."

The positive benefits of these redesign efforts are moderated by individual differences in the strength of employees' growth needs. That is, employees with strong need for accomplishment, learning and challenge will respond more positively than those with relatively weak growth needs. In other, more familiar, terms employees who have high need for self-esteem and self-actualization are the more likely candidates for job redesign. Employees forced to participate in job redesign programs but who lack either the need strength or the ability to perform redesigned jobs may experience stress, anxiety, adjustment problems, erratic performance, turnover, and absenteeism.

The available research on the interrelationships between individual differences, job design, and performance are meager. It is apparent, however, that managers must cope with significant problems in matching employee needs and differences and organizational needs. That difficulty is indicated by the finding of one study that of 125 firms included in the survey, only

5 had made any efforts to redesign jobs.[42] The problems associated with job redesign are several including:[43]

1. The program is time consuming and costly.
2. Unless lower level needs are satisfied, people will not respond to opportunities to satisfy upper level needs. And even though our society has been rather successful in providing food and shelter, these needs regain importance when the economy moves through periods of recession and inflation.
3. Job redesign programs are intended to satisfy needs typically not satisfied in the workplace. As workers are told to expect higher order need satisfaction, they may raise their expectations beyond that which is possible. Dissatisfaction with the program's unachievable aim may displace dissatisfaction with the jobs.
4. Finally job redesign may be resisted by labor unions who see the effort as an attempt to get more work with the same pay.

Despite these problems companies have turned to job redesign as a way to improve productivity and satisfaction.

SOME APPLICATIONS OF JOB REDESIGN

■ In this section we will review a number of actual attempts to implement job redesign. Terms such as *job enrichment, job enlargement,* and *quality of work-life* are often used interchangeably; yet in most instances the terms refer to efforts to change job range and depth. The most publicized efforts have occurred in the Volvo and General Motors automobile manufacturing plants.

The Volvo Experience

When Pehr Gyllenhammar joined Volvo in 1971 as its managing director, performance indicators such as productivity, absenteeism, and turnover were unsatisfactory.[44] The company is the largest employer in Sweden with some 65,000 employees and in 1976 it ranked 61st on *Fortune's* international 500 list. Gyllenhammar took a keen interest in the experiments of Ingvar Barrby, head of the upholstery department, in job rotation (termed job alternation in Volvo). The reduction in turnover from 35 percent to 15 percent encouraged the new managing director to adopt other aspects of job redesign.[45] For example group management and work modules are used at the Torslanda car assembly plant. Employees, in groups, follow the same

[42] Fred Luthans and W. E. Reif "Job Enrichment: Long on Theory, Short on Practice," *Organizational Dynamics,* Fall 1974, pp. 30–43.

[43] Chung, *Motivational Theories and Practices,* pp. 211–12.

[44] John M. Roach, "Why Volvo Abolished the Assembly Line," *Management Review,* September 1977, p. 50.

[45] William F. Dowling, "Job Redesign on the Assembly Line: Farewell to Blue-Collar Blues?" *Organizational Dynamics,* Autumn 1973, pp. 51–67.

auto body for seven or eight work stations along the line for a total period of 20 minutes.

The concepts of group management and natural work modules are more highly developed at a truck assembly plant. Here groups of 5 to 12 people with common work assignments, elect their own supervisors, schedule their output, distribute work to their own members, and are responsible for their own quality control. Group piecerates, rather than individual piecerates, are the bases for wages and everyone earns the same amount except the elected supervisor. Subsequently absenteeism and turnover decreased and quality improved—due, in Gyllenhammar's opinion, to the effects of the job redesign program.

Job redesign at Volvo reached a major milestone in 1974 when the then new, Kalmar assembly plant opened. Gyllenhammar had been personally and visibly behind the design and construction phases of the new plant to assure that opportunities to provide job enrichment were parts of the physical and technological layout. The plant incorporates a technology of assembly in which overhead carriers move the auto body, chassis, and subassemblies to assembly team areas. There, work teams of 20 to 25 employees complete major segments of auto assembly-electrical systems, instrumentation, finishing and so on. Each group is responsible for a whole piece of work. They function as autonomous units much as those at the truck assembly plant.[46]

The General Motors Experience

General Motors became involved with job redesign in 1971.[47] The company was formulating plans for building the GM mobile home, a new product in a rapidly growing market. GM management believed that the new product was amenable to new design concepts as well as innovative approaches to work organization. After analyzing several factors including the expected production rate, technological complexity, and size of the new operation, management determined that the work team concept would be applicable.

The plan called for the eventual creation of 8 six-person teams to produce 32 vehicles per shift in the body-upfit area; 14 three-person teams would complete the same number of chassis; and 4 four-person teams would install air conditioning. Implementing the plan began with the selection of a nucleus of 30 hourly employees who would build the pilot vehicles and later be the team leaders and trainers of the expanded work force. The pilot phase ended in December 1972, and additional employees were recruited to fill out the work teams.

Problems arose shortly thereafter. Efficiency and quality never reached acceptable levels. Teams were unable to maintain discipline and some

---

[46]See Pehr Gyllenhammar, *People at Work* (Reading, Mass.: Addison-Wesley Publishing, 1977), for a full account of the Volvo experience.

[47]This discussion is based upon Noel M. Tichy and Jay N. Nisberg, "When Does Job Restructuring Work?" *Organizational Dynamics*, Summer 1976, pp. 63–80.

team members did not carry their fair share of the load. Absenteeism, turnover, and job dissatisfaction increased. Some team members were unable to keep pace, due in large part to inadequate training and poor work layout. Management had underestimated the complexity of the assembly process and the training required to complete work cycles of up to 18 half-hour sequences.

The discouraging outcomes resulted in the team concept being phased out, beginning in 1973. Three years later only a few people continued to work in teams. In this instance the failure of job design was the consequence of flaws in implementing the concept rather than the concept itself. Here we see the importance of *management skill at coordinating work* to be a crucial moderator of the effects of job redesign on organizational effectiveness and job satisfaction.

Other Experiences with Job Redesign

These two case histories are not the only instances of experiences, positive and negative, with job redesign. Early attempts were undertaken in IBM (1944) and Detroit Edison Company (1950s).[48] In both of these cases, job redesign, specifically job enlargement, resulted in lower costs, fewer absences, and increased productivity. AT&T, Arapahoe Chemical Company, the Internal Revenue Service, and Saab-Scandia of Norway have in some ways implemented job redesign. All these experiences have not been equally successful as we noted in the GM mobile home discussion. Another example of negative results ensuing from job enrichment was the Internal Revenue Service experience.[49]

In general the conclusions one reaches, when considering the experience of job redesign approaches, are that they are relatively successful in increasing quality of output, but not quantity. This conclusion pertains, however, only if the reward system already satisfies lower level needs. If it presently does not satisfy lower level needs, employees cannot be expected to experience upper level need satisfaction (intrinsic rewards) through enriched job content.

Since a primary source of organizational effectiveness is job performance, managers should design jobs according to the best available knowledge. At present, the strategies for designing and redesigning jobs have evolved from scientific management approaches to work design with emphasis on quality of work-life issues. Job enlargement and job enrichment are important, but often incomplete strategies. Strategies which take into account individual differences probably have the greatest probability of success, assuming compatible environmental, situational, and management conditions. Managers must diagnose their own people and organizations to determine the applicability of specific job design approaches.

---

[48] Peter Schoderbek and W. Rief, *Job Enlargement* (Ann Arbor: University of Michigan Press, 1969).

[49] Harold F. M. Rush, *Job Design for Motivation* (New York: The Conference Board, 1971), pp. 52–53.

MAJOR MANAGERIAL ISSUES

A. Micro-organization design involves managerial decisions and actions which specify objective job scopes and relationships to satisfy organizational requirements as well as the social and personal requirements of the jobholders.

B. Contemporary managers must consider the issue of quality of work life when designing jobs. This issue reflects society's concern for work experiences which contribute to the personal growth and development of employees.

C. Strategies for increasing the potential of jobs to satisfy the social and personal requirements of jobholders have gone through an evolutionary process. Initial efforts were directed toward job rotation and job enlargement. These strategies produced some gains in job satisfaction, but did not change primary motivators such as responsibility, achievement, and autonomy.

D. During the 1960s, job enrichment became a widely recognized strategy for improving quality of work-life factors. This strategy is based upon Herzberg's motivation theory and involves increasing the *depth* of jobs through greater delegation of authority to jobholders. Despite some major successes, job enrichment is not universally applicable because it does not consider individual differences.

E. Individual differences are now recognized as crucial variables to consider when designing jobs. Experience, cognitive complexity, needs, values, valences, and perceptions of equity are some of the individual differences which influence the reactions of jobholders to the scope and relationships of their jobs. When individual differences are combined with environmental, situational, and managerial differences, job design decisions become increasingly complex.

F. The most recently developed strategy of job design emphasizes the importance of core job characteristics as perceived by jobholders. Although measurements of individual differences remain a problem, managers should be encouraged to examine ways to increase positive perceptions of variety, identity, significance, autonomy, and feedback. By doing so, the potential for high-quality work performance and high job satisfaction is increased given that jobholders possess relatively high growth need strength.

G. Many organizations including Volvo, Saab, General Motors, and General Foods have attempted job redesign with varying degrees of success. The current state of research knowledge is inadequate for making broad generalizations regarding the exact causes of success and failure in applications of job redesign. Managers must diagnose their own situations to determine the applicability of job redesign in their organizations.

DISCUSSION AND REVIEW QUESTIONS

1. Explain the difficulties that management would encounter in attempting to redesign existing jobs as compared to designing new jobs.

2. Explain the relationships between job depth and perceived autonomy and significance.

3. It is possible to increase the depth of job without decreasing managers' authority? Explain.

4. What are the characteristics of individuals who would respond favorably to job enlargement, but not to job enrichment?

5. Explain why it is necessary to enlarge a job before it can be enriched.

6. Explain the relationships between feedback as a job content factor and personal goal setting.

Is personal goal setting possible without feedback? Explain.

7. What specific core dimensions of jobs could be changed to increase employees' perceptions of instrumentalities and expectancies?

8. Which of the core dimensions do you now value most highly? Explain and list them in rank order of importance to you.

9. Compare the Volvo and General Motors experiences with job redesign and explain why Volvo's experience is relatively more successful.

10. In your opinion, was the General Foods experience with job redesign a success or a failure? Explain.

ADDITIONAL REFERENCES

Aldag, R. J., and A. P. Brief. *Task Design and Employee Motivation.* Glenview, Ill.: Scott, Foresman, 1979.

Brief, A. P., and R. J. Aldag. "Employee Reactions to Job Characteristics: A Constructive Replication." *Journal of Applied Psychology,* 1975, pp. 182–86.

Cummings, L. L.; D. P. Schwab; and M. Rosen. "Performance and Knowledge of Results as Determinants of Goal-Setting." *Journal of Applied Psychology,* 1971, pp. 526–30.

Davis, L. E. "Optimizing Organizational Plant Design: A Complementary Structure for Technical and Social Systems." *Organizational Dynamics,* 1979, pp. 3–15.

Dubin, R. "Industrial Workers' Worlds: A Study of the Central Life Interests of Industrial Workers." *Social Problems,* 1956, pp. 131–42.

Fein, M. "Job Enrichment: A Reevaluation." *Sloan Management Review,* 1974, pp. 69–88.

Ford, R. N. "Job Enrichment Lessons from AT&T." *Harvard Business Review,* 1973, pp. 96–106.

Foy, N., and H. Gadon. "Worker Participation: Contrasts in Three Countries." *Harvard Business Review,* 1976, pp. 71–83.

Hackman, J. R., and G. R. Oldham. "Motivation through the Design of Work: Test of a Theory." *Organizational Behavior and Human Performance,* 1976, pp. 250–79.

Hulin, C. L. "Individual Differences and Job Enrichment—The Case against General Treatments." In *New Perspectives in Job Enrichment,* edited by J. R. Maher. New York: Van Nostrand Reinhold, 1971.

King, N. "Clarification and Evaluation of the Two-Factor Theory of Job Satisfaction." *Psychological Bulletin,* 1970, pp. 18–31.

Konz, S. *Work Design.* Santa Monica, Calif.: Goodyear Publishing, 1979.

Lawler, E. E. "Job Design and Employee Motivation." *Personnel Psychology,* 1969, pp. 415–44.

————; J. R. Hackman; and S. Kaufman. "Effects of Job Design: A Field Experiment." *Journal of Applied Social Psychology,* 1973, pp. 46–62.

O'Connor, E. J.; C. J. Rudolph; and L. H. Peters. "Individual Differences and Job Design Reconsidered: Where Do We Go from Here? *Academy of Management Review,* 1980, pp. 249–54.

Scott, W. E. "Activation Theory and Task Design." *Organizational Behavior and Human Performance,* 1966, pp. 3–30.

Shaw, J. B. "An Information-Processing Approach to the Study of Job Design," *Academy of Management Review,* 1980, pp. 41–48.

Staw, B. M. *Intrinsic and Extrinsic Motivation.* Morristown, N.J.: General Learning Press, 1976.

Steers, R. M. "Effects of Need for Achievement on the Job Performance-Job Attitude Relationship." *Journal of Applied Psychology,* 1975, pp. 678–82.

————. "Factors Affecting Job Attitudes in a Goal-Setting Environment." *Academy of Management Journal,* 1976, pp. 6–16.

————, and L. W. Porter. "The Role of Task-Goal Attributes in Employee Performance." *Psychological Bulletin,* 1974, pp. 434–52.

Umstot, D. D.; C. H. Bell; and T. R. Mitchell. "Effects of Job Enrichment and Task Goals on Satisfaction and Productivity: Implications for Job Design." *Journal of Applied Psychology,* 1976, pp. 379–94.

WORK REDESIGN IN AN INSURANCE COMPANY

The executive staff of a relatively small life insurance company was considering a proposal to install an electronic data processing system. The proposal to install the equipment was presented by the assistant to the president, John Skully. He had been charged with studying the feasibility of the equipment after a management consultant had recommended a complete overhaul of the jobs within the company.

The management consultant had been engaged by the company to diagnose the causes of high turnover and absenteeism. After reviewing the situation and speaking with groups of employees, the management consultant recommended that the organization structure be changed from functional to client basis. The change in departmental basis would enable management to redesign jobs to reduce the human costs associated with highly specialized tasks.

The present organization included separate departments to issue policies, collect premiums, change beneficiaries, and process loan applications. Employees in these departments complained that their jobs were boring, insignificant, and monotonous. They stated that the only reason they stayed with the company was because they liked the small company atmosphere. They believed the management had a genuine interest in their welfare, but felt that the trivial nature of their jobs contradicted that feeling. As one employee said, "This company is small enough to know almost everybody. But the job I do is so boring that I wonder why they even need me to do it." This and similar comments led the consultant to believe that the jobs must be altered to provide greater motivation. But he also recognized that work redesign opportunities were limited by the organization structure. He therefore recommended that the company change to a client basis. In such a structure each employee would handle every transaction related to a particular policyholder.

When the consultant presented his views to the executive staff, they were very much interested in his recommendations. And, in fact, the group agreed that his recommendation was well founded. They noted, however, that a small company must pay particular attention to efficiency in handling transactions. The functional basis enabled the organization to achieve the degree of specialization necessary for efficient operations. The manager of internal operations stated: "If we move away from specialization, the rate of efficiency must go down because we will lose the benefit of specialized effort. The only way we can justify redesigning the jobs as suggested by the consultant is to maintain our efficiency; otherwise there won't be any jobs to redesign because we will be out of business."

The internal operations manager explained to the executive staff that despite excessive absenteeism and turnover, he was able to maintain acceptable productivity. The narrow range and depth of the jobs reduced training time to a minimum. It was also possible to hire temporary help to meet peak loads and to fill in for absent employees. "Moreover," he said, "changing the jobs our people do means that we must change the jobs our managers do. They are experts in their own functional areas but we have never attempted to train them to oversee more than two operations."

The majority of the executive staff believed that the consultants' recommendations should be seriously considered. It was at that point that the group directed John Skully to evaluate the potential of electronic data processing (EDP) as a means to obtain efficient operations in combination with the redesigned jobs. He had completed the study and presented his report to the executive staff.

"The bottom line," Skully said, "is that EDP will enable us to maintain our present efficiency, but with the redesigned jobs, we will not obtain any greater gains. If my analysis is correct, we will have to absorb the cost of the equipment out of earnings because there will be no cost savings. So it comes down to what price we are willing and able to pay for improving the satisfaction of our employees."

Questions for Consideration

1. What core characteristics of the employees' jobs will be changed if the consultants' recommendations are accepted? Explain.

2. What alternative redesign strategies should be considered? For example, job rotation and job enlargement are possible alternatives; what are the relevant considerations for these and other designs in the context of this company?

3. What would be your decision in this case? What should the management be willing to pay for employee satisfaction? Defend your answer.

EXPERIENTIAL EXERCISE

PERSONAL PREFERENCES

Objectives

1. To illustrate individual differences in preferences about various job design characteristics.
2. To illustrate how *your* preferences may differ from those of others.
3. To examine the most important and least important job design characteristics and how managers would cope with them.

Related Topics

This exercise will be related to intrinsic and extrinsic reward topics. The job design characteristics considered could be viewed as either intrinsic or extrinsic job issues.

Starting the Exercise

First you will respond to a questionnaire asking about your job design preferences and how you view the preferences of others. After working through the questionnaire *individually*, small groups will be formed. In the groups discussion will focus on the individual differences in preferences expressed by group members.

The Facts

Job design is concerned with a number of attributes of a job. Among these attributes are the job itself, the requirements of the job, the interpersonal interaction opportunities on the job, and performance outcomes. There are certain attributes that are preferred by individuals. Some prefer job autonomy, while others prefer to be challenged by different tasks. It is obvious that individual differences in preferences would be an important consideration for managers. An exciting job for one person may be a demeaning and boring job for another individual. Managers could use this type of information in attempting to create job design conditions that allow organizational goals and individual goals and preferences to be matched.

The Job Preference form is presented below. Please read it carefully and complete it after considering each characteristic listed. Due to space limitations not all job design characteristics are included for your consideration. Use only those that are included on the form.

Job Design Preferences

A. *Your Job Design Preferences*

Decide which of the following is most important to you. Place a 1 in front of the most important characteristic. Then decide which is the second most important characteristic to you and place a 2 in front of it. Continue numbering the items in order of importance until the least important is ranked 10. There are no right answers since individuals differ in their job design preferences. Do not discuss your individual rankings until the instructor forms groups.

_____ Variety in tasks
_____ Feedback on performance from doing the job
_____ Autonomy
_____ Working as a team
_____ Responsibility
_____ Developing friendships on the job
_____ Task identity
_____ Task significance
_____ Having the resources to perform well
_____ Feedback on performance from others (e.g., the manager, co-workers)

B. *Others Job Design Preferences*

In the A section you have provided your preferences, now number the items as you think others would rank them. Consider others who are in your course, class, or program. That is, those who are also completing this exercise. Rank the factors from 1 (most important) to 10 (least important).

_____ Variety in tasks
_____ Feedback on performance from doing the job
_____ Autonomy

> **Job Design Preferences** (continued)
> _____ Working as a team
> _____ Responsibility
> _____ Developing friendships on the job
> _____ Task identity
> _____ Task significance
> _____ Having the resources to perform well
> _____ Feedback on performance from others (e.g.,
> the manager, co-workers)

Exercise Procedure

Phase I: 15 minutes
1. Individually complete the A and B portions of the Job Design Preference form.
Phase II: 45 minutes
1. The instructor will form groups of four to six students.
2. Discuss the differences in the rankings individuals made on the A and B parts of the form.
3. Present each of the A rank orders of group members on a flip chart or the blackboard. Analyze the areas of agreement and disagreement.
4. Discuss what implications the A and B rankings would have to a *manager* who would have to supervise a group such as the group you are in. That is, what could a manager do to cope with the individual differences displayed in steps 1, 2, and 3 above.

Chapter 13

Macro-Organization Design

AN ORGANIZATIONAL ISSUE FOR DEBATE
The Technological Imperative*

ARGUMENT FOR

Since the pathbreaking studies of Joan Woodward the view that technology *determines* structure has been debated. According to the view, an optimal organization design exists for each technological type; managers, therefore, should match the design with the technology. Woodward's studies indicated that the design strategy proposed by classical theorists is optimal only for mass-production-type technology; System 4 design strategy is appropriate for job order and process technologies. Her studies cast considerable doubt on the view that there is a universal one best way to organize.

The evidence that technology is the compelling force behind design decisions accumulated as other researchers tested Woodward's findings in other settings. Although subsequent research studies differed in some respects, the conclusions were consistent. Studies of industrial organizations in the Minneapolis-St. Paul area, for example, confirmed that when management failed to match structure with technology, additional costs were incurred which resulted in lower than potentially attainable organizational performance.

*Based upon John H. Jackson and Cyril P. Morgan, *Organization Theory* (Englewood Cliffs, N.J.: Prentice-Hall, 1978), pp. 175–98.

ARGUMENT AGAINST

The argument against the technology imperative is based upon research which indicates that while technology is important, other considerations must be taken into account. The most compelling counterargument is that technology is the important variable for designing organization *units* which directly produce the product or service. Thus the production department or division should be designed to meet technological demands, but other units in the organization face different, nontechnological demands. This view is based upon the theory that organizations must deal with various subenvironments each posing different constraints.

The view that technology is the primary influence on structure is not borne out by studies of very large organizations. Woodward's studies, and those of supportive researchers, included firms of relatively small size. The impact of technology is more noticeable in small firms than in larger ones since larger firms create staff units to deal with nonproduction environments—research, marketing, information, for example. Thus, the larger the organization, the less influential technology becomes. Size, then, according to the counter argument is the principal determinant of structure, not technology.

ARGUMENT FOR (continued)

The findings that technology determines structure prompted theorists to devise explanations for the relationship. Their theories attempt to provide general frameworks for thinking about the relationships between structure and technology. Thus in manufacturing as well as nonmanufacturing business firms it is possible to argue that technology is the most important determinant, indeed the imperative.

Managers must choose among several macro-organization design theories to guide their decisions. Macro-organization refers to the overall characteristics of an organization structure. Some theories stress that there is "one best way" to design the organization, and these we term *universal* theories; others state that the optimal structure can vary from situation to situation depending upon such factors as technology and environmental differences, and these we term *contingency* theories. The competing theories also differ in the manner in which they have been devised. For example, some design theories result from logical deduction, others from research investigations. Some theories seek solely to provide the bases for describing organizations, while others seek to prescribe the "best" organization. Finally, some theories focus on the task unit as the important unit of analysis, while others attempt to analyze the total organizational entity. These differences in approach, intent, and unit of analysis impair attempts to devise a general theory of macro-organization design.

UNIVERSAL DESIGN THEORIES

■ Organization design theories which suggest that there is "one best way" to organize include classical organization theory, bureaucratic theory, and System 4 theory. In this section these three important ideas are presented as bases for understanding the modern approach, contingency design theory. Figure 13–1 indicates the relationship among the important theories of macro-organization design. Classical organization theory and bureaucratic theory are much alike. Each arrives at the same recommendations regard-

FIGURE 13–1
Development of Macro-Organization Design Theories

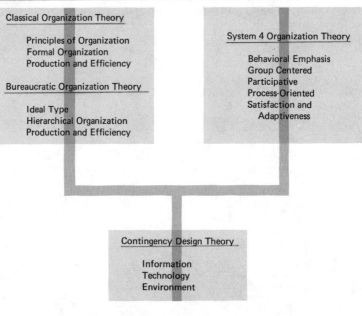

ing the one best way to organize. In contrast, System 4 organization theory proposes that the one best way to organize is in the opposite direction from that of classical organization and bureaucratic theory. Contingency organization design theory, the more recent approach, rests on the idea that either classical or System 4-type organization can be optimal depending upon factors in the situation, that is, contingencies.

Classical Organization Theory

A body of literature emerged during the early part of the 20th century which considered the problem of designing the structure of an organization as but one of a number of managerial tasks, including planning and controlling. The objective of these writers was to define *principles* which could guide managers in the performance of their tasks. To this end, an early writer, Henri Fayol, proposed a number of principles which he had found useful in the management of a large coal mining company in France.[1] Fayol believed that these principles had served him in good stead, yet he recognized their tentative nature. He viewed the art of management as consisting of selecting the appropriate principle for a given situation.

These principles provide guidelines for designing a system of interrelated tasks and authority. If we understand that the organizing function involves dividing a task into successively smaller subtasks, regrouping these tasks into related departments, appointing a manager of each department and delegating authority to that manager, and, finally linking the departments through a chain of command, then we can understand the logic of Fayol's five structural principles.

The Principle of Division of Work. Through specialization, the number of objects to which attention and effort must be directed is reduced, and as Fayol stated, specialization "has been recognized as the best means of making use of individuals and groups of people." At the same time that Fayol stated the general case for specialization, he also recognized that there is an optimum point. As he stated, "division of work has its limits which experience and a sense of proportion teach us may not be exceeded." At the time of Fayol's writings, the limit of specialization, that is, the optimal point, had not been definitively determined. The work of industrial engineers, particularly Taylor and his followers, had resulted in the bases for work simplification methods. These methods, such as work standards and motion and time study, emphasized technical (not behavioral) dimensions of work.

The Principle of Unity of Direction. Activities which have the same objective should operate according to one plan and should be directed by one manager. The principle accounts for the necessity to appoint a manager to coordinate the related activities, but it says nothing about the scope of the manager's role.

---

[1]Henri Fayol, *General and Industrial Management,* trans. J. A. Conbrough (Geneva: International Management Institute, 1929). The more widely circulated translation is that of Constance Storrs (London: Pitman Publishing, 1949).

The Principle of Centralization. There exists for each situation an optimal balance between centralization and decentralization. That balance cannot be determined without reference to the capabilities of managers who are appointed to coordinate the departments. Contrary to some interpretations, this principle does not state that authority for all decisions should be centralized at the top of the organization. Rather, it states that managers' responsibilities should reflect their capacity to meet the responsibilities. Once responsibility is assigned, commensurate authority must also be assigned.

The Principle of Authority and Responsibility. There must be some relationship between the responsibilities of managers and the authority that they exercise; the desired relationship is equality between the two. Yet there is no easy way to assess the relationship, particularly as one examines the tasks of upper level managers. Fayol understood that "as work grows more complex, as the number of workers involved increases, as the final result is more remote, it is increasingly difficult to isolate the share of the initial act of authority in the ultimate result and to establish the degree of responsibility of the manager." The principle states no formula by which one can equate authority and responsibility, and, in fact, no such formula may exist. Yet this recognition does not violate the basic premise of the principle, which is that if one is expected to direct the efforts of subordinates, one should also be delegated "the right to give orders and the power to exact obedience."

The Scalar Chain Principle. The natural result of the implementation of the preceding four principles is a graded chain of superiors from the "ultimate authority to the lowest ranks." The scalar chain is the route for all vertical communications in an organization. Accordingly, all communications from the lowest level must pass through each superior in the chain of command. Correspondingly, communications from the top must pass through each subordinate until it reaches the appropriate level.

These five principles define the major issues to be resolved in creating the structure of tasks and authority. They do not specify fixed rules of conduct or precise answers. Instead they define the major considerations and propose guidelines for managerial action.

Fayol's writings became part of a literature which, although each contributor made unique contributions, had a common thrust. Writers such as Mooney and Reiley,[2] Follett,[3] and Urwick[4] all shared the common objective of defining the principles which should guide the design and management of organizations. A complete review of their individual contributions will not be attempted here; the reader can consult numerous sources for

[2]James D. Mooney and Allan C. Reiley, *Onward Industry* (New York: Harper & Row, 1939). Subsequently revised under the authorship and title, James D. Mooney, *The Principles of Organization* (New York: Harper & Row, 1947).

[3]Henry C. Metcalf and Lyndall Urwick, eds., *Dynamic-Administration: The Collected Papers of Mary Parker Follett* (New York: Harper & Row, 1940).

[4]Lyndall Urwick, *The Elements of Administration* (New York: Harper & Row, 1944).

elaboration of classical organization theory. The major contribution of these writers *is to point out the importance of a rationally designed organization.*

Bureaucratic Organization Theory

Bureaucracy has various meanings. The traditional usage is the political science concept of government by bureaus but without participation by the governed. In laymen's terms, bureaucracy refers to the negative consequences of large organizations, such as excessive "red tape," procedural delays, and general frustration.[5] In Max Weber's analyses, bureaucracy refers to the sociological concept of rationalization of collective activities.[6] It describes a form, or design, of organization which assures predictability of the behavior of employees in the organization.

The inherent logic of the bureaucratic structure led Weber to believe that it is "superior to any other form in precision, in stability, in the stringency of its discipline and its reliability. It thus makes possible a high degree of calculability of results for the heads of the organization and for those acting in relation to it."[7] The bureaucracy compares to other organizations "as does the machine with nonmechanical modes of production."[8]

To achieve the maximum benefits of the bureaucratic form, Weber believed that the organization must adopt certain design strategies. Specifically:

1. All tasks necessary for the accomplishment of goals are divided into highly specialized jobs. This strategy is the familiar division-of-labor principle, and Weber argued its importance in the usual ways, namely, that jobholders could become expert in their jobs and could be held responsible for the effective performance of their duties.

2. Each task is performed according to a "consistent system of abstract rules"[9] to assure uniformity and coordination of different tasks. The rationale for this practice is that the manager can eliminate uncertainty in task performance due to individual differences.

3. Each member or office of the organization is accountable to a superior. The authority wielded by superiors is based upon expert knowledge and it is legitimized by the fact that it is delegated from the top of the hierarchy. A chain of command is thereby created.

4. Each official in the organization conducts business in an impersonal formalistic manner, maintaining a social distance with subordinates and clients. The purpose of this practice is to assure that personalities

[5] Michael Crozier, *The Bureaucratic Phenomenon* (Chicago: The University of Chicago Press, 1964), p. 3.

[6] Max Weber, *The Theory of Social and Economic Organization,* trans. A. M. Henderson and Talcott Parsons (New York: Oxford University Press, 1947).

[7] Ibid., p. 334.

[8] *From Max Weber: Essays in Sociology,* trans. H. H. Gerth and C. W. Mills (New York: Oxford University Press, 1946), p. 214.

[9] Weber, *Theory of Social and Economic Organization,* p. 330.

do not interfere with the efficient accomplishment of the office's objectives; there should be no favoritism resulting from personal friendships or acquaintances.

5. Employment in the bureaucratic organization is based on technical qualifications and is protected against arbitrary dismissal.[10] Similarly, promotions are based on seniority and achievement. Employment in the organization is viewed as a lifelong career, and a high degree of loyalty is engendered.

To the extent that these characteristics are highly articulated in an organization, the organization approaches the "ideal type" of bureaucracy. Obviously few organizations exhibit all the characteristics of the ideal type, yet in some way, all organizations exhibit some degree of one or more of the characteristics. For example, all organizations practice some degree of division of labor, have superior-subordinate relationships, and some kind of procedures.

System 4 Organization

The research which Likert has carried out at the University of Michigan has led him to argue that effective organizations differ markedly from ineffective organizations along a number of structural dimensions.[11] According to Likert an effective organization is one which encourages supervisors to "focus their primary attention on endeavoring to build effective work groups with high performance goals."[12] In contrast, less effective organizations encourage supervisors to:

1. Break the total operation into simple component parts or tasks.
2. Develop the best way to carry out each of the component parts.
3. Hire people with appropriate aptitudes and skills to perform each of these tasks.
4. Train these people to do their respective tasks in the specified best way.
5. Provide supervision to see that they perform their designated tasks, using the specified procedure and at an acceptable rate as determined by such procedures as timing the job.
6. Where feasible, use incentives in the form of individual or group piece-rates.[13]

The foregoing six points summarize the responsibilities of the manager in classical design theory. Yet Likert found through extensive research that these prescriptions did not result in effective organizations, thus substantiating the findings of other human relations researchers. He goes on to argue that organizations can be described in terms of eight dimensions,

---

[10] Peter M. Blau, *Bureaucracy in Modern Society* (Chicago: The University of Chicago Press, 1956), p. 30.

[11] See Rensis Likert, *New Patterns of Management* (New York: McGraw-Hill, 1961); and Rensis Likert, *The Human Organization* (New York: McGraw-Hill, 1967).

[12] Likert, *New Patterns of Management*, p. 7.

[13] Ibid., p. 6.

TABLE 13–1
Classical Design and System 4 Organization

Classical Design Organization	*System 4 Organization*
1. *Leadership process* includes no perceived confidence and trust. Subordinates do not feel free to discuss job problems with their superiors, who in turn do not solicit their ideas and opinions.	1. *Leadership process* includes perceived confidence and trust between superiors and subordinates in all matters. Subordinates feel free to discuss job problems with their superiors, who in turn solicit their ideas and opinions.
2. *Motivational process* taps only physical, security, and economic motives through the use of fear and sanctions. Unfavorable attitudes toward the organization prevail among employees.	2. *Motivational process* taps a full range of motives through participatory methods. Attitudes are favorable toward the organization and its goals.
3. *Communication process* is such that information flows downward and tends to be distorted, inaccurate, and viewed with suspicion by subordinates.	3. *Communication process* is such that information flows freely throughout the organization—upward, downward, and laterally. The information is accurate and undistorted.
4. *Interaction process* is closed and restricted; subordinates have little effect on departmental goals, methods, and activities.	4. *Interaction process* is open and extensive; both superiors and subordinates are able to affect departmental goals, methods, and activities.
5. *Decision process* occurs only at the top of the organization; it is relatively centralized.	5. *Decision process* occurs at all levels through group process; it is relatively decentralized.
6. *Goal-setting process* is located at the top of the organization, discourages group participation.	6. *Goal-setting process* encourages group participation in setting high, realistic objectives.
7. *Control process* is centralized and emphasizes fixing of blame for mistakes.	7. *Control process* is dispersed throughout the organization and emphasizes self-control and problem solving.
8. *Performance goals* are low and passively sought by managers who make no commitment to developing the human resources of the organization.	8. *Performance goals* are high and actively sought by superiors, who recognize the necessity for making a full commitment to developing, through training, the human resources of the organization.

Source: Adapted from Rensis Likert, *The Human Organization* (New York: McGraw-Hill, 1967), pp. 197–211.

each of which is a continuum with classical design organizations being at one extreme and System 4 organizations at the opposite end. The eight dimensions and their extreme points are described in Table 13–1.

The organization described in the left side of Table 13–1 is one which results from the implementation of classical design theory, although Likert does not identify it as such. He initially termed it "Exploitive-Authoritative," but later named it simply "System 1." He states that System 1 organizations are ineffective because they no longer reflect the changing character of the environments within which organizations must operate. System 1, that is, classical design organizations, tend toward status quoism and conservatism.

The major changes which Likert identifies as creating an environment that does not support classical design organizations include:

1. Increased competition from foreign countries with comparatively lower production costs, but with equal technology.
2. A trend in American society toward greater individual freedom and initiative and, concomitantly, less supervision from others.
3. A generally higher level of education resulting in persons more able and willing to accept responsible positions.
4. An increasing concern for mental health and the full development of the individual personality.
5. Increasingly complex technologies requiring expertness beyond the ability of any one person to comprehend. Consequently, the supervisor of specialists in these technologies often knows less about the unit's activities than subordinates.[14]

These environmental changes are creating pressures on managers to discover organizational designs which are able to adapt to these changes. And, according to Likert, System 4 is the direction toward which the more productive and profitable firms are moving.

As suggested in Table 13–1, the System 4 organization is more adaptable because its structural design encourages greater utilization of the human potential. Managers are encouraged to adopt practices which tap the full range of human motivations; decision making, control, and goal-setting processes are decentralized and shared at all levels of the organization. Communications flow throughout the organization, not simply down the chain of command as is the case in bureaucracies. These practices are intended to implement the basic assumption of System 4 which states that an organization will be optimally effective to the extent that its processes are "such as to ensure a maximum probability that in all interactions and in all relationships with the organization, each member, in the light of his background, values, desires, and expectations, will view the experience as supportive and one which builds and maintains his sense of personal worth and importance."[15]

To facilitate the realization of these processes, the organization design must implement three concepts: (1) the principle of supportive relationships, (2) group decisions making and group methods of supervision, and (3) high performance goals.[16] Structurally, the organization is viewed as a set of groups which are linked by managers. This view can be contrasted with the bureaucratic relationship. Figure 13–2 illustrates the System 4 organization design.

As shown in Figure 13–2 the groups consist of all persons reporting to a manager. Some managers are in the position of being members of two groups. In this dual capacity, these managers serve, in Likert's terms, as

---

[14] Ibid., pp. 1–3.

[15] Ibid., p. 103.

[16] Likert, *Human Organization*, p. 47.

FIGURE 13–2
The System 4 Organization

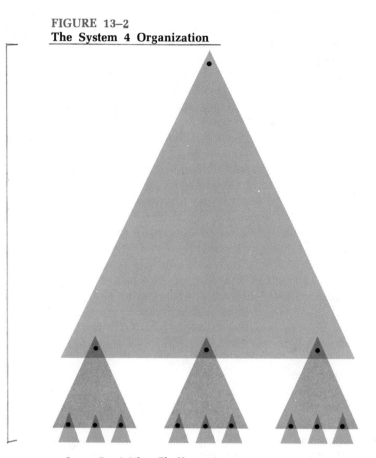

Source: Rensis Likert, *The Human Organization* (New York: McGraw-Hill, 1967), p. 50.

linking pins—they connect each group with its immediate superior's group. In this capacity they represent their groups to higher-ups and coordinate their groups with other dependent groups. The overlapping group structure, combined with the manager's use of group decision making, "represent an optimum integration of the needs and desires of the members of the organization, the shareholders, customers, suppliers, and others who have an interest in the enterprise or are served by it."[17]

There is no question that Likert's views are widely shared by researchers and practitioners. The literature is filled with reports of efforts to implement System 4 in actual organizations.[18] Likert himself reports many of

---

[17] Ibid., pp. 51–52.

[18] See particularly A. J. Marrow, D. G. Bowers, and S. E. Seashore, eds., *Strategies of Organization Change* (New York: Harper & Row, 1967); and William F. Dowling, "At General Motors: System 4 Builds Performance and Profits," *Organizational Dynamics*, Winter 1975, pp. 23–28.

these studies.[19] There is, likewise, no question that the proponents of the System 4 organization believe it is universally applicable; that is, the theory is proposed as the "one best way" to design an organization.

Thus, in retrospect, System 4 theory is the result of the studies which tested the claims of classical design theory. As we have seen, the two approaches are diametrically opposed, yet each claims to be the most effective organization design.

CONTINGENCY DESIGN THEORIES

■ The current trend in management research and practice is to design organizations to fit the situation. Accordingly, neither classical theory nor System 4 is necessarily the more effective organization design; either can be the better approach depending upon the situation. The contingency point of view provides the opportunity to get away from the dilemma of choosing between classical theory and System 4. As such, it is an evolution of ideas, the bases for which can be found in the work of earlier writers.

The essence of the contingency design approach is expressed by the question: Under what circumstances and in what situations is either classical theory or System 4 organization more effective. The answer to this question requires the manager to specify the factors in a situation which influence the relative effectiveness of a particular design. Obviously, the contingency approach is considerably more complicated than the universalistic approach.

Two important lines of thought have attempted to determine the key situational factors. The first proposes that differences in *technology* determine the most effective organization design. The second suggests that differences in *environment and requisite information processing* are the crucial factors. As we will see, these two approaches are compatible and can be integrated into a general model of organization design.

TECHNOLOGY AND ORGANIZATION DESIGN

■ The effects of technology on organization structure can be readily understood at an abstract level of analysis. Although various definitions of technology exist, it is generally understood as "the *actions* that an individual performs upon an object with or without the aid of tools or mechanical devices, in order to make some *change* in that object."[20] A compatible, yet even broader definition is that "technology is the application of knowledge to perform work."[21] Thus organization structures reflect technology in the ways that jobs are designed (the division of labor) and grouped (departmentalization). In this sense, the current state of knowledge regarding the appropriate actions to change an object acts as a constraint on management.

---

[19]Likert, *New Patterns of Management and Human Organization.*

[20]Charles Perrow, "A Framework for the Comparative Analysis of Organizations," *American Sociological Review*, April 1967, p. 195.

[21]Denise M. Rousseau, "Assessment of Technology in Organizations: Closed versus Open Systems Approaches," *Academy of Management Review*, October 1979, p. 531.

Technology, broadly defined, can be analyzed in a variety of institutional and cultural settings, despite the tendency to think of technology only in its limited sense of manufacturing. Knowledge is applied to work wherever work is done, whether in hospitals, universities, or social-service agencies. This is not to say that technology is the only factor to affect organizational structure, or that it is even the most important factor in a specific instance. It is to say that technology cannot be ignored in organization design.

The organization theory literature includes a number of studies which examine the relationship between technology and organization structure. We cannot possibly survey all these studies in this section; to do so would take considerable space and would go beyond the intent of our discussion. Rather, we will briefly review one study which stimulated a number of follow-up studies and has become quite important in the literature of organization design.

The Woodward Research Findings

The findings are based upon analyses of the organization structures of 100 manufacturing firms in southern England. The researchers collected information from each firm regarding:

1. History, background, and objectives.
2. Description of the manufacturing processes and methods.
3. Forms and routines through which the firm was organized and operated.
4. Facts and figures that could be used to make an assessment of the firm's commercial success.[22]

The research team used this information to identify interfirm differences in organization structure, operating procedures, and relative profitability. At the outset, some obvious differences in structure were identified:

1. The number of managerial levels varied from 2 to 12 with a median of 4.
2. The spans of control of chief executives varied from 2 to 18 with a median of 6.
3. The spans of control of first-line supervisors varied from 10 to 90 with a median of 38.
4. The ratios of individual workers to staff personnel varied from less than 1:1 to more than 10:1, and the ratios of direct to indirect labor varied from less than 1:1 to more than 10:1.[23]

These variations in structure stimulated the research team to seek out the causes. The team found that when the type of manufacturing was held constant, that is, "controlled," structural variations still appeared. Thus, the type of manufacturing could not explain the variations. The team then examined the relationship between size, as measured by the number of employees, and structural variations. Again, the team was perplexed by the absence of a relationship—size of firm did not account for differences in organization structure.

---

[22]Joan Woodward, *Industrial Organization: Theory and Practice* (London: Oxford University Press, 1965), p. 11.

[23]Ibid., pp. 25–34.

The researchers sought to determine if there were structural differences between the more and less effective firms. The effectiveness of the firms was judged on the basis of their share of the market, the rate of change in market shares, profitability, capital expansion, and other less objective standards such as reputation of the firm and employee attitudes. The researchers classified the firms into three categories of effectiveness: above average, average, and below average. When the organization structures were compared within each category, no consistent pattern emerged. Thus, there was no relationship between effectiveness as defined by the researchers and organization structure.

It was then that the team began analyzing the information relating to technology—"the methods and processes of manufacture."[24] The team measured technology in terms of three related variables: "(1) stages in the historical development of production processes, (2) the interrelationship between the items of equipment used for these processes, and (3) the extent to which the operations performed in the processes were repetitive or comparable from one production cycle or sequence to the next."[25] The application of the measure to the information about the firm's manufacturing methods resulted in a continuum with job-order manufacturing and process manufacturing methods at the extremes, separated by mass-production manufacturing.

The three-way classification resulted in the identification of 24 job-order manufacturing firms, 31 mass-production firms, and 25 process manufacturing firms. The researchers then analyzed the differences in organization structure *within* each of the three groups and among the three groups. These differences are shown in Table 13–2.

The number of managerial levels varied both within and among the three groups. Clearly the effect of advanced technology is to increase the

TABLE 13–2

The Relationships between Certain Organizational Characteristics and Technology

	Job Order	Mass Production	Process Manufacturing
Median levels of management	3	4	6
Median executive span of control	4	7	10
Median supervisory span of control	23	48	15
Median direct to indirect labor ratio	9:1	4:1	1:1
Median industrial to staff worker ratio	8:1	5.5:1	2:1

Source: Joan Woodward, *Industrial Organization: Theory and Practice* (London: Oxford University Press, 1965), pp. 52–62.

[24] Ibid., p. 35.

[25] J. J. Rackham, "Automation and Technical Change—The Implications for the Management Process," in Gene W. Dalton, Paul R. Lawrence, and Jay W. Lorsch, eds., *Organizational Structure and Design*, ed. (Homewood, Ill.: Richard D. Irwin, Inc., and Dorsey Press, 1970), p. 299. © 1970 by Richard D. Irwin, Inc.

number of managerial levels, that is, to lengthen the chain of command. Furthermore, the above-average firms in terms of success in each group tended to have the median number of managerial levels. The below-average and average firms had either more than, or less than, the median number of levels. Thus, though there are obvious differences among the three groups, the more effective firms within each group shared the common characteristic of having the median managerial levels.[26]

The spans of control of the chief executive varied in relation to technology. The effect of advanced technology was to increase the chief executive's span of control. The researchers also found that spans of control for the chief executive of the above-average firms tended toward the median, whereas the executive spans of below-average and average firms tended toward the extremes.

The spans of control of the first-line supervisor also varied with type of technology, but not linearly. In contrast with executive spans of control which increased with technological complexity, the supervisory spans of control were actually smaller in process manufacturing than in job-order production. The explanation lies partially in the different compositions of the work force, but also in the fact that machines are substituted for people at the production level in process manufacturing.

The ratio of direct to indirect workers varied with technology. The data showed the effect of technology on the composition of the work force and indicated clearly the increasing use of clerical and administrative personnel in more advanced technologies.

The ratio of industrial to staff workers decreased along the technology continuum. The data bear out the importance of technology for explaining variation in personnel composition and organization structure. The data indicated the shift of control away from the work force and toward machines and specialists in staff positions as manufacturing becomes more complex.

The differences in organization structures due to differences in technology are evident in Table 13–2. In addition to these differences, the research team noted other differences due to technology.[27]

1. The organizations at each end of the continuum were more flexible, that is, System 4, with "duties and responsibilities being less clearly defined." Organizations in the middle of the continuum were more rigid, that is, bureaucratic with detailed duties and responsibilities.

2. The organizations at each end of the continuum made greater use of verbal than written communications; organizations engaged in mass-production manufacturing made greater use of written communications. This

---

[26] Woodward, *Industrial Organization*, pp. 68–80, discusses the relationship between technology, organization, and success.

[27] Joan Woodward, *Management and Technology, Problems of Progress in Industry*, no. 3 (London: Her Majesty's Stationery Office, 1958), pp. 4–30; and in Gary A. Yukl and Kenneth N. Wexley, eds., *Readings in Organizational and Industrial Psychology* (New York: Oxford University Press, 1971), p. 19.

pattern is consistent with distinctions between System 4 and bureaucratic theory.

3. The managerial positions were more highly specialized in mass production than in either job-order or process manufacturing. Consequently, the mass-production firms relied heavily on the traditional line-staff type of organization with the predictable conflict between the two groups. First-level supervisors engaged primarily in direct supervision, leaving the technical decisions to staff personnel. In contrast, managers in job-order firms were expected to have greater technical expertise and managers in process manufacturing were expected to have greater scientific expertise.

4. Consistent with the above point, the actual control of production in the form of schedule-making and routing was separated from *supervision of production* in mass-production firms. The two functions were more highly integrated in the role of the first level supervisor in organizations at the extremes of the continuum.

Thus the data indicated sharp organization and managerial differences due to technological differences. But how is it that technology affects organization? We offer our interpretation in the next section.

An Interpretation of Woodward's Findings

The relationship between technology and organizations can be understood with reference to the natural business functions—product development, production, and marketing. The job-order firm produces according to customer specifications; the firm must secure the order, develop the product, and manufacture it. The cycle begins with marketing and ends with production.

This sequence requires the firm to be especially adept at sensing market changes and being able to adjust to those changes. But more importantly, the product development function holds the key to the firm's success. This function must convert customer specifications into products which are acceptable to both the customer and the production personnel. The System 4 structure is most effective for promoting the kinds of interactions and communication patterns which are able to meet the market and product development problems associated with job-order or unit production.

At the other extreme of the technological continuum is the process manufacturer. In these firms the cycle begins with product development. The key to success is the ability to discover a new product through scientific research—a new chemical, gasoline additive, or fabric—which can be produced by already existing facilities or by new facilities once a market is established. The development, marketing, and production functions in process manufacturing all tend to demand scientific personnel and specialized competence at the highest levels in the organization. This concentration of staff expertise accounts for the higher ratios of staff and indirect to direct personnel in process manufacturing. Since the success of these firms depends upon adjustment to new scientific knowledge, the System 4 design is more effective than the bureaucratic design.

The bureaucratic design is effective for firms which use mass-production technology. The market exists for a more or less standardized product—autos, foods, clothing—and the task is to manufacture the product through fairly routine means, efficiently and economically. The workers tend machines which are designed and paced by engineering standards. The actual control of the work flow is separated from the supervision of the work force. In such organizations the ideas of scientific management and classical organization theory are most applicable.

Subsequent research to test the effect of technology on structure has produced mixed results. The most complete replication was undertaken by Zwerman.[28] His findings were generally supportive of the "technological imperative" in that he found similar relationships between technology and executive spans of control and number of managerial levels. Another supportive study was completed by Harvey. He found that as technological diffuseness decreased, that is, fewer product changes occurred over time, there was an *increase* in the number of specialized subunits, the number of managerial levels, the ratio of managerial to nonmanagerial personnel, and the extent of formalized rules and communication channels.[29]

The fact that studies attempting to discern the effects of technology produce mixed results can be explained, at least partially. Recent critical reviews of the literature on technology and structure have noted a number of explanations. First is the confusion over level of analysis. Some studies focus on the effects of technology on the individual task, while other studies focus on effects of technology on groups and organizations.[30] Second is the tendency of researchers to define technology only in terms of the conversion phases of a technical system with little regard to either the input or output phases.[31] Finally, there is the inherent difficulty of distinguishing between technology as a *cause* of structural differences, rather than as the *effect* of such differences. For example, by increasing the degree of participation in decision making (decentralization of authority), a human service organization changed the manner in which clients are treated (technology).[32] These research and theoretical issues must be taken into account when attempting to reconcile studies of technology and structure.

Recent studies have indicated that at least two factors moderate the relationship between technology and structure, *size* and *managerial choice.* The effect of size is to reduce the impact of technology on the total orga-

[28] William L. Zwerman, *New Perspectives in Organization Theory* (Westport, Conn.: Greenwood Publishing, 1970).

[29] Edward Harvey, "Technology and the Structure of Organizations," *American Sociological Review*, 1968, pp. 247–59.

[30] Donald Gerwin, "The Comparative Analysis of Structure and Technology: A Critical Appraisal," *Academy of Management Review*, January 1979, pp. 41–51.

[31] Rousseau, "Assessment of Technology," pp. 531–42.

[32] Charles A. Glisson, "Dependence of Technological Routinization on Structural Variables in Human Service Organizations," *Administrative Science Quarterly*, September 1978, pp. 383–95.

nization structure. This relationship was noted in the Aston studies[33] and subsequently in those by Blau and his associates.[34] The structures of small organizations have not reached the stage of growth which permits the creation of support units such as engineering, research and development, product development, public relations, and the like. Consequently, the effect of technology on structure is more apparent in firms which consist of a larger number of subunits whose goals and functions are related to the production process.[35]

The effect of *managerial choice* takes into account the range of choices that managers have in designing an organization.[36] The choices are constrained by factors such as technology and economies of scale, but managers have considerable discretion within those constraints.[37] This point of view reconfirms the importance of management decision making for organizational performance. More important, it identifies technology as only one, albeit important, factor in the organization's *environment*.

ENVIRONMENT AND ORGANIZATION DESIGN

■ The relationship between technology and effective organization design was firmly established in the Woodward study. Yet, as we saw, the interpretation of these relationships required that the *environment* of the organizations be taken into account. Thus the more basic explanation for differences in organization is differences in the environment. This line of reasoning has been pursued by a number of researchers, notably Lawrence and Lorsch. We shall review some of their theory and research findings in this section.

The Lawrence and Lorsch Findings

The data base of the Lawrence and Lorsch findings consisted of detailed case studies of firms in the plastics, food, and container industries.[38] The

---

[33]The original Aston studies were carried out from 1961 to 1973 by the Industrial Administration Unit of the University of Aston in Birmingham. The significant papers of this research are presented in Derek S. Pugh and David J. Hickson, *Organizational Structure in its Context* (Westmead, England: Saxon House, D. C. Heath, 1976); and Derek S. Pugh and Charles R. Hinings, *Organizational Structure: Extensions and Replications* (Westmead, England: Saxon House, D. C. Heath, 1976).

[34]Peter M. Blau, Cecilia M. Falbe, William McKinley, and K. Tracy Phelps, "Technology and Organization in Manufacturing," *Administrative Science Quarterly*, March 1976, pp. 20–30.

[35]Bernard C. Reimann, "Organizational Structure and Technology in Manufacturing: System versus Work Flow Level Perspectives," *Academy of Management Journal*, March 1980, pp. 61–77; and Steven K. Paulson, "Organization Size, Technology, and Structure: Replication of a Study of Social Service Agencies among Small Retail Firms," *Academy of Management Journal*, June 1980, pp. 341–47.

[36]John R. Montanari, "An Expanded Theory of Structural Determination: An Empirical Investigation of the Impact of Managerial Discretion on Organization Structure" (D.B.A. dissertation, University of Colorado, 1976).

[37]H. Randolph Bobbitt and Jeffrey D. Ford, "Decision-Maker Choice as a Determinant of Organizational Structure," *Academy of Management Review*, January 1980, pp. 13–23.

[38]Paul R. Lawrence and Jay W. Lorsch, "Differentiation and Integration in Complex Organizations," *Administrative Science Quarterly*, June 1967, pp. 1–47; Jay W. Lorsch, *Product Innovation and Organization* (New York: Macmillan, 1965); Paul R. Lawrence and Jay W. Lorsch, *Organization and Environment* (Homewood, Ill.: Richard D. Irwin, 1969).

initial study consisted of case studies of six firms operating in the plastics industry. Lawrence and Lorsch analyzed these studies to answer the following questions.

1. How are the environmental demands facing various organizations different and how do environmental demands relate to the internal functioning of effective organizations?
2. Is it true that organizations in certain or stable environments make more exclusive use of the formal hierarchy to achieve integration, and, if so, why? Is it because less integration is required, or because in a certain environment these decisions can be made more effectively at higher organization levels or by fewer people?
3. Is the same degree of differentiation in orientation and in departmental structure found in organizations in different industrial environments?
4. If greater differentiations among functional departments is required in different industries, does this influence the problems of integrating the organizations' parts? Does it influence the organizations' means of achieving integration?[39]

These four questions not only summarize the thrust of the research, but also introduce three key concepts: *differentiation, integration,* and *environment.*

Differentiation. The "state of segmentation of the organizational system into subsystems, each of which tends to develop particular attributes in relation to the requirements posed by its relevant external environment" is termed *differentiation.*[40] This concept refers in part to the idea of specialization of labor, specifically to the degree of departmentalization. But it is broader and also includes the behavioral attributes of employees of these subsystems, or departments. The researchers were interested in three behavioral attributes:

1. They believed that the employees of some departments would be more or less task- or person-oriented than employees in other departments.
2. They proposed that the employees of some departments would have longer or shorter time horizons than members of other departments. They hypothesized that these differences could be explained by different environmental attributes, specifically the length of time between action and the feedback of results.
3. They expected to find some employees more concerned with the goals of their department than with the goals of the total organization.

The organization of each department in the six firms was classified along a continuum from bureaucratic to System 4. They employees in bureaucratically organized departments were expected to be more oriented toward tasks and have shorter time horizons than employees in System 4-type departments.

---

[39] Lawrence and Lorsch, *Organization and Environment,* p. 16.

[40] Lawrence and Lorsch, "Differentiation and Integration in Complex Organizations," pp. 3–4.

Integration.   The "process of achieving unity of effort among the various subsystems in the accomplishment of the organization's task" is defined as integration, and it can be achieved in a variety of ways.[41] The classical theorists argued for integration through the creation of rules and procedures to govern the behavior of the subsystem members. As observed by Thompson, this means of integration can be effective only in relatively stable and predictable situations.[42] He observes that rules and procedures lose their appeal as the environment becomes more unstable and that integration by *plans* takes on greater significance. But as we approach the highly unstable environment, coordination is achieved by mutual adjustment.[43] Coordination by mutual adjustment requires a great deal of communication through open channels throughout the organization. In terms of the Lawrence and Lorsch research, the type of integrative devices which managers use should be related to the degree of differentiation. It would be expected that highly differentiated organizations would tend to use mutual adjustment as a means of achieving integration.

Environment.   The independent variable, environment, was conceptualized from the perspective of the organization members as they looked outward. Consequently, the researchers assumed that a basic reason for differentiating into subsystems is to deal more effectively with subenvironments. Following the lead of Brown, Lawrence and Lorsch identified three main subenvironments: the *market* subenvironment, the *technical-economic* subenvironment, and the *scientific* subenvironment.[44] These three subenvironments correspond to the sales, production, and research and development functions within organizations.

The researchers hypothesized that the degree of differentiation within each subsystem would vary depending upon certain attributes of the relevant subenvironment. Specifically, the subenvironment could vary along three dimensions: (1) the rate of change of conditions over time, (2) the certainty of information about conditions at any particular time, and (3) the time span of feedback on the results of employee decisions.[45] Thus, in terms of this conceptualization, we can state the principal hypothesis as follows:

> The greater the rate of change, the less certain the information; and the longer the time span of feedback within the relevant subenvironment, the greater the differentiation among the subsystems. Furthermore, the greater the differentiation among the subsystems, the greater the need for, and the difficulty of, achieving integration.

---

[41] Ibid., p. 4.

[42] James D. Thompson, *Organizations in Action* (New York: McGraw-Hill, 1967), p. 56.

[43] Ibid.

[44] Wilfred B. D. Brown, *Exploration in Management* (Middlesex, England: Penguin Books, 1965), pp. 143–45.

[45] Lawrence and Lorsch, "Differentiation and Integration in Complex Organizations," pp. 7–8.

The three concepts and the principal hypotheses are depicted in Figure 13–3. There we see that the Lawrence and Lorsch model recognizes that parts of the organization must deal with parts of the environment. The organizational parts, or subsystems, are identified as marketing, production, and research. The environmental parts, or subenvironments, are identified as market, technical-economic, and science. The subsystems must be organized in such a way as to deal effectively with their relevant subenvironments. The greater the differences among the three subenvironments in terms of rate of change, certainty of information, and time span of feedback, the greater will be the differences among the three subsystems in terms of organization structure and behavioral attributes. The greater these differences, that is, the more differentiated are the three subsystems, the more important is the task of integrating the three subsystems.

FIGURE 13–3
A Conceptualization of the Lawrence and Lorsch Model

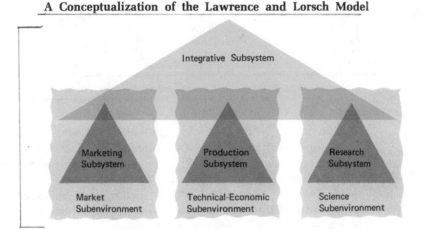

Differentiation, Integration, and Effectiveness

The fact that departments within a single organization are differentiated in terms of organization and behavioral attributes is well established in the Lawrence and Lorsch research. Furthermore, the differentiation is in response to the departments' efforts to cope with their relevant subenvironments. The issue which must now be considered is the relationship between differentiation, integration, and effectiveness.

Lawrence and Lorsch propose that the relative effectiveness of an organization is directly related to the extent to which it achieves required differentiation. In other words, given the state of the subenvironment, there exists an optimal degree of differentiation that the organization should seek to achieve. Furthermore, given the attainment of optimal differentiation, the departments must then be integrated to the degree necessitated by the total environment. As noted earlier, the techniques employed to achieve the required integration range from rules and procedures to mutual adjustment.

The analysis which Lawrence and Lorsch used to examine these issues will not be elaborated here. Let us simply say that they calculated three scores for each of the six organizations: a score to measure the degree of attainment of required differentiation, a score to measure the degree of attainment of required integration, and a score to measure the effectiveness of the total organization.[46] Since the six firms operated in the same industry, the researchers could assume that required integration and differentiation were the same for all firms. Table 13–3 summarizes these findings. The scores were rank-ordered and placed into high, median, and low categories.

TABLE 13–3
Differentiation, Integration, and Effectiveness for the Six Organizations

Organization	Differentiation Score	Integration Score	Effectiveness Score
I	High	High	High
II	High	High	High
III	Low	High	Median
IV	High	Low	Median
V	High	Low	Low
VI	Low	Low	Low

Source: Adapted from Paul R. Lawrence and Jay W. Lorsch, "Differentiation and Integration in Complex Organizations," *Administrative Science Quarterly*, June 1967, p. 27, Figure 1.

The data in Table 13–3 indicate that effectiveness is related to the degree of required differentiation and integration. Clearly the two high performance organizations, I and II, have achieved high differentiation *and* integration, whereas the median and low performance organizations failed to achieve this relationship. The lowest performance organization, VI, achieved low differentiation *and* integration. Thus the findings are consistent with the researchers' expectations.

An Interpretation of Lawrence and Lorsch's Findings

The differentiation-integration approach is based upon the fundamental viewpoint that there is no one best way to organize. But this approach goes further to show that a number of different types of organizations can exist within a single large organization. As Lawrence and Lorsch have shown, a large firm may find it necessary to organize its production department quite differently from its research department. One department may tend toward the bureaucratic design, the other toward the System 4 design. The differences in the organizations are due to the differences in the environments to which the two departments must adapt. The more stable and certain the subenvironment the more bureaucratic should be the departmental organization structure; the more dynamic and uncertain the subenvironment the more System 4 should be the departmental structure.

---

[46] The effectiveness score was based upon "change in profits over the five years prior to the study, change in sales volume over the same period, and percentage of current sales volume accounted for by products developed within the last five years. . . ." Ibid., p. 25.

The process of departmentalizing creates the necessity for integrating the activities of the departments. The integration of separate, yet interdependent, activities is a familiar problem in the management of organizations. The classical writers proposed that the problem could be solved through the creation of rules, procedures, plans, and a hierarchical chain of command which placed managers in the position of integrators or coordinators. The solutions of System 4 proponents, however, differ in that they espouse teams, integrators, and group-centered decision making. Lawrence and Lorsch observe that either the bureaucratic or the System 4 approach is appropriate depending upon the situation. The techniques of the classical writers are appropriate in those organizations which confront relatively homogeneous and certain environments. Thus, organizations which confront stable and certain market, technical-economic, and scientific subenvironments can use classical integrative techniques.

Organizations which confront relatively diverse and uncertain environments, such as the chemical and foods industry, must rely upon integrative techniques espoused by System 4 proponents. Group-centered decision making, mutual adjustment through network communications, and integrative teams are necessary to integrate highly differentiated departments. The relatively more successful firms are those which recognize and adopt the appropriate organization designs for their departments, and the appropriate methods to integrate their departments.

Other studies have established the relationship of environmental factors to organizational structure.[47] But there are inconsistencies and contradictions in these studies. The causes of these inconsistencies are much like those associated with studies of technology. For example, some studies use qualitative measures of environmental uncertainty, others use quantitative measures; still other studies use questionnaire responses as completed by participants in the organization, others use objective indexes of uncertainty.[48] It is necessary to evaluate critically the studies reporting environmental effects before drawing any final conclusions.

ENVIRONMENTAL UNCERTAINTY, INFORMATION PROCESSING, AND ADAPTIVE DESIGN STRATEGIES

■ The relationships among environment, technology, and organization structure can be synthesized. The key concept is *information* and the key idea is that organizations must effectively receive, process, and act on information to achieve performance. Information flows into the organization from the subenvironments. The information enables the organization to respond to market, technological, and resource changes. The more rapid the

---

[47]Lawrence G. Hrebiniak and Charles C. Snow, "Industry Differences in Environmental Uncertainty and Organizational Characteristics Related to Uncertainty," *Academy of Management Journal*, December 1980, pp. 750–59.

[48]H. Kirk Downey and R. Duane Ireland, "Quantitative versus Qualitative Environmental Assessment in Organizational Studies," *Administrative Science Quarterly*, December 1979, pp. 630–37.

changes, the greater the necessity for, and availability of, information.[49]

As Lawrence and Lorsch observed, organizations existing in relatively certain and unchanging environments rely upon hierarchical control, rules and procedures, and planning to integrate the behavior of subunits. These integrative methods are fundamental features of classical organization designs and are effective as long as the environment remains stable and predictable. The information-processing requirements are relatively modest in such environments. For example firms manufacturing and selling paper containers can plan production schedules with relative assurance that sudden shifts in demand, resource supply, or technology will not disrupt the schedule. Information requirements consist almost solely of projections from historical sales, cost, and engineering data.

Organizations existing in dynamic and complex environments, however, are unable to rely upon traditional information-processing and control techniques. Changes in market demand, resource supplies, and technology disrupt plans and require adjustments *during* task performance. On-the-spot adjustments to production schedules and task performance disrupt the organization. Coordination is made more difficult because it is impossible to preplan operations and to devise rules and procedures. It is imperative to acquire information which reflects environmental changes; "the greater the uncertainty, the greater the amount of information that must be processed among decision makers during task completion in order to achieve a given level of performance."[50]

From a managerial perspective, the effect of environmental uncertainty and increased flow of information is to overload the organization with exceptional cases. As a greater number of nonroutine, consequential events occur in the organization's environment, managers are more and more drawn into day-to-day operating matters. Problems develop as plans become obsolete and as the various functions' coordinative efforts break down. Some organizations are designed from their inception to deal with information-processing demands; most, however, must confront the problem at a point in time subsequent to their creation. For these organizations which discover that their present design is incapable of dealing with the demands of changing environments, the problem becomes one of selecting an appropriate adaptive strategy. The two general approaches are (1) reduce the need for information and (2) increase capacity to process information.

---

[49] The development of theory relating information-process and organization structure has been discussed in various sources. The more recent and most publicized sources are Jay Galbraith, *Designing Complex Organizations* (Reading, Mass.: Addison-Wesley Publishing, 1973); and Jay Galbraith, *Organization Design* (Reading, Mass.: Addison-Wesley Publishing, 1977).

[50] Jay Galbraith, "Organization Design: An Information Processing View," *Interfaces*, May 1974, p. 28.

Strategies to Reduce the Need for Information

Managers can reduce the need for information by reducing the (1) number of exceptions that occur and (2) number of factors to be considered when the exceptions do occur. These two ends can be achieved by creating slack resources or by creating self-contained units.[51]

Creating Slack Resources. Slack resources include stockpiles of materials, manpower, and other capabilities which enable the organization to respond to uncertainty. Other examples include lengthening planning periods, production schedules, and lead times. These practices limit the number of exceptional cases by increasing the time span within which a response is necessary. For example, job-order manufacturers can intentionally overestimate the time required to complete a customized product, thus allowing time to deal with any difficulties that arise.

An additional effect of slack resources is to reduce the interdependence between units within the organization. If inventory is available to meet unexpected sales, no interaction is required between production and sales units. If inventory is not available, production and sales units must necessarily interact and coordinate their activities.

It is obvious that creating slack resources has cost implications. Excess inventory (safety stocks, buffer stocks) represents money that can be invested; thus carrying costs will increase. Extended planning, budgeting, and scheduling time horizons lower expected performance. Whether the strategy of creating slack resources is optimal depends upon careful balancing of the relevant costs and benefits.

Creating Self-Contained Units. Creating slack resources can be undertaken within the present organization structure. Creating self-contained units involves a complete reorganization away from functional, toward product, customer or territorial bases. Each unit is provided its own resources—manufacturing, personnel, marketing, and engineering. Ordinarily accounting, finance, and legal functions would remain centralized and made available to the new units on an "as needed" basis. Reorganization around products, customers, or territories enables the organization to achieve desired flexibility and adaptability, but at the cost of lost efficiency.

In terms of information processing, self-contained units inherently face less environmental uncertainty than the larger whole. They deal with a complementary grouping of products or customers and do not have to coordinate activities with other units. With reduced required coordination, the units do not have to process as much information as before the reorganization.

Strategies to Increase Capacity to Process Information

Instead of reducing the amount of information needed, managers may choose to increase the organization's capacity to process it. Two strategies accomplish this objective, (1) invest in vertical information systems or (2) create lateral relationships.

---

[51]Based upon Galbraith, "Organization Design."

__Investing in Vertical Information Systems.__ The result of increased environmental uncertainty is information overload. Managers are simply inundated with information which requires action of some kind. A strategic response to the problem is to invest in information-processing systems, such as computers, clerks, and executive assistants. These resources process information more quickly, and format the data in more efficient language.

Creating Lateral Relationships. As the necessity for increased coordination among functional units intensifies, decisions must be made which cross authority lines. In Chapter 11, we discussed the process by which management can move in successive steps from cross-functional task forces to matrix organization structure. The effect of introducing lateral relationships is to facilitate joint decision making among the functional units, but without the loss of efficiency due to specialization. The cost of the strategy is an increase in the number of managers who deal with the environment. The roles of managers in *boundary spanning* positions are particularly demanding; the success of this strategy depends upon how effectively the role occupants perform. The following section reviews some of the issues associated with these key jobs.

Boundary-Spanning Roles

Boundary-spanning roles perform two functions: (1) to gather information and (2) to represent the organization.[52] Sales personnel, purchasing agents, salespersons, lobbyists, public relations personnel, market researchers, and personnel recruiters are a few of the job titles which gather information and represent the organization. Roles of this type exist at the interface between the organization and its environments; they can be termed *external boundary roles*.

Internal boundary roles, in contrast, exist within the organization at the interface between subunits such as functional and product departments. Product managers, expediters, integrators, and liaison personnel are examples of roles which exist between subunits. As we have seen, organizations cope with environmental uncertainty and increase information by establishing these types of roles. They perform tasks that are similar to those performed by external boundary roles, except that they gather information which facilitates joint decision making.

The demands on those who perform boundary spanning positions are qualitatively different from others in the organization. These unique demands result from the fact that the role occupant must deal with often conflicting expectations, but without the authority to settle the disagreement.[53]

---

[52] Howard Aldrich and Diane Herker, "Boundary Spanning Roles and Organization Structure," *Academy of Management Review*, April 1977, p. 218.

[53] The following discussion is based upon Dennis W. Organ, "Linking Pins between Organizations and Environment," in *The Applied Psychology of Work Behavior*, ed. Dennis W. Organ (Plano, Tex: Business Publications, 1978), pp. 509–19. © 1978 by Business Publications, Inc.

Role Conflict. Boundary spanners are often caught between people who expect different, and often incompatible, behaviors. Product managers in matrix organizations for example, must balance the interests of marketing personnel who want high-quality products and production personnel who desire manufacturing efficiency. The product manager has authority over neither group; and consequently must balance these interests and reach effective decisions through informal influence based upon expertise. The company negotiator must deal simultaneously with the demands of fellow managers as well as union spokespersons. Each segment of the environment or the organization has its own set of goals, beliefs, and values. To the extent that there are great differences among these sets, the boundary spanning role is made more difficult. People having high tolerance for ambiguity and desire for relative freedom from close supervision, that is, autonomy, would have the greatest chance of performing effectively because they would be able to cope with the conflict.

Lack of Authority. Boundary spanners do not have position power; that is, authority is not delegated to them. They must achieve their performance levels through other means. An industrial salesperson, for example, can attempt to influence customer demand by becoming extremely knowledgeable about the customers' technical and production methods. By doing so, he or she is able to influence the customers' decisions with respect to purchasing the organizations' products.

Agents of Change. Some boundary spanning positions are created to facilitate change and innovation. For example, key roles in research and development labs are those which link the lab to the various informational sources in the environment.[54] We have already noted the manner in which organizations respond to the necessity for new product innovation by creating product task forces, teams, and managers. Indeed the need to innovate arises coincidentally with environmental and technological pressures and demands. Yet the fact that boundary spanners are advocates for change places them in conflict with organizational subunits which desire stable operations, such as manufacturing, data processing, and personnel departments. An example of internal boundary spanning roles is provided in the following close-up.

ORGANIZATIONS: CLOSE-UP

Product Managers at General Mills

The concept of product (or brand) managers was first introduced in 1927 when Procter & Gamble assigned a man to oversee Camay soap. Today product managers exist in a variety of multiproduct firms. Although the role of a

---

[54] Michael L. Tushman, "Special Boundary Roles in the Innovation Process," *Administrative Science Quarterly*, December 1977, pp. 587–605.

ORGANIZATIONS: CLOSE-UP (continued)

product manager differs from company to company, at General Mills he or she acts as a business manager, collecting all the necessary information that might affect the product and setting goals and establishing strategies for achieving those goals. Seemingly a product manager at General Mills is a full-fledged manager. Such, however, is not the case. A product manager *represents* the product in the organization and must obtain internal resources by means other than formal authority. In a real sense the product manager has considerable responsibility but no authority over the production and marketing functions necessary to carry out that responsibility.

Product managers compete with one another for financial and staff support for their products. They also compete for promotions to the next tier of management—marketing director. At present there are 33 product managers at General Mills; only 8 or 9 of them will be promoted to the next level. About half of those not promoted will go to another company; the other half will move to other positions in General Mills. The system at General Mills does a good job of preparing future general managers in the marketing aspects of the business, but it is less successful in providing training and experience in the production and finance areas.

Basically, product management is management by persuasion. For example, if a product manager needs special support from the sales force and additional output from manufacturing to implement an aggressive advertising campaign, he or she must sell the idea to people who report to the managers of marketing and manufacturing. If the product manager believes that the product needs different packaging, new recipe testing, or a reformulation of basic ingredients, he or she must persuade the appropriate support personnel to take action on the product. To be effective in the role of product manager, the individual must be effective in dealing with people up and down the line. The individual must be able to cross the boundaries of the various functional areas and obtain the support needed to carry out the plans for the product.

Source: Ann M. Morrison, "The General Mills Brand of Managers," *Fortune,* January 12, 1981, pp. 99–107.

Thus we see that the adaptation of organizations to increasing uncertainty, and need for information involves changes in organization structure at the micro and macro levels. Managers can choose to cope with information processing demands by either reducing the need or by increasing the organization's capability to process it. If managers choose to cope with informational needs by creating lateral relationships, the cost of the strategy must be calculated to include the behavioral demands of employees in boundary-spanning roles.

AN ENVIRONMENTAL-CONTINGENT MODEL OF ORGANIZATION DESIGN

■ The state of knowledge regarding the managerial function of organizing is sufficient to outline a general model of organization design. Such a model would propose guidelines for the design of an organization in any institutional setting—business firms, universities, hospitals, governmental agencies, or any other setting in which people join together to accomplish a task. These guidelines must necessarily be stated in relatively broad terms since we are discussing the general problem of organization design as confronted in any institution. The starting point in the general model of organization design is systems theory.

FIGURE 13–4
The Four Subenvironments of an Organization

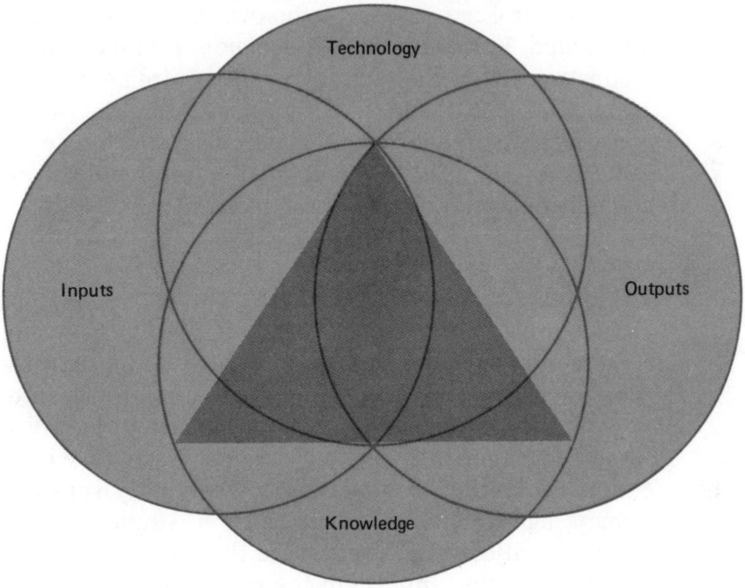

As was first discussed in Chapter 2 where we considered the problem of organization effectiveness, systems theory suggests that we should conceptualize an organization as one element of a larger set of elements; the total set of interacting and interdependent elements is termed a system. We can combine systems theory and the analyses of Woodward and Lawrence and Lorsch to arrive at an understanding of the relationship between an organization and the larger system, or *environment*, in which it exists. Figure 13–4 illustrates <u>this conceptualization in which the organization is viewed as interacting within a total environment which consists of four subenvironments: input, technology, knowledge, and output</u>.

The effective organization design is one which is consistent with the demands of each of these subenvironments; but the relationship between and among the subenvironments and the organization is very complex.

**The Output
Subenvironment**

The most critical managerial decision is the selection of the output market which the organization will serve. This decision determines in large measure the nature and type of input, technology, and knowledge subenvironments which will, in turn, serve the organization. The decision to supply packing cartons rather than petrochemicals involves a simultaneous decision to utilize a certain kind of input, technology, and knowledge. Similarly, the decisions to train physicians, rather than accountants; to treat critically—rather than chronically—ill people; and to solve water pollution rather than solid waste problems involve simultaneous decisions to use certain inputs and technologies in the context of a prevailing state of knowledge.

These interrelationships among the four parts of the subenvironment are implied in Figure 13–4 by the overlapped sets. Some interrelationships can be noted. For example, the decision to enter into certain output markets is constrained by the technological requirement. A decision to enter the automobile, petroleum, and chemical industries involves a decision to make costly investments in the machines and processes required to produce these outputs. The technological requirement can be so great as to discourage firms from entering these markets.

**The Input
Subenvironment**

Inputs can consist of raw materials, people, and problems. Business firms process raw materials; schools and hospitals process people; and governmental agencies process problems. If the inputs are stable and unchanging over time, we would expect the organization and its subunits to tend *(& vice versa)* toward the bureaucratic design. For example, a firm which processes corrugated paper into packing cartons, a school which has a selective admissions policy, a hospital which treats only selected patients, or a government agency which deals with a single problem, say unemployment compensation, would all share the common characteristic of dealing with an unchanging input. On the other hand many organizations seek to take on larger tasks involving more diverse and changeable inputs. Examples of such organizations include chemical and plastic manufacturers, land-grant universities with open admissions policies, municipal hospitals, and multiproblem government agencies, such as the Department of Health and Human Services. These organizations confront a more diverse and uncertain input subenvironment than those which restrict their range of activities to the completion of one task.

The intrinsic characteristics of all inputs regardless of setting is the extent to which they are homogeneous, that is, uniform from unit to unit. In a sense, the homogeneity of inputs is related to the output. But there are instances in which homogeneous inputs are transformed into several different outputs; the textile, petroleum, and chemical industries reflect this situation. The interaction of inputs and outputs is critical for the technological decision.

The Technology Subenvironment

The technology of business firms consists primarily of man-machine operations. Furthermore, a range of technology is available to business firms from single job order to process manufacturing. The choice of technology is related not only to the type of input which the firm processes, but also to the output which is to be returned to the environment. Constant, unchanging inputs which are to be processed into fairly homogeneous outputs require mass-production techniques; varied and changeable inputs which are to be processed into many different outputs demand job-order production; constant and unchanging inputs which are to be processed into many different outputs require process production techniques. Thus the relationship between the output required, the nature of technology, and inputs is straightforward.

Nonbusiness organizations can be analyzed in a similar manner keeping in mind that the concept of technology in these settings refers to the application of analytical techniques, mainly knowledge, rather than the application of machines and tools. A school which permits the enrollment of many different kinds of students, undergraduate and graduate, and which seeks to process these students into a variety of specialties, must use a technology very similar to the job-order printer: each student is more or less under direct supervision of the faculty who teach the specialty the student pursues. The curriculum will be quite flexible with courses tailor-made to the student's needs. A school which enrolls a homogeneous student body which pursues a single specialty, say engineering or accounting, will use "assembly-line technology." That is, the curriculum is specified and there is little deviation from the prescribed norms. We can also see how the "assembly-line technology" would be appropriate for hospitals which specialize in the treatment of tuberculosis and for governmental agencies which specialize in tax collection.

The general characteristic of technology which is relevant for the organization design decision is the extent to which it is routine. That is, routine technology involves the same actions to be performed each time the person acts on the object, on input. Nonroutine technology occurs when the same action cannot be performed each time the person acts on the object, or input. The more routine the actions, the more bureaucratic is the appropriate organization since the actions of each person can be prescribed in detail by staff specialists. The techniques of scientific management (motion and time study, work simplification, and time standards) are most applicable in routine technology. But if one must use nonroutine technology, the organization must be oriented toward System 4 since all actions cannot be prescribed prior to performance.

The Knowledge Subenvironment

The knowledge subenvironment pervades the input, technology, and output environments. Each of these subenvironments is subject to considerable change. Knowledge about inputs may be quite stable, yet be dynamic in the technology and output subenvironments. For example, the scientific knowledge in the petroleum industry is very dynamic in the technology and output subenvironments. New products and new processes are constantly being developed in the research laboratories of oil companies. The reverse is true for the textile industry in which the input subenvironment is constantly providing new fabrics, such as polyester knits. In other industries the technology subenvironment may be more dynamic than either the input or output subenvironments. For example, the printing, railroad, and mining industries have introduced new technology over time, with little change in inputs and outputs.

The knowledge subenvironments in nonbusiness organizations can also be identified. The technology in hospitals is the treatment process and in universities it is the teaching process. A comparison of these two examples suggest considerable difference in the rate of change in the two technologies. Medical research is continuously devising new treatment technologies, and the success of a hospital depends upon the adoption of these new approaches as they appear; the inputs and outputs remain constant. The university is quite different in that it is experiencing considerable change in inputs and outputs but little change in the technology. Certainly new knowledge is being produced by the research faculty, yet the traditional classroom approach remains the basic technology for passing on that new knowledge to the students. Consequently, universities create departments which attempt to learn more about the student body, present and prospective, and about what society is demanding in the form of new careers; yet comparatively little effort is expended to identify new technologies of teaching.

The recognition that managerial decision making plays a key role in organizational design is firmly established in the business policy literature.[55] In fact, much of what was been stated in this section can be summarized in the idea that structure follows strategy[56] and that maximum performance is achieved when there is *congruence* between strategy and structure.[57] Managerial strategy involves the choice of what products and services the organization will supply to specific customers and markets. This choice of output determines, as noted above, a whole range of input, technological, and knowledge factors. Thus managers who decide to supply a single product to a specific set of customers can be expected to design a far simpler organizational structure than a manager of a highly diversified company serving multiple markets with multiple products and services.[58]

---

[55] L. J. Bourgeois, "Strategy and Environment: A Conceptual Integration," *Academy of Management Review*, January 1980, pp. 25–39.

[56] Alfred Chandler, *Strategy and Structure* (Cambridge, Mass.: MIT Press, 1962).

[57] A series of studies have analyzed this relationship including Richard Rumelt, *Strategy, Structure and Economic Performance* (Boston, Mass.: Division of Research, Harvard Business School, 1974) and, more recently, Peter Grinyer, Shawki Al-Bazzaz, and Masoud Yasai-Ardekani, "Strategy, Structure, the Environment, and Financial Performance in 48 United Kingdom Companies," *Academy of Management Journal*, June 1980, pp. 193–220.

[58] Jay R. Galbraith and Daniel A. Nathanson, *Strategy Implementation: The Role of Structure and Process* (St. Paul, Minn.: West Publishing, 1978).

Moreover the strategic choice affects not only the macro aspects of organizational structure, but the micro aspects (job design)[59] and, apparently, leadership behavior[60] as well. The following close-up illustrates vividly the important role of management decision making in structuring organizations.

ORGANIZATIONS: CLOSE-UP

One Governor's View of Organization Structure

When John Y. Brown, Jr. became governor of the state of Kentucky in 1980, he stated that he intended to apply business management principles to state government. In the first 13 months of his four-year term, he has enacted a series of reorganization steps that have substantially changed the structure of Kentucky state government. In the month of January 1981, alone, Governor Brown took the following steps:

Established a new Personnel and Management Cabinet that includes the old Department of Personnel.

Reorganized the old Development Cabinet into a new Commerce Cabinet.

Merged the Tourism and Public Information departments.

Created a new Energy and Agriculture Cabinet and transferred a number of programs from the Agriculture Department to the new Cabinet.

Transferred the Kentucky Housing Corporation from the Finance Department to the Transportation Department.

According to Governor Brown, his reorganization decisions reflect his views regarding the purposes of organization: "We had a slogan in my last business. We called it 'KISS'—Keep it simple, stupid.' Really, that's what we are trying to do: Simplify government. After a year [in office] we have had time to analyze and consolidate in those areas we thought would be most beneficial. I was able to see what needed to be done and match that with the people we had available." To Brown, matching people with tasks is what organization is all about. That idea accounts for the seemingly incongruous grouping of Energy and Agriculture, and of Transportation and the Housing Corporation.

"I am a believer you don't fit people to an organization chart," Brown has said. "An organization chart is just a bunch of marks on a piece of paper. You fit the chart to your people. When I was at Kentucky Fried Chicken, we didn't have an organizational chart until the last year." Acting on his belief has meant that reorganization is a possibility whenever there is a change in the governor's Cabinet.

---

[59] Jon L. Pierce, Randall B. Dunham, and Richard S. Blackburn, "Social System Structure, Job Design, and Growth Need Strength: A Test of the Congruence Model," *Academy of Management Journal*, June 1979, pp. 223–40.

[60] Ricky W. Griffin, "Relationships among Individual, Task Design, and Leader Behavior Variables," *Academy of Management Journal*, December 1980, pp. 665–83.

AN INTEGRATIVE FRAMEWORK

■ Managers must consider many complex factors and variables to design an optimal organization structure. The most important of these considerations are shown in Figure 13–5. The material presented in Chapters 11, 12, and 13 reflects the current state of knowledge regarding the micro and macro issues of organization design. As we have seen, the key design decisions are division of labor, departmentalization, spans of control, and delegation of authority. These decisions reflect *environmental* and *managerial* *factors* as well as the actual and contemplated *size* of the organization. The interactions of these factors and the key decisions are complex; managers do not have the luxury of designing a one best way structure. Instead the optimal design depends upon the situation as determined by the interaction of size, environmental, and managerial factors. Matching the appropriate structure to these factors is the essence of *contingency design* theory and practice.

The overall structure of tasks and authority which results from the key decisions is a specific *organization design*. The alternative designs range along a continuum with functional organizations at one extreme and prod-

FIGURE 13–5
An Integrative Framework for Organization Design

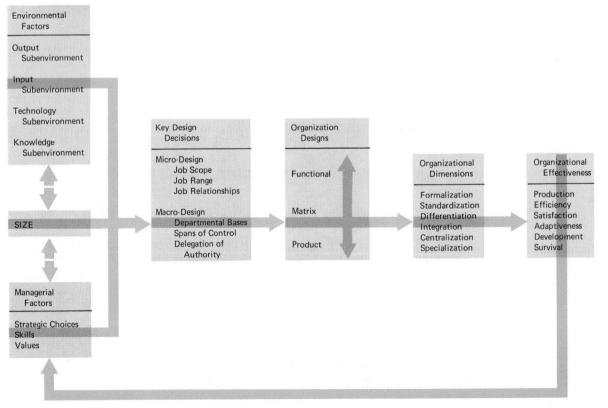

uct at the other. The matrix design, at the midpoint, represents a balance between the two extremes.

Organization structures differ on many dimensions, the more important being shown in Figure 13–5. In general, functional organizations are more formalized, standardized, centralized, and specialized than product organizations. They are also less differentiated and achieve integration through hierarchy, rules and procedures, and planning. Product organizations, however, must achieve integration through lateral relationships and mutual adjustment. The effect of these dimensions is to channel behavior of individuals and groups into patterns which contribute to effective organization performance.

MAJOR MANAGERIAL ISSUES

A. The task and authority relationships among jobs and groups of jobs must be defined and structured according to rational bases. Historically, practitioners and theorists have recommended two specific, yet contradictory, theories for designing organization structures.

B. One theory, termed *classical design,* is based upon the assumption that the more effective organization structure is characterized by highly specialized jobs, homogeneous departments, narrow spans of control, and relatively centralized authority. The bases for these assumptions are to be found in the historical circumstances within which this theory developed. It was a time of fairly rapid industrialization which encouraged public and private organizations to emphasize the production and efficiency criteria of effectiveness. To achieve these ends, classical design theory proposes a single one best way to structure an organization.

C. In recent years, beginning with the human relations era of the 1930s and sustained by the growing interest of behavioral scientists in the study of management and organization, an alternative to classical design theory has been developed. This theory, termed *System 4 design* proposes that the more effective organization has relatively despecialized jobs, heterogeneous departments, wide spans of control, and decentralized authority. Such organization structures, it is argued, not only achieve high levels of production and efficiency, but also satisfaction, adaptiveness, and development.

D. The design of effective organizational structure cannot be guided by a single "one best way" theory. Rather, the manager must adopt the point of view that either the bureaucratic or System 4 design is more effective for the total organization or for subunits within the organization.

E. The manager must identify and describe the relevant subenvironments of the organization in terms of outputs, inputs, technology, and knowledge. These subenvironments determine the relationships within units, among units, and between units and their subenvironments.

MAJOR MANAGERIAL ISSUES (*continued*)

F.   The manager must evaluate each subenvironment in terms of its rate of change, relative certainty, and time span of feedback. These conditions are the key variables for determining the formal structure of tasks and authority.

G.   Each subunit structure is designed along the bureaucratic-System 4 continuum in a consistent manner with the state of environmental conditions. Specifically, slower rates of change, greater certainty, and shorter time spans of feedback are compatible with the bureaucratic design; the converse is true for the System 4 design.

H.   Concurrently with the design of subunit structures is the design of integrative techniques. The appropriate techniques, whether rules, plans, or mutual adjustment, depend upon the degree of subunit differentiation. The greater the differentiation the greater the need for mutual adjustment techniques. At the other extreme, the greater the need for rules and plans.

DISCUSSION AND REVIEW QUESTIONS

1.   Explain the rationale for the argument that there is "one best way" to design an organization.

2.   "Any time a group forms to accomplish a task, a hierarchy of authority *must* be created." Comment.

3.   All organizations have elements of bureaucracy. Can you think of any instance for which this statement is not true?

4.   What is the basis of the argument that bureaucracies tend to become conservative in their actions?

5.   What is the basis of the argument that System 4 organization is the one best way to organize? Do you agree?

6.   Do you believe it would be easier to change an organization from a bureaucracy to a System 4, or from a System 4 to a bureaucracy? Explain.

7.   Do you believe that any real-world organizations can be termed System 4? Do you believe there are any "ideal type" bureaucracies? If not, of what use are these theories?

8.   What are the basic flaws in the arguments of those who propose that there is "one best way" to organize?

9.   Use the characteristics of bureaucratic and System 4 organization to describe two different organizations which you know about. After you have determined the organizational differences, see if you can relate the differences to technological and environmental differences.

10.   What are the counterparts to the market, technical-economic, and scientific subenvironments of a university? A hospital? A professional football team?

11.   What criteria of effectiveness were used in the Woodward research? Compare these with the criteria used in the Lawrence and Lorsch research.

12.   Discuss the manner in which technology and environmental certainty interact to determine the most effective organization.

13.   Although not the main focus of this chapter, we have suggested ways in which the structure of an organization is related to such processes as communications, interactions, and time orientations. As a general rule, are you prepared to accept the argument that the structure does, in fact, determine important aspects of these processes? Discuss your reasoning.

14. Based upon whatever information is at your disposal, rank from high to low the environmental uncertainty of a college of arts and sciences, a college of engineering, a college of business, and a college of education. What does your ranking suggest about the integration techniques which would be appropriate in each college?

ADDITIONAL REFERENCES

Blau, P. M. "A Formal Theory of Differentiation in Organizations." *American Sociological Review,* 1970, pp. 201–18.

————, and Scott, W. R. *Formal Organizations.* San Francisco: Chandler Publishing, 1962.

Burack, E. H. "Industrial Management in Advanced Production Systems." *Administrative Science Quarterly,* 1967, pp. 479–500.

Burns, T., and G. W. Stalker. *The Management of Innovation.* London: Tavistock Publications, 1961.

Corey, E. R., and S. H. Star. *Organization Strategy: A Marketing Approach.* Boston: Division of Research, Harvard Business School, 1971.

Davis, K. "Evolving Models of Organizational Behavior." *Academy of Management Journal,* 1968, pp. 27–38.

Gordon, L. V. "Correlates of Bureaucratic Orientation." *Manpower and Applied Psychology,* 1969, pp. 54–59.

Harvey, E. "Technology and Structure in Organizations." *American Sociological Review,* 1968, pp. 247–49.

Hunt, R. G. "Technology and Structure in Organizations." *American Sociological Review,* 1968, pp. 247–49.

Jurkovich, R. "A Core Typology of Organization Environments." *Administrative Science Quarterly,* September 1974, pp. 380–94.

Lynch, B. P. "An Empirical Assessment of Perrow's Technology Construct." *Administrative Science Quarterly,* 1974, pp. 338–56.

Miewald, R. D. "The Greatly Exaggerated Death of Bureaucracy." *California Management Review,* 1970, pp. 65–69.

Mohr, L. B. "Organizational Technology and Organizational Structure." *Administrative Science Quarterly,* 1970, pp. 444–59.

Osborn, R. N., and J. G. Hunt. "Environment and Organizational Effectiveness." *Administrative Science Quarterly,* 1974, pp. 231–46.

Pennings, J. M. "The Relevance of the Structural-Contingency Model for Organizational Effectiveness." *Administrative Science Quarterly,* 1975, pp. 393–410.

Perrow, C. *Organizational Analysis: A Sociological View.* Belmont, Calif.: Wadsworth, 1970.

Pheysey, D. C.; R. L. Payne; and D. S. Pugh. "Influence of Structure on Organizational and Group Levels." *Administrative Science Quarterly,* 1971, pp. 61–73.

Reimann, B. D. "Dimensions of Structure in Effective Organizations." *Academy of Management Journal,* 1974, pp. 693–708.

Segal, M. "Organization and Environment: A Typology of Adaptability and Structure." *Public Administration Review,* 1974, pp. 212–20.

Sherman, H. *It All Depends: A Pragmatic Approach to Organization.* Tuscaloosa: University of Alabama Press, 1966.

Stevenson, T. E. "The Longevity of Classical Theory." *Management International Review,* 1968, pp. 77–94.

Tannenbaum, A. S.; S. Mozina; J. Jerorsek; and R. Likert. "Testing a Management Style." *European Business,* 1970, pp. 60–68.

Thompson, J. D., ed. *Approaches to Organizational Design.* Pittsburgh: University of Pittsburgh Press, 1966.

Urwick, L. *Notes on the Theory of Organization.* New York: American Management Association, 1952.

CASE FOR ANALYSIS

**DEFINING THE
ROLE OF A
LIAISON OFFICER**

Recently the governor of a southeastern state created the Department for Human Resources. It was in fact a combination of many formerly distinct state agencies which carried out health and welfare programs. The organization chart of the department is shown in Exhibit 1. The functions of each of the bureaus as noted in the governor's press release are as follows:

> *The Bureau for Social Insurance* will operate all income maintenance and all income supplementation programs of the Department for Human Resources. That is, it will issue financial support to the poor, unemployed, and needy, and will issue food stamps and pay for medical assistance.
>
> *The Bureau for Social Services* will provide child welfare services, foster care, adoptions, family services, and all other general counseling in support of families and individuals who require assistance for successful and adequate human development.
>
> *The Bureau for Health Services* will operate all programs of the Department that provide health service including all physical and mental health programs. This bureau will take over the functions of the Department of Health, the Department of Mental Health, and the Commission for Handicapped Children.

EXHIBIT 1
Department for Human Resources

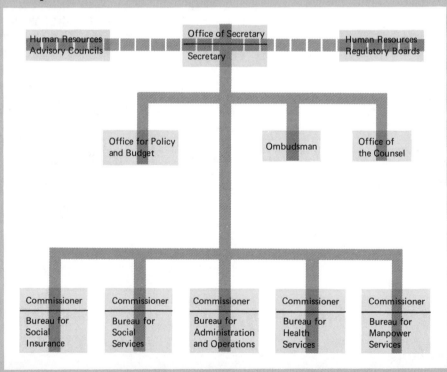

The Bureau for Manpower Services will operate all manpower development and job placement programs of the Department, including all job recruitment and business liaison functions, job training, and worker readiness functions and job counseling and placement.

The Bureau for Administration and Operations will consolidate numerous support services now furnished by 19 separate units such as preaudits, accounting, data processing, purchasing, duplicating, for all the Departments.

Very soon after the department began to operate in its reorganized form, it became apparent that major problems were traceable to the Bureau of Administration and Operations (BAO). Prior to reorganization each department had had its own support staffs—data processing, accounting, personnel, and budgeting. Those staffs and equipment had all been relocated and brought under the direction of the BAO Commissioner. Employees who had once specialized in the work of one area, such as mental health, were now expected to perform work for all the bureaus. In addition, it was necessary to revise forms, procedures, computer programs, accounts, and records to conform to the new department's policies.

Consequently the department began to experience administrative problems. Payrolls were late and inaccurate, payments to vendors and clients were delayed, and personnel actions got lost in the paperwork. Eventually the integrity of the department service programs was in jeopardy.

The executive staff of the department, consisting of the secretary, commissioner, and administrator of the Office for Policy and Budget, soon found itself spending more time dealing with these administrative problems then with policy formulation. It was apparent that the department's effectiveness would depend upon its ability to integrate the functions of BAO with the needs of the program bureaus. It was also apparent that the executive staff was not the appropriate body to deal with these issues. Aside from the inordinate amount of time being spent on the administrative problems, a great deal of interpersonal conflict was generated among the commissioners.

The BAO commissioner was instructed by the secretary to give his full-time attention to devising a means for integrating the administrative functions. After consultation with his staff, the idea of an administrative liaison officer was formulated. The staff paper which described this new job is shown in Exhibit 2. The BAO commissioner presented the paper to the

EXHIBIT 2
Description of Responsibilities, Administrative Liaison Officer

---

Introduction

Executive Order 78–777 abolished the former Human Resources agencies and merged their functions into a new single department. A prime element in the organizational concept of the new department is the centralization of administrative and support activities into a Bureau for Administration and Operations which supports the four program bureaus of the Department. While the centralization of these

EXHIBIT 2 (continued)

administrative and support activities only included those functions that were located in centralized administrative units in the former Human Resources agencies, the size of the Department for Human Resources dictates that extra levels of effort be applied to ensure close coordination and cooperation between the four program bureaus and the Bureau for Administration and Operations.

As one element in the comprehensive range of efforts now being applied to ensure a high level of responsiveness and cooperation between the Bureau for Administration and Operations and each program bureau, there will be created within the Office of the Commissioner for Administration and Operations four positions for administrative liaison officers, one of which will be assigned responsibility for liaison with each program bureau.

Responsibilities

1. Each administrative liaison officer will provide assistance to the program bureau commissioner and other officials of the program bureau to which assigned in the:
   a. Identification and definition of the administrative and operational support needs of that program bureau.
   b. Determination of the relative priorities of those needs for services.
   c. Identification of programmatic and operational requirements of the program bureau that may be assisted by the enforcement of administrative regulations by the Bureau for Administration and Operations.
   d. Identification of resources available within the Bureau for Administration and Operations that may be of value to the program bureau.
   e. Coordination of the delivery of services by the various divisions of the Bureau for Administration and Operations to the program bureau.
   f. Interpretation of data and information provided by the Bureau for Administration and Operations.
   g. Interpretation and distribution of administrative regulations and procedures issued by the Bureau for Administration and Operations with respect to its responsibilities under policies delineated by the secretary and the commissioners of the Department for Human Resources.
2. Each administrative liaison officer will provide assistance to the Commissioner for Administration and Operations and other officials of the Bureau for Administration and Operations in the:
   a. Development of strategies for providing the maximum possible quality and quantity of support services that can be made available to the officer's particular program bureau within budgetary and policy constraints.
   b. Understanding of special needs and problems of respective program bureaus.
   c. Identification of new procedures and systems whereby services rendered to the program bureau can result in improved coordination between all organizational units of the Department for Human Resources.
   d. Identification of inadequacies or gaps in presently available services provided by the Bureau for Administration and Operations.
   e. Direction and/or coordination of task forces and other temporary organizational units created within the Bureau for Administration and Operations assigned to provide resources specific to the program bureau.

EXHIBIT 2 (concluded)

     f. Supervision of all personnel of the Bureau for Administration and Operations that may be on a temporary duty assignment to the program bureau to which the officer is assigned.

Operational Arrangement

1. The administrative liaison officer will be appointed to a position within the Office of the Commissioner for Administration and Operations.
2. The assignment of an administrative liaison officer to a program bureau will require the concurrence of the commissioner of that program bureau.
3. The Office of the Administrative Liaison Officer will be physically located within the suite of offices of the program bureau commissioner to whom the officer is assigned.
4. The administrative liaison officer will attend all staff meetings of the commissioner of the program bureau to which assigned and all staff meetings of the Commissioner for Administration and Operations.

---

executive staff for discussion and adoption. According to the BAO commissioner, there was simply no procedural or planning means for integrating the administrative functions. Rather, it would continue to be a conflict-laden process which would require the undivided attention of an individual assigned to each of the four bureaus.

Questions for Consideration

1. Evaluate the concept of "administrative liaison officer" as a strategy for achieving integration. Is this an example of the mutual adjustment strategy?
2. How will the officers achieve integration when they will have no authority over either the administrative functions or the programs which are to be integrated?
3. What would be the most important personal characteristics to look for in an applicant for these positions?

EXPERIENTIAL EXERCISE

**ORGANIZING A
NEW BUSINESS**

Objectives

To increase the readers' understanding of the organizational design problem in the context of a new business.

Related Topics

Chapters 11, 12, and 13 provide the reader sufficient information.

**Starting the
Exercise**

Form groups of five to eight individuals toward the end of a class meeting. Each group will meet for 5–10 minutes and identify a specific type of business that will be the focus of their exercise. For convenience the groups can be encouraged to select one of the fast-food franchise restaurants. Most readers are familiar with these businesses and have sufficient knowledge of their operations to complete the exercise.

In the interim, before the next meeting, each group member will complete the six steps of the exercise. The groups will meet during class time to share answers and to prepare a group report. The reports will be presented at the second class meeting.

**Instructions for
the Exercise**

1. State the primary mission of your business. What functions must be performed to accomplish the mission.
2. Describe the environment in which your business must operate in terms of the relevant subenvironments. Identify the relative certainty with which information about these subenvironments will be received.
3. Write job descriptions for each class of jobs for each function, including managerial and nonmanagerial jobs.
4. Draw an organization chart and describe how the roles and functions will be integrated.
5. What important knowledge and skills will be required for each of the key roles in the organization?
6. What crucial decisions are to be made which will determine the success of the business?
7. Meet in assigned groups and share your work. Prepare a group plan which embodies the best ideas generated by the group members. Compare your plan with those of other groups and modify if you think necessary.

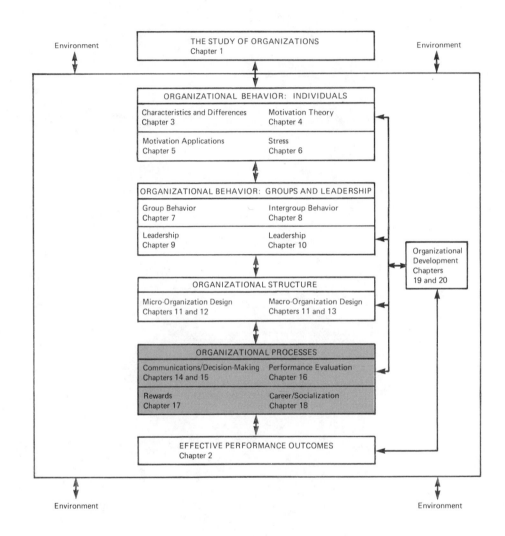

Part Five

THE PROCESSES OF ORGANIZATIONS

Chapter 14

Communication Processes

AN ORGANIZATIONAL ISSUE FOR DEBATE
The Value of Upward Communication*

ARGUMENT FOR

While the classical organization structure formally provides for downward and upward communication, the downward system seems to dominate the upward system in most organizations. As a result, most organizational communication is one way, from higher to lower levels without obtaining any reactions and/or questions from subordinates. In addition, traditional systems—grievance procedures, suggestion systems, employee publications, and "open-door" policies—instituted in many organizations have not worked.

As a result, managers must encourage the free flow of upward communication and encourage subordinates to express their opinions and offer suggestions for improvement. They must seek to develop an atmosphere of trust between them-

ARGUMENT AGAINST

The studies indicating that two-way communication is more effective have always involved complex problems requiring two-way communication for solution. They have also been conducted mostly in laboratory situations and involved problems which have nothing to do with those faced by individuals in most organizations.

In the majority of situations, understanding is easy to achieve and two-way communication is not critical. Besides, it takes time and that is a cost most organizations cannot afford. Time is a valuable resource in most organizations. In highly structured organizations, where the problems are routine, one-way communication is more than adequate if care is taken. This is not to say that the situation might be different in a scientific laboratory than in a police or fire department.

We must also remember the realities of organizational life. Subordinates often purposely withhold information which they think is unpleasant or would displease their superior. Also, distortions and cover-ups occur because a subordinate wants to avoid looking incompetent to a superior.

---

*For research and discussion on this issue, see H. J. Leavitt and R. A. H. Mueller, "Some Effects of Feedback on Communications," *Human Relations*, 1951, pp. 401–10; W. V. Haney, "A Comparative Study of Unilateral and Bilateral Communication," *Academy of Management Journal*, June 1964, pp. 128–36; W. V. Haney, *Communication in Organizational Behavior* (Homewood, Ill.: Richard D. Irwin, 1973)and K. H. Roberts and C. A. O'Reilly III, "Failures in Upward Communication in Organizations: Three Possible Culprits," *Academy of Management Journal*, June 1974, pp. 205–15.

ARGUMENT FOR (continued)

selves and subordinates. Research has indicated that two-way communication is more accurate than one-way communication. However, how accurate it is depends a great deal on the amount of trust the subordinate has in the superior. Under the right conditions communication could take the form of summaries, proposals, and recommendations from subordinates. This will not only improve decision making and organizational performance, but also the attitudes and satisfaction of subordinates.

One of the important purposes of an organization *structure* is to facilitate the *processes* of *communication* and *decision making*. This chapter will focus on communication, while the process of decision making will be the subject of the next chapter. However, both processes are similar in that they pervade everything managers do. The managerial functions of planning, organizing, and controlling all involve managers in specific decisions and communication. In fact, the management functions of planning, organizing, and controlling become operationalized only through communicative activity. When making decisions, managers must both acquire and disseminate information. Thus, communication is critical since managers rarely work with "things" but rather with "information about things."

THE IMPORTANCE OF COMMUNICATION

■ "You said to get to it as soon as I could, how did I know you meant now!" "How did I know she was really serious about resigning!" In these and similar situations, someone usually ends up saying "What we have here is a failure to communicate." This statement has meaning to everyone because each of us has faced situations in which the basic problem was communication. Whether on a person-to-person basis, nation-to-nation, in organizations, or in small groups, breakdowns in communication are pervasive.

It would be extremely difficult to find an aspect of a manager's job that does not involve communication. Serious problems arise when directives are misunderstood, casual kidding in a work group leads to anger, or when informal remarks by a top-level manager are distorted. Each of these is a result of a breakdown somewhere in the process of communication.

Accordingly, the pertinent question is not whether managers engage in communication or not, because communication is inherent to the functioning of an organization. Rather, the pertinent question is whether managers will communicate well or poorly. In other words, communication itself is unavoidable to an organization's functioning; only *effective* communication is avoidable. *Every manager must be a communicator.* In fact, everything a manager does communicates something in some way to somebody or some group. The only question is, "with what effect?" While this may appear an overstatement at this point, it will become apparent as you proceed through the chapter. Despite the tremendous advances in communication and information technology, communication between people in organizations leaves much to be desired. Communication between people does not depend on technology but rather on forces in people and their surroundings. It is a "process" that occurs "within" people.

THE COMMUNICATION PROCESS

■ The general process of communication is presented in Figure 14–1. The process contains five elements—the communicator, the message, the medium, the receiver, and feedback. It can be simply summarized as: Who

FIGURE 14–1
The Communication Process

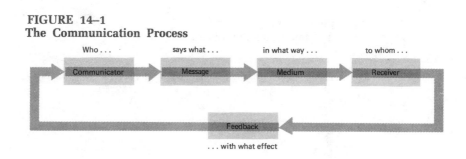

. . . says what . . . in what way . . . to whom . . . with what effect?[1] To appreciate each element in the process we must examine how communication works.

<table>
<tr><td>**How Communication Works**</td><td>Communication experts tell us that effective communication is the result of a common understanding between the communicator and the receiver. In fact, the word *communication* is derived from the Latin (*communis*), meaning common. The communicator seeks to establish a "commonness" with a receiver(s). Hence we can define communication as the *transmission of information and understanding through the use of common symbols.* The common symbols may be verbal or nonverbal. We shall see later that in the context of an organization structure information can flow up and down (vertical), across (horizontal), and down and across (diagonal).</td></tr>
</table>

The most widely used contemporary model of the process of communication has evolved mainly from the work of Shannon and Weaver, and Schramm.[2] These researchers were concerned with describing the general process of communication which could be useful in all situations. Despite its technical jargon, the model which evolved from their work is useful for understanding communication. The basic elements include a communicator, an encoder, a message, a medium, a decoder, a receiver, feedback, and noise. The model is presented in Figure 14–2 (see following page). Each element in the model can be examined in the context of an organization.

The Elements of Communication

Communicator. In an organizational framework, the communicator is an employee with ideas, intentions, information, and a purpose for communicating.

Encoding. Given the communicator, an encoding process must take place which translates the communicator's ideas into a systematic set of symbols—into a language expressing the communicator's purpose. The ma-

---

[1]These five questions were first suggested by H. D. Lasswell, *Power and Personality* (New York: W. W. Norton, 1948), pp. 37–51.

[2]Claude Shannon and Warren Weaver, *The Mathematical Theory of Communication* (Urbana: University of Illinois Press, 1948); and Wilbur Schramm, "How Communication Works," in *The Process and Effects of Mass Communication*, ed. Wilbur Schramm (Urbana: University of Illinois Press, 1953), pp. 3–26.

FIGURE 14–2
A Communication Model

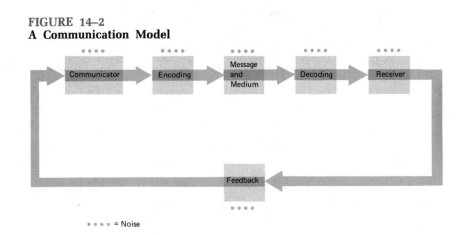

● ● ● ● = Noise

jor form of encoding is language. For example, accounting information, sales reports, and computer data are translated into a message. The function of encoding then is to provide a form in which ideas and purposes can be expressed as a message.

Message.   The result of the encoding process is the message. The purpose of the communicator is expressed in the form of the message—either verbal or nonverbal. Managers have numerous purposes for communicating such as to have others understand their ideas, to understand the ideas of others, to gain acceptance of themselves or their ideas, or to produce action. The message then is what the individual hopes to communicate to the intended receiver, and the exact form it takes depends to a great extent on the medium used to carry the message. Decisions relating to the two are inseparable.

Medium.   The medium is the carrier of the message. Organizations provide information to members in a variety of ways, including face-to-face, telephone, group meetings, computers, memos, policy statements, reward systems, production schedules, and sales forecasts.

Not as obvious, however, are *unintended messages* that can be sent by silence or inaction on a particular issue as well as decisions of which goals and objectives *not* to be pursued and which methods *not* to utilize. Finally, such nonverbal message senders as facial expressions, tone of voice, and body movements also communicate. For example, a decision to utilize one type of performance evaluation rather than another, or a smile from a superior, are types of information. This is what was meant earlier by the statement that everything a manager does communicates.[3]

Decoding-Receiver.   In order for the process of communication to be completed, the message must be decoded in terms of relevance to the re-

---

[3]See George W. Porters, "Non-verbal Communications," *Training and Development Journal,* June 1969, pp. 3–8.

ceiver. *Decoding is a technical term for the receiver's thought processes.* Decoding then involves interpretation. Receivers interpret (decode) the message in light of their own previous experiences and frames of reference. The closer the decoded message is to the intent desired by the communicator, the more effective is the communication. This underscores the importance of the communicator being "receiver-oriented."

Feedback. The provision for feedback in the communication process is desirable.[4] *One-way communication processes are those which do not allow receiver-to-communicator feedback. This may increase the potential for distortion between the intended message and the received message.*[5] A feedback loop provides a channel for receiver response which enables the communicator to determine whether the message has been received and has produced the intended response. *Two-way communication processes provide for this important receiver-to-communicator feedback.* For the manager, communication feedback may come in many ways. In face-to-face situations *direct* feedback through verbal exchanges is possible as well as such subtle means as facial expressions of discontent or misunderstanding. In addition, *indirect* means (such as declines in productivity, poor quality of production, increased absenteeism or turnover, and a lack of coordination and/or conflict between units) may indicate communication breakdowns.

Noise. In the framework of human communication, noise can be thought of as those factors that distort the intended message. They may occur in each of the elements of communication. For example, a manager may be under a severe time constraint and may be forced to act without communicating or may communicate hastily with incomplete information. A subordinate may attach a different meaning to a word or phrase than intended by the manager.

The elements discussed in this section are essential for communication to occur. They should not, however, be viewed as separate. They are, rather, descriptive of the acts which have to be performed for any type of communication to occur. The communication may be vertical (superior-subordinate, subordinate-superior) horizontal (peer-peer), or involve one individual and a group, but the elements discussed here must be present.

COMMUNICATING WITHIN ORGANIZATIONS

■ The design of an organization should provide for communication in four distinct directions: downward, upward, horizontal, and diagonal. Since they establish the framework within which communication in an or-

---

[4]For a theoretical discussion of feedback, see D. M. Herold and M. M. Greller, "Feedback: The Definition of a Construct," *Academy of Management Journal*, March 1977, pp. 142–47.

[5]For the classic experimental study comparing one-way and two-way communications, see Harold J. Leavitt and R. A. H. Mueller, "Some Effects of Feedback on Communications," *Human Relations*, 1951, pp. 401–10. Also see H. J. Leavitt, *Managerial Psychology* (Chicago: University of Chicago Press, 1978).

ganization takes place, let us briefly examine each one. This will enable us to better appreciate the barriers to effective organizational communication and means to overcome these barriers.[6]

Downward Communication.   Downward communication flows from individuals in higher levels to those in lower levels of the hierarchy. The most common forms are job instructions, official memos, policy statements, procedures, manuals, and company publications. In many organizations downward communication is often both inadequate and inaccurate. This is seen in the often-heard statement among organization members that "We have absolutely no idea what's happening." Such complaints are indicative of inadequate downward communication and the need of individuals for information relevant to their jobs. The absence of job-related information can create unnecessary stress among organization members.[7]

Upward Communication.   An effective organization needs upward communication as much as it needs downward communication. In such situations, the communicator is at a lower level in the organization than the receiver. We shall see later that effective upward communication is difficult to achieve, especially in larger organizations. However, successful upward communication is often necessary for sound decision making. Some of the most common upward communication flows are suggestion boxes, group meetings, and appeal or grievance procedures. In the absence of these, people somehow find ways to adapt to nonexistent or inadequate upward communication channels. This has been evidenced by the emergence of "underground" employee publications in many large organizations.[8]

Horizontal Communication.   Often overlooked in the design of most organizations is the provision for horizontal flow of communication. When the chair of the accounting department communicates with the chair of the marketing department concerning course offerings in a College of Business Administration, the flow of communication is horizontal. Although vertical (upward and downward) communication flows are the primary considerations in organizational design, effective organizations also need horizontal communication. Horizontal communication is necessary for the coordination and integration of diverse organizational functions—for example, between production and sales in a business organization and different departments or colleges within a university.

Since mechanisms for assuring horizontal communication ordinarily do not exist in an organization's design, its facilitation is left to individual

---

[6]For a recent general discussion, see S. B. Bacharach and M. Aiken, "Communication in Administrative Bureaucracies," *Academy of Management Journal*, September 1977, pp. 365–77.

[7]J. M. Ivancevich and J. H. Donnelly, Jr., "A Study of Role Clarity and Need for Clarity in Three Occupational Groups," *Academy of Management Journal*, March 1974, pp. 28–36.

[8]See J. S. Lublin, "Underground Papers in Corporations Tell It Like It Isn't," *The Wall Street Journal*, November 3, 1971, p. 9, S.W. ed.

managers. Peer to peer communication is often necessary for coordination and can also provide social need satisfaction.

Diagonal Communication. While probably the least used channel of communication in organizations, diagonal communication is important in those situations where members cannot communicate effectively through other channels. For example, a comptroller of a large organization may wish to conduct a distribution cost analysis. One part may involve the sales force sending a special report directly to the comptroller rather than going through the traditional channels in the marketing department. Thus, the flow of communication would be diagonal as opposed to vertical (upward) and horizontal. In this case a diagonal channel would be the most efficient in terms of time and effort for the organization.

BARRIERS TO EFFECTIVE ORGANIZATIONAL COMMUNICATION

■ A good question at this point is "Why does communication break down?" The answer on the surface is relatively easy. The necessary elements for communication have been identified as the communicator, encoding, the message, the medium, decoding, the receiver, and feedback. If *any one* of these elements is defective *in any way,* clarity of meaning and understanding will not occur. Many barriers can impede the process of communication, resulting in "noise" and an eventual communication breakdown. The barriers identified are by no means the only ones that exist. They are, however, common barriers which are prevalent in both face-to-face communication and in nonverbal communication within organization structures. Let us examine some of these major barriers.

Frame of Reference

Different individuals can interpret the same communication differently depending on their previous experience. This results in variations in the encoding and decoding processes. Communication specialists agree that this is the most important factor that breaks down the "commonness" in communications. When the encoding and decoding processes are alike, communication is most effective. When they become different, communication tends to break down. Thus, while the communicator is actually speaking the "same language" as the receiver, the message conflicts with the way the receiver "catalogs" the world. This problem is depicted in Figure 14–3. The interior areas in this diagram represent the accumulated experiences of the participants in the communication process. If a large area is shared in common, effective communication is facilitated. If a large area is not shared in common—if there has been no common experience—then communication becomes impossible, or at best highly distorted. The important point is that communicators can encode and receivers can decode, only in terms of their experiences.

As a result, distortion often occurs because of differing frames of reference. Teenagers perceive things differently than their parents, and college deans perceive problems differently than faculty members. People in var-

FIGURE 14–3
Overlapping Fields of Experience

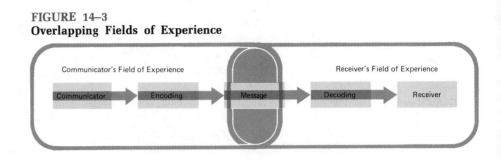

ious organizational *functions* interpret the same situation differently. A business problem will be viewed differently by the marketing manager than the production manager. An efficiency problem in a hospital will be viewed by the nursing staff from their frame of reference and experiences which may result in different interpretations than those of the physician staff. Different *levels* in the organization will also have different frames of reference. First-line supervisors have frames of reference that differ in many respects from those of vice presidents. They are in different positions in the organizations structure and this influences their frames of reference. As a result, their needs, values, attitudes, and expectations will differ and often result in unintentional distortion of communication. This is not to say that either group is wrong or right. All it means is that, in any situation, individuals will choose a part of their own past experiences that relates to the current experience and that is helpful in forming conclusions and judgments. Unfortunately, these incongruencies in encoding and decoding result in barriers to effective communication. We shall see that many of the other barriers examined in this section are also the result of variations in encoding and decoding.

Selective Listening   This is a form of selective perception in which we tend to "block out" new information, especially if it conflicts with what we believe. Thus, when we receive a directive from management we notice only those things that reaffirm our beliefs. Those things that conflict with our preconceived notions we either do not note at all or we distort to confirm our preconceptions.

For example, a notice may be sent to all operating departments that costs must be reduced if the organization is to earn a profit. The communication may not achieve its desired effect because it conflicts with the "reality" of the receivers. Thus, operating employees may ignore or be amused by such information in light of the large salaries, travel allowances, and expense accounts of some executives. Whether or not they are justified is irrelevant; what is important is that such preconceptions result in breakdowns in communication. In other words, if we only hear what we want to hear, we cannot be disappointed.

Value Judgments

In every communication situation, value judgments are made by the receiver. This basically involves assigning an overall worth to a message prior to receiving the entire communication. Value judgments may be based upon the receiver's evaluation of the communicator, previous experiences with the communicator, or the message's anticipated meaning. Thus, a hospital administrator may pay little attention to a memorandum from a nursing team leader because "she's always complaining about something." A college professor may consider a merit evaluation meeting with the department chair as "going through the motions" because the faculty member perceives the chair as having little or no power in the administration of the college. A cohesive work group may form negative value judgments concerning all actions by management.

Source Credibility

Source credibility is the trust, confidence, and faith the receiver has in the words and actions of the communicator. The level of credibility that the receiver assigns to the communicator in turn directly affects how the receiver views and reacts to words, ideas, and actions of the communicator.

Thus, how subordinates view a communication from their manager is affected by their evaluation of the manager. This of course is heavily influenced by previous experiences with the manager. Again we see that everything a manager does, communicates. A group of hospital medical staff who view the hospital administrator as less than honest, manipulative, and not to be trusted are apt to assign nonexistent motives to any communication from the administrator. Union leaders who view management as exploiters and managers who view union leaders as political animals are likely to engage in little real communication.

Semantic Problems

Communication has been defined as the transmission of *information* and *understanding* through the use of *common symbols*. Actually, we cannot transmit understanding. We can only transmit information in the form of words, which are the common symbols. Unfortunately, the same words may mean entirely different things to different people. The understanding is in the receiver, not in the words.

Because different groups use words differently, communication can often be impeded. This is especially true with abstract or technical terms or phrases. A "cost-benefit study" would have meaning to those involved in the administration of the hospital but probably mean very little to the staff physicians. In fact, it may even carry a negative meaning. Concepts like "trusts," "profits," and "Treasury bills" may have concrete meaning to bank executives but little or no meaning to bank tellers. Thus, because words mean different things to different people, it is possible for a communicator to speak the same language as a receiver but still not transmit *understanding*.

Filtering

Filtering is a common occurrence in upward communication in organizations. It refers to the "manipulation" of information so that it is perceived as positive by the receiver. Subordinates "cover up" unfavorable information in messages to their superiors. The reason for such "filtering" should be clear; this is the direction (upward) which carries control information to management. Management makes merit evaluations, grants salary increases, and promotes individuals based on what it receives by way of the upward channel. The temptation to "filter" is likely to be strong at every level in the organization.

In-Group Language   Each of us has undoubtedly had associations with experts and been subjected to highly technical jargon, only to learn that the words or phrases describe very simple procedures or very familiar objects. Many students are asked by researchers to "complete an instrument as part of an experimental treatment." The student soon learns that this involves nothing more than filling out a pencil-and-paper questionnaire.

Often, occupational, professional, and social groups develop their own words or phrases which have meaning only to members. Such special language can serve many useful purposes. It can provide members with feelings of belongingness, cohesiveness, and, in many cases, self-esteem. It can also facilitate effective communication *within* the group. The use of in-group language can, however, result in severe communication breakdowns when outsiders or other groups are involved. This is especially the case when groups use such language in an organization, not for the purpose of transmitting information and understanding, but rather to communicate a "mystique" about the group or its function.

Status Differences   Organizations often express hierarchical rank through a variety of symbols—titles, offices, carpets, secretaries, and so on. Such status differences can result in the perception of a threat on the part of someone lower in the hierarchy which can prevent or distort communication. Rather than look incompetent, a nurse may prefer to remain quiet instead of expressing an opinion or asking a question of the nursing team leader.

Many times, superiors in their quest to utilize their time efficiently enhance this barrier. The governmental administrator or bank vice president may only be accessible by advanced appointment or by passing the careful quizzing of a secretary. This widens the communication gap between superiors and subordinates.

Time Pressures   The pressure of time is an important barrier to communication. An obvious problem is that managers do not have the time to communicate frequently with every subordinate. However, time pressures can often lead to far more serious problems than this. *Short-circuiting* is a failure of the formally prescribed communication system which often is the result of time pressures. What it means simply is that someone has been left out of the formal channel of communication who normally would be included.

For example, suppose a salesperson needs a rush order for a very important customer and goes directly to the production manager with the request since the production manager owes the salesperson a favor. Other members of the sales force get word of this and become upset over this preferential treatment and report it to the sales manager. Obviously, the sales manager would know nothing of the "deal" since the sales manager has been short-circuited. However, in some cases the necessity to go through formal channels is extremely costly or impossible from a practical standpoint. Consider the impact on a hospital patient if a nurse had to report a malfunction in some critical life support equipment in an intensive care unit to the nursing team leader who in turn reported it to the hospital engineer who instructed a staff engineer to make the repair.

Communication Overload

One of the vital tasks performed by a manager is decision making. One of the necessary conditions for effective decisions is *information*. Because of the advances in communication technology, the difficulty is not in generating information. In fact, the last decade has often been described as the "Information Era" or the "Age of Information." Managers often feel "buried" by the deluge of information and data they are exposed to. As a result, people cannot absorb or adequately respond to all of the messages directed to them. They "screen out" the majority of messages, which in effect means they are never decoded. Thus, the area of organizational communication is one in which "more" is not always "better."[9]

The barriers to communication discussed here, while common, are by no means the only ones which exist. Figure 14–4 illustrates the impact of these barriers on the process of communication. Examining each barrier indicates that they are either *within individuals* (e.g., frame of reference,

FIGURE 14–4
Barriers to Effective Communication

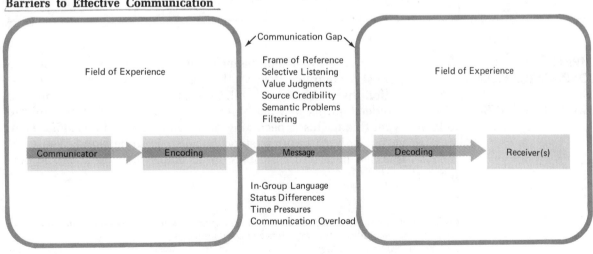

[9] See Charles A. O'Reilly, III, "Individuals and Information Overload in Organizations: Is More Necessarily Better?" *Academy of Management Journal*, December 1980, pp. 684–96.

value judgments), or *within organizations* (e.g., in-group language, filtering). This point is important because attempts to improve communication must by necessity focus on changing people and/or changing the organization structure.[10] This is clearly illustrated in the following *close-up.*

ORGANIZATIONS: CLOSE-UP

Improving Communication at International Paper Co.

Recently, International Paper Company successfully negotiated several labor agreements that included numerous critical changes in the operations of its pulp and paper mills. The firm credits much of the success in reaching the agreements to its revamped approach to employee communication.

One reason for the breakthrough is that both employees and union officials now receive realistic information about the company long before they enter negotiations. A company executive stated that "objectives can only be met with the constructive and active support of employees. Management's chief means for getting that support is effective communication."

International Paper has made employee communication a top priority for line managers. Managers must hold regular meetings with subordinates to inform them of new developments, their decisions and the reasons for them, or any changes in objectives, and to answer all questions.

To support the line managers, the company has strengthened its employee communication department. It has also developed tighter controls over communications flow within the organization, so that it is better coordinated, more consistent, and produced more efficiently. The result, according to the company, has been relevant, timely, and honest information.

Source: Gerard Tavernier, "Using Employee Communications to Support Corporate Objectives," *Management Review*, November 1980, pp. 8–13.

IMPROVING COMMUNICATION IN ORGANIZATIONS

■ Managers striving to become better communicators have two separate tasks they must accomplish.[11] First, they must improve their *messages*—the information they wish to transmit. Second, they must seek to improve their own *understanding* of what other people are trying to communicate to them. What this means is becoming better encoders and decoders. *They must strive not only to be understood but also to understand.* The techniques discussed here will contribute to accomplishing these two important tasks.

---

[10] See P. M. Muchinsky, "Organizational Communication: Relationships to Organizational Climate and Job Satisfaction," *Academy of Management Journal*, December 1977, pp. 592–607, for a recent study on the importance of communication.

[11] For a different discussion that is based on similar ideas, see Leonard R. Sayles and George Strauss, *Human Behavior in Organizations* (Englewood Cliffs, N.J.: Prentice-Hall, 1966), p. 246.

Following Up

This involves assuming you are misunderstood and, whenever possible, attempting to determine if the intended meaning was actually received. As we have seen, meaning is often in the mind of the receiver. An accounting unit leader in a government office passes on notices to the accounting staff members of openings in other agencies. While this may be understood among long-time employees as a friendly gesture on the part of the department head, a new employee might interpret it as an evaluation of poor performance and a suggestion to leave.

Regulating Information Flow

This involves the regulation of communication to ensure an optimum flow of information to managers, thereby eliminating the barrier of "communication overload."[12] Communication is regulated in terms of both quality and quantity. The idea is based on the *exception principle* of management which states that only significant deviations from policies and procedures should be brought to the attention of superiors. In terms of formal communication, then, superiors should be communicated with only on matters of exception and not for the sake of communication.

As we saw in the section on the structure of organizations, certain types of organization structures would be more amenable to this principle than others. Certainly, in Likert's System 4 organization with its emphasis on free flowing communication, this principle would not apply. However, those organizations more toward the bureaucratic end of the "bureaucratic-system 4 continuum" would find this principle useful.

Utilizing Feedback

Earlier in the chapter, feedback was identified as an important element in effective two-way communication. It provides a channel for receiver response which enables the communicator to determine whether the message has been received and produced the intended response.

In face-to-face communication, direct feedback is possible. However, in downward communication, inaccuracies often occur because of insufficient opportunity for feedback from receivers. Thus, a memorandum addressing an important policy statement may be distributed to all employees but this does not guarantee that communication has occurred. One might expect that feedback in the form of upward communication would be encouraged more in System 4 organizations but the mechanisms discussed earlier which can be utilized to encourage upward communication are found in many different organizational designs. A healthy organization needs effective upward communication if its downward communication is to have any chance of being effective. The point is that developing and supporting mechanisms for feedback involves far more than following up on communications.

---

[12]This is described as the principle of "sufficiency" by William G. Scott and Terence R. Mitchell, *Organizational Theory: A Structural and Behavioral Analysis* (Homewood, Ill.: Richard D. Irwin, 1972), p. 161.

Empathy

This involves being receiver-oriented rather than communicator-oriented. The form of the communication should depend largely on what is known about the receiver(s). Empathy requires communicators to figuratively place themselves in the receivers' shoes for the purpose of anticipating how the message is likely to be decoded.

It is vital that a manager understands and appreciates the process of decoding. Decoding involves perceptions, and the message will be "filtered" through the person. Empathy is the ability to put oneself in the other person's role and to assume the viewpoints and emotions of that individual. For vice presidents to communicate effectively with supervisors, for faculty to communicate effectively with students, and for government administrators to communicate effectively with minority groups, empathy is often an important ingredient. Many of the barriers to effective communication discussed can be reduced with empathy. Remember that the greater the gap between the experiences and background of the communicator and receiver, the greater the effort which must be made to find a common ground of understanding—where there are overlapping fields of experience.[13]

Repetition

Repetition is an accepted principle of learning. Introducing repetition or redundancy into communication (especially that of a technical nature) ensures that if one part of the message is not understood, there are other parts which carry the same message. New employees are often provided the same basic information in several different forms when first joining an organization. Likewise, students receive much redundant information when first entering a university. This is to ensure that registration procedures, course requirements, and such new terms as matriculation and quality points are communicated.

Encouraging Mutual Trust

We know that time pressures often negate the possibility that managers can follow up communication and encourage feedback or upward communication every time they communicate. Under such circumstances, an atmosphere of mutual confidence and trust between managers and their subordinates can facilitate communication.[14] Subordinates judge for themselves the quality of the relationship they perceive with their superior. Managers who develop a climate of trust will find following up on each communication less critical and without a loss in understanding among

---

[13] A technique known as *sensitivity training* has been utilized for many purposes in organizations, one of which is to improve the ability of managers to empathize. It will be discussed in Chapter 18.

[14] See Karlene H. Roberts and Charles A. O'Reilly III, "Failures in Upward Communication in Organizations: Three Possible Culprits," *Academy of Management Journal*, June 1974, pp. 205–15; and Leland P. Bradford, Jack R. Gibb, and Kenneth D. Benne, eds., *T-Group Theory and Laboratory Method: Innovation in Re-Education* (New York: John Wiley & Sons, 1965), pp. 285–86.

subordinates. This is because they have fostered high "source credibility" among subordinates.

Effective Timing

Individuals are exposed to thousands of messages daily. Many are never decoded and received because of the impossibility of taking them all in. It is important for managers to note that while they are attempting to communicate with a receiver, other messages are being received simultaneously. The message sent may not be "heard." Messages are more likely to be understood when they are not competing with other messages.

Many organizations use "retreats" when important policies or changes are taking place. A group of executives may be sent to a resort to undertake an important corporate policy issue, or a group of college faculty may "retreat" to an off-campus site to design a new curriculum. On an everyday basis, effective communication can be facilitated with the proper timing of major announcements. Many of the barriers discussed earlier are often the result of poor timing which results in distortions and value judgments.

Simplifying Language

Complex language has been identified as a major barrier to effective communication. Students often suffer when their teachers use technical jargon that transforms simple concepts into complex puzzles.

Universities are not the only place, however, where this occurs. Government agencies are also known for their often incomprehensible communications. We have already noted instances where professional people attempt to communicate with individuals outside of their group using the in-group language. Managers must remember that effective communication involves transmitting *understanding* as well as information. If the receiver does not understand, then there has been no communication. In fact, many of the techniques discussed in this section have as their sole purpose the promotion of understanding. Managers must encode messages in words, appeals, and symbols that are meaningful to the receiver.

Effective Listening

It has been said that to improve communication, managers must seek to be understood, but also to *understand*. This involves listening. One method of encouraging someone to express true feelings, desires, and emotions is to listen. Just listening is not enough; one must listen with understanding. Can managers develop listening skills? There are numerous pointers for effective listening that have been found to be effective in organizational settings. For example, one writer cites cites "Ten Commandments for Good Listening": stop talking, put the speaker at ease, show the speaker you want to listen, remove distractions, empathize with the speaker, be patient, hold your temper, go easy on argument and criticism, ask questions, and stop talking.[15] Note that to stop talking is both the first and the last com-

---

[15] Keith Davis, *Human Behavior at Work* (New York: McGraw-Hill, 1972), p. 394.

mandment. Another writer lists five "Guides for Listening": avoid making value judgments, listen to the full story, recognize feelings and emotions, restate the other's position, and question with care.[16]

Such lists of guidelines can be potentially useful for managers. However, more important than these lists is the *decision to listen*. The above guidelines are useless unless the manager makes the conscious decision to listen. The realization that effective communication involves being understood as well as understanding is probably far more important than lists of guidelines. Then and only then can such guidelines become useful. The importance of listening skills is illustrated in the following close-up.

ORGANIZATIONS: CLOSE-UP

Developing Listening Skills at Sperry Corporation

The Sperry Corporation has initiated an ongoing series of programs designed to heighten the listening skills of its managers. They deal with both internal corporate situations and responding effectively to outsiders.

The training concentrates on specific on-the-job applications showing how Sperry employees in various real-life situations can do a better job of responding—the end product of the listening process. R. L. Robertson, staff vice president—public affairs, states that "listening occurs in four stages—sensing (hearing the message), understanding (interpreting it), evaluating (appraising it), and responding (doing something with it). The ultimate point of the training is that the fourth of these stages—the intelligent, sincere, response—is the basic commitment we are making and provides a valuable payoff to both the sender and the receiver."

Source: *Management Review*, April 1980, p. 40.

Using the Grapevine

The grapevine is an important informal communication channel that exists in all organizations. It basically serves as a bypassing mechanism, and in many cases is faster than the formal system it bypasses. It has been aptly described in the following manner: "With the rapidity of a burning train, it filters out of the woodwork, past the manager's office, through the locker room and along the corridors."[17] Because it is flexible and usually involves face-to-face communication, the grapevine transmits information rapidly. The resignation of an executive may be common knowledge long before it is officially announced.

For management, the grapevine may frequently be an effective means of

---

[16] Henry L. Sisk, *Organization and Management* (Cincinnati: South-Western Publishing, 1977), pp. 350–74.

[17] Davis, *Human Behavior at Work*, p. 267.

communication. It is likely to have a stronger impact on receivers because it is face-to-face and allows for feedback. Because it satisfies many psychological needs, the grapevine will always exist. No manager can do away with it. Research indicates that over 75 percent of the information in the grapevine is accurate.[18] Of course, the 25 percent which is distorted can be devastating. The point, however, is that if the grapevine is inevitable, managers should seek to utilize it or at least attempt to increase its accuracy. One way to minimize the undesirable aspects of the grapevine is to improve other forms of communication. If information exists on issues relevant to subordinates, then damaging rumors are less likely to develop.

In conclusion, it would be hard to find an aspect of a manager's job that does not involve communication. If everyone in the organization had common points of view, communicating would be easy. Unfortunately this is not the case. Each member comes to the organization with a distinct personality, background, experience, and frame of reference. The structure of the organization itself influences status relationships and the distance (levels) between individuals, which in turn influence the ability of individuals to communicate.

In this chapter, we have tried to convey the basic elements in the process of communication and what it takes to communicate effectively. These elements are necessary whether the communication is face-to-face or written and communicated vertically, horizontally, or diagonally within an organization structure. Several common communication barriers were discussed as well as several means to improve communication. Figure 14–5 illustrates the means that can be used to facilitate more effective commu-

FIGURE 14–5
Improving Communication in Organizations (narrowing the communication gap)

Field of Experience

Following Up
Principle of Sufficiency
Empathy
Repetition

Field of Experience

| Communicator | Encoding | Message | Decoding | Receiver(s) |

Encouraging Mutual Trust
Effective Timing
Simplifying Language
Utilizing Feedback
Effective Listening
Using the Grapevine

---

[18] Ibid.

nication. We realize that often there is not time to utilize many of the techniques for improving communication, and that skills such as empathy and effective listening are not easy to develop. The figure does, however, illustrate the challenge of communicating effectively and suggests what is required. It shows that communicating is a matter of transmitting and receiving. Managers must be effective at both. They must understand as well as be understood.

NONVERBAL COMMUNICATION

■ A relatively recent area of research among behavioral scientists is the information sent by a communicator that is unrelated to the verbal information; that is, *nonverbal communication*. The major interest is in *physical cues* which are the characteristics of the communicator's physical presentation; for example, hand movements, facial expressions, eye movements. These are viewed as important influences on the receiver's interpretations of the message. Figure 14–6 presents the factors which research has shown to provide nonverbal information.

Research indicates that generally facial expressions and eye contact and movements provide information about the *type* of emotion, while such physical cues as distance, posture, and gestures indicate the *intensity* of the emotion. These conclusions are important to managers. They indicate that a communicator often sends a great deal more information than is contained in the message. To increase the effectiveness of our communication, we must be aware of the verbal as well as nonverbal content of our messages.

FIGURE 14–6
Factors Transmitting Nonverbal Information

1. Distance. In some situations it indicates attraction or nonattraction while in others it may indicate status differences.
2. Orientation. Face-to-face, back-to-back, or side-by-side orientations may transmit specific information. Cooperating individuals often sit side-by-side while those in competition usually face each other.
3. Posture. This may transmit messages of formality or relaxation.
4. Physical contact. Touching, shaking hands, holding often convey messages. They may convey feelings of attraction or nonattraction or intimacy.
5. Facial expressions. Smiles, frowns, yawns, raised eyebrows, and so on continually transmit information during face-to-face communication.
6. Gestures. Body and hand movements transmit information often reflecting attitudes and feelings.
7. Looking. Eye movement and eye contact transmit information regarding interest, noninterest, attraction, sexual interest.

Source: Summarized from Michael Argyle, "Nonverbal Communication in Human Social Interaction," in *Nonverbal Communication*, ed. R. Hinde (New York: Cambridge University Press, 1972).

MAJOR MANAGERIAL ISSUES

A. Communication is one of the vital processes which breathe life into an organization structure. Communication is unavoidable in an organization's work; only *effective* communication is avoidable.

B. The quality of managerial decisions depends in large part on the quality of information available. Communication is the transmission of information and understanding through the use of common symbols.

C. Everything a manager does communicates. The only question is, with what effect? Every manager is a communicator.

D. The process of communication consists of several basic elements which must always be present if effective communication is to result.

E. Organization design and the communication process are inseparable. The design of an organization must provide for communication in three distinct directions: vertical, horizontal, and diagonal.

F. When the encoding and decoding processes are homogeneous, communication is most effective. When they become heterogeneous, communication tends to break down. Numerous barriers exist which contribute to communication breakdowns. Managers must be aware of those barriers which are relevant to their situations.

G. Numerous techniques exist which aid in improving communication and can be utilized by managers. However, a prerequisite to their use is the conscious realization by the individual manager that communication involves understanding as well as being understood. An effective communicator must also be an effective receiver.

DISCUSSION AND REVIEW QUESTIONS

1. What do we really mean when we say that everything a manager does communicates?

2. Discuss why organizational design and communication flow are so closely related.

3. Discuss how communication flow and the contingency view of organization design are related.

4. Think of a classroom situation in terms of the basic elements of communication: communicator, encoding, message, medium, decoding, receiver, and feedback. Identify each element and discuss the activities involved. For example, who is the communicator, what is the message, who is the receiver, etc. Is effective communication occurring? Why? Identify where, if at all, breakdowns are occurring and why.

5. Think of a situation from your own life in which communication between yourself and another individual or group was not possible. Identify the barriers. What might you have done to overcome these barriers?

6. Discuss what the following statement means to you. "To communicate effectively, one must be understood but also must understand."

7. Think of a situation in which you have been the receiver in a one-way communication process. Describe it. Can you think of some reasons why certain individuals might not like it? Think of reasons why some people might prefer it.

8. Choose a technique discussed in the chapter that you believe can help you become a more effective communicator. Why have you chosen it? How do you plan to implement it?

ADDITIONAL REFERENCES

Beckett, J. A. *Management Dynamics: The New Synthesis.* New York: McGraw-Hill, 1971.

Carlson, R. O. "Is Business Really Facing a Communication Problem?" *Organizational Dynamics,* 1973, pp. 35–52.

Dewherst, H. D. "Influence of Perceived Information-Sharing Utilization." *Academy of Management Journal,* 1971, pp. 305–15.

Ellis, D. S. *Management and Administrative Communication.* New York: Macmillan, 1978.

Ericson, R. F. "Organizational Cybernetics and Human Values." *Academy of Management Journal,* 1970, pp. 49–66.

Gibb, J. R. "Communication and Productivity." *Personnel Administration,* 1964, pp. 485–87.

Goldhaber, G. M. *Organizational Communications.* Dubuque, Iowa: Wm. C. Brown Co., 1974.

Greenbaum, H. H. "The Audit of Organizational Communication." *Academy of Management Journal,* 1974, pp. 139–54.

———. "Management's Role in Organizational Communication Analysis." *Journal of Business Communication,* 1972, pp. 39–52.

Guetzkow, H. "Communication in Organizations." In *Handbook of Organizations,* edited by J. G. March. Chicago: Rand McNally, 1965.

Lewis, G. H. "Organization in Communication Networks." *Comparative Group Studies,* 1971, pp. 149–60.

Mears, P. "Structuring Communication in a Working Group." *Journal of Communication,* 1974, pp. 71–79.

Poole, M. S. "An Information-Task Approach to Organizational Communication." *Academy of Management Review,* 1978, pp. 493–504.

Roberts, K. H. and C. A. O'Reilly, III. "Some Correlates of Communication Roles in Organizations." *Academy of Management Journal,* 1979, pp. 42–57.

Rockey, E. H. *Communicating in Organizations.* Cambridge, Mass.: Winthrop Publishers, 1977.

Rodgers. C. *On Becoming a Person.* Boston: Houghton Mifflin, 1961.

Schemerhorn, J. R. "Information Sharing as an Interorganizational Activity." *Academy of Management Journal,* 1977, pp. 148–53.

Schneider, A. E.; W. C. Donaghy; and P. J. Newman. *Organizational Communication.* New York: McGraw-Hill, 1975.

Tushman, M. L. "Impacts of Perceived Environmental Variability on Patterns of Work Related Communication." *Academy of Management Journal,* 1979, pp. 482–500.

Wiener, N. *Cybernetics: or, Control and Communication in the Animal and the Machine.* New York: John Wiley & Sons, 1948.

———. *The Human Use of Human Beings.* New York: Anchor Books, 1954.

CASE FOR ANALYSIS

LEIGH RANDELL

Leigh Randell is supervisor of In-Flight Services at the Atlanta base of Omega Airlines. Omega Airlines is a very successful regional air carrier with routes throughout the South and Southwest. In addition to Atlanta, it has bases in six other major cities.

Ms. Randell's job involves supervision of all in-flight services and personnel at the Atlanta base. She has been with the airline for seven years and in her present job for two years. For five years she was a flight attendant and was asked by management to assume her present management position. While actually preferring flying to a permanent ground position, she decided to try the management position. In her job, she reports directly to Kent Davis, vice president of In-Flight Services.

During the last year, Leigh has observed what she believes is a great deal of duplication of effort between flight attendants and passenger-service personnel (in-terminal personnel) with respect to the paperwork procedures for boarding passengers. This she believes has often resulted in unnecessary delays in departures of many flights. This especially appears to be the case with through flights, those which do not originate or terminate in Atlanta. Since the majority of Omega's flights are of this type in Atlanta, she believes that it is probably not a major problem at Omega's other bases or at smaller airports. Thus, she has decided to try to develop a more efficient procedure for coordinating the efforts of flight attendants and passenger-service personnel which would simplify the boarding procedures, thereby reducing ground time and increasing passenger satisfaction through closer adherence to departure times.

In this respect she has, on three occasions during the last two months, written memos to Tom Ballard, passenger services representative for Omega at the Atlanta base. Tom's job involves supervision of all passenger service personnel. He has been with Omega for five years, having joined their management training program immediately after graduating from college. He reports directly to Alan Brock, vice president of Passenger Services at the Atlanta base. Exhibit 1 presents the organization structure for the Atlanta base. Each time, Leigh has requested information regarding specific procedures, time, and costs for the boarding of passengers on through flights. She has received no reply from Tom Ballard.

Last week Leigh wrote a memo to Kent Davis in which she stated:

> For several months I have been trying to develop a new method for facilitating the boarding of passengers on through flights by more closely coordinating the efforts of In-Flight Services and Passenger Services. The results would be a reduction in clerical work, costs, ground time, and closer adherence to departure times for through flights. Unfortunately, I have received no cooperation at all in my efforts from the Passenger Services Representative. I have made three written requests for information each of which has been ignored. Needless to say this has been very frustrating to me. While I realize that my beliefs may not always be correct, in this intance I am only trying to initiate

EXHIBIT 1

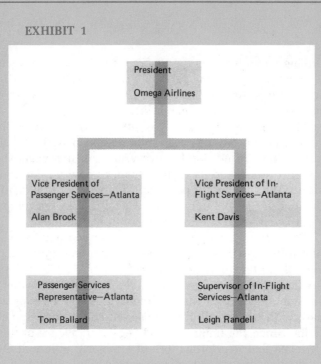

something that will be beneficial to everyone involved: Passenger Services, In-Flight Services, and most important, Omega Airlines. I would like to meet with you to discuss this matter and the possibility of my transferring back to flight duty.

A telephone call by Kent Davis to Alan Brock and then to Tom Ballard summoned them all to a hastily called conference. Tom Ballard was mildly asked why he had not furnished the information to Leigh that she had requested.

"Too busy," he said. "Her questions were out of sight. There was no time for me to answer this sort of request. I've got a job to do. Besides, I don't report to her."

"But Tom, you don't understand," Kent Davis said. "All Ms. Randell is trying to do is improve the present system of boarding passengers on through flights. She has taken the initiative to work on something that might benefit everyone."

Tom Ballard thought for a moment. "No," he replied, "it didn't look like that to me. You know I've also had ideas on how to improve the system for quite some time. Anyway, she's going about it all wrong."

Questions for Consideration

1. What barriers to effective communication do you detect in this case?
2. Is anyone "wrong" in this situation? By what other means could Leigh have requested the information from Tom Ballard? What do you think of Tom Ballard's reaction? Why?

3. While communicating information vertically up or down the organization does not present a major problem, why is it that horizontal and diagonal communication are more difficult to attain? What would you recommend to the management of Omega Airlines to remedy this situation? Why do you believe your recommendations would improve communication in the organization?

EXPERIENTIAL EXERCISE

**FRUSTRATION,
CLARITY,
ACCURACY**

Objectives

1. To display the features of the communication process.
2. To identify the differences between one-way and two-way communications.
3. To examine the reactions of individuals to one- and two-way communications.

Related Topics

The communication process is pervasive in any organization. Therefore, communication is related to any topic discussed in organizational behavior, organizational theory, or management.

Starting the Exercise

The instructor will give the same message to two separate groups. These groups will receive the private message only one time. They are not permitted to ask the instructor any questions about the message.

The Facts

The instructor will serve as the initiator of a message to two separate groups of three or four students. The groups will attempt to develop a clear understanding of what the instructor said. They will then return to the main classroom where other students will serve as communication chains for the message. Both a one-way and two-way chain will be used. To complete both the one- and two-way communication versions of this exercise, a minimum of 22 students will be needed. If a class does not have 22 students, the instructor will need to make some modifications.

Exercise Procedure

Phase I: Group Communication: 10 minutes

Group 1 and Group 2, consisting of three or four students will be selected. The groups should be isolated from each other to receive the message. The instructor will read *one time* the same message to the two groups in their separate rooms or isolated areas. Each group will discuss the message for no more than five minutes.

Phase II: One-Way Communication: 10 minutes

Four students who are not in Groups 1 or 2 will serve as the *chain* for one of the groups and four other students will serve as the chain for the other group. A representative of Group 1 will whisper the message to the first person in the four-person chain, who, in turn, will pass on the private message to the second member and so on. Talking between members in the chain is not permitted. Only one person, the transmitter, is permitted to speak. The last person in the chain will write the message down and hand it to the instructor. The same one-way communication process will be followed in Group 2.

Phase III: Two-Way Communication: 20 minutes

Four new students who have not participated in either Phases 1 or 2 will serve as the Group 1 chain. A representative of Group 1 will discuss the message with the first person in the chain. The representative and the first person can discuss the message privately from other members in the chain. When the discussants are ready and within the allocated time limit, the first person in the chain will then discuss privately the message with the second person in the chain. These private two-way discussions will continue until time has expired or the last person in the chain hears the message and writes it for the instructor. The same two-way communication process will be followed in Group 2.

Phase IV: Analysis of the Exercise: 20 minutes

Each participant should evaluate the exercise. Some of the issues to consider area.

    a. One-way versus two-way communication accuracy.

    b. Attitudes of the different participants—Were any participants frustrated? About what?

    c. What were some of the barriers to effective communication?

Chapter 15

Decision-Making Processes

AN ORGANIZATIONAL ISSUE FOR DEBATE
The Decision Participation Controversy*

ARGUMENT FOR

Many researchers and managers believe that most organization members desire opportunities to participate in the process of decision making. They believe that increased decision participation increases commitment to the organization, job satisfaction, personal growth and development, and acceptance of change. Thus, rather than authority, the manager's mode of influence is based more on reciprocity and collaboration.

Besides leading to greater satisfaction, and as a result, greater effort, performance, and effectiveness, the supporters of this viewpoint have an additional rationale for decision participation. They point out that many problems faced by organizations are becoming increasingly complex, requiring knowledge in sophisticated areas, and are of the type that the organization has not faced in the past. These problems may be technological, human or societal. As a result knowledge and expertise in many different areas are needed to solve these problems. Since knowledge and expertise are widely distributed throughout the organization, wider participation will likely increase the quality of managerial decisions.

ARGUMENT AGAINST

Many practicing managers and researchers believe that in organizational settings people prefer a great amount of clarity in what is expected of them. This need for security in knowing what behavior is expected results in a great deal more respect for the manager who acts decisively. These individuals believe that trying to achieve consensus in a group is upsetting to the group and a waste of organizational resources and time. Since managers are a dominant mode of influence in the organization, they must recognize this and act upon it. The world of a decision maker may be a lonely one but managers must accept the responsibility that the "buck stops" with them. Nothing is more dysfunctional than the "participation ritual" which many managers engage in. Here managers go through the process of participation for the purpose of selling decisions which have already been made, by making them look like group decisions. If managers fail to take charge of group activities, they abdicate their role as manager and performance will be negatively effected.

---

*Much research and opinion exists on this issue. For comprehensive reviews, see V. H. Vroom and P. W. Yetton, *Leadership and Decision-making* (Pittsburgh: University of Pittsburgh Press, 1973); and P. Blumberg, *Industrial Democracy: The Sociology of Participation* (New York: Schocken Books, 1974). Also see J. W. Driscoll, "Trust and Participation in Organizational Decision Making as Predictors of Satisfaction," *Academy of Management Journal*, March 1978, pp. 44–56; and R. S. Schuler, "A Role and Expectancy Perception Model of Participation in Decision Making," *Academy of Management Journal*, June 1980, pp. 331–,40.

The focus of this chapter is decision making. The quality of the decisions managers reach is the yardstick of their effectiveness. Thus, the flow of the preceding material leads logically to a discussion of decision making: that is, people behave *as individuals* and as members *of groups, within* an *organization* structure and *communicate* for many reasons, an important one of which is to *make decisions.* This chapter, therefore, will describe and analyze decision making in terms which reflect the way in which people decide as a consequence of the information they receive both through the organization *structure* and also through the *behavior* of important other persons and groups.

In the last three decades, the systematic analysis of decision making has become known as *decision theory.* Decision theory is firmly rooted in the fields of statistics and the behavioral sciences and has as its goal to make decision making less of an art and more of a science. Since World War II operations researchers, statisticians, computer scientists, and behavioral scientists have sought to identify those elements in decision making which are common to all decisions and thus provide a framework for decision makers to enable them to more effectively analyze a complex situation containing numerous alternatives and possible consequences. We shall see in this chapter that much progress has been made in analyzing and describing certain important aspects of decision making. In other equally important aspects, however, much progress remains to be made.

TYPES OF DECISIONS

■ While managers in various kinds of organizations may be separated by background, lifestyle, and distance, they all sooner or later must make decisions. That is, they face a situation involving several alternatives and their decision involves a comparison between the alternatives and an evaluation of the outcome. In this section our purpose is to move away from a general definition of a decision and present a classification system into which various kinds of decisions can be placed.

Specialists in the field of decision theory have developed several ways of classifying different types of decisions. For the most part these classification systems are similar, differing mainly in terminology. We shall use the widely adopted distinction suggested by Herbert Simon.[1] Simon distinguishes between two types of decisions:

1. *Programmed Decisions.* If a particular situation occurs often, a routine procedure will usually be worked out for solving it. Thus, decisions are programmed to the extent that they are repetitive and routine and a definite procedure has been developed for handling them.

2. *Nonprogrammed Decisions.* Decisions are nonprogrammed when they are novel and unstructured. As such there is no established procedure for handling the problem, either because it has not arisen in exactly the

[1]Herbert Simon, *The New Science of Management Decision* (New York: Harper & Row, 1960), pp. 5–6.

same manner before or because it is complex or extremely important. Such decisions deserve special treatment.

While the two classifications are broad, they point out the importance of differentiating between programmed and nonprogrammed decisions. The managements of most organizations face great numbers of programmed decisions in their daily operations. Such decisions should be treated without expending unnecessary organizational resources on them. On the other hand, the nonprogrammed decision must be properly identified as such since it is this type of decision making that forms the basis for allocating billions of dollars worth of resources in our economy every year. Unfortunately, it is this type of human decision process that we know the least

TABLE 15–1
Types of Decisions

	Programmed Decisions	Nonprogrammed Decisions
Type of problem	Frequent, repetitive, routine, much certainty regarding cause and effect relationships	Novel, unstructured, much uncertainty regarding cause and effect relationships
Procedure	Dependence upon policies, rules, and definite procedures	Necessity for creativity, intuition, tolerance for ambiguity, creative problem solving
Examples	*Business firm:* Periodic reorders of inventory	*Business firm:* Diversification into new products and markets
	University: Necessary grade-point average for good academic standing	*University:* Construction of new classroom facilities
	Health care: Procedure for admitting patients	*Health care:* Purchase of new experimental equipment
	Government: Merit system for promotion of state employees	*Government:* Reorganization of state government agencies

about.[2] Table 15–1 presents a breakdown of the different types of decisions with examples of each type in different kinds of organizations. It indicates that programmed and nonprogrammed decisions require different kinds of procedures and apply to distinctly different types of problems.

Traditionally, programmed decisions have been handled through rules, standard operating procedures, and the structure of the organization which develops specific procedures for handling them. More recently, operations researchers through the development of mathematical models have facilitated the handling of these types of decisions.

---

[2] See Peer Soelberg, "Unprogrammed Decision Making," *Proceedings,* 26th Annual Meeting, The Academy of Management, 1966, pp. 3–16; also see Stephen A. Stumpf, Dale E. Zand, and Richard D. Freedman, "Designing Groups for Judgmental Decisions," *Academy of Management Review,* October 1979, pp. 589–600.

On the other hand, nonprogrammed decisions have traditionally been handled by general problem-solving processes, judgment, intuition, and creativity. Unfortunately, modern management techniques have not made nearly the advances in improving nonprogrammed decision making as they have with programmed decision making.[3]

Ideally, the main concern of top management should be nonprogrammed decisions, while first-level management should be concerned with programmed decisions. Middle managers in most organizations concentrate mostly on programmed decisions, although in some cases they will participate in nonprogrammed decisions. In other words, the nature, frequency, and degree of certainty surrounding a problem should dictate at what level of management the decision should be made.

Obviously, problems arise in those organizations where top management expends much time and effort on programmed decisions. One unfortunate result of this practice is a neglect of long-range planning. In such cases, long-range thinking is subordinated to other activities whether the organization is successful or is having problems. If the organization is successful, this justifies continuing the policies and practices that achieved it. If the organization experiences difficulty, these current problems enjoy first priority and occupy the time of top management.[4]

Finally, the neglect of long-range planning usually results in an over-emphasis on short-run control. This results in a lack of delegation of authority to lower levels of management which often has adverse effects on motivation and satisfaction.

THE DECISION-MAKING PROCESS

Decisions should be thought of as *means* rather than ends. They are the *organizational mechanisms* through which an attempt is made to achieve a desired state. They are, in effect, an *organizational response* to a problem. Every decision is the outcome of a dynamic process which is influenced by a multitude of forces. This process is presented diagrammatically in Figure 15–1. The reader should not, however, interpret this to mean that decision making is a fixed procedure. Instead, it is presented here as a sequential process rather than a series of steps. This enables us to examine each element in the normal progression that leads to a decision.

Examination of Figure 15–1 reveals that it is more applicable to nonprogrammed decisions than to programmed decisions. Problems that occur infrequently with a great deal of uncertainty surrounding the outcome require that the manager utilize the entire process. For those problems which occur frequently it is not necessary to consider the entire process. If a pol-

---

[3] See Herbert A. Simon, *The Shape of Automation* (New York: Harper & Row, 1965).

[4] See A. D. H. Kaplan, *Big Enterprise in a Competitive System* (Washington, D.C.: Brookings Institution, 1954), for the classic study on the importance of long-range strategic planning. For example, it notes that of the 100 largest business organizations in 1909, only 36 remained in 1948.

FIGURE 15–1
The Decision-Making Process

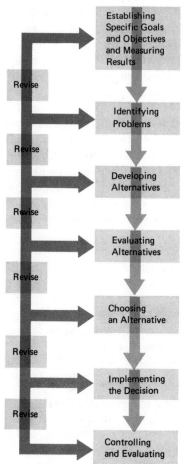

icy is established to handle such problems it will not be necessary to develop and evaluate alternatives each time the problem arises.

Establishing Specific Goals and Objectives and Measuring Results

Organizations need goals and objectives in each area where performance influences the effectiveness of the organization. If goals and objectives are adequately established they will dictate what results must be achieved and what measures will indicate whether or not they have been achieved.

Identifying Problems

A necessary condition for a decision is a problem. That is, if problems did not exist, then there would be no need for decisions.[5] This underscores

_____

[5]Two excellent references on this and related problems are W. E. Pounds, "The Process of Problem Finding," *Industrial Management Review*, Fall 1969, pp. 1–19; and C. E. Watson, "The Problems of Problem Solving," *Business Horizons*, August 1976, pp. 88–94.

the importance of establishing goals and measurable objectives. How critical a problem is for the organization is measured by the difference between levels of performance specified in the organization's goals and objectives and the levels of performance attained. Of course, if performance does not meet a predetermined objective, the problem may be with the objective. In order for objectives to be useful, they must permit the establishment of meaningful standards for effective control. For example, assume that, based on valid indicators, a university projects its enrollment in five years to be 15,000 students. If at the end of five years its enrollment is 11,500 students the school has a problem if the original objective was realistic. Assuming the objective was realistic, then the next phase is the development of alternatives to solve the problem. Otherwise the original objective must be revised. This is indicated by the darker lines in Figure 15–1.

The more volatile the subenvironments faced by the organization, the more complex is this phase of decision making. The following close-up presents one organization's response to such a situation.

ORGANIZATIONS: CLOSE-UP

Threat Analysis at IBM

IBM is one organization that formally trains managers to anticipate what the future may hold in the relevant environments that influence the manager's area of performance. This "threat analysis" or "what if?" type of thinking, it is believed, fosters a future orientation whereby various possible situations or states of nature are identified, analyzed, and incorporated into the decision-making process.

Thus it is true that many of the problems faced by managers may be the result of external forces beyond their control. However, many organizations like IBM train managers how to make decisions and solve problems in the present, but also train them to anticipate future problems.

Developing Alternatives

Before making a decision, feasible alternatives should be developed (actually these are potential solutions to the problem) and the potential consequences of each considered. This is really a search process where the relevant internal and external environments of the organization are investigated to provide information that can be developed into possible alternatives. Obviously, this search is conducted within certain time and cost constraints since only so much effort can be devoted to developing alternatives. Thus in the example above the university president would examine such factors as educational programs offered, faculty performance, the economic environment in the state, and competition from other learning institutions. Based upon this, various alternatives would be developed to solve the problem.

**Evaluating
Alternatives**

Once alternatives are developed they must be evaluated and compared. In every decision situation the objective in making a decision is to select the alternative that will produce the most favorable outcomes and the least unfavorable outcomes. This once again points up the necessity of objectives and goals, since in selecting from among alternatives the decision maker should be guided by the previously established goals and objectives. The alternative-outcome relationship is based on three possible conditions:

1. *Certainty*—The decision maker has complete knowledge of the probability of the outcomes of each alternative.
2. *Uncertainty*—The decision maker has absolutely no knowledge of the probability of the outcomes of each alternative.
3. *Risk*—The decision maker has some probabilistic estimate of the outcomes of each alternative.

Decision making under conditions of risk is probably the most common situation. It is in evaluating alternatives under these conditions that statisticians and operations researchers have made important contributions to decision theory.[6] Their methods have proved especially useful in the analysis and ranking of alternatives.

**Choosing an
Alternative**

The purpose in selecting an alternative is to solve a problem in order to achieve predetermined goals and objectives. This point is an important one. It means that a decision is not end in itself but only a means to an end. While the decision maker chooses the alternative that hopefully will result in the achievement of the objective, the actual selection should not be viewed as an isolated act. If this occurs, it is likely that the factors that led to and lead from the decision will be excluded. Specifically, those following the decision include implementation, control, and evaluation. The critical point is that decision making is *more* than an act of choosing, it is a dynamic process.[7]

Unfortunately for most managers, situations rarely exist in which one alternative singularly achieves the objective without having some impact either positively or negatively on some other objective. Often situations exist where two objectives cannot be optimized simultaneously. If one is optimized, the other is suboptimized. For example, in a business organization, if production is optimized, employee morale may be suboptimized or vice versa. Another example would be where a hospital superintendent optimizes a short-run objective such as maintenance costs at the expense of a long-run objective such as high-quality patient care. Thus, the multi-

(handwritten margin note: similar to Pareto optimality)

---

[6]For a study, see F. Luthans and R. Koester, "The Impact of Computer-Generated Information on the Choice Activity of Decision Makers," *Academy of Management Journal*, June 1976, pp. 328–32.

[7]This important point is discussed in detail in E. F. Harrison, *The Managerial Decision-Making Process* (Boston: Houghton Mifflin, 1975). This is an excellent comprehensive work on the subject of managerial decision making.

plicity of organizational objectives complicates the real world of the decision maker.[8]

A situation could also exist where attainment of an organizational objective would be at the expense of a societal objective. The reality of this situation is clearly seen in the rise of ecology groups, environmentalists, and the consumerism movement. Apparently these groups question the priorities (organizational as against societal) of certain organizational decision makers. In any case, whether an organizational objective conflicts with another organizational objective or a societal objective, the values of the decision maker will influence strongly the alternative chosen. Individual values were discussed earlier and their influence on the decision-making process should be clear.

Thus, in most managerial decision making, *optimal* solutions are often impossible. This is because the decision maker cannot possibly know all available alternatives, the consequences of each, and their probability of occurrence. Thus, rather than being an *optimizer*, the decision maker is a *satisficer*, selecting the alternative that meets an acceptable standard of acceptance.

Implementing the Decision

Any decision is little more than an abstraction if it is not implemented. In other words, the choice must be effectively implemented in order to achieve the objective for which it was made. It is entirely possible that a "good" decision may be hurt by poor implementation. Thus, in this sense, implementation may be more important than the actual activity of choosing the alternative.

Since in most situations implementing decisions involves people, the actual test of the soundness of a decision is their behavior relative to the decision. While a decision may be technically sound, it can easily be undermined by dissatisfied subordinates. Subordinates cannot be manipulated in the same manner as other resources. Thus, a manager's job is not limited to skill in choosing good solutions, but also includes the knowledge and skill necessary to transform the solution into behavior in the organization.[9] This is done by effectively communicating through individuals and groups.

Control and Evaluation

Effective management involves periodic measurements of actual results. Actual results are compared to planned results (the objective) and if deviations exist, changes must be made. Here again, we see the importance of measurable objectives. If they do not exist then there is no way to judge performance. If actual results do not match planned results then changes must be made in the solution chosen, its implementation, or in the original

---

[8] See R. L. Daft, "System Influence on Organizational Decision Making: The Case of Resource Allocation," *Academy of Management Journal*, March 1978, pp. 6–22.

[9] Alvar O. Elbing, *Behavioral Decisions in Organizations* (Glenview, Ill.: Scott, Foresman, 1970), p. 322.

objective if it is deemed unattainable. Let us return again to the college president referred to earlier whose school is facing declining enrollments. Assume the president decides to hire professional recruiters to recruit new freshmen from all states in the union. The president's objective is a 10 percent increase in enrollment over a two-year period. If at the end of the period enrollment has increased only 3 percent, either the original objective was overstated, the use of professional recruiters (the chosen alternative) to achieve the objective was not wise, or the wrong recruiters were chosen (implementation of the chosen alternative). If the original objective must be revised, then the entire decision-making process will be reactivated. The important point is that once a decision is implemented, a manager cannot assume that the outcome will meet the original objective. Some system of control and evaluation is necessary to make sure the *actual results* are consistent with the *planned-for results* when the decision was made.

From the discussion of the decision-making process, the reader should see why there are some people who argue that *what managers do is make decisions.* There is some truth in this argument because the steps in the decision-making process are much like the *functions and activities of managers* presented in Chapter 2.

BEHAVIORAL INFLUENCES ON INDIVIDUAL DECISION MAKING

■ Several behavioral factors influence the decision-making process. Some influence only certain aspects of the process while others influence the entire process. The important point, however, is that each may have an impact and, therefore, must be understood in order to fully appreciate decision making as a process in organizations. Four individual behavioral factors—values, personality, propensity for risk, and potential for dissonance—will be discussed in this section. Each has been shown to have a significant impact on the decision-making process.

Values

The reader has already been introduced to the role of values in Chapter 3. In the context of decision making they can be thought of as guidelines a person uses when confronted with a choice situation. They are acquired early in life and are a basic (often taken for granted) part of an individual's thoughts. The influence of values on the decision-making process is profound:

In *establishing objectives*, value judgments are necessary regarding the selection of opportunities and the assignment of priorities.

In *developing alternatives*, it is necessary to make value judgments about the various possibilities.

When *choosing an alternative*, the values of the decision maker influence which alternative is chosen.

When *implementing the decision*, value judgments are necessary in choosing the means for implementation.

In the *evaluation and control* phase, value judgments cannot be avoided when taking corrective action.[10]

It is clear that values pervade the decision-making process. They are reflected in the decision maker's behavior prior to making the decision, making the actual choice, and putting it into effect.

Personality

Decision makers are influenced by many psychological forces both conscious and subconscious. One of the most important is their personality, which is strongly reflected in the choices they make. One study has attempted to determine the effect of selected personality variables on the process of decision making.[11] The study did not focus solely on a set of personality variables but included three sets of variables.

1. *Personality variables.* These include the attitudes, beliefs, and needs of the individual.
2. *Situational variables.* These pertain to the external, observable situations in which individuals find themselves.
3. *Interactional variables.* These pertain to the momentary state of the individual as a result of the interaction of a specific situation with characteristics of the individual's personality.

The study's conclusions concerning the influence of personality on the decision-making process were as follows:

It is unlikely that one person can be equally proficient in all aspects of the decision-making process. Results suggested that some people will do well in one part of the process, while others will do better in another part.

Different characteristics such as intelligence are associated with different phases of the decision-making process.

The relation of personality to the decision-making process may vary for different groups on the basis of such factors as sex and social status.[12]

An important contribution of this study was that it determined that the personality traits of the decision maker combine with certain situational and interactional variables to influence the decision-making process.

Propensity for Risk

From personal experience the reader is undoubtedly aware that decision makers vary greatly in their propensity to take risks. This one specific aspect of personality strongly influences the decision-making process. A decision maker with a low aversion to risk will establish different objectives,

---

[10]Harrison, *Management Decision-Making Process*, p. 42.

[11]Orville C. Brun, Jr. et al., *Personality and Decision Processes* (Stanford Calif.: Stanford University Press, 1962).

[12]For a study on the effects of sex on decision making, see P. A. Renwick and H. Tosi, "The Effects of Sex, Martial Status, and Educational Background on Selected Decisions," *Academy of Management Journal*, March 1978, pp. 93–103.

evaluate alternatives differently, and select different alternatives than another decision maker in the same situation who has a high aversion to risk. The latter will attempt to make choices where the risk or uncertainty is low or where the certainty of the outcome is high. We shall see later in the chapter that in many cases, individuals are more bold, innovative, and advocate greater risk-taking following participation in a group than they display individually. Apparently, individuals are more willing to accept risk as members of a group.

Potential for Dissonance

While much attention has been focused on the forces and influences on the decision maker prior to making a decision, and on the actual decision, only recently has attention been given to what happens after a decision has been made. Specifically, behavioral scientists have focused attention on the occurrence of postdecision anxiety.

The occurrence of postdecision anxiety is related to what Festinger calls "cognitive dissonance."[13] His theory states that there is often a lack of consistency or harmony among an individual's various cognitions (for example, attitudes, beliefs, and so on) after a decision has been made. That is, there will be a conflict between what the decision maker knows and believes and what was done, and as a result the decision maker will have doubts and second thoughts about the choice that was made. In addition, there is a likelihood that the intensity of the anxiety will be greater when any of the following conditions exist:

1. The decision is an important one psychologically and/or financially.
2. There are a number of foregone alternatives.
3. The foregone alternatives have many favorable features.[14]

Each of these conditions is present in many decisions in all types of organizations. We can expect, therefore, that postdecision dissonance will be present among many decision makers, especially those at higher levels in the organization.

When dissonance occurs, it can, of course, be reduced by admitting that a mistake had been made. Unfortunately, it has been found that many individuals are reluctant to admit they have made a wrong decision. These individuals will more likely use one or more of the following methods to reduce their dissonance:

1. Seek information that supports the wisdom of their decision.
2. Selectively perceive (distort) information in a way to support their decision.
3. Change their attitudes to a less favorable view of the foregone alternatives.

---

[13]Leon Festinger, *A Theory of Cognitive Dissonance* (New York: Harper & Row, 1957), chap. 1.

[14]Ibid.

4. Avoid the importance of the negative aspects and enhance the positive elements.[15]

While each of us may resort to some of this behavior in our personal decision making, it is easy to see how a great deal of it could be extremely harmful in terms of organizational effectiveness. The potential for dissonance is influenced heavily by one's personality, specifically one's self-confidence and persuasibility. In fact, all of the behavioral influences are closely interrelated and are only isolated here for purposes of discussion. For example, what kind of a risk-taker you are and your potential for anxiety following a decision are very closely related, and both are strongly influenced by your personality, perceptions, and value system. Before managers can fully understand the dynamics of the decision-making process, they must appreciate the behavioral influences upon themselves and other decision makers in the organization when they make decisions.

GROUP DECISION MAKING

■ The first parts of this chapter focused on individuals making decisions. However, a great deal of decision making in most organizations is achieved through committees, teams, task forces, and other forms of groups. This is because managers frequently face situations where they must seek and combine judgments in group meetings. This is especially true for nonprogrammed problems which are novel with much uncertainty regarding the outcome. In most organizations it is unusual to find decisions of this type made by one individual on a regular basis. This is because the increased complexity of many organizational problems requires specialized knowledge in numerous fields usually not possessed by one person. This, coupled with the reality that the decision must eventually be accepted and implemented by many units throughout the organization, has increased the use of the collective approach to the decision-making process. The result for many managers has been an endless amount of time spent in committee and other group meetings. It has been found that as much as 80 percent of many managers' working time is spent in committee meetings[16]

Individual versus Group Decision Making

There is considerable debate over the relative effectiveness of individual versus group decision making. For example, groups usually take more time to reach a decision than individuals do, but the bringing together of individual specialists and experts also has its benefits since the mutually rein-

---

[15] W. J. McGuire, "Cognitive Consistency and Attitude Change," *Journal of Abnormal and Social Psychology*, 1960, pp. 345–53. Also see J. S. Adams, "Reduction of Cognitive Dissonance by Seeking Consonant Information," *Journal of Abnormal and Social Psychology*, 1961, pp. 74–78; J. Mills, E. Aronsen, and H. Robinson, "Selectivity in Exposure to Information." *Journal of Abnormal Psychology*, 1959, pp. 250–53; and D. S. Holmes and B. K. Houston, "Effectiveness of Situation Redefinition and Affective Isolation in Coping with Stress," *Journal of Personality and Social Psychology*, 1974, pp. 212–18.

[16] A. H. Van de Ven, *An Applied Experimental Test of Alternative Decision-Making Processes* (Kent, Ohio: Center for Business and Economic Research Press, Kent State University, 1973).

forcing impact of their interaction results in a better decision being made. In fact, a great deal of research has shown that consensus decisions with five or more participants are superior to individual decision making, majority vote, and leader decision.[17] Unfortunately, open discussion has been found to be negatively influenced by such behavioral factors as the pressure to conform, the influence of a dominant personality type(s) in the group, "status incongruity" where lower status participants are inhibited by higher status participants and "go along" even though they believe their ideas are superior, and finally, when certain participants attempt to influence others because they are perceived to be expert in the problem area.[18]

Certain decisions appear to be better made by groups while others appear better suited for individual decision making. Nonprogrammed decisions appear to be better suited for group decision making. The nature of such problems usually calls for pooled talent in arriving at a solution; decisions are of such importance that they are usually made by top managers and to a somewhat lesser extent by middle managers.

In terms of the decision-making process itself, the following points concerning group processes for nonprogrammed decisions can be made:

1. In *establishing objectives* groups are probably superior to individuals because of the greater amount of knowledge available.
2. In *identifying alternatives*, individual efforts of group members are necessary to ensure a broad search in the various functional areas of the organization.
3. In *evaluating alternatives*, the collective judgment of the group, with its wider range of viewpoints, seems superior to that of the individual decision maker.
4. In *choosing an alternative* it has been shown that group interaction and achievement of consensus usually results in groups accepting more risk than an individual decision maker. In any event, the decision is more likely to be accepted as a result of the participation of those affected by its consequences.
5. *Implementation* of a decision, whether or not it is made by a group, usually is accomplished by individual managers. Thus, since a group

---

[17]For examples, see Charles Holloman and Harold Henrick, "Adequacy of Group Decisions as a Function of Decision-Making Process," *Academy of Management Journal*, June 1972, pp. 175–84; and Andrew H. Van de Ven and Andre Delbecq, "Normal versus Interacting Group Processes for Committee Decision-Making Effectiveness," *Academy of Management Journal*, June 1972, pp. 203–12.

[18]For examples, see Soloman Asch, "Studies of Independence and Conformity," *Psychological Monographs*, 1956, pp. 68–70; Norman Dalkey and Olaf Helmer, "An Experimental Application of Delphi Method to Use of Experts," *Management Science*, April 1963, pp. 458–67; E. M. Bridges, W. J. Doyle, and D. J. Mahan, "Effects of Hierarchical Differentiation on Group Productivity, Efficiency, and Risk-Taking," *Administrative Science Quarterly*, Fall 1968, pp. 305–39; Victor Vroom, Lester Grant, and Timothy Cotten, "The Consequences of Social Interaction in Group Problem-Solving," *Organizational Behavior and Human Performance*, February 1969, pp. 77–95; and P. A. Collaras and L. R. Anderson, "Effect of Perceived Expertise upon Creativity of Members of Brainstorming Groups," *Journal of Applied Psychology*, April 1969, pp. 159–63.

cannot be held responsible, responsibility necessarily rests with the individual manager.[19]

Figure 15–2 summarizes the research on group decision making. It presents the relationship between the probable quality of the decision and the method utilized to reach the decision. It indicates that as we move from "individual" to "consensus," the quality of the decision increases. Note also that each successive method involves a higher level of mutual influence by group members. Thus, for a complex problem requiring pooled knowledge, the quality of the decision is likely to be higher as the group moves toward achieving consensus.

FIGURE 15–2

Probable Relationship between Quality of Group Decision and Method Utilized

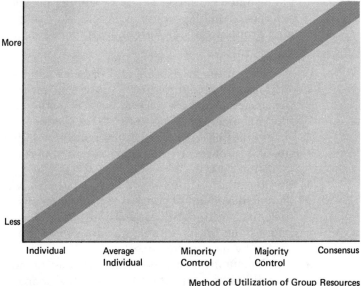

Source: Adapted from J. Hall and V. O'Leary, "The Utilization of Group Resources in Decision Making," National Training Laboratories, PSOTD, 1967, p. 4.

Creativity in Group Decision Making

If groups are better suited for nonprogrammed decisions then it is important that an atmosphere which fosters creativity be created. In this respect group decision making might be similar to brainstorming in that discussion must be free flowing and spontaneous. All group members must participate and the evaluation of individual ideas suspended in the beginning to encourage participation. However, a decision must be reached and this is where it differs from brainstorming. Figure 15–3 presents guidelines

[19]Based on Harrison, *Management Decision-Making Process*, p. 211.

FIGURE 15–3
Creative Group Decision Making

Group Structure
The group is composed of heterogeneous, generally competent personnel who bring to bear on the problem diverse frames of reference, representing channels to each relevant body of knowledge (including contact with outside resource personnel who offer expertise not encompassed by the organization), with a leader who facilitates creative process.

Group Roles
Behavior is characterized by each individual exploring with the entire group all ideas (no matter how intuitively and roughly formed) that bear on the problem.

Group Processes
The problem-solving process is characterized by:

1. Spontaneous communication between members (not focused on the leader).
2. Full participation from each member.
3. Separation of idea generation from idea evaluation.
4. Separation of problem definition from generation of solution strategies.
5. Shifting of roles, so that interaction which mediates problem solving (particularly search activities and clarification by means of constant questioning directed both to individual members and the whole group) is not the sole responsibility of the leader.
6. Suspension of judgment and avoidance of early concern with solutions, so that emphasis is on analysis and exploration, rather than on early solution commitment.

Group Style
The social-emotional tone of the group if characterized by:

1. A relaxed, nonstressful environment.
2. Ego-supportive interaction, where open give-and-take between members is at the same time courteous.
3. Behavior that is motivated by interest in the problem, rather than concern with short-run payoff.
4. Absence of penalties attached to any espoused idea or position.

Group Norms
1. Are supportive of originality and unusual ideas, and allow for eccentricity.
2. Seek behavior that separates source from content in evaluating information and ideas.
3. Stress a nonauthoritarian view, with a realistic view of life and independence of judgment.
4. Support humor and undisciplined exploration of viewpoints.
5. Seek openness in communication, where mature, self-confident individuals offer "crude" ideas to the group for mutual exploration without threat to the individual for "exposing" himself.
6. Deliberately avoid credence to short-run results, or short-run decisiveness.
7. Seek consensus, but accept majority rule when consensus is unobtainable.

Source: Andre L. Delbecq, "The Management of Decision Making within the Firm: Three Strategies for Three Types of Decision Making," *Academy of Management Journal,* December 1967, pp. 334–35.

for developing the permissive atmosphere so important for creative group decision making.

Techniques for Stimulating Creativity

It seems safe to say that in many instances group decision making is preferable to individual decision making. But we have all heard the statement, "A camel is a racehorse designed by a committee." Thus while the necessity of group decision making and its benefits are recognized, there are also numerous problems associated with it, some of which have already been noted. Practicing managers are in need of specific techniques which will enable them to increase the benefits from group decision making while reducing the problems associated with it.

We shall examine three techniques which, when properly utilized, have been found to be extremely useful in increasing the creative capability of a group in generating ideas, understanding problems, and, hopefully, reaching better decisions. This is especially necessary when individuals from diverse groups in the organization must pool their judgments in order to create a satisfactory course of action for the organization. The three techniques are known as brainstorming, the Delphi technique, and the nominal group technique.

Brainstorming. In many situations, groups are expected to produce creative or imaginative solutions to organizational problems. In such instances, brainstorming has often been found to enhance the creative output of the group. The technique of brainstorming was developed by an advertising executive and includes a strict series of rules.[20] The purpose of the rules is to promote the generation of ideas while at the same time avoiding the inhibitions on members usually caused by face to face groups. The basic rules are:

> No idea is too ridiculous. Group members are encouraged to state any extreme or outlandish idea.
>
> Each idea presented belongs to the group not to the person stating it. In this way it is hoped that group members will utilize and build upon the ideas of others.
>
> No idea can be criticized. The purpose of the session is to generate, not evaluate, ideas.

Brainstorming is widely used in advertising and some other fields and is apparently effective. In other situations it has been less successful because there is no evaluation or ranking of the ideas generated. Thus, the group never really concludes the problem-solving process.[21]

The Delphi Technique. This technique involves the solicitation and comparison of anonymous judgments on the topic of interest through a set

---

[20]A. F. Osborn, *Applied Imagination* (New York: Charles Scribner's Sons, 1957).

[21]For a review of research on brainstorming, see T. J. Bouchard, "Whatever Happened to Brainstorming?" *Journal of Creative Behavior*, Fall 1971, pp. 182–89.

of sequential questionnaires interspersed with summarized information and feedback of opinions from earlier responses.[22]

The Delphi process retains the advantage of several judges while removing the biasing effects which might occur during face-to-face interaction. The basic approach has been to collect anonymous judgments by mail questionnaire. For example, the members independently generate their ideas to answer the first questionnaire and return it. The staff members summarize the responses as the group consensus, and feed this summary back along with a second questionnaire for reassessment. Based on this feedback, the respondents independently evaluate their earlier responses. The underlying belief is that the consensus estimate will result in a better decision after several rounds of anonymous group judgment. While it is possible to continue the procedure for several rounds, studies have shown essentially no significant change after the second round of estimation.[23]

The Nominal Group Technique (NGT). NGT has gained increasing recognition in health, social service, education, industry, and government organizations.[24] The term *nominal* was adopted by earlier researchers to refer to processes which bring people together but do not allow them to communicate verbally. Thus, the collection of people is a group "nominally," or "in name only." We shall see, however, that NGT in its present form actually combines both verbal and nonverbal stages.

Basically, NGT is a structured group meeting that proceeds as follows: A group of individuals (7 to 10) sit around a table but do not speak to each other. Rather, each person writes ideas on a pad of paper. After five minutes, a structured sharing of ideas takes place. Each person around the table presents one idea. A person designated as recorder writes the ideas on a flip chart in full view of the entire group. This continues until all participants indicate they have no further ideas to share. There is still no discussion.

The output of this phase is a list of ideas (usually between 18 and 25). The next phase involves structured discussion in which each idea receives attention before voting. This is achieved by asking for clarification, or stating the degree of support for each idea listed on the flip chart. The next stage involves independent voting in which each participant, in private, selects priorities by ranking or voting. The group decision is the mathematically pooled outcome of the individual votes.

Both the Delphi technique and NGT are relatively new, but each has had an excellent record of successes. Basic differences between them are:

1. Delphi participants are typically anonymous to each other, while NGT participants become acquainted.

---

[22]Norman Dalkey, *The Delphi Method: An Experimental Study of Group Opinion* (Santa Monica, Calif.: Rand Corporation, 1969).

[23]Norman Dalkey, *Experiments in Group Prediction* (Santa Monica, Calif.: Rand Corporation, 1968).

[24]See Andre L. Delbecq, Andrew H. Van de Ven, and David H. Gustafson, *Group Techniques for Program Planning* (Glenview, Ill.: Scott, Foresman, 1975). The discussion here is based on this work.

2. NGT participants meet face to face around a table, while Delphi participants are physically distant and never meet face to face.
3. In the Delphi process, all communications between participants is by way of written questionnaires and feedback from the monitoring staff. In NGT, communication is direct between participants.[25]

Practical considerations, of course, often influence which technique is used. For example, such factors as the number of working hours available, costs, and the physical proximity of participants will influence which technique is selected.

Our discussion here is not designed to make the reader an expert in the Delphi process or NGT.[26] Our purpose throughout this section has been to indicate the frequency and importance of group decision making in every type of organization. The three techniques discussed are practical devices with the purpose of improving the *effectiveness* of group decisions.

The use of creativity-generating techniques in organizations is growing and is expected to continue during the next decade. However, their use among European organizations appears to be even greater as the following close-up suggests.

ORGANIZATIONS: CLOSE-UP

Stimulating Creativity in European Firms

European companies—struggling with stagnant economies, stiff competition, and complex labor-management problems—have been using creativity-generating techniques to a far greater extent than many of their American counterparts. Battelle Institute in Frankfurt indicates that brainstorming—the freewheeling, anything goes technique—is still the most popular method for stimulating creativity and generating ideas among the managements of European companies.

Another method, often called Delphi, is based on the assumption that an honest consensus cannot be reached when people attempt to resolve a problem face to face. Using Delphi, individual members anonymously provide their suggestions, which are then compared. The process is repeated until a true consensus is reached.

Third is a method known as morphological analysis, which is the most popular method among the research and development organizations in Europe. A team using this approach begins by breaking a problem down into all of its independent variables. A solution derives from scrutinizing every possible question any of the variables may raise.

Source: *Management Review,* January 1980, p. 4.

---

[25] Ibid., p. 18.

[26] The reader desiring to learn more about each of these techniques is encouraged to consult Delbecq, Van de Ven, and Gustafson, *Group Techniques for Program Planning.* For a recent study, see Frederick C. Miner, Jr., "A Comparative Analysis of Three Diverse Groups' Decision-Making Approaches," *Academy of Management Journal,* March 1979, pp. 81–93.

Decision making is a common responsibility shared by all executives, regardless of functional area or management level. Managers are required, every day, to make decisions that shape the future of their organization as well as their own futures. The quality of these decisions is the yardstick of their effectiveness. Some of these decisions may have strong impact on the organization's success, while others will be important but less crucial. The important point, however, is that *all* will have some effect (positive or negative, large or small) on the organization.

MAJOR MANAGERIAL ISSUES

A. Decision making is a fundamental process in organizations. Managers make decisions as a consequence of the information (communication) they receive through the organization structure and the behavior of individuals and groups within it.

B. Decision making distinguishes managers from nonmanagers. The quality of decisions managers make determines their effectiveness as managers.

C. Decisions may be classified as programmed or nonprogrammed depending on the type of problem. Most programmed decisions should be made at the first level in the organization while nonprogrammed decisions should be made mostly by top management.

D. Decision making should not be thought of as an end but as a *means* to achieve organizational goals and objectives. They are organizational responses to problems.

E. Decision making should be viewed as a multiphased *process* of which the actual choice is only one phase.

F. The decision-making process is influenced by numerous environmental and behavioral factors. Different decision makers may select different alternatives in the same situation because of different values, perceptions, and personalities.

G. A great deal of nonprogrammed decision making is carried on in group situations. Much evidence exists to support the claim that in most instances, though problems do exist, group decisions are superior to individual decisions. Three relatively new techniques (brainstorming, the Delphi technique, and the nominal group technique) exist which have the purpose of improving the effectiveness of group decisions. The management of collective decision making must be a vital concern for future managers.

DISCUSSION AND REVIEW QUESTIONS

1. In terms that are satisfactory to you, define a decision.

2. Describe two situations you faced which called for programmed decisions on your part and two which called for nonprogrammed decisions. What were some of the differences between them? Did this influence your decision-making approach? In what way(s)?

3. Think of a decision you made recently in response to a problem you faced. Describe it in terms of the decision-making process presented in Figure 15–1.

4. For decision-making purposes, why are goals and objectives so important?

5. Think of a major decision you made recently. It may have involved your personal life, a major purchase, etc. Do you believe there were any behavioral influences upon your decision? Discuss them.

6. What is your attitude toward risk? Has it ever influenced a decision you made? Discuss it. What are the implications of this discussion?

7. Have you ever been a member of a committee or task force which was charged with making some type of decision? Describe it in terms of your satisfactions, dissatisfactions, problems, and so forth.

ADDITIONAL REFERENCES

Alutto, J., and D. Vredenburgh. "Characteristics of Decisional Participation by Nurses." *Academy of Management Journal,* 1977, pp. 341–47.

Bouchard, R. J., and M. Hare. "Size, Performance, and Potential in Brainstorming Groups." *Journal of Applied Psychology,* 1970, pp. 51–55.

Collins, B. E., and H. Guetzkow. *A Social Psychology of Group Processes for Decision Making.* New York: John Wiley & Sons, 1964.

Dalkey, N. C. *The Delphi Method: An Experimental Study of Group Opinion.* Santa Monica, Calif.: Rand Corporation, June 1969.

Delbecq, A. L. "The Management of Decision Making within the Firm: Three Strategies for Three Types of Decision Making." *Academy of Management Journal,* 1967, pp. 329–39.

Drucker, P. *The Effective Executive.* New York: Harper & Row, 1967.

Eells, R., and C. Walton. *Conceptual Foundations of Business.* Homewood, Ill.: Richard D. Irwin, 1974.

Gerwin, D., and F. D. Tuggle. "Modeling Organizational Decisions Using the Human Problem-Solving Paradigm." *Academy of Management Journal,* 1978, pp. 762–73.

Gifford, W. E.; H. R. Bobbitt; and J. W. Slocum, Jr. "Message Characteristics and Perceptions of Uncertainty by Organizational Decision Makers." *Academy of Management Journal,* 1979, pp. 458–81.

Gustafson, D. H.; R. M. Shukla; A. Delbecq; and G. W. Walster. "A Comparative Study of Differences in Subjective Likelihood Estimates Made by Individuals, Interacting Groups, Delphi Groups, and Nominal Groups." *Organizational Behavior and Human Performance,* 1973, pp. 280–91.

Hall, E. J.; J. Mouton; and R. R. Blake. "Group Problem-Solving Effectiveness under Conditions of Pooling versus Interaction." *Journal of Social Psychology,* 1963, pp. 147–57.

Halter, A. N., and G. W. Dean. *Decisions under Uncertainty with Research Applications.* Cincinnati: South-Western Publishing, 1971.

Huber, G., and A. L. Delbecq. "Guidelines for Combining the Judgment of Individual Members in Decision Conferences." *Academy of Management Journal,* 1972, pp. 161–74.

Kahn, H., and A. H. Weiner. *The Year 2000: A Framework for Speculation on the Next Thirty-Five Years.* New York: Macmillan, 1967.

Kogan, N., and M. A. Wallach. *Risk-Taking: A Study in Cognition and Personality.* New York: Holt, Rinehart & Winston, 1964.

Lang, J. R.; J. E. Dittrich; and S. E. White. "Managerial Problem Solving Models: A Review and a Proposal." *Academy of Management Review,* 1978, pp. 854–66.

Lindley, D. V. *Making Decisions.* New York: John Wiley & Sons, 1971.

Miller, D. W. and M. K. Starr. *The Structure of Human Decisions,* Englewood Cliffs, N.J.: Prentice-Hall, 1967.

Rosen, B., and T. H. Jerdee. "Effects of Decision

Performance on Managerial Willingness to Use Participation." *Academy of Management Journal,* 1978, pp. 722–24.

Schmidt, W. H. *Organizational Frontiers and Human Values.* Belmont, Calif.: Wadsworth, 1970.

Sharkansky, I. *Public Administration: Policy Making in Government Agencies.* Chicago: Markham Publishing, 1972.

Shull, F. A.; A. L. Delbecq; and L. L. Cummings. *Organizational Decision Making.* New York: McGraw Hill, 1970.

Simon, H. A. *Models of Man.* New York: John Wiley & Sons, 1957.

————. *Sciences of the Artificial.* Cambridge, Mass.: MIT Press, 1969.

Tersine, R. J., and W. E. Riggs. "The Delphi Technique: A Long-Range Planning Tool." *Business Horizons,* 1976, pp. 51–56.

Van de Ven, A. H. *Group Decision Making and Effectiveness: An Experimental Study.* Kent, Ohio: Kent State University Press, 1974.

White, J. K. "Generalizability of Individual Difference Moderators of the Participation in Decision Making—Employee Response Relationship." *Academy of Management Journal,* 1978, pp. 36–43.

Tom Madden slipped into his seat at the meeting of the faculty of the College of Business Administration of Longley University. He was 10 minutes late because he had come completely across campus from another meeting which had lasted 1¼ hours. "Boy!" he thought, "if all of these meetings and committee assignments keep up, I won't have time to do anything else."

"The next item of importance," said the Dean, "is consideration of the feasibility report prepared by the Assistant Dean, Dr. Jackson, for the establishment of our Latin American MBA Program."

"What's that?" Tom whispered to his friend Jim Lyon sitting next to him.

"Ah, Professor Madden," winked Lyon, "evidently you've not bothered to read this impressive document," passing Tom the 86-page report, "otherwise you'd know."

"Heck, Jim, I've been out of town for two weeks on a research project and have just come from another meeting."

"Well, Tom," chuckled Jim, "the report was circulated only three days ago to, as the Dean put it, 'insure we have faculty input into where the college is going.' Actually, Tom, I was hoping you'd read it because then you could have told me what was in it."

"Dr. Jackson," said the Dean, "why don't you present a summary of your excellent report on what I believe is an outstanding opportunity for our college, the establishment of an MBA program in Latin America."

"Hey, Jim," said Tom, "they've got to be kidding, we're not doing what we should be doing with the MBA we've got here on campus. Why on earth are we thinking about doing another one 3,000 miles away?"

Jim shrugged. "Some friend of the Dean's or Jackson's from down there must have asked them, I guess."

While the summary was being given, Tom thumbed through the report. He noted that they were planning to offer the same program they offered in the United States. "Certainly," he thought, "their students' needs are different from ours." He also noted that faculty were going to be sent from the United States on one- to three-year appointments. "You would think that whenever possible they would seek local instructors who were familiar with the needs of local industry," Tom thought. He concluded in his own mind, "Actually, why are we even getting involved in this thing in the first place? We don't have the resources."

When Jackson finished the summary, the Dean asked, "Are there any questions?"

"I wonder how many people have had the time to read this report in three days and think about it," Tom thought to himself.

"Has anybody thought through this entire concept?" Tom spoke up. "I mean. . . ."

"Absolutely, Professor Madden," the Dean answered. "Dr. Jackson and I have spent a great deal of time on this project."

"Well, I was just thinking that. . . ."

"Now, Professor Madden, surely you don't question the efforts of Dr. Jackson and myself. Had you been here when this meeting started, you would know all about our efforts. Besides, it's getting late and we've got another agenda item to consider today, the safety and security of final examinations prior to their being given."

"No further questions," Tom said.

"Wonderful," said the Dean. "Then I will report to the president that the faculty of the College of Business Administration unanimously approves the Latin American MBA program. I might add, by the way, the president is extremely pleased with our method of shared decision making. We have made it work in this college while other colleges are having trouble arriving at mutually agreed-upon decisions.

"This is a great day for our college. Today we have become a multinational university. We can all be proud."

After the meeting, as Tom headed for the parking lot, he thought, "What a way to make an important decision. I guess I shouldn't complain though, I didn't even read the report. I'd better check my calendar to see what committee meetings I've got the rest of the week. If I've got any more I'll. . . ."

Questions for Consideration

1. Analyze this exercise and outline as many factors as possible which influenced the faculty decision in this case—either positively or negatively.

2. Does this exercise indicate that shared decision making cannot be worthwhile and effective? How could it be made more effective in the College of Business Administration?

3. Do you believe decision making of this type may be more worthwhile and effective in some types of organizations than in others? Discuss.

Chapter 16

Performance Evaluation Processes

AN ORGANIZATIONAL ISSUE FOR DEBATE
Using a Trait-Oriented Performance Evaluation*

ARGUMENT FOR

An important decision that managers make is to determine how performance evaluation will be used. Performance evaluation programs have been used to assess an employee's traits, behavior, and output. Many organizations make decisions using systems that evaluate traits such as dependability, technical competence, commitment, and initiative.

The assumption made by some individuals using traits is that there is a relationship between these selected traits and individual job performance. The trait-oriented evaluation system is assumed by some users to be relatively inexpensive to implement, informative, and as accurate as behavioral- or results-oriented programs. Since subjectivity cannot be completely eliminated from any performance evaluation system, there is sufficient reason to employ the least expensive program.

Another argument supporting a trait-oriented system focuses on the overemphasis on results. The negative consequences of overemphasizing results are dysfunctional and not conducive to the actual development of employees. It can be reasoned that if quality of work-life improvements are to occur, there must be less emphasis on bottom-line results.

ARGUMENT AGAINST

Opponents of trait-oriented performance evaluation programs believe that results-oriented evaluations are needed. They agree that certain traits are important in performing some jobs. However, their argument is that traits are so ingrained and difficult to determine that few managers can successfully evaluate or alter them significantly. Traits are also considered less helpful for use in coaching and feedback sessions involving a rater and ratee. The rater is not able to cite examples of specific job behaviors that can be corrected or modified to improve performance.

To serve judgmental and developmental purposes, performance evaluation must emphasize those job-related behaviors and results over which the individual employee has control. Individualized goal setting evaluations between a superior and subordinate with feedback of results and behaviorally anchored rating scales (BARS) are two programs that can, if used correctly, provide some information on job-related behaviors and results. Of course, these two evaluation methods also have limitations and problems.

---

* The issues of performance evaluation are discussed in W. J. Kearney, "Performance Appraisal: Which Way to Go?" *MSU Business Topics,* Winter 1977, pp. 58–64.

This chapter focuses on the uses, types, and applications of formal performance evaluation systems. The challenge facing managers involves finding an evaluation approach that provides an equitable, legally correct, and informative basis for evaluating the performance of employees. This is not a small challenge because every system has strengths, weaknesses, and costs that need to be evaluated carefully. In some organizations there may be a need to use more than one evaluation approach. The important theme of the chapter is not whether formal evaluation programs should be used, but what programs should be used and how they should be used.

Since performance evaluation is inevitable and is to some degree subjective, managers need to gather information that is relevant, accurate, and sufficiently complete. Managers that gather this type of information eventually will have to address the following questions: (1) What is the purpose of the evaluation; (2) What criteria should be evaluated; (3) What are some of the pitfalls of evaluation to avoid; (4) What method(s) of evaluation is best suited to accomplish the purpose?; and (5) How can evaluation become a development experience for subordinates?

PURPOSES OF PERFORMANCE EVALUATION

■ Many varieties of performance evaluation programs are now being used in organizations. In most organizations the evaluation program is designed to provide both the ratee and rater (manager) with information about job performance. However, before any performance evaluation program is selected there should be a clear understanding among raters and ratees about the objectives of the system. Two broadly stated purposes of performance evaluation are to reach an *evaluative* or *judgmental* conclusion about job performance and to *develop* employees through the program.[1] These two broadly stated purposes are compared in Table 16–1. Notice the differences in time orientation, objectives, and roles of the ratee and rater.

Organizations are becoming increasingly aware that raters must clearly identify the purpose of the performance evaluation program. The judgmental and developmental purposes are certainly not mutually exclusive. In fact, surveys of performance evaluation practices indicate that many organizations have both a judgmental and developmental purpose.

Specific Purposes

Managers are continually faced with making judgments concerning the job performance of subordinates. For example, judgments are made about promotions and pay raises. Most experts recommend that evaluation sessions that address salary or promotion should be kept separate from those dealing with personal and career development. The rationale for the separation is based on the differences in the judgmental and developmental purposes of performance evaluation illustrated in Table 16–1.

A well-designed and implemented performance evaluation program can

---

[1]L. L. Cummings and Donald P. Schwab, *Performance in Organizations* (Glenview, Ill.: Scott, Foresman, 1973), p. 5.

TABLE 16-1
Two Major Purposes of Performance Evaluation: A Comparison

Points of Comparison	*Broad Evaluation Purposes*	
	Judgmental	*Developmental*
Time orientation	Past performance	Preparation for future performance
Objective	Improving performance by changing behavior through reward system	Improving performance through self-learning and personal growth
Method	Use of rating scales, comparisons, and distributions	Counseling, mutual trust, goal setting, and career planning
Supervisor's role .... (rater)	A judge who appraises	A supportive counseling and encouraging person who listens, helps, and guides
Subordinate's role .... (ratee)	Listener, reacts and attempts to defend past performance	Actively involved in charting out future job performance plans

Source: Adapted from L. L. Cummings and Donald P. Schwab, *Performance In Organizations* (Glenview, Ill.: Scott, Foresman, 1973), p. 5, Table 1–1.

have a motivational impact upon ratees. It can encourage improvement, develop a sense of responsibility, and increase organizational commitment. Performance evaluation can also be motivational if it can provide ratees with some understanding of what is expected of them.

Another specific purpose of performance evaluation is the improvement of managerial understanding. A formal program encourages managers to observe the behavior of subordinates. Through increased and more thorough observations, improved mutual understanding between supervisors and subordinates can result.

Performance evaluation information also provides a basis for planning, training, and development. Such areas of weakness in technical competence, communication skills, and problem-solving techniques can be identified and analyzed.

A research purpose can also be accomplished through performance evaluation. The accuracy of selection decisions can be determined by comparing performance evaluations with such selection devices as test scores and interviewers' ratings.

Although the two broad purposes of performance evaluation are judgmental and developmental, the specific reasons for using it transcend the organization. Some of these more *specific* purposes are summarized in Table 16–2.

One other important and often forgotten purpose of performance evaluation is to reduce favoritism in making important managerial decisions. This reason is not shown in Table 16–2, but it is extremely important to many employees. It is not shown in Table 16–2 because it is a subjective factor, while the other purposes cited are specific and related to the broad

TABLE 16–2
Specific Purposes of Performance Evaluation

Motivation	Identifying training and development needs
Promotion	
Dismissal	Evaluating effectiveness of selection and placement decisions
Salary increases	
Wage increases	Transfer
Improved managerial awareness of subordinate job tasks and problems	Human Resource Planning
	Layoff
Improved subordinate understanding of management's view of his/her performance	

judgmental and developmental categories. The negative effects of perceived favoritism include strained supervisor-subordinate relationships, low morale, and dissatisfaction with company policies.[2]

THE PERFORMANCE CRITERION ISSUE OF EVALUATION

■ The performance evaluation program at any level within the organization hierarchy must at some point focus on the criterion issue. A *criterion* is a variable that has dimensionality.[3] It may be a physiological variable, such as an increase in blood pressure when being asked to speed up production. It may be an economic variable, such as cost per unit, or a psychological variable such as commitment toward an organization. In performance evaluation the *criterion* is the dependent or predicted measure for appraising the effectiveness of an individual employee. This definition applies to the individual level of analysis. At the organizational level of analysis, the point of discussion centers on evaluating organizational effectiveness. The majority of our discussion of performance evaluation will concentrate on the individual level.

Requirements of a Performance Criterion

There are a number of requirements that should be met before a variable qualifies as a performance criterion. First, a criterion should be *relevant* to the individual and the organization. Determining what is relevant is itself controversial. Some person or group must make a judgment about what constitutes relevance. Once the relevant criterion has been selected, there must be an effort to develop a sound and valid measure of the variable.

Second, the criterion must be *stable* or *reliable*. This involves agreement between evaluations, at different points in time. If the results from the two

---

[2]P. Pigors and C. A. Myers, *Personnel Administration* (New York: McGraw-Hill, 1977), p. 270.

[3]Robert M. Guion, *Personnel Testing* (New York: McGraw-Hill, 1965), p. 90.

different evaluations show little agreement, there would be some uncertainty about whether the criterion was stable.

Third, a performance criterion may be relevant and reliable and still be useless in evaluating employees. A criterion is useful only if it can *discriminate* between good performers and poor performers. If all employees are good performers then there is no need to discriminate. If, however, there are good, average, and poor performers then the evaluation criterion must discriminate.

Finally, the criterion must be *practical.* The criterion must mean something to the rater and ratee. If the criterion serves no useful or practical function, then it becomes something that is evaluated but offers no meaning.

Meeting these four requirements does not provide the answer to two questions: (1) Should one criterion be used to measure job performance? and (2) Should the criterion be an economic, physiological, or some other variable?

Criterion or Criteria?

The use of the term *criterion,* a single noun, has resulted from the search for years to find the "ultimate criterion." Thorndike stated:

> . . . The ultimate criterion for a production line worker might be that he perform his task, maintaining the tempo of the line, with the minimum of defective products requiring rejection upon inspection, that he be personally satisfied with the task. . . .[4]

This statement adequately represents the view of those who believe that a single criterion exists for every job.

In general, there is ample evidence to support either the single criterion or multiple criteria arguments. In some situations, especially at the policy-making level, a single criterion is needed to reach a managerial decision. In other cases, involving promotion, salary and wage decisions, transfer, and counseling, multiple criteria can be useful in illustrating why a particular decision is made or a specific development program recommended. It would be extremely difficult to explain a promotion decision on the basis of a single criterion. Of course, if the employee receives the promotion, he or she may not mind the use of an ultimate criterion for reaching the decision.

Some Other Issues Involving Criteria

Selecting appropriate criteria to use in performance evaluation is further complicated by the fact that they are often dynamic. That is, criteria that are valid, reliable, and practical at one point in an employee's career may become inappropriate over a period of time. For example, during the first year or so on the job various criteria may be applied and have meaning to

---

[4]R. L. Thorndike, *Personnel Selection* (New York: John Wiley & Sons, 1949), p. 11.

the rater and ratee. However, as the employee acquires experience, confidence, and career goals, these original criteria may not be appropriate.

Another controversial issue concerning criteria involves the activities versus results debate. The job performance of any one person can be viewed in terms of the activities performed and the effort made by the individual.[5] Any performance evaluation program that concentrates on either activities or results to the exclusion of the other, often produces problems because employees learn what is important and work at this aspect of the job. For example, if production output is a major criterion for assessing performance, assembly-line workers may produce as many units as possible so that they receive a good evaluation. The production quantity orientation may result in poor quality products being manufactured at high costs because of the excessive amount of rejects.

On the other hand, a program of performance evaluation which appraises only activities has some limitations. First, it would encourage only activities and disregard accomplishments. For example, if our assembly-line worker is only evaluated on whether safety rules were followed and his or her work area was properly prepared for production, there may be too few units made for eventual sale.

It seems appropriate to suggest that whenever possible, performance evaluation criteria should be established for both activities and results. If any performance evaluation program addresses either activities or results. If any performance evaluation program addresses either activities or results criteria at the exclusion of the other, there may be little attention paid to organizational and personal goal accomplishment. Organizations often focus on results, while activities seem to be important to groups and individuals. Therefore, so that all parties can benefit as much as possible from the performance evaluation program, results and activities criteria should be developed when possible.[6]

PERFORMANCE CRITERIA AND THE LAW

■ The Equal Employment Opportunity Commission (EEOC), the federal agency responsible for administering and enforcing the Civil Rights Act of 1964, issued the Uniform Guidelines on Employment Selection Procedures in 1978. These guidelines have an impact on performance evaluation because evaluations are viewed as a selection procedure.[7] The guidelines state that a procedure such as a performance evaluation must not adversely impact any group protected by the Civil Rights Act.

Most performance evaluation procedures rely on paper-and-pencil methods to identify specific work behavior. Management uses the outcomes of

---

[5]Lyman W. Porter, Edward E. Lawler III, and J. Richard Hackman, *Behavior in Organizations* (New York: McGraw-Hill, 1975), pp. 324–25 has an excellent discussion of the activities versus results controversy.

[6]Ibid., p. 326.

[7]Richard Henderson, *Performance Appraisal* (Reston, Va.: Reston Publishing, 1980), p. 217.

the evaluation to make promotion, pay, transfer, and other human resource decisions (see Table 16–2). In making these decisions there is the potential for bias and poor judgment in many parts of the evaluation process. For example, managers who are serving as raters could use criteria that are not important in performing a job or place too little weight on significant job performance criteria.

Since employers have been winning only about 5 percent of the race, sex, and age discrimination cases, understanding the law seems to be a major concern. Court rulings provide managers with guidelines on the issues of criteria, validity, and reliability. These three concepts are extremely important if a case reaches the courts.

For example, performance evaluation criteria must provide a representative sampling of an employee's job performance. If the evaluation is used for estimating a person's promotion potential, the system must provide data about such potential. It must be valid or measure what it is suppose to measure—potential.

The principal kinds of validity that are relevant for making performance evaluations are briefly presented in Table 16–3. As shown, numerous types of validity exist.[8] The important point to note is that validity is inferred and not directly measured. The manager has to make a judgment about the adequacy of the validity of the criteria he or she is using. The federal courts now are insisting that proper consideration be given to the validity and reliability of performance evaluation instruments.

In order to comply with federal laws regarding performance evaluation, the criteria, validity, and reliability issues must be carefully considered. Managers need also to review previous court rulings. In addition to addressing the validity and reliability issues managers must make sure that:

The overall performance evaluation process is standardized and as objective as possible.

The performance evaluation is as job related as possible.

A thorough, formal job analysis for all positions is carefully done.

Subjective ratings are considered as only one input in the evaluation decisions.

Raters are trained to use the performance evaluation instruments and process.

Raters have daily contact with and are able to frequently observe ratees.

The evaluation is conducted independently by more than one rater for each ratee.[9]

---

[8]For an excellent and brief discussion of validity and reliability of performance criteria, see Henderson, *Performance Appraisal*, pp. 221–24; and Richard I. Henderson, *Compensation Management* (Reston, Va.: Reston Publishing, 1979), pp. 389–91.

[9]Duane E. Thompson, Charles R. Klasson, and Gary L. Lubben, "Performance Appraisal and the Law: Policy and Research Implications of Court Cases" (Paper presented at Academy of Management Meetings, Atlanta, Georgia, August 9, 1979), pp. 5–6.

TABLE 16–3
Types of Validity Used in Determining Acceptability of Performance Evaluation Criteria

Type of Validity	*Brief Description*
Concurrent	Statistical correlation between a predictor (an item on the evaluation form) and actual job performance.
Content	The degree to which scores or ratings on the evaluation are a representative sample of all job behaviors required to perform the job.
Criterion-related	Whenever individual difference measures are used, criterion-related validity should be examined. Scores or ratings on the evaluation are related to some criterion (e.g., expert judgment). If the criterion is available at the same time that predictor is measured, concurrent validity is being assessed
Predictive	In contrast to concurrent validity, if criterion data are not available until after predictor scores are obtained, then predictive validity is being measured. Thus, predictive validity is oriented toward the future, while concurrent validity is oriented toward the present.
Construct	The degree to which scores may be interpreted as measuring a property such as potential, motivation, commitment. It is important to obtain a degree of objectivity in assessing the property.
Convergent	The correlation between the same properties or traits rated by different raters is significantly different from zero.
Discriminant	The correlation between the same traits rated by different raters should be higher that the correlation between different traits rated by the same rater. Also, the correlation between the same traits as rated by different raters should be higher than the correlation between different traits rated by different raters.

The law and the need for a formal performance evaluation system have greatly affected what organizations are now using. In essence, no matter what process is used managers or raters must make judgments about ratees. Furthermore, these judgments need to be based on scientifically derived criteria. Figure 16–1 displays the central importance of criteria in the performance evaluation process. Furthermore, the importance of the law, the role of the rater in providing feedback to and developing ratees, and the part played by the ratee in understanding responsibilities, criteria, and goals are emphasized.

FIGURE 16–1
The Four Main Phases of Performance Evaluation

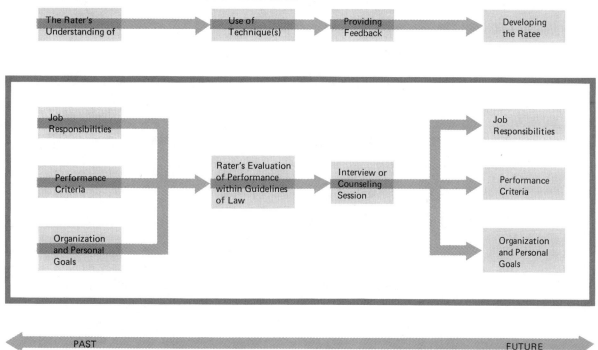

JOB ANALYSIS AND PERFORMANCE EVALUATION

■ In Figure 16–1 the importance of criteria development in performance evaluation is identified. One needs to examine jobs and how the organization divides its tasks into individual jobs before criteria that are reliable, valid, and practical emerge. The description of how one job differs from another in terms of demands, activities, and skills required is *job analysis*.

Broadly stated, job analysis is devoted to the gathering and analysis of job-specific information. The job analyst is interested in specifying the unique characteristics or structure of characteristics which differentiates one job from another. By careful analysis of the job's characteristics, a summary statement of what an employee on the job actually does is developed. This is called a *job description*. Furthermore, a dollar value is attached to the job, enabling the organization to relate the dollar value of the job to the value of other jobs. The assignment of dollar values is called *job evaluation*. Performance evaluation distinguishes the performance and potential among employees on the basis of various criteria. Figure 16–2 presents the relationships between job analysis and performance evaluation.

Through job analysis a manager is provided with clues about which criteria can be used to evaluate successful performance of the job. There are several kinds of criteria commonly used in organizations. The type of cri-

FIGURE 16–2
Job Analysis and Performance Evaluation: A Relationship

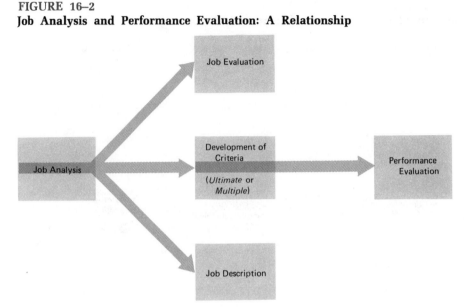

Source: Adapted from Frank J. Landy and Don A. Trumbo, *Psychology of Work Behavior* (Homewood, Ill.: Dorsey Press, 1980), p. 104.

teria used depends on such factors as the type of job, the time period covered by the evaluation, and the purposes to be served by the evaluation program. The criteria used for the research and development scientist working in an organizational laboratory are different than criteria used to evaluate the first-line supervisor or the salesperson.

PERFORMANCE EVALUATION METHODS: TRADITIONAL

■ If pressed for an answer most managers could offer a general description of the job performance of subordinates. However, a more formal and systematic procedure than asking for managerial or supervisor opinions is usually used.[10] Managers usually attempt to select a performance evaluation procedure that will minimize conflict with ratees, provide relevant feedback to ratees, and contribute to the achievement of organizational goals. Basically, the manager attempts to find, develop, and implement a performance evaluation program that can benefit the employee, other managers, the work group, and the organization.

As is the case with most managerial procedures and applied organizational behavior practices, there are no universally accepted methods of performance evaluation that fit every purpose, person, or organization. What is effective in IBM will not necessarily work in General Mills. In fact what

[10]For an excellent discussion of performance evaluation methods, see Frank J. Landy and James L. Fair, "Performance Rating," *Psychological Bulletin*, February 1980, pp. 72–107.

is effective within one department or for one group in a particular organization will not necessarily be right for another unit or group within the same company. The only important point agreed upon by managers and organizational researchers is that some type of measuring device or procedure be used to record data on a number of performance criteria so that subjectivity in reward, development, and other managerial decisions is minimized.

Graphic Rating Scales

The oldest and most widely used performance evaluation procedure, the scaling technique, appears in many forms. Generally, the rater is supplied with a printed form, one for each subordinate to be rated. The form contains a number of job performance qualities and characteristics to be rated. The rating scales are distinguished by (1) how exactly the categories are defined; (2) the degree to which the person interpreting the ratings can tell what response was intended by the rater, and (3) how carefully the performance dimension is defined for the rater.

Figure 16–3 presents samples of some of the common rating scale formats. The first distinguishing feature between rating scales, the meaning of the possible response categories, is usually handled by the use of anchor statements or words placed at points along a scale. Rating scales (a), (b), (c), (d), and (h) use anchors.

The second distinguishing feature among rating scales is the degree to which the person interpreting the ratings can tell what response was intended. The clarity of response intention is exemplified in scales (e), (f), and (g).

Quality of work can be interpreted differently by various raters. Therefore, a performance dimension needs to be defined for each rater. Scales (a), (b), (e), and (g) give the rater little dimension definition. Scales (c) and (h) provide the rater with a fairly good definition of the performance dimension.

Ranking Methods

Some managers use a rank order procedure to evaluate all subordinates. The subordinates are ranked according to their relative worth to the company or unit on one or more performance dimensions. The procedure followed usually involves identifying the best performer and the worst performer. They are ranked in the first and last positions on the ranking list. The next best and next poorest performers are then filled in on the list. This rank ordering continues until all subordinates are placed on the list. The rater is forced to discriminate by the rank ordering performance evaluation method.

There are some problems with the ranking method. It is likely that ratees in the central portion of the list will not be much different from each other on the performance rankings. Another problem involves the size of the group of subordinates being evaluated. It becomes more difficult to rank large groups of subordinates.

There are other forms of performance evaluation ranking programs that

FIGURE 16–3
Some Samples of Rating Scale Formats

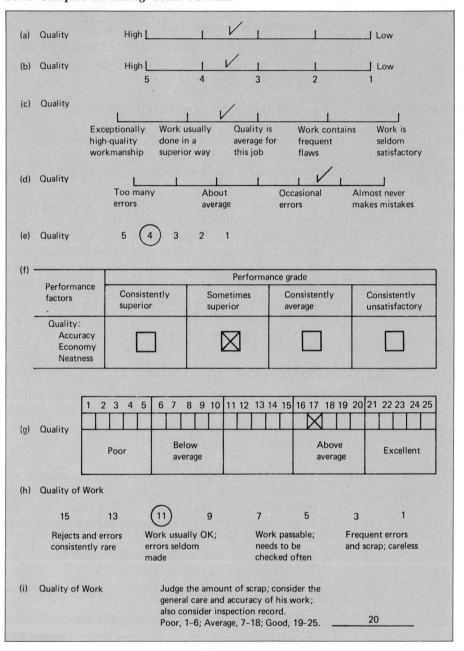

Variations on a graphic rating scale; each line represents one way in which a judgment of the quality of a person's work may be given. (From *Personnel Testing*, p. 98, by Guion. Copyright 1965, McGraw-Hill Book Company.)

are used. For example, in the *paired comparison* method, every subordinate is compared with every other. The supervisor is asked to identify the best performer from each pair. If a supervisor had eight subordinates he or she would have:

$$\text{Pairs} = \frac{N(N-1)}{2}$$

or

$$\frac{8(8-1)}{2} = 28$$

Weighted Checklists

The weighted-checklist rating consists of a number of statements that describe various types and levels of behavior for a particular job or group of jobs. Each statement has a weight or value attached to it. The rater evaluates each subordinate by checking those statements that describe the behavior of the individual. The check marks and the corresponding weights are summated for each subordinate.

The weighted checklist makes the rater think in terms of specific job behavior. However, this procedure is difficult to develop and very costly. Separate checklists are usually established for each different job or group of jobs.

Descriptive Essays

The essay method of performance evaluation requires the rater to describe each ratee's strong and weak points. Some organizations require every rater to discuss specific points in the evaluation, while others allow the rater to discuss whatever he or she believes is appropriate. One problem of the descriptive essay evaluation is that it provides little opportunity to compare ratees on specific performance dimensions. Another limitation is the writing skills of raters.

RATING ERRORS

◼ The descriptions of just four of the traditional performance evaluation methods point out problems and potential errors of each. The major problems and errors can be *technical* in the form of poor reliability, validity, and practicality or rater misuse. In some situations raters are extremely harsh or easy in their evaluations. These are referred to as *strictness or leniency rater errors.* The harsh rater gives ratings which are lower than the average ratings usually given to subordinates. The lenient rater tends to give higher ratings than the average level given to subordinates. Figure 16–4 illustrates the distribution of lenient and harsh ratings. These kinds of rating errors typically result because the rater is applying personal standards to the particular performance evaluation system being used. For example, the words outstanding or average may mean different things to different raters.

Another problem is called the *halo error.* The term *halo* suggests that

FIGURE 16–4

Example of Leniency and Harshness in Performance Ratings

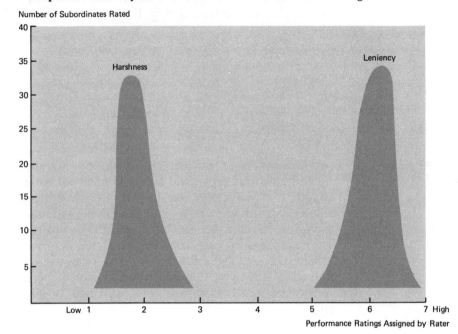

Number of Subordinates Rated

Performance Ratings Assigned by Rater

there is a positive or negative aura around an individual employee. This aura influences the rater's evaluation in about the same way for all performance dimensions considered. Halo error is due to the rater's inability to discriminate between the different dimensions being rated. It is also caused by the rater assuming that a particular dimension is extremely important. The rating on this dimension influences all of the other dimension evaluations.

Central tendency error occurs when a rater fails to assign either extremely high or extremely low ratings. That is, the rater tends to rate almost all ratees around the average. A graphic illustration of the central tendency error is shown in Figure 16–5. This type of evaluation error provides little information for making promotion, compensation, training, career planning, and development decisions. Everyone is about the same—average. Playing it safe by rating everyone average does not enable the manager to integrate performance evaluation with reward or employee development programs.

In many performance evaluation programs the most recent behaviors of ratees tend to color ratings. Using only the most recent behaviors to make evaluations can result in what is called the *recency of events* error. Forgetting to include important past behaviors can introduce a strong bias into the evaluation. Ratees usually are aware of this tendency and become visi-

FIGURE 16–5

Example of Central Tendency Error in Performance Ratings

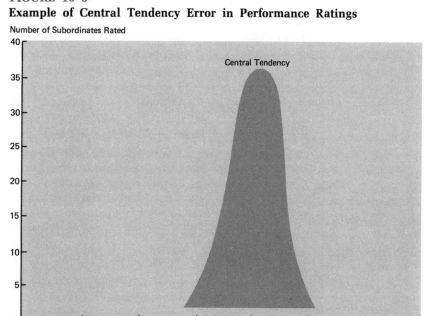

ble, interested, productive, and cooperative just before the formal evaluation occurs.

According to research findings,[11] rating errors are likely to be minimized if

1. Each dimension addresses a single job activity rather than a group of activities.
2. The rater on a regular basis can observe the behavior of the ratee while the job is being accomplished.
3. Terms like *average* are not used on a rating scale, since different raters have various reactions to such a term.
4. The rater does not have to evaluate large groups of subordinates. Fatigue and difficulty in discriminating between ratees become major problems when large groups of subordinates are evaluated.
5. Raters are trained to avoid such errors as leniency, harshness, halo, central tendency, and recency of events.

---

[11]For discussions of minimizing rating errors, see H. J. Bernardin and C. S. Walter, "The Effects of Rater Training and Diary Keeping on Psychometric Error in Ratings," *Journal of Applied Psychology*, February 1977, pp. 64–69; and R. G. Burnaska and T. D. Hollman, "An Empirical Comparison of the Relative Effects of Rater Response Bias on Three Rating Scale Formats," *Journal of Applied Psychology*, June 1974, pp. 307–12.

6. The dimensions being evaluated are meaningful, clearly stated, and important.

The following close-up portrays how Syborn Corporation attempts to improve its performance evaluation system.

ORGANIZATIONS: CLOSE-UP

Performance Evaluation at Syborn Corporation

Syborn Corporation was like most firms—not very satisfied with its performance evaluation program. It appeared that most raters did not know how to evaluate subordinates effectively and objectively. There seemed to be a preference to rush through the evaluations in a matter of minutes. Rushing led to making more errors and more dissatisfaction with the program.

Syborn decided to provide the managers doing the rating with a training program designed to improve rating skills and the motivation to set objectives. The first part of the training involved managers in interpersonal skill exercises and in learning procedures for setting evaluation reviews and substantiating goals. The firm used lectures, discussions, and videotaping in this part of the program.

The second part of the training presented to the managers involved five general principles to improve their managerial performance. The five principles were presented, discussed, and critiqued. They were:

1. Maintain and enhance self-esteem.
2. Focus on behavior, not personality.
3. Use reinforcement techniques to shape behavior.
4. Listen actively.
5. Maintain communication and set specific follow-up dates.

So far more than 250 Syborn managers have participated in the course—one full day a week for four weeks. Since only 8 or 10 managers participate in each course there is time for total involvement, thus reinforcing the goals of the program.

Source: "Syborn Trains Managers to Improve Performance Appraisals," *Management Review*, January 1981, pp. 32–33.

In addition to these guidelines there are other forms of performance evaluation that attempt to minimize rating errors. Two of the more recently developed approaches are the use of behaviorally anchored rating scales (BARS) and management by objectives (MBO).

PERFORMANCE EVALUATION METHODS: BARS AND MBO

In an effort to improve on the reliability, validity, and practicality of traditional performance evaluations, some organizations have used various behaviorally based and goal-setting programs. The behaviorally based programs attempt to examine what the employee does in performing the job.

The objective or goal-oriented programs typically examine the results or accomplishments of the employee.

Behaviorally Anchored Rating Scales

Smith and Kendall developed a procedure which is referred to as behaviorally anchored rating scales (BARS) or behavioral expectation scales (BES).[12] The BARS approach relies on the use of "critical incidents" to construct the rating scale. Critical incidents are examples of specific job behaviors which determine various levels of performance. Once the important areas of performance are identified and defined by employees who know the job, critical incident statements are used as anchors to discriminate between high, moderate, and low performance. The BARS rating form usually covers 6 to 10 specifically defined performance dimensions each with various descriptive anchors. Each dimension is based on observable behaviors and is meaningful to employees being evaluated.

An example of a BARS for engineering competence is presented in Figure 16–6. The dimension is defined for the rater, the anchors define the particular response categories for the rater, and the response made by the rater is specific and easy to interpret. The feedback provided by the BARS is specific and meaningful. If the ratee is given a 1.5 on this dimension, he or she is provided with the specific performance incident that the rater used to make such a rating.

Proposed Advantages of BARS

Some thorough reviews of the literature have concluded that BARS are (1) costly to construct, (2) require significant time to put into use, and (3) are not much better in improving rating errors than graphic rating scales or weighted checklists.[13] Despite some discouraging research findings and constructive criticisms, BARS are still being used by numerous organizations. The remaining popularity of BARS is based on various proposed advantages. It is assumed that since job knowledgeable employees participate in the actual development steps, the final form will be reliable, valid, and meaningful. It should also cover the full domain of the job. A common problem of traditional performance evaluation programs is that they do not tap the full domain of the job.[14]

The use of BARS is also valuable for providing insights when developing training programs. The skills to be developed are specified in terms of actual behavioral incidents rather than abstract or general skills. Trainees in a BARS-based program could learn expected behaviors and how job performance is evaluated.[15]

---

[12] P. C. Smith and L. M. Kendall, "Retranslation of Expectations: An Approach to the Construction of Unambiguous Anchors for Rating Scales," *Journal of Applied Psychology*, April 1963, pp. 149–55.

[13] Landy and Fair, "Performance Rating."

[14] J. P. Campbell, M. D. Dunnette, R. D. Arvey, and L. W. Hellervik, "The Development and Evaluation of Behaviorally Based Rating Scales," *Journal of Applied Psychology*, February 1973, pp. 15–22.

[15] M. R. Blood, "Spin-offs from Behavioral Expectation Scale Procedures," *Journal of Applied Psychology*, August 1974, pp. 513–15.

FIGURE 16–6
A BARS Performance Dimension

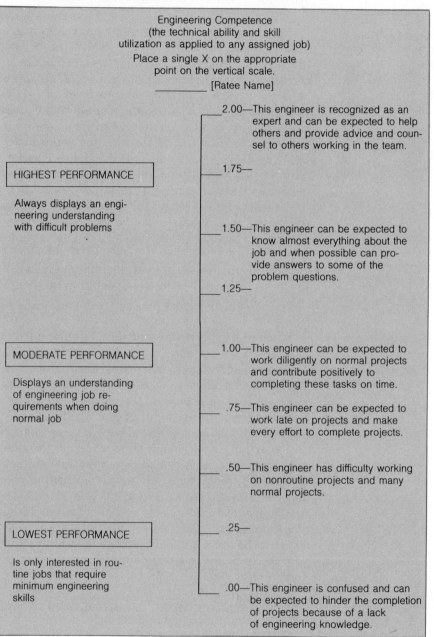

Engineering Competence
(the technical ability and skill
utilization as applied to any assigned job)
Place a single X on the appropriate
point on the vertical scale.
_____ [Ratee Name]

2.00—This engineer is recognized as an expert and can be expected to help others and provide advice and counsel to others working in the team.

1.75—

HIGHEST PERFORMANCE

Always displays an engineering understanding with difficult problems

1.50—This engineer can be expected to know almost everything about the job and when possible can provide answers to some of the problem questions.

1.25—

MODERATE PERFORMANCE

Displays an understanding of engineering job requirements when doing normal job

1.00—This engineer can be expected to work diligently on normal projects and contribute positively to completing these tasks on time.

.75—This engineer can be expected to work late on projects and make every effort to complete projects.

.50—This engineer has difficulty working on nonroutine projects and many normal projects.

LOWEST PERFORMANCE

Is only interested in routine jobs that require minimum engineering skills

.25—

.00—This engineer is confused and can be expected to hinder the completion of projects because of a lack of engineering knowledge.

The literature also implies that through the use of a behaviorally anchored system, leniency, halo, and central tendency errors will be reduced. These errors are assumed to be minimized because of the independence between dimensions rated and the reliability of the BARS.[16] However, some critics of the BARS present results that indicate that this approach is not always the most reliable, valid, and practical. They also suggest that more research is needed comparing BARS with other traditional evaluation methods.[17]

It is suggested that a BARS program can minimize subordinate or ratee defensiveness toward evaluation. By being involved in the development of a BARS, subordinates can make their inputs known. These inputs can be incorporated in the final BARS. As McGregor pointed out, many superiors are uncomfortable about judging someone and acting out the role of an evaluator.[18] The BARS development steps could include both superiors and subordinates. In a sense then, all parties involved can contribute to the creation of the evaluation criteria (dimensions) and the behavioral incidents used as anchors.

Management by Objectives

In the traditional and BARS evaluation programs, the rater is making judgments about the performance of subordinates. There are behavioral scientists, organizational researchers, and managers who believe that a results-based program is more efficient and informative. One popular results-based program is called management by objectives (MBO). An MBO program typically involves the establishment of objectives (also referred to as goals) by the supervisor alone or jointly by the supervisor and subordinate.

MBO is far more than just an evaluation approach. It is usually a part of an overall motivational program, planning technique, or organizational change and development program. More details on MBO will be presented later in Chapter 20.

An MBO performance evaluation program focuses on what an employee achieves. The key features of a typical MBO program are as follows:

1. Superior and subordinate meet to discuss and jointly set goals for subordinates for a specified period of time (e.q., six months or one year).
2. Both the superior and subordinate attempt to establish goals that are realistic, challenging, clear, and comprehensive. The goals also should be related to organizational and personal needs.
3. The criteria for measuring and evaluating the goals are agreed upon.

[16]S. Zedeck and H. T. Baker, "Nursing Performance as Measured by Behavioral Expectation Scales: A Multitrait-Multirater Analysis," *Organizational Behavior and Human Performance*, June 1972, pp. 457–66.

[17]D. P. Schwab, H. G. Henneman Ill., and T. A. DeCotiis, "Behaviorally Anchored Rating Scales: A Review of the Literature," *Personnel Psychology*, Winter 1975, pp. 549–62.

[18]D. McGregor, "An Uneasy Look at Performance Appraisal," *Harvard Business Review*, May–June 1957, pp. 89–94.

4. The superior and subordinate establish some intermediate review dates when the goals will be reexamined.
5. The superior plays more of a coaching, counseling, and supportive role and less the role of a judge and jury.
6. The entire process focuses upon results accomplished and counseling subordinates, and not upon activities, mistakes, and organizational requirements.

MBO-type programs have been used in organizations throughout the world.[19] Approximately 40 percent of Fortune's 500 largest industrial firms report using MBO-type programs.[20] Like each of the performance evaluation programs already discussed, there are both benefits and potential costs associated with using MBO. The assumed benefits include better planning, improved motivation because of knowledge of results, basing evaluation decisions on results instead of on traits, improving commitment through participation, and improving supervisory skills in such areas as listening, counseling, and evaluating. These are certainly significant benefits, but they are not always accomplished in MBO programs. Using MBO is no sure way to improve upon the problems associated with performance evaluation programs. It too, has some potential and real problems. The fact that MBO stresses results is a benefit that can also be a problem. Focusing only on results may take attention away from how to accomplish the goals. A subordinate receiving feedback about what has been achieved may still not be certain about how to make performance corrections.

Other problems that have been linked to MBO programs include: improper implementation, lack of top management involvement, too much emphasis on paperwork, failing to use an MBO system that best fits the needs of the organization and employees, and inadequate training preparation for employees who are asked to establish goals.[21]

A final limitation or cost of MBO is that comparisons of subordinates are difficult. In traditional performance evaluation programs, all subordinates are rated on common dimensions. In MBO, each individual usually has a different set of goals that is difficult to compare across a group of subordinates. The superior must make reward decisions not only on the basis of goals achieved, but also on his or her conception of the kind of goals that were accomplished. The feeling of achieving goals will generally wear thin among subordinates if the accomplishment is not accompanied by meaningful rewards.

---

[19] G. P. Latham and G. A. Yukl, "A Review of Research on the Application of Goal Setting in Organizations," *Academy of Management Journal*, December 1975, pp. 824–43.

[20] J. Singular, "Has MBO Failed?" *MBA* October 1975, pp. 47–50.

[21] J. M. Ivancevich, "Different Goal Setting Treatments and Their Effects on Performance and Job Satisfaction, *Academy of Management Journal*, September 1977, pp. 406–19; and J. M. Ivancevich, J. H. Donnelly, Jr. and J. L. Gibson, "Evaluating MBO: The Challenges Ahead," *Management by Objectives*, Winter 1976, pp. 15–24.

PERFORMANCE EVALUATION: THE ASSESSMENT CENTER

■ The assessment center technique was pioneered by Douglas Bray and his associates at American Telephone and Telegraph Company in the mid-1950s. In the 1970s, it had become a popular evaluation technique used in organizations of all sizes. The foundation of this technique is a series of situational exercises in which candidates for promotion, training, or other managerial programs take part over a two- to three-day period while being observed and rated. The exercises are simulated management tasks and include such techniques as role playing and case analysis. In some assessment centers, personal interviews and psychological tests are also used to make evaluations.[22] The assessment center is unique as an evaluation technique. It is unique in that it focuses on the future instead of on past performance. Thus, it is a technique that attempts to evaluate a ratee's potential.

Purposes of Assessment Centers

Since individual ratees are observed in a controlled setting (the center), raters can compare the performances of candidates or employees on a first-hand basis. Today it is estimated that over 4,000 organizations use assessment centers.[23] The centers are used:

1. To identify individuals who are suited for a particular type or level of management job.
2. To determine individual and group training and development needs.
3. To identify individuals for promotion to positions that are quite different from their current positions; for example, salespeople, technicians, or engineers being considered for managerial positions. Because the new managerial jobs would require such different skills and abilities than a sales or engineering job, it is difficult to determine a candidate's ability before the promotion. The assessment center attempts to identify some indicators of managerial ability before the decision is made.

Dimensions Measured by Assessment Centers

There are different dimensions measured in assessment centers depending upon the purpose of the evaluation. Such dimensions as interpersonal skills, communication ability, creativity, quality of problem-solving skills, tolerance for stress and ambiguity, and planning ability are some of the commonly assessed dimensions.

IBM has conducted studies of its assessment center programs. All show a positive relationship between center ratings and various criteria of success.[24] Such variables as energy level, communication skills, aggressiveness, and self-confidence were rated in the IBM program.

---

[22]R. B. Finkle, "Managerial Assessment Centers," in *Handbook of Industrial and Organizational Psychology*, ed. M. D. Dunnette (Chicago: Rand McNally, 1976), pp. 861–88.

[23]Joyce D. Ross, "A Current Review of Public Sector Assessment Centers: Cause for Concern," *Public Personnel Management*, January–February 1979, p. 41.

[24]W. E. Dodd, "Summary of IBM Assessment Validations" (Paper presented as part of the symposium: "Validity of Assessment Centers," at the 79th Annual Convention of the American Psychological Assn., 1971).

Chevrolet Sales Divisions select candidates for assessment centers by using nine dimensions for measuring managerial potential. Some of these are: judgment, use of time, job knowledge, and interpersonal communications. The candidates that are rated the highest on these nine dimensions are selected for the assessment center evaluation. In the center, potential for higher-level position responsibility is rated.[25]

A Typical Program

There is no universally used set of exercises applied in assessment centers. An example of an assessment center schedule is presented in Figure 16–7.

FIGURE 16–7
Format for a Typical Two-and-half-Day Assessment Center

Day 1	*Day 2*	*Day 3*
A. Orientation of Approximately 12 Ratees.	A. Individual Decision-Making Exercise—Ratees are asked to make a decision about some problem that must be solved. (*Raters* observe fact finding skill, understanding of problem-solving procedures, and risk-taking propensity.)	A. Individual Case Analysis and Presentation. (*Raters* observe problem-solving ability, method of preparation, ability to handle questions, and communication skills.)
B. Break-up into Groups of Six or Four to Play Management Simulated Game. (*Raters* observe: planning ability, problem-solving skill, interaction skills, communication ability.)		B. Evaluation of Other Ratees. (Peer evaluations.)
C. Psychological Testing—Measure verbal and numerical skills.	B. In-Basket Exercise. (*Raters* observe decision making under stress, organizing ability, memory, and ability to delegate.)	
D. Interview with Raters. (*Raters* discuss goals, motivation, and career plans.)	C. Role-Play of Performance Evaluation Interview. (*Raters* observe empathy, ability to react, counseling skills, and how information is used.)	
E. Small Group Discussion of Case Incidents. (*Raters* observe confidence, persuasiveness, decision-making flexibility.)	D. Group Problem Solving. (*Raters* observe leadership ability and ability to work in a group.)	

[25] F. M. McIntyre, "Unique Program Developed by Chevrolet Sales," *Assessment and Development*, January 1975.

After the assessment program, the raters meet to discuss and evaluate all candidates. The assessment center raters are usually managers two or more levels above the ratees. They are used because they are familiar with the jobs for which ratees are being considered and because by participating they can improve their evaluation skills and techniques.

Problems of Assessment Centers

Again it must be stated that evaluating employee performance in any setting is extremely difficult. One of the potential problems of the assessment center evaluation procedure is that it is so pressure packed. Outstanding employees who have contributed to the organization may simply not perform well in the center. Raters may be embarrassed by not being able to justify ratings or because of their limited ability to identify key behaviors.

Another problem involves the feelings of individuals who receive mediocre or poor evaluations. Employees who receive a poor evaluation may leave the organization or be demoralized for an extended period of time. It is natural for the highly rated participants in centers to be identified as "comers" or individuals to develop. The poorly rated participants may be viewed as "losers."

Basing promotion decisions or identifying individuals with high potential on the results of a single assessment center experience is questionable. The research evidence on the reliability and validity of assessment centers is still somewhat mixed.[26] Until more evidence is available, the assessment center may be useful for only some situations and some evaluation decisions. It is another evaluation procedure that has both potential benefits and problems.

A REVIEW OF POTENTIAL PERFORMANCE EVALUATION PROGRAMS

■ Table 16–4 summarizes the main points of the various approaches discussed. The usefulness of each method is debatable. In some organizations one system is more useful because of the type of individuals doing the rating or the criteria being used. Every program discussed thus far has both costs and benefits. Since performance evaluation is such an integral part of managing within organizations, recognizing the strengths, weaknesses, and best uses for a particular program is an important job for managers.

DEVELOPING EMPLOYEES THROUGH PERFORMANCE EVALUATION FEEDBACK

■ An evaluation program solely for the sake of rating employees will soon lose any potential value or motivational impact unless it becomes integrated with the main emphasis of the organization. The judgment and development purposes will show through when both the ratees and raters understand each others roles in the process. The rater must clarify, coach, counsel, and provide feedback. On the other hand, the ratee must understand rater expectations, his or her own strengths and weaknesses, and the

---

[26]R. J. Klimoski and W. J. Strickland, "Assessment Centers—Valid or Merely Prescient," *Personnel Psychology* Autumn 1977, pp. 353–61.

TABLE 16–4
Managerial Points of Interest when Selecting a Performance Evaluation Program

Point of Interest	Programs						
	Graphic Rating Scales	Ranking	Checklists	Essay	BARS	MBO	Assessment Centers
Acceptability to subordinates	Fair	Fair/poor	Fair	Poor	Good	Generally good	Generally good
Acceptability to management	Fair	Fair/poor	Fair	Poor	Good	Generally good	Generally good
Useful in reward allocations	Poor	Poor	Fair	Fair	Good	Good	Fair/good
Useful in counseling and developing subordinates	Poor	Poor	Poor	Fair	Good	Good	Good
Meaningful dimensions	Rarely	Rarely	Sometimes	Rarely	Often	Often	Often
Ease of developing actual program	Yes	Yes	Yes	No	No	No	No
Development costs	Low	Low	Low	Moderately high	High	High	High

goals that need to be accomplished. These various roles can become clear if the performance evaluation program is considered a continual process that focuses both on task accomplishment and personal development.

Regardless of how individual job performance information is collected—whether by a BARS, an assessment center, or a rating scale—the rater must provide formal feedback to the ratee. An example of how feedback is used is presented in the following close-up.

ORGANIZATIONS: CLOSE-UP

Performance Evaluation in Greensboro, North Carolina, City Government

The city of Greensboro, North Carolina, implemented a performance planning and appraisal system (PPA) for managers and subordinates. A main feature of PPA was to acquire and provide information to subordinates about performance. The first step in PPA was the establishment of a work plan for each subordinate. This plan identified the job responsibilities of each subordinate and then required the supervisor and subordinate mutually to set challenging goals.

Another part of PPA called for the supervisor to provide regular feedback to employees. There were quarterly and annually scheduled feedback sessions. The basis of these feedback sessions is the work plan objectives that were set at the beginning of the cycle and the actual accomplishments of the subordinates. The feedback sessions provided a forum to examine the progress of subordinates in three areas: new projects, routine tasks, and personal development. The supervisor and subordinate in the feedback sessions exchanged comments, expectations, and concerns about the progress being made and not being made in the three target areas.

The Greensboro PPA program is an example of a program that incorporated feedback sessions from the outset. Unfortunately, many performance evaluation programs fail to emphasize or even use formal feedback sessions. Without formal feedback it is difficult to imagine ratees making the necessary modifications in their activities and behaviors to improve performance accomplishments.

Source: Richard Henderson, *Performance Appraisal* (Reston, Va.: Reston Publishing, 1980), pp. 205–6.

The performance evaluation feedback interview should be a part of any program from the beginning. It should focus on the job performance of the ratee. Generally, raters feel uncomfortable about discussing ratee weaknesses or problems. On the other hand, ratees often become defensive when personal weaknesses or failures are pointed out by a rater. Kay, Meyer, and French reviewed the relationship between comments focusing on subordinate weaknesses in a feedback interview and defensive comments made by the ratees.[27] They found that as critical comments increased, subordinate defensiveness increased. Furthermore, they concluded that praise in the feedback sessions was ineffective. They assumed that since most raters first praise then criticize and finally praise to end the feedback session, ratees become conditioned to this sequence. In essence, praise becomes a conditioned stimulus preceeding the arrival of criticism.

If the performance evaluation program is acceptable to the rater and ratee, there is a higher probability that the feedback interview can be more than a praise-criticism-praise sequence. The acceptability of any program depends upon such factors as: (1) how the evaluation will be used; (2) who developed the program; (3) whether the criteria are fair; (4) how good the rater is in evaluating performance; and (5) whether the rater has sufficient time to spend planning for, implementing, and providing feedback in the program? It should be noted that providing effective feedback information requires skill time, and patience. Feedback has both positive and negative consequences. Poorly presented performance evaluation feedback can result in distrust, hostility, dissatisfaction, and turnover. Effective evaluation feedback can be motivational and encourage the development of ratees.

Too often performance evaluation interviews focus on the past year or on plans for the short run. Rarely do a manager and subordinate discuss careers.[28] Recall that in our presentation of the performance evaluation process (Figure 16–1) the future development of the ratee is considered extremely important. It is important for managers to have knowledge about the various career tracks and requirements available within the organization. The manager should be able to view the job performance of subordinates and be able to help create tasks that are challenging. This also means that the creation of challenging tasks will help prepare subordinates for future jobs which require the use of more skills and abilities. Basically, it seems worthwhile for managers to consider and be prepared to discuss the lifelong sequence of job experiences and jobs of subordinates, as part of the evaluation interview. Only through managerial consideration of career goals can the evaluation process in reality become a development experience as well as a judgmental analysis of job performance.

MAJOR MANAGERIAL ISSUES

A. Performance evaluation occurs in most organizations. It is a formal process that systematically involves the evaluation of subordinates' job performance and potential for future development.

B. Performance evaluation is used in a broad sense to make judgments and to develop subordinates. In a more specific sense it has motivational,

---

[27]E. Kay, H. Meyer, and J. R. P. French, "Effects of Threat in a Performance Appraisal Interview," *Journal of Applied Psychology*, October 1965, pp. 311–17.

[28]G. W. Dalton, P. H. Thompson, and R. L. Price, "A New Look at Performance by Professionals," *Organizational Dynamics*, Summer 1977, pp. 19–42.

MAJOR MANAGERIAL ISSUES (continued)

improved knowledge, research, promotion, and training and development purposes.

C. Federal laws play a major role in performance evaluation. Managers are advised to examine carefully the validity and reliability of the techniques and programs they use to evaluate subordinate performance.

D. An important step in developing any performance evaluation program involves the establishment of criteria. A criterion is a dependent or predicted measure for appraising the effectiveness of employees. A good criterion must be relevant, stable, able to discriminate between ratees, and practical.

E. A few of the widely used performance evaluation programs are graphic rating scales, ranking procedures, weighted checklists, and descriptive essays. These procedures often result in raters making rating errors. The most common errors are harshness and leniency, halo effect, central tendency, and recency of events. Some methods available for reducing these errors include eliminating terms such as *average* on the scales, having raters rate a small number of individuals instead of many people, and training raters to recognize the most common error tendencies.

F. The behaviorally anchored rating scale (BARS) is a form of evaluation that uses critical incidents or examples of specific job behaviors to determine various levels of performance. The development of the BARS is time consuming and costly, but can involve the joint participation of raters and ratees. This joint effort can result in more acceptance of the evaluation program by raters and ratees.

G. A results-based performance evaluation program is called management by objectives (MBO) or goal setting. The program typically involves a superior/subordinate meeting to discuss and jointly set goals for subordinates for a specified period of time. The superior plays more of a coaching and supportive role in this results-based program.

H. The assessment center technique has become a popular evaluation technique in the past two decades. The foundation of this program is a set of exercises in which candidates for promotion, training, or other managerial programs take part—over a two- to three-day period—while being observed and rated. One major problem with this program involves the participants who are rated low. They can become extremely demoralized about their future careers in the organization.

I. The performance evaluation feedback interview(s) is an essential part of any program. Feedback provides information about how others view the ratee's job performance. Without feedback, knowledge about progress, development, and clarity about expectations is difficult to attain. Another important part of feedback involves relating performance and progress to career development. Feedback of recent results and activities plus events for the near future should be combined with discussions about organizational career tracks and requirements for the long run.

DISCUSSION AND REVIEW QUESTIONS

1. How can common rating errors result in problems in a performance evaluation program?

2. What are the main differences between a behaviorally anchored rating scale (BARS) and a graphic rating scale?

3. What role can subordinates play in developing the evaluation system that will be used by their superiors?

4. Why is it important for the rater to be able to observe behavior in most performance evaluation programs?

5. It is often stated that any performance evaluation program contains some degree of subjectivity. Do you agree?

6. Why is development considered an important purpose of performance evaluation?

7. Some claim that the assessment center is a pressure packed experience or a "fishbowl" exercise. Why are these statements made?

8. Why is job analysis an important antecedent to the development of criteria and the actual performance evaluation program used?

9. Why is the performance evaluation feedback interview such an important part of the process of appraisal?

ADDITIONAL REFERENCES

Anthony, W. P., and E. A. Nicholson. *Management of Human Resources: A Systems Approach to Personnel Management.* Columbus, Ohio: Grid, 1977.

Beatty, R. W., and C. E. Schneier. *Personnel Administration: An Experiential Skill-Building Approach.* Reading, Mass.: Addison-Wesley Publishing, 1981.

Beer, M. "Performance Appraisal: Dilemmas and Possibilities." *Organizational Dynamics,* 1981, pp. 24–36.

Burack, E. H. "Career Path—Why all the Confusion?" *Human Resource Management,* 1977, pp. 21–27.

Buzzotta, V. R.; R. E. Lefton; and M. Sherberg. "Coaching and Counseling: How You Can Improve the Way It's Done," *Training and Development Journal,* 1977, pp. 50–60.

Ciminero, A. R.; K. S. Calhoun; and H. E. Adams eds. *Handbook of Behavioral Assessment.* New York: John Wiley & Sons, 1977.

Coleman, C. J. *Personnel.* Cambridge, Mass.: Winthrop Publishers, 1979.

Haynes, M. G. "Developing an Appraisal Program" Parts I and II. *Personnel Journal,* 1978, pp. 14–19, 66–67, 104, 107.

Ivancevich, J. M. "Longitudinal Study of the Effects of Rater Training on Psychometric Error in Ratings." *Journal of Applied Psychology,* 1979, pp. 502–8.

———— "A Longitudinal Study of Behavioral Expectation Scales: Attitudes and Performance." *Journal of Applied Psychology,* 1980, pp. 139–46.

Jacobs, R.; D. Kafry; and S. Zedeck. "Expectations of Behaviorally Anchored Rating Scales." *Personnel Psychology,* 1980, pp. 595–640.

Jaffee, C. O.; F. D. Frank; and J. B. Rollins. "Assessment Centers: The New Method for Selecting Managers." *Human Resource Management,* 1976, pp. 5–11.

Latham, G. P.; L. M. Saari; E. D. Purcell; and M. A. Campion. "The Situational Interview." *Journal of Applied Psychology,* 1980, pp. 425–27.

Locher, A. M., and K. S. Teel. "Performance Appraisal—A Survey of Current Practices." *Personnel Journal,* 1977, pp. 245–47, 54.

McAfee, F., and B. Green. "Selecting a Performance Appraisal Method." *Personnel Administrator* 1977, pp. 61–64.

McCormick, E. J. *Job Analysis: Methods and Applications.* New York: AMACOM, 1979.

Maier, N. R. F. *The Appraisal Interview: Three Basic Approaches.* La Jolla, Calif.: University Associates, 1976.

Mollenhoff, D. V. "How to Measure Work by Professionals." *Management Review* 1977, pp. 39–43.

Sashkin, M. "Appraising Appraisal: Ten Lessons from Research for Practice." *Organizational Dynamics,* 1981, pp. 37–50.

THE EVALUATION OF A PERFORMANCE EVALUATION PROGRAM

Mike Pecaro, the project manager for a new power plant being constructed for the Atlanta, Georgia, area was called into the vice president's office to discuss some complaints about the company's performance evaluation program. In order to determine whether the complaints of engineers, technicians, and machinists were justified, Mike was asked to critique the present evaluation system. The system used eight dimensions that were assumed to be associated with good performance. The rating scale being used ranged from one to seven, with seven being a rating given for the highest level of performance. The three highest rated engineers in Mike's group were used as reference points for purposes of discussion. The ratings are presented in Exhibit 1.

EXHIBIT 1
Ratings for Three Best Performers in Mike Pecaro's Group

Performance Dimension	Bob Lowry	Tony Nelson	Randy Anderson
Quality of work	6	6	7
Dependability	6	7	7
Cooperation	7	6	7
Customer interaction	7	7	7
Meeting budget requirements	6	7	7
Development of subordinates	7	6	6
Problem-solving skill	6	7	6
Technical competence	7	7	7
Total score	52	53	54

Don Baker, the vice president, wanted Mike to critique the soundness of the overall performance evaluation program. He was interested in whether the performance dimensions were meaningful to the engineers, technicians, and machinists. The same dimensions were being used for each group. One of the major and loudest complaints had to do with the relevance of some of the dimensions. Listed below are some of the complaints received from employees:

Machinist: The evaluation dimensions mean nothing since I have no control over some of them. I never interact with customers. Why am I rated on this dimension?

Technician: Everyone is rated about average so the rating system is really a failure.

Technician: The performance dimensions are a mystery to all of us. What does dependability mean? What is an example of problem solving skill?

Engineer: My supervisor never provides me with any feedback on progress. I have to guess at how I am doing. I have no idea of where I am going in the company.

Engineer: The performance evaluation never covers the long run. It only focuses on the short run or yesterday's results. I do not like this emphasis.

Engineer: My supervisor really doesn't know how to use the evaluation program. He uses it just to exercise tighter control of my activities. Shouldn't it be used to help me make improvements?

Mike was not surprised to hear these kinds of complaints since he also felt uneasy about the performance evaluation program. He told Don that most of the comments were on target. He rated the present system unreliable, inaccurate, and uninformative. The present rating system had some flaws that could be eliminated. Based on the seemingly endless list of complaints, Mike recommended that the present system be reevaluated by a committee of supervisors and subordinates. Don wanted some time to think about the possible solutions to the growing negative reactions to the present system.

Questions for Consideration

1. What type of system is presently being used to evaluate performance?
2. What problems and errors with the present system of evaluation are displayed in the list of complaints?
3. What are some of the possible solutions available for correcting the shortcomings of the present program?

EXPERIENTAL EXERCISE

THE FACTS OF ORGANIZATIONAL LIFE

Objectives

1. To illustrate how difficult it is to use performance evaluation when making promotion choices.
2. To emphasize the impact of outside forces on performance evaluation programs.
3. To consider how a performance evaluation decision may become complex.

Related Topics

The government's role in performance evaluation will be illustrated in this exercise. The difficulty of informing individuals that they will not be promoted is considered.

Starting the Exercise

Set up groups of five to eight students for the 40- to 60-minute first phase of the exercise. If possible include men and women in all groups. The groups should be separated from each other and asked to reach a decision within the group. Before the groups are established, each person should read the facts of the situation.

The Facts   The Sebring Electronics Corporation is located in Baton Rouge, Louisiana. The company has, over the past five years, incorporated a performance evaluation program for operating employees that is generally viewed as a fair system. The company has maintained a steady rate of growth and has reached a point where two new supervisors are needed. Since the company motto is to "hire, develop, promote, and reward from within," it is now the job of a management committee to locate the best two new supervisors.

The performance evaluation program was designed to provide needed information to make promotion, wage and salary, training and development, and career planning decisions. Recently, there has been pressure applied by the federal government to play down the role of performance evaluation in making various decisions. The government wants Sebring to initiate affirmative action to promote more females, blacks, and Chicanos. Presently, of the 96 managerial personnel in the Baton Rouge facility, only 6 were female, 3 were black, and 2 were Chicano.

The six employees being considered for the two supervisory vacancies are considered the best within the company for the promotions. They are:

Tony Santos: Chicano; age 37; married; 4 children; 2 years college;
    9 years with Sebring.

Barbara Golding: White, age 32; married; 1 child; 3 years college;
    6 years with Sebring.

Mark Petro: White; age 38; married; 2 children; 1 year college;
    7 years with Sebring.

Denny Slago: White; age 39; single; high school graduate;
    10 years with Sebring.

Bobby Green: Black; age 38; married; 2 years college;
    8 years with Sebring.

George Nelson: White; age 40; single; 3 years college;
    7 years with Sebring.

The performance records of these six individuals have been carefully scrutinized. Average performance over a two-year period is presented in Exhibit A. These data are being weighed heavily by the committee to make the final choices.

Exercise Procedures   Phase I: 40 to 60 minutes
1. Each group is to select two employees for the promotions. A group consensus should be the final step in reaching agreement. The group should also develop a statement supporting their decision.
2. The group decisions should be placed on a board or chart in front of all class members and discussed.

EXHIBIT A

Two-Year Performance Evaluation of Six Top Candidates for Promotion

Candidate for Promotion	Objective Performance Dimensions*				Subjective Performance Dimensions			
	Quantity†	Quality‡ %	Cost§	Absences‖ (unexcused %)	Develops Assistants	Potential for Promotion	Cooperative Attitude	Communication Skills
Tony Santos	138.7	87.4	1.61	5.1	Good	Good	Fair	Good
Barbara Golding	106.4	85.8	1.74	8.1	Good	Good	Good	Fair
Mark Petro	110.8	89.6	1.39	6.2	Good	Good	Good	Excellent
Denny Slago	165.7	94.6	1.02	3.0	Excellent	Excellent	Good	Good
Bobby Green	120.8	86.8	1.41	5.9	Excellent	Good	Fair	Good
George Nelson	169.7	95.1	1.00	2.1	Good	Good	Excellent	Good

*The quantity, quality, and cost measures are weekly averages. The absence indicator is the average of four six-month periods of review.
† Higher mean score indicates more quantity.
‡ Higher mean score indicates better quality.
§ Lower mean score indicates better cost control.
‖ Lower mean score indicates better absence record.

Phase II: 40 minutes

1. Assume that Barbara Golding and Bobby Green were selected for the promotion.

2. Select two people from the class to role play an interview between the chairperson of the promotion committee and Denny Slago.

3. Denny is concerned about the decision and is very upset about not being selected. The committee chairperson's role is to explain to Denny why he was not selected.

4. If possible, use two different role-play groups. Have one group wait outside of the room during the first role play. In one role play have a woman play the role of the chairperson. In the second role play, have a woman act out the role of Denny.

5. As a class, consider the impact of any promotion decision at Sebring on the four employees who were not selected. Also consider whether any performance evaluation program would make the Sebring decision any easier.

Chapter 17

Reward Processes

AN ORGANIZATIONAL ISSUE FOR DEBATE
The Pay for Performance Controversy

ARGUMENT FOR

Merit pay or "pay for job performance" as a basis for rewarding employees is a widely accepted management practice. Although some argue about the relative importance of pay compared with other extrinsic and intrinsic rewards, there is general agreement in management circles that pay is an important reward for most employees. If two employees are hired to perform the same job and one is a better performer, surely the high performer should be paid more for his or her superior performance.

Almost all managerial employees and many non-managers are paid using a merit pay system. One alternative is to set a minimum level of pay for each job and then provide incremental increases until an upper level of compensation is reached. This approach is criticized because it has little motivational power. Under such a plan an employee is rewarded with pay increases simply for attending and staying on the job. Under a pay for performance plan, the highest performers receive the largest increases and the poorest performers receive the smallest or no increases at all. Thus, management has available a "carrot" or a "'stick" to motivate better performance. The "carrot" is used for high performers and the "stick" is applied to low performers.

ARGUMENT AGAINST

Despite the logical attractiveness of the pay for performance plan, experience shows clearly that it is a pipe dream. Typically, managers do not discriminate and give small rewards to individuals in the same job, regardless of performance differences.

A major problem with merit pay plans is the fact that an employee's increases are based primarily on supervisory judgments. It is assumed that a supervisor can make reliable and valid distinctions between individual job performances. Who actually accepts the judgments of others about personal matters such as job performance? Are the judgments really reliable and valid?

Another problem with the pay for performance approach is that it forces employees to compete for rewards. Since pay dollars are limited, a system of paying for performance forces employees to think in win-lose terms. "If I win a raise, someone else loses a raise." Unfortunately, this mentality is usually detrimental to organizational effectiveness.

After performance evaluation occurs, managers distribute various rewards to employees. The manner and timing of distributing rewards are important issues that managers must address almost daily. Managers distribute such rewards as pay, transfers, promotions, praise, and recognition. They can also help create the climate that results in more challenging and satisfying jobs. Because these rewards are considered important by employees, they have significant effects on behavior and performance. In this chapter we are concerned with how rewards are distributed by managers. The reactions of people to rewards are also discussed. We also examine the response of employees to rewards received in organizational settings. Administrating rewards is another topic reviewed. The role of rewards in organizational membership, absenteeism, turnover, and commitment is presented.

To attract people to join the organization, to keep coming to work, and to motivate them to perform at high levels, managers reward employees. Employees exchange their time, ability, skills, and effort for valued rewards. This relationship between the organization and its employees has been called the psychological contract. Schein states the psychological contract as follows.

> The individual has a variety of expectations of the organization and the organization a variety of expectations of him or her. These expectations not only cover how much work is to be performed for how much pay, but also involves the whole pattern of rights, privileges, and obligations between the worker and the organization.[1]

A MODEL OF INDIVIDUAL REWARDS

■ A model that illustrates how rewards fit into the overall policies and programs of an organization could prove useful to managers. The main objectives of reward programs are (1) to attract qualified people to join the organization; (2) to keep employees coming to work, and (3) to motivate employees to achieve high levels of performance. Figure 17–1 presents a model that attempts to integrate satisfaction, motivation, performance, and rewards. Reading the model from left to right suggests that the motivation to exert effort is not enough to cause acceptable performance. Performance results from a combination of effort and the level of ability, skill, and experience of an individual. The performance results of the individual are evaluated either formally or informally by management. As a result of the evaluation, two types of rewards can be distributed, intrinsic, or extrinsic. The rewards are evaluated by the individual. To the extent that the rewards are satisfactory and equitable, the individual achieves a level of satisfaction.

---

[1]Edgar H. Schein, *Organizational Psychology* (Englewood Cliffs, N.J.: Prentice-Hall, 1970), p. 12.

FIGURE 17–1
The Reward Process

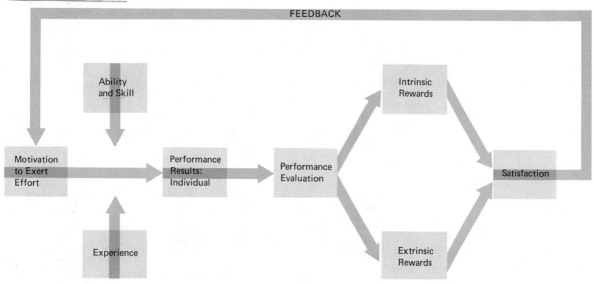

REWARDS AND	■ A significant amount of research has been done on what determines
SATISFACTION	whether individuals will be satisfied with rewards. Lawler has concisely

summarized five conclusions based on the behavioral science research literature. They are:

1. *Satisfaction with a reward is a function of both how much is received and how much the individual feels should be received.* This conclusion has as its basis the comparisons that people make. When individuals receive less than they feel they should there is some dissatisfaction.

2. *An individual's feelings of satisfaction are influenced by comparisons with what happens to others.* People tend to compare their efforts, skills, seniority, and job performance with those of others. They then attempt to compare rewards. That is, they examine inputs (their own) with inputs of others relative to the rewards received.

3. *Satisfaction is influenced by how satisfied employees are with both intrinsic and extrinsic rewards.* There is some debate among researchers whether intrinsic or extrinsic rewards are more important in determining job satisfaction. The debate has not been settled because most studies suggest that both types of rewards are important. One clear message from the research is that extrinsic and intrinsic rewards satisfy different needs.

4. *People differ in the rewards they desire and in how important different rewards are to them.* Individuals differ on what rewards they prefer. In fact, at different points in a person's career, at different ages, and in various situations preferred rewards vary.

5. *Some extrinsic rewards are satisfying because they lead to other rewards.* There are some extrinsic rewards that lead to other more preferred re-

wards. For example, the size of a person's office or whether the office has carpet or drapes often is considered a reward because it indicates the individual's status and power. Money is a reward that leads to other things such as prestige, autonomy and independence, security, and shelter.[2]

The relationship between rewards and satisfaction is not perfectly understood, nor is it static in nature. It changes because people and the environment change. There are, however, some important considerations that managers could use to develop and distribute rewards. First, there must be enough rewards available so that basic human needs are satisfied. Federal legislation, union contracts, and managerial fairness have provided at least minimal rewards in most work settings. Second, individuals tend to compare their rewards with others. If inequities are perceived, dissatisfaction will occur. Regardless of the quantity of rewards individuals receive, people make comparisons. Finally, managers distributing rewards must recognize individual differences. Unless individual differences are considered, it is likely that the reward process will invariably be less effective than desired. Any reward package should be sufficient to (1) satisfy basic needs (e.g., food, shelter, clothing), (2) be considered equitable, and (3) be individually oriented.[3] An interesting approach to rewarding employees is presented in the following close-up.

ORGANIZATIONS: CLOSE-UP

Sheraton's "Superstar" Program

The Sheraton Corporation is in the hotel business. Management of the firm knows that when employees do not perform, guests do not receive necessary services. Thus management wanted to identify the employees who were superperformers and reward them. They wanted these employees to know that management cared about them and recognized when they did a good job.

The result of management's concern was the Superstar program. Hotel guests are given a "star card" when they check in, at the food and beverage outlets, and in their rooms so they can vote for the most efficient and pleasant employees. The votes are totaled monthly, and a total of 20 superstars are chosen. The winners are announced at a monthly meeting and awarded a certificate and $100.

A super, superstar employee of the month is chosen from the 20 finalists and is awarded a $100 check and a trophy. At the end of the year 1 of the 12 monthly winners is selected as the employee of the year and receives a $1,000 check and a trophy.

In addition to the monthly employee meetings, superstar winners are announced in the superstar newsletter. This again calls specific attention to the

[2]Edward E. Lawler III. "Reward Systems," in *Improving Life at Work*, eds. J. Richard Hackman and J. Lloyd Suttle (Santa Monica, Calif.: Goodyear Publishing, 1977), pp. 163–226.

[3]Ibid., p. 168.

> **ORGANIZATIONS: CLOSE-UP** (continued)
>
> best performers at Sheraton. The superstar performance and special reward program is now in its second year of operation and going strong. Management is satisfied with the results, and most employees are satisfied that the program is fair and meaningful.
>
> Source: "Superstars at Sheraton," *Personnel Journal*, February 1981, p. 104.

INTRINSIC AND EXTRINSIC REWARDS

■ The rewards shown in Figure 17–1 are classified into two broad categories, *extrinsic* and *intrinsic*. Whether we are discussing extrinsic or intrinsic rewards it is important to first consider the rewards *valued* by the person. An individual will put forth little effort unless the reward has *value*. Both extrinsic and intrinsic rewards can have value.[4]

Extrinsic Rewards

Financial Rewards: Salary and Wages. Money is a major extrinsic reward. It has been said that "although it is generally agreed that money is the major mechanism for rewarding and modifying behavior in industry . . . very little is known about how it works."[5] To really understand how money modifies behavior, the perceptions and preferences of a person being rewarded must be understood. Of course, this is a challenging task for a manager to complete successfully. It requires careful attention and observation of the person. In addition, the manager must be trusted so that the person will communicate his or her feelings about financial rewards.

Many organizations utilize some type of incentive pay plan to motivate employees. Lawler presents the most comprehensive summary of various pay plans and their effectiveness as motivators.[6] Each plan is evaluated on the basis of the following questions:

1. How effective is it in creating the perception that pay is related to performance?
2. How well does it minimize the perceived negative consequences of good performance?
3. How well does it contribute to the perception that important rewards other than pay (e.g., praise and interest shown in the employee by a respected superior) result in good performance? A summary of Lawler's ideas is presented in Table 17–1.

---

[4]Richard A. Guzzo, "Type of Rewards, Cognitions, and Work Motivation," *Academy of Management Review*, January 1979, pp. 75–86.

[5]R. L. Opsahl and M. D. Dunnette, "The Role of Financial Compensation in Industrial Motivation," *Psychological Bulletin*, August 1966, p. 114.

[6]Edward L. Lawler III, *Pay and Organizational Effectiveness* (New York: McGraw-Hill, 1971), pp. 164–70.

TABLE 17–1
Evaluation of Pay-Incentive Plans in Organizations

Type of Pay Plan	Performance Criteria	Perceived Pay Performance Linkage	Minimization of Negative Consequences	Perceived Relationship between Other Rewards and Performance
Salary plan				
For individuals	Productivity	Good	Neutral	Neutral
	Cost effectiveness	Fair	Neutral	Neutral
	Superiors' rating	Fair	Neutral	Fair
For group.................	Productivity	Fair	Neutral	Fair
	Cost effectiveness	Fair	Neutral	Fair
	Superiors' rating	Fair	Neutral	Fair
For total organization	Productivity	Fair	Neutral	Fair
	Cost effectiveness	Fair	Neutral	Fair
	Profits	Neutral	Neutral	Fair
Bonus plan				
For individuals	Productivity	Excellent	Poor	Neutral
	Cost effectiveness	Good	Poor	Neutral
	Superiors' rating	Good	Poor	Fair
For group.................	Productivity	Good	Neutral	Fair
	Cost effectiveness	Good	Neutral	Fair
	Superiors' rating	Good	Neutral	Fair
For total organization	Productivity	Good	Neutral	Fair
	Cost effectiveness	Good	Neutral	Fair
	Profits	Fair	Neuttal	Fair

Source: Adapted from Edward E. Lawler III, *Pay and Organizational Effectiveness* (New York: McGraw-Hill, 1971). Table 9–3, p. 165.

By looking at each criteria separately, some interesting patterns evolve. The individual salary and bonus plans seem to be best if management is attempting to link pay and performance. The least effective way of accomplishing this is to implement a total organizational salary plan. This makes sense because the individual may not perceive his or her impact on organizational outcomes such as productivity, cost effectiveness, and profits.

The bonus plans are generally more effective than the salary plans. This is especially noticeable for the first objective of linking pay and performance. Bonus plans typically are related to the current performance of employees. Salary plans, on the other hand, are often related to past performance. Neither pay plan minimizes the potential negative consequences of linking pay and performance. Perhaps it is futile to think about developing a perfect pay plan.

If management is attempting to relate nonpay rewards to performance, the group and total organization plans seem better suited than individual plans. In essence, if people believe that other rewards stem from performance, they would tend to encourage improved performance among peers throughout the organization.

This discussion should clearly illustrate that no one plan can accomplish every desirable objective. The evidence indicates that bonus plans, where they can be used, are generally the best type of salary or wage plan. Individually based plans also seem to be superior to group and organizational plans.

Financial Rewards: Fringe Benefits. In most cases fringe benefits are primarily financial. There are some cases, however, such as IBM's recreation program for employees and General Mills' picnic grounds that are not entirely financial. The major financial fringe benefit in most organizations is the pension plan. For most employees, the opportunity to participate in the pension plan is a valued reward. Fringe benefits such as pension plans, hospitalization, and vacations are not usually contingent on the performance accomplishments of employees. In most cases fringe benefit plans are based on seniority or attendance.

Interpersonal Rewards. The manager has some power to distribute such interpersonal rewards as status and recognition. By assigning individuals to prestigious jobs, the manager can attempt to improve or remove the status a person possesses. However, if co-workers do not believe a person merits a particular job, it is likely that status will not be enhanced. Managers by reviewing performance can grant what they consider to be improved status job changes in some situations. The manager and co-workers both play a role in granting job status.

Much of what was just stated about status applies also to recognition. In a reward context *recognition* refers to acknowledging employee achievement that could result in improved status. Recognition from a manager could include public praise, expressions of a job well done, or receiving special attention. The extent to which recognition is motivating depends, as do most rewards, on its perceived value and on the connection the individual sees between it and behavior.[7]

Promotions. For many employees, promotion does not happen often; some never experience it in their careers. The manager making a promotion reward decision attempts to match the right person with the job. The criteria that are often used to reach promotion decisions are performance or seniority. Performance, if it can be accurately assessed, is often given significant weight in promotion reward allocations.

Intrinsic Rewards

Completion. The ability to start and finish a project or job is important to some individuals. These people value what is called *task completion*. The completion of a task and its effect on a person is a form of self-reward. Some people have a need to complete tasks. Opportunities that allow such people to complete tasks can have a powerful motivating effect.

Achievement. Achievement is a self-administered reward that is derived when a person reaches a challenging goal. McClelland has found that

---

[7]Lyman W. Porter, "Turning Work into Nonwork: The Rewarding Environment," in M. D. Dunnette, *Work and Nonwork in the Year 2001* (Belmont, Calif.: Wadsworth, 1973), p. 113.

there are individual differences in striving for achievement.[8] Some individuals seek challenging goals, while others tend to accomplish moderate or low goals. In goal-setting programs it has been proposed that difficult goals result in a higher level of individual performance than do moderate goals. However, even in such programs individual differences must be considered before reaching conclusions about the importance of achievement rewards.

Autonomy. There are some people who want jobs that provide them with the right and privilege to make decisions and operate without being closely supervised. A feeling of autonomy could result from the freedom to do what the employee considers best in a particular situation. In jobs that are highly structured and controlled by management, it is difficult to create tasks that employees would consider as leading to a feeling of autonomy.

Personal Growth. The personal growth of any individual is a unique experience. A person who is personally growing senses his or her development and can see how capabilities are being expanded. By expanding capabilities a person is able to maximize or at least satisfy skill potential. If some people are not allowed or encouraged to develop their skills they often become dissatisfied with their jobs and organizations.

Those rewards included in this section are distributed or created by managers, work groups, or the individual. Table 17–2 summarizes the rewards we have discussed. As the table indicates the manager can play either a direct and an indirect role in developing and administering the rewards.

REWARDS AND JOB PERFORMANCE

■ There is agreement among behavioralists and managers that extrinsic and intrinsic rewards can be used to motivate job performance. It is also clear that certain conditions must exist if rewards are to motivate good job performance: they must be *valued* by the person and they must be related to the level of job performance that is to be motivated.[9]

In Chapter 4 expectancy motivation theory was presented. It was stated that according to the theory, every behavior has associated with it (in a person's mind), certain outcomes or rewards or punishments. In other words, an assembly-line worker believes that if he or she behaves in a certain way, he or she will get certain things. This is a description of the *performance-outcome expectancy.* The worker may expect that a steady performance of 10 units a day will eventually result in a transfer to a more challenging job. On the other hand, a worker may expect that the steady 10 units a day performance will result in being considered a "rate buster" by co-workers.

Each outcome has a *valence* or value to the person. Outcomes such as pay, promotion, a reprimand, or a better job have different values for dif-

---

[8]David C. McClelland, *The Achieving Society* (New York: D. Van Nostrand, 1961).

[9]Lyman W. Porter, Edward E. Lawler III, and J. Richard Hackman, *Behavior in Organizations* (New York: McGraw-Hill, 1975), p. 352.

TABLE 17–2

Types and Sources of Some Popular Extrinsic and Intrinsic Rewards

Type	Source of Reward		
	Manager	Group	Individual
I. Extrinsic			
A. Financial			
1. Salary and wages	D		
2. Fringe benefits	D		
B. Interpersonal	D	D	
C. Promotion	D		
II. Intrinsic			
A. Completion	I		D
B. Achievement	I		D
C. Autonomy	I		D
D. Personal growth	I		D

D = The direct source of the reward.
I = The indirect source of the reward.

ferent people. This occurs because each person has different needs and perceptions. Thus, in considering which rewards to use, a manager has to be astute at considering individual differences. If valued rewards are used to motivate they can result in the exertion of effort to achieve high levels of performance.

ADMINISTERING REWARDS

■ Managers are faced with the decision of how to administer rewards. Three major theoretical approaches to reward administration are: (1) positive reinforcement, (2) modeling and social imitation, and (3) expectancy.[10]

Positive Reinforcement

As discussed in Chapter 5, in administering a positive reinforcement program, the emphasis is on the desired behavior that leads to job performance, rather than performance alone. The basic foundation of administering rewards through positive reinforcement is the relationship between behavior and its consequences. Consequences are viewed as outcomes in an employee's environment related to the demonstration of certain behaviors. If the consequence increases the occurrence of a behavior it is called a reinforcer. If a manager can identify behavior that leads to high levels of performance, select the most effective positive reinforcers that shape the behavior, and distribute the reinforcers on some form of effective schedule, job performance can be improved.

While positive reinforcement can be a useful method to shape desired behavior, other considerations concerning the type of reward schedule to

---

[10]Porter, "Turning Work into Nonwork," p. 122, suggests three approaches. He introduces operant conditioning. We believe that when rewards are being discussed positive reinforcement should be used.

use are also important. We have already discussed schedules of positive reinforcement in both Chapters 4 and 5. Suffice it to say that managers should explore the possible consequences of different types of reward schedules for individuals. It is important to know how employees respond to continuous, fixed interval, and fixed ratio schedules. In addition, managers could benefit from understanding how individuals respond to different forms of monetary and nonmonetary positive reinforcers.

Modeling and Social Imitation [11]

There is little doubt that many human skills and behaviors are learned by observational learning or, simply, imitation. This form of learning was presented in Chapter 3.[12] Observational learning equips a person to duplicate a response, but whether it is actually imitated depends on whether the model person was rewarded or punished for particular behaviors. If a person is to be motivated he or she must observe models receiving reinforcements that are valued.

In other to use modeling to administer rewards, managers would need to determine who responds to this approach. In addition, selecting appropriate models would be a necessary step. Finally, the context in which modeling occurs needs to be considered. That is, if high performance is the goal and it is almost impossible to achieve because of limited resources, the manager should conclude that modeling is not appropriate. Some managers using modeling have attempted to force it on employees when the situation did not warrant such an approach. Managers must judge the appropriateness of using modeling to administer rewards.

Expectancy Theory

Expectancy-theory is incorporated in Figure 17–1. It states that the effort expended by an employee to perform a job is a joint function of both the *value* the person attaches to obtaining rewards (extrinsic and intrinsic) and the expectation (perceived chance or probability) that a specific level of energy will be enough to receive the reward.

The expectancy approach like the other two methods of administering rewards requires managerial action. Managers must determine the kinds of rewards employees desire and do whatever is possible to distribute them or create conditions so that what is available in the form of rewards can be applied. In some situations it is just not possible to provide the rewards that are valued and preferred. Therefore, managers often have to increase the desirability of other available rewards.

A manager can and often will use principles from each of the three methods of administering rewards—positive reinforcement, modeling, and expectancy. Each of these methods indicates that job performance of employees is a result of the application of effort. To generate the effort to

---

[11] The discussion of Porter, "Turning Work into Nonwork," stimulated the development of this section.

[12] A. Bandura and R. H. Walters, *Social Learning and Personality Development* (New York: Holt, Rinehart & Winston, 1963).

perform, managers could use positive reinforcers, modeling, and expectations to get the job done. It should be remembered that performance may never be satisfactorily accomplished if employees are deficient in problem-solving skills, specific abilities, and experience. To get the most from administering rewards a manager needs to have employees that have the ability, skill, and experience to perform.

REWARDS AND ORGANIZATIONAL MEMBERSHIP

■ As stated earlier a major objective of a reward system is to attract people to join or become members of an organization. This involves people making organizational and job choices. The notion of how an individual moves from outside to inside an organization is called *organizational entry*.[13] There are a number of research studies that examine the organizational entry decisions of employees. Most of these studies indicate that people are attracted to organizations which are rated highest on the individuals' expectations about what the organization will be like and their goals and values. It appears that people will choose the organization which they believe will result in the best set of outcomes or rewards. This behavior seems reasonable because being able to obtain valued rewards leads to high levels of satisfaction.

In an interesting study of job choice, individuals were asked to rate the jobs they were considering in terms of their chances of achieving a number of goals. These individuals were also asked to rank the goals in order of importance. The data showed that these individuals were attracted to organizations that were seen as being instrumental for the attainment of their preferred goals.[14]

The attraction of members to an organization depends to some extent on how people in the external market view the possible rewards offered by the organization. If the reward image of the company is clear and people value the potential rewards there will be attraction. Just as rewards can be used to attract people to join, they can and are used to motivate individuals to remain with the organization.

REWARDS AND TURNOVER AND ABSENTEEISM

■ Some managers assume that low turnover is a mark of an effective organization. This view is somewhat controversial because a high quit rate means more expense for an organization. However, some organizations would benefit if disruptive and low performers quit. Thus, the issue of turnover needs to focus on the *frequency* and on *who* is leaving.

---

[13] John P. Wanous, "Organizational Entry: The Individual's Viewpoint," in *Perspectives on Behavior in Organizations*, ed. J. Richard Hackman, Edward E. Lawler III, and Lyman W. Porter (New York: McGraw-Hill, 1977), pp. 126–35; and John P. Wanous, *Organizational Entry* (Reading, Mass.: Addison-Wesley Publishing, 1979).

[14] Victor H. Vroom, "Organizational Choice: A Study of Pre- and Post-Decision Processes," *Organizational Behavior and Human Performance*, December 1966, pp. 212–25.

Ideally if managers could develop reward systems that retained the best performers and caused poor performers to leave, the overall effectiveness of an organization would improve. To approach this ideal state an equitable and favorably compared reward system must exist. The feeling of *equity* and *favorable comparison* has an external orientation. That is, the equity of rewards and favorableness involves comparisons to external parties. This orientation is used because quitting most often means that a person leaves one organization for an alternative elsewhere. Of course, if an organization had an endless stream of extrinsic and intrinsic rewards and could increase the level of rewards distributed, high performers could usually be retained. This is a very costly reward strategy that most organizations are not able to afford.

There is no perfect means for retaining high performers. It appears that a reward system that is based on *merit* should encourage most of the better performers to remain with an organization. There also has to be some differential in the reward system that discriminates between high and low performers. The point being that the high performers must receive significantly more extrinsic and intrinsic rewards than the low performers.

Absenteeism, no matter for what reason, is a costly and disruptive problem facing managers. It is costly because it reduces output and disruptive because schedules and programs must be modified. It is estimated that absenteeism in the United States results in over 400 million workdays lost per year, or about 5.1 days per employee.[15] Employees attend work because they are motivated to do so. The level of motivation will remain high if an individual feels that attendance will lead to more valued rewards and fewer negative consequences than alternative behaviors.

There has been some research on reward systems and attendance. In an interesting study, researchers used a poker incentive plan to improve attendance. Each day as an employee came to work and was on time, he was allowed to select one card from a regular playing deck. At the end of a five-day week, the employees who attended every day on time would have a regular five-card hand. The highest hand won $20.[16] There were eight winners, one for each department. This plan seemed to result in a decrease of absenteeism of 18.7 percent. This study did not compare the poker incentive plan with any other system, so whether it would be better than some other reward system is not known. However, it was better than when no bonus or prize was distributed for attendance.

Another study reported the effects of an employee-developed bonus plan on attendance. Three work groups developed a plan that offered a cash bonus to workers who attended work regularly.[17] The result indicated that

---

[15] Richard M. Steers and Susan R. Rhodes, "A New Look at Absenteeism," *Personnel*, November–December 1980, pp. 60–65.

[16] E. Pedalino and V. Gamboa, "Behavior Modification and Absenteeism: Intervention in One Industrial Setting," *Journal of Applied Psychology*, December 1974, pp. 694–98.

[17] Edward E. Lawler III and J. Richard Hackman, "The Impact of Employee Participation in the Development of Pay Incentive Plans: A Field Experiment," *Journal of Applied Psychology*, December 1969, pp. 467–71.

job attendance improved significantly. Further data from the study showed what happens when a plan developed by some individuals is imposed on other people. The plan developed by the three groups was applied to two other groups in the organization. The findings indicated that it was not effective in reducing absenteeism. The success of a reward plan involving employee participation was linked to where the plan was developed.

Managers appear to have some influence over attendance behavior. They have the ability to punish, establish bonus systems, and allow employee participation in developing plans. Whether any of these or other approaches will reduce absenteeism is determined by the value of the rewards perceived by employees, the amount of the reward, and whether employees perceive a relationship between attendance and rewards. These same same characteristics appear every time we analyze the effects of rewards on organizational behavior.

REWARDS AND ORGANIZATIONAL COMMITMENT

■ There is little research on the relationship between rewards and organizational commitment. *Commitment* to an organization involves three attitudes: (1) a sense of identification with the organization's goals; (2) a feeling of involvement in organizational duties; and (3) a feeling of loyalty for the organization.[18] There are indications that commitment, or rather its absence, can reduce organizational effectiveness. People who are committed are less likely to quit and accept other jobs. Thus, the costs of high turnover are not incurred. In addition, committed and highly skilled employees require less supervision. A system of close supervision and rigid monitoring control process is time consuming and costly. Furthermore, a committed employee perceives the value and importance of integrating individual and organizational goals. The employee thinks of his or her goals and the organization's in personal terms.

A study of upper middle managers in large organizations reported some of the organizational rewards that significantly influence commitment. Some of these rewards were:

> **Personal Importance.**   The experience of being considered a valuable and productive member of an organization.
>
> **Realization of Expectations.**   Those managers who were able to fulfill expectations because the organization fulfilled its promises reported more commitment.
>
> **Job Challenge.**   Challenging, interesting, and self-rewarding job assignments appeared to strengthen commitment. The study also found that the job experience in the first year continued to shape the attitudes of managers into the future.

Intrinsic rewards are important for the development of organizational commitment. Organizations able to meet employee needs by providing achievement opportunities and by recognizing achievement when it occurs

---

[18]Bruce Buchanan, "To Walk an Extra Mile: The Whats, Whens, and Whys of Organizational Commitment," *Organizational Dynamics*, Spring 1975, pp. 67–80.

have a significant impact on commitment. Thus, managers need to develop intrinsic reward systems which focus on personal importance or self-esteem, integrating individual and organizational goals, and designing jobs that are challenging.

SELECTED REWARD SYSTEMS

■ The typical list of rewards that managers can and do distribute in organizations has been discussed above. We all know that pay, fringe benefits, and opportunities to achieve challenging goals are considered rewards by most people. It is also generally accepted that rewards are administered by managers through such processes as reinforcement, modeling, and expectancies. What are some of the newer, yet largely untested reward programs which some managers are experimenting with? Three different and largely untested approaches to rewards are cafeteria fringe benefits, banking time off, and paying all employees a salary.

Cafeteria-Style Fringe Benefits

A cafeteria-style fringe benefit plan involves management placing an upper limit on how much the organization is willing to spend. The employee is then asked to decide how he or she would like to receive the total fringe benefit amount. The employee is able to develop a personally attractive fringe benefit package. Some employees take all of the fringes in cash or purchase special medical protection plans. The cafeteria plan provides individuals with the benefits they prefer rather than what someone else establishes for them. A cafeteria-style program is discussed in the following close-up.

ORGANIZATIONS: CLOSE-UP

American Can's Benefits Program

American Can Company now has nearly 9,000 salaried employees who design their own personal benefits package. The company provides a core of nonoptional benefits and then employees can select from a group of options on the basis of flexible "credits" that are allocated to each participant in the plan. Employees enrolled in the program are also able to buy additional benefits through payroll deductions.

American Can keeps a close watch on how employees spend their money. Management at first feared that they would find employees making foolish choices. However, the profile of how the benefits are selected is really fairly predictable. Young single employees take more time off. So do married women, who usually want the same number of vacation days as their husbands. Those with young families tend to choose more medical and life insurance coverage. Older employees are more concerned with savings, first for their children's education and later, as their children leave home, for their retirement.

Benefit options can be changed once a year. In September, every employee

```
┌─────────────────────────────────────────────────────────────────┐
│ ORGANIZATION: CLOSE-UP (continued)                                │
```

ORGANIZATION: CLOSE-UP (*continued*)

receives a form stating his or her existing program and the credits earned. Employees may then choose to remain with the same options or elect completely different options. Changes go into effect January 1.

Since the program has been in effect employees seem to understand their benefits much more than they used to. A survey conducted before the flexible benefits program was introduced showed little understanding among the employees about benefits. Many employees believed that the benefits had little value. However, since the plan was implemented employees now recognize the significant value of their benefits. They also discuss the fringe benefits thoroughly with spouses. The American Can program has certainly made employees aware of and interested in fringe benefits.

Source: Gerard Tavernier, "How American Can Manages Its Flexible Benefits Program," *Management Review*, August 1980, pp. 9–13.

There are some administrative problems associated with cafeteria plans.[19] Because of the different preferences of employees, records become more complicated. For a large organization with a cafeteria plan, a computer system is almost essential to do the record keeping. Another problem involves receiving group insurance premium rates. Most life and medical insurance premiums are based on the number of employees participating. It is difficult to determine what the participation level will be under a cafeteria plan.

TRW Corporation has placed approximately 12,000 employees on a cafeteria plan. It allows employees to rearrange and redistribute their fringe benefit packages every year. Over 80 percent of the TRW participants changed their benefit packages since the plan was initiated.[20]

Banking Time Off

A *time-off* feature is attractive to most people. In essence, most companies have a time-off system built into their vacation programs. Employees receive different amounts of time off based on the number of years worked for the organization. An extension of such a time-off reward could be granted for certain levels of performance. That is, a bank of time-off credits could be built up contingent on performance achievements. Some organizations today are selecting their best performers to attend educational and training programs.

One company in Houston selects the best performers and provides them with an opportunity to attend an executive educational program. Being el-

---

[19]James H. Shea, "Cautions about Cafeteria-Style Benefit Plans," *Personnel Journal*, January 1981, pp. 37.

[20]Lawler, "Reward Systems," p. 182.

igible is largely contingent on the performance record of the individual. Those finally selected are given two Fridays off a month to attend classes.

The All-Salaried Team

In most organizations managers are paid salaries and nonmanagers receive hourly wages. The practice of paying all employees a salary is supposed to improve loyalty, commitment, and self-esteem. The notion of being a part of a team is projected by the salary-for-everyone practice. One benefit of the all-salary practice considered important by nonmanagers is the elimination of punching a time clock. To date rigorous investigations of the influence, if any, of an all-salary practice are not available. It does seem to have promise when applied to some employees.

The link between the performance evaluation system and reward distribution was shown in Figure 17–1. The discussion of this and other linkages in the reward process suggest the complexity of using rewards to motivate better performance. Managers need to use judgment, diagnosis, and the resources available to reward their subordinates. As shown, administering rewards is perhaps one of the most challenging and frustrating tasks that managers must perform.

MAJOR MANAGERIAL ISSUES

A. The major objectives of the reward processes are to attract people to join the organization, to keep them coming to work, and to motivate them to perform at high levels.

B. It is general knowledge that there are certain reward process issues that should be addressed if any objectives are to be accomplished. Namely, there must be enough rewards to satisfy basic needs, people make comparisons between what rewards they receive and what others receive, and individual differences in reward preferences are important issues for consideration.

C. Management can and must distribute both extrinsic and intrinsic rewards. *Extrinsic* rewards are those that are external to the job such as promotions, fringe benefits, and pay. *Intrinsic* rewards are associated with doing the job. They include responsibility, challenge, and meaningful work.

D. If extrinsic and/or intrinsic rewards are to motivate good job performance, they must be *valued* by the employee and linked to the level of performance that is expected.

E. Managers have many means available for administering extrinsic and intrinsic rewards. Three of the most popular methods include positive reinforcement, modeling, and applying expectancy theory principles.

F. Rewards, if used effectively, can affect such organizational behaviors as membership, turnover, absenteeism, and commitment. The research evidence showing how rewards influence these behaviors is still rather limited.

> **MAJOR MANAGERIAL ISSUES** (continued)
>
> G. Some newer and different reward strategies used by managers include cafeteria-style fringe benefits, banking time off, and an all-salaried work force.
>
> H. The reward process is complex but extremely important in encouraging, sustaining, and developing organizational effectiveness and individual job performance.

DISCUSSION AND REVIEW QUESTIONS

1. Most managers use an array of rewards and punishment to accomplish desired outcomes. However, most systems are designed around a number of features such as merit, seniority, or attendance. Why is it almost impossible to distribute rewards on the basis of merit?

2. Develop a list of extrinsic and intrinsic rewards that are important to you. What kind of organization and job would be able to provide you with these rewards?

3. Have you ever been rewarded by modeling? Present a personal experience that shows how modeling influenced you.

4. The timing of receiving a reward is especially important when implementing positive reinforcement? Why?

5. Herzberg contends that pay is basically an extrinsic reward. Do you now agree with this premise? Why?

6. What managerial skills and abilities are needed to derive the most benefit from administering rewards?

7. It has been said that distributing rewards carefully and equitably is an investment in the most important organizational resource, people. Do you agree?

8. Some of the newer reward plans like cafeteria fringe benefits and banking time off have not really met the test of science. What type of research is needed to determine whether these kinds of plans are organizationally successful?

9. There are some who believe that no matter how attractive an organization's extrinsic and intrinsic rewards, there will be some employees who remain dissatisfied. What could account for this?

10. If equity and favorable comparisons are so important in reward systems, how can an organization develop a program that is generally viewed as equitable and favorable?

ADDITIONAL REFERENCES

Cook, C. W. "Guidelines for Managing Motivation." *Business Horizons*, 1980, pp. 61–69.

Crystal, G. S.   Pay for Performance—Even If It's Just Luck." *The Wall Street Journal*, March 2, 1981, p. 16.

Ellig, B. R. "Perquisites: The Intrinsic Form of Pay." *Personnel*, 1981, pp. 23–31.

Flamion, A. "The Dollars and Sense of Motivation." *Personnel Journal*, 1980, p. 51–52, 61.

Hammer, T. H., and S. D. Bacharach, eds. *Reward Systems and Power Distribution in Organizations: Searching for Solutions.* New York: Cornell University, 1977. "How to Earn Well— Pay." *Business Week*, June 12, 1978, pp. 143–46.

Kerr, S. "On the Folly of Rewarding A, While Hoping for B." *Academy of Management Journal,* 1975, pp. 769–83.

Latham, G. P.; L. L. Cummings; and T. R. Mitchell. "Behavioral Strategies to Improve Productivity." *Organizational Dynamics,* 1981, pp. 4–23.

Macy, B. A., and P. H. Mirvis. "Measuring Quality of Work and Organizational Effectiveness in Behavioral Economic Terms." *Administrative Science Quarterly,* 1976, pp. 212-26.

Mirvis, P. H., and E. E. Lawler III. "Measuring the Financial Impact of Employee Attitudes." *Journal of Applied Psychology,* 1977, pp. 1–8.

Mobley, W. H.; R. W. Griffeth; H. H. Hand; and B. H.

Meglino. "Review and Conceptual Analysis of the Turnover Process." *Psychological Bulletin,* 1979, pp. 493–522.

Mowday, R. T.; R. M. Steers; and L. W. Porter. "The Measurement of Organizational Commitment." *Journal of Vocational Behavior,* 1979, pp. 224–47.

Pritchard, R. D.; K. M. Campbell; and D. J. Campbell. "Effects of Extrinsic Financial Rewards on Intrinsic Motivation." *Journal of Applied Psychology,* 1977, pp. 9–15.

Salancik, G. R. "Commitment Is Too Easy!" *Organizational Dynamics,* 1977, pp. 62–80.

Smith, C. A. "Lump Sum Increases—A Creditable Change Strategy." *Personnel,* 1979, pp. 59–63.

THE EFFORT, PERFORMANCE, PAY DILEMMA AT JUSTIS CORPORATION

John Hankla is a generator assembler working for the Justis Manufacturing Corporation. The company employes approximately 4,200 nonunionized workers and 495 managerial personnel. Justis manufacturers repair parts and generators which are used for construction equipment.

The assemblers in what has become known as the Arco unit work the day shift and have worked for the company an average of 15 years. Each of the assemblers has worked for the company for at least eight years and is paid an hourly wage. The wage program for assemblers is related primarily to seniority and performance. The new plant manager, Paul Slanker, wants to continue integrating the performance of assemblers with the wage increases that are granted every 12 to 15 months.

The performance of assemblers in the Arco unit is evaluated by the shift foremen, Randy Jones and Paul. They use an evaluation form that focuses on quantity of output, quality control, promptness of completing task assignments, and intragroup aid provided by idle assemblers. The intragroup factor is concerned with the steps taken by assemblers who have completed their work on the generator to help others on the line who have fallen behind for some reason.

The line is a straight flow processing arrangement with six work stations. These stations are arranged as shown in Exhibit 1.

The wages of the 12 assemblers range from $3.98 to $6.25 an hour. Each assembler is trained and able to work at any of the six work stations. They typically work at one station for periods of up to four months and then rotate to another station on the line. Randy and Paul believe that John is without doubt the best performer. He has continually helped others on conveyor 1 and 2 to reduce the backlogs that often occur.

Paul and Randy believe that with current inflationary conditions an increase in pay would be a desirable reward for any of the assemblers. They further believe that competition is a force which needs to be examined carefully, especially with regard to productivity per person. Although Justis has much the same equipment as its two competitors, it is top management's opinion that the performance and the effort expended by Justis's employees are not up to the level of the competition. They want supervisors to improve the effort and performance of their subordinates.

The plan for improving performance focuses on wages. Paul and Randy have decided to raise John's merit increase by 10 percent above any of the other assemblers. They believe that Joyce, Marko, and Tom have the same ability and skill as John, but do not exert the effort needed to perform as well. Pete, Alice, Al, and Mick are just slightly less skilled than the high-skill group but do not seem to be motivated to improve their skill levels. Tony, Mike, Dot, and Will just do not have the same level of skills as the others.

EXHIBIT 1

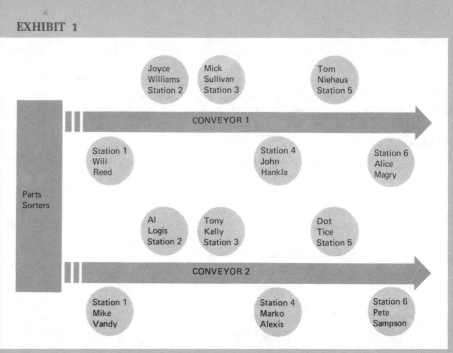

The assemblers, because of their close proximity to each other, often exchange thoughts about the job, the company, the management, and the pay-performance-ability linkage in the organization. This has led to comparisons and in some instances arguments about who is the best worker, the best company person, and the most likely to be promoted to the supervisory level of management. In the past eight years, four people have been promoted to management positions from the Arco unit.

The first person notified about this year's merit increase was Joyce Williams. She received a raise of 4.8 percent. Next, was Tom Niehaus who received a raise of 5.0 percent. The third person was Al Logis who received a raise of 4.4 percent. John was the fourth person notified of the merit increase plus his supplemental increase for superior performance which resulted in a total merit increase of 16.4 percent. The other raises ranged from 4.0 to 6.4 percent.

The notification of merit increases took five weeks to complete. The assembly-line gossip immediately identified a difference between most of the increases and John's. Almost immediately the Arco unit's productivity decreased and its backlogs increased. Its monthly production over the past two years is shown in Exhibit 2; current production is shown by the darker line, last year production is shown by the lighter line.

Although Paul knew he was no statistician the decrease in productivity and the sustained lower level of output between June and October worried him. He called Randy in to discuss the problems in the Arco unit. Paul wanted to work out a motivation plan that would get the unit "pointed in the right direction" again.

EXHIBIT 2

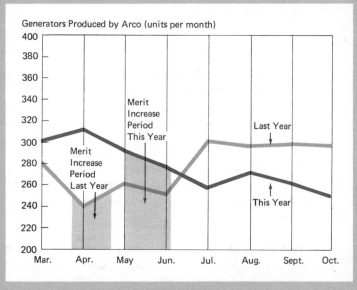

Generators Produced by Arco (units per month)

Questions for Consideration

1. Do you believe that it is possible to think about the problems identified in this situation in terms of a need satisfaction model? Explain.

2. Should the decrease in productivity have been expected by Paul and Randy? Why?

3. Is the type of work performed by the Arco unit suited for the type of performance evaluation and pay plan used by management? Explain.

EXPERIENTIAL EXERCISE

MAKING CHOICES ABOUT REWARDS

Objectives

1. To illustrate individual differences in reward preferences.
2. To emphasize how both extrinsic and intrinsic rewards are considered important.
3. To enable people to explore the reasons for reward preferences of others.

Related Topics

Since rewards are so pervasive in organizational settings, they tend to be linked to merit, seniority, and attendance. In fact, they are so related to organizational behavior that few issues of work life can be discussed without mentioning rewards.

Starting the Exercise

Initially individuals will work alone establishing their own list of reward preferences after reviewing Exhibit A. Then the instructor will set up groups of four to six students to examine individual preferences and complete the exercise.

The Facts

It is possible to develop an endless list of on-the-job rewards. Presented in a random fashion in Exhibit A are some of the rewards that could be available to employees.

EXHIBIT A
Some Possible Rewards for Employees

Company picnics	Recognition	Participation in decisions
Watches	Smile from manager	Stock options
Trophies	Feedback on performance	Vacation trips for
Piped-in music	Feedback on career progress	performance
Job challenge	Larger office	Manager asking for advice
Achievement opportunity	Club privileges	Informal leader asking for
Time-off for performance	More prestigious job	advice
Vacation	More job involvement	Office with a window
Autonomy	Use of company recreation	The privilege to complete a
Pay increase	facilities	job: Start to finish

Exercise Procedures

Phase I: 25 minutes

1. Each individual should set up from Exhibit A a list of extrinsic and intrinsic rewards.
2. Each person should then rank order from most important to least important the two lists.
3. From the two lists rank the *eight* most important rewards. How many are extrinsic and how many are intrinsic?

Phase II: 30 minutes

1. The instructor will set up groups of four to six individuals.
2. The two lists in which the extrinsic and intrinsic categories were developed should be discussed.
3. The final rank orders of the eight most important rewards should be placed on a board or chart at the front of the room.
4. The rankings should be discussed within the groups. What are the major differences displayed?

Chapter 18

Socialization and Career Processes

AN ORGANIZATIONAL ISSUE FOR DEBATE

The Socialization Process Is a Major Contributor to Individual, Group, and Organizational Performance

ARGUMENT FOR *

Proponents of the idea that socialization is a major influence on individual and, consequently, group and organizational performance argue that "socialization shapes the person." The point is made that through socialization activities such as orientation programs, apprenticeships, and job training, individuals learn the skills, behaviors, and attitudes that are necessary to satisfy the organization's demands. They, the proponents, note that socialization activities go on regardless of whether management encourages or discourages the process. They also point out that socialization in organizations is but a special case of learning socially accepted modes of behavior. Socialization is a condition of social living; it occurs in families, schools, and on street corners. It is a natural process and must therefore make significant contributions or else the process would not be so pervasive.

Specifically, the argument that socialization is an important factor rests on three assumptions. First is the assumption that individuals taking on new jobs or positions are in a state of anxiety and

ARGUMENT AGAINST †

The antagonists of socialization do not refute its pervasiveness as a social process. Nor do they deny that socialization is the source of considerable role-related and job-relevant learning. The point to be made is that the impact of socialization on organizational performance variables cannot be generally stated. Considerable empirical research is required to specify the relationship between socialization activities and performance criteria.

Recent research undertaken in a hospital setting indicated that the effects of socialization varied across occupational groups. The sample included engineers, accounting clerks, radiology technicians, nurses' aides, and registered nurses. Each group responded uniquely to the socialization activities it experienced. Generally, however, none of the groups reported any association between specific performance criteria such as work motivation and job involvement and socialization experience. These two criteria are ordinarily considered important aspects of individual performance, and many managerial practices are di-

---

* Based on John Van Maanen, "People Processing: Strategies of Organizational Socialization," *Organizational Dynamics*, Summer 1978, pp. 19–36.

† Based on Daniel C. Feldman, "A Practical Program for Employee Socialization," *Organizational Dynamics*, Winter 1976, pp. 64–80.

ARGUMENT FOR (continued)

desire and seek opportunities for learning the requirements of their new roles. Second, socialization processes go on regardless of management intent; they occur in social settings, and peers actively participate in teaching the newcomer the ways of the organization. Third, the performance of the organization depends upon the contributions of individuals, and as individuals come and go, their roles must be passed on to their successors.

ARGUMENT AGAINST (continued)

rected toward improving them. Yet socialization activities do not seem to affect them significantly.

On the positive side, socialization experiences are related in the study to general satisfaction. This finding has important implications because there is a general relationship between satisfaction and absenteeism and turnover. Thus the argument against socialization reflects not a complete dismissal of its importance; rather it reflects a more modest viewpoint as to what can and should be expected from it.

Socialization is an extremely important organizational process. Through socialization the organization attempts primarily to achieve high levels of individual performance, although group and organizational performance are also enhanced by effective socialization efforts. Specifically, organizational socialization "is the process by which an individual comes to appreciate the values, abilities, expected behaviors, and social knowledge essential for assuming an organizational role and for participating as an organization member."[1] The specific activities of socialization vary among organizations, yet the purpose remains the same: to integrate individual and organizational interests.

From the perspective of the individual, the socialization process is related to career development. That is to say, the individual looks to the organization for opportunities to achieve satisfying work experiences which comprise a satisfying career. The socialization process attempts to focus an individual's perception of satisfying work activities on those which lead to effective group and organizational performance. Thus individual career development and organizational socialization processes are interrelated. Because of this interrelatedness, the two are discussed in this chapter. We will consider first the meaning and importance of careers in organizational settings.

ORGANIZATIONAL CAREERS

■ The popular meaning of career is reflected in the idea of moving upward in one's chosen line of work. Moving upward implies commanding larger salaries, assuming more responsibility, and acquiring more status, prestige, and power. Although typically restricted to lines of work which involve gainful employment, we can certainly relate the concept of career to homemakers, mothers, fathers, volunteer workers, civic leaders, and the like. These people also advance in the sense that their knowledge and skills grow with time, experience, and training. Here we will restrict our attention to careers of those in organizations, yet to do so does not deny the existence of careers in other contexts.

The definition of career as used in this discussion is as follows:

> The career is the individually perceived sequence of attitudes and behaviors associated with work-related experiences and activities over the span of the person's life.[2]

This definition emphasizes that *career* does not imply success or failure except in the judgment of the individual, that a career consists of both

---

[1]Meryl R. Louis, "Surprise and Sense Making: What Newcomers Experience in Entering Unfamiliar Organizational Settings," *Administrative Science Quarterly*, June 1980, pp. 229–30. This definition of socialization in organizational settings is generally accepted and reflects the view of Edgar H. Schein, "Organizational Socialization and the Profession of Management," *Industrial Management Review*, January 1968, pp. 1–16.

[2]Douglas T. Hall, *Careers in Organizations* (Santa Monica, Calif.: Goodyear Publishing, 1976), p. 4.

attitudes and behaviors, and that it is an ongoing sequence of work-related activities. Yet even though the concept of career is clearly work related, it must be understood that a person's nonwork life and roles play a significant part in it. For example, a mid-career manager 50 years old can have quite different attitudes about a job advancement involving greater responsibilities than a manager nearing retirement. A bachelor's reaction to a promotion involving relocation is likely to be different from that of a father of school-age children.

Although careers have typically been thought of in terms of upward mobility, recent ideas have enlarged the concept. For example, it is evident that an individual can remain in the same job, acquiring and developing skills, but without moving upward in an organizational or professional hierarchy. It is also possible for an individual to move among various jobs in different fields and organizations.[3] Thus the concept of career must be broad enough to include not only traditional work experiences, but also the emerging work and lifestyles.

Career Effectiveness
In organizational settings career effectiveness is judged not only by the individual, but also by the organization itself. But what is meant by career effectiveness? Under what circumstances will individuals state that they have had "successful" or "satisfying" careers? And will the organization share the individuals' views about their careers? Although numerous characteristics of career effectiveness could be listed, four are often cited. They are performance, attitude, adaptability, and identity.

Career Performance. Salary and position are the more popular indicators of career performance. Specifically, the more rapidly one's salary increases and one's advancement up the hierarchy, the higher the level of career performance. As one advances (is promoted), the greater is the responsibility in terms of employees supervised, budget allocated, and revenue generated. The organization is, of course, vitally interested in career performance since it bears a direct relation to organizational effectiveness. That is, the rate of salary and position advancement reflects in most instances the extent to which the individual has contributed to the achievement of organizational performance.

Two points should be made. First to the extent that the organization's performance evaluation and reward processes do not fully recognize performance, individuals may not realize this indicator of career effectiveness. Thus individuals may not receive those rewards, salary, and promotion, associated with career effectiveness because the organization either does not or cannot provide them. Second, the organization may have expectations for the individual's performance which the individual is unwilling or unable to meet. The organization may accurately assess the individual's potential as being greater than present performance, yet because the indi-

---

[3]Meryl R. Louis, "Career Transitions: Varieties and Commonalities," *Academy of Management Review,* July 1980, p. 330.

vidual has interests beyond his or her career (for example, family, community, religious) performance does not match potential. In such instances the individual may be satisfied with career performance, yet the organization is disappointed. This mismatch occurs as a consequence of the individual's *attitudes* toward the career.

Career Attitudes. This aspect of career effectiveness refers to the way individuals perceive and evaluate their careers. The more positive are these perceptions and evaluations, the more effective are the careers. Positive attitudes have important implications for the organization as well in that individuals with positive attitudes are more likely to be committed to the organization and to be involved in their jobs. The manner in which individuals come to have positive career attitudes is a complex psychological and sociological process; a full development of that process is beyond the scope of this discussion. However it is evident that positive career attitudes are maintained to the extent that career demands and opportunities are consistent with an individual's interests, values, needs, and abilities.

Career Adaptability. Few professions are stagnant and unchanging. On the contrary, the condition of change and development more accurately describes contemporary professions. Changes occur in the profession itself requiring new knowledge and skills to practice it; for example, medicine and engineering have and will continue to advance in the utilization of new information and technology. Other professions likewise have changed markedly. Individuals unable to *adapt* to these changes and to *adopt* them in the practice of their careers run the risk of early obsolescence. It goes without saying that organizations benefit through the *adaptiveness* of its employees. An expression of the mutual benefits derived from career adaptability is the dollars expended by organizations for employee training and development. Thus career adaptability implies the application of the latest knowledge, skills, and technology in the work of a career.

Career Identity. Two important components comprise career identity. First is the extent to which individuals have clear and consistent awareness of their interests, values, and expectations for the future. Second is the extent to which individuals view their lives as consistent through time, the extent to which they see themselves as extensions of their pasts. The idea expressed in this concept is, "What do I want to be and what do I have to do to become what I want to be?"[4] Individuals who have satisfactory resolutions to this question are likely to have effective careers and to make effective contributions to the organizations which employ them.

Effective careers in organizations, then, are likely to occur for individuals with high levels of performance, positive attitudes, adaptiveness, and identity resolution. Moreover, effective careers are without doubt linked to organizational performance.

Figure 18–1 suggests some possible relationships between the character-

---

[4]Erik H. Erikson, "The Concept of Identity in Race Relations: Notes and Queries," *Daedalus* 95 (1966): 148, as cited in Hall, *Careers*, p. 95.

FIGURE 18–1

Suggested Relationships between Characteristics of Career Effectiveness and Criteria of Organizational Effectiveness

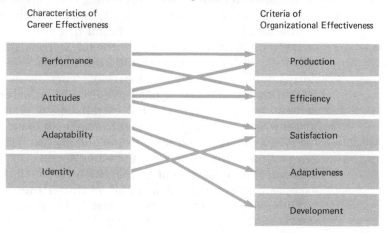

istics of career effectiveness and criteria of organizational effectiveness. The degree to which these relationships are generally valid cannot be stated with certainty, yet some suggestions are warranted.

Career performance would seem to be related to organizational production and efficiency. In most organizations the performance evaluation process places primary emphasis on these two criteria, and career performance effectiveness is judged accordingly. Positive career attitudes would imply commitment to production and efficiency and, perhaps by definition, satisfaction. Individuals with positive career attitudes working in organizations which place emphasis on employee growth and development would no doubt be effective; thus arrows could also be drawn from attitudes to adaptiveness and development. Career adaptability is directly related to organizational adaptiveness and development, particularly for those occupations and organizations which are subject to rapid change. Finally, career identity is directly related to satisfaction; it may be related to other criteria, but one can reach a level of identity resolution which excludes production and efficiency activities.

Career Stages

The idea that individuals go through distinct but interrelated stages in their careers is widely recognized. The simplest version would include four stages: (1) prework stage (attending school), (2) initial work stage (moving from job to job), (3) stable work stage (maintaining one job), and (4) retirement stage (leaving active employment). Most people prepare for their occupations by undergoing some form of organized education in high school, trade school, vocational school, or college. They then take a first job, but chances are they will move to other jobs in the same organization. The degree of movement among jobs (job mobility) varies according to a number of factors, including organizational policy, labor market conditions, and individual differences.[5] Eventually they settle into a position in which they remain until retirement. The duration of each stage varies among individuals, but in general they each go through them.

Studies of career stages have found that needs and expectations change as the individual moves through them.[6] Managers in American Telephone and Telegraph (AT&T) expressed considerable concern for security needs during the initial years on their jobs. This phase, which the researchers termed the *establishment* phase, ordinarily lasts during the first five years of employment. Following the establishment phase is the *advancement* phase which lasts approximately from age 30 to age 45. During this period the AT&T managers expressed considerably less concern for security needs satisfaction and more concern for achievement, esteem, and autonomy. Promotions and advancement to jobs with responsibility and opportunity to exercise independent judgment are characteristics of this phase.

Following the advancement phase is the *maintenance* phase. This period is marked by efforts to stabilize the gains of the past. In some respects this phase is analogous to a plateau—no new gains are made, yet it can be a period of creativity since the individual has satisfied many of the psychological and financial needs associated with earlier phases. Although each individual and career will be different in actuality, it is reasonable to assume that esteem and self-actualization would be the most important needs in the maintenance phase. Many people experience what is termed the *mid-career* crisis during the maintenance phase. Such people are not successfully achieving satisfaction from their work and may, consequently, experience physiological and psychological discomfort.

The maintenance phase is followed by the *retirement phase*. The individual has, in effect, completed one career and may move on to another one.[7] During this phase the individual may have opportunities to experience self-actualization through activities that were impossible to pursue while working. Painting, gardening, volunteer service, and quiet reflection are some of the many positive avenues available to retirees. But depending upon the individual's financial and health status, the retirement years can be spent satisfying security and physiological needs.

Some of the important characteristics of career stages are summarized in Figure 18–2. This figure depicts a simple three-stage model of careers in context of organizations. It also reflects the passage of an individual along a traditional career path.

---

[5] Yoav Vardi, "Organizational Career Mobility: An Integrative Model," *Academy of Management Review*, July 1980, pp. 341–55.

[6] Douglas T. Hall and Khalil Nougaim, "An Examination of Maslow's Need Hierarchy in an Organizational Setting," *Organizational Behavior and Human Performance* 3 (1968): 12–35.

[7] James B. Shaw, "The Process of Retiring: Organizational Entry in Reverse," *Academy of Management Review* January 1981, pp. 41–47.

FIGURE 18–2
Characteristics of Three General Career Stages

	Stage 1	Stage 2	Stage 3
Age	18-24	24-44	45-65/70
Primary Work-Related Activities	Obtaining Job-Related Skills and Knowledge	Becoming an Independent Contributor to the Organization's Performance	Assuming Responsibility for the Work of Others
Primary Psychological Demands	Being Dependent upon Others for Rewards	Being Dependent upon Self-Generated Rewards	Being Independent of Others or Self for Rewards
Primary Need Satisfaction	Security	Achievement, Esteem, Autonomy	Esteem, Actualization

Career Paths

Effective advancement through career stages involves moving along career paths. From the perspective of the organization, career paths are important inputs into manpower planning. An organization's future manpower needs depend upon the projected passage of individuals through the ranks. From the perspective of the individual a career path is the sequence of jobs which he or she desires to undertake to achieve personal and career goals. It is virtually impossible to integrate completely the needs of both the organization and the individual in the design of career paths, yet systematic career planning has the potential for closing the gap.

In the traditional sense career paths emphasize upward mobility in a single occupation or functional area, as reflected in Figure 18–3. When recruiting personnel, the organization's representative will speak of engineers', accountants', or marketers' career paths. In these contexts the recruiter will describe the different jobs typical individuals will hold as they work progressively upward in an organization. Each job, or rung, is reached when the individual has accumulated the necessary experience and ability and has demonstrated that he or she is ready for promotion. Implicit in such career paths are attitudes that failure results whenever an individual does not move on up after an elapsed time.

Organizational Careers in Perspective

Upon reflection, the achievement of career effectiveness is a complex process. At minimum the following complexities can be noted:

1. Career effectiveness consists of four criteria (performance, attitudes, adaptability, and identity) which are interrelated in different ways for different individuals. It cannot be said with certainty that, for example, achieving high levels of performance will lead to or is the result of positive career attitudes. Individual differences in perception and personality account for differences in career effectivensss criteria.

2. The relative importance of career effectiveness criteria varies among

FIGURE 18–3
Career Path, General Management

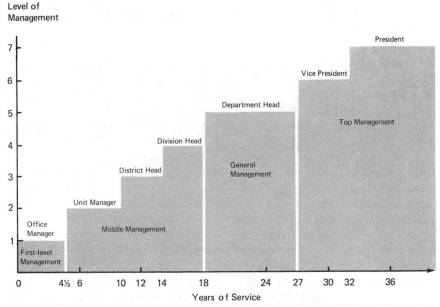

Source: Based on William F. Glueck, *Personnel: A Diagnostic Approach* (Plano, Tex: Business Publications, 1978) pp. 272–73. © 1978 by Business Publications, Inc.

individuals, but also among organizations. Some individuals (and organizations) may value performance at the expense of adaptability while other individuals (and organizations) may value adaptability over performance. Thus career effectiveness requires individual and organizational agreement as to the importance of criteria.

3. The organization provides opportunities in the form of career paths for the realization of career effectiveness. The passage of individuals along career paths coincides with the passage of career stages. Thus the coincidence of career paths and career stages reinforces the interrelationship and interdependence between the individual and the organization. An important linkage between the individual and the organization is the socialization process.

SOCIALIZATION: A LINKAGE BETWEEN CAREER EFFECTIVENESS AND ORGANIZATIONAL EFFECTIVENESS

■ The socialization process goes on throughout an individual's career. As the needs of the organization change, for example, its employees must adapt to those new needs; that is, they must be socialized. But even as we recognize that socialization is ever present, we must also recognize that it is more important at some times than at others. For example, socialization is most important when an individual first takes a job or takes a different job in the same organization. The socialization process occurs throughout the career stages and at every step along career paths, but individuals are more aware of it when they change jobs or change organizations.[8] The parallelism between careers and socialization efforts implies the existence of socialization stages corresponding to career stages.

Socialization Stages

The stages of socialization coincide generally with the stages of a career. For convenience, three stages sufficiently describe the socialization process: (1) anticipatory socialization, (2) accommodation, and (3) role management.[9] Each stage involves specific activities which if undertaken properly increase the individual's chances of having an effective career. Moreover, these stages occur continuously and often simultaneously.

Anticipatory Socialization. The first stage involves all those activities which the individual undertakes prior to entering the organization or taking a different job in the same organization. The primary purpose of these activities is to acquire information about the new organization and/or new job. This stage of socialization corresponds to the prework career stage, and the information-gathering activities include formal schooling, actual work experience, and recruiting efforts of organizations attempting to attract new employees.

People are vitally interested in two kinds of information prior to entering a new job or organization. First, they want to know as much as they can about what working for the organization is really like. Second, they want to know whether they are suited for the jobs available in the organization. Individuals seek out this information with considerable effort when they are faced with the decision to take a job, whether it be their first one or one which comes along in the way of transfer or promotion. At these times the information is specific to the job or the organization. But we should understand that we also form impressions about jobs and organizations in less formal ways. For example, our friends and relatives talk of their experiences. Parents impart both positive and negative information to their offspring regarding the world of work. Thus we continually receive information about this or that job or organization, but we are more receptive to it when faced with the necessity to make a decision.

It is desirable, of course, that the information transmitted and received during the anticipatory stage be such that the organization and the job are accurately and clearly depicted. Yet we know there are considerable differences among individuals in the way they decode and receive information. Yet if the fit between the individual and the organization is to be optimal, two conditions are necessary. The first condition is *realism*. That is to say, both the individual and the organization must portray themselves to be

---

[8] Stuart M. Klein and Richard R. Ritti, *Understanding Organizational Behavior* (Boston: Kent Publishing, 1980), pp. 122–23.

[9] These stages are identified by Daniel C. Feldman, "A Contingency Theory of Socialization," *Administrative Science Quarterly*, September 1976, pp. 434–35. The following discussion is based heavily upon this work as well as Daniel C. Feldman, "A Practical Program for Employee Socialization," *Organizational Dynamics*, Autumn 1976, pp. 64–80.

realistic. The second condition is *congruence*. This condition is present when the individual's skills, talents, and abilities are fully utilized by the job. Either over utilization or underutilization of them results in incongruence and, consequently, poor performance.[10]

The necessity to obtain realism and congruence during the anticipatory socialization stage places special emphasis on the organization's recruitment efforts. It is through recruitment that the organization attracts the kinds and types of people on whom it depends for future performance. All too often the recruitment process is undertaken from the perspective of "getting warm bodies" or "filling slots." The result of these perspectives is that the organization is portrayed unrealistically. The recruitees are simply not told the whole story, only the good parts. The predictable outcome is the creation of unrealistic expectations. Individuals are led to believe that certain things will happen to them, and when they do not, the natural outcome is lowered satisfaction and production.

One way to counteract the unrealistic expectations of new recruits is to provide realistic information during their recruiting process. This practice is based on the idea that people should know both the bad and the good things to expect from their jobs and their organizations. Through *realistic job previews* (RJPs), recruits are given opportunities to learn not only the benefits that they may expect, but also the nonbenefits. Studies have shown that the recruitment rate is the same for those who receive RJPs as for those who do not. More important, those who receive RJPs are more likely to remain on the job and to be satisfied with it than are those who have been selected in the usual manner. The practice of "telling it like it is" is used by a number of organizations, including the Prudential Insurance Company, Texas Instruments, and the U.S. Military Academy.[11]

Accommodation. The second stage of socialization occurs after the individual becomes a member of the organization, after he or she takes the job. During this stage the individual sees the organization and the job for what they actually are. Through a variety of activities the individual attempts to become an active participant in the organization and a competent performer on the job. This breaking-in period is ordinarily stressful for the individual because of anxiety created by the uncertainties inherent in any new and different situation. Apparently the closer the individual reached realism and congruence during the anticipatory stage, the greater the likelihood that some of the stress will be lessened. Nevertheless, the demands on the individual do indeed create situations which induce stress.

There are four major activities comprising the accommodation stage. All individuals, to a degree, must engage in (1) establishing new interpersonal relationships with both co-workers and supervisors, (2) learning the tasks required to perform the job, (3) clarifying their role in the organization and

---

[10]Feldman, "A Practical Program," pp. 65–66.

[11]See John P. Wanous, *Organizational Entry* (Reading, Mass.: Addison-Wesley Publishing, 1980).

the formal and informal groups relevant to that role, and (4) evaluating the progress which they are making toward satisfying the demands of the job and the role. Readers who have been through the accommodation stage will recognize these four activities and will recall more or less favorable reactions to them.

If all goes well in this stage, the individual will feel a sense of acceptance by co-workers and supervisors and will experience competence in performing the tasks of the job. The breaking-in period will, if successful also result in role definition and congruence of evaluation. These four outcomes of the accommodation (acceptance, competence, role definition, and congruence of evaluation) are experienced by all new employees to a greater or lesser extent. However the relative "value" of each of these outcomes varies from person to person. Acceptance by the group may be a less-valued outcome for an individual whose social need is satisfied off the job, for example. Regardless of these differences due to individual preferences, each of us will experience the accommodation stage of socialization and will ordinarily move on to the third one.

Role Management. The third stage of socialization, role management, coincides with the third stage of careers, stable work. In contrast to the accommodation stage which requires the individual to adjust to demands and expectations of the immediate work group, the role management stage takes on a broader set of issues and problems. Specifically, the third stage requires the individual to resolve two types of conflicts. First, there is the conflict which arises between the individual's work and home lives. For example, the individual must allocate time and energy between the job and his or her role in the family. Since the amount of time and energy are fixed and the demands of work and family seemingly insatiable, conflict is inevitable. Employees who are unable to resolve these conflicts are often forced to leave the organization or to perform at an ineffective level. In either case the individual and the organization are not well served by unresolved conflict between work and family.

The second source of conflict which arises during the role management stage is between the individual's work group and other work groups in the organization. This source of conflict can be more apparent for some employees than for others. For example, as an individual moves up in the organization's hierarchy, he or she is required to interact with various types of groups both inside and outside the organization. Each group can and often does place different demands on the individual, and to the extent that these demands are beyond the ability of the individual to meet, stress will result. The tolerance for the level of stress induced by these conflicting and irreconcilable demands varies among individuals, but generally it can be assumed that the existence of unmanaged stress works to the disadvantage of the individual and the organization.

The Outcomes of Socialization

If an individual moves through each stage of the socialization process in a positive manner, then the groundwork is laid for an effective career. Note that it is the groundwork, or beginnings, that result from socialization. Socialization processes contribute to some aspects of one's reaction to a job and organization, but not to all reactions. For example, general satisfaction, the degree to which an individual is satisfied and happy in his or her work, is related to high congruence, role definition, resolution of conflicting demands of work groups, and resolution of work-family conflicts. Congruence is an activity of the anticipatory stage, role definition occurs during the accommodation stage, and the conflict resolution activities are the primary characteristics of the role-management stage. Thus each stage of the socialization process contributes to general satisfaction.

The same research which found the relationships noted above also found that socialization activities are unrelated to two very important variables: internal work motivation and job involvement. Thus an individual may have positive or negative experiences with an organization's socialization processes and have, coincidentally, positive or negative work motivation and job involvement. The most likely explanation for this finding is that motivation and involvement are the results of the nature of the work itself. Our discussion of job design in Chapter 12 noted the importance of job-related factors such as task identity, task significance, job freedom, and feedback to employees' sense of job satisfaction. Thus while organizational socialization processes can contribute to building a solid foundation for effective careers, they cannot guarantee them. It is possible to incorporate motivating factors into the socialization process, and organizations which are committed to providing maximum career opportunities will do so.

CHARACTERISTICS OF EFFECTIVE SOCIALIZATION AND CAREER PROCESSES

■ Organization socialization processes vary in form and content from organization to organization. Even within the same organization, different individuals experience different socialization processes. For example, the accommodation stage for a college-trained management recruit is quite different from that of a member of the lowest-paid occupation in the organization. As Van Maanen has pointed out, socialization processes are not only extremely important in shaping the individuals who enter an organization, they are also remarkably different from situation to situation.[12] This variation reflects either the lack of attention by management to such an important process or it reflects the uniqueness of the process as related to organizations and individuals. Either explanation permits the suggestion that while uniqueness is apparent, some general principles can be implemented in the socialization process.[13]

---

[12]J. Van Maanen, "People Processing: Strategies for Organizational Socialization," *Organizational Dynamics*, Summer 1978, pp. 18–36.

[13]The following discussion reflects the research findings of Feldman, "A Practical Program."

Effective Anticipatory Socialization

The organization's primary activities during the first stage of socialization are *recruitment* and *selection and placement* programs. If these programs are effective, then new recruits in an organization should experience the feeling of *realism* and *congruence*. In turn, accurate expectations about the job result from realism and congruence.

Recruitment programs are directed toward new employees, those not now in the organization. It is desirable to give these prospective employees information not only about the job, but also about those aspects of the organization which will affect the individual. It is nearly always easier for the recruiter to stress job-related information to the exclusion of organization-related information. Job-related information is usually specific and objective, whereas organization-related information is usually general and subjective. Nevertheless the recruiter should, to the extent possible, convey factual information about such matters as pay and promotion policies and practices, objective characteristics of the work group the recruit is likely to work with, and other information which reflects the recruit's concerns.

Selection and placement practices, in the context of anticipatory socialization, are important conveyers of information to employees already in the organization. Of prime importance is the manner in which individuals view career paths in the organizations. As noted earlier the stereotypical career path is one which involves advancement up the managerial hierarchy. Yet this concept does not take into account the differences among individuals toward such moves. Greater flexibility in career paths would require the organization to consider the following alternatives.[14]

Lateral transfers involve moves at the same organizational level from one department to another. A manager who has plateaued in production could be transferred to a similar level in sales, engineering, or some other area. The move would require the manager to learn quickly the technical demands of the new position, and there would be a period of reduced performance as this learning occurred. But once qualified, the manager would bring the perspectives of both areas to bear on decisions.

Downward transfers are associated in our society with failure; an effective manager simply does not consider a move downward to be a respectable alternative. Yet downward transfers are in many instances not only respectable alternatives, but entirely acceptable alternatives, particularly when one or more of the following conditions exist:

The manager values the quality of life afforded by a specific geographic area and may desire a downward transfer if this is required in order to stay in or move to that area.

The manager views the downward transfer as a way to establish a base for future promotions.

---

[14]Douglas T. Hall and Francine S. Hall, "What's New in Career Management," *Organizational Dynamics,* Summer 1976, pp. 21–27.

The manager is faced with the alternatives of dismissal or a downward move.

The manager desires to pursue autonomy and self-actualization in non-job-related activities—such as religious, civic, or political activities—and for that reason may welcome the reduced responsibility (and demands) of a lower-level position.

The use of *fallback positions* is a relatively new way to reduce the risk of lateral and downward transfers. The practice involves identifying in advance a position to which the transferred manager can return if the new position does not work out. By identifying the fallback position in advance, the organization informs everyone who is affected that some risk is involved but that the organization is willing to accept some of the responsibility for it and that returning to the fallback job will not be viewed as failure. Companies such as Heublein, Procter & Gamble, Continental Can, and Lehman Brothers have used fallback positions to remove some of the risk of lateral and upward moves. The practice appears to have considerable promise for protecting the careers of highly specialized technicians and professionals who make their first move into general management positions.

An alternative to traditional career pathing is to base career progression on real-world experiences and individualized preferences. Such paths would have several characteristics:[15]

1. They would include lateral and downward as well as upward possibilities, not tied to "normal" rates of progress.
2. They would be tentative and responsive to changes in organizational needs.
3. They would be flexible enough to take into account the qualities of individuals.
4. Each job along the path would be specified in terms of acquirable skills, knowledge, and other specific attributes—not merely educational credentials, age, or work experience.

Realistic career paths, rather than traditional ones, are necessary for effective anticipatory socialization. In the absence of such information the employee can only guess at what is available.

Effective Accommodation Socialization

Five different activities comprise effective accommodation socialization. They are (1) designing orientation programs, (2) structuring training programs, (3) providing performance evaluation information, (4) assigning challenging work, and (5) assigning demanding bosses.

Orientation programs are seldom given the attention they deserve. The

---

[15]James W. Walker, "Let's Get Realistic about Career Paths," *Human Resource Management,* Fall 1976, pp. 2–7.

first few days on the new job can have either very strong negative or positive impacts on the new employee. Taking a new job involves not only new job tasks, but also new interpersonal relationships. The new person comes into an ongoing social system which has evolved a unique set of values, ideals, frictions, conflicts, friendships, coalitions, and all the other characteristics of work groups. If left alone, the new employee must cope with the new environment in ignorance, but if given some help and guidance he or she can cope more effectively.

Thus the organization should design orientation programs which enable the new employee to meet the rest of the employees as soon as possible. Moreover, specific individuals should be assigned the task of orientation. These individuals should be selected for their social skills and be given time off from their own work to spend with the new people. The degree to which the orientation program is formalized will vary, but in any case, the program should not be left to chance.

Training programs are invaluable in the breaking-in stage. There is no question that training programs are necessary to instruct new employees in proper techniques and to develop requisite skills. Moreover effective training programs provide frequent feedback as to progress in acquiring the necessary skills. What is not so obvious is the necessity to integrate the formal training with the orientation program.

Most jobs involve not only the use of technical skills, but also the use of social skills. Most of us must work with other people to get our work done. But the people that we have to work with have unique personalities that must be understood. For example, nurses must learn about the personalities and preferences of physicians with whom they work in order to perform their nursing duties effectively. Yet it takes nurses considerably longer to learn about physicians than it takes to learn the technical skills of their jobs. Thus to the extent possible, training programs should include both the technical as well as the social information required to perform specific jobs. Career development training programs need not be elaborate as the following organizational close-up illustrates.

ORGANIZATIONS: CLOSE-UP

Career Development at the University of Minnesota

William C. Thomas is assistant vice president for administration and personnel at the University of Minnesota. He implemented a career development program in the University of Minnesota personnel department which has as its primary purpose the development of people in the jobs they now hold and, secondarily, the preparation of these people for advancement to other jobs. The program itself contains no particularly unique features. Its basic characteristic is the annual discussion between supervisors and employees at which time career development objectives are mutually agreed upon.

ORGANIZATION: CLOSE-UP (*continued*)

However it is the translation of these objectives into developmental activities that sets this effort apart from other career development programs. The budget of the University of Minnesota contains no provision for employee career development activities. Therefore any unit wishing to undertake such efforts must come up with the money through cost cutting and increased efficiency. Thomas stresses low-cost techniques such as one-to-one supervisory coaching, internal small-group workshops, individual self-help reading courses, training seminars taught by the unit's own employees, and job rotation. The strength of the program is the involvement of the employees in their own development activities and the discussion which is annually held between each employee and his or her supervisor. Perhaps as important is the fact that the program demonstrates that career development need not be an expensive fringe benefit, but rather can be undertaken through the combined efforts of both the employees and the organization. The University of Minnesota program therefore puts into practice the idea that career development involves benefits to the individual and the organization and that each should be expected to share in the cost of the program.

Source: W. C. Thomas, "A Career Development Program that Works," *Management Review*, May 1980, pp. 38–40.

Performance evaluation, in the context of socialization, provides important feedback about how well the individual is getting along in the organization. Inaccurate or ambiguous information regarding this important circumstance can only lead to performance problems. To avoid these problems, it is imperative that performance evaluation sessions take place in face-to-face meetings between the individual and manager and that the performance criteria be as objective as possible in the context of the job. Management by objectives and behaviorally anchored rating scales are particularly applicable in these settings.

Feedback on performance is an important managerial responsibility. Yet many managers are inadequately trained to meet this responsibility. They simply do not know how to evaluate the performance of their subordinates. This management deficiency is especially damaging to new managers. They have not been in the organization long enough to be socialized by their peers and other employees. They are not as yet sure of what they are expected to believe, what values to hold, or what behaviors are expected of them. They naturally look to their own managers to guide them through this early phase. But when their managers fail to evaluate their performance accurately, they remain ignorant and confused as to whether they are achieving what the organization expects of them. The following close-up depicts one approach to the integration of performance evaluation and career development.

ORGANIZATIONS: CLOSE-UP

Career Development at Exxon Corporation

The executive succession plan at Exxon Corporation has been developed over the past 30 years. It has produced nearly everyone now on the board of directors and the top 200 executives.

At least once each year each of Exxon's 50,000 management and professional employees from 13 organizations in 100 countries is assessed by at least four different superiors. According to Frank Gaines, Jr., Exxon's executive development coordinator, the pooling of these judgments results in considerable consistency. Evidently, although executive potential is difficult to define, it is easy to recognize.

The heart of the system is a process by which each individual is ranked in order of potential and performance at each managerial level. The rankings are filed on standardized forms which include suggested training, recommended additional experience, and ultimate potential. For example, a particular manager may, as a result of the annual review, be advised that he or she needs additional training in human relations and experience in an overseas branch and has the potential for reaching the level of director or higher. Also included on the form is the individual's projected career path over the next five years.

The system attempts to take into account the wishes and needs of the individuals themselves. For example, a manager with a child in school may not be amenable to a career move involving geographic relocation. However, it is possible that one with a child in difficulty in the present school system might view a relocation as a means to get the youngster into a new school situation. At present Exxon has not experienced too many difficulties with the dual-career family. But Gaines expects that problems will arise in the next 10 to 15 years. He predicts that many people will opt to change companies rather than to relocate for career purposes, particularly when the move would create hardships for one of the dual careerists.

Source: *The Career Development Bulletin*, The Center for Research in Career Development, 2, no. 1 (1980).

Assigning challenging work to new employees is a principal feature of effective socialization programs. The first jobs of new employees often demand far less of them than they are able to deliver. Consequently, they are unable to demonstrate their full capabilities, and in a sense they are being stifled. This is especially damaging if the recruiter had been overly enthusiastic in "selling" the organization when they were recruited.

Some individuals are able to *create* challenging jobs even when their assignments are fairly routine. They do this by thinking of ways to do their jobs differently and better. They may also be able to persuade their managers to give them more leeway and more to do. Unfortunately, many recent college graduates are unable to create challenge. Their previous experiences in school were typically experiences in which challenge had been given to them by their teachers. The challenge had been created *for* them, not *by* them.

Job enrichment is an established practice for motivating employees with strong growth and achievement needs. If the nature of the job to be assigned is not intrinsically challenging, the newly hired individual's manager can enrich the assignment. The usual ways to enrich a job include giving the new employee more authority and responsibility, permitting the new employee to interact directly with customers and clients, and enabling the new employee to implement his or her own ideas (rather than merely recommending them to the boss).

Assigning demanding bosses is a practice which seems to have considerable promise for increasing the retention rate of new employees. In this context, "demanding" should not be interpreted as "autocratic." Rather, the type of boss most likely to get new hirees off in the right direction is one who has high but achievable expectations for their performance. Such a boss instills the understanding that high performance is expected and rewarded and, equally important, that the boss is always ready to assist through coaching and counseling. Apparently, 9, 9 leaders—according to managerial grid theory—would be effective for this purpose, but if these are unavailable, task-oriented leaders would be more effective than person-oriented leaders.

The socialization programs and practices that are intended to retain and develop new employees can be used separately or in combination. A manager would be well advised to establish policies which would be most likely to retain those recent hirees who have the highest potential to perform effectively. The likelihood of that result is improved if the policies include realistic orientation and training programs, accurate performance evaluation feedback, and challenging initial assignments supervised by supportive, performance-oriented managers. Although such practices are not perfect, they are helpful not only in retaining employees but also in avoiding the problems which may arise during the role management stage of socialization.

Effective Role Management Socialization

Organizations which effectively deal with conflicts associated with the role management stage recognize the impact of such conflicts on job satisfaction and turnover. Even though motivation and high performance may not be associated with socialization activities, satisfaction and turnover are, and organizations can ill-afford to lose capable employees.

Retention of employees beset by off-job conflicts is enhanced in organizations which provide professional counseling services and which schedule and adjust work assignments for those with particularly difficult conflicts at work and home. Of course these practices do not guarantee that the employee will be able to resolve or even cope with the conflict. The important point, however, is for the organization to show good faith and make a sincere effort to adapt to the problems of its employees.

SOCIALIZATION AS AN INTEGRATION STRATEGY

■ Our discussion has emphasized the interrelationships between socialization processes and career effectiveness. Yet it is possible to view socialization as a form of organizational integration. Specifically, socialization from the integration perspective is a strategy for achieving congruence of organizational and individual goals.[16] The content of socialization strategies are practices and policies which have appeared in a number of different places throughout this text. Here we can summarize not only our discussion of career and socialization processes but also cast some important organization behavior concepts and theories in a different framework.

Organizational integration is achieved primarily by aligning and integrating the goals of individuals with the objectives of organizations. The greater the congruity between individual goals and organization objectives the greater the integration. The socialization process achieves organizational integration by, in effect, undoing the individual's previously held goals and creating new ones which come closer to those valued by the organization. In its most extreme form, this "undoing" process involves debasement techniques such as those experienced by Marine Corps recruits, military academy plebes, and fraternity pledges. Such instances are, as noted, extreme.

More frequently and more applicable in organizational settings are the activities of leaders and peers (the immediate work group). A leading spokesperson for the use of leader and peer socialization is Rensis Likert. In the presentation of his ideas on leadership theory, Likert stresses the importance of the leader who maintains high performance standards and group-centered leadership techniques. The leader sets high standards for his or her own behavior and performance and through group-centered leadership encourages the group to follow the example. If successful, the leader will have created a group norm of high performance which is made apparent to a new employee assigned to the group.

Finally the 9, 9 theory of leadership involves the development of mutual understanding of objectives through discussions between the group's leader and its members. The understanding, when reached, would represent a balanced, but high concern for both people and production concerns. The group would then act to achieve the objectives of the group and represent the legitimacy of the objectives to new group members.

The common thread running throughout leadership theories is the active role played by the leader and the group members in achieving integration of goals and objectives. Effective socialization, particularly during the accommodation and role management stages, requires joint and supportive efforts of leaders and peers alike.

---

[16] See Jon H. Barrett, *Individual Goals and Organizational Objectives* (Ann Arbor: Institute for Social Research, University of Michigan, 1970), pp. 4–14.

MAJOR MANAGERIAL ISSUES

A. Effective organizational socialization practices can have positive effects on the development of effective careers.

B. The concept of career in organizations must be broad enough to include emerging patterns of work and nonwork life.

C. Effective careers include the characteristics of performance, attitudes, adaptability, and identity. These characteristics can be related to criteria of organizational effectiveness to the extent that individual and organizational goals are congruent.

D. Most individuals move through their careers in generally predictable patterns. Each career stage involves specific activity, psychological, and behavioral demands. Moreover the relative importance of specific needs changes as the individual progresses through each stage.

E. Organizational socialization processes coincide with the stages of careers. Anticipatory socialization occurs with the prework career stage. Accommodation occurs with the establishment and advancement career stages, and role management occurs with the maintenance stage.

F. The success of organizational socialization depends upon how well the socialization activities meet the career needs of individuals at each career stage.

G. Effective socialization efforts reflect the diverse career orientations of contemporary society. No longer can it be said that careers follow predictable, traditional paths.

H. From a broad perspective, organizational socialization can be viewed as a means for achieving organizational integration.

DISCUSSION AND REVIEW QUESTIONS

1. "Socialization in organizations will occur regardless of what managers do, one way or the other." Comment on this statement.

2. Describe the ways in which socialization and career processes are interrelated.

3. What factors in contemporary society do you think have contributed to the increasing interest in nontraditional career paths?

4. Rank the relative importance of the four characteristics of effective careers from the perspective of the individual, the organization. Explain your rankings.

5. What in your opinion is the ethical responsibility of organizations in the area of providing career counseling to employees?

6. Which of the three socialization stages is most important for developing high-performing employees? Explain your answer.

7. What are the characteristics of the role management stage which create difficulties for an organization which desires to help its employees through the stage?

8. Why are leaders and peers considered the most important actors in socialization processes?

9. Based upon your own work experience, have managers or peers been more important in socializing you into an organization?

10. If there is validity to the finding that socialization contributes to satisfaction but not production or efficiency, how can an organization justify expending resources for formal socialization programs?

ADDITIONAL REFERENCES

Bolles, R. *What Color Is Your Parachute? A Practical Manual for Job Hunters and Career Changers.* Rev. ed. Berkeley, Calif.: Ten Speed Press, 1977).

Bradford, L. P. "Emotional Problems in Retirement and What Can Be Done." *Group and Organizational Studies,* 1979, pp. 429–39.

Driver, M. "Career Concepts and Career Management in Organizations." In *Behavioral Problems in Organizations,* edited by C. L. Cooper. Englewood Cliffs, N.J.: Prentice-Hall, 1979.

Hamner, W. C. *Organizational Shock.* New York: John Wiley & Sons, 1980.

Kotter, J.; V. Faux; and C. McArthur. *Self-Assessment and Career Development.* Englewood Cliffs, N.J.: Prentice-Hall, 1978.

Schein, E. *Career Dynamics: Matching Individual and Organizational Needs.* Reading, Mass.: Addison-Wesley Publishing, 1978.

Sheehy, G. *Passages: Predictable Crises of Adult Life.* New York: E. P. Dutton, 1976.

Souerwine, A. H. *Career Strategies: Planning for Personal Achievement.* New York: AMACON, 1978.

Wanous, J. P. *Organizational Entry: Recruitment, Selection and Socialization of Newcomers.* Reading, Mass.: Addison-Wesley Publishing, 1980.

**REFUSING A
PROMOTION**

Ron Riddell, 36 years old, is a project manager for the Dowling Products Corporation and has established a reputation as a conscientious, prompt, and creative manager. He presently is working on a new cleansing product that can be used to clean sink tops. The cleanser is expected to generate gross sales of $3 million the first year it is on the market.

Ron has a permanent team of eight men and three women and a temporary team of two women and two men assigned to him only for the important cleansing product. The team plans, organizes, and controls the various project phases from development to pilot marketing testing. The team must work closely with engineers, chemists, production managers, sales directors, and marketing research specialists before a quality product can be finally marketed.

Ron, in the past eight years, has directed four projects that have been considered outstanding market successes and one that has been considered a "superloser" financially. His supervisor is Norma Collins, Ph.D., a chemical engineer. Norma has direct responsibility for seven projects, three of which are considerably smaller than Ron's and three of which have about the same potential and size as Ron's.

Norma has recently been selected to be the overseas divisional coordinator of research and development. She and three top executives have met for the past two weeks and have decided to offer Norma's present position to Ron. They believe that the new job for Ron will mean more prestige and authority, and certainly an increase in salary.

Norma is given the task of offering the position to Ron. This is the discussion that occurs in Norma's office:

Norma: Ron, how is the cleansing project going?

Ron: As good as could be expected. I sometimes think that Joe Rambo is trying to slow down our progress. He is just a "bear" to get along with.

Norma: Well, everyone has been a little concerned because of the main competitor's progress on their cleansing product. I'm sure we can put everything together and effectively compete in the market.

Ron: I know we can.

Norma: I wanted to talk to you about a new job that is becoming vacant in 30 days. The executive selection committee unanimously believes that Ron Riddell is the right person for the job.

Ron: What new job are you talking about?

Norma: My job, Ron. I have been promoted to overseas divisional coordinator of research and development. We want to begin turning over my job to you as soon as possible. If we drag our feet, the cleansing project may not be the success that we need to bolster our financial picture.

Ron: I am flattered by this opportunity and really believe that professionally I can handle the challenge. My real concern is the personal problems I'm having.

Norma: Do you mean personal problems here at Dowling?

Ron: No, I mean problems in my family that have led to sleepless nights, arguments with my wife, and hostility between myself and my best neighbor. My brother Mark has been arrested two times recently, once for vagrancy and once for possession of narcotics. As you know, my Dad died four years ago and my mother just can't handle the kid. So I have pitched in and am trying to straighten the kid out. Connie, my wife, is fed up with the time I spend here at work and my meddling into my brother's problems. She has even threatened to leave me and take the kids with her to Denver. The new job is really interesting, but I'm afraid it would be the "straw that breaks the camel's back."

Norma: I'm sorry to hear about these problems Ron. I know that it is hard to separate outside problems and pressures from Dowling problems and pressures. If you are going to become a more important part of the management team it will mean that separation is mandatory. The new job is the challenge that we have trained you for and is a reward for your outstanding past performance. Please think over the job offer and let me know in three days. We need your talents, experience, and leadership.

Ron left Norma's office with a sick feeling in his stomach. He had worked hard for years and the goal he was striving for was within his reach. All he had to do was to say yes to Norma. He thought about the additional money, status, and authority attached to the new job. Then he thought about his wife who had become more depressed about his working on Saturdays and Sundays; his daughter whom he really had not talked to for six months; his mother who had helped pay for his college education; and his brother who always called and asked him to play golf or shoot pool only to be told, "I have to work Steve, sorry."

After thinking over the offer for three days Ron walks into Norma's office.

Norma: Come on in, Ron, and relax.

Ron: I can't relax, because I am extremely nervous. I really want the job, but my family must come first. My daughter, wife, and mother have helped me get to my present position. I just feel that taking on this new job will lead to so many problems that I must turn it down.

Norma: I sympathize with your dilemma and wish you the best of luck. I want you to understand, however, that this type of opportunity may never happen again. The company needs your talents now. Can't you get your wife and mother to understand the importance of this job in your career? I just can't believe that they would not understand.

Ron: Norma, we all have priorities and personal backgrounds that just can't be ignored.

Norma: Ron, you are sounding like a behavioral scientist. I know this just as well as you. What I'm saying is that you have worked this long and hard and now decide not to accept the challenge. This is what puzzles me.

Questions for Consideration

1. What organizational responsibilities does Norma believe that Ron is shirking by turning down the new job offer?

2. Why would the behavioral orientations of Ron and Norma differ?

3. Do you consider personal needs and problems as more important than organizational needs and problems? Why?

4. Should organizations force an employee like Ron to fit their plans for him? Why?

EXPERIENTIAL EXERCISE

**REORIENTING AN
EXCELLENT
PERFORMER**

Objectives

1. To examine the process of reviewing career planning decisions.
2. To illustrate some of the major problems facing individuals involved in the career planning process.

Related Topics

Career planning is related to organizational behavior topics such as goal setting, individual growth, and group development.

Starting the
Exercise

Each student should first consider his or her own career and plans for the future. This will set the theme for participating in the exercise.

The Facts

Roger Belhurst is a 50-year-old district sales manager for Rockhurst Corporation. He has been in his present position for 10 years. His superior rates Roger as outstanding in every area in the performance evaluation program. Unfortunately, order cutbacks and the lack of promotion opportunities have kept Roger in his current position. In addition, Roger's superior has stated that, "Roger is in a position that uses his skills and abilities optimally." Roger disagrees and believes that he is being put on the shelf and will not be promoted. His present attitudes about the company, his job, and the future are poor.

Exercise Procedures

Phase I: Group Analysis: 15 minutes

The instructor will select two groups of five to seven people. Each group will analyze the Roger Belhurst case. The groups should develop a career plan which would result in an improvement in Roger's overall attitudes. Each group will make five-minute presentations to the class.

Phase II: Evaluation: 15 minutes

A third group of three to five people will serve as evaluators of the analysis presented by the two groups. The evaluators should develop a set of criteria and apply these to the two *five*-minute presentations. They should then decide which presentation is better. When one group is presenting the solution to Roger's career plan, the second group should not be present in the room.

Phase III: Critique: 20–30 minutes

The entire class should reflect and critique the presentations and the evaluations. During the critique the following questions should be answered:

a. Why was one group's analysis and career plan better than the other group's?

b. What criteria were used by the evaluators to rate the two group presentations?

c. What would be Roger's reaction to the career plan?

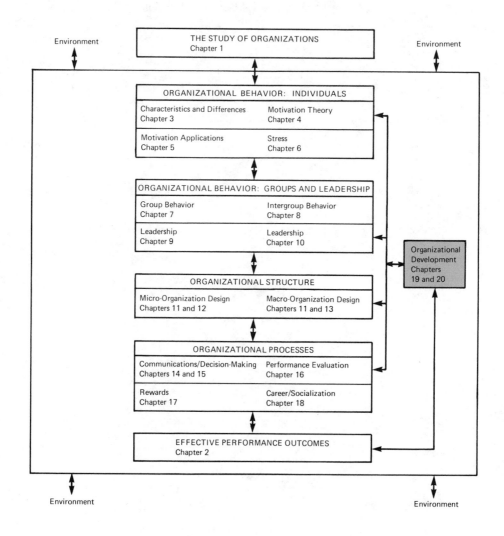

Part Six

DEVELOPING ORGANIZATIONAL EFFECTIVENESS

Chapter 19

Organizational Development: Improving Performance

AN ORGANIZATIONAL ISSUE FOR DEBATE
External Change Agents Are Necessary for Successful OD

ARGUMENT FOR

Successful instances of organization development (OD) are always (or at least usually) the result of intervention by a person or group external to the organization itself. The rationale for this position is that external persons are not caught up in the day-to-day operations of the organization and are able to see problems and causes of problems more clearly than those who must work within it. The change agent is able to see the issues because he or she is neutral and impartial, having no vested interest or personal stake in the organization. Managers and staff personnel already in the organization are unable to see clearly the problems, and indeed, may be part of them.

Moreover, so the argument goes, external change agents are solely able to undertake the necessary steps which bring about development. They alone are able to present unbiased information which indicates the necessity to change attitudes and behaviors. Through attitude defreezing and refreezing, successful organizational development occurs. But managers whose attitudes require change cannot themselves be the catalyst for changing the attitudes of others.

Support for the position is to be found in research studies and case histories. One researcher documented the differences to be found in the strategies associated with successful versus unsuccessful OD efforts. He concluded that successful OD strategy invariably was associated with the use of an external change agent.

ARGUMENT AGAINST

The argument against is based on the idea that organization development efforts vary from company to company. In some instances the developmental effort may involve nothing more than changes in job descriptions and departmental bases. In other instances the OD effort may involve fundamental changes in personal and interpersonal variables. Thus the necessity for an external change agent rests in part on the depth of intervention.

Alternatives to the exclusive use of external change agents include establishing a corporate-level organization-development department, hiring an OD specialist, training a member of the personnel department, and assigning OD responsibility to the management-development department. Each of these alternatives has advantages and disadvantages. Although the existence of internal change agents does not preclude the use of external change agents their existence provides reasonable alternatives to the exclusive use of external parties.

The process by which managers sense and respond to the necessity for change has been the focus of much research and practical attention in recent years. If managers were able to design perfect sociotechnical organizations and if the scientific, market, and technical environments were stable and predictable, there would be no pressure for change. But such is not the case. The statement that "we live in the midst of constant change" has become a well-worn but relevant cliché. Of course, the need for change affects organizations differently; those which operate in relatively certain environments need to be less concerned with change than those which operate in less certain environments. But, even managers in certain environments must continually combat the problems of complacency.[1]

The literature and practice which deal with the process of organizational change cannot be conveniently classified because of the yet unsettled nature of this aspect of organizational behavior. Various conceptualizations and theories and their meanings and interpretations are subject to considerable disagreement. The current trend is to use the term *organizational development* (OD) to refer to the process of preparing for and managing change. Since we will use the term in this and the next chapter, it is important that we clarify our meaning and interpretation.

In its most restrictive usage, OD refers to *sensitivity training*.[2] In this context, OD stresses the process by which people in organizations become more aware of themselves and others. The emphasis is on the psychological states of employees which inhibit their ability to communicate and interact with other organizational members. The assumption is that organizational effectiveness can be increased if people can engage in honest and open discussion of issues. We will have more to say about sensitivity training in the following chapter.

A slightly more encompassing definition of OD states:

> Using knowledge and techniques from the behavioral sciences, organizational development is a *process* which attempts to increase organizational effectiveness by integrating individual desires for growth and development with organizational goals. Typically, this process is a planned change effort which involves a total system over a period of time, and these change efforts are related to the organization's mission.[3]

This definition acknowledges the existence of methods other than sensitivity training. For example, participative management, job enrichment, management by objectives, and the managerial grid are some alternative meth-

---

[1] Chris Argyris, *Management and Organizational Development* (New York: McGraw-Hill, 1971), p. 20.

[2] See Stanley M. Herman, "What Is This Thing Called Organizational Development?" *Personnel Journal*, August 1971, pp. 595–603.

[3] W. Warren Burke and Warren H. Schmidt, "Management and Organizational Development," *Personnel Administration*, March 1971, p. 45, and Alan Sheldon, "Organizational Paradigms: A Theory of Organizational Change," *Organizational Dynamics*, Winter 1980, pp. 61–80.

ods for integrating individual and organizational objectives.[4] This definition also acknowledges the fact that OD is a planned process over time which must be justified in terms of organizational effectiveness. The definition, however, is still incomplete for our purposes.

The concept of OD must be broad enough to include not only the behavioral approach, but others as well. The following definition identifies all the significant aspects of OD:

> The term "Organization development" . . . implies a normative, re-education strategy intended to affect systems of beliefs, values, and attitudes within the organization so that it can adapt better to the accelerated rate of change in technology, in our industrial environment and society in general. It also includes formal organizational restructuring which is frequently initiated, facilitated and reinforced by the normative and behavioral changes.[5]

The three subobjectives of OD are "changing attitudes or values, modifying behavior, and inducing change in structure and policy."[6] However, it is conceivable that the strategy might well emphasize one or another of these subobjectives. For example, if the structure of an organization is optimal in management's view, the OD process might attempt to educate personnel to adopt behaviors consistent with the structure. Such would be the case of leadership training in participative management in an organization which already has a System 4 structure.

Moreover the concept of OD must include the possibility of programs aimed at providing personnel with technical skills. It is entirely possible that effective change is not forthcoming simply because people in the organization do not have technical skills to cope with it. Management may determine that attitudes, behavior, and structure are appropriate yet the organization cannot respond to change because key personnel simply do not have the skills to respond. The skill training programs of industry and government are as important a part of OD as are the more fashionable programs such as sensitivity training.

Organizational development as the term is used in contemporary management practice has certain distinguishing characteristics:

1. *It Is Planned.* OD is a data-based approach to change which involves all of the ingredients that go into managerial planning. It involves goal setting, action planning, implementation, monitoring, and taking corrective action when necessary.

---

[4] William B. Eddy, "Beyond Behavioralism? Organization Development in Public Management," *Public Personnel Review*, July 1970, p. 171.

[5] Alexander Winn, "The Laboratory Approach to Organizational Development: A Tentative Model of Planned Change" (Paper read at the Annual Conference, British Psychological Society, Oxford, September 1968), p. 1, and cited in Robert T. Golembiewski, "Organizational Development in Public Agencies: Perspectives on Theory and Practice," *Public Administration Review*, July/August 1969, p. 367.

[6] Ibid., p. 367.

2. *It Is Problem-Oriented.* OD attempts to apply theory and research from a number of disciplines, including behavioral science, to the solution of organization problems.

3. *It Reflects a Systems Approach.* OD is both systemic and systematic. It is a way of more closely linking the human resources and potential of an organization to its technology, structure, and management processes.

4. *It Is an Integral Part of the Management Process.* OD is not something that is done to the organization by outsiders. It becomes a way of managing organizational change processes.

5. *It Is Not a "Fix-It" Strategy.* OD reflects a continuous and ongoing process. It is not a series of ad hoc activities designed to implement a specific change. It takes time for it to become a way of life in the organization.

6. *It Focuses on Improvement.* The emphasis of OD is on improvement. It is not just for "sick" organizations or for "wealthy" ones. It is something that can benefit almost any organization.

7. *It Is Action Oriented.* The focus of OD is on accomplishments and results. Unlike some other approaches to change which tend to describe how organizational change takes place, the emphasis is on getting things done.

8. *It Is Based upon Sound Theory and Practice.* OD is not a gimmick or a fad. It is solidly based upon the theory and research of a number of disciplines.[7]

These characteristics of contemporary organizational development indicate that managers who implement OD programs are committed to making fundamental changes in organizational behavior. The following close-up illustrates one company's commitment to organizational development.

ORGANIZATIONS: CLOSE-UP

Organizational Development at B. F. Goodrich

Roger J. Howe, Mark G. Mindell, and Donna L. Simmons are members of the organizational development staff of the B. F. Goodrich Tire and Rubber Company, a major multinational corporation. They represent the commitment of the company to implement permanent and ongoing organizational development efforts in the corporation. B. F. Goodrich's commitment to ongoing organizational development is reflected in its statement of operating principles, a public statement which defines and directs management in the development of strategic plans. The statement of principles includes the following: "the company will stress the technology of management and organization development, with specific focus on interpersonal relationships among individuals and business groups."

The program at B. F. Goodrich involves training some 60 individuals in

---

[7]Newton Margulies and Anthony P. Raia, *Conceptual Foundations of Organizational Development* (New York: McGraw-Hill, 1978), p. 25.

> **ORGANIZATIONS: CLOSE-UP** (continued)
>
> the process and methods of organization development. These individuals are then located throughout the organization, in both line and staff departments. The primary function of these trained individuals is to assist the managers of the departments in the diagnosis and identification of organizational development needs. The basic idea is that internal people will have a better chance of gaining acceptance for OD efforts and will also be able to diagnose problems in terms that are consistent with the problems of the specific manager and the department. As practiced at B. F. Goodrich, organization development is an integral part of the organization's practices and policies. It represents not only a commitment to the development of individuals and groups, but also the recognition that a major internal innovation requires much the same commitment as a new product innovation. The OD program at B. F. Goodrich enables the line manager to call upon the OD personnel whenever a new process or policy is to be introduced that will affect the way the individuals or groups perform their assigned tasks.
>
> Source: Roger J. Howe, Mark G. Mindell, and Donna L. Simmons, "Introducing Innovation through OD," *Management Review*, February 1978, pp. 52–56.

LEARNING PRINCIPLES IN THE CONTEXT OF OD PROGRAMS

■ To better understand how changes are brought about in individuals it is essential to comprehend the various principles of learning discussed in Chapter 3. Managers can design a theoretically sound OD program and not achieve any of the anticipated results because they overlooked the importance of providing reinforcement or continuous feedback to employees. These are principles of learning, and they should be tailored to the needs of the group that is affected by the program.

Expectations and Motivations

People must want to learn. They may want more skill in a particular job or more understanding of the problems of other units of the firm. Some people recognize this need and are receptive to experiences which will aid them in developing new skills or new empathy. Others reject the need or play it down, because learning is to them an admission that they are not completely competent in their jobs. These kinds of people face the prospect of change with different expectations and motivations. Determining the expectations and motivations of people is not an easy task. It is, however, a task which must be undertaken. The point to remember is that not everyone wants to participate in a change program and it is management's responsibility to show employees why they should want to change.

Reinforcement and Feedback

An important principle of learning is that of reinforcement. This principle suggests that when people receive positive rewards, information, or feelings for doing something, it becomes more likely that they will do the same thing in the same or similar situation.[8] The other side of the coin involves the impact of punishment for a particular response. It is assumed that punishment will decrease the probability of doing the same or similar thing at another time. The principle then implies that it would be easier to achieve successful change through the use of positive rewards. It can also be said that reinforcement can occur when the knowledge or skill acquired in a training program is reinforced through a refresher course.

A major problem associated with reinforcement is the determination of reinforcers. That is, what will serve as the appropriate reinforcer of desired behavior? For some people, money or praise is an effective reinforcer, while others respond more to a refresher type of training experience. Once again situations and individuals determine effective reinforcement. The feedback concept is similar to the principle of reinforcement. Employees generally desire knowledge on how they are doing. This is especially true after a change program has been implemented. Providing information about the progress of a unit or group of employees lets the employees take corrective action. A number of studies indicate that employees perform more effectively on a variety of tasks when they have feedback than when it is absent.[9] The timing of feedback is a factor that should be considered. Most college students want to know their course grade as soon as possible after the final examination. The same need to know exists for managers who have set objectives for the next year. They want to know immediately if their objectives are acceptable. Thus the immediacy of feedback is an issue to consider. Feedback provided a long time after a personal action has occurred will probably not be as effective as providing feedback immediately after the action. As one might anticipate, individuals differ in their receptivity to feedback concerning their actions. In general, it is more favorably received by employees who have motivation to improve themselves and/or their unit.

Transfer of Learning

Management must guard against the possibility that what was learned at a training site is lost when transferring a person to the actual work site. If things have gone well, only a minumum amount will be lost in this necessary transfer. A possible strategy for keeping the loss to a minimum is to make the training situation similar to the actual workplace environment. Another procedure is to reward the newly learned behavior. If the colleagues and superiors approve new ideas or new skills, newly trained people will be encouraged to continue to behave in the new way. If they behave negatively they will be discouraged from persisting with attempts to use what has been learned. This is one of the reasons that it has been suggested that superiors be trained before subordinates. The superior, if

---

[8]For the most recent statement by the most widely recognized spokesperson for the principle of reinforcement, see B. F. Skinner, *About Behaviorism* (New York: Alfred A. Knopf, 1974).

[9]Victor Vroom, *Work and Motivation* (New York: John Wiley & Sons, 1964), pp. 242–43.

trained and motivated, can serve as a reinforcer and feedback source for the subordinate who has left the training confines and is now back on the job.

There are numerous other principles of learning that will prove invaluable when attempting to manage OD programs. Those noted above, however, are current issues discussed in the OD literature. The manager who fails to consider them when introducing an OD program will have a difficult time improving organizational effectiveness.

An OD program must be designed systematically. This argues for an analytical approach which breaks down the process into constituent steps, logically sequenced. For this purpose a model is proposed which identifies the key elements and decision points which managers can follow. This model is described in the next section and the remainder of this chapter elaborates on each of the steps in the model.

A MODEL FOR MANAGING ORGANIZATIONAL DEVELOPMENT

■ The model which we propose is described in Figure 19–1 and consists of eight steps which are linked in a logical sequence. A manager considers each of them, either explicitly or implicitly, to undertake an OD program. The prospects of initiating successful change can be enhanced when the manager explicitly and formally goes through each successive step.[10]

The model presumes that forces for change continually act upon the organization; this assumption reflects the dynamic character of the modern world. At the same time it is the manager's responsibility to sort out the information that he receives from the organization's information system and other sources which reflect the magnitude of change forces. The information is the basis for recognizing the need for change; it is equally desirable to recognize when change is *not* needed. But, once the manager recognizes that something is malfunctioning he must then diagnose the problem and identify relevant alternative techniques. The selected technique must be appropriate to the problem, as constrained by limiting conditions. One example of a limiting condition which we have discussed in an earlier chapter is the prevailing character of group norms. The informal groups may support some change techniques but may sabotage others. Other limiting conditions include leadership behavior, legal requirements, and economic conditions.

Finally, the manager must implement the change and monitor the change process and change results. The model includes feedback to the implementation step and to the forces for change step. These feedback loops suggest that the change process itself must be monitored and evaluated. The mode of implementation may be faulty and lead to poor results, but responsive action could correct the situation. Moreover, the feedback

---

[10]Equivalent models for managing organizational development are discussed in Eric L. Herzog, "Improving Productivity via Organizational Development," *Training and Development Journal*, April 1980, pp. 36–39, and Roland L. Warren, *Social Change and Human Purpose: Toward Understanding and Action* (Chicago: Rand McNally, 1977).

FIGURE 19–1

A Model for the Management of Organizational Development

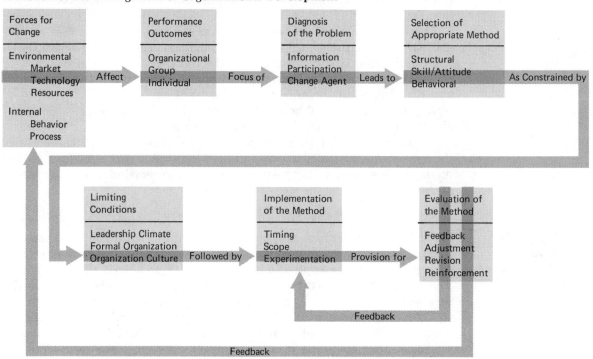

loop to the initial step recognizes that *no* change is final. A new situation is created within which problems and issues will emerge; a new setting is created which will itself become subject to change. The model suggests no "final solution," rather it emphasizes that the modern manager operates in a dynamic setting wherein the only certainty is change itself.

FORCES FOR CHANGE

■ The forces for change can be classified conveniently into two groups. They are: (1) environmental forces and (2) internal forces. Environmental forces are beyond the control of the manager. Internal forces operate inside the firm and are generally within the control of management.

Environmental Forces

The manager of a business firm has historically been concerned with reacting to changes in the *marketplace*. Competitors introduce new products, increase their advertising, reduce their prices, or increase their customer service. In each case, a response is required unless the manager is content to permit the erosion of profit and market share. At the same time changes occur in customer tastes and incomes. The firm's products may no longer have customer appeal; customers may be able to purchase less expensive, higher quality forms of the same product.

The enterprise system generally eliminates from the economic scene those firms which do not adjust to market conditions. The isolated-from-reality manager who ignores the signals from the market will soon confront the more vocal (and louder) signals of discontented stockholders. But, by that time, the appropriate change may well be dissolution of the firm—the final solution.

A second source of market forces are those which supply the firm with its resources. A change in the quality and quantity of human resources can dictate changes in the firm. For example, the adoption of automated processes can be stimulated by a decline in the supply of labor. The techniques of coal mining and tobacco farming have greatly changed during recent years due to labor shortages. We can also understand how changes in the materials supply can cause the firm to substitute one material for another. Rayon stockings and synthetic rubber tires were direct outgrowths of war-induced shortages in raw materials. We need not catalog the whole range of possible changes in the resource markets which stimulate organizational change. The potential is great, however, and must be recognized.

The second source of environmental change forces is *technology*. The knowledge explosion since World War II has introduced new technology for nearly every business function. Computers have made possible high-speed data processing and the solution to complex production problems. New machines and new processes have revolutionized the way many products are manufactured and distributed. Computer technology and automation have affected not only the technical conditions of work, but the social conditions as well. New occupations have been created and others have been eliminated. The slowness to adopt new technology which reduces costs and improves quality will show itself in the financial statements sooner or later. Technological advance is a permanent fixture in the business world and, as a force for change, it will continue to demand attention.

Finally the third environmental force is *social and political* change. Business managers must be "tuned in" to the great movements over which they have no control but which, in time, influence their firm's fate. Sophisticated mass communications and international markets create great potential for business, but also pose great threat to those managers unable to understand what is going on. Concurrently, the drive for social equality poses new issues for managers which had not been previously confronted. Finally, to add to the scene, the relationship between government and business becomes much closer as new regulations are imposed. These pressures for change reflect the increasing complexity and interdependence of modern living. The traditional functions of organizations are being questioned and new objectives are being advanced. No doubt, the events of the future will intensify external environmental forces for change.

Internal Forces

The forces for change which occur within the organization can be traced to *process* and to *behavioral* causes. Process forces include breakdowns in decision making and communications. Decisions are either not being made, are made too late, or are of poor quality. Communications are short-circuited, redundant, or simply inadequate. Tasks are not undertaken or not completed because the person responsible did not "get the word." A customer order is not filled, a grievance is not processed, or an invoice is not filed and the supplier is not paid because of inadequate or nonexistent communications. Interpersonal and interdepartmental conflicts reflect breakdowns in organizational processes.

Low levels of morale and high levels of absenteeism and turnover are symptoms of behavioral problems that must be diagnosed. A wildcat strike or a walkout may be the most tangible sign of a problem, yet such tactics are usually employed because they arouse the management to action. In most organizations a certain level of employee discontent exists and a great danger is to ignore their complaints and suggestions. But the process of change includes the *recognition* phase and it is at this point that management must decide to act or not to act.

No doubt in many organizations, the need for change goes unrecognized until some major catastrophe occurs. The employees strike or seek the recognition of a union before the management finally recognizes the need for action. Whether it takes a whisper or a shout, by some means the need for change must be recognized; and once recognized, the exact nature of the problem must be diagnosed.

**DIAGNOSIS OF
A PROBLEM**

■ Appropriate action is necessarily preceded by diagnosis of the symptoms of the problem. Experience and judgment are critical to this phase unless the problem is readily apparent to all observers. Ordinarily, however, managers can disagree on the nature of the problem. There is no formula for accurate diagnosis, but the following three questions point the manager in the right direction:

1. What is the problem as distinct from the symptoms of the problem?
2. What must be changed to resolve the problem?
3. What outcomes (objectives) are expected from the change and how will such objectives be measured?

The answers to these questions can come from information ordinarily found in the organization's information system. Or it may be necessary to generate ad hoc information through the creation of committees or task forces. Meetings between managers and employees provide a variety of points of view which can be sifted through by a smaller group. Technical operational problems may be easily diagnosed, but more subtle behavioral problems usually entail extensive analysis. One approach for diagnosing the problem is the attitude survey.

Attitude surveys can be administered to the entire work force or to a representative sample. The survey permits the respondents to evaluate and rate—management, pay and pay-related items, working conditions, equipment, and other job-related factors. The appropriate use of such surveys requires that the questionnaire be completed anonymously so that employees can express their views freely and without threat, whether real or imagined. The objective of the survey is to pinpoint the problem or problems as perceived by the members of the organization. Subsequent discussions of the survey results, at all levels of the organization, can add additional insights into the nature of the problem.[11]

The survey is a useful diagnostic approach if the potential focus of change is the total organization. If smaller units or entities are the focus, the survey technique may not be a reliable source of information. For example, if the focus is a relatively small work group, diagnosis of the problem is better accomplished through individual interviews followed by group discussion of the interview data. In this approach the group becomes actively involved in sharing and interpreting perception of problems.

Problem identification of individual employees comes about through interviews and personnel department information. Consistently low performance evaluations are indicators that problems exist., but it is often necessary to go into greater detail. Identification of individuals' problems is far more difficult than identification of organizational problems. Thus the diagnostic process must stress the use of precise and reliable information.

Managers must make two key decisions prior to undertaking the diagnostic phase. They must determine the degree to which subordinates will participate in the process and they must decide whether a change agent will be used. These two decisions have implications not only for the diagnosed process but also for the eventual success of the entire program.

The Degree of Subordinate Participation

The degree to which subordinates participate in decisions which affect their activities has been the subject of much practical and theoretical discusion. Fayol, for example, spoke of the principle of centralization in terms of the extent to which subordinates contribute to decision making. The researchers at the Hawthorne plant discovered the positive impact of supervisory styles which permit employees some say in the way they do their work. In fact, the Hawthorne studies produced the first scientific evidence of the relationship between employee participation and production. Other studies followed, including the influential Coch and French,[12] and Lewin[13] research which provided evidence that participation by subordinates could lead to higher levels of production, satisfaction, and efficiency.

Despite the considerable research, many unanswered questions remain regarding the relationships between subordinate participation, production,

---

[11]Ernest C. Miller, "Attitude Surveys: A Diagnostic Tool," *Personnel* May/June 1978, pp. 4–10.

[12]Lester Coch and John R. P. French, Jr., "Overcoming Resistance to Change," *Human Relations*, August 1948, pp. 512–32.

[13]Kurt Lewin, "Frontiers in Group Dynamics," *Human Relations*, June 1947, pp. 5–41.

Table 19–1
The Transition of Values Underlying OD Strategy

Away from:	*Toward:*
1. A view of man as essentially bad.	1. A view of man as basically good.
2. Avoidance or negative evaluation of individuals.	2. Confirming them as human beings.
3. A view of individuals as fixed.	3. Seeing rthem as being in process.
4. Resisting and fearing individual differences.	4. Accepting and utilizing them.
5. Utilizing an individual primarily with reference to his job description.	5. Viewing him as a whole person.
6. Walling off the expression of feelings.	6. Making possible both appropriate expression and effective use.
7. Maskmanship and game-playing	7. Authentic behavior.
8. Use of status for maintaining power and personal prestige.	8. Use of status for organizationally relevant purposes.
9. Distrusting people.	9. Trusting them.
10. Avoiding facing others with relevant data.	10. Making appropriate confrontation.
11. Avoidance of risk taking.	11. Willingness to risk.
12. A view of process work as being unproductive effort.	12. Seeing it as essential to effective task accomplishment.
13. A primary emphasis on competition.	13. Much greater emphasis on collaboration.

and acceptance of change. Moreover, whether actual participation or perceived participation is the more important factor bearing on organizational effectiveness, is not completely settled. It may be that all subordinates do not aspire to participate, but do desire the *opportunity* to do so when the occasion arises.[14] Nevertheless, the tendency in much of the current literature on development methods and strategies is to take the position that active participation is a cardinal requirement for successful OD programs. This position is much more a matter of espousing a set of values than a matter of scientific evidence.

Changing Values. The values which are held by those who espouse participative management are an expanded version of McGregor's Theory Y assumptions. As reflected in Table 19–1, these values are in transition and though not completely accepted in managerial practice, they are being adopted by ever-increasing numbers of managers. These values reflect the growing importance of the humanistic point of view. One can see that if the new set of values is adopted; that is, if one accepts the idea that subordinates are basically good with untapped abilities which can be used in

---

[14] See T. O. Jacobs, *Leadership and Exchange in Formal Organizations* (Alexandria, Va.: Human Resources Research Organization, 1971), pp. 204–9, for a review of research bearing on this issue.

active problem solving for the organization's benefit, important implications follow. For example, subordinates will be actively involved in the development program from its very inception. Not only will they participate in the identification of jobs to be enlarged, but they will also participate in determining whether, for example, job enrichment is the proper method to use.

The *degree* to which subordinates are actively involved in the development program can be constrained by situational factors. But the strategic decision regarding subordinate participation is not simply an either-or decision. A continuum more aptly describes the decision, as shown in Figure 19–2. The figure identifies two extreme positions (unilateral and delegated) and a middle-of-the-road approach (shared) to change.[15]

FIGURE 19–2
Strategies for Introducing Major and/or Minor Changes

Unilateral (emphasis on management reaching decisions)	Shared (emphasis on interaction and sharing of authority between manager and subordinates)	Delegated (emphasis on subordinates reaching decisions)

Unilateral Approach.   At one extreme, subordinates make no contribution to the development, or change, program. The definition and solution to the problem are proposed by management. The use of unilateral authority can appear in three forms:

1. *By Decree.*   This is simply a situation in which the superior dictates a program. There is little upward communication and subordinates are expected to accept the program without asking questions. This form assumes that subordinates will accept the program because it is being stated by authority figure that they deal with—the "boss."
2. *By Replacement.*   This form involves the replacement of personnel and it is based upon the premise that key personnel are the crucial factors in developing the organization. The replacement decision is a top-down decision since top-level executives develop the plan for replacing personnel.
3. *By Structure.*   This form attempts to alter the organizational structure by administrative fiat. An example is when a manager's span of control is increased or decreased.

Delegated Approach.   At the other extreme from the unilateral approach is the delegated approach. In this approach the subordinates actively participate in the development program, in one of two forms.[16]

---

[15] Larry E. Greiner, "Patterns of Organization Change," *Harvard Business Review*, May–June 1967, pp. 119–30.

[16] Ibid., pp. 121–22.

1. *The Discussion Group.* Managers and their subordinates meet, discuss the problem, and identify the appropriate development method. The managers refrain from imposing their own solution upon the group. The assumption of this approach is that two-way discussion and problem solving among subordinates and managers results in more motivated groups.

2. *The T-Group.* The emphasis of the T-group is on increasing an individual's self-awareness. The T-group is less structured than the discussion approach, but in this context the T-group is designed to initiate the development program and it is not the central focus. For example, the T group could identify MBO as the development method to be implemented.

The delegated approach focuses on having the subordinates interact with the superior and eventually work out a development approach. It is a major step, if used correctly, in creating a climate of full subordinate participation.

Shared Approach. This approach is built upon the assumption that authority is present in the organization and must be exercised after, and only after, giving careful consideration to such matters as the magnitude of the development effort, the people involved, and the time available for introducing the method. This approach also focuses upon the sharing of authority to make decisions. This approach is employed in two slightly different formats:

1. *Group Decision Making.* The problem is defined by management and communicated to the subordinates. The subordinates are then free to develop alternative solutions and to select what they believe is the best method to be implemented. It is assumed that the subordinates will feel a greater commitment to the solution because they participated in selecting a course of action.

2. *Group Problem Solving.* This form stresses both the definition of the problem and the selection of a possible solution. Here authority is shared throughout the process from problem identification to problem solution. It is assumed that the group, because it is involved in the entire decision process, will have increased insight into understanding the development program that is finally implemented.

A report which surveyed published cases of organizational change notes that the shared approach was relatively more successful than the unilateral or delegated approaches.[17]

The Shared Approach: Some Preconditions. Before the shared strategy can be successful, certain preconditions with respect to employees must exist. They are:

1. An intuitively obvious factor is that employees must want to become

---

[17]Ibid., pp. 119–30.

involved. They may for any number of reasons reject the invitation. They may have other needs, such as getting on with their own work, for example. Or they may view the invitation to participate as a subtle (but not too subtle) attempt by managers to manipulate them toward an already predetermined solution. If the organizational climate includes perceptions of mistrust and insincerity, any attempt to involve workers will be viewed by them in cynical terms.

2. The employees must be willing and able to voice their ideas. Even if they are willing and able, they must have some expertise in some aspect of the analysis. Certainly the technical problems associated with computer installation or automated processes are beyond the training of typical employees, yet they may have valuable insights into the impact of the machinery on their jobs. But even if they have knowledge, they must be able to articulate their ideas.

3. Managers must feel secure in positions. If insecure, then they will perceive any participation by employees as a threat to their authority. They may view employee participation as a sign of weakness or as undermining their status. They must be able to give credit to good ideas and to give explanations for ideas of questionable merit. As is evident, managers' personalities and leadership styles must be compatible with the shared authority approach if it is to be a successful strategy.

4. Finally, managers must be open-minded to employees' suggestions. If they have predetermined the solution, the participation by employees will soon be recognized for what it is. Certainly managers have final responsibility for the outcome, but they can control the situation by specifying beforehand the latitude of the employees. They may define objectives, establish constraints, or whatever, so long as the participants know what is expected of them.[18]

Successful organizational development strategies emphasize sharing authority among managers and employees. The shared approach involves the personnel in a process which not only minimizes resistance to change, but which also maximizes acceptance through the application of basic learning principles.

The Role of Change Agents

Because there is a tendency to seek answers in traditional solutions, the intervention of an outsider is usually necessary. The intervener, or change agent, brings a different perspective to the situation and serves as a challenge to the status quo.

The success of any change program rests heavily on the quality and workability of the relationship between the change agent and the key decision makers within the organization. Thus, the form of intervention is a crucial phase.

To intervene is to enter into an ongoing organization, or among persons,

---

[18] Arnold S. Judson, *A Manager's Guide to Making Changes* (New York: John Wiley & Sons, 1966), pp. 109–13.

or between departments for the purpose of helping them improve their effectiveness.[19] There are a number of forms of intervention that are used in organizations. First, there is the *external change agent* who is asked to intervene and provide recommendations for bringing about change. Second, there is the *internal change agent*. This is the individual who is working for the organization and knows something about its problems. Finally, a number of organizations have used a combination *external-internal* change team to intervene and develop programs. This approach attempts to use the resources and knowledge base of the external and internal change agents.

Each of the three forms of intervention has advantages and disadvantages. The external change agent is often viewed as an outsider. This belief when held by employees inside the company results in the need to establish rapport between the change agent and decision makers. The change agent's views on the problems faced by the organization are often different from the decision maker's views and this leads to problems in establishing rapport. The differences in viewpoints often result in the mistrust of the outsider (external change agent) by the policy makers or a segment of the policy makers.

The internal change agent is often viewed as being more closely associated with one unit or group of individuals than any other. This perceived favoritism leads to resistance to change on the part of others not included in the circle of close friends. The internal interventionist, however, is familiar with the organization and its personnel and this knowledge can be valuable in preparing for and implementing change.[20]

The third type of intervention, the combination external-internal team, is the rarest but seems to have an excellent chance for success. In this type of intervention the outsider's objectivity and professional knowledge are blended with the insider's knowledge of the organization and its human resources. This blending of knowledge often results in increased trust and confidence among the parties involved. The ability to communicate and develop a more positive rapport is communicated throughout the organization and can reduce the resistance to any change which is forthcoming.

The change agent, whether internal or external to the organization can relate to the organization according to one or more models.[21]

The Medical Model.   Perhaps the most basic of all models, the medical model places the change agent in the role of adviser. The organization requests the change agent to assist in clarifying the problems, diagnosing the causes, and recommending courses of action. The organization retains the responsibility for accepting or rejecting the change agents' recommenda-

[19] See Chris Argyris, *Intervention Theory and Method* (Reading, Mass.: Addison-Wesley Publishing, 1970); and Fritz Steele, *Consulting for Organizational Change* (Amherst: University of Massachusetts Press, 1975).

[20] Jerome Adams and John J. Sherwood, "An Evaluation of Organizational Effectiveness: An Appraisal of How Army Internal Consultants Use Survey Feedback in a Military Setting," *Group and Organization Studies*, June 1979, pp. 170–82.

[21] Based upon Margulies and Raia, *Conceptual Foundations*, pp. 108–14.

tions. The relationship is analogous to the physician-consultant arrangement; that is, the physician may seek opinions from other experts, but the choice of therapy remains with the physician.

The Doctor-Patient Model. The application of this model places the organization in the position of a "patient" who suspects that something is wrong. The change agent—the "doctor"—diagnoses and prescribes a solution which, of course, can be rejected by the patient. Yet by virtue of the relationship, the organization will usually adopt the change agent's recommendations. The change agent engages in diagnostic and problem-identification activities jointly with the organization. To the extent that the organization is totally involved in the process, the more likely will management accept the recommended solution.

The Engineering Model. This model is used when the organization has performed the diagnostic work and has decided upon a specific solution. For example, management desires to implement a MBO or job enrichment program and it seeks the services of experts to aid in the implementation. An alternative form of the model is when the organization has defined the problem-excessive turnover, intergroup competition, or ineffective leadership behavior, for example—and requests the change agent to specify a solution. The general characteristic of the model, however, is that the diagnostic phase is undertaken by management.

The Process Model. The process model is widely used by OD consultants. It involves the actual *collaboration* of the change agent and the organization through which the management is encouraged to see and understand organizational problems. Through joint efforts managers and change agents try to comprehend the factors in the situation which must be changed to improve performance. The change agent avoids taking sole responsibility for either diagnosis or prescription; rather, the emphasis is placed upon enabling management to comprehend the problems. The change agents' emphasis is teaching management *how* to diagnose, rather than doing it for management.

The choice of appropriate model depends upon characteristics of the change agent, the organization, and the situation. It is not a matter of one model being superior in all instances, rather for any given circumstance an appropriate model exists. The following close-up illustrates the model used in one situation.

ORGANIZATIONS: CLOSE-UP

Organizational Development at Johnson & Johnson

Organizational change and development efforts often fail because managers and consultants fail to integrate their efforts and activities. At the Johnson & Johnson manufacturing plant in Chicago change efforts have been suc-

ORGANIZATION: CLOSE-UP (continued)

cessful because the program made a conscious effort to involve not only the department managers and their work groups, the objects of change, but also the department manager's manager, the superintendent. Productivity improvements recorded by the participating work groups included: a 600 percent increase in earnings above previous standards, a 30 percent productivity gain, and a reduction in downtime from 15 to 6 percent.

The role of the consultants is to help break down the barriers to change and to bring the groups into the overall organization system. The consultants diagnose the situation and select a change technique based upon the diagnosis. MBO, behavior modification, transactional analysis, group and individual training, job redesign, and confrontation meetings have been used from time to time.

The role of the department manager is to stay involved in the process throughout the duration and to develop new relationships with the first-line supervisors as they develop their new skills and motivation. The department manager also serves as a positive reinforcer of the change efforts.

The role of the superintendent is to integrate the efforts of the focal department with other departments within the organization. Of special concern is the necessity to coordinate the changes in rates of production that usually accompany a change effort. Ordinarily there is a sudden upturn in productivity followed by a downturn due to the disruptive effects of the change effort. The superintendent must explain these changes to other departments and at the same time maintain faith in the eventual success of the program despite the negative signs. The superintendent must sell other departments on the necessity to alter their plans to accommodate the changing department. Moreover the superintendent takes a visible part in the process by providing periodic feedback to the supervisors and crews undergoing change.

Source: Richard D. Babcock and William B. Alton, "A Systematic Approach to Managing Corporate Change," *Management Review*, December 1979, pp. 24–27.

Change agents facilitate the diagnostic phase by gathering, interpreting, and presenting data. Although the accuracy of data is extremely important, of equal importance is the way in which the data are interpreted and presented. There are generally two ways in which this is accomplished. First, the data are discussed with a group of top managers, who are asked to make their own diagnosis of the information; or, second, change agents may present their own diagnoses without making explicit their frameworks for analyzing the data. A problem with the first approach is that top management tends to see each problem separately. Each manager views his or her problem(s) as being the most important and fails to recognize other problem areas. The second approach has inherent problems of communication. External change agents often have difficulty in the second approach because they become immersed in theory and various conceptual frameworks which are less realistic than the managers would like.[22]

A more general difficulty with either of these approaches derives from the close relationship between diagnosis and action.[23] One important guideline for managers of OD programs is that the method should not be separated from the diagnosis. In many OD programs the emphasis appears to be on the implementation of a particular method with little concern for whether it is appropriate. For example, Blake and Mouton concentrate on implementing the managerial grid across different companies,[24] and Seashore and Bowers designed an action program for the Banner organization based on participative management prior to the diagnosis of specific problem areas.[25] Instead of a "canned" approach in which the diagnosis and method are the same for different companies, a more "tailored" approach to change is needed. That is, interventions which fit the particular problems of an organization are needed. This belief is supported by Mann when he states, "Change processes organized around objective new social facts about one's own organizational situation have more force for change than those organized around general principles about human behavior."[26]

ALTERNATIVE DEVELOPMENT TECHNIQUES

■ The choice of the particular technique depends upon the nature of the problem which management has diagnosed. Management must determine which alternative is most likely to produce the desired outcome, whether it be improvement in the skills, attitudes, behavior, or structure. As we have noted, diagnosis of the problem includes specification of the outcome which management desires from the change. In the following chapter we will describe a number of change methods, some of which have been discussed in previous chapters. They will be classified according to whether the major focus of the technique is to change skills and attitudes, behavior, or structure. This classification of approaches to organizational change in no way implies a distinct division among the types. On the contrary, the interrelationships among skills, attitudes, behavior, and structure must be acknowledged and anticipated.

An important contribution of behavioral research is the documentation of the impact of structure on attitudes and behavior. Overspecialization and

---

[22] Stanley Seashore and David Bowers, *Changing the Structure and Functioning of an Organization: Report of a Field Experiment* (Ann Arbor: Survey Research Center, University of Michigan, 1963).

[23] Jay W. Lorsch and Paul Lawrence, "The Diagnosis of Organizational Problems," in *Organizational Development*, ed. Margulies and Raia, p. 219.

[24] Robert R. Blake and Jane S. Mouton, *The Managerial Grid* (Houston: Gulf Publishing, 1964).

[25] Seashore and Bowers, *Changing the Structure and Functioning of an Organization.*

[26] Floyd Mann, "Studying and Creating Change," in *The Planning of Change*, ed. W. Bennis, K. Benne, and R. Chin (New York: Holt, Rinehart, & Winston, 1961), pp. 605–13.

narrow spans of control can lead to low levels of morale and low production. At the same time, the technology of production, distribution, and information processing can affect the structural characteristics of the firm; as well as attitudes and behaviors. The fact that these interrelationships are so pronounced might suggest a weakness in our classification scheme; but, in defense of it, the techniques can be distinguished on the basis of their major thrust or focus—whether skills, attitudes, behavior, or structure.

RECOGNITION OF LIMITING CONDITIONS

■ The selection of any developmental technique should be based upon diagnosis of the problem, but the choice is tempered by certain conditions that exist at the time. Scholars identify three sources of influence on the outcome of management development programs which can be generalized to cover the entire range of organizational development efforts, whether attitudinal, behavioral, or structural. They are leadership climate, formal organization, and organizational culture.

Leadership climate refers to the nature of the work environment which results from "the leadership style and administrative practices" of superiors. Any OD program which does not have the support and commitment of management has a slim chance of success.[27] We can also understand that the style of leadership may itself be the subject of change; for example, the managerial grid and System 4 are direct attempts to move managers toward a certain style—open, supportive, and group-cenetered. But, it must be recognized that the participants may be unable to adopt such styles if the styles are not compatible with their own superior's style.

The formal organization must also be compatible with the proposed change. The formal organization includes the effects on the environment resulting from the philosophy and policies of top management, as well as "legal precedent, organizational structure, and the systems of control." Of course, each of these sources of impact may itself be the focus of a change effort; the important point is that a change in one must be compatible with all others. For example, a change in structure which will eliminate employees contradicts a policy of guaranteed employment.

The organizational culture refers to the impact on the environment resulting from "group norms, values, and informal activities." The impact of traditional behavior which is sanctioned by group norms, but not formally acknowledged, was first documented in the Hawthorne studies. A proposed change in work methods or the installation of an automated device can run counter to the expectations and attitudes of the work group and, if such is the case, the OD strategy must anticipate the resulting resistance.

The implementation of OD, which does not consider the constraints imposed by prevailing conditions within the present organization, may of

---

[27] Bernard J. White and V. Jean Ramsey, "Some Unintended Consequences of 'Top Down' Organizational Development," *Human Resources Management*, Summer 1978, pp. 7–14, note potential problems associated with extensive involvement of top management in the diagnostic phase of organizational development.

course amplify the problem that initiated the process. Even if implemented, the groundwork for subsequent problems is made more fertile than what could ordinarily be expected. Taken together, these conditions constitute the climate for change and they can be positive or negative.

IMPLEMENTING THE METHOD

■ The implementation of the OD method has two dimensions—*timing and scope*. Timing refers to the selection of the appropriate point in time to initiate the method and scope refers to the selection of the appropriate scale. The matter of timing is strategic and depends upon a number of factors, particularly the organization's operating cycle and the groundwork which has preceded the program. Certainly if a program is of considerable magnitude, it is desirable that it not compete with day-to-day operations, thus, the change might well be implemented during a slack period. On the other hand, if the program is critical to the survival of the organization, then immediate implementation is in order. The scope of the program depends upon the strategy. The program may be implemented throughout the organization. Or, it may be phased into the organization level by level, department by department. The shared strategy makes use of a phased approach, which limits the scope but provides feedback for each subsequent implementation.

The method which is finally selected is usually not implemented on a grand scale; rather it is implemented on a small scale in various units throughout the organization. For example, an MBO program can be implemented in one unit or at one level at a time. The objective is to experiment with the method; that is, to test the validity of the diagnosed solution. As the management learns from each successive implementation, the total program is strengthened. Not even the most detailed planning can anticipate all the consequences of implementing a particular method. Thus it is necessary to experiment and to search for new information that can bear on the program.

As the experimental attempts provide positive signals that the program is proceeding as planned, there is a reinforcement effect. The personnel will be encouraged to accept the change required of them and to enlarge the scope of their own efforts. The acceptance of the change is facilitated by the positive results.

EVALUATING THE PROGRAM

■ An OD program represents an expenditure of organizational resources in exchange for some desired end result. The resources take the form of money and time which have alternative uses. The end result is in the form of increased organizational effectiveness—production, efficiency, and satisfaction in the short run; adaptiveness and development in the intermediate run; survival in the long run. Accordingly, some provision must be made to evaluate the program in terms of expenditures and results. The evaluation phase has two problems to overcome: the acquisition of data which measure the desired objectives,[28] and the determination of the expected trend of improvement over time.

The acquisition of information which measures the sought-after objective is the relatively easier problem to solve, although it certainly does not lend itself to naive solutions. As we have come to understand, the stimulus for change is the deterioration of performance criteria which management traces to structural and behavioral causes. The criteria may be any number of effectiveness indicators, including profit, sales volume, absenteeism, turnover, scrappage, or costs. The major source of feedback for those variables is the organization's information system. But if the change includes the expectation that employee satisfaction must be improved, the usual sources of information are limited, if not invalid. It is quite possible for a change to induce increased production at the expense of declining employee satisfaction. Thus, if the manager relies on the naive assumption that production and satisfaction are directly related, the change may be incorrectly judged successful when cost and profit improve.

To avoid the danger of overreliance on production data, the manager can generate ad hoc information which measures employee satisfaction. The benchmark for evaluation would be available if an attitude survey had been used in the diagnosis phase. The definition of acceptable improvement is difficult when evaluating attitudinal data, since the matter of "how much more" positive the attitude of employees should be is quite different than the matter of "how much more" productive they should be. Nevertheless, if a complete analysis of results is to be undertaken, attitudinal measure-

FIGURE 19–3
Three Patterns of Change in Results through Time

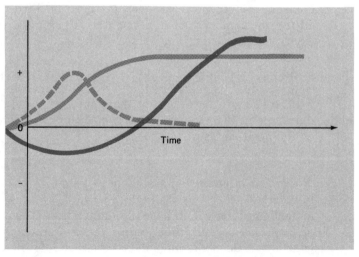

_____

[28] Arthur G. Bedeian, Achilles A. Armenakis, and Robert W. Gibson, "The Measurement and Control of Beta Change," *Academy of Management Review*, October 1980, pp. 561–66.

ments must be combined with production and other effectiveness measurements.

The second evaluation problem is the determination of the trend of improvement over time. The trend itself has three dimensions: (1) the first indication of improvement, (2) the magnitude of improvement, and (3) the duration of the improvement. In Figure 19–3 three different patterns of change for a particular effectiveness criterion are illustrated.

In the change illustrated by the lighter solid line, improvement is slight during the early periods of time, but rises and maintains itself at a positive level. The dashed line illustrates a marked increase, but followed by deterioration and a return to the original position. The darker solid line describes a situation in which the early signs indicate a decrease, but followed by a sharp rise toward substantial improvement. The patterns demonstrate only three of a number of possible relationships. A well-devised OD program would include an analysis of what pattern can be expected. The actual pattern can then be compared to the expected.

Ideally, the pattern would consist of an index which measures both the attitudinal and performance variables. Figure 19–4 illustrates a model which describes the necessary information for such an index. The solid line is the expected pattern through time. It shows a movement into acceptable behavior prior to a movement into acceptable performance. The expected pattern may, of course, assume any configuration. The dashed

FIGURE 19–4
Expected and Actual Pattern of Results

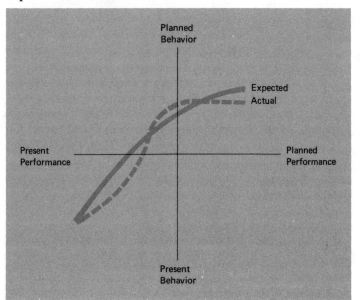

Source: Jeremiah J. O'Connell, *Managing Organizational Innovation* (Homewood, Ill.: Richard D. Irwin, 1968), p. 156. © 1968 by Richard D. Irwin, Inc.

line is the plot of actual change through time. It reflects not only what is happening, but also the impact of corrective action which management takes to keep the change on course. If the expected pattern is valid as originally conceived, then management's objective is to minimize the oscillations around the planned results.

In a practical sense, the effectiveness of an OD program cannot be evaluated if objectives have not been established before it was implemented. A program which was undertaken to make the organization "a better place to work," or to develop the "full potential of the employees," cannot be evaluated. If on the other hand measurable criteria which are valid indicators of "better places to work" and "full potential" are collected during the diagnostic phase and subsequently tracked as the program is undertaken, bases for evaluation exist. A considerable body of literature exists which describes methods of evaluation, and managers of OD programs should consult it for guidance in program evaluation.[29]

Generally, an evaluation model would follow the steps of evaluative research. The steps include:

1. Determining program objectives.
2. Describing the activities undertaken to achieve the objectives.
3. Measuring effects of the program.
4. Establishing baseline points against which changes can be compared.
5. Controlling extraneous factors, preferably through the use of a control group.
6. Detecting unanticipated consequences.

The application of this model will not always be possible. For example, managers do not always specify objectives in precise terms and control groups are difficult to establish in some instances. Nevertheless, the difficulties of evaluation should not discourage attempts to evaluate.[30]

This chapter has discussed the steps in the organizational development model. The reader should recognize that each step is important not only in its own right, but also as it affects each subsequent step. For example, an incorrect diagnosis of the problem could result in the selection of an inappropriate technique. Actual experience documents the fact that no amount of organizational restructuring will resolve problems which are rooted in attitude and skill deficiencies. Similarly, the development of attitudes and behaviors cannot have long-lasting effects if the structure of tasks and au-

---

[29] Achilles A. Armenakis, Hubert S. Feild, and Don C. Mosely, "Evaluation Guidelines for the OD Practitioner," *Personnel Journal*, Spring 1975, pp. 39–44; and William M. Evan, ed., *Organizational Experiments* (New York: Harper & Row, 1971).

[30] Henry W. Reicken, "Memorandum on Program Evaluation," in *Organization Development*, ed. Wendell L. French, Cecil H. Bell, Jr., and Robert A. Zawacki (Plano, Tex.: Business Publications, 1978), pp. 416–20. © 1978 by Business Publications, Inc.; James A. Terborg, George S. Howard, and Scott E. Maxwell, "Evaluating Planned Organizational Change: A Method for Assessing Alpha, Beta and Gamma Changes," *Academy of Management Review*, January 1980, pp. 109–22.

thority relationships are hostile to the newly learned attitudes and behaviors.

There are no guarantees that correct managerial decisions are forthcoming from the use of any model. Much is left to managerial judgment. Nevertheless, the model presented in this chapter does introduce the appropriate questions and issues.

MAJOR MANAGERIAL ISSUES

A. The necessity to consider organizational development arises from changes in the inter- and extra-organizational environment. Changes in input, output, technological, and scientific subenvironments may indicate the need to consider the feasibility of a long-term, systematically managed program for changing the structure, process, and behavior of the organization. Even in the absence of environmental changes, organizational processes and behavior may become dysfunctional for achieving organizational effectiveness.

B. The diagnosis of present and potential problems involves the collection of information which reflects the level of organizational effectiveness. Data which measure the current state of production, efficiency, satisfaction, adaptiveness, and development must be gathered and analyzed. The purpose of diagnosis is to trace the causes of the problem to one or more formal and informal components.

C. In addition to serving as the bases for problem identification, the diagnostic data also establish the basis for subsequent evaluation of the organizational development effort.

D. The problem must be diagnosed and managers can undertake the analysis by considering three questions:

   1. What is the problem as distinct from its symptoms?
   2. What must be changed to resolve the problem?
   3. What outcomes are expected and how will these outcomes be measured?

   The managerial response to these questions should be stated in terms of criteria which reflect organizational effectiveness. Measurable outcomes such as production, efficiency, satisfaction, adaptiveness, and development must be linked to skill, attitudinal, behavioral, and structural changes which are necessitated by the problem identification.

E. Managers must evaluate the impact of limiting conditions. For example, if the organizational climate is conducive to the shared strategy, the employees would have been brought into the diagnostic process and participated with management from that point on. Through shared authority, the problem would be associated with skill, attitude, behavioral, and structural causes and the appropriate method selected. If employee participation is inappropriate because the necessary preconditions do not exist, management must unilaterally define the problem and select the

MAJOR MANAGERIAL ISSUES (*continued*)

appropriate method. Whether the problem is related to skill, attitude, behavioral, or structural causes, the strategy must include provision for the learning principles of feedback, reinforcement, and transfer.

F. The logical step of the OD process is the decision to provide for an evaluation procedure. The ideal situation would be to structure the procedure in the manner of an experimental design. That is, the end results should be operationally defined and measurements should be taken, before and after, in both the organization undergoing development and in a second organization (the "control group"). Or, if the scope of the program is limited to a subunit, a second subunit could serve as a control group. The purpose of an evaluation is not only necessitated by management's responsibility to account for its use of resources, but also to provide feedback. Corrections can be taken in the implementation phase based upon his feedback.

DISCUSSION AND REVIEW QUESTIONS

1. Is it correct to argue that if either Maslow's or Herzberg's theory of motivation is valid then management should expect employees to have a need to participate in decision making? Explain your answer.

2. Is it correct to argue that if employees desire to participate they should be permitted to do so? Explain your answer.

3. Critique your instructor's teaching approach in terms of his or her utilization of learning principles.

4. Under what circumstances would the unilateral strategy be appropriate for implementing an OD method? Use the concept of leadership climate in your answer.

5. Assume that you are responsible for implementing a MBO system in an organization and that a unilateral strategy has been used. What problems of employee commitment can you anticipate, and how would you overcome these problems?

6. "The benefits derived from traditional training programs are so intangible that it makes little sense to measure them." Comment on this statement made by the training officer of a large corporation.

7. Identify the learning principles that are implemented in the shared strategy.

8. What OD strategy would likely be used in an organization that tends toward a bureaucracy? Explain your answer in terms of alternative strategies that are available.

9. Explain the difficulties you would encounter in attempting to obtain diagnostic information from the members of two groups who believe that they compete for scarce resources.

10. Describe the factors which would sustain the process model of change agent behavior.

ADDITIONAL REFERENCES

Armenakis, A. A., and H. S. Feild. "Evaluation of Organizational Change Using Non-Independent Criterion Measures." *Personnel Psychology*, 1975, pp. 39–44.

Bennis, W. G. *Changing Organizations.* New York: McGraw-Hill, 1966.

Burke, W., ed. *Contemporary Organizational Development.* Washington, D.C.: NTL Institute for Applied Behavioral Science, 1972.

Friedlander, F., and L. Brown. "Organizational Development." *Annual Review of Psychology,* 1974, pp. 219–341.

Greiner, L. E. "Evolution and Revolution as Organizations Grow." *Harvard Business Review,* 1972, pp. 37–46.

Halal, W. "Organizational Development in the Future." *California Management Review,* 1974, pp. 35–41.

Havelock, R. G., and M. G. Havelock. *Training for Change Agents.* Ann Arbor, Mich.: Center for Research on Utilization of Scientific Knowledge, 1973.

Herman, S. M., and M. Korenich. *Authentic Management: A Gestalt Orientation to Organizations and Their Management.* Reading, Mass.: Addison-Wesley Publishing, 1977.

House, R. J. *Management Development: Design, Evaluation, and Implementation.* Ann Arbor: University of Michigan, 1967.

Kilmann, R. H., and R. P. Herden. "Toward a Systemic Methodology for Evaluating the Impact of OD Interventions on Organization Effectiveness." *Academy of Management Review,* 1976, pp. 87–98.

King, A. S. "Expectation Effects in Organizational Change." *Administrative Science Quarterly,* 1974, pp. 221–30.

Lippitt, G. L. *Organization Renewal.* New York: Appleton-Century-Crofts, 1969.

Lippitt, R.; J. Watson; and B. Westely. *The Dynamics of Planned Change.* New York: Harcourt Brace Jovanovich, 1958.

Miles, R. E., and J. B. Ritchie. *Participative Management: Quality vs. Quantity." California Management Review,* 1971, pp. 48–56.

O'Connell, J. J. *Managing Organizational Innovation.* Homewood, Ill.: Richard D. Irwin, 1968.

Partain, J., ed. *Current Perspectives on Organizational Development.* Reading, Mass.: Addison-Wesley Publishing, 1973.

Patten, T. H., and L. E. Dorey. "Long-Range Results of a Team Building OD Effort." *Public Personnel Journal,* 1977, pp. 31–50.

Schein, V. E. "Political Strategies for Implementing Change." *Group and Organizational Studies,* 1977, pp. 42–48.

Sirota, D., and A. D. Wolfson. *Pragmatic Approach to People Problems." Harvard Business Review,* 1973, pp. 120–28.

Sofer, C. *The Organization from Within.* London: Quadrangle Books, 1962.

Tichy, N. M. "How Different Types of Change Agents Diagnose Organizations." *Human Relations,* 1975, pp. 771–79.

Varney, G. *An Organization Development Approach to Management Development.* Reading, Mass.: Addison-Wesley Publishing, 1976.

EVALUATION OF AN MBO PROGRAM

Attitude survey data which a State Health Department collected as a part of its OD program served as a basis for evaluating the program. The program was based upon the MBO method and it was designed to develop the managerial capabilities of program directors, among other objectives. The initial diagnosis had indicated the program directors were by and large not involved in decision making because division directors, their immediate supervisors, preferred the directive style of management. One of the consequences of this style was the relatively short supply of program directors who were promotable to more responsible positions.

The OD program was designed to develop, through training and experience, the division directors' ability to work with their program directors in less directive, more participative ways. It was also anticipated that program directors would need training in how to accept and implement the increased authority. The external change agent also believed, and the top management agreed with him, that the program must build in the opportunities for division and program directors to meet and make decisions.

Accordingly, the program provided for the division directors and the commissioner's office to meet as a group on a regular basis. During these meetings they studied the literature on participative management and MBO. Equally important, they also learned the commissioner's philosophy and attitudes toward management. Training materials containing journal articles and case studies were provided and discussed during the sessions. And to focus the discussion of the group on real, rather than hypothetical problems, the attitude survey data were analyzed and evaluated by the division directors.

During this period division directors were expected to train the program directors of their respective divisions. They were to meet the first or second day after each of their sessions with their program directors and discuss, interpret, and elaborate the materials which they themselves had been studying. In this manner the division directors not only assumed the roles of coaches, but the program directors were also made aware of the commissioner's intent to develop a climate which encouraged and supported participative management and increased delegation of authority.

The training period preceded by six months the development of goal statements for each division. These statements would serve as the bases for allocating the department's budget among the divisions. It was expected that the division directors would develop these statements jointly with program directors and that this experience would reinforce the learning presumed to have occurred during the training sessions.

Two months after the completion of the training sessions and funding decisions, a second attitude survey was undertaken. The questionnaire was completed by all employees. The respondents remained anonymous except for the designation of certain demographic and job information, including level in the managerial hierarchy. Thus it was possible to combine the responses of program and division directors to obtain group means. The change agent presented the data from the second attitude survey to the division directors. He noted one result that he believed they should discuss and analyze. That result seemed to indicate that one of the objectives of the program had not been attained, that being the intended downward delegation of authority to program directors.

A number of questions on the questionnaire measured the perceived amount of authority. Generally, the program directors indicated that their authority had declined since the first attitude survey. One particularly interesting question to which all the directors responded on both occasions was stated as follows:

How much "say" do you think each of the following people usually has in deciding work objectives of the departmental program? *Circle one in each line across.*

	Usually Has a Great Deal of Say	*Quite a Bit of Say*	*Some Say*	*Just a Little Say*	*Usually Has no Say at All*
Program directors	1	2	3	4	5
Division heads	1	2	3	4	5
The commissioner's office	1	2	3	4	5

Exhibits 1 and 2 present the group means to this question for the division directors (solid line) and program directors (dashed line). Plainly the program directors' perceptions of what had happened during the previous year were contrary to what was supposed to happen. They believed, as indi-

EXHIBIT 1

Group Means for Response of Division and Program Directors prior to OD Program

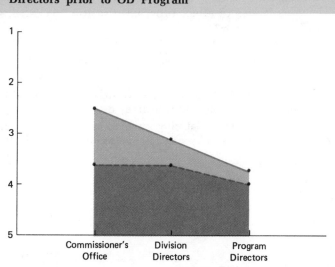

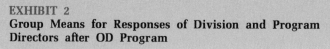

EXHIBIT 2
**Group Means for Responses of Division and Program
Directors after OD Program**

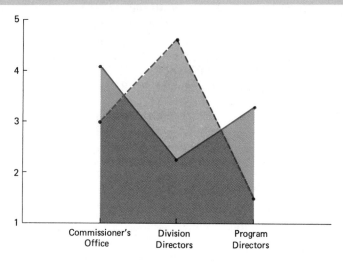

cated by their responses, that not only did they have less say in their programs, but that division directors had considerably more than before. And the division directors reported that they had considerably less and that program directors had more "say" in deciding work objectives.

The division directors were confused by the questionnaire results. How could it be, they asked the change agent, that despite our efforts they believe that we have more and they have less authority? Are the data reliable? Is there any other evidence to indicate that the program has backfired, at least as it was to affect program directors? What do we do now? Scrap it and start all over?

Questions for Consideration

1. What would be your answers to the division directors if you were the change agent?

2. What other kinds and sources of information would be useful in determining the validity of the attitude survey data?

3. How likely is it that efforts which managers undertake to delegate authority will be perceived by subordinates as efforts to centralize authority?

Chapter 20

Methods and Applications of Organizational Development

AN ORGANIZATIONAL ISSUE FOR DEBATE
Sensitivity Training Is an Effective OD Technique

ARGUMENT FOR *

Sensitivity training is a learning experience which emphasizes human relations skills. "The training is designed to help good managers become better managers." The proponents of sensitivity training believe that the inability to deal with others—subordinates, superiors, peers, and clients—is a major cause of organizational problems. The learning that occurs in sensitivity training sessions provides managers with greater awareness of their own values, motives, and assumptions.

The evidence for the effectiveness of sensitivity training is testimonial in nature. That is, participants state that they have learned to cope with frustrations, anxieties, and stress in their jobs as a consequence of their training. As one participant stated: "Through becoming more aware of others' problems, I found that my problems were not unique. As a result, I achieved more inner peace and ability to face some of the problems of our team."

ARGUMENT AGAINST †

The arguments which support those who believe that the claims of sensitivity training are overstated rest upon research findings. The research efforts attempt to evaluate the impact of sensitivity training on participants. The conclusion of the research is that there is little evidence to indicate changes in participants' "standings on objective measures of attitudes, values, outlooks, interpersonal perceptions, self-awareness, or interpersonal sensitivity." Thus even though participants often report that they believe that these changes have occurred as a consequence of sensitivity training, there are no objective facts to support their beliefs.

Another claim of sensitivity training is that participants are better able to analyze problems, synthesize information, face and resolve interpersonal conflict, and implement solutions. At present no research evidence exists to support these claims, largely because researchers have spent

---

* Based upon Leland P. Bradford, "How Sensitivity Training Works" in *The Failure of Success*, ed Alfred J. Marrow (New York: AMACOM, 1972) pp. 241–56.

† Based upon Marvin D. Dunnette and John P. Campbell, "Laboratory Education: Impact on People and Organizations" in *Concepts and Controversy in Organizational Behavior*, ed. Walter Nord (Santa Monica, Calif.: Goodyear Publishing, 1972), pp. 455–82.

ARGUMENT FOR (continued)

Wives of executives often participate with their husbands. As one executive's wife stated: "I gained a deeper understanding of the tremendous stress and strain my husband is constantly under. I had not understood his problems before and tended to blame him for poor communication. Now we both realize our joint responsibility for communication, and more importantly, how we can go about it." This wife's reaction to the training is shared by many others who have gone through it.

ARGUMENT AGAINST (continued)

their efforts to evaluate the human relations effects of sensitivity training. Thus even though much personal testimonial evidence supports sensitivity training, empirical research data support the counter argument.

The management of organizational development requires the designation of an end result, the selection of a method to achieve that end result, and the implementation of the method. The desired end result can be stated in terms of improved production, efficiency, satisfaction, adaptiveness, and development, separately or in some combination. Furthermore, a variety of methods are available to assist the manager in achieving the end results. These range from changing structure to changing behavior. This chapter continues the discussion by elaborating upon the issues and problems associated *with alternative development methods.*

DEPTH OF INTENDED CHANGE

■ The diagnostic process is critical to the eventual success of the OD program, yet there are no easily mastered approaches which guarantee accurate diagnosis. Managers can, however, undertake diagnosis in a systematic manner by recognizing that the problem may be rooted in either the formal or informal components of the organization. In Figure 20–1 the organization is depicted as an iceberg. The formal components of an organization are analogous to that part of an iceberg which is above water; the informal components lie "below water." As indicated in Figure 20–1, the formal components are observable, rational, and oriented to structural factors. The informal components are, on the other hand, not observable to all people, affective, and oriented to process and behavioral factors.

The problems of the organization as indicated by ineffective levels of production, efficiency, satisfaction, adaptiveness, and development can be traced to one or more formal and informal components. And even though the diagnostic information may indicate that the source of the problem is a formal component, the manager must recognize the potential impact of a change in an informal component if the formal component is changed.

Generally speaking, the greater the scope and magnitude of the problem, the more likely it is that the problem will be found in the informal components. At the same time, the greater the problem, the greater the magnitude and extent of intended change. That is, as the "target" of the OD program lies deeper in the "organizational iceberg," the more fundamental is the intended change. At one extreme are problems which lie with the *structure* of the organization. Job definitions, departmentalization bases, spans of control, and delegated authority can be manipulated. At the other extreme are problems which lie with the *behavior* of groups and individuals. These problems are related to personal views, value orientations, feelings, and sentiments as well as activities, sentiments, and roles within and among groups. And while these behaviors can certainly be affected by changes in structure, they are ordinarily deep-seated and must be directly confronted.

The relationship between source of problem and degree of intended change is illustrated in Figure 20–2; it suggests that there are 10 levels, or targets, of an OD program.[1] As we noted above, as the target moves from

---

[1]The relationship between depth of organization and intended change is more popularly

FIGURE 20–1
The Organizational Iceberg

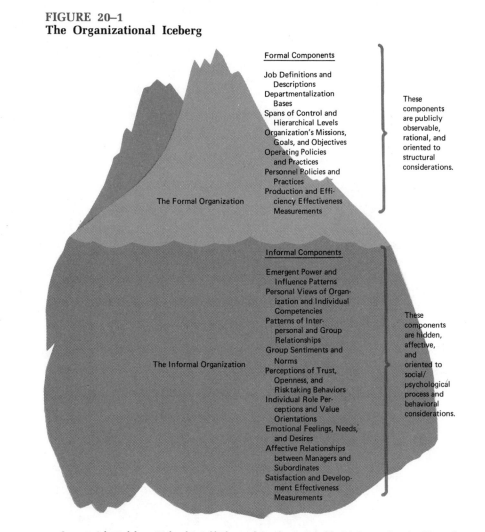

Source: Adapted from Richard J. Selfridge and Stanley L. Sokolik, "A Comprehensive View of Organizational Development," *MSU Business Topics*, Winter 1975, p. 47.

left to right and, consequently, deeper into the organization the OD program can be expected to be more person- and group-centered. It will rely more upon socio-psychological and less upon technical-economic knowledge. Levels I through IV involve the formal structure, policies, and practices of the organization; levels V and VI involve skills and attitudes of managerial and nonmanagerial personnel; and levels VII through X involve

termed *depth of intervention*. We have chosen to term it *degree of intended change* to highlight the issues associated with change, rather than those related to intervention. See Roger Harrison, "Choosing the Depth of Organizational Intervention," *Journal of Applied Behavioral Science*, April–May 1970, pp. 181–202, for an original discussion of the concept.

FIGURE 20–2
Model of Organizational Development Targets

STRUCTURAL TARGETS ←						→BEHAVIORAL TARGETS			
Level I	Level II	Level III	Level IV	Level V	Level VI	Level VII	Level VIII	Level IX	Level X
Organizational Structure	Operating Policies and Practices	Personnel Policies and Practices	Job Performance Appraisal and Improvement	Management Attitudes and Skills	Non-management Attitudes and Skills	Intergroup Behavior	Intragroup Behavior	Individual Behavior	Individual-Group Behavior

Depth of intended → change

LOW ——————————————————→ HIGH

Adapted from Richard J. Selfridge and Stanley L. Sokolik, "A Comprehensive View of Organizational Development," *MSU Business Topics*, Winter 1975, p. 49.

the behavior of groups and individuals. For each of these levels, one or more OD *methods* exist as possible solutions. Only after the problem and its level are diagnosed should the method be selected.

Despite an ever-increasing knowledge base, organizational development practitioners are not absolutely certain that a specific method will have its intended effects. In fact there are many instances of failure, and some of these instances will be discussed in the sections to follow. Recently a number of reviews have been undertaken to discern the relative success of OD methods, particularly in terms of whether they have affected the intended target in the intended manner. These reviews suggest that OD methods do not always obtain the desired changes in the targets of intervention. Thus even though there is growing sophistication in the OD theory and practice, there is yet room for caution,[2] as suggested by the following close-up.

ORGANIZATIONS: CLOSE-UP

Failure at Rushton

Paul S. Goodman, in his book *Addressing Organizational Change: The Rushton Quality of Work Experiment*, traces the history of a QWL experiment which allowed three eight-member crews in one section of a coal mine to direct their own work, subject only to safety regulations. The experiment was an attempt to enrich the work of coal miners by providing increased autonomy, self-direction, and team problem solving. The experiment was concerned not only with improving the quality of work life but also improving productivity. For a period of about three years the experiment was deemed successful: indicators of morale, safety, and productivity all improved. Then the experiment began to fail and now is virtually disbanded. The causes for the failure have little to do with the experiment itself, according to Goodman.

The failure was due to a series of union walkouts over issues that were unrelated to the experiment but which nevertheless produced tensions between management and labor. But there were difficulties that could be traced to the experiment. For example, the external consulting team failed to train adequately the miners so that they could continue the program after the consultants left; a program that would share the gains from the program with the miners was promised but never implemented; and there were basic antagonisms that developed between members of the experimental and control work teams. Nevertheless and despite the failure of the Rushton experiment, Goodman believes that management should not hesitate to attempt quality of work-improvement programs. If managed properly the results can be positive for both management and labor.

---

[2] Robert Blake and Jane Mouton, "Why the OD Movement Is Stuck and How to Break It Loose," *Training and Development Journal*, September 1979, pp. 12–20; William A. Pasmore and Donald C. King, "Understanding Organizational Change: A Comparative Study of Multifaceted Interventions," *The Journal of Applied Behavioral Sciences*, October–November–December 1978, pp. 455–68; Jerry I. Porras, "The Comparative Impact of Different OD Techniques and Intervention Intensities," *The Journal of Applied Behavioral Science*, April–May–June 1979, pp. 156–78.

**STRUCTURAL
DEVELOPMENT
METHODS**

■ Structural development in the context of organizational change refers to managerial action which attempts to improve effectiveness through a change in the formal structure of task and authority relationships. At the same time we must recognize that the structure creates human and social relationships which over time can become ends for the members of the organization. These relationships, once defined and made legitimate by management, introduce an element of stability.[3] Members of the organization may resist efforts to disrupt these relationships.

Structural changes affect some aspect of the formal task and authority definitions. As we have seen, the design of an organization involves the definition and specification of job range and depth, the grouping of jobs in departments, the determination of the size of groups reporting to a single manager, and the delegation of authority. Within this framework, the communication and decision-making processes occur. Three methods designed to change all or some aspect of the organization structure are discussed in this section. They are management by objectives (MBO), System 4, and MAPS. These methods are appropriate for consideration when the problem is diagnosed as being in levels I through IV.

**Management by
Objectives**

Management by objectives (MBO) has been widely applied and evaluated during the last two decades.[4] One of the early proponents of MBO, Peter Drucker, proposed a process which would allow managers to participate in the establishment of goals and objectives for their units. The process can also include the participation of nonmanagers in the determination of their specific objectives. According to Drucker the only conditions which must be satisfied are that the objectives must be defined in terms of their contribution to the total organization and that the person who establishes them must have sufficient control to accomplish them.

The original work of Drucker and subsequent writings by others[5] provide the basis for three guidelines for implementing MBO:

1. Superiors and subordinates meet and discuss objectives which if met would contribute to overall goals.
2. Superiors and subordinates jointly establish attainable objectives for the subordinates.

---

[3] R. K. Ready, *The Administrator's Job* (New York: McGraw-Hill, 1967), pp. 24–30.

[4] Mark L. McConkle, "Classifying and Reviewing the Empirical Work on MBO: Some Implications," *Group and Organization Studies*, December 1979, pp. 461–75.

[5] Peter Drucker, *The Practice of Management* (New York: Harper & Row, 1954); George Odiorne, *Management by Objectives* (New York: Pitman Publishing, 1965); and W. J. Reddin, *Effective Management by Objectives* (New York: McGraw-Hill, 1970). For two recent reviews, see Henry Tosi, "Effective and Ineffective MBO," *Management by Objectives* 4 (1975): 7–14; and John M. Ivancevich, James H. Donnelly, Jr., and James L. Gibson, "Evaluating MBO: The Challenge Ahead," *Management by Objectives* 4 (1975): 15–23. For specific discussions and case studies of applications of MBO in health-care and governmental organizations, see *First Tango in Boston: A Seminar on Organizational Change and Development* (Washington, D.C.: National Training and Development Services, 1973); and "Management by Objectives in the Federal Government," *The Bureaucrat*, Winter 1974.

3. Superiors and subordinates meet at a predetermined later date to evaluate the subordinates' progress toward the objectives.

The exact procedures employed in implementing MBO vary from organization to organization and from unit to unit. However, the basic elements of objective setting, participation of subordinates in objective setting, and feedback and evaluation are usually parts of any MBO program. The intended consequences of MBO include improved contribution to the organization, improved attitudes and satisfaction of participants, and greater role clarity. MBO is highly developed and widely used in business organizations, but its applicability in health-care and governmental organizations has not been completely tested. In this section we will describe an OD project which was undertaken in a state department of health and which resulted in the implementation of an MBO system.

The project began with the administration of an attitude questionnaire to all employees in the department. The purpose of the attitude survey was twofold: To provide information for pinpointing attitudinal problems and to provide base-line measurements for follow-up studies. The same attitude questionnaire was administered to the state department of mental health employees, the "control group." The two departments are quite similar in mission and employee characteristics such as age, educational level, and length of service. Subsequent comparisons of the attitude data would indicate problems as they arose in the department as related to the OD program.

The attitude data became the focus of discussion in training sessions attended by the division directors and the commissioner of health. The discussions focused on the problems identified in the attitude survey. It was found, for example, that there was considerable ambiguity in the minds of employees about the goals and means for achieving goals. This finding substantiated the judgment of management that MBO should be implemented in the health department.

The group identified their own training needs as the discussions continued and the trainer, a university professor, supplied the appropriate literature and materials. The division directors read the technical literature on MBO and participative management. They also held periodic informal discussions with the program directors of their own divisions. In this manner the entire management cadre was involved in the OD program.

Subsequent to the training sessions the division directors, in consultation with their own subordinates, prepared goal statements which became the basis for subsequent discussions with the commissioner and his staff. The goal statements listed in order of priority the major objectives of each division. The number of objectives depended upon the scope of each division's activities and ranged from 5 to 15. In addition, the resource requirement for each objective was estimated and indicated in the statements. The outcome of the discussion between each division director and the commissioner was mutually agreed-upon sets of objectives and resource allocations.

The management group met periodically to discuss the problems that they had experienced in the first phase of the MBO cycle. Among the problems it identified was the difficulty of obtaining accounting data pertaining to their objectives. The typical governmental accounting procedures as used in the health department emphasized the determination of program cost and included allocations of administrative cost on rather arbitrary bases. These cost data were not compatible with or pertinent to divisional goals. A second problem was more fundamental to the MBO method and not so easily resolved as the accounting problem: the identification of effectiveness criteria for divisional objectives. The discussions indicated that the management group tended to overemphasize production criteria at the expense of efficiency and satisfaction criteria. Some attention was given to development and adaptiveness criteria, but it was relatively little. These issues were confronted and the discussion shifted to the matter of reporting progress at the six-month review date.

The six-month review discussions between the commissioner and each of the division directors indicated the necessity for revisions in light of revised priorities and planning premises. The revised objectives prevailed during the next six months and the cycle began anew.

The program undertaken in the health department reflected the main features of OD as we have defined it here:

1.   The program was long-term and systematically planned.
2.   The managerial personnel at all levels confronted organizational problems as revealed by diagnostic data.
3.   The training sessions were designed to facilitate the discussion of mutual problems with technical literature serving as a source of help in the resolution of these problems.
4.   The MBO method was integrated into the organization only after careful experimentation and consideration.

System 4 Organization

According to Likert, an organization can be described in terms of eight operating characteristics. They are: (1) leadership, (2) motivation, (3) communication, (4) interaction, (5) decision making, (6) goal setting, (7) control, and (8) performance. Furthermore, the nature of each of these characteristics can be located on a continuum through the use of a questionnaire which members of the firm (usually managers) complete. The means of each response category are calculated and plotted to produce an organizational profile as shown in Figure 20–3.

To diagnose the extent to which a particular organization approximates the System 4 structure, Likert has devised a 51-item questionnaire which is completed by the employees of an organization. The employees indicate their perceptions of the extent to which the characteristics which define the System 4 organization are present in their own organization. The

FIGURE 20–3
Organizational Profiles for Two Manufacturing Firms

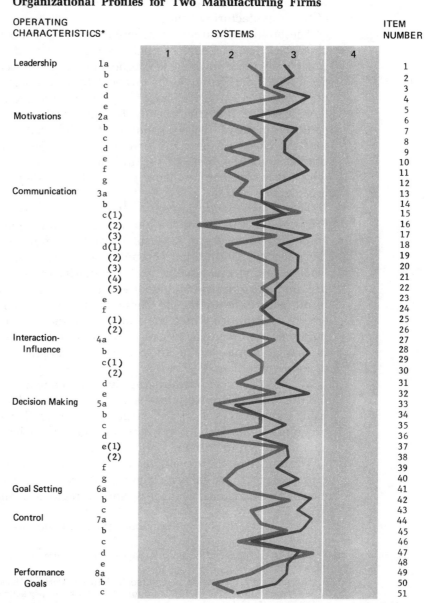

OPERATING CHARACTERISTICS*		SYSTEMS	ITEM NUMBER

Leadership	1a		1
	b		2
	c		3
	d		4
	e		5
Motivations	2a		6
	b		7
	c		8
	d		9
	e		10
	f		11
	g		12
Communication	3a		13
	b		14
	c(1)		15
	(2)		16
	(3)		17
	d(1)		18
	(2)		19
	(3)		20
	(4)		21
	(5)		22
	e		23
	f		24
	(1)		25
	(2)		26
Interaction-Influence	4a		27
	b		28
	c(1)		29
	(2)		30
	d		31
	e		32
Decision Making	5a		33
	b		34
	c		35
	d		36
	e(1)		37
	(2)		38
	f		39
	g		40
Goal Setting	6a		41
	b		42
	c		43
Control	7a		44
	b		45
	c		46
	d		47
	e		48
Performance Goals	8a		49
	b		50
	c		51

Each of the eight characteristic is measured by a number of items. Leadership, for example, is measured by five questionnaire items (ia–e).

means of the responses are calculated and plotted along the continua which describe the eight characteristics. Figure 20–3 illustrates the profiles of two manufacturing firms.

The profiles illustrate the differences which can occur in organizational characteristics. In Likert's terms, the organization described by the lighter line clearly tends toward the classical design, whereas the organization defined by the darker line tends toward a System 4 organization. If the theory of System 4 is valid, we should expect the organization on the right to be more effective than the one to the left. Furthermore, both organizations could be improved by a developmental plan that would move each organization closer to the right, or closer to System 4. This result would be predicted on the basis of the universalistic nature of System 4 theory, which is to say that the theory predicts that System 4 is the most effective organization design.

The change toward System 4 involves measuring the present state of the firm through the use of the questionnaire. Subsequent training programs emphasize the concepts of System 4 and the application of the concepts to the present organization. Through the use of supportive, group-oriented leadership and the equalization of authority to set goals, implement control, and make decisions, higher earnings and efficiency should ordinarily result (according to Likert).[6] These results derive from positive changes in employee attitudes which are induced by the structural changes.[7] As the point has been made by others, "To obtain lasting change, one does not try to change people, but rather to change the organizational constraints that operate upon them."[8]

Various OD programs utilizing System 4 concepts have been reported in the literature.[9] Here we will describe a program which combined management training (Level V) and structural change (Level I). Essentially, the program was designed to develop attitudes and behaviors which would be compatible with a System 4 organization.[10]

The target of the development effort was the sales unit of a business firm, specifically 16 sales managers. The group consisted of a national sales manager, 2 divisional managers, and 13 regional managers. The short-run

---

[6]Rensis Likert, *The Human Organization* (New York: McGraw-Hill, 1967).

[7]Ibid., p. 47.

[8]Eliot D. Chapple and Leonard R. Sayles, *The Measure of Management* (New York: Macmillan, 1961), p. 202.

[9]An important illustration is reported in Alfred J. Marrow, David G. Bowers, and Stanley E. Seashore, *Management by Participation* (New York: Harper & Row, 1967). This report documents the effort of the Harwood company management to transform the Weldon company, which it purchased in 1961, into a System 4 organization. A follow-up study of the Harwood experience is reported in Stanley E. Seashore and David G. Bowers, "Durability of Organizational Change," *American Psychologist*, March 1970, pp. 227–33. Also see W. F. Dowling, "At General Motors: System 4 Builds Performance and Profits," *Organizational Dynamics*, Winter 1975, pp. 23–28.

[10]This OD program is reported in Robert T. Golembiewski and Stokes B. Carrigan, "Planned Change in Organization Style Based on the Laboratory Approach," *Administrative Science Quarterly*, March 1970, pp. 79–93.

goals of the program were (1) to integrate the 16 managers into an effective team following the appointment of a new national sales manager, a divisional manager, and three regional managers, (2) to facilitate the development and acceptance of new roles for the regional managers who, with the introduction of a new product line, would have to spend 90 percent of their time in managerial work, rather than the present 40 percent, and (3) to confront and resolve certain communication and interpersonal problems which remained as a result of the personnel changes. The main difficulty was the regional managers' perception that the new national head was so aggressive that he would dominate the divisional managers.

The long-run goals of the program were (1) to make more congruent actual and preferred behaviors (the managers feared that mistrust and secrecy would be required to succeed in the organization, but they preferred trusting and open relationships), (2) to move the organization more toward the System 4 end of the continuum, and (3) to experiment with a "bottom-up" approach to OD (the usual approach is "topdown," as in the case of the health department OD program).

To get at these objectives, the sales managers engaged in training during which they experimented with the kinds of behaviors appropriate for a System 4 organization. Learning exercises which emphasized interpersonal and intergroup relations were an important part since these are the key relationships involved in building integrated work teams. The training sessions culminated in a confrontation between regional and divisional managers and between the division and the national sales manager. These confrontations encouraged the managers to share and to test the value of openness and problem solving in the organization. However, the real test of openness and problem solving would come in the context of the everyday work of the organization; that is, whether the behavior learned in the training sessions could be transferred back to the workplace.

To obtain some indication of the lasting effects of the training session and to gauge progress toward the development of a System 4 organization, the managers completed the organizational profile questionnaire prior to the training session and again four months later. There was no control group available. Obviously the absence of a control group limits the analysis and the results must be validated by other means such as observation of actual workplace behavior. Given these limitations, the differences between the before and after measures indicated that movement had been made toward the System 4 organization and that this movement had been facilitated by the training methodology. Thus the behavior learned in the training sessions appears to have been made a part of the organization structure.

MAPS Design Technology

Organization development, as we have noted, involves management in a long-term, collaborative process to improve the performance of organizations, groups, and individuals. Moreover, typical OD methods are based upon specific humanistic values and assumptions. MAPS is a relatively recent development which embodies the ideas of organization development in the design of organization structure. MAPS—an acronym for multivariate analysis, participation, and structure, attempts to apply humanistic theories of motivation to create organization structures.[11]

Although the method has not fully evolved, at present its proponents suggest that an organization structure can be designed (or redesigned) by going through the following steps. These steps should be undertaken by members of the organization with the aid of an external consultant familiar with the MAPS approach.[12]

1. Diagnosing the organization to determine whether organization structure is a cause of performance problems.
2. Determining the focus, or target, of the change effort; determining whether the total organization structure or selected work-group structures should be changed and developed.
3. Specifying the objectives to be accomplished by the effort; these objectives would be related to performance criteria and to the diagnosed problems.
4. Matching the specific MAPS approach to the diagnosed problems and objectives. The approach varies depending upon the change target, problem diagnosis, and stated objectives.[13]
5. Developing a questionnaire which specifies the various specific tasks that the organization or group must accomplish and which lists the members of the organization or group. The list of tasks is produced in a participative collaborative effort by all the members of the organization *and*, in some instances, by customers and/or clients. The purpose of this step is to account fully for the total range of tasks necessary to achieve effective organizational or group performance.
6. Administering the questionnaire to all members of the target organization or group. Each member indicates his/her strength of preference to work on specific tasks as well as preference of other individuals with whom to work on these preferred tasks.
7. Analyzing the questionnaire data through multivariate statistics (and a computer) to identify "clusters" of tasks and people. These clusters reflect the preferences of individuals to work on specific tasks with specific other people. Thus the MAPS design technology is a modern-day application of the concept of sociometric choice.[14]

---

[11] Ralph H. Kilmann, *Social System Design: Normative Theory and the MAPS Design Technology* (New York: North-Holland Publishing, 1977), p. 23.

[12] Ralph H. Kilmann, "On Integrating Knowledge Utilization with Knowledge Development: The Philosophy behind the MAPS Design Technology," *Academy of Management Review*, July 1979, pp. 420–21.

[13] See Kilmann, *Social System Design*, for a complete discussion of this quite technical aspect of MAPS.

[14] See J. L. Moreno, "Contributions of Sociometry to Research Methodology in Sociology," *American Sociological Review*, June 1947, pp. 287–92, for a classic discussion of sociometry.

8. Selecting a specific set of clusters of tasks and people. It is inevitable that different combinations of tasks and people clusters will result from the application of different rules for combining them. The ultimate decision is based upon discussion among all those individuals vitally affected by the outcome, thus providing additional opportunity for participation.

9. Implementing the selected set of clusters—the organization design—by providing resources and support which enable the members of the newly formed groups to learn to work together.

10. Monitoring the entire implementation process to detect problems which can be resolved at early stages.

11. Evaluating the realized results of the change in terms of the objectives originally set forth during the diagnostic stage.

12. Rediagnosing the new structure in recognition of the fact that solutions to old problems become sources of new problems.

A careful reading of the 12 steps of the MAPS method indicates the manner in which it implements effective OD strategy. Steps 1–4 and 8–12 apply the change strategy discussed in Chapter 19 and which has been associated with instances of successful change efforts. Thus MAPS represents an integration of a specific method with a more general OD strategy.

The MAPS Design Technology is a relatively new development in organizational development. The first reported application was in the redesign of a university departmental structure.[15] Since that first application several other attempts have been reported.[16] Although it is too early to establish the potential significance of MAPS, its initial effects are promising.

SKILL AND ATTITUDE DEVELOPMENT METHODS

■ The development of skills and attitudes requires training programs of a periodic or continuing nature. These programs are designed to improve participants' knowledge, skills, and attitudes toward their jobs and the organization. The training may be part of a larger effort such as MBO, job enrichment, or System 4 programs, or it may be directed toward the development of specific objectives. In the usual case, managerial training is directed toward the development of communication and decision-making skills, thus developing the organization's fundamental processes.

Because of the multiplicity of training programs we will only describe some of the more representative and widely publicized types in this section. Some of the advantages and disadvantages associated with each program will be described. The attainment of desired objectives such as knowledge acquisition or improvement in job performance will also be examined.

---

[15] Bill McKelvey and Ralph H. Kilmann, "Organization Design: A Participative Multivariate Approach," *Administrative Science Quarterly*, March 1975, pp. 24–36.

[16] See Kilmann, "On Integrating Knowledge Utilization," for a review of these studies.

On-the-Job Training

A popular philosophy over the years has been to train employees on the job. It is assumed that if training occurs off the job there will be a loss in performance when trainees are transferred back to the job. It is also proposed that from an economic standpoint the on-the-job training is best since employees are producing while they undergo training. There are, however, a number of shortcomings in on-the-job training. First, employees may be placed in a stress-laden situation even before learning the job. This may result in accidents or poor initial attitudes about the job. Second, the area in which a person is being trained is often congested. Finally, if a number of trainees are learning in various job locations, the trainer must move around constantly to monitor their performance.

Job-Instruction Training. Formulated during World War II by the War Manpower Board, this program provides a set of guidelines for undertaking on-the-job training for white- and blue-collar employees. After trainees are introduced to the job, they receive a step-by-step review and demonstration of the job functions. When trainees are sufficiently confident that they understand the job they demonstrate their ability to perform the job. This demonstration continues until the trainees reach a satisfactory level of performance.

The objective of this approach is to bring about a positive change in performance which is reflected in higher production, lower scrap costs, and so on. This type of training is best suited for jobs that have specific content. Variations of this program are used in universities in preparing doctoral candidates for teaching and research careers and in hospitals in preparing nurses for new job duties. A crucial point to recognize is that the trainer must have the technical skill to perform the job which the trainee is performing. Note also that the trainer must understand the importance of repetition, active participation, and immediate constructive feedback.

Junior Executive Boards. This technique, popularized by the McCormick Company, concentrates on providing junior-level (middle- and lower level managers) with top-level management problem-solving experience. The junior executive may serve on a committee or junior board that is considering some major decision concerning investments or personnel planning. The assumption in this type of training is that the trainee will acquire an appreciation for decisions being made "upstairs" and this can be translated into a better overall view of the organization's direction and difficulties. In addition, the ability of the junior executive to contribute to problem solving can be assessed. In effect management is teaching the trainee and determining the trainee's ability to cope with major problems. The value of such a program depends upon the trainee's readiness to cope with these problems and the feedback received about performance.

Off-the-Job Training

Traditionally organizations have found that it is necessary to provide training that supplements on-the-job efforts. Some of the advantages of off-the-job training are:

1. It lets executives get away from the pressures of the job and work in a climate in which "party-line" thinking is discouraged and self-analysis is stimulated.
2. It presents a challenge to executives that, in general, enhances their motivation to develop themselves.
3. It provides resource people and resource material—faculty members, fellow executives, and literature—that contribute suggestions and ideas for the executives to "try on for size" as they attempt to change, develop, and grow.

The theme of the advantages cited above is that trainees by being away from job pressures are more stimulated to learn. This is certainly debatable since it is questionable whether much of what is learned can be transferred back to the job. Attending a case problem-solving program in San Diego is quite different from facing irate customers in Detroit. Despite the difficulty of transferring knowledge from the classroom-type environment to the office plant, or hospital, these programs are still very popular and widely utilized.

The Lecture Method. This is probably the most widely used method of training because it is a relatively inexpensive way to distribute information to a large audience. The effectiveness of the lecture method is best achieved in programs in which knowledge acquisition by participants is the objective. Thus, if changing attitudes is the primary objective of a training program, it would seem that the lecture method could not accomplish this objective by itself.

A main attraction of the lecture method is its simplicity and the control it is supposed to give to the trainer. The lecture can be prepared weeks or months ahead of time and the material can be used again. Despite the advantage of preparing the lecture before presentation, the procedure doesn't ensure that learning will occur. A critical point often forgotten is that the audience must be motivated to learn. In training programs that participants are required to attend, their presence doesn't ensure motivation. The best developed and planned lecture may not achieve any impact if the participants are not ready to learn.

The Discussion or Conference Approach. This method provides the participants with opportunities to exchange ideas and recollections of experience. Through the interaction in the sessions the participants stimulate each other's thinking, broaden their outlook, and also improve their communicative abilities.

The role of participants is relatively passive in the lecture method, while in the discussion group trainees have many opportunities to participate. The trainer serves as a resource person and provides immediate feedback. Because of the active interaction between trainer and participants the trainer must be highly skilled. If interpersonal skills are to be improved and/or knowledge acquired, the trainer must understand the importance of reinforcing positive behavior and feeding back clearly the contribution of each participant to the group discussion.

The Case Study and Role-Playing Method. This method provides trainees with a description of some events that actually occurred in an organization. The case may describe the manner in which a nursing supervisor is trying to motivate subordinates or the type of wage and salary program implemented in a retail store. Trainees read the case, identify the problems, and reach solutions.

In role playing, trainees are asked to participate actively in the case study. That is, they act out a case as if it were a play. One participant may be the nurse supervisor and three other participants may play the roles of subordinates. The rationale is that by role playing the participants can actually "feel" what the cases are all about.

BEHAVIORAL DEVELOPMENT METHODS

■ Levels VII through X require methods which delve deeply into group and individual behavior processes. Intergroup, intragroup, individual-group, and individual behavior are often confounded by emotional and perceptual processes which interfere with effective organizational functioning. These development targets have received the greatest amount of attention from OD experts and, consequently, a considerable number of methods have been devised for attacking them. Instead of cataloging these methods, only four will be discussed in detail—the managerial grid, sensitivity training, team building, and life planning. They are the more readily used methods since they tend to span at least two and potentially three levels of targets.

The Managerial Grid

The managerial grid program is based upon a conceptualization of a particular style of leadership behavior.[17] The two dimensions which the developers of the program, Blake and Mouton, identify are concern for production and concern for people. A balanced concern for production and people is the most effective leadership style according to Blake and Mouton and is termed 9, 9. The program requires not only the development of this style, *but also the development of group behavior which supports and sustains it.* The entire program consists of six sequential phases which are undertaken over a three- to five-year period.

The six phases can be separated into two major segments.[18] The first two phases provide the foundation for the later four phases. The latter four phases build on the beginning foundation.

---

[17]Robert R. Blake and Jane S. Mouton, *The Managerial Grid* (Houston: Gulf Publishing, 1964).

[18]The descriptions of the six phases are based primarily upon Robert R. Blake, Jane S. Mouton, Louis B. Barnes, and Larry E. Greiner, "Breakthrough in Organization Development," *Harvard Business Review,* November–December 1964, pp. 133–35; and Robert R. Blake, Jane S. Mouton, Richard L. Sloma, and Barbara P. Loftin, "A Second Breakthrough in Organization Development," *California Management Review,* Winter 1968, pp. 73–78.

1. Laboratory-Seminar Training. This is typically a one-week conference designed to introduce the manager of the grid philosophy and objectives. From 12 to 48 managers are assigned as members of problem-solving groups. These seminars are conducted by line managers of the company who have already been through this initial grid training phase.

The seminar begins by determining and reviewing each participant's style of behavior concerning production and people. It continues with 50 hours of problem solving, focusing upon situations involving interpersonal behavior and its influences on task performance. Each group regularly assesses its problem-solving performance. This immediate face-to-face feedback sets the stage for phase 2.

2. Intragroup Development. This begins after phase 1 when superiors and immediate subordinates explore their managerial styles and operating practices as a group. It is anticipated that the climate of openness and candor which was established in phase 1 will carry over into the second phase. Taken together the first two phases provide conditions which are designed to:

> . . . enable managers to learn managerial grid concepts as an organizing framework for thinking about management practices;
> . . . build improved relationships between groups, among colleagues at the same level, and between superiors and subordinates;
> . . . make managers more critical of outworn practices and precedents while extending their problem-solving capacities in interdependent situations. Words like "involvement" and "commitment" become real in terms of day-to-day tasks.[19]

3. Intergroup Development. This phase involves group-to-group working relationships and focuses on building 9, 9 group roles and norms beyond the single work group. Situations are established whereby tensions that typically exist between groups are identified and discussed by group members.

The objective of this phase is to move the groups from the usual "we win–you lose" patterns to a joint problem-solving activity. This procedure also helps to link managers who are at the same management level but belong to different work units.

4. Organizational Goal Setting. The immediate objective of the fourth phase is to set up a model of an effective organization for the future. The development of a future organization blueprint involves developing convictions about ideal management practices by testing existing ones and setting practical attainable objectives within a time framework. Through the use of the total organization, planned goals at each level will hopefully be linked.

---

[19] Blake, Mouton, Barnes, and Greiner, "Breakthrough in Organization Development," p. 137. The development of effective group behavior can be the central focus of an OD program. For example, see John R. Kimberly and Warren R. Nielsen, "Organizational Development and Change in Organizational Performance," *Administrative Science Quarterly*, June 1975, pp. 191–206.

5. Goal Attainment. This phase uses some of the same group and educational procedures as phase 1 but the major concern is the total organization. Once the special task groups define the problem areas other groups are set up throughout the organization. These groups are given a written "task paragraph" which describes the problem and the goal. Group members are given packets of information on the issue under discussion. The group members study the packets and then are given a test on its content. Once the information is understood and agreement is reached within the group, it begins to work on corrective steps.

6. Stabilization. The final phase is a period of stabilizing the changes brought about in prior phases. A period of time, perhaps as long as a year, is necessary after the first five phases to identify weaknesses and take corrective actions in the goals set and the plans implemented. This phase also enables management to evaluate the total program.

The longevity of the managerial grid method suggests that it is more than a fad to practicing managers. Thus, it would appear that more rigorous studies of what it can and cannot accomplish are required. Only by properly studying this approach can those interested in implementing it as a developmental method generally understand how it can change employee behavior.

Team Building

The managerial grid attempts to develop a group structure to support and sustain a particular leadership style. It is not necessary, however, to develop group behavior around 9, 9 or any other leadership model. Rather group behavior can be developed to perform more effectively through an intervention technique termed team building. Whereas the managerial grid is a comprehensive technique, the focus of team building is the work group as illustrated by the following close-up.

ORGANIZATIONS: CLOSE-UP

Quality of Work-Life at Tarrytown

Organizational efforts to be effective in unionized organizations must involve the union as well as management. In 1973 General Motors and the United Auto Workers established the National Committee to Improve the Quality of Work Life. The committee consists of two high-placed union officials and two top-management people. The purpose of the committee is to encourage and sponsor efforts at the local plant level which are designed to improve and develop the quality of work life.

An example of the results produced by the joint committee is the improvement in performance at the Tarrytown, New York, plant where the company assembles the front-wheel-drive Chevrolet Citation. The plant had a history of union-management adversity, excessive costs, and poor overall performance. Gus Beirne, former superintendent of the plant, recalls: "Workers and bosses were constantly at each others' throats." Something had to be done. With the

---

ORGANIZATION: CLOSE-UP (*continued*)

support and encouragement of the national committee, the Tarrytown plant established its own joint committee and began discussions regarding ways to overcome the difficulties which beset the plant.

A significant outcome of the local committee's deliberations was the initiation of a three-day training program for all employees at Tarrytown. The primary focus of the training program was the development of skills in team problem solving. But the training sessions also enabled management and union officials to talk to the participants about the plant and how their jobs were related to other jobs in the plant. Attendance at the program was voluntary, but nearly all of the 3,800 employees attended during its year and a half duration.

The effort is credited with much of the improvement in the Tarrytown plant's performance indicators. Morale is improved, absenteeism has dropped, and grievances are only a fraction of what they were before the training sessions. Top management now considers Tarrytown to be one of the best performing assembly plants in General Motors. The clear lesson in the Tarrytown experience is that management and labor can cooperate to their mutual advantage to increase both job satisfaction and productivity.

Source: "Stunning Turnaround at Tarrytown," *Time*, May 5, 1980, p. 87.

The purpose of team building is to enable work groups to more effectively get their work done, to improve their performance.[20] The work group may be existing, or relatively new, command and task groups. The specific aims of the intervention include setting goals and priorities, analyzing the ways the group does its work, examining the group's norms and processes for communicating and decision making, and examining the interpersonal relationships within the group. As each of these aims is undertaken, the group is placed in the position of having to recognize explicitly the contributions, positive and negative, of each group member.[21]

The process by which these aims is achieved begins with *diagnostic meetings*. Often lasting an entire day, the meetings enable each group member to share with other members his or her perceptions of problems. If the group is large enough, subgroups engage in discussion and report their ideas to the total group. The purpose of these sessions is to obtain the views of all members and to make these views public. That is, diagnosis, in this context, implies the value of "open confrontation" of issues and problems that previously were talked about in relative secrecy.

Problem identification, and consensus as to their priority, is an initial

---

[20]Richard W. Woodman and John J. Sherwood, "Effects of Team Development Intervention: A Field Experiment," *The Journal of Applied Behavioral Science*, April–May–June 1980, pp. 211–17.

[21]Richard Beckhard, "Optimizing Team-Building Efforts," *Journal of Contemporary Business*, Summer 1972, p. 24.

and important step. However *a plan of action* must be agreed upon. The action plan should call on each group member or members to undertake a specific action to alleviate one or more of the problems. If for example, an executive committee agrees that one of its problems is lack of understanding and commitment to a set of goals, a subgroup can be appointed to recommend goals to the total group at a subsequent meeting. Other group members can work on other problems. For example, if problems are identified in the relationship among the members, a subgroup initiates a process for examining the roles of each member.[22]

Team-building interventions do not always require a complex process of diagnostic and action meetings. For example, the chief executive of a large manufacturing firm recognized that conflict within his executive group was creating defensiveness between the functional departments. He also recognized that his practice of dealing on a one-to-one basis with each of the executive group members, each of whom headed a functional department, contributed to the defensiveness and conflict. Rather than viewing themselves as team members having a stake in the organization, the functional heads viewed each other as competitors. The chief executive's practice of dealing with them individually confirmed their beliefs that they managed relatively independent units.

To counteract the situation, the chief executive adopted the simple expedient of requiring the top group to meet twice weekly. One meeting focuses on operating problems, the other on personnel problems. The ground rule for these meetings is that the group must reach consensus on decisions. After one year of such meetings, company-oriented decisions were being made and the climate of interunit competition was replaced by cooperation.[23]

Team building is also effective when new groups are being formed. Problems often exist when new organizational units, project teams, or task forces are created. Typically such groups have certain characteristics which must be overcome if they are to perform effectively. For example:

1. Confusion exists as to roles and relationships.
2. Members have a fairly clear understanding of short-term goals.
3. Group members have technical competence which puts them on the team.
4. Members often pay more attention to the tasks of the team than to the relationship among the team members.

The result of these characteristics is that the new group will focus initially on task problems, but ignore the relationship issues. By the time relationship problems begin to surface, the group is unable to deal with them and the performances begin to deteriorate.

---

[22]Wendell L. French and Cecil H. Bell, Jr., *Organization Development* (Englewood Cliffs, N.J.: Prentice-Hall, 1973), pp. 112–20.

[23]Virginia E. Schein and Larry E. Greiner, "Can Organization Development Be Fine-Tuned to Bureaucracies?" *Organizational Dynamics*, Winter 1977, p. 54.

To combat these tendencies, the new group should schedule team-building meetings during the first weeks of its life. The meetings should take place away from the work site; one- or two-day meetings are often sufficient. The format of such meetings varies, but essentially the purpose is to provide time for the group to work through its timetable and the roles of members in reaching the groups objectives. An important outcome of the meeting is to establish understanding about each member's contribution to the team and the reward for that contribution.[24]

Life Planning

Problems at the individual level are often diagnosed as the result of mismatches between what people want out of life and what they get. People grow and change, they develop skills, attitudes, and beliefs throughout their lives which may be incompatible with their lifestyles, including their work lives. Life situations change away from the workplace as children come and go, as marriages strengthen or decay. The intertwining of work and living creates dynamic forces which effect in strong measure job performance.

Initial career choices reflect a person's interests, personality, self-identity, and social background at the time. But these factors change. Life-planning techniques are not only a reflection of an organization's commitment to the aspirations of its employees, but are also valid responses to ineffective individual performance.[25]

Life planning and development involves an intervention process which encourages individuals to focus on their past, present, and future states. Specifically the process enables individuals to consider the following points:[26]

1. An assessment of one's life at the present time, including important events and choices as well as personal strengths and weaknesses.
2. A formulation of future goals related to desired lifestyle and career path.
3. The establishment of a plan which specifies goals, action steps, and target dates.

These points are considered by each individual after engaging in exercises which require explicit analyses. Although the specific format of the exercise may vary, the following is representative:

First Phase

1. Draw a straight line from left to right to represent your life span. The length represents your total life experience and future expectations.
2. Indicate on the line where you are now.

[24] Richard Beckhard, *Organization Development* (Reading, Mass.: Addison-Wesley Publishing, 1969), pp. 28–29.

[25] Douglas T. Hall, *Careers in Organizations* (Santa Monica, Calif.: Goodyear, 1976), pp. 11–22.

[26] French and Bell, *Organization Development*, pp. 144–46.

3. Prepare an inventory of important happenings, including:
    a. Peak experiences you have had.
    b. Things you do well.
    c. Things you do poorly.
    d. Things you would like to stop doing.
    e. Things you would like to learn to do well.
    f. Peak experiences you would like to have.
    g. Values you want to achieve.
    h. Things you would like to start doing now.
4. Discussion of each person's statements in subgroups.

Second Phase

1. Write your own obituary.
2. Form pairs and write a eulogy for your partner.
3. Discussion in subgroups.[27]

The value of providing opportunities for employees to assess their lives depends largely upon the commitment of organizations. The forms of that commitment are money and time—money to sponsor the training and time of employees to participate. But if done properly, benefits can accrue to individuals and organizations. For example, life planning:

> Demonstrates the larger social responsibility of a mature organization.
> Indicates to adult employees that the organization cares about them.
> Prepares individuals to change in society, organizations, and themselves.
> Releases the potential of the individual on behalf of the organization.[28]

Life planning is closely related to management by objectives, but it focuses on life, rather than job, accomplishments. This technique commits the organization to a process which recognizes the value of each individual and to an effort to integrate individual and organizational aspirations.

Sensitivity Training   This highly publicized development method focuses on individual and individual-group problems. "Sensitivity" in this context means sensitivity to self and self-other relationships. An assumption of sensitivity training is that the causes of poor task performance are the emotional problems of people who must collectively achieve the goal. If these problems can be removed, a major impediment to task performance is consequently eliminated. Sensitivity training stresses "the *process* rather than the *content* of training and focuses upon *emotional* rather than *conceptual* training."[29] Thus, we can see that this form of training is quite different from tradi-

---

[27] Ibid., pp. 144–45.

[28] Gordon L. Lippitt, "Developing Life Plans: A New Concept and Design for Training and Development," *Training and Development Journal*, May 1970, p. 3.

[29] Henry C. Smith, *Sensitivity to People* (New York: McGraw-Hill, 1966), p. 197. Emphasis added.

tional forms of training which stress the acquisition of a predetermined set of concepts with immediate application to the workplace.

The process of sensitivity training includes a group (a T-group) which in most cases meets at some place away from the job. The group, under the direction of a trainer, can engage in a group dialogue which has no agenda and no focus. The objective is to provide an environment which produces its own learning experiences.[30] As group members engage in the dialogue they are encouraged to learn about themselves as they deal with others. They explore their needs and their attitudes as revealed through their behavior toward others in the group and through the behavior of others toward them. The T-group may be highly unstructured. As one who participated in sensitivity training points out, "It [sensitivity training] says 'Open your eyes. Look at yourself. See how you look to others. Then decide what changes, if any, you want to make and in which direction you want to go.' "[31]

The role of trainers in the T-group is to facilitate the learning process: according to Kelly, they are "to observe, record, interpret, sometimes to lead, and always to learn."[32] The artistry and style of trainers are critical variables in determining the direction of the T-group's sessions. They must walk the uneasy path of unobtrusive leadership. They must be able to interpret the role of participants and encourage them to analyze their contributions without being perceived as a threat themselves. Unlike the group therapist, the T-group trainers deal with people who are considered normal, but who have come together to learn. The usually described role of trainers is that of "permissive, nonauthoritarian, sometimes almost nonparticipative" leadership.

The critical test of sensitivity training is whether the experience itself is a factor leading to improvement in task performance. It is apparent that even if the training induces positive changes in the participant's sensitivity to self and others, such behavior may be either not possible or not permissible back in the workplace. The participant must deal with the same environment and the same people as before the training. The open, supportive, and permissive environment of the training sessions is not likely to be found on the job. Even so, the proponent of sensitivity training would reply that the participants are better able to deal with the environment and to understand their own relationship to it. We would also recognize that sensitivity training may well induce negative changes in some participants' ability to perform their organizational task; the training sessions can be occasions of extreme stress and anxiety. The capacity to deal effectively

---

[30]L. P. Bradford, J. R. Gibb, and K. D. Benne, *T-Group Theory and Laboratory Method* (New York: John Wiley & Sons, 1964).

[31]Alfred J. Marrow, *Behind the Executive Mask* (New York: American Management Association, 1964), p. 51.

[32]Joe Kelly, *Organizational Behavior*, rev. ed. (Homewood, Ill.: Richard D. Irwin, 1974), p. 664. © 1974 by Richard D. Irwin, Inc.

with stress varies among individuals, and the outcome may be dysfunctional for some participants.

The scientific evidence to date suggests mixed results for the effectiveness of sensitivity training as a change method.[33] Managers must critically examine this technique in terms of the kinds of changes they desire and those which are possible given the existence of conditions which limit the range of possible changes. In this light the manager must determine whether the changes induced by sensitivity training are instrumental for organizational purposes and whether prospective participants are able to tolerate the potential anxiety of the training.

The current thinking of OD specialists is that, while sensitivity training may have a "significant impact on most participants," it is not enough "from the standpoint of organizational improvement." More and more we see the use of sensitivity training as one aspect of a total program. A now-famous application of sensitivity training at TRW Systems is illustrative of the way in which the total organization is the target of change. As Davis has observed:

> The notion very early in the TRW Systems effort was to focus on changes in the on-going culture itself: the norms, rewards, systems, and processes. If all we did was to have a lot of people attend sensitivity training, this might indeed be useful to them as individuals, but its usefulness would be quite limited with respect to the total organization.[34]

The inconclusive results regarding the relationships between sensitivity training and organizational effectiveness have caused managers to become skeptical about its continual use.[35] That skepticism and the concern of OD experts to improve their methods have led to a number of variations on the basic sensitivity approach. These variations tend to delve less deeply into the nonwork-related feelings and sentiments of the participants and instead focus only on task-relevant behavior. These variants have not been fully evaluated in terms of organizational effectiveness, yet their existence suggests a continuing place for sensitivity training-type methods in organizational development literature and practice.

AN OVERVIEW

■ This and the preceding chapter comprise an integral unit which, for sake of presentation, has been separated. We should now bring the two

---

[33] See Robert J. House, "T-Group Education and Leadership Effectiveness: A Review of the Empirical Literature and a Critical Evaluation," *Personnel Psychology*, Spring 1967, pp. 1–32; and John P. Campbell and Marvin D. Dunnette, "Effectiveness of T-Group Experiences in Managerial Training and Development," *Psychological Bulletin*, August 1968, pp. 73–104.

[34] S. Davis, "An Organic Problem-Solving Method of Organizational Change," *Journal of Applied Behavioral Science*, January–February 1967, pp. 3–21 as quoted in Fred I. Steele, "Can T-Group Training Change the Power Structure?" *Personnel Administration*, November 1970, p. 50.

[35] William J. Kearney and Desmond D. Martin, "Sensitivity Training: An Established Management Development Tool?" *Academy of Management Journal*, December 1974, pp. 755–60.

chapters together by restating the model to emphasize the key decisions which managers must make.

Forces for Change

The forces for change are either external or internal. No management decision is required in this step of the model except to provide for the information system which senses the external and internal environment. Of particular concern is the necessity for continually monitoring the organizational climate. Problems associated with low morale, communication breakdowns, and ineffective leadership are associated with climate variables.

Recognition of the Need for Change

This step is crucial to the entire development process. It is at this point that managers decide to act. If in management's judgment the forces for change are significant, the process moves to the next step, diagnosis.

Diagnosis of the Problem

The key decision in this step is whether the stimulus for change should be acted upon. This decision can be approached by making three related decisions:

1. What is the problem as distinct from its symptoms?
2. What must be changed to resolve the problem?
3. What outcomes are expected and how will these outcomes be measured?

The managerial response to these questions should be stated in terms of criteria which reflect organizational effectiveness. Measurable outcomes such as production, efficiency, satisfaction, adaptiveness, and development must be linked to skill, attitudinal, behavioral, and structural changes which are necessitated by the problem identification.

If the organizational climate is conducive to the shared strategy, the employees would have been brought into the process at the recognition of need step and participated with management from that point on. Through shared authority, the problem would be associated with skill, attitude, behavioral, and structural causes and the appropriate technique selected.

If the climate is not conducive to employee participation because the necessary preconditions do not exist, management must unilaterally define the problem and select the appropriate method. Whether the problem is related to skill, attitude, behavioral, or structural causes, the strategy must include provision for the learning principles of feedback, reinforcement, and transfer. Without these principles none of the development methods, whether sensitivity training, managerial grid, management by objectives, job enrichment, or System 4 organization has a maximum chance of success.

The model therefore, emphasizes that the OD program be specifically tailored to the problems and personnel of the organization. It recommends against the implementation of "canned" approaches which are the current rage in the literature. Throughout our discussions of organizational design, motivation, and leadership, we have stressed the situational approach. This point of view is fundamental to the process of organizational development and change.

**Recognition of
Limiting Conditions**

Inherent in the situational approach is the understanding that each organization must adapt in unique ways to its environment. Accordingly, conditions are created which limit the range of development methods and strategies available to management. The leadership style, the formal organization, and group norms all come together and are reflected by the organizational climate. A development method such as sensitivity training or System 4 organization will fail if the climate does not support the behavioral changes induced by the OD program. The learning cannot be transferred to the workplace.

Selection of Method

The analysis of the problem, identification of alternatives, and recognition of constraints lead to the selection of the most promising method. The selection is based upon the principle of maximizing expected returns to the organization if the decision is characterized by risk or by one of the principles of uncertainty.

**Implementation
of the Method**

The implementation decision involves scope and timing. The shared approach prescribes a limited scope accompanied by feedback to participants. Timing relates to when the method will be implemented and there are no specific guidelines except that the method should be initiated when it is least disruptive to the day-to-day routine.

**Evaluating
the Method**

The logical last step of the OD process is the decision to provide for an evaluation procedure. The ideal situation would be to structure the procedure in the manner of an experimental design. That is, the end results should be operationally defined and measurements should be taken before and after in both the organization undergoing development and an organization not undergoing development. Or if the scope of the program is limited to a subunit, a second subunit could serve as a control group.

The purpose of the evaluation is not only necessitated by management's responsibility to account for its use of resources, but also to provide feedback. Corrections can be taken in the implementation phase based upon this feedback. Subsequent implementations can benefit from the feedback.

We have now concluded the section which deals with organizational development. Much of the discussion in previous chapters has been mentioned in our elaboration of the development model. Concepts such as organizational design, structure, decision making, communications, motivation, groups, and leadership are apparent and important for the management of development and change.

MAJOR MANAGERIAL ISSUES

A. After diagnosing the problem and identifying the target for change, management must select the most promising development method. The philosophy of OD emphasizes that the correct order of analysis is problem to method, not method to problem.

B. Management must tailor the OD program to the problems and personnel of the organization. Throughout our discussions of organizational design, motivation, and leadership, we have stressed the contingency approach. This point of view is fundamental to the process of organizational development and change.

C. Inherent in the situational approach is the understanding that each organization must adapt in unique ways to its environment. Accordingly, conditions are created which limit the range of development methods and strategies available to management. A development method such as sensitivity training or System 4 will fail if management does not support the behavioral changes induced by the OD program.

D. The analysis of the problem, identification of alternatives, and recognition of constraints lead to the selection of the most promising method and strategy. The selection is based upon the principle of maximizing expected returns to the organization.

E. Although there is by nature considerable overlap among the levels for which a particular method is appropriate, each has a primary focus. One should not expect, for example, that MBO will be effective in changing behaviors at level X, although it may affect to a degree the behavior at levels VII and VIII.

F. The number of OD methods is considerable and ever-increasing. Only a few of the more widely used ones have been discussed. Managers considering the possibility of OD should consult a more detailed description of them. Several such descriptions appear in the citations and additional references to this chapter.

DISCUSSION AND REVIEW QUESTIONS

1. Do you believe that changes are required in processes, behaviors, or structure in the college you attend?

2. Which organizational development method described in the chapter would you recommend to your university's president for implementation? Why?

3. What are the implicit value judgments of the oganizational development techniques described in this chapter? Do you agree with them?

4. Could professors use the approaches of MBO and job enrichment in the management of their classrooms; that is, could they, for example, "enrich" the roles of students? What difficulties might they encounter?

5. Describe how you would go about designing a managerial grid training program for a group of campus student leaders.

6. What are the differences between job enrichment and System 4 organization? Are the differences

simply matters of emphasis, or are there fundamental differences?

7. What would be the most serious limiting condition for each of the development methods discussed in this chapter?

8. What specific motivation theories explain the apparent success of MBO? Develop fully your answer.

9. Explain how team-building exercises apply group-development theory as explained in Chapter 7.

ADDITIONAL REFERENCES

Beckhard, R. *Organizational Development: Strategies and Models.* Reading, Mass.: Addison-Wesley Publishing, 1969.

Bennis, W. G. *Organizational Development: Its Nature, Origins, and Prospects.* Reading, Mass.: Addison-Wesley Publishing, 1969.

Burke, W. W. "Management and Organizational Development: What Is the Target of the Change?" *Personnel Administration,* 1971, pp. 44–56.

Connor, P. E. "A Critical Inquiry into Some Assumptions and Values Characterizing OD." *Academy of Management Review,* 1977, pp. 635–44.

Corprew, J., and H. Davis. "An Organization Development Effort to Improve Instruction at a University." *Educational Technology,* 1975, pp. 44.

Crockett, W. J. "Team Building: One Approach to Organizational Development." *Journal of Applied Behavioral Science,* 1970, pp. 291–306.

Cummings, G.; E. S. Molloy; and R. H. Glen. "Intervention Strategies for Improving Productivity and the Quality of Work Life." *Organizational Dynamics,* 1975, pp. 52–68.

Davis, H. J., and K. M. Weaver. *Alternate Workweek Patterns: An Annotated Bibliography of Selected Literature.* Washington, D.C.: National Council for Alternative Work Patterns, 1978.

Eddy, W. B. "From Training to Organization Change." *Personnel Administration,* 1971, pp. 37–43.

Filley, A. C. *Interpersonal Conflict Resolution.* Glenview, Ill.: Scott, Foresman, 1975.

Fink, S. L.; J. Beak; and K. Taddeo. "Organizational Crisis and Change." *Journal of Applied Behavioral Science,* 1971, pp. 15–37.

Fordyce, J. D., and R. Weil. *Managing with People: A Manager's Handbook of Organizational Development Methods.* Reading, Mass.: Addison-Wesley Publishing, 1979.

French, W. L., and C. H. Bell, Jr. *Organization Development.* Englewood Cliffs, N.J.: Prentice-Hall, 1973.

Heller, F. A. "Group Feed-Back Analysis as a Change Agent." *Human Relations,* 1970, pp. 319–33.

Herman, S. M. "What Is This Thing Called Organizational Development?" *Personnel Journal,* 1971, pp. 595–603.

Hornstein, H. A., and N. M. Tichy. "Developing Organization Development for Multinational Organizations." *Columbia Journal of World Business,* 1976, 11. 124–37.

Kaufman, R. "Organizational Improvement: A Review of Models and an Attempted Synthesis." *Group and Organizational Studies,* 1976, pp. 474–95.

Lawrence, P. R., and J. W. Lorsch. *Developing Organizations: Diagnosis and Action.* Reading, Mass.: Addison-Wesley Publishing, 1969.

Lindell, M. K., and J. A. Drexler. "Equivocality of Factor Incongruence as an Indicator of Type of Change in OD Interventions." *Academy of Management Review,* 1980, pp. 105–8.

Lippitt, R.; J. Watson; and B. Westley. *The Dynamics of Planned Change.* New York: Harcourt, Brace Jovanovich, 1958.

Luthans, F., and R. Kreitner. *Organizational Behavior Modification.* Glenview, Ill.: Scott, Foresman, 1975.

McClelland, D. C. "Toward a Theory of Motive Acquisition," *American Psychologist,* 1965, pp. 321–33.

Margulies, N., and J. Wallace. *Organizational Change: Techniques and Applications.* Glenview, Ill.: Scott, Foresman, 1973.

Nadler, D. A. "The Use of Feedback for Organizational Change." *Group and Organizational Studies*, 1976, pp. 177–86.

Plovnick, M., and R. Fry. "New Developments in OD Technology." *Training and Development Journal*, 1975, pp. 19–25.

Schein, V. E.; E. H. Maurer; and J. F. Novak. "Impact of Flexible Working Hours on Productivity." *Journal of Applied Psychology*, 1977, pp. 463–65.

Schneier, C. E. "Behavior Modification in Management: A Review and Critique." *Academy of Management Journal*, 1974, pp. 528–48.

Scott, D. "Productive Partnership Coupling MBO and TA." *Management Review*, 1976, pp. 12–19.

Seashore, S. E., and D. G. Bowers. *Changing the Structure and Functioning of an Organization.* Ann Arbor: Survey Research Center, University of Michigan, 1963.

Stephenson, T. E. "Organization Development—A Critique." *Journal of Management Studies*, 1975, pp. 249–65.

Taylor, J. C. "Some Effects of Technology in Organization Change." *Human Relations*, 1971, pp. 105–23.

Umstot, D. D. "Organization Development Technology and the Military: A Surprising Merger?" *Academy of Management Review*, 1980, pp. 189–201.

Warrick, D. D. "Applying OD to the Public Sector." *Public Personnel Management*, 1976, pp. 186–90.

White, S. E., and T. R. Mitchell. "Organization Development: A Review of Research Content and Design." *Academy of Management Review*, 1976, pp. 57–73.

Winn, A. "Social Change in Industry: From Insight to Implementation." *Journal of Applied Behavioral Science*, 1966, pp. 170–84.

**DEVELOPING
EFFECTIVE
WORK TEAMS***

The Saga Administrative Corporation was created in the 1940s to provide food service to universities and other institutions. The organization of the company was along territorial lines; the food service managers at institutions reported to district managers who in turn reported to regional managers. The vice president for food service, located in Menlo Park, California, had responsibility for food service operations and was the ultimate source of authority for all decisions regarding food service.

The rapid expansion of the company caused considerable upheaval in the way Saga had typically functioned. The philosophy of the chairman of the board reflected that of the company's founders; it stated, essentially, that the "Saga way" was to prosper by promoting within the company a sense of respect for the dignity of each individual employee and by encouraging a spirit of entrepreneurism. Employees throughout the organization, should be made to feel that they had contributions to make and that they should exercise initiative and independent action. The company's top management knew from experience that the food service manager at a particular institution faced unique problems and must be willing and able to make decisions. But apparently this philosophy had been lost during the expansion period. More and more, it seemed to top management, managers all down the line looked to headquarters for decisions. Attitude surveys were undertaken and they indicated that managers viewed headquarters as a "Big Daddy," which always knew best.

In response to their own views of the situation and the results of the attitude surveys, Saga's executives met with two OD experts from the UCLA faculty. That meeting was the initial step in the development of an OD program in Saga. But at that time there was no commonly held view as to exactly what was wrong or what was required to correct it. The executives simply felt that a more effective organization was needed and that they wanted to do whatever was required to develop it.

As a first step the executive group appointed one of their own members to direct the program. His first task was to diagnose the problems and then select a method or set of methods which would be appropriate for Saga. He held meetings throughout the country with managers from all levels of the hierarchy. The focus of the meetings was the data from the attitude surveys. The managers were encouraged to express their interpretations of the meanings of the attitudes reflected in the data. The issues which continually emerged from these meetings centered on feelings of isolation and aloneness. The food service managers at institutions simply felt that they no longer were parts of the organization. Resentment and frustration were prevalent emotions. The institutional food service managers were particu-

---

*This case is based upon William J. Crockett, Robert E. Gaernter, and Sam Farry, "Humanistic Management in a Fast-Growing Company," in *The Failure of Success*, ed. Alfred J. Marrow (New York: AMACOM, 1972), pp. 275–85.

larly vocal and stated that if they bucked decisions up the line it was because headquarters wanted it that way.

The director of the OD effort listened carefully to the discussions at these meetings. It was apparent that the OD method must focus on building mechanisms which would restore the philosophy of Saga and make it real in the company's operations. A concept was needed and it seemed that Likert's idea of interlocking work teams would fit Saga's situation. The geographical dispersion of the company made it possible to think of teams of food service managers and their district managers which would function as decision-making groups. But to build these teams required more than simply stating that they existed and defining their authority. It was necessary to restore the confidence of managers and in the good intentions of top management.

The team-building program was thus defined as a method for developing individual, group, and individual-group behavior. The mechanics of the program were as follows:

1. The vice president for food services and his four area managers met first and confronted the issues and problems which kept it from functioning effectively.
2. Area managers met with their district managers. Like the initial meetings held with the vice presidents, these meetings created a renewed sense of trust and confidence. The group confronted its problems, and communication was more frank and open than in previous meetings.
3. Finally, district managers and institutional food service managers met. The meetings were based upon materials and experience obtained from earlier sessions between upper level management.

The process of team-building began at the top and moved successively down into the organization. Information was shared at every level; expectations, attitudes, and feelings were confronted and discussed. The underlying assumption was that these teams could function effectively only if they were able to communicate authentically. As one manager observed: "What's changed is not that problems go away, but that we can now find out about them for ourselves, we can discuss them openly, and we don't have to conduct an attitude survey to know how we feel."

Questions for Consideration

1. What were the fundamental problems which the Saga OD program sought to resolve?
2. Must any rapidly expanding company experience problems similar to those of Saga?
3. What value orientation underlies the "Saga Way" philosophy?

Part Seven

EPILOGUE

CHAPTER 21
Epilogue: Organizations: Behavior,
Structure, Processes

Chapter 21

Epilogue: Organizations: Behavior, Structure, Processes

We have now completed our presentation of *Organizations: Behavior, Structure, Processes*. As mentioned at the outset, we live in an organized society. It is now virtually impossible to escape organizations. Most of us work in organizations and will spend the remainder of our working years in them. Therefore, the intent of this book was to study, examine, and review organizations and what takes place within them. The theme of the book was three characteristics of organizations—behavior, structure, and processes.

The main actors throughout our presentation have been people; specifically the employees of organizations. It is *people* who conduct the affairs, transactions, and productive work in organizations. It is *people* who perform well or slow down production or who quit to join other organizations. It is *people* who make decisions. It is *people* who lead and appraise others, distribute rewards, and personally grow and develop. Thus, this book actually focuses on the behavior of people in organizations.

As you know by now theories of human behavior are numerous, sometimes confusing, and often contradictory. Nevertheless, theorists, researchers, and managers continue the search to become more knowledgeable about people. In fact, the field of study now called organizational behavior has evolved because managers and society want to know more about people within organizations.

PEOPLE IN ORGANIZATIONS

■ The concern for people performing jobs in organizations is not new. What is relatively new, however, is that we are finally becoming more scientific in our study of people within organizations. The importance and use of the scientific approach has been introduced in each chapter of the book.

The scientific approach to the study of people in organizations is the result of such factors as (1) the managers' need for more than simple, intuitive opinions to make decisions and solve problems, (2) the contributions of a number of behavioral disciplines, (3) a trend away from a "one-best-way" philosophy and prescription about people toward a more contingency-based approach, and (4) shifts in the political, economic, international, and competitive environments in which organizations are attempting to survive.

THE MANAGER: THEORIST, RESEARCHER, AND PRACTITIONER

■ As indicated throughout the book, the managers today are expected to know and use theories, understand relevant research findings, and apply techniques that work. Furthermore, managers also need to have diagnostic skills. They must diagnose such things as perceptions, attitudes, group norms, intergroup conflict, noncompliance with requests, creativity, low morale, exceptional performance, rating errors, and other topics covered throughout the book. As suggested, these are difficult factors to diagnose.

Managers must perform their diagnostic tasks in organization settings that are occasionally turbulent, ambiguous, and nonreceptive. This suggests that the managers' lives are challenging but also potentially troublesome. For example, research findings indicate that managers:

Work long hours.

Are extremely busy.

Perform work that is fragmented.

Have numerous tasks to perform.

Are primarily involved with oral communication.

Use a lot of interpersonal contact.

Are not the best reflective planners.

Are not generally aware of how they use their time.[1]

A manager described by these findings will be hard pressed to be a theorist, researcher, practitioner, and diagnostician. However, this is what makes the job exciting for many individuals. It is dynamic, filled with challenges and uncertainty, and involves people. This is what we hope was portrayed in the book. We admit that managing people in organizations is difficult, but we also know that managers are extremely important in our society.

ORGANIZATIONAL BEHAVIOR: REVISITED

■ We pointed out early that many of the theories, research findings, and practical applications that managers review, use, and modify have evolved from the behavioral disciplines. As a result of this evolution we have now reached a point where the field of organizational behavior is recognized as an integrative attempt to apply the behavioral sciences.

---

[1] Morgan W. McCall, Jr., Ann M. Morrison, and Robert L. Hannan, *Studies of Managerial Work: Results and Methods* (Greensboro, N.C.: Center for Creative Leadership, 1978).

In Chapter 1 we defined organizational behavior (OB) as:

> The study of human behavior, attitudes, and performance within an organizational setting; drawing on theory, methods, and principles from such disciplines as psychology, sociology, and cultural anthropology to learn about employee perceptions, values, learning capacities, and actions while working in groups and within the total organization, analyzing the external environments effect on the organization and its human resources, missions, objectives, strategies.

Each part of this definition was covered in the book. However, as we noted in Chapter 1 it is valuable to consider OB as: (1) a way of thinking, (2) an eclectic field of study, (3) humanistic, (4) performance oriented, (5) concerned about how the environment affects people, and (6) scientifically based. These features spell out why OB is now considered an applied field of study.

The integration of the behavioral sciences into OB has significant value to practicing managers. It provides them with theories, research, and techniques that they can use and modify in their unique organizational context. Figure 21–1 presents many of the topics discussed in the chapters in the context of OB.

The Trend away from Simple Answers

The prominence of the contingency theme indicates that simple, universally accepted answers do not exist. There are simple explanations that can provide some insight about people in organizations, but they are often incomplete, misleading, and unrealistic. For example, the trait theories of leadership are concise but are considered unrealistic and nonpredictive. In their place have emerged more complex, yet unproven theories of leadership such as the path-goal and Vroom-Yetton models.

The trend away from the simple toward the more complex is found at every level of analysis—individual, group, and organizational—and for most organizational behavior topics from individual perception to goal setting to team building to career planning. Unfortunately, many theorists and researchers have failed to explain their more complex theories and models to managers. In many cases they have instead added jargon and complexity at the expense of clarity, practical utility, and meaningfulness. This is unfortunately a verdict reached by too many managers. Consequently, managers in many cases have refused to permit the testing of these theories and models in their organizations. If additional knowledge is to be gained from scientifically testing more complex theories and models, there will be a need to improve the clarity of these approaches.

Certainly, simple answers are not sufficient for most organizational problem areas. However, there is nothing sacred about a more complex approach. Each approach will have to meet three tests: (1) is it understandable, (2) is it better than the simpler approaches, and (3) can it be applied by managers? Conduct your own evaluation of some of the more complex theories and models that we presented. Do they pass or fail these three

FIGURE 21–1
The Manager's Guide to Applied Organizational Behavior

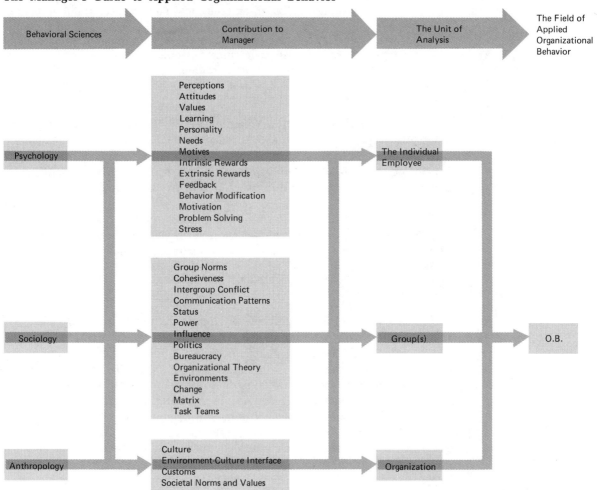

tests?—behavior modification, matrix design, BARS, career planning, superordinate goals, attribution theory of leadership. Being understandable means that the approach can be explained.

The Environment

In this era of inflation, international conflict, increasing foreign competition, and growing concern about the quality of life, managers are searching for better insight and answers to problems. These shifting environmental forces have led to the growth of interest in the kind of environmental topics covered in *Organizations: Behavior, Structure, Processes*. In addition, more and more organizations are scientifically monitoring environmental forces. This monitoring provides a source of information that is so vitally needed to make changes within organizations.

Managers now realize that environmental forces operate on the internal functioning of an organization—the individuals, groups, and total system. There is acceptance of the thesis that multiple forces interacting together cause people, groups, and the organization to behave. The exact nature of this causality is not yet clear. However, now managers accept the premise that environmental forces must be considered when examining the behaviors occurring within organizations. Studying how people behave within organizations without considering the environment results in unrealistic, incomplete, and misleading conclusions.

ADDITIONAL WORK TO BE DONE

■ Instead of offering just another set of predictions about what the future holds for managers, organizations, and society, we prefer to spell out some areas for additional theorizing, research, and application. We have tried to provide in the book an analysis of people working in organizations. Hopefully, you can distill from the chapters, cases, exercises, and actual organizational situations a sense of (1) what organizations are, (2) what organizations have (i.e., behavior, structure, processes), and (3) what organizations do. Furthermore, the book should have pointed out many areas that need to be developed further. Some of these areas in need of additional work will be briefly identified.

Theories

Well-articulated theories that are relevant to managerial practice need to be developed more completely for understanding individual, group, and organizational characteristics. These theories must be coherent, use managerial language, be testable, and possess reasonable generalizability from one setting to the next. The theories will have to incorporate the changing nature of society, the labor force, and economic conditions.

For example, Maslow's need hierarchy has a commonsense appeal, but does it apply to women, blacks, handicapped employees, overworked managers, and employees in dangerous occupations? Is it possible to develop or use a more complex explanation of motivation? We believe it is possible if more effort is made to expand the domain of a theory without increasing its jargon. Clarity of presentation should be a major criterion in the development of theories in the field of organizational behavior.

History

We propose that more attention needs to be paid to an organization's history. The way organizations operate today and will operate tomorrow is significantly influenced by past events. We need to take a closer view of the actions of key managers and leaders, how strategic policy decisions were reached, how managers responded to various crises, and what skills seemed valuable in solving problems. There seems to be a reluctance to even consult history, and what is lost is some of the explanation of how an organization became what it is today. We need a historical branch in the field of organizational behavior as much as we need a theoretical, research, and application orientation.

Measurement

The measurement techniques for studying behavior and testing theories need to be improved. Reliance solely on self-report surveys is questionnable and not advisable. We now have the theoretical, psychometrical, and statistical capabilities to develop more valid, reliable, and practical techniques than the self-report survey. We need people to work on measurement in conjunction with managers so that measuring procedures are developed that not only have psychometric power but also appeal to managers. We are not suggesting the elimination of self-report surveys, only the redirection of effort toward other techniques such as observation, interviewing, and the use of documents and records.

Cost versus Benefits

The economic and psychological costs versus benefits of such techniques as goal setting, leadership training, career pathing, job enrichment, and matrix organizational structures need to be seriously evaluated. Few studies even estimate the costs of such techniques. We need to begin evaluating techniques in terms of costs (economic and noneconomic) and benefits (economic and noneconomic). Accountants and economists have much to offer the field of organizational behavior in terms of methods for analyzing costs and benefits. Since managers are held accountable for their actions, it seems important to work more systematically on the issue of costs versus benefits.

The Stress Connection

There exists a need to study the effects of work stress and its interaction with nonwork stress. To understand the relevance of stress at work in industrialized societies we must analyze the stress concept and evaluate it in terms of its impact on:

Health and longevity.
Quality of life.
Economic costs.
Humanistic values.

Unfortunately, much of the available stress research fails to look at the interaction of work stress and nonwork stress. The work to be done in the area needs to look at stress in terms of work, leisure, homelife, and societal values. From this broader perspective knowledge can be gained to benefit organizations, government, and unions. Each of these parties should be concerned about the *individual* who experiences stress.

Training and Development

The training of managers to recognize important contingencies and appropriate responses needs to be undertaken. Managers need to be trained in problem-solving and decision-making skills to make the most efficient use of organizational resources. Unless managers are properly trained, goal attainment will be placed in serious jeopardy, productivity will suffer, and the quality of work-life will decrease. Not only must formal training occur, but there must also be scientific evaluation of its effectiveness. Are managers more successful, more responsive to contingency factors, more aware of the environment, more thorough problem solvers after training? These questions can only be answered if the training is evaluated with valid and reliable measures.

Studying Foreign Management Practices

The economic development and growth of such nations as Japan, West Germany, and Australia are the result of many factors such as government policies, favorable trade pacts with other nations, sound planning and forecasting, and effective managerial practices. The classic view of an economic miracle is the story of Japan. "Made in Japan" was once the mark of shoddy merchandise. However, it is now a badge of quality for everything from compact automobiles to videotape recorders. Are there any lessons for those interested in people working in organizations? We believe so.

There is a need in the field of OB to learn from the experience of other organizations in other countries as well as in domestic organizations. Study and analysis of the relationship between workers and their companies in Japan can provide insight into the managerial techniques being used. Why do Japanese workers have a sense that the company is the base of their lives? Can this feeling be generated for the U.S. worker? These and similar questions need to be studied at the individual, group, and organizational levels. We are suggesting that the application of OB can be improved by examining what has been successfully used and how it was used in other organizations around the world.

Some American companies have begun experimenting with Japanese-style management techniques. What is now needed are careful and long-term analyses of these experiments. There are major differences in the economic and political systems and cultures of nations like Japan, Canada, West Germany, and the United States. However, some of the managerial techniques that are successful in one country are exportable to other nations. We need to find out what is exportable, what needs to be modified, and why some things work and others fail. These studies should be conducted by using the scientific approach encouraged in this book. Furthermore, inquiring into what works and what doesn't should proceed at three levels of analysis—the individual, the group, and the organization.

Studying Women and Minorities

Since the early 70s, more and more women and minorites have moved into managerial careers. This development has led to the following kinds of questions being asked: Do women fear success? Can blacks effectively manage white subordinates? How do Mexican-Americans feel about working for women managers? Do men and women differ in aggressiveness, risk-taking propensity, commitment, and the work ethic?

It would be foolish to deny that women and minorities working as managers in organizations is as of now relatively misunderstood. What is needed are sound, scientific investigations of men, women, blacks, Mexican-Americans, and others performing managerial jobs in organizational settings. We need reliable and valid data to examine and locate differences in style and characteristics if they do exist. Preconceptions, tacit assumptions, and personal opinions should be replaced with comparative research that is based on scientific procedures.

These are only a few of the areas that are ready for more dialogue, debate, theory building, research, and experimentation. Instead of requesting construction of *the* model of organizational behavior as the foremost need, we have elected to call attention to specific areas of interest and concern. Of course, work must procede in integrating concepts, variables, and causal linkages in the field of organizational behavior. However, just as important is the need to study and analyze more thoroughly people working within organizations. We need theories, frameworks, and techniques to manage, but one should never lose sight of the people as individuals, working in groups, and as part of the total organization.

Appendix A

Experimentation in the Behavioral Sciences

INTRODUCTION

■ In Chapter 1 we noted that the experimental method is the prototype of the scientific approach. It is the ideal toward which we strive but unfortunately do not always achieve. In this appendix we shall examine a number of different approaches which can be used in designing experiments. To illustrate the various approaches we shall use an example of a training program being offered to a group of first-line supervisors. The task of the researcher is to design an experiment which will permit the assessment of the degree to which the program influenced the performance of the supervisors. We will use the following symbols in our discussion:

S = The subjects, the supervisors participating in the experiment
O = The observation and measurement devices used by the researcher (that is, ratings of supervisors' performance by superiors).
X = The experimental treatment, the manipulated variable (that is, the training program).
R = The randomization process.[1]

We shall examine six different designs which vary in degree of sophistication and point out the problems associated with each one. In each design the training program (X) is the independent variable, and performance is the dependent variable.

One-Shot Design

If we assume that all supervisors go through the training program it will be difficult for the researchers to evaluate it. This is because the researchers cannot compare performance scores with earlier scores before the training program. In addition they cannot compare the group with another group

---

[1]R. H. Helmstader, *Research Concepts in Human Behavior* (New York: Appleton-Century-Crofts, 1970); William G. Scott and Terence R. Mitchell, *Organization Theory: A Structural and Behavioral Analysis* (Homewood, Ill.: Richard D. Irwin, 1976); and D. W. Emory, *Business Research Methods* (Homewood, Ill.: Richard D. Irwin, 1980).

which did not undergo the training program. Thus, this design is called a *one-shot* design and is diagrammed as follows:

$$X \quad O$$

The letter X stands for the experimental treatment (that is, the training program) and O for the observation. This is the measure of performance on the job and would probably be presented in the form of an average score based on ratings of superiors. However, the researchers can in no way determine whether performance was influenced at all by the training program. This experimental design is rarely used because of its weaknesses.

One-Group Pretest-Posttest Design

The previous design can be improved upon by first gathering performance data on the supervisors, instituting the training program, and then remeasuring their performance. This is diagrammed as follows:

$$O_1 \quad X \quad O_2$$

Thus, a pretest is given in time period one, the program is administered, and a posttest is administered in time period two. If $O_2 > O_1$, the differences can be attributed to the training program.

There are numerous factors which can confound the results obtained with this design. For example, suppose new equipment has been installed between O_1 and O_2. This could explain the differences in the performance scores. Thus, a *history* factor may have influenced our results. There are numerous other factors which also could influence our results. The most recurring ones are listed along with the definition of each one in Table 1.[2] Examination of Table 1 indicates that results achieved in this design may also be confounded by *maturation* (supervisors may learn to do a better job between O_1 and O_2 which would increase their performance regardless of training), *testing* (the measure of performance in O_1 may have made the supervisors aware that they were being evaluated which may make them work harder and increase their performance), and *instrumentation* (if the performance observations were made at different times of the day when fatigue could play a role, the results could be influenced). Each of these factors offers other explanations for changes in performance than the training program. Obviously, this design can be improved upon.

Static-Group Comparison Design

In this design, half of the supervisors would be allowed to sign up for the training. Once the enrollment reached 50 percent of the supervisors, the training program would begin. After some period of time the group of supervisors who enrolled in the program would be compared with those who did not enroll. This design is diagrammed as follows:

$$X \quad O$$
$$O$$

---

[2] Ibid.

TABLE 1
Some Sources of Error in Experimental Studies

Factor	Definition
1. History	Events other than the experimental treatment (X) which occurred between premeasurement and postmeasurement.
2. Maturation	Changes in the subject group with the passage of time which are not associated with the experimental treatment (X).
3. Testing	Changes in the performance of the subjects because previous measurement of their performance made them aware they were part of an experiment (that is, measures often alter what is being measured).
4. Instrumentation	Changes in the measures of participants' performance that are the result of changes in the measurement instruments or conditions under which the measuring is done (for example, wear on machinery, boredom, fatigue on the part of observers).
5. Selection	When participants are assigned to experimental and control groups on any basis other than random assignment. Any other selection method will result in systematic biases which will result in differences between groups which are unrelated to the effects of the experimental treatment (X).
6. Mortality	If some participants drop out of the experiment before it is completed, the experimental and control groups may not be comparable.
7. Interaction effects	Any of the above factors may interact with the experimental treatment, resulting in confounding effects on the results. For example, the types of individuals withdrawing from a study (mortality) may differ for the experimental group and the control group.

Since the supervisors were not randomly assigned to each group it is highly possible that the group that enrolled are the more highly motivated or more intelligent supervisors. Thus, *selection* is a major problem with this design. However, note that the addition of a *control group* (comparison group) has eliminated many of the error factors associated with the first two designs. The problem here is that the subjects were not randomly assigned to the experimental group (undergoing training) and the control group (no training). Therefore, it is possible that differences may exist between the two groups that are not related to the training.

The three designs discussed thus far (one-shot, one-group pretest-posttest, static-group comparisons) have been described as "pseudo-experimental" or "quasi-experimental designs. When true experimentation cannot be achieved, these designs (especially the last two) are preferred over no research at all or over relying on personal opinion. The following three designs can be considered "true" experimental designs because the researcher has complete control over the situation in the sense of determining precisely who will participate in the experiment and which subjects will or will not receive the experimental treatment.

Pretest-Posttest Control Group Design

This design is one of the simplest forms of true experimentation used in the study of human behavior. It is diagrammed as follows:

$$R \quad O_1 \quad X \quad O_2$$
$$R \quad O_1 \quad\quad O_2$$

Note that this design is similar to the one-group pretest-posttest design except that a control group has been added and the participants have been randomly assigned to both groups. Which group is to receive the training (experimental group) and which will not (control group) is also randomly determined. The two groups may be said to be equivalent at the time of the initial observations, and when the final observations are made, and different only in that one group has received training while the other has not. In other words if the change from O_1 to O_2 is greater in the experimental than from O_1 to O_2 in the control group we can attribute it to the training program rather than selection, testing, maturation, and so forth.

The major weakness of the pretest-posttest control group design is one of *interaction* (selection and treatment), where individuals are aware they are participating in an experiment. In other words, being observed the first time makes all participants work more diligently, both those who are in the training program and those who are in the control group. Here the participants in the training program will be more receptive to training because of the pretest. This problem of interaction can be overcome by using a posttest-only control group design.

Posttest-Only Control Group Design

In this design, participants are randomly assigned to two groups, the training is administered to one group, and scores on posttests are compared (performance evaluated). It is diagrammed as follows:

$$R \quad X \quad O$$
$$R \quad\quad O$$

This eliminates the problem of the previous design by not administering a pretest. However, the dependent variable (performance) is an ultimate rather than a relative measure of achievement. The researcher also does not have a group which was pretested and posttested without receiving the experimental treatment (training program). Such a group can provide valuable information on the effects of history, maturation, instrumentation, and so on. However, where a pretest is difficult to obtain or where its use is likely to make the participants aware that an experiment is being carried on, this approach may be much preferred to the pretest-posttest control group design.

Solomon Four-Group Design

This design is a combination of the previous two designs and is diagrammed as follows:

Group 1	R	O_1	X	O_2
Group 2	R	O_1		O_2
Group 3	R		X	O_2
Group 4	R			O_2

Where gain or change in behavior is the desired dependent variable, this design should be used. This design is the most desirable of all of the designs examined here. While it does not control any more sources of invalid results, this does permit the estimation of the extent of the effects of some of the sources of error. In our example here, the supervisors are randomly assigned to four groups two of which will receive the training, one with a pretest and one without. Therefore, the researcher can examine among other things the effects of history (Group 2), testing (Group 2 to Group 4), and testing-treatment interaction (Group 1 to Group 3). Clearly, this design is the most complex, utilizing more participants, and will be more costly. The added value of the additional information will have to be compared to the additional costs.

This appendix has examined a number of different approaches to designing experiments. While there are other approaches, these are widely used. Our purpose has been to familiarize the reader with experimentation in the behavioral sciences. A complete treatment of the subject is beyond the scope of this text.[3]

---

[3] For a complete coverage of this area, see Fred N. Kerlinger, *Foundations of Behavioral Research* (New York: Holt, Rinehart, & Winston, 1973), pp. 300–76; Helmstader, *Research Concepts in Human Behavior*, pp. 91–121; and Emory, *Business Research Methods*, pp. 330–65.

— Appendix B ————————

Selected Comprehensive Cases

Glenn Taylor

Dick Spencer

Excelsior Bakeries, Inc.

A Case of Misunderstanding:
Mr. Hart and Mr. Bing

GLENN TAYLOR *

Glenn Taylor, age 50, held the position of vice president for finance and controller of the Sage Electronics Company.

Sage was a large and profitable electronics company which manufactured and marketed its products on a worldwide basis; its stock was listed on a major stock exchange. Mr. Taylor had joined the company 10 years earlier as an assistant treasurer. Prior to joining Sage he had had a very successful career in the field of public accounting. Sage in fact used to be one of his clients when he worked for a large public accounting firm.

Taylor's work at Sage was impressive, and James Johnson, Sage's president, considered him one of the ablest men in top management. On several occasions James Johnson had credited Taylor for playing a valuable role in the rapid growth and success of the company. In recent years Sage had made a number of acquisitions, and Taylor had played a key role in negotiating the purchase terms. In addition, and almost single-handedly, Taylor had introduced most of the planning and control systems which guided the company. These systems included a management-by-objectives program and both long and short-term profit planning systems involving budgeting of sales and expenses which were used for control purposes. They had been introduced as part of a major reorganization of Sage which took place several years ago. Taylor had designed the systems for use by line managers at the request of James Johnson, who had hired him originally.

Glenn Taylor was born and raised in the Presbyterian faith. He considered himself a religious person, and tried to practice his religious principles in business. Business associates respected his high moral and ethical standards and his sense of fair play. Discussing his job, Glenn stated: "Central to the idea of controllership, it seems to me, are the ideas of responsibility, controls, and defining the rules of the game. The rules have to be administered fairly."

In the spring of 1970, Mr. Taylor hired Philip Hawkins as a special staff assistant. Hawkins started work on July 1, just three weeks after he had received his M.B.A. degree from a well-known eastern school of business administration. Hawkins had been in the top third of his graduating class; and although he had concentrated in finance and accounting, he had taken several courses in the organizational behavior area as part of his second-year program. During his second year Hawkins had written a research report on the behavioral aspects of control systems which Taylor considered "quite interesting." Though Hawkins viewed his staff assignment with excitement, he considered it as a stepping stone to a line position within 12 to 15 months in one of Sage's divisions. When Hawkins accepted the job in early May, Taylor said that he would have a real problem for him when he started work, and he would appreciate hearing his views on it then. "In

---

* Reproduced by permission of the President and Fellows of Harvard College.

fact," Taylor said, "I'll write it out in case form on a confidential basis and give it to you on your first day of work." Without inquiring about the nature of the problem, Hawkins replied that he would look forward to tackling Taylor's case problem when he returned to Sage.

Glenn Taylor had been thinking long and hard about the problem he would write out for Philip Hawkins, for it had been bothering him for a considerable length of time. While he had talked about the problem with his wife and with Kenneth Johnson, who was both vice president for domestic operations of Sage and a close friend, he had never talked about it to anyone else inside or outside of the company. He did say, however, that he had informed the president, James Johnson, "in general" about the situation. James Johnson and Kenneth Johnson were brothers and major stockholders of the company. (See Exhibit 1 for an abbreviated organization chart.)

EXHIBIT 1

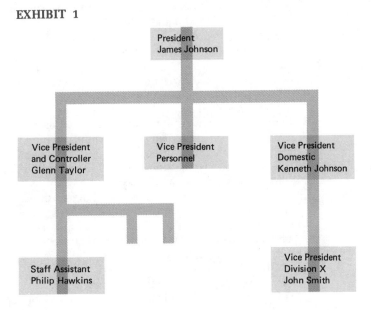

Before giving his written case to Philip after they had lunched together on July 1, Glenn emphasized the confidential nature of this problem. "Confidentially," said Glenn, "the biggest damn problem I have is John Smith. Sometimes I think I should say the hell with it and forget it, but I'm afraid if I do that it will hurt the company too much." He suggested that Philip read the case that evening and that they get together to discuss it the following day. Philip thought his approach made sense and was flattered that Taylor was willing to confide in him. Before departing for a meeting Glenn said, "John Smith is the problem, and if you can solve this problem you will go a long way in Sage." The written case which Glenn gave to Philip appears below:

John Smith is one of the key executives in charge of operations for a significant geographical area of my company. He has been an employee for over 15 years, first in the role of a production supervisor, then division production manager. There were other position changes until his present position as a divisional domestic vice president.

He has enjoyed a succession of promotions and is highly regarded by all those who have worked for him. In part, this is a reflection of his personality, as the other side of the coin is being reflected in difficulties I am encountering with him.

First, John is a law unto himself and gives favorite treatment to those working for him. He freely disregards company personnel practices and procedures and administers to his people as he chooses. His secretary gets the highest salary of any secretary in the company, works on a time schedule ignoring regular office hours, etc. This situation is widely recognized and resented by many others, but he has always gotten away with it and as a result he considers this his prerogative.

As he has progressed, this disregard for policy has become more noticeable on a higher level, even to the point of disregarding presidential requests or responding to them in such a way that they have been disregarded for all practical purposes. For example, he has never chosen to completely comply with annual profit-plan requests. He will present location plans without review and personal commitment, or at times he will submit data sufficiently different from standard forms to make collation and comparison difficult.

This has been accompanied by attempts to impose an iron curtain over the flow of information. This occurs with him personally and with operations under his supervision. When I request a meeting to discuss mutual problems, it rarely takes place unless forced by me.

Communications with others working under him become most troublesome, and strong measures are sometimes required to keep avenues of communication open to operations. Relationships with an operating location become noticeably different when he is in charge of it or when his responsibility no longer covers. it.

This can be very unfortunate since many of our mutual areas of responsibility frequently overlap into areas with which he has no knowledge. To date we have been fortunate in preventing any serious losses, but solely by accident.

He works hard—long hours—travels a large part of his time—is unstinting as to his time on company affairs. He has a keen, analytical mind, but tends to let small things prevent his deciding on major things.

Personally, away from the office we get along fine. He is affable, good company, and there is a free, open conversation without strain.

These relationships also appear to apply to others at his level and above.

When Philip entered Glenn's office late in the afternoon on July 2, Glenn offered him a seat and then closed his office door. He told his secretary they were not to be disturbed.

Taylor (*laughing*): Well, Phil, I bet you didn't run into any cases like my case in your business school studies. Believe me, Phil, this guy is getting away with murder over there. I sure would like to know what to do about it next. . . .

Hawkins: Glenn, I don't know whether I can be of any help, but I would like to try. I wonder, though, if. . . .

Taylor (*excitedly*): The whole trouble is this guy thinks he's a law unto himself . . . he runs his damned division the way *he* wants to and says to *hell* with everybody else! I don't know, maybe the best thing for me to do is. . . .

Hawkins: Excuse me, Glenn, but frankly I'm still not clear just on some of the facts here. For example, just what is the background history on this problem?

Taylor: Every since John was promoted to the vice presidency several years ago the relations between our people have become more and more difficult. It's gotten to the point now where my people come to me and say they can't get any information out of that division, and they're supposed to get reports as a matter of course. . . . They're spending so much time trying to pry things loose there that other divisions and problems are suffering. When we finally do get stuff from him it's likely to be scratched on the back of an envelop or something—absolutely no thought has gone into it, obviously. I tell you, he has no regard for the problems we're trying to deal with here.

Hawkins: Glenn, do you think a part of this problem may be explained by the image of your office? We had a lot of case studies about that at the B School, and I found that to be the case in my research report.

Taylor: You have put your finger on something there. There can be no doubt about it. We're known as the checkers, the probers, and the spies. The office of the controller does not have a good image, and it is part of the problem. But we have a job to do, too, and I am responsible for developing full reports that go to the board of directors.

Hawkins: I wonder what it's like working for a guy like Smith. . . .

Taylor: Oh, I can tell you he gets tremendous loyalty—his people just love him. He goes to bat for them, too . . . his secretary is the highest paid in the entire company. And this is pretty well true of many of his people—they get more pay and benefits and sometimes even faster promotions than any other division—I tell you, after John's been in a slot for a while it begins to close up to any kind of corporate-wide control. . . . The guy is really getting away with murder. . . .

Hawkins: What do you think Smith himself thinks about all this?

Taylor: Well, he's convinced he's doing what he should. He's a real seat-of-the-pants manager—he just doesn't take any time for the systems we've introduced. He's been around a long time—he's 46 now—and he knows this business inside out. It's like pulling eye teeth to get any information out of him. He doesn't pay any attention to routine requests of mine for meetings—and he certainly never takes the initiative to arrange one or ever try to find out what our procedures are. The only time we get together is when I *force* a meeting.

Hawkins: He must be difficult to deal with.

Taylor: That's for sure. But it's funny, you know, he's not an angry type. Off the job, as I wrote in the case, we get together occasionally at a party at Jim or Ken Johnson's club and everything's fine—we get along fine. . . . I've only seen him mad about something once. That was when he was trying to protect another secretary of his after she had caused all kinds of trouble over in another division getting information she had no business getting—those people wanted Smith's head! Well, the personnel director and I put our foot down. Smith got mad, I got mad and I held firm. I said, "That girl has to go, and that's the way it's going to be!" He backed down at that point.

Hawkins: What does Smith's boss—Kenneth Johnson—know about all this?

Taylor: Oh, Ken is very aware of all this. He knows the whole story, but he says he has the same trouble with John as I do. He can't get any information either. He's wringing his hands over this guy running his division like it was his own company.

Hawkins: Well, what about the president? Does he know about it? Can't he get action?

Taylor: Yeah, he knows about it too . . . we've *had* to tell him why there are gaps in our reports or where the unlikely estimates come from.

Hawkins: Why doesn't he crack down?

Taylor: Well, the trouble is, Smith does turn in the results—he gets the profits. Last year he turned in the most profits of any division in the company. It's been like that just about every job he has. He's always gotten the promotions, all along the line since he came to Sage 15 years ago.

Hawkins: Oh, I see. . . .

Taylor: I'll tell you, though, something has got to be done. I think Jim is beginning to see more and more the problems Smith is causing—and *could* cause. He told me last week he was going to look into this whole thing again.

Hawkins: You mentioned there were problems he *could* cause. What kinds of things?

Taylor: Why, my God, he's writing contracts with suppliers and making sales agreements all the time with nobody around here knowing about it! A year ago he was about to sign a licensing agreement with another manufacturer that would have put us smack into a lot of trouble because of a new product being developed by another division! He just charges ahead, thinking only for himself. The key point is that Smith could hurt the long-run profitability of the company in the area of trademarks, patents, and taxes. He almost gave away the company's patents in one horror case, and if he changed one licensing agreement the way he wanted to it would have cost the company $25,000 in taxes. There is a need for close cooperation between Smith and me, otherwise there will be lost profits.

Hawkins: Who runs his division while he's away? You say he travels a great deal and he's away now on a long business trip.

Taylor: Ken Johnson is trying to run it, and he's asked me for help. As a matter of fact, I have a meeting with him tomorrow to see what we can do. Apparently, Smith's people are tighter than ever since he's been away—Ken says they won't tell him any more now than they ever did.

Hawkins: What kinds of things have you thought of doing?

Taylor: I've beat my head on this one so much with so little results to show for it that I've just about decided to say "to hell with it." I don't know. . . . I suppose if I didn't care what happened to the company I would just sit back and do my job and let the chips fall where they may, but I'm not like that; I couldn't do that after all the effort that's gone into building up the new organization.

Continuing, Taylor stated:

> Smith and I have never competed. He always gets promoted, yet he is a complete nonconformist who gets away with murder. He causes serious morale problems with his peers who try to follow our team management concepts. Here is a good question for you: What do you do when a guy rejects management concepts (management by objectives, long-range planning, and budgets, for example) and still makes better than average profits? Top management has worked hard to develop what it considers the best available management and control techniques. To be honest, Phil, it may be that the best thing for me to do is to say "the hell with it," but I find it hard to accept defeat and admit that "seat-of-the-pants" management is best after all.

As Taylor talked about his case, Philip noted that he got red in the face on several occasions and appeared quite nervous. Philip knew that this was a serious matter for Glenn Taylor, and he truly wanted to help him with his problem.

DICK SPENCER *

After the usual banter when old friends meet for cocktails, the conversation between a couple of university professors and Dick Spencer, a former student who was now a successful businessman, turned to Dick's life as a vice president of a large manufacturing firm.

"I've made a lot of mistakes, most of which I could live with, but this one series of incidents was so frustrating that I could have cried at the time," Dick said in response to a question. "I really have to laugh at how ridiculous it is now, but at the time I blew my cork."

Spencer was plant manager of Modrow Company, a Canadian branch of the Tri-American Corporation. Tri-American was a major producer of primary aluminum with integrated operations ranging from the mining of bauxite through the processing to fabrication of aluminum into a variety of products. The company also made and sold refractories and industrial chemicals. The parent company had wholly owned subsidiaries in five separate U.S. locations and had foreign affiliates in 15 different countries.

Tri-American mined bauxite in the Jamaican West Indies and shipped the raw material by commercial vessels to two plants in Louisiana where it was processed into alumina. The alumina was then shipped to reduction plants in one of three locations for conversion into primary aluminum. Most of the primary aluminum was then moved to the companies' fabricat-

---

* This case was developed and prepared by Dr. Margaret Fenn, Graduate School of Business Administration, University of Washington. Reprinted by permission.

ing plants for further processing. Fabricated aluminum items included sheet, flat, coil, and corrugated products; siding; and roofing.

Tri-American employed approximately 22,000 employees in the total organization. The company was governed by a board of directors which included the chairman, vice chairman, president, and 12 vice presidents. However, each of the subsidiaries and branches functioned as independent units. The board set general policy which was then interpreted and applied by the various plant managers. In a sense, the various plants competed with one another as though they were independent companies. This decentralization in organizational structure increased the freedom and authority of the plant managers, but increased the pressure for profitability.

The Modrow branch was located in a border town in Canada. The total work force in Modrow was 1,000. This Canadian subsidiary was primarily a fabricating unit. Its main products were foil and building products such as roofing and siding. Aluminum products were gaining in importance in architectural plans, and increased sales were predicted for this branch. Its location and its stable work force were the most important advantages it possessed.

In anticipation of estimated increases in building product sales, Modrow had recently completed a modernization and expansion project. At the same time, their research and art departments combined talents in developing a series of 12 new patterns of siding which were being introduced to the market. Modernization and pattern development had been costly undertakings, but the expected return on investment made the project feasible. However, the plant manager, who was a Tri-American vice president, had instituted a campaign to cut expenses wherever possible. In his introductory notice of the campaign, he emphasized that cost reduction would be the personal aim of every employee at Modrow.

Salesman. The plant manager of Modrow, Dick Spencer, was an American who had been transferred to this Canadian branch two years previously, after the start of the modernization plan. Dick had been with the Tri-American Company for 14 years, and his progress within the organization was considered spectacular by those who knew him well. Dick had received a Master's degree in Business Administration from a well-known university at the age of 22. Upon graduation he had accepted a job as salesman for Tri-American. During his first year as a salesman, he succeeded in landing a single, large contract which put him near the top of the sales-volume leaders. In discussing his phenomenal rise in the sales volume, several of his fellow salesmen concluded that his looks, charm, and ability on the golf course contributed as much to his success as his knowledge of the business or his ability to sell the products.

The second year of his sales career, he continued to set a fast pace. Although his record set difficult goals for the other salesmen, he was considered a "regular guy" by them, and both he and they seemed to enjoy the few occasions when they socialized. However, by the end of the second year of constant travelling and selling, Dick began to experience some doubt about his future.

His constant involvement in business matters disrupted his marital life, and his wife divorced him during the second year with Tri-American. Dick resented her action at first, but gradually seemed to recognize that his career at present depended on his freedom to travel unencumbered. During that second year, he ranged far and wide in his sales territory, and successfully closed several large contracts. None of them was as large as his first year's major sale, but in total volume he again was well up near the top of salesmen for the year. Dick's name became well known in the corporate headquarters, and he was spoken of as "the boy to watch."

Dick had met the president of Tri-American during his first year as a salesman at a company conference. After three days of golfing and socializing they developed a relaxed camaraderie considered unusual by those who observed the developing friendship. Although their contacts were infrequent after the conference, their easy relationship seemed to blossom the few times they did meet. Dick's friends kidded him about his ability to make use of his new friendship to promote himself in the company, but Dick brushed aside their jibes and insisted that he'd make it on his own abilities, not someone's coattail.

By the time he was 25, Dick began to suspect that he did not look forward to a life as a salesman for the rest of his career. He talked about his unrest with his friends, and they suggested that he groom himself for sales manager. "You won't make the kind of money you're making from commissions," he was told, "but you will have a foot in the door from an administrative standpoint, and you won't have to travel quite as much as you do now." Dick took their suggestions lightly, and continued to sell the product, but was aware that he felt dissatisfied and did not seem to get the satisfaction out of his job that he had once enjoyed.

By the end of his third year with the company Dick was convinced that he wanted a change in direction. As usual, he and the president spent quite a bit of time on the golf course during the annual company sales conference. After their match one day, the president kidded Dick about his game. The conversation drifted back to business, and the president, who seemed to be in a jovial mood, started to kid Dick about his sales ability. In a joking way, he implied that anyone could sell a product as good as Tri-American's, but that it took real "guts and know-how" to make the products. The conversation drifted to other things, but this remark stuck with Dick.

Sometime later, Dick approached the president formally with a request for a transfer out of the sales division. The president was surprised and hesitant about this change in career direction for Dick. He recognized the superior sales ability that Dick seemed to possess, but was unsure that Dick was willing or able to assume responsibilities in any other division of the organization. Dick sensed the hesitancy, but continued to push his request. He later remarked that it seemed that the initial hesitancy of the president convinced Dick that he needed an opportunity to prove himself in a field other than sales.

Troubleshooter. Dick was finally transferred back to the home office of the organization and indoctrinated into productive and administrative roles in the company as a special assistant to the senior vice president of production. As a special assistant, Dick was assigned several troubleshooting jobs. He acquitted himself well in this role, but in the process succeeded in gaining a reputation as a ruthless headhunter among the branches where he had performed a series of amputations. His reputation as an amiable, genial, easy-going guy from the sales department was the antithesis of the reputation of a cold, calculating headhunter which he earned in his troubleshooting role. The vice president, who was Dick's boss, was aware of the reputation which Dick had earned but was pleased with the results that were obtained. The faltering departments that Dick had worked in seemed to bloom with new life and energy after Dick's recommended amputations. As a result, the vice president began to sing Dick's praises, and the president began to accept Dick in his new role in the company.

Management Responsibility. About three years after Dick's switch from sales, he was given an assignment as assistant plant manager of an English branch of the company. Dick, who had remarried, moved his wife and family to London, and they attempted to adapt to their new routine. The plant manager was English, as were most of the other employees. Dick and his family were accepted with reservations into the community life as well as into the plant life. The difference between British and American philosophy and performance within the plant was marked for Dick who was imbued with modern managerial concepts and methods. Dick's directives from headquarters were to update and upgrade performance in this branch. However, his power and authority were less than those of his superior, so he constantly found himself in the position of having to soft pedal or withhold suggestions that he would have liked to make, or innovations that he would have liked to introduce. After a frustrating year and a half, Dick was suddenly made plant manager of an old British company which had just been purchased by Tri-American. He left his first English assignment with mixed feelings and moved from London to Birmingham.

As the new plant manager, Dick operated much as he had in his troubleshooting job for the first couple of years of his change from sales to administration. Training and reeducation programs were instituted for all supervisors and managers who survived the initial purge. Methods were studied and simplified or redesigned whenever possible, and new attention was directed toward production which better met the needs of the sales organization. A strong controller helped to straighten out the profit picture through stringent cost control; and, by the end of the third year, the company showed a small profit for the first time in many years. Because he felt that this battle was won, Dick requested transfer back to the United States. This request was partially granted when nine months later he was awarded a junior vice president title, and was made manager of a subsidiary Canadian plant, Modrow.

Modrow Manager. Prior to Dick's appointment as plant manager at Modrow, extensive plans for plant expansion and improvement had been approved and started. Although he had not been in on the original discussions and plans, he inherited all the problems that accompany large-scale changes in any organization. Construction was slower in completion than originally planned, equipment arrived before the building was finished, employees were upset about the extent of change expected in their work routines with the installation of additional machinery and, in general, morale was at a low ebb.

Various versions of Dick's former activities had preceded him, and on his arrival he was viewed with dubious eyes. The first few months after his arrival were spent in a frenzy of catching up. This entailed constant conferences and meetings, volumes of reading of past reports, becoming acquainted with the civic leaders of the area, and a plethora of dispatches to and from the home office. Costs continued to climb unabated.

By the end of his first year at Modrow, the building program had been completed, although behind schedule, the new equipment had been installed, and some revamping of cost procedures had been incorporated. The financial picture at this time showed a substantial loss, but since it had been budgeted as a loss, this was not surprising. All managers of the various divisions had worked closely with their supervisors and accountants in planning the budget for the following year, and Dick began to emphasize his personal interest in cost reduction.

As he worked through his first year as plant manager, Dick developed the habit of strolling around the organization. He was apt to leave his office and appear anywhere on the plant floor, in the design offices, at the desk of a purchasing agent or accountant, in the plant cafeteria rather than the executive dining room, or wherever there was activity concerned with Modrow. During his strolls he looked, listened, and became acquainted. If he observed activities which he wanted to talk about, or heard remarks that gave him clues to future action, he did not reveal these at the time. Rather he had a nod, a wave, a smile, for the people near him, but a mental note to talk to his supervisors, managers, and foremen in the future. At first his presence disturbed those who noted him coming and going, but after several exposures to him without any noticeable effect, the workers came to accept his presence and continue their usual activities. Supervisors, managers, and foremen, however, did not feel as comfortable when they saw him in the area.

Their feelings were aptly expressed by the manager of the siding department one day when he was talking to one of his foremen: "I wish to hell he'd stay up in the front office where he belongs. Whoever heard of a plant manager who had time to wander around the plant all the time. Why doesn't he tend to his paperwork and let us tend to our business?"

"Don't let him get you down," joked the foreman. "Nothing ever comes of his visits. Maybe he's just lonesome and looking for a friend. You know how these Americans are."

"Well, you may feel that nothing ever comes of his visits, but I don't. I've been called into his office three separate times within the last two months. The heat must really be on from the head office. You know these conferences we have every month where he reviews our financial progress, our building progress, our design progress, etc.? Well, we're not really progressing as fast as we should be. If you ask me we're in for continuing trouble."

In recalling his first year at Modrow, Dick had felt constantly pressured and badgered. He always sensed that the Canadians he worked with resented his presence since he was brought in over the heads of the operating staff. At the same time he felt this subtle resistance from his Canadian work force, he believed that the president and his friends in the home office were constantly on the alert, waiting for Dick to prove himself or fall flat on his face. Because of the constant pressures and demands of the work, he had literally dumped his family into a new community and had withdrawn into the plant. In the process, he built up a wall of resistance toward the demands of his wife and children who, in turn, felt as though he was abandoning them.

During the course of the conversation with his university friends, he began to recall a series of incidents that probably had resulted from the conflicting pressures. When describing some of these incidents, he continued to emphasize the fact that his attempt to be relaxed and casual had backfired. Laughingly, Dick said, "As you know, both human relations and accounting were my weakest subjects during the Master's program, and yet they are two fields I felt I needed the most at Modrow at this time." He described some of the cost procedures that he would have liked to incorporate. However, without the support and knowledge furnished by his former controller, he busied himself with details that were unnecessary. One day, as he describes it, he overheard a conversation between two of the accounting staff members with whom he had been working very closely. One of them commented to the other, "For a guy who's a vice president, he sure spends a lot of time breathing down our necks. Why doesn't he simply tell us the kind of systems he would like to try, and let us do the experimenting and work out the budget?" Without commenting on the conversation he overheard, Dick then described himself as attempting to spend less time and be less directive in the accounting department.

Another incident he described which apparently had real meaning for him was one in which he had called a staff conference with his top-level managers. They had been going "hammer and tongs" for better than an hour in his private office, and in the process of heated conversation had loosened ties, taken off coats, and really rolled up their sleeves. Dick himself had slipped out of his shoes. In the midst of this, his secretary reminded him of an appointment with public officials. Dick had rapidly finished up his conference with his managers, straightened his tie, donned his coat, and had wandered out into the main office in his stocking feet.

Dick fully described several incidents when he had disappointed, frustrated, or confused his wife and family by forgetting birthdays, appointments, dinner engagements, etc. He seemed to be describing a pattern of behavior which resulted from continuing pressure and frustration. He was setting the scene to describe his baffling and humiliating position in the siding department. In looking back and recalling his activities during this first year, Dick commented on the fact that his frequent wanderings throughout the plant had resulted in a nodding acquaintance with the workers, but probably had also resulted in foremen and supervisors spending more time getting ready for his visits and reading meaning into them afterwards than attending to their specific duties. His attempts to know in detail the accounting procedures being used required long hours of concentration and detailed conversations with the accounting staff, which were time-consuming and very frustrating for him, as well as for them. His lack of attention to his family life resulted in continued pressure from both wife and family.

The Siding Department Incident.   Siding was the product which had been budgeted as a large profit item of Modrow. Aluminum siding was gaining in popularity among both architects and builders, because of its possibilities in both decorative and practical uses. Panel sheets of siding were shipped in standard sizes on order; large sheets of the coated siding were cut to specifications in the trim department, packed, and shipped. The trim shop was located near the loading platforms, and Dick often cut through the trim shop on his wanderings through the plant. On one of his frequent trips through the area, he suddenly became aware of the fact that several workers responsible for the disposal function were spending countless hours at high-speed saws cutting scraps into specified lengths to fit into scrap barrels. The narrow bands of scrap which resulted from the trim process varied in length from 7 to 27 feet and had to be reduced in size to fit into the disposal barrels. Dick, in his concentration on cost reduction, picked up one of the thin strips, bent it several times and fitted it into the barrel. He tried this with another piece, and it bent very easily. After assuring himself that bending was possible, he walked over to a worker at the saw and asked why he was using the saw when material could easily be bent and fitted into the barrels, resulting in saving time and equipment. The worker's response was, "We've never done it that way, sir. We've always cut it."

Following his plan of not commenting or discussing matters on the floor, but distressed by the reply, Dick returned to his office and asked the manager of the siding department if he could speak to the foreman of the scrap division. The manager said, "Of course, I'll send him up to you in just a minute."

After a short time, the foreman, very agitated at being called to the plant manager's office, appeared. Dick began questioning him about the scrap disposal process and received the standard answer: "We've always done it that way." Dick then proceeded to review cost-cutting objectives. He talked about the pliability of the strips of scrap. He called for a few pieces of scrap to demonstrate the ease with which it could be bent, and ended what he thought was a satisfactory conversation by requesting the foreman to order heavy-duty gloves for his workers and use the bending process for a trial period of two weeks to check the cost saving possible.

The foreman listened throughout most of this hour's conference, offered several reasons why it wouldn't work, raised some questions about the record-keeping process for cost purposes, and finally left the office with the forced agreement to try the suggested new method of bending, rather than cutting, for disposal. Although he was immersed in many other problems, his request was forcibly brought home one day as he cut through the scrap area. The workers were using power saws to cut scraps. He called the manager of the siding department and questioned him about the process. The manager explained that each foreman was responsible for his own processes, and since Dick had already talked to the foreman, perhaps he had better talk to him again. When the foreman arrived, Dick began to question him. He received a series of excuses, and some explanations of the kinds of problems they were meeting by attempting to bend the scrap material. "I don't care what the problems are," Dick nearly shouted, "when I request a cost-reduction program instituted, I want to see it carried through."

Dick was furious. When the foreman left, he phoned the maintenance department and ordered the removal of the power saws from the scrap area immediately. A short time later the foreman of the scrap department knocked on Dick's door reporting his astonishment at having maintenance men step into his area and physically remove the saws. Dick reminded the foreman of his request for a trial at cost reduction to no avail, and ended the conversation by saying that the power saws were gone and would not be returned, and the foreman had damned well better learn to get along without them. After a stormy exit by the foreman, Dick congratuled himself on having solvied a problem and turned his attention to other matters.

A few days later Dick cut through the trim department and literally stopped to stare. As he described it, he was completely nonplussed to discover gloved workmen using hand shears to cut each piece of scrap.

EXCELSIOR BAKERIES, INC.*

Upon completing my junior year in college in early June, I returned to my hometown, Pottersville, New York. The next day I went to see Roger Farnum, the plant superintendent of the local branch of Excelsior Bakeries, Inc., to find out when I should report for work. I had worked at the Excel-

---

*Reproduced by permission of the President and Fellows of Harvard College.

During the winter following the events described in this case, the writer submitted it as a report for a course in administration he was taking in a graduate school of business.

sior plant the previous summer as a general helper on the slicing and wrapping crew for hamburger and hot dog rolls. Since I was a union member and had spoken to Farnum during spring vacation about a job for this summer, I was positive of being rehired.

When I walked into the office, Farnum said jokingly: "Hi, George! Ready to go to work for a change after all that book learning?" I was rather surprised to see Farnum so jovial and cordial. I remembered him as always having a long face and never saying more than two words at a time. I finally answered: "Yes, sir, any time you say and as soon as possible."

"Well, on the recommendation of Murphy, you're going to run the hamburger and hot dog machine this summer. Murphy wants to work on the ovens; and since we don't want to change a regular worker over to the wrapper just for a couple of months, we figured you would accept the added responsibility and could handle the job."

Phil Murphy, a regular employee of the plant, had run the wrapping machine last summer and had been leader of a crew of three other summer workers and me. I had visited Murphy at the plant during spring vacation, and he had told me he was going to work on the ovens this year because it was daywork and paid more. I had casually mentioned to him at that time to try to get me the wrapping machine job, but I hadn't thought of it again, since it had always been assigned to a regular worker.

I was extremely pleased to accept the job, for I knew it meant 6 cents more an hour, and it would entail some leadership responsibility. I thought to myself: "Now I will be part of management and not just another worker."

Farnum told me to report for work that following Sunday, a week earlier than I had expected, so I could familiarize myself with the machine before the "rush season" started.

Excelsior Bakeries, Inc., was a large firm with many plants spread across the entire United States. The Pottersville branch produced mainly white, rye, whole wheat, and French bread, but supplemented these major lines with hamburger and hot dog rolls, dinner rolls, doughnuts, and other bakery products. It also distributed, in its area of operation, pies, cakes, crackers, and other specialties produced in the Boston plant.

Pottersville was located in a region noted for its many summer resorts, camps, and hotels, which are open from June until September. During the summer season, production and sales of the local Excelsior plant increased tremendously as the summer population swelled the normal demand. This seasonal rise was especially significant in hot dog and hamburger rolls, whose sales increased over the winter months by approximately 100–150 percent in June, 150–250 percent in July, and 250–300 percent in August. Because of this great seasonal increase, the company had to hire about 15 employees just for the 3 summer months. Five of the "extra help" were needed on the wrapping crew for hot dog and hamburger rolls. These workers were usually drawn from college students on vacation, employment agencies, and transients. In the past several years the extra help had been predominantly college students, because they were more dependable and willing to remain on the job right up to Labor Day.

After I reported to work, I spent the first week with the regular employees. Ed Dugan, a past operator of the wrapping machine, worked with me, teaching me all the techniques of operating the machine efficiently. The machine was rather old and had to be tended carefully at all times so that the cellophane wrapping paper would not jump off the rollers. The wrapping paper was expensive, and Joe McGuire, the night foreman, "blew his top" whenever a lot of paper was wasted.

Exhibit 1 shows the working area and the positions of each operator on the slicing and wrapping crew. Worker No. 1 took the pans of rolls from the racks and fed the rolls out on a conveyor, which carried them into the slicing machine. Worker No. 2 stacked the sliced rolls into two rows, one on top of the other, making groups of eight or one dozen. Worker No. 3 slid the groups of rolls down the table to worker No. 4, who fed them into the wrapping machine. Worker No. 5, the wrapping machine operator and crew leader, placed the wrapped packages in a box, keeping count of the actual number packaged. The work was rather routine and extremely monotonous and boring. Workers No. 1 through No. 4 continually exchanged positions in order to break the monotony.

EXHIBIT 1
Wrapping Machine Layout

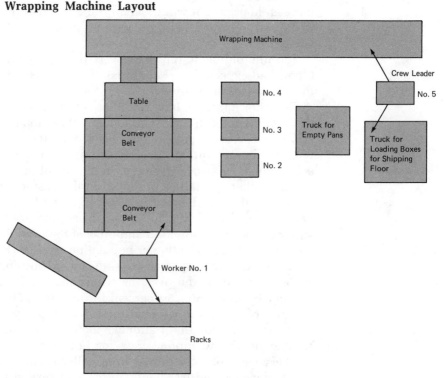

The plant employees worked on a five-day week—working on Sunday and Monday; off on Tuesday; working Wednesday, Thursday, and Friday; and off again on Saturday. Production was on daily orders from the various sales routes. The salesmen left the plant early in the morning with their loaded trucks and, after making their deliveries, returned in the afternoon with the orders for the next day. The volume varied from day to day, and the rolls were ready for wrapping at varying times. Therefore, the wrappers generally reported for work at a different time each day, being notified by the plant superintendent. Usually, the crew began about 6:00 to 8:00 P.M. and worked until all the orders were filled for that night. The number of hours worked ranged from 7 to 15 or even more. All time over eight hours was overtime and paid for as time and a half. If a worker was a union member, the company had to guarantee him seven hours' pay for any night on which it called him in. If there were not seven hours of slicing and wrapping, the foreman found something else for the men to do, such as thoroughly cleaning the machines, greasing the pans, or doing other odd jobs. If a man wished, though, he could ask to punch out before seven hours were up, thereby forfeiting the guaranteed seven hours' pay for that night and receiving pay only for the hours he had worked.

Four different types of packages were wrapped on the machine: hamburger and hot dog dozen-roll packages, and hamburger and hot dog packages of eight rolls. A different size and type of paper was used for each package. Different-sized plates had to be used in the machine also. On an average night a complete changeover of the machine had to be made about six times, each alteration taking about 10 minutes. In addition, it took about five minutes to replace a roll of paper when it ran out, and two to three minutes to replace the labels and seals. During these changeovers and replacements, which were made by the machine operator, the rest of the crew smoked cigarettes out on the shipping dock or else folded boxes for the operator if he needed them. I never asked anyone to make boxes if he wanted to have a cigarette or wanted to get a drink of water. But if a man was just sitting around or "goofing off," I would ask him to fold boxes, as the crew is supposed to do during these breaks. McGuire hated to see anyone sit around, but he never begrudged anyone a cigarette.

With the start of my second week, orders rose, and the rest of the summer help was called in. I was very pleased when three of my close friends were assigned to my crew. Art Dunn, a student at Williams, had worked on the wrapping crew with me the previous summer, as had Jack Dorsey, a student at the University of Vermont. Bill Regan, a Fordham student, had not worked for Excelsior the previous summer; but he had lived next door to me, and we had grown up together. The four of us had been close friends during high school days and since graduation, even though we went to different colleges. Harry Hart, the fourth man, was also new to the wrapping crew. Hart had graduated from high school a year before the rest of us and was attending the University of Massachusetts. We old-timers were already union members. The new men joined soon after they began work.

With the help of Dunn and Dorsey, I was able to train Regan and Hart quickly; and within a couple of nights, they were thoroughly proficient in all four positions. During these first two nights, Dunn and Dorsey thoroughly indoctrinated Regan and Hart into the "code" of the wrapping crew.

Excelsior Bakeries offered college students an excellent opportunity to make a considerable amount of money during the summer, paying an hourly rate of $1.63 and providing plenty of overtime. The code of the wrapping crew was a concerted group action to set the number of hours to be worked on a certain night. At the beginning of the night's work, the crew could fairly well estimate from the production orders just how long it should take to put the work out. If it was estimated to take about eight hours, the crew would purposely slow down to stretch it to nine or nine and a half hours, so they could get overtime pay. On almost any night the work could be stretched out by an hour or so. Only on big nights of 12 or more hours did the crew work at normal speed. As an indication of the effectiveness of this slowdown, there were several occasions when a seven- or eight-hour night was estimated, but the crew "pushed the stuff through" and finished in six hours in order to have a few beers before the local bar closed at 3:00 A.M.

As a member of this crew the previous summer, I was one of the strong advocates of this code. If a new worker or a temporary replacement from somewhere else in the plant appeared on the crew, he had to conform, or the group gave him much verbal abuse or the even worse "silent treatment." These were unbearable conditions, and the new man always accepted the code.

Murphy, the previous year's leader, although a regular employee of the plant, had cooperated with the group and never complained. He used to say: "After all, I want the overtime, too!"

After the first few nights of work, I noticed the code had begun to operate. I had never stopped to think of the effects this slowdown had on management and the operations of the plant. It raised labor production costs, delayed the salesmen in leaving for their routes, and raised other problems as well. At first, I was rather confused as to whether I should allow this practice to continue or, as "part of management," put my foot down and take action to stop it. Because I could not think of any satisfactory course of action which would satisfy everyone, I allowed the code to operate. I rationalized myself into believing: "Well, if management isn't going to do anything about it, why the hell should I worry about it?"

The first couple of weeks went smoothly. The only problems I had to face were minor arguments among the crew and the usual horseplay and "goofing off" in the middle hours of the morning.

McGuire, the night foreman, occasionally would say to me, smiling: "Took you guys a pretty long time to get those rolls out tonight, didn't it?" or, on a really short night: "You can really shove those rolls through when you feel like having a few brews!" McGuire could not see us working from his office, as the line of racks blocked his view, but he regularly walked over to check on us. When he appeared, the man feeding the slicing machine would place the rolls on the conveyor belt "back to back" with no space in between, the maximum rate at which the crew could operate. When he was in his office or "up front," a space of about 6 to 12 inches was allowed between rolls, thereby reducing the speed of production by 10 to 15 percent.

Occasionally, a "little war" would break out between the wrapping crew and two doughnut men across the aisle from the wrapping machine. The members of each group would throw doughnuts or hot dog and hamburger rolls at the others. One night, one of these battles was beginning to get out of hand to the point where the boys had stopped work. I reprimanded them and told them to "knock it off" and get back to work. Regan called me a "company man," and Dunn said something about the "lieutenant with the gold-plated bars."

I was trying to ignore the comments when suddenly I heard the paper snap. I stopped the machine and adjusted it; but even after the machine had been adjusted, package after package kept coming through unwrapped or "crippled." I tried everything I knew to find the cause of the trouble; but just when I thought I had the machine running properly, something else would go wrong. By this time, I was ready to give up and call McGuire for his advice.

Then I noticed the four crewmen having a good laugh for themselves. I had been so concerned about trying to change the adjustments on the machine that I had not noticed Regan tinkering with the machine at the other end. He was also feeding the hotdog rolls improperly, breaking them before putting them in the machine so they would slide off and get caught, thereby drawing unevenly on the paper. I lost my temper completely and was in the process of a real argument with Regan and the rest of the crew when McGuire came down to see why the machine was shut down. When he asked, I stuttered: "Hell, Joe, these—ah—this damn machine isn't drawing right. I've tried everything, but I think I've finally found the real reason. Let's try it now, fellas!"

That night, when I was making my final count with McGuire and the shipping foreman, I was considerably short on hot dog rolls, because of the many losses caused by Regan's tampering with the machine. McGuire gave me quite a reprimand and said I'd better "watch it."

The next night, when I came to work, Farnum stopped me and asked why I had lost so much paper the night before. I told him it was a breakdown in the machine. He gave me orders to weigh each roll of paper before we started wrapping each night and to weigh it again when we finished. I was to record the weights on tabulation control sheets kept in his office.

That night, before starting work, I told the crew what had happened and what McGuire and Farnum had said to me. I told them that I was being held responsible for paper and production control, and that I would tolerate no more "horsing around," especially tampering with the machine. I emphasized that I would not go "on the carpet" again for *anyone*. Relations between me and the crew, with the exception of Hart, were rather strained for a couple of nights. None of them said very much to me. Also, I did not go swimming or play golf with them for a couple of days, as we usually did every afternoon. However, I had no more incidents of this sort, and the crew continued to meet the output schedule as they had previously. Gradually, the incident was forgotten, and relations among us became what they had been before.

During the latter part of August, the annual Excelsior clambake was held. In the late afternoon, McGuire called me over to the bar to have a drink. Mr. Farnum and Mr. Sommers, the plant general manager, were with him. McGuire threw his arm around me and said to Farnum: "George did a great job this summer on the wrapper, didn't he, Rog?"

"Best season we've had so far, Joe."

A CASE OF MISUNDERSTANDING: MR. HART AND MR. BING *

In a department of a large industrial organization there were seven workers (four men and three women) engaged in testing and inspecting panels of electronic equipment. In this department one of the workers, Bing was having trouble with his immediate supervisor, Hart, who had formerly been a worker in the department. Had we been observers in this department we would have seen Bing carrying two or three panels at a time from the racks where they were stored to the bench where he inspected them together. For this activity we would have seen him charging double or triple set-up time. We would have heard him occasionally singing at work. Also we would have seen him usually leaving his work position a few minutes early to go to lunch, and noticed that other employees sometimes accompanied him. And had we been present at one specific occasion, we would have heard Hart telling Bing that he disapproved of these activities and that he wanted Bing to stop doing them. However, not being present to hear the actual verbal exchange that took place in this interaction, let us note what Bing and Hart each said to a personnel representative.

What Bing Said

In talking about his practice of charging double or triple setup time for panels which he inspected all at one time, Bing said:

> This is a perfectly legal thing to do. We've always been doing it. Mr. Hart, the supervisor, has other ideas about it, though; he claims it's cheating the company. He came over to the bench a day or two ago and let me know just how he felt about the matter. Boy, did we go at it! It wasn't so much the fact that he called me down on it, but more the way in which he did it. He's a sarcastic

*Reproduced by permission of the President and Fellows of Harvard College.

bastard. I've never seen anyone like him. He's not content just to say in a manlike way what's on his mind, but he prefers to do it in a way that makes you want to crawl inside a crack in the floor. What a guy! I don't mind being called down by a supervisor, but I like to be treated like a man, and not humiliated like a school teacher does a naughty kid. He's been pulling this stuff ever since he's been promoted. He's lost his friendly way and seems to be having some difficulty in knowing how to manage us employees. He's a changed man over what he used to be like when he was a worker on the bench with us several years ago.

When he pulled this kind of stuff on me the other day, I got so damn mad I called in the union representative. I knew that the thing I was doing was permitted by the contract, but I was intent on making some trouble for Mr. Hart, just because he persists in this sarcastic way of handling me. I am about fed up with the whole damn situation. I'm trying every means I can to get myself transferred out of this group. If I don't succeed and I'm forced to stay on here, I'm going to screw him in every way I can. He's not going to pull this kind of kid stuff any longer on me. When the union representative questioned him on the case, he finally had to back down, because according to the contract an employee can use any time-saving method or device in order to speed up the process as long as the quality standards of the job are met.

You see, he knows that I do professional singing on the outside. He hears the people talking about my career in music. I guess he figures I can be so cocky because I have another means of earning some money. Actually, the employees here enjoy having me sing while we work, but he thinks I'm disturbing them and causing them to "goof-off" from their work. Occasionally, I leave the job a few minutes early and go down to the washroom to wash up before lunch. Sometimes several others in the group will accompany me, and so Mr. Hart automatically thinks I'm the leader and usually bawls me out for the whole thing.

So, you can see, I'm a marked man around here: He keeps watching me like a hawk. Naturally, this makes me very uncomfortable. That's why I'm sure a transfer would be the best thing. I've asked him for it, but he didn't give me any satisfaction at the time. While I remain here, I'm going to keep my nose clean, but whenever I get the chance, I'm going to slip it to him, but good.

What Hart Said   Here, on the other hand, is what Hart told the personnel representative:

Say, I think you should be in on this. My dear little friend Bing is heading himself into a show-down with me. Recently it was brought to my attention that Bing has been taking double and triple set-up time for panels which he is actually inspecting at one time. In effect, that's cheating, and I've called him down on it several times before. A few days ago it was brought to my attention again, and so this time I really let him have it in no uncertain terms. He's been getting away with this for too long and I'm going to put an end to it once and for all. I know he didn't like me calling him on it because a few hours later he had the union representative breathing down my back. Well, anyway, I let them both know I'll not tolerate the practice any longer, and I let Bing know that if he continues to do this kind of thing, I'm inclined to think the guy's mentally deficient, because talking to him has actually no meaning to him whatsoever. I've tried just about every approach to jar some sense into that guy's head, and I've just about given it up as a bad deal.

I don't know what it is about the guy, but I think he's harboring some deep feelings against me. For what, I don't know, because I've tried to handle that bird with kid gloves. But his whole attitude around here on the job is one of indifference, and he certainly isn't a good influence on the rest of my group. Franklin, I think he purposely tried to agitate them against me at times, too. It seems to me he may be suffering from illusions of grandeur, because all he does all day long is sit over there and croon his fool head off. Thinks he's a Frank Sinatra! No kidding! I understand he takes singing lessons and he's working with some of the local bands in the city. All of which is OK by me; but when his outside interests start interfering with his efficiency on the job, then I've got to start paying closer attention to the situation. For this reason I've been keeping my eye on that bird and if he steps out of line any more, he and I are going to part ways.

You know there's an old saying, "You can't make a silk purse out of a sow's ear." The guy is simply unscrupulous. He feels no obligation to do a real day's work. Yet I know the guy can do a good job, because for a long time he did. But in recent months he's slipped, for some reason, and his whole attitude on the job has changed. Why, it's even getting to the point now where I think he's inducing other employees to "goof off" a few minutes before the lunch whistle and go down to the washroom and clean up on company time. I've called him on it several times, but words just don't seem to make any lasting impression on him. Well, if he keeps it up much longer, he's going to find himself on the way out. He's asked me for a transfer, so I know he wants to go. But I didn't given him an answer when he asked me, because I was storming mad at the time, and I may have told him to go somewhere else."

Glossary of Terms

ABC Analysis. A term to describe the analysis of antecedents, behavior, and consequences when investigating work- or job-related issues.

Accommodation Stage Socialization. Socialization activities undertaken or experienced after an individual takes a job or enters an organization.

Adaptiveness. A criterion of effectiveness which refers to the ability of the organization to respond to change which is induced by either internal or external stimuli. An equivalent term is *flexibility*, although adaptiveness connotes an intermediate time frame whereas flexibility is ordinarily used in a short-run sense.

Anticipatory Stage Socialization. Socialization activities undertaken or experienced prior to taking a job or entering an organization.

Assembly-Line Technology. A form of manufacturing in which component parts are brought together and combined into a single unit of output. It is used to produce relatively standard products which have a mass market.

Assessment Centers. An evaluation technique that uses situational exercises to identify promotable, trainable, and high potential employees.

Attitudes. Mental states of readiness for need arousal.

Attribution Leadership Theory. A theory of the relationship between individual perception and interpersonal behavior. The theory suggests that understanding and predicting how people will react to events around them is enhanced by knowing what their causal explanation for those events are.

Authority. Authority resides in the relationship between positions and in the role expectations of the position occupants. Thus, an influence attempt based on authority is generally not resisted because when joining an organization individuals become aware that the exercise of authority is required of supervisors and compliance is required of subordinates. The recognition of authority is necessary for organizational effectiveness and is a cost of organizational membership.

Banking Time Off. A reward practice of allowing employees to build up time off credits for such things as good performance or attendance. The employee

629

would then receive the time off in addition to the regular vacation time granted by the organization because of seniority.

Baseline. The period of time before a change is introduced.

Behavior Modification. An approach to motivation that uses the principles of operant conditioning.

Behaviorally Anchored Rating Scales (BARS). A rating scale developed by raters and/or ratees that uses critical behavioral incidents as interval anchors on each scale. Approximately 6 to 10 scales with behavioral incidents are used to derive the evaluation.

Boundary Spanning Role. The role of an individual who must relate to two different systems, usually an organization and some part of its environment.

Bureaucrcratic Theory. The theory developed by Max Weber that defined the characteristics of an organization which maximizes stability and controllability of its members. The ideal-type bureaucracy is an organization which contains all the elements to a high degree.

Cafeteria Fringe Benefits. The employee is allowed to develop and allocate a personally attractive fringe benefit package. The employee is instructed what the total fringe benefits allowed will be and then distributes the benefits according to his or her preferences.

Career. The individually perceived sequence of attitudes and behaviors associated with work-related experiences and activities over the span of the person's life.

Career Effectiveness. The extent to which the sequence of career attitudes and behaviors are satisfying to the individual.

Career Paths. Different jobs and/or positions associated with a specific career.

Career Stages. Distinctly different, yet related, stages in the progression of a career.

Case Study. Examination of numerous characteristics of one person or group, usually over an extended time period.

Central Tendency Error. The tendency to rate all ratees around an average score.

Centralization. A dimension of organization structure which refers to the extent to which authority to make decisions is retained in top management.

Classical Design Theory. A body of literature which evolved from scientific management, classical organization, and bureaucratic theory. The theory emphasizes the design of a preplanned structure for doing work. It minimizes the importance of the social system.

Classical Organization Theory. A body of literature which developed from the writings of managers who proposed principles of organization. These principles were intended to serve as guidelines for other managers.

Coercive Power. An influence over others based upon fear. A subordinate perceives that failure to comply with the wishes of a superior would lead to punishment or some other negative outcomes.

Cognition. This is basically what individuals know about themselves and their environment. Cognition implies a conscious process of acquiring knowledge.

Cognitive Dissonance. A mental state which occurs when there is a lack of consistency or harmony among an individual's various cognitions (for example, attitudes, beliefs, and so on) after a decision has been made.

Command Group. The command group is specified by the formal organization chart. The group of subordinates who report to one particular manager constitutes the command group.

Commitment. A sense of identification, involvement, and loyalty expressed by an employee toward the company.

Communication. The transmission of information and understanding through the use of common symbols.

Complexity. A dimension of organization structure which refers to the number of different jobs and/or units within an organization.

Confrontation Conflict Resolution. A strategy which focuses on the conflict and attempts to resolve it through such procedures as rotation of key group personnel, the establishment of superordinate goals, improving communications, and similar approaches.

Conscious Goals. The main goal a person is striving toward and is aware of when directing behavior.

Consideration. Leader acts which imply showing supportive concern for the followers in a group.

Content Motivation Theories. Theories which focus on the factors within the person that energize, direct, sustain, and stop behavior.

Contingency Design Theory. An approach to designing organizations which states that the effective structure depends upon factors in the situation.

Continuous Reinforcement. A schedule that is designed to reinforce behavior every time the exhibited behavior is correct.

Counterpower. Leaders exert power on subordinates and subordinates exert power on leaders. Power is a two-way flow.

Criterion. The dependent or predicted measure for appraising the effectiveness of an individual employee.

Decentralization. Basically this entails pushing the decision-making point to the lowest managerial level possible. It involves the delegation of decision-making authority.

Decision Acceptance. Important criterion in Vroom-Yetton model that refers to the degree of subordinate commitment to the decision.

Decision Quality. Important criterion in Vroom-Yetton model that refers to the objective aspects of a decision that influence subordinates' performance aside from any direct impact on motivation.

Decisions. Decisions are the organizational mechanisms through which an attempt is made to achieve a desired state. They are organizational responses to a problem.

Decoding. This is the mental procedure which a receiver of a message goes through to decipher a message.

Defensive Behavior. When an employee is blocked in attempts to satisfy needs to achieve goals, one or more defense mechanisms may be evoked. They include withdrawal, aggression, substitution, compensation, repression, and rationalization.

Delegated Strategy. An OD strategy which precludes participation by management. The employees through case discussion or sensitivity training determine the OD program.

Delegation. The process by which authority is distributed downward in an organization.

Delphi Technique. A technique for improving group decisions. It involves the solicitation and comparison of anonymous judgments on the topic of interest through a set of sequential questionnaires interspersed with summarized information and feedback of opinions from earlier responses.

Departmentalization. The manner in which an organization is structurally divided. Some of the more publicized divisions are by function, territory, product, customer, and project.

Development. A criterion of effectiveness which refers to the ability of the organization to increase its capacity to respond to current and future environmental demands. Equivalent or similar terms include institutionalization, stability, and integration.

Differential Piecerate System. An incentive wage system that pays a fixed rate for all production up to standard, but a higher rate for all pieces once the standard is met.

Differentiation. An important concept in the Lawrence and Lorsch research which refers to the process by which subunits in an organization develop particular attributes in response to the requirements imposed by their particular subenvironments. The greater the differences among the subunits' attributes, the greater the differentiation.

Dominant Competitive Strategy. A concept defined in the Lawrence and Lorsch research to refer to the subenvironment which is crucial to the organization's success. The dominant strategy may be production, marketing, or product development depending upon the industry.

Downward Communication. Downward communication flows from individuals in higher levels of organization structure to those in lower levels. The most common type is job instructions and related information from superior to subordinate.

Dysfunctional Intergroup Conflict. Any confrontation or interaction between groups that hinders the achievement of organizational goals.

Effectiveness. In the context of organizational behavior effectiveness refers to the optimal relationship among five components: production, efficiency, satisfaction, adaptiveness, and development.

Efficiency. A short-run criterion of effectiveness which refers to the ability of the organization to produce outputs with minimum use of inputs. The measures of efficiency are always in ratio terms, such as benefit/cost, cost/output, and cost/time.

Encoding. This is the converting of an idea into an understandable message by a communicator.

Environmental Certainty. A concept in the Lawrence and Lorsch research which refers to three characteristics of a subenvironment that determine the subunit's requisite differentiation. The three characteristics are rate of change, certainty of information, and time-span of feedback or results.

Environmental Diversity. A concept in the Lawrence and Lorsch research which refers to the differences among the three subenvironments in terms of certainty.

Equity Theory of Motivation. A theory which examines discrepancies within a person after the individual has compared his or her input/output ratio to a reference person.

ERG Theory of Motivation. A theory developed and tested by Alderfer which categorizes needs as existence, relatedness, and growth.

Eustress. This is a term made popular by Dr. Hans Selye to describe good or stimulating stress.

Expectancy. The perceived likelihood that a particular act will be followed by a particular outcome.

Expectancy Theory. In this theory the employee is viewed as faced with a set of first-level outcomes. The employee will select an outcome based upon how this choice is related to second-level outcomes. The preferences of the individual are based upon the strength (valence) of desire to achieve a second-level state and the perception of the relationship between first- and second-level outcomes.

Experiment. An investigation to be considered an experiment must contain two elements—manipulation of some variable (independent variable) and observation of the results (dependent variable).

Expert Power. Capacity to influence related to some expertise, special skill, or knowledge. It is a function of the judgment of the less powerful individual that the other person has ability or knowledge that exceeds his own.

Extinction. The decline in response rate because of nonreinforcement.

Extrinsic Rewards. Those rewards such as pay, promotion, or fringe benefits which are external to the job.

Field Experiment. In this type of experiment the investigator attempts to manipulate and control variables in the natural setting rather than in a laboratory.

Fixed Interval Reinforcement. A situation in which a reinforcer is applied only after the passage of a certain period of time since the last reinforcer was applied.

Formal Groups. The demands and processes of the formal organization lead to the formation of different types of groups. Specifically, two types of groups specified by the formal organization are: the command group and the task group.

Formalization. A dimension of organization structure which refers to the extent to which rules, procedures, and other guides to action are written and enforced.

Friendship Group. An informal group that is established in the workplace because of some common characteristic and may extend the interaction of members to include activities outside the workplace.

Functional Intergroup Conflict. A confrontation between groups that enhances and benefits the achievement of organizational goals.

General Adaptation Syndrome (G.A.S.). A description of the three phases of the defense reaction a person establishes when stressed. These phases are called alarm, resistance, and exhaustion.

Goal. This is a specific target that an individual is trying to achieve; it is the target (object) of an action.

Goal Approach to Effectiveness. A perspective on effectiveness which emphasizes the central role of goal achievement as the criterion for assessing effectiveness.

Goal Commitment. This is the amount of effort actually used to achieve a goal.

Goal Difficulty. This is the degree of proficiency or level of goal performance being sought.

Goal Orientation. A concept which refers to the focus of attention and decision making among members of a subunit.

Goal Participation. The amount of involvement a person has in setting task and personal development goals.

Goal Setting. The process of establishing goals. In many cases goal setting involves a superior and subordinate working together setting the subordinate's goals for a specified period of time.

Goal Specificity. The degree of quantitative precision of the goal.

Graicunas' Model. Proposition that an arithmetic increase in the number of subordinates results in a geometric increase in the number of relationships under the jurisdiction of the superior. Graicunas set this up in a mathematical model

$$C = N\left(\frac{2^N}{2} + N - 1\right)$$

Grapevine. An informal communication network that exists in organizations and short-circuits the formal channels.

Grid Training. A leadership development method proposed by Blake and Mouton which emphasizes the necessary balance between production and person-orientation.

Group. Two or more employees who interact with each other in such a manner that the behavior and/or performance of a member is influenced by the behavior and/or performance of other members.

Group Cohesiveness. The attraction of members to the group in terms of the desirability of group membership to the members. In a straightforward manner, this is the "stick-togetherness" quality of a group.

Halo Error. A positive or negative aura around a ratee that influences a rater's evaluation.

Hawthorne Studies. A series of studies undertaken at the Chicago Hawthorne Plant of Western Electric from 1924 to 1933. The studies made major contributions to the knowledge of the importance of the social system of an organization. They provided the impetus for the human relations approach to organizations.

History. One of the sources of error in experimental results. It consists of events other than the experimental treatment which occur between pre- and post-measurement.

Horizontal Communication. Horizontal communication occurs when the communicator and the receiver are at the same level in the organization.

Incentive Plan Criteria. To be effective in motivating employees incentive plans should (1) be related to specific behavioral patterns (for example, better performance), (2) be immediately received after displaying the behavior, and (3) reward the employee for consistently displaying the desired behavior.

Informal Groups. Informal groups are natural groupings of people in the work situation since they appear in response to man's social need to associate with others. Two specific types are interest groups and friendship groups.

Information Flow Requirements. The amount of information which must be processed by an organization, group or individual to perform effectively.

Initiating Structure. Leadership acts which imply structuring job tasks and responsibilities for followers.

Instrumentality. The relationship between first- and second-level outcomes.

Instrumentation. One of the sources of error in experimental results. It is changes in the measure of participants' performance that are the result of changes in the measurement instruments or conditions under which the measuring is done (for example, wear on machinery, fatigue on the part of observers).

Integration. A concept in the Lawrence and Lorsch research which refers to the process of achieving unity of effort among the organization's various subsystems. Techniques for achieving integration range from rules and procedures and plans to mutual adjustment.

Interaction. Refers to any interpersonal contact in which one individual can be observed acting and one or more other individuals responding to the action.

Interaction Effects. When any of the sources of errors in experimental results interact with the experimental treatment resulting in confounding results. For example, the types of individuals withdrawing from any experiment (mortality) may differ for the experimental group and the control group.

Interest Group. A group that forms because of some special topic of interest. Generally, when the interest declines or a goal has been achieved, the group disbands.

Intergroup Conflict. The conflict between groups which can be functional or dysfunctional.

Interpersonal Orientation. A concept which refers to whether a person is more concerned with achieving good social relations as opposed to achieving a task.

Interpersonal Rewards. Extrinsic rewards such as receiving recognition or being able to socially interact on the job.

Interrole Conflict. This type of conflict is the result of facing multiple roles. It occurs because individuals simultaneously perform many roles, some of which have conflicting expectations.

Intervention. The process by which either outsiders or insiders assume the role of a change agent in the OD program.

Intrapersonal Conflict. The conflict which a person faces internally, as when an individual experiences personal frustration, anxiety, and stress.

Intrarole Conflict. This type of conflict is more likely to occur when a given role has a complex role set. It occurs ehen different individuals define a role according to different sets of expectations, making it impossible for the person occupying the role to satisfy all.

Intrinsic Rewards. Those rewards which are part of the job itself. The responsibility, challenge, and feedback characteristics of the job are examples.

Job Analysis. The description of how one job differs from another in terms of demands, activities, and skills required.

Job Content. The perception of factors which define the general nature of a job.

Job Definition.   The first subproblem of the organizing decision. It involves the determination of the task requirements of each job in the organization.

Job Depth.   This refers to the amount of control which an individual has to alter or influence the job and the surrounding environment.

Job Description.   A summary statement of what an employee actually does on the job.

Job Enlargement.   An administrative action that involves increasing the range of a job. Supposedly this action results in better performance and a more satisfied work force.

Job Enrichment.   An approach developed by Herzberg that seeks to improve task efficiency and human satisfaction by means of building into people's jobs greater scope for personal achievement and recognition, more challenging and responsible work, and more opportunity for individual advancement and growth.

Job Evaluation.   The assignment of dollar values to a job.

Job-Order Technology.   A form of production in which products are tailor-made to customer specifications.

Job Range.   This designates the number of operations a job occupant performs to complete a task.

Job Relationships.   The interpersonal relationships required of or made possible by a job.

Job Rotation.   A form of training which involves moving an employee from one to another work station. In addition to the training objective, this procedure is also designed to reduce boredom.

Laboratory Experiment.   The key characteristic of laboratory experiments is that the environment in which the subject works is created by the researcher. The laboratory setting permits the researcher to control closely the experimental conditions.

Leader-Member Relations.   A factor in the Fiedler contingency model which refers to the degree of confidence, trust, and respect followers have in the leader.

Learning.   The process by which a relatively enduring change in behavior occurs as a result of practice.

Learning Transfer.   An important learning principle which emphasizes the carry-over of learning into the workplace.

Legitimate Power.   Capacity to influence derived from the position of a manager in the organizational hierarchy. Subordinates believe they "ought" to comply.

Linking-Pin Function.   An element of System 4 organization which views the major role of managers to be that of representative of the group they manage to higher level groups in the organization.

Lockheed Model.   A span of control model that identifies relevant variables for establishing spans of control. Some of the variables included are the complexity of functions, the coordination of subordinates required, and the direction and control required by subordinates.

Locus of Control.   A personality characteristic that specifies people who see the control of their lives as coming from inside themselves as *internalizers*. People who believe that their lives are controlled by external factors are *externalizers*.

MAPS Design Technology. An acronym for multivariate analysis, participation, and structure, a method for designing and implementing an organization structure through organizational development.

Maturation. One of the sources of error in experimental studies. It results from changes in the subject group with the passage of time which are not associated with the experimental treatment.

Maturity. An important life cycle leadership concept which includes achievement motivation, the willingness and ability to take responsibility, task relevant education, and experience of an individual or a group.

MBO. A process that specifies that superiors and subordinates will jointly set goals for a specified time period and then meet again to evaluate the subordinates' performance in terms of the previously established goals.

Merit Rating. A formal rating system that is applied to hourly paid employees.

Modeling. A method of administering rewards that relies on observational learning. An employee learns the behaviors that are desirable by observing how others are rewarded. It is assumed that behaviors will be imitated if the observer views a distinct link between performance and rewards.

Modified or Compressed Workweek. A shortened workweek. In many cases it involves working four days a week, 10 hours each day. This form of the modified workweek is called a 4/40. There are also 3/36 and 4/32 schedules being used.

Mortality. One of the sources of error in experimental studies. It occurs when participants drop out of the experiment before it is completed, resulting in the experimental and control groups not being comparable.

Motion Study. The process of analyzing work to determine the preferred motions to be used in the completion of a task.

Motivator-Hygiene Theory. The Herzberg approach that identifies conditions of the job which operate primarily to dissatisfy employees when they are not present (hygiene factors—salary, job security, work conditions, and so on). There are also job conditions that when present lead to high levels of motivation and job satisfaction. However, if these conditions are not present, they do not prove highly dissatisfying. They include achievement, growth, and advancement opportunities.

Multiple Roles. This concept describes the notion that most individuals play many roles simultaneously because they occupy many different positions in a variety of institutions and organizations.

Need Hierarchy Model. Maslow assumed that man is a wanting animal whose needs depend on what he already has. This in a sense means that a satisfied need is not a motivator. Man's needs are organized in a hierarchy of importance. The five need classifications are—physiological, safety, belongingness, esteem, and self-actualization.

Needs. The deficiencies that an individual experiences at a particular point in time.

Noise. Interference in the flow of a message from a sender to a receiver.

Nominal Group Technique. A recent technique for improving group decisions. It is a structured group meeting that includes both verbal and nonverbal stages.

Nonprogrammed Decisions. Decisions are nonprogrammed when they are novel and unstructured. As such there is no definite procedure for handling the problem either because it has not arisen in exactly the same manner before or because it is complex or extremely important.

Operant. Behaviors amenable to control by altering consequences (rewards and punishments) which follow them.

Optimal Balance. The most desirable relationship among the criteria of effectiveness. Optimal, rather than maximum, balance must be achieved in any case of more than one criterion.

Organizational Climate. A set of properties of the work environment, perceived directly or indirectly by the employees, assumed to be a major force in influencing employee behavior.

Organizational Development. A planned process of reeducation and training designed to facilitate organizational adaptation to changing environmental demands.

Organizational Profile. A diagram which shows the responses of members of an organization to the questionnaires which Likert devised to measure certain characteristics of an organization.

Organizations. Organizations are differentiated from other collections of people by their goal-directed behavior. That is, they pursue goals and objectives that can be more effectively achieved by the concerted action of individuals. They possess three important characteristics: behavior, structure, and processes.

Participative Management. Is not a specific motivation technique but is a concept of managing that encourages employee's participation in decision making and on matters that affect their jobs.

Path-Goal Leadership Model. A theory which suggests that it is necessary for a leader to influence the followers' perception of work goals, self-development goals, and paths to goal attainment. The foundation for the model is the expectancy motivation theory.

Perception. The process by which an individual gives meaning to the environment. It involves organizing and interpreting various stimuli into a psychological experience.

Performance Evaluation. The systematic, formal evaluation of an employee's job performance and potential for future development.

Person-Role Conflict. This type of conflict occurs when role requirements violate the basic values, attitudes, and needs of the individual occupying the position.

Personal-Behavioral Leadership Theories. A group of leadership theories that are based primarily on the personal and behavioral characteristics of leaders. They focus on *what* leaders do and/or *how* they behave in carrying out the leadership function.

Personality. A stable set of characteristics and tendencies that determine commonalities and differences in the behavior of people.

Personality Test. Instruments used to measure emotional, motivational, interpersonal, and attitude characteristics that make up a person's personality.

Pooled Interdependence. This type of work interdependence occurs when it is not necessary for the groups to interact except through the total organization which supports them.

Position Power. A factor in the Fiedler contingency model which refers to the power inherent in the leadership position.

Power.   The ability to influence another person's behavior.

Process.   In systems theory, the process element consists of technical and administrative activities which are brought to bear on inputs in order to transform them into outputs.

Process Motivation Theories.   Theories which provide a description and analysis of the process of how behavior is energized, directed, sustained, and stopped.

Process Principles.   The organization principles as defined by Fayol which define the desirable behavior of managers as they deal with subordinates.

Process Technology.   An advanced form of manufacturing in which a homogeneous input is converted into a relatively standardized output having a mass market.

Production.   A criterion of effectiveness which refers to the organization's ability to provide the outputs which the environment demands of it.

Programmed Decisions.   Decisions are programmed to the extent that they are repetitive and routine and a definite procedure has been developed for handling them.

Punishment.   Presenting an uncomfortable consequence for a particular behavior response or removing a desirable reinforcer because of a behavior response. Managers can punish by application or punish by removal.

Qualitative Overload.   A situation in which a person feels that he or she lacks the ability or skill to do the job or that performance standards are set too high.

Quantitative Overload.   When a person feels that he or she has too many things to do or insufficient time to complete a job.

Ranking Methods.   The ranking of ratees on the basis of relevant performance.

Recency of Events Error.   The tendency to be biased in ratings by recent events.

Reciprocal Causation of Leadership.   The argument that follower behaviors have an impact on leader behavior and that leader behavior influences follower behaviors.

Reciprocal Interdependence.   In this type of work interdependence the output of each group serves as input to other groups in the organization.

Referent Power.   Power based on a subordinate's identification with a superior. The more powerful individual is admired because of certain traits, and the subordinate is influenced because of this admiration.

Reward Power.   An influence over others based on hope of reward; the opposite of coercive power. A subordinate perceives that compliance with the wishes of a superior will lead to positive rewards, either monetary or psychological.

Role.   Role relates to the expected behavior patterns attributed to a particular status position.

Role of Money.   The potential roles of money are (1) a conditioned reinforcer, (2) an incentive which is capable of satisfying needs, (3) an anxiety-reducer, and (4) serves to erase feelings of dissatisfaction.

Role Ambiguity.   A person's lack of understanding about the rights, privileges, and obligations of a job.

Role Conflict.   Because of the multiplicity of roles and role sets, it is possible for an individual to face a situation of the simultaneous occurrence of two or more role requirements for which the performance of one precludes the performance of the other. This situation is described as role conflict.

Role Management Socialization. Socialization activities undertaken or experienced during the stable career/work stage.

Role Set. This refers to those individuals who have expectations for the behavior of the individual in the particular role. The more expectations the more complex the role set.

Satisfaction. A criterion of effectiveness which refers to the organization's ability to gratify the needs of its participants. Equivalent terms include morale and voluntarism.

Scalar Chain. The graded chain of authority which is created through the delegation process.

Scientific Management. A body of literature which emerged during the period 1890–1930 and which reports the ideas and theories of engineers concerned with such problems as job definition, incentive systems, and selection and training.

Selection. One of the sources of error in experimental studies. It occurs when participants are assigned to experimental and control groups on any basis other than random assignment. Any other selection method will result in systematic biases which will result in differences between groups which are unrelated to the effects of the experimental treatment.

Sensitivity Training. A form of educational experience which stresses the process and emotional aspects of training.

Sequential Interdependence. This type of work interdependence occurs when one group must complete some task before another group can complete its task.

Shared Approach. An OD strategy which involves managers and employees in the determination of the OD program.

Situational Theory of Leadership. This approach to leadership advocates that leaders understand their own behavior, the behavior of their subordinates, and the situation before utilizing a particular leadership style. It requires diagnostic skills in human behavior on the part of the leader.

Socialization Processes. Activities by which an individual comes to appreciate the values, abilities, expected behaviors, and social knowledge essential for assuming an organizational role and for participating as an organization member.

Span of Control. This is the number of subordinates reporting to a superior. The span is a factor that affects the shape and height of an organization structure.

Status. In an organizational setting it relates to positions in the formal or informal structure. In the formal organization it is designated while in informal groups it is determined by the group.

Status Consensus. The agreement of group members about the relative status of members of the group.

Stress. An adaptive response, mediated by individual differences and/or psychological processes, that is, a consequence of any environmental action, situation, or event that places excessive psychological and/or physical demands upon a person.

Stressor. An external event or situation that is potentially harmful to a person.

Strictness or Leniency Rater Errors. The harsh rater gives ratings that are lower than the average ratings usually given. The lenient rater is just the opposite. He or she tends to give higher ratings than the average level.

Structural Principles. The principles which can guide the manager in designing the formal task and authority relationships in an organization.

Structure. The established patterns of interacting and coordinating the technology and human assets of an organization.

Structure (in group context). The term structure used in the context of groups refers to the standards of conduct applied by the total group, the communication system, and the reward and sanction mechanisms of the group.

Survey. A survey usually attempts to measure one or more characteristics in many people, usually at one point in time. Basically they are used to investigate current problems and events.

System 4 Organization. The universalistic theory of organization design which is proposed by Likert. The theory is defined in terms of overlapping groups, "linking pin" management, and the principle of "supportiveness."

Systems Theory. An approach to the analysis of organizational behavior which emphasizes the necessity for maintaining the basic elements of input-process-output and for adapting to the larger environment which sustains the organization.

Task Group. A group of individuals working as a unit to complete a project or job task.

Task Structure. A factor in the Fiedler contingency model which refers to how structured a job is with regard to requirements, problem-solving alternatives, and feedback on the correctness of accomplishing the job.

Technology. An important concept which can have many definitions in specific instances but which refers generally to actions, physical and mental, which an individual performs upon some object, person, or problem in order to change it in some way.

Testing. One of the sources of error in experimental studies. It occurs when changes in the performance of the subject occur because previous measurement of his performance made him aware he was part of an experiment.

Thematic Apperception Test (TAT). A projective test that uses a person's analysis of pictures to evaluate such individual differences as need for achievement, need for power, and need for affiliation.

Time Orientation. A concept which refers to the time horizon of decisions. Employees may have relatively short- or long-term orientations depending upon the nature of their tasks.

Time Study. The process of determining the appropriate elapsed time for the completion of a task.

Tolerance of Ambiguity. The tendency to perceive ambiguous situations or events as desirable. On the other hand, intolerance of ambiguity is the tendency to perceive ambiguous situations or events as sources of threat.

Trait Theory of Leadership. An attempt to identify specific characteristics (physical, mental, personality) which are associated with leadership success. It relies on research which relates various traits to certain success criteria.

Type A Personality. Associated with research conducted on coronary heart disease. The Type A person is an aggressive driver who is ambitious, competitive, task oriented, and always on the move. Rosenman and Friedman, two medical researchers, suggest that Type As have more heart attacks than Type Bs.

Type B Personality. A pattern exhibited by a relaxed, patient, steady, even-tempered individual. The opposite of the Type A.

Unilateral Strategy. An OD strategy which precludes participation by employees. The management hierarchy exercises authority to determine the OD program.

Universal Design Theory. A point of view which states that there is "one best way" to design an organization.

Upward Communication. Upward communication flows from individuals in lower levels of organization structure to those in higher levels. Some of the most common upward communication flows are suggestion boxes, group meetings, and appeal or grievance procedures.

Valence. The strength of a person's preference for a particular outcome.

Vroom-Yetton Model. A leadership model that specifies which leadership decision-making procedures will be most effective in each of several different situations. Two leadership styles proposed are autocratic (AI, and AII), two are consultative (CI and CII), and one is joint decision oriented (leader and the group, GII).

Weighted Checklist. A rating system consisting of statements that describe various types and levels of behavior for a particular job. Each of the statements is weighted according to importance.

Woodward Research. A path-breaking research project which documented the association between technology and organization structure and stimulated a wide range of subsequent studies which contribute to the contingency design point of view.

— Name Index —

Subject Index

This book has been set VIP in 10 and 9 point Melior leaded 2 points. Part numbers are 30 point Melior Bold and chapter numbers are 30 point Melior Bold; part and chapter titles are 24 point Melior. The size of the type page is 38 by 48 picas.